DISSOLVE TO

DISSOLVE TO

DISSOLVE TO

SATYAJIT
RAY

SATYAJIT RAY

THE INNER EYE

Andrew Robinson

ANDRE DEUTSCH

First published in Great Britain
1989 by André Deutsch Limited
105–106 Great Russell Street, London WC1B 3LJ

British Library Cataloguing in Publication Data
Robinson, Andrew
    Satyajit Ray : the inner eye.
    1 .   Indian cinema films. Directing. Ray, Satyajit,
    1921 –
    I .   Title
    791 .43'0233
ISBN 0 – 233 – 98473 – 9

Typesetter: Quorn Selective Repro Ltd
Printed and bound in Great Britain by
WBC Ltd, Bristol & Maesteg

For Krishna and for my parents

'The eye, which is said to be the window of the soul, is the primary means by which the brain may most fully and magnificently contemplate the infinite works of nature . . .'

Leonardo da Vinci

'All great civilisations have been based on loitering.'

Jean Renoir

'I do not put my faith in institutions, but in the individuals all over the world who think clearly, feel nobly and act rightly. They are the channels of moral truth.'

Rabindranath Tagore

CONTENTS

ACKNOWLEDGEMENTS

My first debt is to Satyajit Ray, who has been a reserve of help and refreshment throughout the research and writing of this book, despite his suffering a period of poor health. Non-Bengalis now have at least two good reasons for wishing to learn that beautiful but elusive language: to read Rabindranath Tagore in the original, and to follow Satyajit Ray's films. I am grateful to him for reading my typescript quickly and correcting a number of factual errors without in any way seeking to influence my judgments.

Those who have known Ray have contributed through interviews, correspondence and conversations, especially Alex Aronson, Norman Clare, Saeed Jaffrey, and the late Marie Seton. Their names are listed at the back under Notes. I should like to acknowledge the assistance of the Marie Seton Collection at the British Film Institute, from which I have quoted Ray's letters to Seton, and of Pamela Cullen, Seton's executor.

Nemai Ghosh, Ray's photographer for about twenty years, was an invaluable and generous source of stills and production photographs. Ray's son Sandip turned up some fine unpublished photographs by the late Bansi Chandragupta, Ray's first art director.

Two people in Calcutta, Ujjal Chakravarti and Dhruba Gupta, looked after me in their homes, thereby helping me to understand Bengali life better. Ujjal was uniquely helpful in analysing Ray's films with me over a warm Steenbeck at the Film and Television Institute in Pune.

Anita Desai and Adam Low read the typescript in draft and made various perceptive suggestions for improvement, for which I am grateful. Raghubir Singh 'goaded' me to rewrite the Introduction. Ujjal Chakravarti, Debasish Mukherjee and Sandip Ray helped check the Bibliography, Filmography and list of Awards.

I am also grateful for advice and stimulus from Shampa Banerjee, Sukanta Chaudhuri, Uma Das Gupta, George Fenton, Stephen Haggard, Nasreen Munni Kabir, Subrata Lahiri, Iqbal Masud, Hilary Minster, Arghya Kamal Mitra, Partha Mitter, Rajeet Mitter, Russi Mody, Zia Mohyeddin, Rudrangsu Mukherjee, Trilokesh Mukherjee, Muriel Peters, William Radice, Santha Rama Rau, Paritosh Sen, K. G. Subramanyan, E. P. Thompson, Asok Viswanathan and Ronald Warwick.

Other people who have helped me in their various ways are Nirmalya Acharya, Kenneth Ballhatchet, the late Dhiren Bhagat, John Boulton, Dilip Chatarji, Shyamal Chowdhury, Allegra Huston, Pico Iyer, Amarnath Jayatilaka, K. Kawakita, Anita Mehta, Probodh Moitra, Ben Nyce, Kiranmoy Raha, Dilip K. Roy, Hirak Sen, Mrinal Sen, Ramesh Sen, Robert Sykes and D. J. Wenden.

Harris Films kindly made available some of Ray's films in Britain, but I owe a debt to the National Film Archive of India in Pune and to its Director P. K. Nair for his cooperation in allowing me to view Ray's films at length.

The staff of the British Film Institute in the Archive Viewing Service, Library and Stills Library have helped me. Markku Salmi, Leslie Hardcastle, Janet Moat and Anthony Smith, must be singled out for thanks.

Granada Television was an understanding employer during my research and writing. I should like to thank Denis Forman, Don Harker, Brian Lapping and Leslie Woodhead for their support.

I have written about Ray for various magazines and newspapers over the past six or seven years. My thanks to the following editors in three continents: George Brock, Allen Eyles, Stephen Glover, Penelope Houston, Mike Leahy, Vinode Mehta, Charles Moore, Pritish Nandy, Richard Patterson, Sunanda Datta Ray, Alan Ross and Tom Sutcliffe.

Finally, of course, I am grateful to Tom Rosenthal, for commissioning the book in 1983 from a complete unknown, to Laura Morris, one of the most dedicated editors I know, to Michèle Young, an incisive and meticulous copy-editor.

A. R.

ILLUSTRATIONS

All illustrations are identified from left to right.

Nemai Ghosh supplied prints of the frontispiece, 1, 4, 6, 8, 13–16, 19, 20, 22, 25, 27, 30, 33, 35–41, 43, 45, 46, 49, 51, 56, 58, 59, 67, 71, 74, 76–84, 87, 89–92, 94–103, 105–110, 112–129, 131–134, 141–147
The National Film Archive, London, supplied prints of 2, 3, 5, 12, 21, 23, 24, 26, 31, 32, 34, 42, 44, 47, 48, 50, 52–55, 57, 60–66, 68, 72, 73, 75, 85, 86, 88, 93, 111, 135
The National Film Archive, Pune, supplied a print of 104
La Cinémathèque Francaise, Paris, supplied prints of the endpapers, 17
The Academy of Fine Arts, Calcutta, supplied a print of 137 (*left*)
Satyajit/ Sandip Ray supplied prints of 9, 18, 70, 130
Lindsay Anderson supplied a print of 69, Norman Clare a print of 11, J. B. R. Nicholson a copy of 142
Other illustrations were copied from published sources.

A NOTE ON THE PRONUNCIATION AND
SPELLING OF BENGALI

'It's a critical disadvantage to admire a director's work immensely and to know that one can never quite come to terms with pronouncing his name', the editor of *Sight and Sound* once wrote. For readers of this book who wish to know the Bengali pronunciation of 'Satyajit Ray', 'Shottojeet Rye' is about as close as one can get. Almost every 's' in Bengali is a soft 's'. Most Indians who are not from Bengal will pronounce the name 'Sat-y-a-jit Ray', with a hard 's' and his second name rhymed with 'say' – just as a westerner would tend to do. Either pronunciation seems to me equally acceptable outside Bengal.

The same disparity applies, a fortiori, to all the other Bengali names that are unavoidably scattered through the book. If it is any consolation to the western reader, he should at least know that Indians who are not Bengalis face almost the same difficulties with pronunciation as he does.

The spelling of Bengali words and names in English is a tricky matter, since there is no widely accepted system of transliteration. Mostly, I have retained the commonly used spellings with all the inconsistencies that these entail – e.g. Tagore rather than Thakur – rather than adopting the more accurate (but off-putting) spelling used by many academics. I have also arbitrarily chosen to use 'ch' rather than the cumbersome 'chh' throughout, 's' rather than 'sh' in general, except for words ending with an 's' – e.g. I prefer Ghosh to Ghos – and to use a single spelling for each of the names Banerjee, Chakravarti, Chatterjee and Mukherjee. This avoids the confusion inherent in the many transliterations of these names in use, often for the same individual – Banerji, Banerjee, Bannerji, Bannerjee or Bandopadhyay (the direct transliteration), for instance. As the irritable old printer of visiting cards in *The Middle Man* insists, 'There are fourteen ways of spelling Banerjee!', while the Calcutta telephone directory lists at least forty-eight ways of spelling Chakravarti. I hope that those affected by this fiat will be understanding of my reasons.

A. R.

INTRODUCTION

Getting to know Ray

My earliest memory of a Satyajit Ray film is vague but slightly threatening. I must have been watching his ghost-story *The Lost Jewels* on BBC television when I was about ten. I don't remember seeing any others until becoming a member of the university film society at Oxford. By then I had spent some months living and working in India – which might have been expected to focus my interest in Ray rather more sharply. But they had not; perhaps because India is so vast and I had been nowhere near Ray's native city Calcutta.

It took the world première of *The Chess Players* at London's National Film Theatre in late 1977 to awaken my interest properly. I had never enjoyed watching a film so much before, even though we all had to wear headphones to follow the Urdu dialogue in Saeed Jaffrey's mellifluous English reading, which we knew had been arranged at the last minute. The warmth and urbane humour of the film, coupled with its unobtrusively innovative style, suggested that its creator must be a highly civilised individual; and its intriguing range of references showed him to be equally at home in both East and West.

When Ray himself appeared afterwards on stage with Jaffrey he seemed in tune with his film. Standing a foot taller than his actor, dressed in a well-cut suit and tie, he talked briefly and simply in a strong, pleasant, above all musical voice of indefinable accent. His affection for Jaffrey and Jaffrey's devotion to him were transparent, and the capacity audience radiated goodwill towards them both. Much later I learnt that Ray had not heard the commentary that night, because he had handed over his headphones to an usherette who wanted them: an impressive gesture of faith in his actor's ability.

The next time I saw Ray he was dressed in full academic regalia, ready to receive an honorary doctorate from Oxford – only the second film director to be so honoured after his hero Chaplin. He looked much sterner than he had in London the year before, somewhat ill at ease, and carried his mortar-board in his hand rather than wearing it like the others (so scared was he that it would be blown away, as he later told me). Nor had he, unlike his fellows, brought a camera to the ceremony: he thought it would be forbidden in the Sheldonian Theatre.

The incongruity amused me as much as Ray's first biographer Marie Seton when she relayed it to me with her inimitable gusto at our first meeting a few years later. Her pioneering book on Ray, which I had read in the meantime, amply confirmed my first impressions of an unassuming nature. It also contained a graphic description of Ray's struggle to finish *The Chess Players* and have it seen in India. Without exchanging a word with Ray, I had begun to feel I already knew him.

In the spring of 1981 he visited Oxford again, this time to attend a season of his films there. I hoped to meet him at last but his plane was late and I had to leave the screening before he arrived. Instead, I wrote him what amounted to a fan letter. I had a job in a publishing house at the time and asked Ray if he had considered writing his autobiography. Walking away from All Souls after delivering this billet-doux, I noticed a very tall man just getting out of a car, followed by a woman dressed in a sari. They were Ray and his wife of course, and my nerve failed me. The letter would have to serve as my introduction.

A month or two later I received his reply from Calcutta. From reading Seton, I guessed that he had typed it himself – on a ribbon not in its first youth.

> I have long been toying with the idea of writing a book on my experiences as a film-maker, possibly confining myself to the Apu Trilogy ('My Years with Apu'), but·the snag is, as you have yourself guessed, I never seem to have the time. Apart from making a feature film a year, I also jointly edit a children's monthly magazine, doing most of the illustrations, writing stories, poems, devising puzzles etc. This takes up all my free time between films. So you see how difficult it is for me to make any kind of commitment at this stage. Let me, however, thank you for your offer. If and when there is an MS, may I send it to you?

That was all: frank and informal, like all the letters I have received from Ray in the years since then, as well as those he wrote to Marie Seton from 1955 onwards which appear as a body for the first time in this book. Ray has never employed a secretary or personal assistants, preferring to answer his correspondence himself, usually without bothering to keep copies; and nearly everyone who writes to him gets a reply – often prompt and always to the point. I felt even more determined to meet him.

The right moment came in April the following year. Ray was in London again for a few days to see friends and answer questions at the National Film Theatre, following a season of nearly all his films. He spoke well but this time seemed a bit tense. I watched how his normally mobile face would sometimes glaze over at a question that did not engage him. 'Would you ever make a film about Indians in

London who are fifty-fifty?' a London Indian in the audience asked him. There was a pause. 'Fifty-fifty . . . ?' queried Ray in a heavy voice almost a drawl, and then lapsed into silence; he obviously wished to avoid giving offence, but clearly people without roots – whether in London or in Calcutta – did not much interest him as an artist. When I mentioned this interview afterwards to Indians who had been present, I noticed that this response had touched a nerve, and I could guess how Ray's reputation for remoteness had grown up. It made me slightly nervous about our meeting the following morning.

In the event it was enjoyable – I felt for both of us. We met in Ray's room at the Savoy Hotel – the accommodation arranged for him by the NFT. He was wearing what I came to recognise as his directing garb: short-sleeved shirt, slacks and sandals. In a letter he had agreed to give me an interview for a film magazine. We talked for nearly three and a half hours. From time to time he puffed on a pipe, as an alternative to the cigarettes he had been told to give up a few years before. Once, the phone rang: it was Marie Seton. Ray chatted to her amiably for a while.

His mildly wary air of the previous evening was nowhere in evidence now. My questions were mostly very specific, which he seemed to like. His replies came slowly but surely and in complete sentences – a fact that did not surprise me as it should have, because he was the first person I had ever interviewed. They were never glib, and occasionally I felt they would never emerge at all (such as when I asked him 'What is your overall attitude to the British heritage in India?'). He often smiled and chuckled and occasionally burst into the hearty laugh I would later often hear. 'Life itself is full of funny things', he happened to remark at one point. No one who knows Ray well would ever call him solemn; he is the inheritor of a long family tradition of making Bengalis laugh.

At the end I showed him some fine colour artwork for a new edition of Kipling's *Just So Stories* I was involved in publishing. With his love of children's writing and illustrating I had a hunch he would be interested. He was, and studied it carefully for several minutes. At the same time he returned to me a proof copy of his friend Kurosawa's autobiography that I had earlier left at the hotel in the hope of encouraging Ray to write his own. Even on his short visit he had found time to read it, and when I said I did not need it back, he was happy to take it to Calcutta for his son, who had just made his first film there with screenplay and music by his father.

Eight months later I arrived in Calcutta myself. Ray had written to say I was welcome to watch the shooting of *The Home and the World*. My plan was to cover it for *American Cinematographer*. I felt that would give me the ideal excuse to pry into every aspect of its production.

Ray's home city was just as simultaneously depressing and fascinating as other sympathetic foreign visitors have frequently commented, though I was lucky to make my first acquaintance with it during the coolest part

of the year; in the summer it is a humid inferno. Its ramshackle sprawl
and unfathomable levels of human activity overwhelm the mind, at least
to begin with. But, unlike the casual visitor, I had a point of reference;
I did not exactly feel I knew Calcutta in advance as someone might feel
he knew New York after seeing Woody Allen's films, but neither did the
city seem alien. It never struck me either as the 'City of Dreadful Night'
(the phrase made famous by Kipling), or as the 'City of Joy' – the title of a
recent bestseller. It defied labels. I had already read and understood Ray's
1966 comment on it, that 'there is something about creating beauty in the
circumstances of shoddiness and privation that is truly exciting.'

Within a few days I got to know the city from a unique perspective:
Ray on the hunt for props, costumes and materials to suit the lavish
period settings of Tagore's story, in the shops and homes of his intricate
network of relatives, friends and contacts. 'Come any time. We are very
busy shopping around getting props from people's houses,' he had told
me without preliminaries over the phone at my hotel – and he meant
exactly that. Over the next few days I tagged along as he and his assistants,
including his son, went calmly in pursuit of a wind-up gramophone of
c. 1907 vintage, a pistol that originally belonged to Tagore's grandfather,
imitation classical figurines and other *objets d'art*, and bric-a-brac of all
kinds from a shop in central Calcutta stuffed with the relics of a more
expansive age. Everything we collected was put into his Ambassador car
(a version of the 1950s Morris Oxford ubiquitous in India), we all climbed
in too and bumped off through the polluted air towards the studio several
miles away. Once, there was nothing for it but for me and Ray (whose legs
match his six-foot-four-inches height) to cram into the front seat next to
the driver. I could think of no other world-famous film director used to
operating quite like this.

When I first entered his flat in a large, pleasantly shabby mansion-block
dating from the time of Ray's birth in the 1920s, I found him discussing the
exact kind of button required by one of his costume designs with a member
of his production team. He struck me immediately as more animated than
in London – thoroughly at ease with his surroundings. Apart from some
months during his childhood and about six months in Europe in 1950,
Ray's life has been spent in Calcutta. As he later remarked to me, 'I don't
feel very creative when I'm abroad somehow. I need to be in my chair in
Calcutta!' Looking around the room where he likes to work, I could see
why. It has the subdued colours, cavernous ceilings, louvered windows and
revolving fans of the Raj – no air-conditioning. Every day at certain times
which change with the seasons, Ray follows a ritual of opening and closing
windows as the sun moves round. Everywhere, in crammed bookcases and
in mushrooming piles, there are magazines and books, some of them old
and rare, many of them presents from his friends and contacts all over the
world. He has a good record and tape collection too, with a preponderance
of the western classical music he and his wife have loved since their teens,

plus a hi-fi system acquired rather late in life that has replaced its faithful but unsophisticated predecessor since Ray's recent illness. There is also a piano, at which he used to sit and pick out tunes for his background scores (until the arrival of synthesisers in Calcutta), with his doors and windows for once firmly closed to guests and the city's racket to allow him to concentrate fully. On top of it stand some of his many awards and a bust of Beethoven, and on the wall above hangs a photograph of Eisenstein, whose films Ray once compared to Bach's music. But unlike most Bengali homes, Ray's has no image of Rabindranath Tagore, who has influenced him, as well as his father and grandfather, more than anyone else: 'Such a cliché!' he told me when I once mentioned it.

This is the atmosphere that Ray finds congenial and creative. He is one of the most unostentatious men ever to make a film – and in a country renowned for the brashness of its movie industry. There are residences in Calcutta – once known as the 'City of Palaces' – to match the most baroque mansion of a star in Bombay (or Malibu), but Ray has never wanted to live in one, nor to be a VIP Indian-style, with an entourage of flatterers and rumours. (In fact he has yet to own a house or flat.) He 'detests' making public speeches and has given only one lecture on his own work to date. The many generous offers of films he has received from abroad, he has so far eventually turned down because of strings attached. The one time he went against this instinct, and embraced a Hollywood offer to direct a science fiction film in India, the project ran aground in acrimony (though it seems to have influenced E.T.). To work properly, Ray needs to be entirely free, and because he is patient and has relatively few personal wants, he has managed to achieve this freedom and maintain it. He in fact feels himself to be rich and seemed surprised when I once queried this. What I had not realised was just how short of money he had been until his early twenties. 'I mean I have no money worries as such' he said, 'thanks to my writing, not from films really. I'm certainly not as rich as Bombay actors – by no means; but I'm comfortable, I can buy the books and records I want.'

Ensconced in his favourite chair – an intermittently functioning telephone within easy reach and his drawing-board, brushes, pens, inks and paints to hand when he wants them – Ray likes best to recline in loose clothes with his bare feet resting on a convenient low table, and work at the red cloth-bound shooting notebooks that contain literally every aspect of a film, and at his children's magazine. Often he spends a whole day at a stretch in his chair (though bad health has forced him to rest more in recent years). Much of this time he is deaf to the world, absorbed in his thoughts, an ability cultivated by him in the several houses and flats he has passed through in south Calcutta, so as to exclude the increasing blare of car horns, amplified film songs and festivals from the teeming city, the chatter of visitors talking among themselves and, sometimes, unwelcome attempts at conversation. The flat he lives in now with his wife Bijoya and their son Sandip is comparatively spacious and the neighbourhood relatively quiet, but the habit of switching off the outside world has become second nature.

The day I first visited the studio with Ray was typical of life in Calcutta in recent years, even for the well-off. There was an extended power cut (known as 'load-shedding') and we found ourselves driving gingerly through a ghostly, smoky city lit only by hurricane-lamps, cooking-fires and those fortunate premises with electric generators. The studios were lit by hurricane-lamps. Ray, dressed in his home clothes – loose pyjamas and Indian-style shirt (*panjabi* or *kurta*) with a large shawl wrapped boldly around the upper half of his commanding form – examined the almost-finished set and instructed his art director on the precise manner in which the curtains should fall, the shape of the half-moon windows above the doors and other details. 'It looks rather spectral, doesn't it?' he said with a smile.

Seeing the studio in the clear light of day I realised what I had missed on our nocturnal visit. 'Load-shedding', while not the least of Ray's problems, must take second place to the primitive lighting arrangements, the lack of air-conditioning (which made me admire the actors in *The Chess Players* even more, especially Richard Attenborough who had to face a Calcutta summer), and the ineffective soundproofing that means much dialogue has to be dubbed later. There were some very persistent pigeons roosting in the roof of the studio, for instance, which had sometimes to be driven off with stones so that shooting could continue. One of Ray's assistant directors later volunteered, 'We are proof against all hazards.' Ray himself told me, without a trace of affectation, 'After all, we do have the bare essentials – and the rest is here, in my head. I don't think you need any more than that really.'

The day the shooting began I was touched when he suddenly produced some sheets of dialogue from the film script he had translated for me and written out the night before in his forceful handwriting, so that I could get the maximum out of my experience in the studio. Over the next two weeks he produced several more batches as shooting progressed.

The atmosphere on his set was the result of an accumulation of such careful forethought. It was alert, without being tense. There was a stream of visitors – mainly members of Ray's extended family or relatives of his wife, his old friends, or the family and friends of his cast – whom Ray usually greeted and sometimes chatted to between shots without any sign of irritation. I felt that what was taking place inside the studio was not so very different from his life outside it; there was none of the hyped-up artificiality and much less of the boredom of a western film set, or, for that matter, of the sets next-door to Ray's, where other Bengali directors continue to churn out the trashy melodramas that Ray swept aside with *Pather Panchali* in 1955. Ray's film-making, like his films, is never divorced from life.

Whenever he felt he had something to contribute Ray was on the move around the studio, talking volubly, often vociferously in Bengali with occasional phrases in English, indicating what he wanted to his small production team and, once the set was ready, his actors. In general he kept his rehearsals to a minimum, however, to reserve his actors' spontaneity for the camera. Otherwise he sat quietly, on a small wicker stool, pondering with his red shooting notebook in his hands and smoking or just biting his pipe; as his production team went about their jobs I was sometimes hardly aware that Ray was present at all. Only when he perceived that all was ready for him would he then almost shout out in English 'Come on. Taking, taking!' This tendency to withdraw when not needed must be what he had in mind when he once insisted to me that the aristocratic image of him held by many, is a wrong one. 'When I'm working I'm a *complete* democrat. It's when I'm sitting at home alone and doing nothing that it seems aristocratic,' he said, and laughed at the notion. 'Film-making is a democratic undertaking, I think.'

Near the end of my stay I was lucky to be witness to a historic shot: the first full-blooded kiss in a Ray film! He decided to clear the studio of all but his production team and family, who are normally present throughout the production process (his son Sandip as an assistant director, his wife Bijoya to advise on costumes, make-up, music, and anything else that comes to her mind – she is the first to read everything Ray writes). On this occasion his wife's elder sister was there too and told me, with a laugh, that the idea of watching a kiss in front of her relatives made her a little embarrassed. Critics of Ray as something of a puritan would have said that he was too, but I didn't feel him to be; nervous yes, in case his actors muffed the scene, but not embarrassed. Outwardly he looked calm and very focused, brows furrowed behind the camera, which had to track rapidly from one side of the couple to the other. Three takes were made – more than average for Ray – but the actors were still not quite right. Swatilekha Chatterjee's hair was getting in her way, and her bangles were not in the correct place. Ray wanted to zoom in on these as she embraced Soumitra Chatterjee and gripped his shoulder. The fourth take was going well when Ray looked up from the camera waving the zoom control – technical malfunction. 'This has betrayed me,' he said to me heavily. Five takes were required in all before Ray was satisfied, and everyone, the actors especially, could unwind. As we left the studio a little later, Ray remarked slightly mischievously, 'There's another kiss tomorrow.'

During 1983 he continued to shoot the film and compose and record the music for it. I saw him again in London in May – this time staying in the rather functional hotel he uses near Russell Square in a box-like room with a bed that can barely have fitted him. I wanted to raise a vital question: how would he feel about me writing a book about him? 'I don't want another foreigner writing a book about me without learning Bengali' was his reply. I gulped a bit, even though I had anticipated the idea after watching him at home and at work in Calcutta. Otherwise he appeared to accept my suggestion.

At the end of September there arrived a characteristic letter beginning 'Important I have to buy a woman's hat (circa '05) in London'. This was for Jennifer Kendal to wear: could I make enquiries in advance of his arrival in early October? He was about to accept a Fellowship of the British Film Institute from the hands of Prince Charles, along with Orson Welles, Marcel Carné, David Lean, Michael Powell and Emeric Pressburger. The idea obviously tickled him, as it did me, and I had sent him a four-line verse on the subject. His letter ended with his improved version of my verse, a proper limerick:

> When Bonnie Prince Charlie met Life-Fellow Ray
> He really couldn't think quite what to say
> Then he thought it'd be dandy
> To ask 'Have you seen Gandhi?'
> But Ray beat him to it to his utter dismay

which has the nice twist to it that only an Englishman would pronounce 'Gandhi' to rhyme with 'dandy' – or an Indian wanting to oblige an Englishman.

To his great regret Ray never made this award ceremony. He had a heart attack just days before his flight was due to depart. The very few remaining scenes in The Home and the World and the post-production had to be completed by Sandip under the close supervision of Satyajit. Both the film and Ray were invited to the Cannes Festival. The film just reached there in time, along with Sandip and others, but not Ray; he was in hospital again following a second attack.

The next time I met him was at Heathrow Airport on his way back to Calcutta from Houston, where he had undergone a heart bypass operation. The experience had been a very unpleasant one and he was still in pain. He was sitting in a wheel-chair and looked much thinner. I couldn't think quite what to say, but Satyajit was not at all put out. 'You've put on weight,' he straightaway remarked with almost his old smile.

He spent some days in London along with his wife and son, recuperating in a hotel off Oxford Street, where I saw him regularly. Just down the road, at the now-defunct Academy Cinema (where Pather Panchali played nearly thirty years previously to lyrical reviews), The Home and the World was about to open. A five-minute taxi-ride would have taken him there. Ray had not yet seen it, and as the days passed, I realised he did not intend to either – until he returned to familiar territory. Considering all that the film meant to him, his restraint was formidable. Instead, we all went to see a Spielberg film – Indiana Jones – which Ray had heard about while convalescing in Houston. Throughout the film he watched impassively, except for when some particularly grotesque 'Indian' priests appeared – 'A brown sacred thread,' he said quizzically with perhaps a touch of disgust. Afterwards, he admitted to feeling somewhat depressed that audiences seemed to enjoy such unrelenting action. Later still, in Calcutta, he remarked that all but the first ten minutes of the film were 'absolutely haywire, unbelievably bad.'

Since then, Ray has stayed inside his flat much more than in the past, recovering his strength to make another feature film – and also, in the early days, waiting for a lift to be installed to give him easy access. Meantime, besides writing, illustrating and editing stories for his children's magazine, writing best-selling novellas about his detective duo for other magazines and for book publication (which provide him with his regular income), and translating some of his stories for publication abroad during 1987, he has written a series of screenplays and music scores for his son's television films under the title *Satyajit Ray Presents*, and made a documentary film about his father, a comic writer and illustrator much-loved in Bengal, whose birth centenary fell in October 1987.

In a sense it was a good time to draw Ray out on the subject of himself and of his work. I was in and out of his flat during visits to Calcutta, catching him in many moods, even loquacious (especially in Bengali). At mealtimes – taken Indian-style of course, with the fingers, but sitting at a table rather than on the floor – his wife and son would be there and maybe a family friend or two. Occasionally there would be some mild disagreement. I remember the kiss in *The Home and the World* was controversial, for instance; Bijoya was convinced it would not get past the censors. 'You've been saying that for years,' replied Satyajit in a quiet, firm voice that spoke volumes for his capacity to outface every kind of convention once he has set his mind on it.

On the whole though, he prefers to listen and watch, rather than talk, just as he did as a solitary child 'imbibing' life – to use his own word – in a houseful of unselfconscious adults. You can feel his powers of observation acting upon you in a manner that goes a long way towards explaining the psychological intensity of his films, 'the pleasure of recognising the familiar pin-pointed by art' (in the words of Ray's closest British friend, now dead). A Bengali friend of mine, who dropped her bag in Ray's room, recalls distinctly the sensation of him studying the movement of her body as she bent to pick the bag up. The moments with him I myself have enjoyed most are his pauses and laughs – neither of which, like the wordless peaks of his films, can really be caught in print. They punctuate the most revealing passages of my many hours of interviews with him. I cannot truthfully say Ray welcomed the prospect of these talks, at least partly because it was a filmed interview he gave that helped to precipitate his first heart attack; but in the event he spoke freely. I got the feeling that he could not resist answering a well-constructed question. Those that were not – such as that question at the NFT a few years earlier – usually elicited a loud request for a repeat, silence, or perhaps a brief response trailing off into a sort of dismissive sniff.

Satyajit is 'very much a private person', as he once volunteered to me. Although he knows himself extremely well, he is 'guarded' about revealing that knowledge to anyone else except obliquely – to use the adjective favoured by Lindsay Anderson, who has been a friend since 1950. Most of those in Bengal who have known him since his youth feel he is at heart a loner, like his own detective hero Felu. Not that he is a snob; he is willing to talk to anyone at any level – hence his unrivalled rapport with children as a director – but he finds it difficult to tolerate insincerity, insensitivity or stupidity in a person or artistic production for very long. That is why he avoids and distrusts politicians and lawyers, for instance, and why he can seem remote, aloof or even cold to some. But I have yet to meet anyone with a genuine feeling for a subject that interests Ray who did not enjoy talking to him about it – whether it was cinema, music, painting, literature, a new scientific theory, cricket, the fast-changing face of Calcutta, someone he admires, or any of a host of other things, often quite unexpected.

In the short time that I have known Satyajit he has constantly surprised me. I knew about his liking for chess, crosswords and Scrabble, for instance; but I never suspected his addiction to one-armed bandits. In the last few years, it turned out, he has several times vanished from Calcutta to Katmandu, where few people recognise him, so that he can play the machines at a casino there to his heart's content. 'He's become a slot-machine freak,' says his son with a grin, who shot a television film in Katmandu during one such visit.

Ray is a rich and multifarious person in an age of impoverished specialisation. As V. S. Naipaul remarked of him to me, 'Ray and Kurosawa are among the most prodigious personalities in the cinema since it came into being.' Or as Satyajit himself replied in 1982 when I asked him if he had felt conscious of the range of eastern and western influences on him as he grew up: 'I never had the feeling of grappling with an alien culture when reading European literature, or looking at European painting, or listening to western music, whether classical or popular.'

To do Ray full justice would take a wide understanding of world cinema of all kinds and western and Indian classical music, as well as an informed appreciation of the language, literature, music, art, religions and history of Bengal, the cultural confluence of India – and especially of Bengal's greatest creative figure Rabindranath Tagore. That is not to mention a grasp of the classical heritage of the Mughals at Lucknow, portrayed in *The Chess Players*, and the history of the British Raj in India. Even the little I have read in Bengali, including much of Ray's own writings (and his charming memoir of his early life), hints at depths and subtleties in his work that most viewers sadly will never appreciate – which helps to account for the common impression that Ray's films are 'slow'. I have seldom felt this myself, even when I first got to know them. Their characters always felt so vivid, so individual, so *real*. In fact my chief credential for writing about Ray is the lasting satisfaction I have had from repeated viewings of his films and from my friendship with him. I hope that some of this pleasure, at least, will engage the reader of what follows.

London (Islington and Palmers Green)
December 1988

THE RAY FAMILY TREE (PATERNAL)

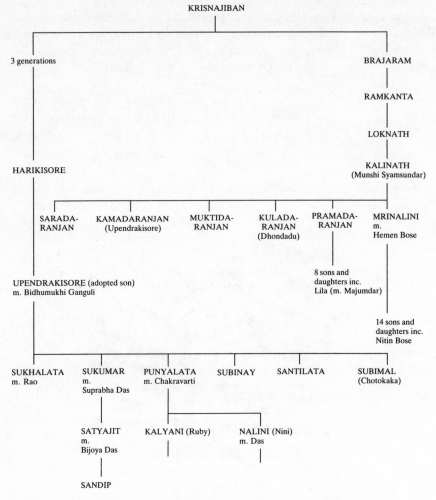

KRISNAJIBAN

3 generations

BRAJARAM

RAMKANTA

LOKNATH

KALINATH
(Munshi Syamsundar)

HARIKISORE

SARADA-RANJAN   KAMADARANJAN   MUKTIDA-RANJAN   KULADA-RANJAN   PRAMADA-RANJAN   MRINALINI
(Upendrakisore)   (Dhondadu)   m.
                                                                          Hemen Bose

8 sons and
daughters inc.
Lila (m. Majumdar)

UPENDRAKISORE (adopted son)
m. Bidhumukhi Ganguli

14 sons and
daughters inc.
Nitin Bose

SUKHALATA   SUKUMAR   PUNYALATA   SUBINAY   SANTILATA   SUBIMAL
m. Rao   m.   m. Chakravarti   (Chotokaka)
            Suprabha Das

SATYAJIT   KALYANI (Ruby)   NALINI (Nini)
m.   m. Das
Bijoya Das

SANDIP

THE RAY FAMILY TREE (MATERNAL)

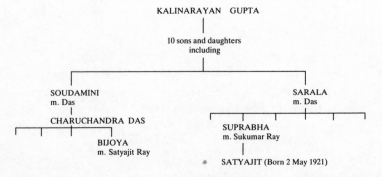

KALINARAYAN GUPTA

10 sons and daughters
including

SOUDAMINI
m. Das

SARALA
m. Das

CHARUCHANDRA DAS

SUPRABHA
m. Sukumar Ray

BIJOYA
m. Satyajit Ray

SATYAJIT (Born 2 May 1921)

1

A Bengali Banyan Tree:
The Ray Family

⸙⸙⸙⸙

UNTIL quite late in Satyajit Ray's life many Bengalis thought of him as 'the son of Sukumar Ray' and 'the grandson of Upendrakisore Ray', rather than as an artist in his own right. Besides indicating their tacit disapproval of the cinema, they were also expressing an engrained reverence for the family. This the Rays more than justified. Upendrakisore was a pioneer of half-tone printing, a musician and composer of songs and hymns, and a writer and illustrator of classic children's literature. His son Sukumar was a writer and illustrator of nonsense literature, the equal of Lewis Carroll and Edward Lear. Both men were also universally considered the epitome of courtesy, artists in their lives as much as in their works.

Their earliest known ancestor was Ramsundar Deo, a Hindu youth who uprooted himself in the mid-sixteenth century from his village in what is now West Bengal and wandered into East Bengal (now Bangladesh). He reached Serpur where, at the house of the local zamindar, he met the ruler of nearby Yasodal, who took a liking to him for his quick intelligence and invited him to Yasodal. There he gave him a house, land and a daughter in marriage. For the rest of his life Ramsundar Deo administered his father-in-law's estates.

Subsequent generations of his family lived at Yasodal and, later, in a village called Masua further east, on the other side of the river Brahmaputra. They steadily gathered wealth and education and acquired the honorific title 'Majumdar', a common Bengali surname today meaning roughly 'revenue accountant', in recognition of their service to the Muslim rulers of Bengal. The name 'Ray', which they later took, is also an honorific. A derivative of 'Raja', it was usually assumed by landowners and showed that the family had moved steadily up the social scale.

At some point in the latter half of the eighteenth century a flood destroyed Masua and divided the family into two branches, one of which became noted for its learning, the other for its wealth and piety. Of the first, Ramkanta Majumdar was fluent in several languages, an expert singer and musician and a man of great physical strength and courage. It is said that he would eat a full basket of parched rice and a whole jackfruit for breakfast, and that once, when he was sitting on his verandah, a wild boar attacked him. He grabbed its snout and held it in his vice-like grip before shouting for help. The boar was done to death with sandals and bare hands. In another story Ramkanta singlehandedly retrieved a cow stolen from him at the behest of a local zamindar, upturning a couple of the zamindar's toughs and sticking their heads in the mud of a river-bank.

The eldest of Ramkanta's three sons had the habit of replying to a question in verse; the youngest became a famous scholar in Persian; but the second son, Loknath, was so fluent in Sanskrit, Arabic and Persian that he was able to read aloud in one language from a book written in another such that his listeners would not know he was translating. In his twenties he began practising certain austerities associated with Tantric yoga and increasingly withdrew from the world. His father, concerned that his son would become a sannyasi, secretly gathered together his books and sacred objects one day and dropped them in a river. Loknath was so shattered that he took to a fast and died within three days. As he lay on his deathbed he told his weeping wife, who held their only child, 'Now you have only one, but from him will come a hundred!' – a family story often repeated in Satyajit Ray's childhood a century later.

This son, Kalinath, father of Upendrakisore Ray, was probably born in the 1830s. He too was a scholar in Sanskrit, Arabic and Persian, but not a sannyasi. Held in high esteem for his integrity, he would be called to adjudicate at the disputations of Hindu pundits – and, remarkably, those of Muslim maulvis too. They regularly appealed to him to interpret *firmans*, the legal documents that formed the basis of administration from the earliest days of the Mughal Empire. In fact, Kalinath Ray became better known as 'Munshi' (Professor) Syamsundar: an unusual distinction for that period when Islam was in retreat all over India.

Apart from Hinduism and Islam, the third major influence in Bengal at this time was of course European, acting initially through the East India Company, under Clive, Hastings, Cornwallis and others, then, after 1857, through the British Government and its representatives in India. Calcutta was their capital and the second city of the British Empire, known as the 'City of Palaces' after the grand mansions of British merchants and their Bengali collaborators lining the banks of the river Hooghly. The intermixing of all three civilisations, but principally the Hindu and the European, produced the cultural upsurge in nineteenth-century Bengal in which the Ray family figured prominently. Conveniently labelled the Bengal Renaissance, it embraces the entire gamut of imaginative response of one culture to another – from the most creative, in the persons of Sir William Jones and Rabindranath Tagore, to the most sterile: those Bengalis who preferred to speak in English, write in English and think in English and who 'would be supremely happy when they could dream in English' (in the famous words of a contemporary Bengali satirist). The Renaissance included perhaps a dozen men of world stature, and one dazzling genius, but its typical representative was an imitator of the West. As David Kopf, an American historian, has recently put it, 'The Bengal Renaissance was the child of eighteenth-century cosmopolitanism and pragmatic British policy built around the need for an acculturated civil-service class.'

The most energetic group of Bengalis to emerge from this colonial interaction were the Brahmos, a small minority within Hindu society who from the late 1820s reacted strongly both to Christianity, western literature and ideas and to the appalling social excesses of that time, such as *sati*. They rejected idolatry and caste and, in due course, the concept of a revealed religion. Founded by Raja Rammohun Roy, a phenomenal linguist and the greatest Indian intellectual of the nineteenth century, who died in Britain in 1833, the Brahmos were subsequently led by Devendranath Tagore, father of Rabindranath. In the 1860s and 70s two schisms took place, leading to the creation of the Sadharan (Low Church) Brahmo Samaj. This was the branch with which the Ray family became associated in the 1880s.

Brahmo beliefs were never clearly distinguished, despite endless debate, either within a 'Samaj', or sect, or between the different Samajes. Throughout the last century and into this one, Christian missionaries continued their efforts to claim Brahmos for Christ, but the attempt was a vain one, as much enmeshed in the political and social differences between Britain and India as in theological controversy. Brahmoism at its highest was more Christian than the religion of the missionaries. Perhaps Rabindranath Tagore put it best years later when he reminded westerners that 'much of the spirit of Christianity runs counter, not only to the classical culture of Europe, but to the European temperament altogether.'

In its heyday Brahmoism was a vigorous movement for social reform motivated by ideas of 'plain living, high principles, industry and perseverance' which bear a resemblance to Victorian values of the time in Britain that is by no means accidental. From the 1860s to the 1890s, Brahmos were 'very powerful figures,' to quote Satyajit Ray, 'very demanding figures with lots of social fervour in them: the willingness, the ability and the eagerness to do good to society, to change society for the better.'

A typical Brahmo protagonist was Dwarkanath Ganguli, Upendrakisore Ray's father-in-law. Born in East Bengal in 1844, he fled his orthodox Hindu home in the 1860s and later founded a journal dedicated to exposing the sexual degradation of women known as 'Kulin Brahminism' – a pioneering expression of male sympathy for female values integral to his great-grandson Satyajit Ray's films. In the 1880s he became a champion of the rights of workers on the British-owned indigo plantations in Assam, where he defeated the sahibs in bare-fisted duels. Meanwhile, after the death of his first wife, he had married again – a student of the school he had founded in Calcutta half his age, the elegant and accomplished Miss Kadambini Bose. In 1882 she had become one of the two earliest women BAs in the British Empire (only three years after Oxford University's first woman BA), which she then capped by becoming the first fully qualified woman physician in India, completing her training in Edinburgh. It was Kadambini who delivered Satyajit and although he never knew her (she died when he was only two), he felt her influence through the profound effect she had on all the Ray women, including his mother.

Upendrakisore, born in 1863, was about the same age as Kadambini. Although his birthplace was in rural Masua, several days' journey from the missionaries, littérateurs and intellectuals in Calcutta, he soon felt the attraction of Brahmoism. His position was rather a peculiar one. The second of Munshi Syamsundar's five sons, he had been adopted at the age of five by a childless relative belonging to the orthodox wealthy branch of the Ray family. This relative, a zamindar and lawyer in Mymensingh, the headquarters of the area, apparently chose Upendrakisore from amongst the brothers because his skin was very fair – a quality still sought after in India today. He changed the boy's name from Kamadaranjan to Upendrakisore, after the style of his own, Harikisore, to which he added the honorific 'Ray Chaudhuri'.

Ironically, he had picked the brother probably least suited to his traditional Hindu outlook. Though not a fanatic, Harikisore was a scrupulous observer of caste taboos and ceremonies, like the zamindar in Ray's *The Goddess* which relates to this period, and President of the Mymensingh association for the upholding of Hindu practices in the face of Brahmo encroachments. He forbade his adopted son to meet a schoolfriend who was sympathetic to Brahmoism. So they met in secret, in some nearby woods with the notes of Upendrakisore's flute for signal.

A love of drawing and of music had made an early appearance in Upendrakisore. When the Governor of Bengal paid a visit to his school in Mymensingh some time in the 1870s, he spotted the boy drawing intently in class. Picking the book up he saw an excellent sketch of himself. The teachers were worried as to how the sahib would react. But he patted Upendrakisore on the back and told him, in English of course, 'You must not let this skill disappear. When you grow up you should follow this line.' In Ray's *Aparajito*, the young Apu in his country school guilelessly recites the poem '*Bangla Desh*' ('Land of Bengal') to a spellbound Bengali inspector. Although the circumstances differ greatly, the spirit of these scenes is similar.

Like Apu half a century later, Upendrakisore won a scholarship to study in Calcutta. Although in later life he paid frequent visits to Mymensingh, it appears he never lived there again after starting at Presidency College, the city's foremost academic institution. Not only was the cosmopolitan atmosphere of India's capital city more congenial to him than that of a zamindari, Harikisore had produced children of his own. Though Upendrakisore retained a share in the land at Mymensingh, he preferred drawing and singing in Calcutta. He began to practise classical Indian styles under the best teachers and to develop his love of Brahmo songs and hymns. Soon he was composing some of his own which were incorporated into the Brahmo repertoire. His singing and playing were much in request at meetings and social gatherings: a performance he gave at Jorasanko, the Tagore family mansion in north Calcutta, led to a lifelong friendship with Rabindranath.

In 1884 he graduated in the arts and the following year he married the daughter of Dwarkanath Ganguli by his first marriage, moving into the large family house at 13 Cornwallis Street in central Calcutta, opposite the main temple of the Brahmo Samaj. Though she was no match in intellect for her young stepmother Kadambini, Upendrakisore's wife was a remarkable woman in her own right who bore him three sons and three daughters. Sukumar, Satyajit's father, was the second child to arrive, born in 1887. The third was Punyalata, author of a vivid memoir of this period in the life of the Ray family – *Chelebelar Dinguli* (*Those Childhood Days*), published in 1957 with exquisite illustrations by her nephew Satyajit. She shows Upendrakisore constantly drawing and painting, or playing his violin or singing, either in performance or in class as the teacher of a great variety of pupils, including non-Indians. Listeners gathered in the street outside when he played, just as they did around him when he took his family to an exhibition or festival and explained things to his children. He was obviously the most affectionate of fathers, with an understanding of young children's minds which enabled him to write with great charm and simplicity for them. Some of his earliest Bengali writings were the *Mahabharata for Children* and the *Ramayana for Children*. His grandson Satyajit thrilled to them as a child in the 1920s and 30s; and as an adult, reading the full versions of these sprawling epics, he was astonished to find that his grandfather had managed to pack 'practically everything' from them into his abridgements.

Sukumar took after his father in very many ways. He was serious, lively and intensely curious, and a natural story-teller. He would show his brothers and sisters pictures of weird and wonderful animals from their father's storybooks and invent his own stories about them. He created his own creatures too, with untranslatable onomatopoeic names – forerunners of the verses and drawings which today are loved wherever Bengali is spoken.

He also dreamed up a novel way of relieving frustration through story-telling – 'Fake Anger', as he called it. Like his son Satyajit, Sukumar was famously even-tempered from early childhood on. If one of his friends felt angry with somebody but could not get back at him, Sukumar would say, 'All right, let's fake some anger!' Then he would begin spinning strange stories about his victim, with everyone else joining in. 'There was no hatred or malice in them,' recalls his sister in her memoir, 'we only imagined the person in a ridiculous situation. We had to think of all the possible ways of making that person look foolish and of all the embarrassing positions he could get into. It soon reduced you to stitches, and the peculiar thing was, that in the course of all this giggling the anger just evaporated, leaving one feeling light and happy.'

When Sukumar was about eight, a new element appeared in the lives of the Ray children which would later have a profound influence on Satyajit's life and films – a printing press. There were already advanced presses in Calcutta in the early 1890s but good quality printing of illustrations simply did not exist. Upendrakisore's illustrations for his *Ramayana for Children* had been ruined as a result. With just the help of technical books published in the West, Upendrakisore acquired the confidence to set himself up as Calcutta's first high-quality process engraver and went on to win international prizes for the quality of his reproduction. He began by ordering a camera and various pieces of half-tone equipment from Britain, which Punyalata remembers arriving by bullock-cart; soon after that, they moved out of 13 Cornwallis Street to a house not far away which Upendrakisore had made into a studio.

The money for this came from selling most of his share in the zamindari at Mymensingh to his foster brother Narendrakisore, who was in charge of it following his father Harikisore's death. Never much inclined towards his childhood milieu of orthodox religion and caste conventions, Upendrakisore had moved still further away from it while in Calcutta, no doubt accelerated by such incidents as a libellous attack on his father-in-law's wife Kadambini Ganguli in 1891 by the editor of a Hindu journal in Calcutta: as a liberated Brahmo woman she was accused of being a whore.

A few years after that the zamindari itself was the focus of trouble. Harikisore's widow, insulted by a Muslim peasant, demanded and was brought the peasant's head – an act of feudal vengeance of a type by no means unheard of in rural India at that time. The subsequent criminal case did much damage to her son Narendrakisore's finances and of course to his estate, which steadily declined like that of the doomed zamindar in Ray's *The Music Room*. The case became a celebrated scandal which the writer Nirad Chaudhuri remembers hearing about in his childhood in East Bengal at the turn of the century.

The printing firm of U. Ray was founded in 1895. Experimentation began immediately. Starting in 1897, Upendrakisore wrote a series of articles for the best-known British printing journal of the time, *Penrose Annual*, based on his researches. Their titles, though technical, are self-explanatory: 'Focussing the screen' (1897), 'The theory of the half-tone dot' (1898), 'The half-tone theory graphically explained' (1899), 'Automatic adjustment of the half-tone screen' (1901), 'Diffraction in half-tone' (1902–3), 'More about the half-tone theory' (1903–4), 'The 60° cross-line screen' (1905–6), 'Multiple stops' (1911–12).

U. Ray, working solo in distant Calcutta, had arrived on the printing scene at the beginning of a revolution in half-tone processes. The rational part of his mind was excited by the possibilities of applying the scientific theory governing the transmission of light as it was then understood, to a very inexact craft. Perhaps, too, the family tradition of scholarship in the subtleties of the ancient Sanskrit texts, with their conception of the dual nature of the universe, gave Upendrakisore insight in advance of the advent of the wave theory of light in the West in the 1920s. An article Upendrakisore wrote in 1903 shows his unusual perspective on the problem, besides demonstrating the clarity of his English prose.

One writer has said that the effect of diffraction is to make the half-tone dot *smaller* than it otherwise would be. Another has said it makes it *larger*. And this has very naturally provoked the remark that 'both can hardly be right'. Yet, strange as it may at first sound, both these contradictory statements are true. The writers in question looked at the subject from different points of view, and were thus, in each case rightly, led to opposite conclusions.

This particular article concludes with some remarks that bear a remarkable resemblance, both in attitude and style, to the unpretentious analyses which the writer's grandson began to write about the making of films more than half a century later. A multiplicity of techniques applied to an art are fine if you have the resources, both Rays make clear, but you cannot do without imagination.

The following year *Penrose Annual* carried no contribution from U. Ray. He had fallen seriously ill and been forced to give up work and retire to a health resort for some time. In his stead, the *Penrose* editor in London (noting that his readers would 'miss an article from the classical pen of Mr. U. Ray B.A.') summarised Upendrakisore's latest researches, and informed the trade that U. Ray had anticipated by some years the important screen just patented by someone in Britain. Unable to prove his theory in Calcutta for lack of resources, Upendrakisore had appealed to his printing colleagues in Britain for help and one of them had plagiarised his ideas. It is difficult to say how much Upendrakisore resented this in private, but his later articles in *Penrose Annual* do have a faintly bitter tang; he was obviously irritated by what he felt to be the sloppiness of most technical writing in the field and an intransigent refusal to give theory its due, coupled to some unscrupulousness. Both his son and his grandson would encounter similar behaviour, but each refused to let such overtones of imperial arrogance cloud their judgment of the West overall.

Like the majority of educated Bengalis Upendrakisore came into direct contact with the British relatively rarely, which minimised the potential for the kind of friction found in Forster's *A Passage to India*. Even when it was unavoidable, Upendrakisore seems to have been able to deflect it with irony somewhat as Satyajit has done in *The Chess Players*. Once, for instance, Upendrakisore was sharing a train compartment with some Englishmen. At a station one of them, a young man, commanded Upendrakisore, 'Call the biscuitwallah here!' Either because he had misheard or because he felt amused, Upendrakisore enquired: 'You want *pani* – water?' The youth became indignant and demanded – 'Are you deaf ? Why don't you listen? Don't you know that we have conquered your country!' 'Is it you who has conquered this country?' asked Upendrakisore mildly, 'Then you must be a very old man by now, though you look so young.' This made the older sahibs laugh and deflated the young man.

Such unfailing courtesy in real life and in his original works may have prompted Upendrakisore's interest in less benign stories, as a form of release. His first collection of retellings of Bengali folk-tales free from their dialect appeared in 1910 and has become a Bengali classic. Satyajit has translated a few of them into English, and someone else has published an edition in Britain. Stupid tigers, foolish weavers and Brahmins, and cunning jackals stalk their pages. Most of the endings, though not all, are notably cruel and there is much cynicism.

Tagore was an enthusiastic advocate of Upendrakisore's writing, encouraging him to translate and adapt stories from abroad as well as from Bengal and from the Indian legends. As a frequent visitor to the house Tagore came to regard Sukumar as one of his favourite young friends. Like everyone else, and especially Sukumar's five brothers and sisters, he fell for Sukumar's open-mindedness and brilliant wit; in later life Tagore apparently tried to outdo Sukumar's nonsense verse but gave up in admiration. His jokes could be reassuringly practical too. Once his sister Punyalata and two other children planted flowering shrubs in tubs. Theirs produced some beautiful blue flowers, but hers showed only white ones. Not long afterwards though, she was delighted to see that her plant had burst into multi-coloured bloom. It was only later that she noticed splashes of paint on the floor and realised that Sukumar had been up early with his brush. One wonders if he knew then of the famous scene in *Alice's Adventures in Wonderland*; the book later influenced him strongly.

At school both the teachers and his classmates liked Sukumar. He had an independent spirit without being rebellious. Once, when he was about thirteen, a master expatiated on the harmful effects of the bioscope – a favourite bugbear of Brahmo puritans, along with the theatre, alcohol and smoking – and then asked Sukumar for his opinion. He declared that among all the trashy pictures there were some good ones too. He also persuaded the master to go and see one with him (*Les Misérables*) – and made a convert: 'You have disabused me of a wrong notion. I had no idea there were such good bioscope pictures,' the master told him afterwards.

As a young man, Sukumar fully supported the movement that swept Bengal from about 1903 in reaction to Lord Curzon's proclaimed intention of partitioning the province (about which Tagore later wrote his novel *The Home and the World*, filmed by Ray). Although Sukumar, like his father and son, was never involved in active politics, he was a patriot. He had earlier snubbed his sister when she greeted a British victory in the Boer War with enthusiasm, by making the rhymed remark (here translated): 'When we ourselves are beat, can you laugh at another's defeat?' It was around this time that he composed his first songs, which were patriotic ones, and his first play, a comedy about a 'brown sahib', an imitation Englishman who gets his comeuppance. But he could also joke about the dreadful quality of the much-vaunted *swadeshi* (Indian-made) products of the time in a song which he called 'Swadeshi Fever'. He dubbed them 'awful-looking, less-lasting, expensive at the price'. Even so, he used them.

In 1906 Sukumar left Presidency College with Double Honours in Physics and Chemistry. His Nonsense Club began around this time. Its inspiration came from one person – Sukumar – but many of his family and friends took part in it. He wrote two plays for it, and produced a hand-written magazine, *Sare Batris Bhaja* – literally, *32½ Delicacies*, a street cry of Calcutta hawkers who sold thirty-two varieties of savoury and half a chilli. According to Punyalata, 'there was no sarcasm in it, only a spirit of pure, effortless wit.' One copy survives with Ray.

The first play *Jhalapala* (a nonsense title) is all word-play, the second, *Laksmaner Saktisel* (*Laksman and the Wonder Weapon*), is a spoof on the *Ramayana*. Funny excerpts from each, staged by Ray, appear in his 1987 documentary film *Sukumar Ray* (made for the centenary of his father's birth). As Ray puts it, 'Characters out of the *Ramayana* descend from the epic heights . . . Unpoetic matters easily find place here . . . Hanuman eats sugar-puffs, the Messenger of Death finds his salary in arrears.'

Sukumar began to make his mark as a critic in his early twenties. His first piece, 'Photography as an art', was based on considerable practical experience; he took photographs from his early teens, developed and printed them himself, and in 1922 became the second Indian to be made a Fellow of the Royal Photographic Society. Another article, which he sent from London two years later, discussed the Post-Impressionist exhibition organised by Roger Fry; and a third – in reply to a pompous art critic – showed that Sukumar could be caustic: 'O.C. Ganguly says that spirituality is the essence of Indian Art . . . Does he mean that if the eyes are half-closed, the figure is meditating and looks limp, then so much the better?'

Upendrakisore Ray never went to Britain, but in October 1911 his son took up a scholarship to study printing and photographic techniques in London, where Satyajit would go in 1950 to study graphic design. He was then twenty-four, a youthful energetic man of few prejudices, wide learning and even wider interests, high-spirited but perhaps a shade pampered by a doting mother and sisters, who was determined to learn as much about his chosen profession as he possibly could, before anything else. This singlemindedness was later shared by Satyajit, with his pursuit of films in London; neither father nor son had much time for conventional sight-seeing.

Sukumar inhabited two distinct worlds during his stay in Britain. One was that of a specialised craft, notoriously inward-looking, located first at the London School of Photo-engraving and Lithography just north of Fleet Street and then at the School of Technology in Manchester, the country's second city and in 1911 the hub of imperial commerce. The other was his social and artistic life – visiting galleries and museums, meeting artistic, literary and religious Englishmen with a sympathy for things Indian, but making only one lasting friendship amongst these new acquaintances. In June 1912 his circle became much wider with the arrival in London of his friend Tagore, then on his third, historic visit to London.

Two lucid articles in English written by Sukumar in this period epitomise these two worlds. It is quite hard to believe that the same person was responsible for both pieces. The first, 'Half-tone facts summarised', is typical of his father's style (and of his son's); it appeared in *Penrose Annual* along with a follow-up entitled 'Standardising the original'. The second, 'The spirit of Rabindranath Tagore', which could never have been written by Satyajit because of its philosophical bent, began life as a lecture and then appeared in a well-known religious journal of the day, the *Quest*. It was the first serious critique of Tagore by an Indian to be published in the West, about a year after W.B. Yeats's ecstatic introduction to Tagore's poems, and it remains today one of the most perceptive because of its writer's uniquely informed empathy with the subject. Besides insight into Tagore, it offers special insight into Sukumar's state of mind, of which there are only a few hints in his many letters home (apart from their tone, which is surprisingly serious for so humorous a man). In Britain Sukumar seems to have been undergoing an inner conflict, accentuated by a growing awareness of the power of imperialism that led to war within a year of his departure from Britain. In the article, too, is the outline of his future clash and disenchantment with the Brahmo Samaj, and even the beginnings of the frightening loss of faith in life that took hold of him seven years later. He shares Tagore's doubt whether organised religions have any answers to the really important questions, but suggests that Tagore himself may point the way:

> Where poetry is coextensive with life itself, where art ceases to be the mere expression of an imaginative impulse, it is futile to attempt a comprehensive analysis. Rabindranath's poetry is an echo of the infinite variety of life, of the triumph of love, of the supreme unity of existence, of the joy that abides at the heart of all things. The whole development of his poetry is a sustained glorification of love.

Sukumar left Britain with Tagore in September 1913, two months before the news of Tagore's Nobel Prize came through. In December he married Suprabha Das, a beautiful girl from a well-known musical Brahmo family whom he had met before his trip to Britain, and soon settled down in the new house-cum-printing press that Upendrakisore had begun building in north Calcutta at 100 Garpar Road during his son's absence abroad. He had also started the magazine for young people which his grandson now edits – *Sandesh*, which means both 'Sweetmeat' and 'Information'. The first issue appeared in May 1913 and included some illustrations by Sukumar – his first to be published – sent from Britain. Upendrakisore published it until his death in December 1915. He was its chief contributor and illustrator; stories, articles, drawings and paintings, riddles and poems streamed from his pen, pencil and brushes. *Sandesh* was the culmination of a quarter of a century's imaginative affection for young people. No doubt it also – along with his violin-playing – helped to take Upendrakisore's mind off his worsening diabetic condition, which appears to have been aggravated by the disruption of drugs from Europe caused by the First World War. In the *Penrose Annual* obituary, delayed because of the war, Upendrakisore is described with moving simplicity as 'an Indian gentleman of remarkable scientific gifts, who probed deeply into the mysteries of half-tone.' To his grandson Satyajit, who is much averse to hyperbole, he has always been an inspiration.

My grandfather was a rare combination of East and West. He played the *pakhwaj* as well as the violin; wrote devotional songs while carrying out research on printing methods; viewed the stars through a telescope from his own roof; wrote old legends and folk-tales anew for children in his inimitably lucid and graceful style and illustrated them in oils, water-colours and pen-and-ink, using truly European techniques. His skill and versatility as an illustrator remain unmatched by any Indian.

His son Sukumar's achievement was not so much his drawings, brilliant though the fantasy ones are, as the creation of a nonsense world unique in Bengali literature. Satyajit still marvels at its originality, while weaving a fantasy world of his own. His father's came into being between 1914 and his premature death in 1923. In some ways it is reminiscent of Carroll's and Lear's – and there is no doubt that he was by then fully aware of Carroll, if not so much of Lear – but, as Ray has pointed out, Sukumar's creatures are not pure fantasies but generally half-known to us, both in the language they speak and in their appearance. They also usually impinge on ordinary human beings, unlike many of Lear's creatures. Much of his humour is also rooted in Bengali behaviour, which means it does not always travel well. In translating Carroll and Lear for *Sandesh*, Ray has invented Bengali 'equivalents' to keep them funny. But whatever the limitations of translation, no non-Bengali speaker can look at the Stortle, the Whalephant or the Porcuduck (to use their paler English names) and miss the fertility of Sukumar's imagination, even if its full flavour eludes him. Some of the most charming of Sukumar's whimsies, they are also some of his earliest, being first spotted in *Sandesh* in 1914. The poem in which they appear is called '*Khichuri*' ('Hotch-potch'). Here it is in Satyajit Ray's 'translation':

> *A duck once met a porcupine; they formed a corporation*
> *Which called itself a Porcuduck (a beastly conjugation!).*

A stork to a turtle said, 'let's put my head upon your torso;
We who are so pretty now, as Stortle would be more so!'
The lizard with the parrot's head thought: Taking to the chilli
After years of eating worms is absolutely silly.
A prancing goat – one wonders why – was driven by a need
To bequeath its upper portion to a crawling centipede.
The giraffe with grasshopper's limbs reflected: Why should I
Go for walks in grassy fields, now that I can fly?
The nice contented cow will doubtless get a frightful shock
On finding that its lower limbs belong to a fighting cock.
It's obvious the Whalephant is not a happy notion:
The head goes for the jungle, while the tail turns to the ocean.
The lion's lack of horns distressed him greatly, so
He teamed up with a deer – now watch his antlers grow!

Some verses must surely have been provoked – at least in part – by the solemnity of Brahmos who surrounded Sukumar in the Samaj. Others are keenly satirical. We can guess that Sukumar is mocking those Bengalis obsessed with using *swadeshi* products instead of foreign ones, those who pigeon-hole life in dogmas, and those who distrust the scientific attitude towards medicine as foreign-inspired. Some of his satires are still acutely topical: one pokes fun at the snobbery and money-mindedness of arranged marriages; another has a go at the timid, office-bound mentality of the Bengali clerk (the Babu Kipling mercilessly lampooned), who believes that his moustache – an important symbol of his status – has been stolen while he was dozing. The mirror that his cringing subordinates are holding up to his face only infuriates him the more. Here are the last three verses in Satyajit's 'translation':

'Know this – in the near future
I ought to – no, I must reduce your wages.'
This he did. And then at random
He composed a memorandum.
Herewith quoted (minus appendages):

'If you think your employees
Deserve your love – correction please:
They don't. They're fools. No common sense.
They're full of crass incompetence.
The ones in my establishment,
Deserve the highest punishment.

'They show their cheek in not believing
Whiskers lend themselves to thieving.
Their moustaches, I predict,
Will soon be mercilessly picked:

And when that happens they will know
What Man is to Moustachio:
Man is slave, Moustache is master,
Losing which Man meets disaster.'

Finally, an example of pure nonsense, is the chant written by Sukumar for a king in one of his plays. Ray, in *The Philosopher's Stone*, puts some of this chant in the mouth of the *nouveau riche* clerk played hilariously by Tulsi Chakravarti; it is supposed to be a secret Sanskrit formula for the stone that turneth all to gold. This is Sukanta Chaudhuri's 'translation':

A green and gold orang-outang,
Rocks and stones that jolt and bang,
A smelly skunk and izzy-tizzy,
No admission, very busy.
Ghost and ghoul, do re mi fa
And half a loaf is better far.
Coughs and colds and peanut plants,
Pussies are the tiger's aunts,
Trouble-shooters, blotted blobs,
City centre vacant jobs.

The nuclei of some of these verses, plays and stories, may have formed at the new club that Sukumar Ray started in 1915 as a successor to his Nonsense Club. Called the Monday Club after the day it met, it soon became known as the Manda Club, for its tendency to indulge in feasts (*'manda'* meaning roughly 'sticky sweet'). It also discussed serious subjects as diverse as the jute industry, Swami Vivekananda, Bengali dialects, Strindberg, Turgenev and Plato, and its members included some of the best and brightest of young Bengal. A note from the Third Annual Meeting of the Club indicates that it could poke fun at itself too: 'Datta Das Babu to move that "In the interests of plain living, high thinking, tea and biscuits" . . .'

The Club also served to bring together a group of like-minded young Brahmos with a passion to reform the Sadharan Brahmo Samaj. They shared a feeling that the Samaj had become puritanical and more concerned with in-fighting than social reform. The burning issue had come to be whether or not Tagore was fit to be an honorary member, given his view that Brahmos were Unitarian Hindus. 'I cannot separate Brahmoism from inner Hinduism,' he had said. This had deeply upset many Brahmos who regarded themselves as neither Christians nor Hindus but as a kind of separate caste. Not only that, Tagore was opposed to the missionary efforts of the Samaj, and was said to favour the subordination of women, to the extent of marrying off his daughter below the age acceptable to Brahmos; he had also written love songs and the novel *Gora*, which was a frontal assault on Brahmo dogmatism. Worst of all, he had made it clear that he had no real

desire to be part of *any* group, whatever its beliefs. Despite the fact that the
Samaj hymnbook contained a very large number of Tagore's songs, many
Brahmos chose to regard him as a somewhat frivolous person, especially
in comparison with his saintly father, Maharsi Devendranath Tagore, the
leader of the Samaj in the nineteenth century.

It is this background of rancour and factionalism that helps to explain
an extraordinary letter written by Sukumar to a friend in the Samaj. In
it he explained that while at a meeting making a speech in memory of a
well-known Brahmo, he had suddenly lost control of his words and found
himself making a very pessimistic speech in complete contradiction to all
that he believed. He had come to the conviction that it was a premonition of
his own death. (The word 'death' is in English and underlined.) He therefore
wanted to withdraw from the Samaj and its squabbles with immediate effect,
to concentrate on his own life in whatever time still remained to him. In
early 1921, six months after writing this letter, he contracted the virulent
malarial disease kala-azar; within three years he was dead, at the age of
only thirty-five.

This psychic experience of Sukumar's, together with others, has
deeply affected his son Satyajit, though he was not born at the time of
the premonition. For many years it was regarded as a family secret. 'This
is something you have to believe,' he says, 'you can't help it.' Thinking
of his great-great-grandfather Loknath he adds 'There's probably some
streak of mysticism or spiritualism in our blood. This whole business of
creation, of the ideas that come in a flash, cannot be explained by science.
It cannot. I don't know what can explain it but I know that the best ideas
come at moments when you're not even thinking of it. It's a very private
thing really.'

Whatever psychological speculation one might indulge to explain
Sukumar's strange experience, he certainly adhered to his resolution and
abandoned his very active role in the Samaj. To all the bitterness and doubt
of that period he responded characteristically – with humour. A friend who
stayed with Sukumar for a week in a sanitorium in Darjeeling during May
1921 – the month Satyajit was born in Calcutta – recalled that neither
of them discussed the controversy; instead, Sukumar read out his latest
poems from *Abol Tabol*, the collection he began publishing in *Sandesh*
in 1914 and which has since become his best-known work. Its preface
contains a typical note of warning to those around Sukumar: 'This book
was conceived in the spirit of whimsy. It is not meant for those who do
not enjoy that spirit.'

'As far as my father's writing and drawing goes, nearly all his
best work belongs to his last two and a half years,' Satyajit thinks
– that is, after he contracted kala-azar. It includes *Ha-Ja-Ba-Ra-La*, a
story with some obvious similarities to *Alice's Adventures in Wonderland*
but infused with Sukumar's own spirit; *Hesoram Husiar's Diary*, a sort of
parody of Conan Doyle's *The Lost World* introducing prehistoric animals

that, says Ray, 'only Sukumar knows about, and only he could have named, in matchless compounds of Latin and Bengali'; and an unfinished attempt to introduce each letter of the Bengali alphabet through long poems using traditional alliterative techniques. He also wrote a history of the Brahmo Samaj for children in the form of a long poem, of which the last few lines are surprisingly pessimistic, considering its readership. 'Obviously the feeling was so strong that he couldn't avoid expressing it,' says Satyajit.

Although he was very ill, and mostly bedridden, Sukumar Ray worked until the very last days of his life; it appears that the disease allowed him periods of lucidity when he could compose, followed by relapses. 'The dummy for *Abol Tabol* was laid out by him,' says Satyajit. 'He was composing little tailpieces where there was room left at the bottom: filling them up with two-liners and four-liners. That was done straight into the dummy itself. That's the only place where you can find these tailpieces.'

In fact he never saw the finished book; it was published by U. Ray and Sons nine days after his death on 10 September 1923. The last poem in it, 'Abol Tabol' itself, was Sukumar's last composition. Here are the first four lines and the last four, in Sukanta Chaudhuri's 'translation':

> *On hazy nights, among the clouds,*
> *Through moonlit veils and rainbow shroud*
> *With crazy rhyme and puckish note*
> *I sing my song with open throat . . .*
> *. . . A keen primordial lunar chill,*
> *The nightmare's nest with bunchy frill –*
> *My drowsy brain such glimpses steep,*
> *And all my singing ends in sleep.*

'I do not know of any other humourist,' his son has written, 'who could jest in this spirit at the meeting-point of life and death.' Tagore, who used to ask Sukumar and his wife to sing his songs privately for him soon after he had composed them, sang some himself at Sukumar's request beside his bed not long before he died. When the news reached him that Sukumar was gone, Tagore said: 'I have seen a great deal of Death, but I have seldom seen such a youthful figure, with such a short span of life behind him, stand before Death and offer so much to the Divine Spirit and with such dedication. At the gate of Death itself he sang a song of praise for eternal life. As I sat beside his death-bed he filled my soul with the note of that music.'

2

Early Years
1921–40

‑‑❦【❦❧❦】❦‑‑

You can never tell in advance which incidents in your childhood
will stick in the mind and which will be wiped away for ever. To
stick or not to stick; these things obey no rule. That is the mystery
of memory. When I was five, I left my birthplace at Garpar Road
for ever and went to Bhowanipur. The day we actually moved from
the old house to the new is gone beyond recall, but I have a distinct
recollection, even today, of a very ordinary dream I had there about
the son of our cook called Haren.

S O BEGINS Ray's introduction to his short memoir of his childhood
Jakhan Choto Chilam (*When I Was Small*), which he originally wrote
in 1981 for *Sandesh* and later revised and published as a small book with his
own pint-sized drawings. Like his aunt Punyalata's memoir *Those Childhood
Days*, which inspired him, Ray's book is a gallery of sketches of family,
friends and teachers, for the most part affectionately drawn, interwoven
with his childish preoccupations – stories and games, magic and magic
lanterns, circuses and cinema – against a serene Calcutta backdrop, and
interspersed with regular visits to Lucknow and Darjeeling, and other
places, to stay with his relatives who had spread over Bengal, and into
neighbouring Bihar and Uttar Pradesh. The book's vision is deliberately
that of a boy growing up but, like the films and stories Ray has created
for children, it can hold an adult reader too.

Satyajit has only one memory of his father Sukumar, who died when
he was about two and a half. It belongs to the courtyard of a house on
the banks of the Ganges outside Calcutta, where the family had gone for
the sake of Sukumar's health. His father is sitting indoors by the window
painting. He suddenly calls out 'Ship coming!' His son remembers running
into the courtyard and seeing a steamer pass by with a loud hoot. As a sort
of private tribute to this memory, the painting Sukumar was then at work
on appears in Satyajit's documentary on his father.

His main memories of those earliest years revolve around his grandfather's
house-cum-press, U. Ray and Sons at 100 Garpar Road, and the relatives

1   Five brothers of Ray family, *c.* 1913: Saradaranjan (with beard), Pramadaranjan,
Upendrakisore (Kamadaranjan), Muktidaranjan, Kuladaranjan ('Dhondadu') (*Ray family*)

2   Dwarkanath Ganguli (*Ray family*)

3   Dr Kadambini Ganguli (*Ray family*)

4   Upendrakisore Ray
(*Ray family*)

5   Sukumar Ray
(*Ray family*)

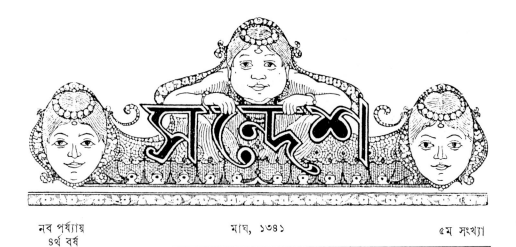

নব পর্য্যায়
৬র্থ বর্ষ

মাঘ, ১৩৪১

৫ম সংখ্যা

6 *Sandesh*: illustrations by Upendrakisore Ray for (a) mast-head, (b) *Ramayana for Children*, (c) 'Dance of the Ghosts' from *Goopy Gyne Bagha Byne*

(b)

(c)

(a)

7 Illustrations by Sukumar Ray: (a) 'Hotch-potch', (b) 'The Missing Whiskers', (c) 'Tagore Worship in Lilliput'

(b)

(c)

(a)

(b)

(c)

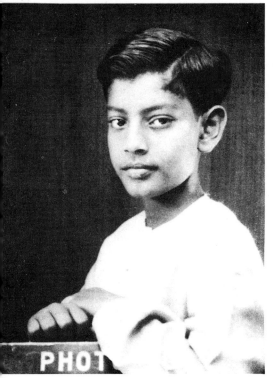

8 Satyajit: (a) aged two, before his father's
death, (b) with cousin, (c) in 1932 (*Ray family*)

9 Subimal Ray ('Chotokaka') (*Ray family*)

10   Illustrations from *When I Was Small* by Satyajit
Ray, including house at 100 Garpar Road

11 Bijoya and Satyajit Ray,
London, 1950 (*Norman Clare*)

12 Ray family, *c*. 1957: Suprabha, Sandip, Satyajit, Bijoya (A. *Huq*)

13   One of a series of advertisements by Ray, *c.* 1949

14   Cover design by Ray for *Sandesh*, 1978

15   Cover design by Ray for *Eksan*, quarterly magazine, 1978

who occupied it. It stood in a peaceful road in north Calcutta with a deaf
and dumb school on one side, a private school on the other which was no
doubt typical of the crammers that Tagore tells us he spent his childhood
years trying to escape in the 1860s and 70s. In the heat of midday, when
Calcutta traffic of all kinds came to a stop, Satyajit would hear the chant
of multiplication tables, of reading out loud and, sometimes, the shouts of
angry masters.

There were three storeys and a fine flat roof, which Upendrakisore
had used for his astronomy. The printing machinery was housed at the
front of the building on the ground floor and directly above that were the
block-making and typesetting rooms. The Ray family lived at the back on
all three floors. To reach them, a visitor entered a small lane to one side
of the house. A door gave on to stairs to the right which led to the family
apartments; those turning left were on press business.

Satyajit was fascinated from the beginning by the whole paraphernalia
of printing, particularly as one of its end products was *Sandesh* with
its three-colour cover. He became a frequent visitor to the first floor.
As he entered, the compositors, sitting side by side in front of their
multi-sectioned typecases, would glance up at him and smile. He would
make his way past them to the back of the room – to the block-making
section with its enormous imported process camera, and its distinctive
smells. 'Even today,' says Ray, 'if I catch a whiff of turpentine, a picture
of U. Ray and Sons' block-making department floats before my eyes.' The
main operator of the camera, Ramdohin, was his friend. He had had no
formal education; Upendrakisore had trained him from scratch and he
was like one of the family. Presenting Ramdohin with a piece of paper
with some squiggles on it, Satyajit would announce: 'This is for *Sandesh*.'
Ramdohin would solemnly wag his head in agreement, 'Of course, Khoka
Babu, of course' and lift Satyajit up to show him the upside-down image
of his drawing in the screen of the camera. But somehow it would never
appear in *Sandesh*.

Satyajit and *Sandesh* were mixed up in two other ways. With his widowed
grandmother he spent hours sorting out and cleaning old picture blocks in
her room on the first floor. And with his uncle Subinay, Sukumar's younger
brother who managed the press after his death, he would discuss *Sandesh*'s
paper requirements. Books of paper samples, sent from Germany, lay in his
uncle's room on the second floor. They had a wonderful range of textures.
His uncle would hand him one and say: 'Take a look inside. Which ones
shall we order?' Running his hand over them like an expert, Satyajit would
tender his advice. 'I really imagined the ones I had chosen would be sent
from Germany.' He is saddened by the look of today's *Sandesh* (which he
revived in 1961); good paper is now unobtainable in Calcutta at a price
the magazine can afford.

He and his mother Suprabha lived in a room on the first floor, below
his uncle Subinay. Besides a hazy recollection of English lessons there

with an aunt, Satyajit recalls his mother reading Conan Doyle stories to him in English, translating them into Bengali as she went along. Two of his horror stories were favourites.

What he has completely forgotten are the early visits of his girl cousin, Kalyani, 'Ruby', the elder daughter of Punyalata, who used to help Suprabha by bathing her little boy while she coped with her invalid husband. Full of affection for him, and a sense of fun too, Ruby liked to offer her charge some *pan* to chew and then ask him for a kiss; the blood-red juice would leave a small mark on her face. Today she says that Satyajit was really 'coddled' and 'adored' as a child, though not spoilt; to begin with because his parents had wanted a child for a long time, afterwards to make up for his lack of a father. A jewel had been born, and the baby soon became 'Manik' – meaning 'jewel' – the name by which Ray's family, friends and co-workers know him (or 'Manikda', if they prefer to add the formal Indian suffix).

The person Ray himself remembers best from this period is undoubtedly the occupant of the ground-floor rooms below his own: his grandfather's younger brother Kuladaranjan – 'Dhondadu' to Manik. It is obvious why from the way Ray describes him in his memoir:

> Dhondadu threw the hammer, he enlarged photographs of those who had died, he introduced me to the ancient stories, and, at one time, he played cricket. As Captain of the Bengali team at the Town Club he had once, in a match against the European team, been stuck at ninety-nine runs right through the match, and then at the end scored a century. I heard the story of how he pulled this off many times from him.

His craft – photographic enlargement – must have been enthralling for a young child. As soon as an acquaintance of Kuladaranjan's died, someone from that household would appear at Garpar Road and place an order. The original would very likely be a small, slightly fuzzy face in a large group, but by the time Dhondadu had finished it felt like the deceased person was actually looking out from the frame. Relatives would now come, the picture would be set upright on a table and unwrapped, and they would gaze at it and wipe their eyes. This was a scene Ray often saw in his childhood; in fact his mother wept before a portrait of Sukumar on the first anniversary of his death and so did the three-and-a-half-year-old Manik (though he does not remember this). Very early on he learnt to treat death as part of life.

He liked to watch the entire process of transformation in his grand-uncle's room. Placing an enlarged photograph on an easel Dhondadu would press a pair of bellows with his foot and spray the photograph with a nozzle held in his hand. The colour used was mainly black or dark brown, but once he finished a photograph of the deceased Maharaja of Natore in green for the background vegetation and red for the drapes of his Kashmir shawl, while the new Maharaja and Manik stood watching.

Upstairs, on the first floor, were stored the storybooks written by Kuladaranjan and published by U. Ray and Sons. He retold the *Iliad* and the *Odyssey* in Bengali, and a great many Indian legends and folk-tales; he also corresponded with Conan Doyle's widow and obtained the rights to translate his works into Bengali gratis.

Where Dhondadu's many activities were purposeful and productive, the eccentricities of Satyajit's youngest uncle – 'Chotokaka' – were pointless but beguiling; they remind one of some of the characters in the films Ray has made for children. 'I doubt if there has ever been anyone at all like him', Ray reckons. He lived first at Garpar Road, in a room on the second floor, later, away from Satyajit (though he regularly visited him) and later still, in Ray's own ménage with Satyajit's mother, wife and son until his death in 1973.

Chotokaka was a master at the City College School all his life and never married. In fact he had something about him of the sannyasis he used to visit for enlightenment – he was introverted and content with very little. Perhaps that is what helped to draw him and Manik together; an unusual degree of self-sufficiency and an indifference to luxury have been marked characteristics of Ray from the very beginning.

Apart from retelling his eccentric dreams (which were reminiscent of the nonsense world of his elder brother Sukumar), dubbing members of the family with incomprehensible names which everyone was expected to understand, and chewing his food thirty-two times like Gladstone which made his meals an hour longer than anyone else's, Chotokaka also kept a diary which intrigued Manik. He began each entry with important head-lines from the day's papers and carried on with an almost hourly account of what he did, what he read, what he ate, where he went and what he saw. Any train journey Chotokaka undertook meant recording precise details of the engine types. Everything was noted in his diary in one of four colours – red, green, blue and black. Manik never understood Chotokaka's code properly but he realised that descriptions of nature were in green, nouns were in red and the rest was in black or blue.

Oddest of all in Manik's eyes was Chotokaka's sudden urge to learn judo, that came when Manik was about thirteen. Until then Chotokaka had been wholly unathletic, but he was quite serious about going through with it and so – to Manik's surprise – was Takagaki, an expert brought over from Japan by Tagore after his visit there. Uncle and nephew stuck at the lessons for quite a while (though Ray now remembers only a couple of the holds), and watched spellbound as Takagaki fought Captain Hughes, the light-weight boxing champion of Calcutta who came regularly to refresh his judo skills.

But all this took place long after Satyajit had left Garpar Road. Besides all the adult company he had there, Manik had a couple of playmates nearer his own age: Haren, son of the family cook (who appears in the dream Ray still recalls), and Chedi, son of the family maid. Chedi was very good with his hands, and together they made a number of absorbing things such as kite strings coated in powdered glass, nail bangers and curd-pot lanterns: skills that Ray would later put to use to make props for his films.

Beyond Garpar Road and Dhondadu, there were the other three grand-uncles, a grand-aunt, and their families. The first two were fine cricketers; in fact the eldest, Saradaranjan Ray, has a place in the history of cricket in India so outstanding that the British dubbed him the 'W.G. of India', after his similarly bearded contemporary W.G. Grace. He was also a Sanskrit scholar and mathematician. The youngest was another fine cricketer, but he was constantly away from the pitch on the borders of Assam and Burma as an officer in the Survey of India. Like many of his generation he was a firm believer in building up the Indian physique (an obsession that Ray would later gently lampoon in his films and stories) and curbing any sign of effeminacy in a man: he even disapproved of Tagore's shoulder-length hair. When Satyajit was in his early teens he was compelled to exercise under this grand-uncle's command, along with his cousins.

Upendrakisore's sister married a remarkable man, Hemendranath Bose, who died before Satyajit was born. He was probably best-known as a perfumer; the jingle for his company was a familiar advertisement in Calcutta newspapers in Satyajit's childhood (here translated):

> Dab Kuntolin on your hair.
> On your hanky sprinkle Delkhosh.
> In your pan try Tambulin.
> That will gratify H. Bose.

But he was also a pioneer of the bicycle in India, one of the first people in Calcutta to own a motor car, and the first to make phonogram recordings, in collaboration with a French company. The atmosphere in the family house, which Manik often visited, was infused with his own love of fun and pleasure. His fourteen children included, in due course, a famous singer, a painter and connoisseur of music, a film sound recordist, four cricketers (one of whom was *the* name of his time), and a well-known film director Nitin Bose, who would later tell Satyajit he should take up art direction and forget directing. (When *Pather Panchali* finally got made, so moved was this uncle that he went to see it over and over again.)

H. Bose was a Brahmo, and so were Kuladaranjan and the brother in the Survey of India, like Upendrakisore; while Saradaranjan and the youngest brother remained Hindus. 'When you went to their houses,' recalls Ray, 'you saw *sindur* [vermilion] on the parting of their wives' hair, saris worn in a different fashion, and amulets on the arms of the men. From the prayer room would come the sounds of conch and bells, and my aunts and grand-aunts would come out with *prasad* [shrine offerings] and make us finish eating it.' But, in spite of such differences, the Brahmo part of the family did not feel different from the Hindu: 'the friendliest of friendly relations existed', says Ray.

Almost the only serious complaint he has against his first fifteen years or so concerns Brahmoism (which by the 1930s had become thoroughly mixed up with socialism and Marxism). As a five-year-old he was obliged to sit for long periods listening to sermons, readings and songs. Some of the songs (which included his grandfather's), if well sung by someone like his mother, he liked very much; but sermons were a chore, particularly as they meant getting up at four in the morning, bathing in cold water and a long bus-ride to reach the Samaj temple in time for the early rituals. His mother insisted on this. Satyajit continued to attend until he was in his late teens, when she accepted his decision to abandon it; no doubt if Sukumar had been alive, he would have encouraged a more sympathetic approach. Today, when asked what his Brahmo background means to him Satyajit replies instantly 'Nothing', and then checks himself.

Well I don't know. I'm myself because of my upbringing I am sure, but I've had to make a great many films about Hindu families believing in Hindu orthodoxy, and therefore the intellectual interest in Hinduism persists. As material for a film I feel Hinduism is much more interesting than Brahmoism. As a child I found Hinduism much more exciting than Brahmoism, and Christianity too. When I think of Brahmoism I think of solemn sermons mainly. I don't think of being free from the shackles of orthodoxy.

Perhaps partly as a reward for having to endure Brahmo rituals, Christmas and Christmas presents were part of Satyajit's childhood. While he was living at Garpar Road his mother took him to the largest department store in Calcutta, Whiteaway Laidlaw (which closed down soon after Independence), a floor of which was done up splendidly at Christmas, mainly for the benefit of the European population. There Manik first rode in a lift and met Father Christmas, and his mother bought him an affordable box of crackers. He got to like Christmas so much that a few years after this, he persuaded an elder cousin to play Father Christmas for him in June.

It was an upbringing lavish in affection, but once Sukumar fell ill his wife and son were in difficult circumstances. Things became much worse after the collapse of U. Ray and Sons in 1926 and the folding of *Sandesh* which, except for a brief revival in 1931, was not published again until 1961. It appears that this collapse was the result of impracticality on the part of Sukumar's brother Subinay who had been managing it, combined with disloyalty by some of the staff Upendrakisore had trained. No one now quite knows. Sound business planning was never one of the priorities of Upendrakisore and his direct descendants, though each has demonstrated an ability to combine quality with commercial viability. In the case of Satyajit, he is simply not interested in business for its own sake.

The firm was finally wound up in January 1927 and the family house

built by Upendrakisore passed into the hands of the more reasonable of
the creditors. The family itself had no option but to separate and at the
end of 1926 Manik was taken by his mother to live with her brothers in
south Calcutta. He did not visit Garpar Road again for nearly forty years.
His mother, though, had to take a daily bus-ride to the area where she used
to live, where now she taught sewing at a school for widows. At a time when
few respectable women worked for a living, she was determined to bring up
her only child without living off her family. The only other financial help she
received was a small monthly sum for Satyajit's education, as part of the
conditions of liquidation of U. Ray and Sons. The adult Ray remembers
many meetings between his mother and lawyers, but she never went into
details with him – then or later.

Although the move to up-and-coming Bhowanipur away from the
heart of the older part of the city was a drastic change, Satyajit did
not feel it as a wrench. 'Adults treat all children in such a situation as
"poor little creatures", but that is not how children see themselves', he
comments in his memoir, articulating his fundamental attitude as perhaps
the most natural director of children in cinema.

Nevertheless, whether he thought of it or not, he was now thrown
back on his own resources. There were no Dhondadus and Chotokakas in
the house in Bhowanipur, and his mother was often away at work. He had
been taken from a world of writers, artists and musicians, where West mixed
freely and fruitfully with East, science with arts, to a typically middle-class
milieu of barristers and insurance brokers, with the exception of an aunt
about to become a famous singer of Tagore songs and, after her father's
death in 1931, a 'cousin' Bijoya, Satyajit's future wife, who was musical
and interested in acting. Most of the people who surrounded Satyajit now,
though not politically active, were emotionally caught up in politics in a
way not true of Sukumar Ray or his relatives. During an early phase of
Gandhian non-cooperation, for instance, the whole household, led by the
driver of their car, caught the craze for spinning – even Satyajit, who in
later life would share Tagore's scepticism about Gandhi's fads. Then, too,
there was a vast Swadeshi Mela (or 'Home-produced Festival') in south
Calcutta which included working wax models (made in Bombay) of the
nationalist leaders – Gandhi on the floor of his jail cell writing, Mother
India holding in her arms the corpse of C.R. Das, one of the most important
Bengali nationalists (and an uncle by marriage of Satyajit's future wife): she
would look at the body, close her eyes, and then shake her head sorrowfully,
over and over again.

But there were no children of Satyajit's age in his uncles' house.
Though he often saw his cousin Ruby (who used to bathe him) and
her younger sister Nini (who now edits Sandesh with him), they were
older than him and he seldom spoke about himself with them. Yet today
he does not think of his childhood as lonely. 'Loneliness and being alone
– bereft of boys and girls of your own age as friends – is not the same

thing. I wasn't envious of little boys with lots of sisters and brothers. I felt I was all right and I had a lot to do. I could keep myself busy doing various things, small things – reading, looking at books and looking at pictures, all sorts of things including sketching. I used to draw a lot as a child.' Like many only children, he was also a close observer of his elders, and noticed that his uncles and their friends in their twenties and thirties did not always behave as if they *were* elders; they had a noisy passion for games like ludo, for instance. He says that he must have been 'imbibing' a great deal about people at this time without being aware of it. Certainly, the twenty years he spent with his maternal uncles gave him an invaluable grounding in the mores of the Bengali middle class, both as characters for films and as an audience.

Like the lonely wife Charu, wandering round her house in the first seven minutes of *Charulata*, Satyajit was highly sensitive as a child to sounds and lighting. Half a century later, he can remember various vanished street cries and the fact that in those days you could spot the make of a car from inside the house by the sound of its horn. He remembers Fords, Chevs, Vauxhalls, Humbers, Wolseleys, Dodges, Buicks, Austins, Studebakers, Morrises, Oldsmobiles and Opal Citroëns. Now they are all extinct in Calcutta, he notes sadly. 'Once in a blue moon one catches sight of a Baby Austin. But that huge Lancia and the La Salle with the snake-mouthed "Boa Horn"? They can only be seen in dreams.' Gone too is the Lancia belonging to the husband of one of his Bhowanipur aunts. It had a glass cricket perched on its bonnet which glowed pink as the car cruised along.

Small holes in the fabric of his uncles' house taught Satyajit some basic principles of light. At noon in summer rays of bright sunlight got in through a chink in the shutters of the bedroom. Satyajit would lie there alone watching the 'free bioscope' created on the wall: a large inverted image of the traffic outside. He could clearly make out cars, rickshaws, bicycles, pedestrians and other things. A small hole in the main door of the house showed similar properties, if not so dramatically.

His favourite reading at this time were the ten copiously illustrated, self-confidently imperial volumes of the *Book of Knowledge* and later, the *Romance of Famous Lives* which his mother bought him; there he first encountered Beethoven, and developed an adolescent taste for western painting from the Renaissance up to the beginning of Impressionism. He also read comics and detective stories, the *Boy's Own Paper* (in which he won a prize for a photograph of Kashmir when he was fifteen), Sherlock Holmes and P.G. Wodehouse, (and came to believe that London was 'perpetually shrouded in impenetrable fog' and that most homes in England had butlers). Throughout his early years, and to a great extent in his adult life too, his taste in English fiction has been light; he has read comparatively few classics.

His interest in Bengali fiction was still less developed, until his early twenties. Instead, he was well read in the ancient stories and in folk-tales, thanks to Upendrakisore and Kuladaranjan and other family story-tellers, and books like Abanindranath Tagore's *Raj Kahini* – a collection of stories of Rajput chivalry based on Colonel James Tod's classic *Annals and Antiquities of Rajasthan*. (Satyajit later illustrated this himself and made two films in Rajasthan.) While Manik was living in Bhowanipur, Dhondadu used to visit him regularly and read aloud a chapter of Upendrakisore's version of the *Mahabharata* each time. There was one particular grisly episode involving severed and exploding heads that Manik made his grand-uncle tell him at least four times.

A performance by a Bengali magician at a wedding at his uncles' house, led to a passion for magic which lasted until he went to college, and which from time to time appears in his films and stories. He had already seen some first-rate stage performances by European magicians visiting Calcutta, but this magician was really startling. One of his many tricks which remain totally inexplicable to Ray to this day, involved giving a pack of cards to one member of the audience and borrowing a stick from another. He then pointed at the pack with the stick and called, 'Out, Ace of Spades!' The Ace slipped swiftly out and sat fluttering on the tip of the stick. A few days later, Manik encountered the magician near his house. Dressed in a shirt and dhoti he looked very ordinary indeed. But Manik already saw himself as this man's disciple. 'Certainly,' the magician said, taking a pack of cards from his pocket, and there and then he taught him a very simple trick. Manik never set eyes on the man again; so thrilled had he been to meet him, he had forgotten to take his address.

Stereoscopes and magic lanterns were popular toys in Bengali homes of the period. The magic lantern was a box with a tube at the front containing a lens, a chimney on top and a handle at the right-hand side. The film ran on two reels with a kerosene lamp for light source. 'Who knows?' writes Satyajit in his memoir. 'Perhaps this was the beginning of my addiction to film?' Visits to the cinema began while Satyajit was still at Garpar Road and continued when he moved to his uncles' house. Until he was about fifteen, when Satyajit took control of the visits, they were comparatively infrequent and each film would be followed by 'weeks of musing on its wonders.' Although his uncles enjoyed going, they did not altogether approve of cinema and for many years they limited him to certain foreign films and ruled out Bengali productions as being excessively passionate for the young mind. This suited him well enough, as he disliked the only Bengali film he saw as a boy. He went to it by accident: an uncle had taken him to see the first Johnny Weissmuller Tarzan film, and the tickets had all been sold. He saw the dismay on Manik's face and took him down the road to a Bengali cinema. The film was *Kal Parinay* (*The Doomed Marriage*) – an 'early example of Indian soft porn', according to Ray, who remembers the hero and the heroine – 'or was it the Vamp?' – newly married and lying in bed, and a close-up showing the woman's leg rubbing against the man's.

'I was only nine then, but old enough to realise that I had strayed into forbidden territory.' His uncle made repeated whispered efforts to take him home, but Manik, already precociously dedicated to the cinema, turned a deaf ear. It was not that he was enjoying the film, simply that he was determined to get to the end.

In Calcutta those were the days of Silents, Partial Talkies and One Hundred Per Cent Talkies and, at the grandest cinema in town, a Wurlitzer played by a sahib called Byron Hopper. The choice of foreign films was quite impressive. Much later, out of curiosity, Ray decided to check the files of the Calcutta *Statesman* for a certain date in 1927, and found seven films playing at the same time: *Moana, Variety, The Gold Rush, Underworld, The Freshman* and *The Black Pirate*.

Chaplin, Keaton and Harold Lloyd made a tremendous and lasting impression on him. So did *The Thief of Baghdad* and *Uncle Tom's Cabin*. Other memories of Hollywood films seen in the 1920s include:

> Lillian Gish, in *Way Down East*, stepping precariously from one floating chunk of ice to another while fiendish bloodhounds nosed along her trail; John Gilbert, as the Count of Monte Cristo, delirious at the sight of gold in a treasure chest; Lon Chaney, as the Hunchback, clutching with dead hands the bell ropes of Notre Dame, and – perhaps the most exciting memory of all – the chariot race in *Ben Hur*, undimmed by a later and more resplendent version, for the simple reason that the new Messala is no match for the old and dearly hated one of Francis X. Bushman.

The equally dearly hated figure of Simon Legree in *Uncle Tom's Cabin* proved a bit too much for another of Manik's uncles on the occasion of a family outing. When Uncle Tom's ghost returns at the end and his erstwhile master lashes his whip at it, this uncle shot up from his seat in front of a packed house and shouted in Bengali something like, 'You bastard, still whipping!? still whipping! You devil! This time you will get your just deserts!'

Stories of romance and passion – even of the foreign variety – were generally out of bounds to Manik, but when he was about eleven he did get to see several of Lubitsch's films: *Love Parade, The Smiling Lieutenant, One Hour with You, Trouble in Paradise* – 'a forbidden world, only half-understood, but observed with a tingling curiosity', as he later described it. The beginning of *Trouble in Paradise* particularly stuck in his memory, showing that Lubitsch's sophisticated wit appealed to Satyajit even then – though typically, the scene he remembers is without words:

> It opened with a moonlit shot of the romantic Grand Canal in Venice. The inevitable gondola appeared, glided up the glistening water, and, as it moved closer, turned out to be filled with garbage. The fat gondolier pulled up the boat in front of the villa, collected some more garbage and, at the point of rowing off, burst into an aria by Verdi.

One kind of film permissible to him as a boy that did *not* appeal, either to Manik or to his family, was the British film. Technical superiority notwithstanding, it was marred by the same faults that Ray would later ridicule in the Bengali cinema of the time – and now, according to Satyajit: stagey settings, theatrical dialogue, affected situations and acting. 'We laughed at Jack Hulbert not mainly because we were tickled, but because we did not want our British neighbours in the theatre to think that we had no sense of humour', he later wrote – and that was as close as he came to the British in Calcutta until he took a job in his early twenties.

As the 1930s wore on, Satyajit saw films more and more frequently, some Bengali ones included. He began keeping a notebook with his own star-ratings, and learned to distinguish the finish of the different Hollywood studios. He even wrote a fan letter to Deanna Durbin (and received a very polite reply). But at no point did he consider that he might direct films himself. That idea did not strike him until his late twenties, well after he had left university, although an astrologer to whom his mother took him when he was twenty-two, had already predicted that he would become internationally famous 'through the use of light'.

Satyajit first visited Tagore's university, where he would become an art student in 1940, when he was seven. It meant he and his mother taking a slow train to Santiniketan, more than a hundred miles north to north-west of Calcutta in the flat, bare countryside of Birbhum. Maharsi Devendranath Tagore had bought some land there in 1863 as a place of retreat and meditation. His son Rabindranath had settled there at the turn of the century and founded a school, followed twenty years later by the university, to which he dedicated his Nobel Prize winnings. Manik had actually been taken there once before, as a small baby by his parents who were hoping for an improvement in Sukumar's failing health from the change of air. This time too Suprabha took him to meet Tagore. Manik had been nurturing the hope of getting a poem inscribed in a new notebook of his. After keeping the notebook for a day, Tagore obliged. As he handed it back to the small son of his late lamented friend he said to both Manik and his mother: 'Let him keep this, and when he is a little older he will understand it.' The eight lines of verse – now familiar to Bengalis – meant roughly that Tagore had travelled the world at great expense and seen every country, the greatest mountains and the vastest oceans, but that he had failed to see the world outside his own door: a single drop of dew upon a stalk of rice – 'a drop which reflects in its convexity the whole universe around it', Ray later commented, admitting its significance to Indian art in general and to his own work.

He and his mother stayed in Santiniketan for about three months, in a little hut set among the trees that cover the campus. He had a playmate about his own age, the foster-daughter of Rabindranath's son. On nights when there was a full moon Manik and his mother would walk out to the Khoyai, a ravine famous for its stark eroded beauty, where she would sing Tagore's songs and Brahmo hymns full-throatedly, giving vent to her sorrow at her husband's tragic death.

Manik was also given a present by Nandalal Bose, the head of the art school at Santiniketan, who was already a famous artist and would later teach Satyajit. He drew four pictures for Manik in his little black notebook: a cow, a cheetah, a bear and a striped tiger with a black mark on the tip of its tail. 'Why this black mark?' asked Manik. 'This tiger is very greedy. He entered a kitchen to steal some meat. And the tip of his tail got caught in a hot oven.'

This trip to Santiniketan took place before Satyajit started school, as did his first visits to Darjeeling and Lucknow, two other places that have influenced his films. In Darjeeling he was able to see the third highest mountain in the world, Kanchenjungha, which gave its name to the film he set in the resort. As in the film, so on this childhood visit: the peak remained obstinately invisible behind clouds for some days after his arrival in Darjeeling. Then, at dawn one morning he was woken by his mother and saw the mountain in all its glory, changing from rose to gold to silver as the sun came up. Now he could compare the real thing to Upendrakisore's painting of it which he knew from their house in Calcutta.

In Lucknow, centre of the nawabi culture Ray depicted in *The Chess Players*, he and his mother stayed with the barrister Atulprasad Sen who had married a cousin of hers. Sen had known Sukumar Ray in London from 1911–3 and had been a member of his Monday Club. He is now the most famous composer of songs in Bengal after Tagore. His house was filled with singing and playing as Upendrakisore's once had been. Allauddin Khan – guru of Ravi Shankar and father of Ali Akbar Khan, both of whom have composed for Ray, and by general consent the finest North Indian classical musician of modern times – happened to be staying during Satyajit's visit, and he would often play the piano and the violin.

On this and subsequent visits to Lucknow, Satyajit came to know the courtliness of the city that had survived from the time of the deposed King Wajid Ali Shah three quarters of a century before. He also explored some of the historic buildings shown in *The Chess Players* which were in varying stages of ruin by the late 1920s. The most fascinating to him was the Bhulbhuliya Maze inside the great mosque, the Bara Imambara. The story went that if you entered the maze without a guide you would never get out. The marks of cannon balls on the walls of the Residency and the marble plaque in the very room where Sir Henry Lawrence was struck by such a shot, conjured up the Sepoy Mutiny of 1857 vividly for Satyajit. When he came to research *The Chess Players* nearly half a century later, these childhood memories were an inspiration to him.

When he was eight and a half Satyajit began school at what was considered to be one of the best Bengali-medium institutions, Ballygunj Government

High, quite close to his uncles' house. Until then he had been taught mainly by his mother, an 'indefatigable worker' who was also a good teacher in both Bengali and English (and whose beautiful handwriting helped Satyajit to form his own). He puts school in a separate compartment in his memoir *When I Was Small* and it is probably right to do so here too, since his formal education contributed little to what he felt to be important in his first twenty years of life: and that despite academic results always above average. His account of his schooldays is largely a catalogue of teachers' and boys' quirks; he used people at school, as he did those at home, to sharpen his powers of observation. Who, after seeing Apu's worthy headmaster and the sarcastic grammarian college teacher in *Aparajito* can doubt this?

He found not a single one of the masters in his six years there really inspiring, but they were not too bad-tempered or sardonic a bunch on the whole. As in any school, their foibles came in for close scrutiny by the boys, but there was an extra dimension for fun: the uneasy coexistence of two languages, Bengali and English, with its limitless scope for mispronunciation and misunderstanding. The masters' ability to speak it and write it – always a sensitive matter in Bengal – varied enormously. One of them, for instance, a Muslim with the telltale rustic accents of someone from East Bengal, took hold of a circular from the school caretaker and announced in his best English that a Charlie Chaplin film was to be shown on a certain day, 'Through the kind courtesy of Messrs Kodok Company' – not recognising it he had assumed Kodak was a Bengali name, rhyming with the word for a particular Bengali sweet. At the opposite extreme stood the assistant headmaster, an almost faultless brown sahib: light-skinned, clean-shaven, correct in jacket, tie and stiff upper lip. During school programmes in the hall he stood with his hands resting on his stomach. Should applause be called for, he would never lift both hands together but keep one of them on his stomach and tap it gently on the back with the other. Needless to say, his English was very pukka. He even knew the correct pronunciation of the French names in *Ivanhoe*. 'Who would have known that "Front-de-Boeuf" should be pronounced "Frodbo"?' asks Ray in his memoir with gentle irony.

Besides their English the masters' apparel was also a source of great amusement. Like the characters in Ray's films, who faithfully reflect the gamut of Bengali sartorial possibilities, the staff wore everything from pressed trousers and a buttoned-up coat, to a voluminous dhoti. The second headmaster of Satyajit's time had trousers which were notably baggy. Their appearance happily coincided with the reading of 'Rip Van Winkle' in Satyajit's class, who soon alighted on the wide hose known as galligaskins as the correct term for the head's trousers.

Satyajit himself was known from his first day as Manik, after unwisely giving the name to a mischievous boy when asked. His cousin Ruby claims today that Manik was 'very shy and withdrawn' at school, but that does not seem to be his own feeling – although he does admit to being labelled a bit of a goody-goody. He certainly had to put up with some teasing about his famous relatives, when the news got out. 'Eh, Manik, Amal says that George the Fifth is your grandad. Is that right?' or 'What relation is Rabi Babu [Rabindranath] to you? Your uncle?' But this was nothing to the suffering of the boy who *was* related to the Tagores but lacked their gifts. Neither he nor Satyajit had quite the confidence to silence their classmates shown by another boy, Anil, who was the nephew of Lord Sinha, the first Indian to sit on the Viceroy's Council and a grand figure.

The most revealing story of school that Ray tells in his memoir concerns an item in the school programme that translates as 'Music Drawing'. One pupil would sing a song while another illustrated its words in harmony, with coloured chalks on a blackboard. The same song, by Tagore, cropped up every year; its words meant roughly 'The gentle sweet breeze fills the spotless white sail, Never before have I seen such a vessel.' The same pupil, Haripadda, would illustrate it each time with flying colours. In 1933 he had passed out of the school, leaving a gap. The drawing master, who had taken a special shine to Satyajit because of his obvious talent, tried his best to persuade him, but he refused to step in. 'The fact of the matter was that stagefright like mine is seldom seen. If I heard that I was to get a prize, my whole body became feverish, because I knew that my name would be called in front of everyone, I would have to leave my place and walk up to receive my prize from some bigwig or other, and then walk all the way back to my seat; the prospect was simply terrifying.' Though he has received scores of awards since those days and appeared on many platforms, Ray still feels the deepest reluctance to take a public role unless he is in total sympathy with an occasion and in firm control of it. This is one reason out of several for his distaste for political life.

Satyajit was able to matriculate when he was just short of fifteen because, by lucky coincidence, the government had just relaxed the age limit. If it had not, Satyajit would have been willing to follow a common practice and have his age altered by a lawyer; but his mother did not approve of the idea. Relations between them were somewhat strained at this time, which is not very surprising given Satyajit's age. When the family went on holiday to Kashmir, for instance, Ruby remembers Manik's mother getting quite annoyed with him because he was more interested in cinemas than scenery. 'I don't think even his mother knew what was going on inside,' she says: a gap in communication that later helped to give the mother–son relationship in *Aparajito* a poignancy that is almost painful to watch. Not that the link is more than 'an echo on a purely psychological plane', as Ray puts it today; in real life his mother did the opposite of Apu's – she pushed him to enter Presidency College like his father and grandfather. His own inclination, like that of the family friend Tagore sixty years before, was to avoid further study and develop his artistic skills, perhaps as a commercial artist. As the straightforward Ruby puts it, 'Manik's mother insisted he become a graduate, not a vagabond.'

Not long before this he had discovered an unusual new interest, also unconnected with academic study: western classical music. It came upon him, as he later wrote, 'at an age when the Bengali youth almost inevitably writes poetry' and quite quickly became an obsession. He already owned a hand-cranked Pigmyphone which had been given to him when he was about five by a relative through marriage, the owner of one of the best record shops in Calcutta. 'Tipperary' (which appears incongruously in *Pather Panchali*) and 'The Blue Danube' were two of the earliest records he played on it. When he was about thirteen he began listening to some other records – mainly by Beethoven – that happened to be in the house. His response, perhaps partly because it had been primed by his earlier reading, was 'immediate and decisive'; he felt excited to be discovering something new, totally unlike the Brahmo hymns and Tagore songs he was surrounded by and the Indian instrumental music he also knew. With what little money he had, he started hunting for bargains in the music shops. According to his school friend Anil who hunted with him, on the day that he found *Eine Kleine Nachtmusik* 'Manik lost his sleep that night.'

He started attending concerts of the Calcutta Symphony Orchestra, and he joined a gramophone club whose members were almost all Europeans and Parsis. The number of Bengalis seriously interested in western class-ical music in Calcutta in the 1930s and 40s could be counted on the fingers of two hands, according to Ray. Apart from himself, his friend Chanchal Chatterjee, and the writer Nirad Chaudhuri, there were those few Brahmos, such as Tagore's niece, who had studied it in some way. It was a very exclusive circle.

Considering his love of music of all kinds, which he believes to be greater than his love of cinema, and given that he has composed most of the background scores for his films along with many songs, it seems odd that Satyajit learnt no instrument in his youth, Indian or western. The main reason seems to be that his musical orientation up to the age of about twenty was western and he was so absorbed in getting to know western music that he did not feel the urge to play it too. It may also be a reflection of his diffidence about any sort of performing role unless he is completely confident of doing himself justice. All his relations say he has a beautiful voice, but he never sings before others, unless it is to demonstrate a point.

Satyajit's years at college (1936–9) were years of deepening understanding of western music, frequent film-going and the beginning of his collection of books, especially art books, culled from his hours of browsing in the rows of second-hand bookstalls in College Street outside Presidency College and in the bazaars of the area. Towards his academic work he felt little enthusiasm, although he took some pride in being at the best college in the city. He was not, by his own admission, 'scholastically inclined', but he recognised that it would help him get a job to have 'BA' after his name, and he was quite anxious to get one as soon as practical, both to help his mother and to achieve some independence.

In his third year at college he even allowed himself to study just about the most uncongenial subject possible for his cast of mind – economics. Encouragement had come from his father's Brahmo friend Professor Mahalanobis, by then India's leading statistician. He promised Satyajit an editorial position on his economics journal as soon as he graduated and at a salary roughly three times what he accepted instead as a graphic artist. One of Ray's cardinal principles has been to apply himself only to that at which he is naturally gifted; he feels that Bengalis have always been inclined to encourage round pegs to try to fit themselves into square holes.

Among the other subjects he studied was English literature, which he enjoyed. One of his professors was very disappointed to discover, on meeting Satyajit by chance two or three years after graduation, that he had gone in for art. As for film-making, that would have been beneath consideration. Satyajit puts his command of English down to this period of his life; not so much to the tuition he received, as to the voracious reading he did: Evelyn Waugh, Aldous Huxley – 'even essays' – but he was also getting to know some of the nineteenth-century writers and Shakespeare, though it is seldom that he refers to them in his own writing and conversation today, even indirectly. Literary language has never interested him as much as the art of story-telling, as his own writing makes plain.

Of the British staff at Presidency College, Humphry House, who had written books on Dickens and Gerard Manley Hopkins, was quite an influence on his students at this time. Like a handful of other renegades in the last decade or so of the Raj, he rebelled against the colonial establishment, not so much as a 'mole in the crown'* as a gadfly. The pamphlet he published in October 1937, 'I spy with my little eye', led to his removal from the college. It is a satirical exposé of police surveillance in Calcutta at the time, littered with coded references – some literary, some not – which have become totally obscure with the passing of time. But a few of his mock-exam questions are worth quoting for the peculiar flavour that they give of the last decade of the Raj in Calcutta:

Either/Or

1. Would you rather be damned with Plato and Lord Bacon than go to Heaven with Marx and Engels?

Would you rather be damned with Marx and Engels than go to Heaven with Plato and Lord Bacon?

2. Compare the Wife of Bath with Mr. Pickwick as bourgeois types.

*In the phrase of Michael Carritt, an ICS official in Bengal in the 1930s who was a Communist sympathiser.

3. 'I can hardly believe my eyes.' (Berkeley) Comment on this statement as relevant to *either* events in Strand Road on the evening of August 14th *or* the value of photography in detective work.

4. Which is better, a code or a cipher? Give examples from other people's letters.

5. Expand the following statement to about twenty-five times its original length, bringing out the implications in such a way as to show that it is seditious: 'I will now discharge my conscience of my political creed, which is contained in two articles and has no reference to any party or persons. My faith in the People governing is, on the whole, infinitesimal; my faith in the People governed is, on the whole, illimitable.' (Dickens)

One can see why House's students, Satyajit among them, liked him. The ironic tone and the distrust of ideology, academic labels, politicians and governments, was and is close to Ray's own feelings on those subjects. He sums them up when he says, 'I would prefer to be judged for what I am rather than whom I resemble', and quotes Tagore in his commentary for the documentary *Rabindranath Tagore*: 'I do not put my faith in institutions, but in the individuals all over the world who think clearly, feel nobly and act rightly. They are the channels of moral truth.'

In the case of Ray such perceptions have been quickened by modern Bengali history and the Renaissance, to which he both does and does not belong. Even at its most fruitful, during the lifetime of Upendrakisore, the Renaissance meant a true synthesis of East and West for but a tiny minority of those caught up in it. Western political and philosophical ideas, however, then and ever since appealed to a great many Bengalis, giving birth to a tribe of quarrelsome, worldly barrister-nationalists, puritanical Brahmos, Marxist theoreticians and professors of philosophy, politics and economics, who prefer the world of punditry and disputation to real life. Nirad Chaudhuri, who knew this world at close quarters while remaining detached from it, has written that 'the Bengali's response to English literature has made him most sensitive, human and creative, while European thought, whether political or social, has invariably desiccated him and led him to sterile dogmatism.'

When Satyajit finally graduated from Presidency College in the summer of 1939, his academic label meant 'almost nothing' to him. As he put it in a lecture on his life and work given over forty years afterwards: 'Erudition is something which I singularly lack. As a student, I was only a little better than average, and in all honesty, I cannot say that what I learnt in school and college has stood me in good stead in the years that followed . . . My best and keenest memories of college consist largely of the quirks and idiosyncracies (sic) of certain professors.'

By coincidence, he stepped into the wider world in the same year as his most famous character at the beginning of *The World of Apu*. In virtually every respect they were different, including Satyajit's height – nearly six foot four inches – but they did have one characteristic in common: deliberate uncertainty about their futures. Satyajit was considering becoming a commercial artist; although he had no formal training, his inherited gifts were obvious to all and he had no particular desire to employ them as a fine artist, especially since he disliked what was then called Oriental Art (as his father and grandfather had too). In fact his whole sensibility, when he left Presidency College, was tuned to the West – its literature, paintings, music and films. They were what excited him the most.

Fortunately for both his life and work, his mother had other ideas. She felt that Tagore and his rural retreat, where the students were intended to have little to do with classrooms and city pleasures if possible, would have a 'therapeutic effect' on her city-bred son – as Satyajit later reflected – 'much as a visit to a hill station or a health resort [is supposed to have] on one's system.' And so, after a longish period of persuasion, Satyajit left crowded Calcutta and arrived in mid-1940 to study fine art in the stillness and space of Santiniketan, Tagore's 'place apart', his 'Abode of Peace'.

3

Santiniketan and Tagore
1940–2

···❈❙【 I ❮·⁂⟨◉⟩⁖·⟩ 】❖❈···

S ATYAJIT'S initial reluctance to study at Tagore's university had two basic causes. First, he loved city life in Calcutta. Although he shared much of Tagore's aversion for Calcutta's westernised educational institutions, he had no wish to try Tagore's pastoral kind either. Secondly, he concurred with the common Calcutta view of graduates from Santiniketan: that they were sentimental, intellectually second-rate and, if they were male, effeminate. Several painters and musicians from Santiniketan used to visit his uncles' house. They had 'long hair, and spoke Bengali in a strange affected sing-song.' To a person like Satyajit, who has always taken pride in the vigour and clarity of his pronunciation (whether in Bengali or in English) and in his appearance, this was very off-putting. He imagined it was true of all Santiniketanites and was pleasantly surprised to find, when he eventually reached there, that not one of his art teachers spoke like that, even though many other people did.

He also connected the place with the reproductions of Oriental Art published in the pages of two important Calcutta journals of the time (the work of U. Ray and Sons until its bankruptcy). These were by artists of the so-called Bengal School trained under Abanindranath Tagore (a distant nephew of Rabindranath) and his former student Nandalal Bose, who had migrated from Calcutta to Santiniketan to run the art school. Their subjects were mainly myths and epic stories, treated in a wan or saccharine manner, thoroughly stylised, with neither the boldness and colour sense of Mughal and Rajput miniatures, nor the vitality of Far Eastern painting. Satyajit regarded them as roughly the equivalent in painting of the Bengali films of the period, without their vulgarity.

Why therefore did Satyajit change his mind about going to Santiniketan? The answer must probably be a mixture of respect for his mother's wishes, a growing conviction during 1939/40 that he needed some basis in Indian art to be a success as a commercial artist, and the lure of Tagore himself, his father's and grandfather's close friend, who had several times requested Satyajit's mother to send her son to his university.

Fifty years later Tagore and Ray are indissolubly bound. If non-Bengalis know Tagore at all today, it is mainly by virtue of Ray's interpretations of him on film, and it is also true that those who suspect Tagore of lacking in substance tend to dismiss Ray as slight too. The differences between them are actually both many and real: Ray's love of cinema and the relative lack of importance he attaches to literature – poetry in particular, his profound love of western music, his preference for city over country, and his distaste for public and political roles (though Tagore came increasingly to share this). But the affinity between them has the deepest of roots. Not only is one of Ray's finest films, *Charulata*, based on one of Tagore's most personal stories, he has adapted one of his best novels, *The Home and the World*, three of his short stories, as *Three Daughters*, another story originating with Tagore though not written by him, as *The Goddess*, and toiled for more than a year to create a documentary about him. In his other films there are countless references to and echoes of Tagore. His songs have moved Ray from the earliest days at Garpar Road and so have his paintings, from Ray's time at Santiniketan onwards. And this is not to speak of his poetry, letters, essays and plays.

The fact is – despite Tagore's eclipse in the West today compared with his household name in the inter-war years – that he is an artist of Shakespearian stature, though Ray himself dislikes such comparisons.

As a poet, dramatist, novelist, short story writer, essayist, painter, song composer, philosopher and educationist Tagore is obviously more *versatile* than Shakespeare. But why compare? With indifferent translations Tagore will never be understood in the West as he is in Bengal. As a Bengali I know that as a composer of songs, he has no equal, not even in the West – and I know Schubert and Hugo Wolf; as a poet, he shows incredible facility, range and development; some of his short stories are among the best ever written; his essays show an amazing clarity of thought and breadth of vision; in his novels he tackled some major themes and created some memorable characters; as a painter starting at the age of nearly seventy, he remains among the most original and interesting India has produced.

Bengalis with far less appreciation of other cultures than Ray, are still more fulsome in their praise. Ray's pugnacious contemporary – and the other Indian film-maker of true originality – Ritwik Ghatak, chose to put it this way in an interview just before his death in 1976:

I cannot speak without Tagore. That man has culled all my feelings long before my birth. He has understood what I am and he has put in all the words. I read him and I find that all has been said and I have nothing new to say. I think all artists, in Bengal at least, find themselves in the same difficulty. It just cannot be helped. You can be angry with him, you can criticise him, you may dislike him, but in the final analysis, you will find that he has the last word.

Beneath such a vast shadow it is easy to become solemn. Perhaps only Sukumar Ray, who knew both the giant and the man, could encapsulate the difficulty exactly. An impish drawing of his shows the prostrate form of Tagore beached like a colossal whale and peopled all over by tiny figures in attitudes similar to a detective or archaeologist, examining different parts of the whole. The Bengali caption means 'Tagore Worship in Lilliput'.

It may be that Satyajit unconsciously avoided taking advantage of his family relationship with Tagore because he feared that proximity to him would turn him into a Lilliputian too. Once at Santiniketan he certainly made no effort to meet Tagore; in the year and a bit that he spent there before Tagore's death in August 1941, Satyajit met him only three or four times. 'One didn't pay him social calls,' he points out today with a laugh. 'One stole up to him with one's heart in one's mouth and touched his feet.' He found himself unable to hold a normal conversation with Tagore. 'He never used a wrong word; I mean if you recorded his normal conversation it would sound like a prepared speech. Everything was so incredibly perfect.' Because of this, and Tagore's prophetic appearance, and the natural distance due to age (Tagore was then just short of eighty), Satyajit felt awkward in his presence; and the atmosphere of adulation surrounding him only heightened this feeling. Nevertheless, some of Ray's drawings of Tagore done later – one somewhat severe, another quite gentle in a Far Eastern manner – suggest that he must have observed his demeanour directly, as well as taking it from other sources like photographs.

Within a few months of Satyajit's arrival, after the long-overdue award of an honorary doctorate to Tagore by representatives of Oxford University at Santiniketan in August 1940, it was clear that Tagore was dying. But he remained creative to the end, like Sukumar. On 14 April 1941, the Bengali New Year, his eightieth birthday message, 'Sabhyater Sankat' ('Crisis in Civilization'), was delivered. As war engulfed the nations of East and West in which he had been made tumultuously welcome between 1912 and 1930, he made this heartfelt plea, which Ray quoted in his documentary on Tagore:

As I look around I see the crumbling ruins of a proud civilisation strewn like a vast heap of futility. And yet I shall not commit the grievous sin of losing faith in Man. I would rather look forward to the opening of a new chapter in his history after the cataclysm is over and the atmosphere rendered clean with the spirit of service and sacrifice.

On 25 July the old poet was taken from Santiniketan to Calcutta for the last time – to Jorasanko, the mansion where he was born (and where Upendrakisore Ray had sung for his family for the first time some sixty years before). After an unsuccessful operation, just before which Tagore dictated his last poem, he lost consciousness and died on 7 August. One in particular of his more than two thousand songs, which Tagore had requested for his final departure, was sung over his body:

> In front lies the ocean of peace,
> launch the boat, Helmsman,
> you will be the comrade ever . . .
> may the mortal bonds perish,
> may the vast universe take him in its arms,
> and may he know in his fearless heart
> the Great Unknown.

Satyajit remembers that day clearly. News reached Santiniketan quite early in the day over the only telephone line. He and a group of friends immediately caught a train to Calcutta and headed for Jorasanko, travelling the entire distance barefoot – the traditional Indian sign of respect for the dead. In the steamy monsoon atmosphere, hundreds of thousands of people were milling around near the Tagore mansion, a sea of humanity that is vividly conveyed by the old footage of the funeral procession with which Ray opens his documentary. Being students at Santiniketan, Satyajit and his friends were allowed inside the courtyard of the house, but they could not get near Tagore. Satyajit caught sight of Nandalal Bose decorating the body with white flowers. It was said that there were tears in Tagore's eyes, which had never been seen before. As the body was raised on to people's shoulders there was a terrible uproar and he saw hairs being pulled from Tagore's beard as souvenirs. Then, as if to spoil the mood completely, someone decided to pickpocket Satyajit of his bus-fare so he had to walk home across Calcutta after escaping the crowd.

There were four individuals at Santiniketan who exerted a direct influence over Satyajit: Alex Aronson, a lively minded young German-Jewish refugee and a pupil of Leavis's at Cambridge, who taught English; Pritwish Neogy, another Bengali art student; and the art teachers Nandalal Bose and Binode Bihari Mukherjee, both already established painters.

It was western music that drew Aronson and Ray together. Even fewer people cared for it in Santiniketan than in Calcutta, despite the atmosphere there being charged with other kinds of music. 'Bengalis', according to Aronson today, 'found most western music a chaotic and intolerable noise.' Manik (as Aronson called Satyajit) was the exception 'who responded wholeheartedly, intelligently, and unreservedly, and with infectious enthusiasm. The most remarkable thing about it all was his devotion to music of any kind, so that he could listen with the same absorption to Indian and western music.' He had simply turned up one day at Aronson's house on the campus with a few records which he hoped to play on Aronson's wind-up gramophone. 'On that occasion he brought Beethoven's opus 132, which we listened to in solemn silence.' Later they discovered a piano in Tagore's house which, though poor, Aronson played while Satyajit listened, sometimes acting as page-turner. Later still, after Aronson left Santiniketan for Dhaka (Dacca), they used to meet in Calcutta at Satyajit's house, listen to music there or go to concerts. A casual comment in a letter Satyajit wrote to Aronson in 1945 catches their shared passion: 'When are you coming down? There is a lot of good music in store for you.'

His relationship with Neogy, with whom he shared his hostel ac-commodation, revolved mainly around painting rather than music. Even then, in his early twenties, Neogy had the extraordinary ability to identify a painting by looking at one square inch of it and, according to Satyajit, he could 'immediately spot the fake from the genuine'. Since Satyajit had reciprocal abilities in music, which Neogy did not, their friendship was a rewarding one. More than anyone else at Santiniketan, Neogy helped to broaden Satyajit's sympathies to include Indian art and sculpture of all kinds, some of the western art of the early Renaissance and the last hundred years, and many other kinds of art.

In late 1941 he and Neogy, along with two other art students at Santiniketan, set off on a tour of India by third-class train to see the great masterpieces of classical Indian art for themselves, at Ajanta, Ellora, Elephanta, Sanchi and Khajuraho (where they slept in a cowshed in bitter cold). Gazing at these works with their fluid forms, hewn out of the living stone or floating free of western inhibitions of perspective or anatomical accuracy, and sometimes attempting to sketch them himself, Satyajit experienced them as both alien and familiar. He began to feel his roots as an Indian artist, intuitively grasping that he was too much inclined towards western music, towards 'the idea of composed music, with its formal beauty and structure.' Although he was already hearing Indian classical music at Santiniketan, there was no instrumentalist of genius playing there and he did not begin to listen seriously to it until he returned to Calcutta during the war. Today he feels that if he were forced to choose between a concert by a first-rate pianist playing some favourite European pieces or a first-rate Indian musician playing or singing an unknown (and improvised) programme, as is customary, he would choose the latter – for the element of surprise, the possibility that the Indian might be at his best (with its attendant risk that he might have drunk too much or simply not be in the mood).

The tour was a consolidation of his growing awareness of the qualities that distinguish eastern art from western art. Generalisations here are exceptionally tricky, given the redundancy of words to express response to the greatest works of art, and especially given the sheer variety of art included within the labels 'eastern' and 'western'. Few people are more aware of this than Ray, but if pressed, he identifies 'a sort of symbolism and a looking for the essence rather than the surface' as a hallmark of Indian, Chinese and Japanese art. His favourite western painters, Cézanne and Giorgione, show this character too: 'There's something very mysterious and poetic in Giorgione which appeals to an Indian,' he says. 'I think he would be liked by people who like Indian art, but are not familiar with western art to the same extent.'

His tour also sharpened his perception of the eloquent use of very small details in Indian art to express something much greater – Tagore's dewdrop – which Ray says is common to great art from every civilisation, but seems to be a *sine qua non* of the greatest Indian art forms. It is found in Rajput miniatures, in the paintings at Ajanta, in the sculptures at Ellora, in the Sanskrit classics, in folk-poetry and folk-singing, in *Bharata Natyam* dancing, in Tagore, and in Ray's films. He cites the five or six slanting parallel lines of dots etched against the sky which stand for rain in a Rajput miniature, or the billowing scarf draped over the heroine that shows the presence of a storm; love, yearning, joy, sorrow, anger, shame, envy and other intense states of mind are apparent simply from the details of the body's postures. 'Film directors can learn a lot from these pictures.'

Ray's art teacher Binode Bihari Mukherjee also displays this quality. Ray regards him as the finest Indian painter of the modern period (not counting Tagore who, being untrained, has a unique status), as well as 'a great intellect with a total lack of flamboyance'. The profound, delicate film Ray made about him, *The Inner Eye*, reveals respect and affection for Mukherjee and his work. The artist, who died in 1980, comes closest to being Ray's guru.

From the beginning of his life Mukherjee suffered from very poor eyesight, and in later life he went blind altogether, though he continued to create art. But when Satyajit arrived in Santiniketan in 1940, Mukherjee was reaching the height of his powers. His was the first painting Satyajit saw on arrival at the new two-storey students' hostel in the art school. As he walked up its stairs to the verandah his gaze went up involuntarily. 'The entire ceiling was a painting, showing a gentle village scene in glowing colours, full of trees, fields, ponds, people, birds and beasts. A village in Birbhum. One could call it a tapestry, or an encyclopedia. Such painting did not seem to bear any relation to Oriental Art as I knew it.'

Ten years after this, Mukherjee created another mural, his finest, on three walls of another building at Santiniketan. Ray calls it the most noble and effective work of art created in India this century. It depicts the lives of the saints and mystics of medieval India such as Kabir, some of whom had lived in the area from which Ray's earliest known ancestor came. Mukherjee had found that many of them were from the lower strata of society: weavers, cotton-cleaners, cobblers, barbers and so on. But, in spite of their handicaps, they had found faith and transmitted it to others, not through exclusive religious doctrines as the Brahmins had, but through a simple philosophy of love and tolerance. Incredibly, Mukherjee painted the whole work without the help of a preliminary tracing on the walls; there was about his endeavour something of the fervent devotion of the craftsmen and artists who built the medieval cathedrals in the West. As Ray says it in *The Inner Eye*,

The whole composition shows a remarkable cohesiveness. Saints and devotees, cities and mountains, rivers and trees and people, all fuse into an organic whole and make it a profoundly original and valid conception of the theme. There are resonances of other styles and other periods. But all the influences have been assimilated into a synthesis that bears the unmistakable hallmark of Binode Bihari Mukherjee.

In his two and a half years at Santiniketan, Ray came to know Mukherjee's work and thinking intimately. His *aperçus* enlightened him. He recorded some of them in 1971–2 while making the film. One in particular recalls Ray's own approach to filming village life in *Pather Panchali* and in fact his overall vision of cinema. As Mukherjee tells it, he had been working outdoors at Santiniketan many years before, just as Ray and the other art students used constantly to do. He had been painting a herd of buffaloes. A group of tribal girls from the area (Santhals like those in Ray's *Days and Nights in the Forest*) stood watching. After a while one of them simply remarked, 'You've put in all these buffaloes, but not a single young one?' In Ray's words elsewhere, 'For a popular medium, the best kind of inspiration should derive from life and have its roots in it.'

Nandalal Bose, 'Mastermosai', was more conscious of discipline and the canons of Indian art tradition than Mukherjee. He belonged, in some ways, to the school of Oriental Art that Satyajit disliked for its divorce from life, but Bose rose above it. Someone who studied under both teachers a little before Ray once commented that while Bose always expected a student to ask for advice on what to do next on completion of an exercise, Mukherjee expected him to have made up his own mind. Satyajit found Bose less imaginative and articulate than Mukherjee. Nevertheless he had much respect for him and has always recognised the value to his films of the formal training Bose insisted on.

He remembers Mastermosai 'stealing up' on him from behind while he was sketching outdoors, for instance, and saying, 'That's a good outline of a cow. But a cow is more than an outline. You must feel the form of the animal – the flesh and bones beneath the skin, and this feeling must show in the way your pencil moves.' Another of his comments, made to someone else, shows Bose's sympathy for the idea that eastern art 'looks for the essence'. It is strikingly reminiscent of *Pather Panchali*: 'Under a limitless sky everything is born, grows, dies and is born again. Incessant change from one form to another moves in an evolutionary cycle. If one can assess these transformations, one can be nature's poet or nature's painter. The great Chinese painters were able to do this aright.'

Bose was in fact notably influenced by Far Eastern art; he had accompanied Tagore on his 1924 visit to China and Japan. He passed on some of his feeling for it to Satyajit, who relished Bose's lessons in Chinese art and calligraphy. 'This was basic – this reverence for life, for organic growth', Ray wrote later. 'While you paint, each stroke of brush, each movement of finger, of wrist, of elbow, contemplates and celebrates this growth. And not just things that live and grow. Everything that comprises perceptible reality is observed, felt, analysed and reduced to its basic form, basic texture, basic rhythm.'

Bose also told Satyajit: 'Consider the Fujiyama. Fire within and calm without. There is the symbol of the true Oriental artist.' Ray was reminded of this dictum when he saw the films of Ozu and Mizoguchi after he had become a film-maker. To what extent he feels it applies to himself – or indeed to Akira Kurosawa whom he feels is half-western – is doubtful, but in this connection his attachment to another, related remark of his old teacher is interesting: if there are two angry men, it is the one who controls his anger who is the more powerful of the two.

Like his father and grandfather, Ray very rarely loses his temper. He may well feel inwardly anguished in his work, as he once said of his difficult collaborations with great instrumentalists on his background scores, but he will not show that he is by displays of emotion. Except for Neogy and one or two others, the other students at Santiniketan remember Ray as an imposing, withdrawn figure. Amartya Sen, for instance, now a world-famous economist, then it is true about ten years Satyajit's junior, thought of him 'mainly as Sukumar Ray's – the *great* Sukumar Ray's! – son, who had some talents too, of diverse kinds (I was told), but I was younger and too low-brow to attempt mixing with him!' Even Dinkar Kowshik, who shared Satyajit's hostel accommodation – in which Nandalal Bose had arranged a special bed because of Satyajit's height – and who travelled with him around India on the art tour, confirms this impression; although Satyajit was by then in love with Bijoya, they never discussed her. Nor would he ever agree to join one of the many gregarious groups singing songs, though he did sometimes sing to illustrate a musical point. (During the big procession in Calcutta in 1961 for the Tagore centenary, people remember Ray walking some distance away and not singing.) The general feeling about him then, according to Kowshik, was that he would be good at whatever he took up, but that there was, as yet, no sign of genius.

Satyajit himself does recall attending some of the impromptu concerts and performances that were a feature of life in Santiniketan, as well as some early morning services in the glass-walled pavilion set aside for this purpose. Besides the Brahmo hymns, which could be enjoyable, and Tagore songs, there was a gifted accompanist of his own age on the *esraj* – the violin-like instrument played with distinction by Upendrakisore. 'Such was his command of the instrument, and so deep and true his feeling for the songs,' Ray wrote of him thirty-five years later on a record-sleeve note, 'that one often found oneself listening to the instrument rather than the singer.' He even liked the sermons – at least, those given by Tagore's friend, the writer and philosopher Ksitimohan Sen (the grandfather of Amartya Sen and an authority on Hinduism). He was witty and down to earth, avoiding the abstract discussion of religion that bores Satyajit.

Most of his time, however, when he was not painting or drawing or chatting to Aronson, Neogy and a few others, was spent alone with the portable HMV gramophone he had brought from Calcutta, or with books. He borrowed from the art department library three of the earliest books on film aesthetics, Rotha's *The film till now* and two books of theory by Arnheim and Spottiswoode, and became fascinated by them, especially by the idea of parallels between music and film. They were instrumental in converting him from film fan to serious student of cinema.

Not that Santiniketan was a promising field for conversion. Tagore was quite interested in the possibilities of film as art, but his interest never developed, partly no doubt because of the abysmal quality of Bengali films during his lifetime. The nearest cinema to Satyajit's hostel was in the village two miles away, had wooden seats and showed the usual hammy mythological films; the nearest Wurlitzer could have been on the moon.

As he had anticipated in Calcutta, he did feel somewhat cut off. He was soon shuttling back and forth to the city at the weekend (which falls on a Tuesday and Wednesday in Santiniketan), visiting his mother and others including Bijoya, going to the cinema, browsing for books and records, and eating his favourite ice-cream Magnolia. He was perfectly happy to return to Santiniketan where his friends were, but, as he puts it, 'I had to have both.' One of his major regrets at that time was that while he had been standing in the wilds of Santiniketan sketching Nature, he had missed *Citizen Kane*, which had played for three days only in the newest and biggest cinema in Calcutta.

In December 1942 Satyajit left Santiniketan for good, without completing his five-year course, to the disappointment of Nandalal Bose. He had come to feel that 'I just didn't have it in me to become a painter', probably as a result of his discussions about art with Mukherjee, Bose and Neogy, as well as the quality of his own work which did not really satisfy him. And with Rabindranath dead, some spark in the place seemed to have died. He also felt the tensions of the times, magnified, in a curious sense, by being out of touch with Calcutta. During August, Gandhi had launched the Quit India Movement, and throughout the latter part of that year the Japanese were expected to bomb Calcutta. When this finally happened on 20 December, Ray, Neogy, Kowshik and one other – the same group as had toured India together – became really anxious. They walked sixteen miles, crossed a river by boat and walked again to catch a train to Calcutta which they just missed. After spending the night on the platform they took the early morning train. In the event, despite a major exodus from the city, they found little real cause for concern there. Nevertheless, Satyajit felt no urge to return to Santiniketan – nor did he follow others into Gandhi's movement, unlike Kowshik, who was later sent to jail.

Alex Aronson says of him today: 'Manik did not fit very well into the somewhat unreal atmosphere of Santiniketan. He was too active, too conscious a mind, too eager to get acquainted with new aspects of eastern and western cultures to stay long at such a place. In spite of his love of the open country, he is basically a city-dweller.' Or as Ray candidly admitted in the Calcutta lecture on his life and work he gave in 1982:

> My relationship with Santiniketan was an ambivalent one. As one born and bred in Calcutta, I loved to mingle with the crowd on Chowringhee, to hunt for bargains in the teaming profusion of second-hand books on the pavements of College Street, to explore the grimy depths of Chor Bazaar for symphonies at throwaway prices, to relax in the coolness of a cinema, and lose myself in the make-believe world of Hollywood. All this I missed in Santiniketan, which was a world apart. It was a world of vast open spaces, vaulted over with a dustless sky, that on a clear night showed the constellations as no city sky could ever do. The same sky, on a clear day, could summon up in moments an awesome invasion of billowing darkness that seemed to engulf the entire universe. And there was the Khoyai, rimmed with the serried ranks of *tal* trees, and the [river] Kopai, snaking its way through its rough-hewn undulations. If Santiniketan did nothing else, it induced contemplation, and a sense of wonder, in the most prosaic and earthbound of minds.
>
> In the two and a half years, I had time to think, and time to realise that, almost without my being aware of it, the place had opened windows for me. More than anything else, it had brought me an awareness of our tradition, which I knew would serve as a foundation for any branch of art that I wished to pursue.

4

Commercial Artist and Critic
1943–50

···◆◆[◦◦◦◦◦◦]◆◆···

ABOUT three months after he left Santiniketan, at the beginning of April 1943, Satyajit took a job. He joined a British-owned advertising agency, D.J. Keymer which had an office in north Calcutta, working as a junior visualiser at a salary of eighty rupees per month (£3–4 today). Within a few years he was its art director. He remained there until 1956, when he took the plunge and became a full-time film-maker after the success of *Pather Panchali*.

It was entirely his own decision to take a job and give up studying; the idea of putting his artistic skills to use and earning money from them had been forming in his mind for several years. His mother agreed quite willingly, happy that he had enjoyed a spell at Santiniketan as she had always wanted. Satyajit had been recommended to Keymer's by someone the family knew. He was interviewed by Assistant Manager D.K. Gupta, who was to play an important part in his life for the next decade or so. 'I see, you're Sukumar Ray's son. Tell me about the books your father wrote,' were his first words on being introduced. Within a day or two Satyajit had an appointment letter.

Although Keymer's was considered more informal than J. Walter Thompson – because it had fewer sahibs – it had its share of tensions, naturally exacerbated by the charged political atmosphere of the 1940s. The position of art director, for instance, had to be shared with an Englishman, 'a nice fellow but a shockingly bad artist', wrote Satyajit to a British friend in London in 1948. 'But he has to be there, being an Englishman, and I have to be there, as part of the Post-Independence Diplomatic Managerial Policy. Of course he gets three times as much as I do.' The managers were all British in the years Satyajit worked there, a succession of Englishmen and Scotsmen. He liked most of them, and did not allow nationalist emotions to cloud his feelings towards them; two or three became friends. They, for their part, treated him with respect and generosity, such was the high standard of design he maintained, calling him Maneck Roy to avoid the tricky 'Satyajit'; in fact, one of them even now believes that 'Satyajit Ray' is a kind of stage name – 'but you can never be quite sure with these Bengalis.' Nicholson, an ex-Indian Army officer whose calligraphy Ray admired, last but one of the managers in his time, probably spoke for most of them when he said that, 'Ray was a man of real integrity. He had no *chalaki* in him' – a word meaning, roughly, 'trickiness'. What Maneck Roy possessed – in Nicholson's sadly outdated word – was 'bottom'.

That is not to say that Satyajit ever relished the work or the life of an advertising office, useful background though it was for such films as *Mahanagar, Days and Nights in the Forest* and, especially, *Company Limited*. A laconic comment in his shooting notebook for this last film seems to do duty for his general feelings towards advertising: 'the usual comments are bandied about' – to describe the scene when the lights go up after the screening of a typical 'ad film' and the assembled executives attempt smart backchat. Satyajit's usual reaction to this had been an aloof silence. He concentrated his attentions on the purely artistic aspects of the job. 'If you had really sat down and thought about what you were doing' he says today, 'you would have found it a dismaying thought. Partly because the clients were generally so stupid. You'd produce an artwork which was admirable, you'd know it was good, and they'd come out with little criticisms that were so stupid that you'd really want to give up immediately.' An office colleague who was also a friend dating from pre-Keymer's days, Subrata Banerjee, recalls this aspect of Satyajit: 'If a change was required, he would frown, toss the layout aside and get on with his work. A gruff "I'll do it" was the only reply one got. He was really not involved.' But he remembers too that when he and some others lost their jobs in 1956, Satyajit gave his help 'ungrudgingly' to their fledgling advertising agency, even though he was in the thick of making *Aparajito*. He believes strongly in that kind of loyalty.

His contribution to the development of advertising imagery in India was certainly distinctive, but hard to define. Like all the best graphic designers, he combined visual flair with a feel for the meaning of words and their nuances. Sometimes this meant changing a headline to fit a layout. According to Banerjee, 'He interpreted the words in such a way that he often gave them a new depth of meaning.' He brought to his work a fascination with typography, both Bengali and English, which he shared with his father and grandfather. It has regularly surfaced in his film credit sequences and book and magazine covers over the past forty-five years. The cover of one established Bengali quarterly consists simply of Ray's permutations of the letters of the Bengali word for 'Now'; his designs for two English typefaces, Ray Roman and Ray Bizarre, won an international competition in 1971.

He also introduced into advertising more calligraphic elements than before (and created the fully calligraphic wedding invitation), as well as genuinely Indian elements – everyday details and motifs from past and present, emphatically not the borrowings from mythology he so disliked in Oriental Art. His series of drawings for ICI, promoting the anti-malaria pill Paludrine, are still remembered in Calcutta. They reflect his love of detail in Indian art forms and prefigure the minute observation of his films. Each shows a domestic scene from Bengali middle-class life such as Satyajit himself was leading; and someone, of course, is handing someone else a Paludrine. They remind one of the 'spot-the-difference' pictures that once appeared on the back of cereal packets in Britain.

But it was design of a more lasting, less mercenary kind that occupied Satyajit's best energies during those years at Keymer's. Around the end of 1943, D.K. Gupta started up a publishing house in both English and Bengali called Signet Press and asked Satyajit to design the books. He was given a completely free hand in a field that was as good as virgin. The very staid typographic covers of Tagore's university press were representative of the kind of publishing Gupta wanted to get away from. 'He definitely wanted to do something original,' says Ray.

The jackets he designed then of which he is proudest today, are those of poetry anthologies by post-Tagore poets like Bisnu Dey and Jibanananda Das. Another notable cover he did was for Jim Corbett's adventure classic *Maneaters of Kumaon*: front and back show a striped pelt with entry and exit wounds – the latter slightly larger to mark the passage of the bullet. Writer, publisher, and blurb appear in the holes. In 1946 he designed two covers for a classically elegant edition of Nehru's *Discovery of India*. For many years, well beyond his entry into cinema in 1955, Ray's name was better known in some circles in Calcutta as a cover designer.

He also at this time began illustrating books. One of the earliest was by his aunt Lila Majumdar, now a successful children's writer, who edits *Sandesh* with Satyajit and his cousin Nini. Satyajit invited her to begin her career with Signet Press. And in 1944 he made some woodcuts of simple vitality for an abridgement for children of the novel *Pather Panchali*. Some of the scenes that appealed to him then, such as the children huddling together during the storm, later found their way onto celluloid.

For the Signet Press bulletin, he drew a series of author portraits – a gallery of famous Bengalis, each done in an appropriate style, including one of Nandalal Bose in Satyajit's imitation of his style. Bernard Shaw, as a Signet author, was there too. So was Bibhutibhusan Banerjee, the author of *Pather Panchali*. A few years later, when the idea of filming *Pather Panchali* first took root in his mind, Satyajit considered approaching Banerjee for the rights to the novel; but he held back, fearful of a rebuff because of his lack of resources.

Fruitful though all this was, and financially rewarding too, Satyajit's relationship with D.K. Gupta suffered from the kind of strain inevitable where a publisher tries to combine quality with commercial viability. The letter Satyajit wrote to Alex Aronson in Dhaka at this time speaks of 'dark and shameful dealings' by a well-known Bengali academic for which Satyajit says Gupta had fallen, leading him to reject a manuscript by Aronson; so rude was Gupta when Satyajit brought the matter up on behalf of his friend, that he thought seriously about breaking with him and Signet.

They had already had one major clash before this one, over some books very close to Satyajit's heart – those by his father Sukumar. Biswas, the purchaser of U. Ray and Sons, had been quietly publishing them since 1927 without paying Satyajit or his mother a *paisa*. Gupta suddenly announced in the Calcutta press at the end of 1943 that Signet had acquired the rights to all works by Sukumar Ray, and began to publish them forthwith, one after the other. Unlike Biswas, he did pay a royalty, if only for the first four years; but he upset both Satyajit and his mother by fast-talking them into changing the distinctive formats of the books; he also, for reasons unknown, decided to have them re-illustrated. Later, after Gupta's death and the decline of Signet Press, some were reissued in their original formats and with the original illustrations, but not, alas, to the same standard of reproduction as that of U. Ray and Sons in the mid-1920s.

On balance though, Satyajit felt grateful to D.K. Gupta for a unique opportunity at a time when it could not have been more welcome to him. Not only did his work for Signet earn him a useful increment to his salary, and enable him to experiment with a wide range of styles and techniques of drawing, painting and typography, it also gave him a growing familiarity with fiction in Bengali to offset his earlier predilection for English. By his mid thirties Satyajit had acquired a clear sense of the strengths and weaknesses of Bengali literature from both a literary and visual point of view.

A novel which appeared around this time and greatly impressed him was Bibhutibhusan's *Asani Sanket*. In 1972 Ray filmed it with restrained pathos as *Distant Thunder*. Through the eyes of a village Brahmin priest and his wife, it shows the beginnings of the Bengal Famine of 1943–4, which killed at least three and a half million people. When it reached Calcutta from the villages, in August 1943, Satyajit had been at Keymer's for nearly six months. To understand his reaction to it, one must understand the scale of the catastrophe. Another eyewitness, editor of the Calcutta *Statesman* Ian Stephens, tried to come to terms with it and his own response in his book *Monsoon Morning*. He begins by saying that: 'Death or suffering if on a vast enough scale seems almost meaningless, like the stars or the waves of the sea. A single person's dying, even of a person one doesn't know, can shock one more than that of millions. And death by famine, anyway in a big Indian city, may from a casual glance be scarcely noticed at first.'

During the spring of 1943 famine approached Calcutta in its 'stealthy, deceptive way', says Stephens. Absorbed in running the *Statesman* short-staffed, he hardly noticed any difference. 'The hot weather passed, the rains began before it was evident that the famine had come: the real thing, the classical Indian famine of the historians, that terrifying ancient scourge. We were in it before we fully knew it.' Its causes were complex and did few groups in British-Indian society much credit, but the government reaction, then and in the months to come, was a matter for shame. Linlithgow, the Viceroy, did not even visit Calcutta. Here is how Stephens reacted in his first editorial on the subject, published in late August:

> Thoughtful Britons in this country must realise that so long as their nation, their Parliament, and their Secretary of State maintain some responsibility for India's welfare, the ultimate blame rests upon themselves ... In Indian public life are elements at least as causative of disaster: the unbridled greed of the mercantile classes, the hatreds among politicians, the widespread lack of civic sense. But India not yet being self-governing, disproportionately many of her people inevitably lack the tradition of public service. Under the present system, responsibility for breakdown rests in the last resort upon Authority in Britain and its representatives here.

Given the extent of official apathy, it is perhaps not surprising that Satyajit, along with most people he knew, did nothing to help the victims; but he still feels a sense of shame about it. 'One gets used to everything ultimately,' he says today after considerable reflection, including corpses lying stinking in the streets and the 'refrain' of their cries for *phyan*, the water usually thrown out once the rice is boiled. The reason that he gives for his general indifference at the time is honest, if somewhat shocking: he felt that he was 'getting established in life. New fields were opening before me, and there was my *intense* absorption into western music which was then at its height. So if one said I was a little callous about the famine, one wouldn't be far wrong; because one just got used to it, and there was nobody doing anything about it. It was too vast a problem for anyone to tackle.'

The period 1943–7 was in fact a most extraordinary one in the history of the second city of the British Empire, with the Partition following hard on the grim aftermath of the Famine. Trains from East Bengal unloaded their contents on to the railway platforms of Calcutta where they remained, whole families taking up just four to six square feet of space, including babies born on the spot. The immediate impact of the Second World War was negligible by comparison. Although Calcutta was bombed by the Japanese and hundreds of thousands left it (including the refuse collectors), damage was slight. It was the influx of American GIs and other Allied servicemen that changed things, and gave a kick to the city's cultural life. GIs used to seek out Satyajit at his house and tell him about a US movie playing in town or at their base – 'Wanna come?' For the first time in Calcutta it became normal to read a review of a US movie *after* seeing the movie – probably in a wafer-thin copy of *Time*. Because of the war, Ray was able to see films that had not been released even in London.

Concerts too were excellent, and there was jazz, which Satyajit enjoyed for a while. Apart from performances of Indian music – especially by the young Ravi Shankar – which Satyajit had begun to attend, he remembers hearing Isaac Stern, for instance. On the BBC he listened to Narayana Menon playing Bach on the *vina*, and on Berlin Radio to some good music broadcast along with Hitler's speeches. And in Bombay, where he had relatives and Bijoya was living for a while, he discovered a source of miniature scores and began buying them and reading them in bed. He taught himself western musical notation by comparing the score with his phenomenal musical memory, which could retain a symphony once he had heard it three times or so.

Until early 1948, he and his mother continued to live in his uncles' house at Rashbehari Avenue in south Calcutta, to which they had moved from Bhowanipur, via another house in the area. Satyajit had been looking for a flat – not an easy task in wartime – as he mentioned in his letter to Aronson in September 1945: 'I propose to have a room of my own which should be a library-cum-studio-cum-concert-room affair.' The place he eventually found was by no means all he had hoped, 'not nearly as much comfort as I used to have in my uncles' house', he lamented in a letter a month or so after moving. 'The noise in the neighbourhood is terrific. Radios, gramophones, yelling babies and what not. The first few days were really nerve racking. But I'm getting used to it slowly. I can play the gramophone only after things have quietened down around half past ten or eleven at night.'

He was writing to the man who had become his first British friend, Norman Clare. Music and war had brought them together while Clare was in the RAF in Calcutta from late 1944 until early 1946. Clare knew an RAF Communist who introduced him to the poet Bisnu Dey who knew Satyajit's concert-going companion, Chanchal Chatterjee, one of the group of Bengalis who knew western classical music. Clare stayed in the house of Satyajit's uncles for three or four months at the end of 1945 just as, about five years on, Satyajit and Bijoya would stay with him in London. India showed him that 'it was possible to respond to people in a different, more intimate way.' He remembers being on a bus reading a book in Bengali when someone called out aggressively, 'You can't read that.' Clare proved he could, whereupon everyone in the bus insisted on signing the book and inviting him to dinner. Yet he was also spat at while out walking in the smartest part of central Calcutta – an equally characteristic experience of the transition years of the Raj.

During the day, while Satyajit was at Keymer's, Clare sometimes went to the cinema with Bijoya: an unusual sight in the Calcutta of that time which Clare remembers provoked considerable gossip. He recalls her beauty and her obvious devotion to Manik. When Ray returned home from Keymer's he would immediately change out of western clothes into a dhoti or pyjama. Then they would chat, go and see a film, listen to music – Furtwängler being their favourite conductor – or play chess. 'There was a long time when I did nothing but play chess in the evening,' Ray says today. After Clare left he had no partner, so he took up solitaire chess; the habit wore off as he became engrossed in film-making, but resurfaced in the form of *The Chess Players*.

Clare remembers Satyajit as a gregarious person, whatever his aloofness in the office. Throughout his life Ray has always been open with people when he is interested in what they are saying or doing; it is only otherwise that he tends to withdraw into himself. For many years from the mid-1940s he used to meet a group of friends at a coffee house near Keymer's for an *adda*, a word that embraces extended gossip on every conceivable subject. 'Do not look down upon the *addas* in the Calcutta tea and coffee shops,' an energetic Bengali professor used to warn those who criticised Bengalis for being all talk and no action. 'They are unrecognised universities where heads clash and ideas emerge' – which is how Ray presented the *adda* in his film *Mahapurush (The Holy Man)*, where a group of friends conspire to nail a fake holy man. During Satyajit's *addas* in the coffee house he taught his friends quite a bit, learnt something himself (especially about how to deal with people), and had a lot of fun which included sharpening his skills on the *Times* crossword, published daily on the back page of the *Statesman*. It is a chatty, relaxed side of him that non-Bengalis seldom see, especially now that old-style *addas* have rather disappeared with the post-war pressures of Calcutta life.

Some of the members of the coffee-house group would play a role in Ray's film career too: apart from the musical Chanchal Chatterjee and Satyajit's old friend Pritwish Neogy from Santiniketan, there was Bansi Chandragupta, a Kashmiri who was then a dissatisfied art director in Bengali cinema and would become Ray's art director, Chidananda Das Gupta, then in advertising, who would become a film critic and father of the actress and film director Aparna Sen, R.P. Gupta, a voluble mine of information, and many others who sometimes turned up. But, by general agreement, the focus of attention was on Satyajit and a polymath called Kamal Kumar Majumdar. In R.P. Gupta's words, which have become an unofficial record of those days, while Majumdar 'gave vent to his views on anything from the sensibility of Mallarmé to the voluptuous rotundity of the *jala* [giant-sized clay jar], Ray provided the counterpoint to Majumdar's verbal pyrotechnics with his clarity of thinking, sharpness of wit and total sensibility.'

Majumdar, who would become Bengal's finest novelist of the post-war period, with a style somewhat akin to James Joyce, was probably the only contemporary of Satyajit's in Calcutta for whose overall artistic judgment he had a thorough respect. After he died in 1979, Ray wrote of him that 'it is beyond me to bring Kamal Babu back to life in a few words for those who did not know him. I have never come across another person who was such a bundle of apparent contradictions.' Of their coffee-house days together, he remembers most clearly Majumdar's acute irony. Once, referring to a certain left-wing poet, he said, 'That gentleman won't even take a pinch of snuff unless it contains social content.' 'Are peasants and labourers aware of the concern for their plight shown by the Marxist *babus* in the cities?' asks Ray. Or as Majumdar mischievously put it, 'Does the frog know it has a Latin name?' He was the first person to refer to sahibs as 'fair-faced gentlemen'. 'There was no rival to him in the oblique humour stakes, nor in the superb timing of his jokes. A friend of ours used to eat a double omelette every day in the coffee house. One day Kamal Babu, unable to restrain himself, said to him "A man who eats so many eggs needs to keep five mistresses." '

Politics and philosophy, except as subjects for humour, were just about the only topics excluded from these *addas*. Neither Majumdar nor Ray found them interesting, though some of the others felt differently. When asked what he was doing on Independence Day – 15 August 1947 – Ray has absolutely no recollection now. 'I remember the death of Gandhi very well,' he says. 'Because that day Chidananda Das Gupta and I had gone to Professor Mahalanobis asking him to be president of the Calcutta Film Society. On the way back in the tram they were selling the special editions of the newspapers and we read of Gandhi's assassination.'

Cinema was endlessly discussed, particularly after Ray and Das Gupta had founded the Film Society in late 1947 and even more after 1951 when Satyajit was at work on *Pather Panchali*. 'I am taking the cinema more and more seriously', he wrote to Clare in May 1948. He would regularly go to the cinema alone, but would also take along his friends after work on Saturdays, paying for them himself. By the time he returned from Santiniketan he had graduated from an admiration of stars and studios to a focus on directors. He began to take 'hieroglyphic' notes in the dark on their various cutting methods, particularly those of the Americans. Through his contacts with GIs, and otherwise, he saw recent films by Capra, Ford, Huston, Milestone, Wilder, and Wyler. He also saw a Hollywood Renoir, *The Southerner*, which he greatly liked.

Russian films too were available: *Alexander Nevsky*, *The Childhood of Gorky*, *Storm Over Asia*, *Ivan the Terrible Part 1*, and others. *Ivan* made a tremendous impression on him, though not entirely for its filmic qualities.

> The Gothic gloom of the film, Cherkasov's grand gestures, and the music of Prokofiev stayed with me all the day and well into the night, until I fell asleep and found them back in a grotesque dream, in the middle of which I woke up gasping for breath. It turned out that a *pan* I had bought from the shop next to the cinema had given me quinsy, swelling the inside of my throat to the point where I could hardly breathe.

He came to the conclusion around this time that Eisenstein reminded him of Bach and Pudovkin of Beethoven.

He continued to see Bengali films too. They had somewhat improved
with the arrival of Bimal Roy and Nitin Bose (his uncle referred to above), but
chiefly in the technical sense; their acting, dialogue and settings remained
theatrical. One exception, which made a virtue of its theatricality, was the
dance fantasy *Kalpana*, the work of the dancer Uday Shankar (Ravi Shankar's
elder brother) which Satyajit saw many times during 1948; 'I never knew
Indian music and dancing could have such an impact on me', he wrote to
Norman Clare in London. The film also contained some daring cutting.
In the darkness of the cinema hall, Satyajit took a series of photographs
of the shots that most appealed to him.

European films were rare then and became rarer still after the war
ended. Satyajit found himself leafing through the pages of *Sight and
Sound* (and *Sequence* slightly later), looking at the stills in frustration. It
was this that led him and Chidananda Das Gupta to think of starting the
Film Society.

Around 1946 he began writing film scripts as a hobby. He acquired
a copy of René Clair's published script *The Ghost Goes West* and also
the 1943 anthology *Twenty Best Film Plays*, compiled by John Gassner
and Dudley Nichols. When plans for a Bengali film were announced he
would write a scenario for it, in fact often two scenarios – 'his' way and
'their' way. In this manner he wrote ten or twelve scenarios. One of them
was for a film Bimal Roy was planning. Satyajit went to him and told him
about his script. It turned out that Roy admired him as a cover designer.
He invited him to the studio. When Satyajit went there he found himself
sitting watching Roy and the writer of the original story discuss the script for
four or five hours; he was entirely ignored. But today he feels no resentment
about this; after all, he says, he had absolutely no credentials.

A slightly later experience, with a screenplay he wrote based on
a very dramatic story by a well-known Bengali Marxist writer, was
much more typical of what he endured in the early 1950s at the
hands of Bengali producers. The story concerned 'an overbearing English
manager' of a zamindari, 'whose dark doings are brought to an end by a
plucky Bengali youth with radical leanings', in Ray's words. Carrying his
script, he was summoned to see the potential producer, a businessman. A
professional cameraman trained at UFA in the days of Pabst and Murnau
and a director with many hits to his credit were also present, among others. They sat down at 'the longest conference table I have ever seen' and
Satyajit began reading. After various comments the well-known director
put his arm round Satyajit's shoulder three-quarters of the way through,
and said to him, 'These words like "fade-out" – do you really know what
they mean?' At the end the producer said he liked it very much but he
had one piece of advice: when the hero finally confronted the cringing
English manager, the punchline should be – 'Quit India!' Ray's comment
today? 'It was a long time before *Pather Panchali* got made.'

The most amusing part of this, at least in retrospect, was that the producer had become interested in Ray after reading an article he had written – his first on the cinema – for the Calcutta *Statesman*, entitled 'What is wrong with Indian films?' Anticipating the polemics of *Cahiers du Cinéma*, he had analysed the failure of Indian directors to grasp the nature of the medium, and concluded with a resounding manifesto: 'The raw material of cinema is life itself. It is incredible that a country that has inspired so much painting and music and poetry should fail to move the film-maker. He has only to keep his eyes open, and his ears. Let him do so.'

The Calcutta Film Society was by then in operation. 'We have acquired a very bad reputation among professionals', wrote Satyajit to Clare, 'as conceited highbrow theorists who do nothing but debunk the Indian Cinema – which is of course very far from the truth.' It was actually India's second film society; Bombay had started one in 1942. Both suffered from crippling official red tape, as would be the case for many years to come. Under the terms of the Indian Cinematograph Act of 1918, and later amendments, nowhere, even the most innocuous gathering, was exempt from censorship. In other words, Independent India retained all the rigidity of colonial India. Besides a fee for films over two thousand feet in length, a complete script, a synopsis in eight copies and texts of songs in eight copies were required by the censors. About the one bright spot was that foreign embassies could show whatever they liked; that was how Satyajit had seen many of the Russian classics.

There were further problems: the predictable antipathy to quality and innovation of the existing industry, and the traditional antipathy of many middle-class Indians to film people. To begin with, Satyajit provided the books and magazines, Chidananda Das Gupta a room in his house that happened to be free. But, lacking a regular meeting place suitable for showing films, they took to doing the rounds of various rooms belonging to members of the Society. 'On one occasion, in the middle of our discussion,' Ray remembers, 'our friend was summoned by the owner of the house and summarily told that he would not put up with film people spoiling the sanctity of his house.'

In fact, for the first five years the membership refused to rise above twenty-five – and not all paid their subscriptions regularly, as Chidananda and Satyajit discovered to their cost. The membership included most of the coffee-house circle, Nemai Ghosh (no relation to Ray's stills photographer), who in 1949/50 made an interesting if melodramatic film *Chinnamul* about the Partition refugees, and Charuprakash Ghosh, a businessman who later part-financed *Aparajito* (and acted in it as the lecherous bachelor in Benares).

Despite its difficulties, the Society did show a lot of good films, some of them new to Satyajit, in the period up to 1952 when it temporarily folded up. They managed to get a print of *Battleship Potemkin* (which Satyajit had already learnt to pronounce correctly from Aronson), and Ray viewed it several dozen times. They also made a discovery at a local distributor: a print of *Un Carnet de Bal* which had been wrongly labelled. Das Gupta remembers Satyajit taking it home hugging the reels and refusing to let anyone else carry them.

They started a bulletin too, which Ray designed, using resources at Keymer's and Signet Press; some of the articles in his book *Our Films Their Films* first appeared in the Film Society Bulletin. Directors and others visiting Calcutta were invited to speak. Cherkasov and Pudovkin, Renoir and Huston all did so at various times. Satyajit asked Cherkasov how he had managed to get his eyes so wide open in *Ivan*, because looking at him it did not seem possible. Cherkasov said that Eisenstein had forced him to do it. 'He was slightly critical of the way he was handled by Eisenstein, made to assume postures that were very difficult, "so that at the end of the day I would have muscle pains all over my body".'

In 1948 the genial Harisadhan Das Gupta (no relation to Chidananda), a wealthy member of the coffee-house *adda* as well as the Film Society, embarked with Satyajit on an attempt to film Tagore's *Ghare Baire* (*The Home and the World*). They were an ill-matched pair, and the whole venture had an air of farce about it, painful though it was for both of them at the time. They had first met when Harisadhan had just returned from a year or so in California where he had gone to study nuclear physics and ended up studying Hollywood cinema. He sought out Satyajit in the three-room flat to which he had moved with his mother that year. Harisadhan had brought the latest model of Chevrolet with him from the USA and had great difficulty negotiating the bends to the flat. At that time, he says today, 'All Satyajit had was a small cot, a big pot of water and one small stool where I used to sit.'

Over the next year or so, they spent a lot of time together, and the idea of Harisadhan directing and Satyajit scripting a film of *Ghare Baire* took shape in their minds. Both of them saw it in Hollywood terms. Today, Das Gupta still does, Ray's 1984 film of the novel notwithstanding. As he rather staggeringly says, 'I consider that the best of Hollywood and British films – John Ford and David Lean – should be the goals for film-makers in this country. We are very much lost.'

Satyajit produced a script and, along with Bansi Chandragupta as art director, they began looking for locations and properties, an actress to play Tagore's Bimala, and a producer. Harisadhan had already bought the rights from the Tagore estate for an enormous sum – twenty thousand rupees, nearly thrice what was paid for *Pather Panchali*. He opened an office with a huge table and very comfortable chairs, and acquired a company name and a letterhead designed by Ray. Friends gathered there for tea and *adda*. A potential producer appeared – another Ghosh. He promised several hundred thousand rupees in backing. 'All we had to do was go to Nepal and collect some gold bars, *then* make the film,' recalls Das Gupta with a wry chuckle.

Another producer then appeared, this time for real. He made a contract with Satyajit and another with Harisadhan. But later he sent for them: he wanted one of his friends, yet another Ghosh, this one a doctor specialising in venereology, to hear the scenario too. After a while, both he and his consultant asked for some changes to be made. Harisadhan was in favour, Satyajit against. As he put it thirty-five years later, 'I was certainly not going to let a compromise sully my maiden contribution to the cinema.' A deadlock ensued and the producer terminated the contracts. The two friends did not speak to each other for quite a while afterwards. Satyajit 'felt like a pricked balloon' but much later, when he read the screenplay again in the mid-1960s, he felt it was 'the greatest good fortune the film was never made.' He could see 'how pitifully superficial and Hollywoodish' his screenplay was.

The following year, 1949, both Harisadhan and Satyajit were able to be of considerable assistance to Jean Renoir when he visited Calcutta in search of locations and actors for *The River*. Meeting Renoir changed Satyajit's life; not in an abrupt manner, which would be uncharacteristic of Ray's response to people, but because Renoir's attitudes to both life and film-making, and to Satyajit's own idea of filming *Pather Panchali* which he discussed with him in outline, appealed to him in their wholeness. It is not that Renoir and Ray were all that similar as personalities, simply that Satyajit recognised in Renoir a real film artist – the first he had come to know – and drew strength for his own work from the knowledge that such a person existed. Forty years later, while receiving the Legion of Honour from the President of France in Calcutta, Ray told him that he had always considered Renoir to be his 'principal mentor'.

They first met at a Calcutta hotel where Renoir and his wife were ensconced. Satyajit nervously sought him out. As he put it, in an excellent article he wrote for Lindsay Anderson in *Sequence* just after, 'Renoir was not only approachable, but so embarrassingly polite and modest that I felt if I were not too careful I would find myself discoursing upon the Future of the Cinema for his benefit.' He subsequently joined him and his wife on several trips to locations outside Calcutta by car and on foot, during which he was able to answer the majority of Renoir's barrage of questions; both his curiosity and his energy, given his size, were amazing. Renoir, for his part, found Satyajit's knowledge of the West 'fantastic', according to Chidananda Das Gupta. A second authority on Bengal who also helped Renoir was Satyajit's coffee-house companion Majumdar, a decided Francophile whose knowledge of Bengali village life was unrivalled. He told Renoir in his flamboyant way that it was impossible for him to make a good film on Bengal by remaining stuck in a hotel. Satyajit's approach to the great man, though he does not admit it in so many words, was quite different: 'very Anglo-Saxon, very correct', according to an amused R.P. Gupta.

Satyajit's erstwhile partner Harisadhan had been taken on by Renoir, to his great delight, as a kind of factotum, and it is he who gave Satyajit a copy of the first script of *The River*, written by Renoir and Rumer Godden (whose book it was) in Hollywood. Ray was quite disappointed by it and tried, very tactfully, to make some suggestions for improvements. 'Renoir would not say "All right, I'm now going to change it",' Ray comments today, 'but in the final script, when he returned after the recce, I saw the changes were there.' One of them referred to a prospective marriage between the American soldier Captain John and the half-caste girl Melanie; Ray advised against this, as it would have been both improbable and sentimental.

When Ray eventually saw the film, with Renoir in Hollywood in 1967, he was not surprised to find that he did not care for it very much, with the exception of the background – the life of the river – and the disappearance, after her little brother's death, of the young English girl who turns to the fishermen for consolation in the face of her parents' apparent indifference. This is a piece of psychology on a par with the central theme of *Aparajito* – a boy's growing indifference to his mother as he becomes a man – that so fascinated Ray. The rest of *The River* is picturesque, in his opinion, but does not carry conviction. Though *The River* is immensely more charming than David Lean's hollow *A Passage to India*, it belongs in the same class, not in that of the Apu Trilogy.

As an authentic picture of Indian life of any kind, *The River* was in fact doomed from the outset, partly because of Hollywood and partly because of Renoir himself, as is clear from his absorbing but slightly sad autobiography, *My Life and My Films*. His backer, a Beverly Hills florist who had served in India in the US Air Force, wanted a vehicle for an elephant hunt, while Renoir's agent preferred instead a tiger hunt. At Renoir's insistence they got neither, but even so he felt bound to play up the picturesque qualities of India to satisfy his American audience.

His own instincts towards the subcontinent were Gallic. Everything he saw made him either exult or fall into gloom; he lacked the ballast of basic knowledge of India's culture and history which counterbalances its immediate impact on the senses. Consequently, where his best work (in which I would include *The Golden Coach*, made after *The River*) is poetic, with the 'fairy-tale element' he said was essential to him – his Indian film is just romantic. There are many clues to this failure of imagination in Renoir's book, such as his swallowing of the insipid 'Santiniketan style' Satyajit so disliked, and his overstatement that 'the most important thing I learnt on that first trip was the reason for the Indians' resentment against the British. It was not because they had conquered them, but because they had ignored them. They treated them as though they weren't there. But the Indians have a longing for human contacts, a need for living warmth.' Renoir seems to have found this in Harisadhan Das Gupta (who, coincidentally, looks uncannily like Renoir), but not in Satyajit Ray whose knowledge of East and West made him reserve his enthusiasm for Renoir's project, while yielding to few in his admiration of the man as a humane genius. From hints dropped by Renoir, Ray realised the false position the director had got into, forced by war and French antipathy to his masterpiece *La Règle du Jeu* to migrate to Hollywood. And Renoir too must have sensed Ray's disapproval, without perhaps grasping its full implications. There seems no other explanation for the fact that Ray does not appear even *once* in Renoir's autobiography. Although he paid Ray some high compliments in Hollywood in 1967, he told the critic Penelope Gilliatt in 1974 that 'Ray is quite alone, of course.' In one important sense – that of Ray as film artist – Renoir was right; but in every other it is a misconception sadly typical of Renoir when speaking of India. He had simply failed to perceive the depth of Ray's Indian roots.

The shooting of *The River* began in late 1949 and continued through the first half of 1950. Bansi Chandragupta assisted Eugene Lourié; Subrata Mitra, later Ray's lighting cameraman, took stills. Satyajit himself was present as an observer on two or three occasions, but was unable to get further involved. There was his job at Keymer's to consider, and the fact that his British boss Broom had offered to send him to London for six months' training. 'Doubtless the management hoped that I would come back a fully-fledged advertising man wholly dedicated to the pursuit of selling tea and biscuits', he later wrote.

He had also at last married the girl he had known since the early thirties. Bijoya was the youngest granddaughter of his mother's aunt, which made her a kind of cousin to Satyajit: a fact that inevitably provoked comment in Calcutta. She had kept up her love of music and her childhood interest in acting had led to a brief unhappy spell in Hindi films in Bombay; she had also been a teacher and government servant in Calcutta. They married in Bombay in October 1948 with the minimum of fuss – just the signing of a register – but Satyajit's mother and his wife's elder sisters later persuaded them to have a, very simple, Brahmo ceremony in Calcutta presided over by Ksitimohan Sen, whom Satyajit had liked at Santiniketan. It had taken Suprabha Ray some years to come round to the idea of a cousin-marriage. As Bijoya put it forty years afterwards: 'My mother-in-law gave in and accepted me as her daughter-in-law gracefully. I am eternally grateful to her for this.'

For many months their plans were uncertain. Satyajit's mother fell very seriously ill. When she recovered, Satyajit and Bijoya had to make sure she would be properly cared for in their absence. Then there was *The River* to consider. Here is an extract from a letter of that time to Norman Clare from Bijoya, apologising for both her long silence and her English:

Would it be possible for you to get hold of a flat at such short notice? The other flats [mentioned in Clare's earlier letter] cannot possibly be vacant now. Please let me know whether I shall be required to take cutlery, crockery and kitchen utensils with me. Manik's boss,

Mr. Broom wanted us to leave earlier, but it was Manik who urged him to postpone it till the end of February. He had two reasons – of course he stated only one to Mr. Broom. To him he said he wanted to avoid the extreme cold weather [in London]. Actually his main reason was to watch Jean Renoir direct Rumer Godden's *The River*. As you know he is here to make the picture in technicolour, and Manik's enthusiasm to get to the bottom of things is boundless . . . Renoir has become very friendly with Manik and seems quite fond of him.

Clare's house in Hampstead had four storeys and a flat was free for Satyajit and Bijoya when they arrived in London in April 1950. For the first few days Clare remembers her standing behind Manik's chair at mealtimes feeding him titbits before taking her own food, as any traditional Indian wife might do. 'I am certainly no gourmet,' says Satyajit today, 'but good cooking has always been important to me.' (During their stay in London, Bijoya was tickled to discover the existence of such a thing as curry powder.)

Keymer's office was near the Strand and Satyajit went there every day by bus. It turned out to be smaller than the Calcutta office, which amused him. After he had been there a month or so an unpleasant incident occurred in which he was provoked into losing control of himself for the first and almost the last time in his life. 'It was a face-to-face confrontation,' says Ray, 'the sort of thing I generally avoid.' He had overheard his boss, a Mr Ball, claiming credit for a poster Keymer's had done for the *Observer* which was in fact Satyajit's work. Without abusing the man, he made it quite clear to him that he could not accept him as a boss, and walked out. Luckily, he was immediately able to join Benson's, another agency nearby, because it was a part of Keymer's. Broom wrote to him from Calcutta expressing full support.

Satyajit remained upset about the incident for days. Discussing it with Marie Seton many years later, he said, 'I had always thought the English in England were better people than the English who come to India.' Probably out of sensitivity for the embarrassment it might cause Clare, he did not even mention the matter to him, but he did tell Clare's mother about it because she asked; she had noticed a persistent scowl on his face.

Satyajit and Bijoya did a lot of walking in London during their five months there. (With his immense height Satyajit wanted nothing to do with Clare's scooter, after one brief run as a pillion passenger.) They were determined to visit as many exhibitions, concerts, plays and, of course, films as they could. Despite the office incident and the rationing, he remembers London as better then than on his many later visits. At exhibitions he used to leave the admission charge in an unattended bowl, for instance – 'I don't think that kind of thing is possible now,' he says. He stuck to the city and visited nowhere outside it, not even Oxford and Cambridge, favourite haunts of educated Indians. Tourism has never much appealed to him. As

Sukumar found on his trip to Britain forty years before, he needed some reason to identify with a place, usually a human one. Again like his father, he made relatively few friends among the English. Apart from Clare and his immediate family, there was really only Gavin Lambert, and Lindsay Anderson at *Sequence* with whom he had exchanged letters about Renoir – and who was born in India. He and Lindsay saw some films together, including the occasional film society viewing session lasting ten or twelve hours, which is where he remembers first seeing *Earth*. Lambert and Ray were never close but Anderson became a friend, though never intimate. 'I always knew Satyajit to be intelligent and sympathetic and I suppose that's fairly rare,' says Anderson reflectively. 'I think I knew instinctively there were areas we wouldn't share, but you didn't worry about them.' Although he encouraged Ray by letter during the long haul to make *Pather Panchali*, and gave it probably the finest review it has had, in the *Observer* in 1956 after the Cannes screening, they never discussed his plans for making the novel into a film in 1950. Anderson is not surprised by this. 'Satyajit is a guarded person; it all goes together with the kind of artist he is after all. He's not someone who would ever make himself easily accessible.'

The real sticking-point between them, then and later, was John Ford's work. Both of them certainly admired it, but where Anderson's admiration bordered on 'deification' (to use Ray's word), Ray's stopped well short of that. He dislikes Ford's 'sentimentality', his 'excessive proneness to nostalgia' and 'his readiness to yield to commercial pressures'. But, he says, 'Lindsay was absolutely up in arms and wouldn't come down. Even in letters we fought, we argued about it; he over-praised certain things in *Sequence* and I had my own view about it.' To which Anderson says today, 'I responded to Ford probably more deeply than he did, because I would probably respond to the emotional quality in Ford more than he would. But it's not something one can be heavy about.'

Of the roughly one hundred films that Satyajit saw while he was in London, including *La Règle du Jeu* which he rates one of the best films ever made, the revelation was unquestionably *Bicycle Thieves*. It 'gored' him. 'I came out of the theatre my mind firmly made up. I would become a film-maker', he said in his 1982 lecture, though characteristically, he did not let on about this even to Clare. 'The prospect of giving up a safe job didn't daunt me any more. I would make my film exactly as De Sica had made his: working with non-professional actors, using modest resources, and shooting on actual locations. The village which Bibhutibhusan had so lovingly described would be a living backdrop to the film, just as the outskirts of Rome were for De Sica's film.'

In the review he wrote on his return for the Film Society Bulletin, in which he largely dismisses the Italian films he saw in London (including *Rome, Open City*), Satyajit seems virtually to be describing his own film to come, when speaking of De Sica's scriptwriter:

[Zavattini's] greatest assets are an acute understanding of human beings and an ability to devise the 'chain' type of story that fits perfectly into the ninety-minute span of the average commercial cinema. Simplicity of plot allows for intensive treatment, while a whole series of interesting and believable situations and characters sustain interest . . . For a popular medium, the best kind of inspiration should derive from life and have its roots in it. No amount of technical polish can make up for artificiality of theme and dishonesty of treatment. The Indian film-maker must turn to life, to reality. De Sica, and *not* DeMille, should be his ideal.

Bicycle Thieves also reminded Ray of an artist in a different medium, whose work helped to inspire both the mood of *Pather Panchali* and the kind of lighting he strove for from the beginning. This was Henri Cartier-Bresson, whose work he had first seen as a teenager in the French magazine *Verve*, and later, in the early forties, in a book of photographs published by the Museum of Modern Art, New York (which happened to be the first place to screen *Pather Panchali* in 1955). Ray's admiration for him is warmly reciprocated by Cartier-Bresson. Ray has commented on his work in an exhibition catalogue of Indian photographs, in a way that also helps to define his own artistic aims. He describes Cartier-Bresson's style as 'unique in its fusion of head and heart, in its wit and poetry . . . The deep regard for people that is revealed in his Indian photographs, as well as in his photographs of any people anywhere in the world, invests them with a palpable humanism. Add to this the unique skill and vision that raise the ordinary and the ephemeral to a monumental level, and you have the hallmark of the greatest photographer of our time.'

But it is from a letter Satyajit wrote to Bansi Chandragupta from London that we get what is probably the most revealing insight into the effect of *Bicycle Thieves* on Satyajit, as well as a pronouncement applying to all his best films, and something close to a definition of his 'Indianness' as an artist:

> The entire conventional approach (as exemplified by even the best American and British films) is wrong. Because the conventional approach tells you that the best way to tell a story is to leave out all except those elements which are directly related to the story, while the master's work clearly indicates that if your theme is strong and simple, then you can include a hundred little apparently irrelevant details which, instead of obscuring the theme, only help to intensify it by contrast, and in addition create the illusion of actuality better.

Satyajit and Bijoya left London in September 1950, heading for the galleries and concert-halls of the Continent before sailing for home about a month later. They visited Lucerne, attended the Music Festival at Salzburg and the Biennale in Venice, and spent a week in Paris where their money ran very low. In Salzburg they were determined to hear Furtwängler conduct the Vienna Philharmonic in Mozart's *The Magic Flute*, which Satyajit feels is 'the most enchanting, the most impudent and the most sublime of Mozart's operas'. The tickets were all sold. Cheated by an usher, who charged them three times the price and then absconded, they stood for half an hour in the aisle until two German youths gave up their seats to them, saying in English, 'You must be from India.' Perhaps it was an unacknowledged tribute to Tagore's tremendous impact on Germany in the 1920s – who knows?

At Venice, Satyajit dropped a line to Chandragupta: 'Venice is a fantastic place – very reminiscent of Benares in some ways, and equally photogenic.' His comment had a curious prescience about it. Seven years later he would come back to Venice for a different reason: to collect the Golden Lion at the Venice Film Festival, for *Aparajito*, a film which opens in Benares.

5

The Making of Pather Panchali
(Song of the Little Road) 1950–5

❖❖[❦ ☙❀☙ ❧]❖❖

THE novel that Ray had mentally committed himself to filming had by 1950 become a classic in Bengal. It first appeared as a serial in a Calcutta journal in 1928, on condition that it could be discontinued if it proved unpopular with readers; both its style and its author were then unknown. In fact, the story of Apu and Durga rapidly established itself in the imagination of Bengal, and the novel appeared in book form the following year. Although Banerjee wrote about fifty published works in all, *Pather Panchali* remains his best known.

It is based, to a great extent, on Banerjee's own impecunious early life. He was born in 1894 in a village north of Calcutta. His father was a priest who also had a good voice for singing traditional songs. His mother was a village girl. The family lived in extreme poverty, as a result of the father's impracticality. Although it included no daughter like Durga in the novel, Banerjee had a cousin who fits the character, judging from the diary he kept, which also mentions an old aunt who lived with the family – the model for Indir Thakrun of *Pather Panchali*.

Somehow, Banerjee managed to matriculate from a local school and obtain a degree in Calcutta. While still at college, he married a girl, but lost her a year later in the great influenza epidemic of 1918. Like his Apu, he was devastated by the loss; though he had several subsequent romantic attachments, he did not marry again until his mid-forties. Meanwhile he became a teacher, living at first in a squalid bazaar near the railway station of a village outside Calcutta, until moving back to the city around 1924.

According to Nirad Chaudhuri, who became a close friend of Banerjee at this time (and helped him to get his novel published in book form), 'his hard life had not embittered him, nor made him a cynic. His sympathy for ordinary people was unlimited, and he was not repelled even by the squalor in which such people had to live in our society. Somehow, he could always make them rise above their surroundings; I would even say – far above the limitations of their world.'

Pather Panchali is a novel with a plethora of characters in it. But the main ones, as in the film, are the growing boy Apu, his elder sister Durga, their mother Sarbajaya and father Harihar Ray who is a priest, and his elderly distant relative Indir Thakrun. There is an extended prologue too about the ancestry of the Ray family, one of whom was a brutal robber; the shadow of his deeds is thought to have fallen on succeeding generations. The sad history of Indir Thakrun, who is about seventy-five when the main story begins, is also described. She is very soon dead, treated with extreme callousness by Sarbajaya, who cannot bear to share with her what meagre food she can scrape together; Durga's affection for the old lady cannot save her. The bulk of the novel is about the small family's struggle to survive in their ancestral home in the village. Durga dies of a fever, and the house decays beyond repair. Eventually Harihar decides to pull up his roots and leave. He, his wife and Apu depart for Benares where their life continues; in fact, nearly a fifth of the novel takes place in the city. Ray incorporated this section into *Pather Panchali*'s sequel, *Aparajito (The Unvanquished)*.

His adaptation involved drastic compression, elision and omission of scenes in the novel, as well as occasional additions. Out of a seemingly random sequence of significant and trivial episodes, Ray had to extract a simple theme, while preserving the loitering impression created by the original. 'The script had to retain some of the rambling quality of the novel,' comments Ray, 'because that in itself contained a clue to the feel of authenticity: life in a poor Bengali village does ramble.' Much of the power of the film lies in this calculated enriching of an elemental situation by contrasts: as Durga delights her old 'auntie' with a stolen fruit, Sarbajaya ticks her off for taking it; as Indir Thakrun goes off to die in the forest, Apu and Durga bubble with life; and as Harihar returns to the village, terribly overdue but happy because he is bearing gifts for his wife and children, Sarbajaya can think only of the child who has left them forever during his absence.

Major changes made to the novel by Ray all have their rationale and do not diminish it. The death of Indir, for instance, takes place well into the film when we have got to know her well, and out in the open so that the two children come across her corpse and appreciate the meaning of Death; in the novel she dies early on at a village shrine in someone's house and only adults are present. Nor, in the novel, do either of the children ever see a train, until Apu boards one after leaving the village – though they attempt to. Nor is Durga's death the direct consequence of getting wet in the monsoon; the cause of her fever in the novel is left mysterious. Finally, there is the ending of the film: Ray felt, as have others who have translated and abridged the novel, that the departure from the village formed a natural break.

The only valid criticism of Ray's approach might lie in the film's attenuated sense of the village as a whole. In the novel we learn more about its history and geography – there is, for instance, a ruined indigo factory with a child's gravestone still visible belonging to the son of a long-departed British planter's family – and thereby gain a deeper feeling of Harihar's roots there, which in turn strengthens our understanding of his reluctance to leave his house after disaster befalls him.

Ray's principal challenge in turning *Pather Panchali* into a film was, ironically enough, to dispel his ignorance of village life. Unlike Tagore, and many other Bengali writers, Ray had very little first-hand knowledge of it apart from what he had seen in the villages around Santiniketan sketching and painting. He had to invent ways to convey on the screen the all-important atmosphere of Banerjee's novel, which is full of descriptions such as this:

> Durga was a big girl now, and her mother would no longer let her go to parties far from home. She had almost forgotten what *luchis* tasted like. Until a little while ago, when the nights were bright with the full moon of September and the path through the bamboo grove was like a thread woven of light and shade, she used to wander all round the village and come back with her sari full of sweets and dried, pressed and toasted rice for the Lakshmi festival. At this time of the year conches were being blown in every house, and all along the path floated the smell of frying *luchis*. She always hoped that somebody in the village would send some as part of the festival offering. Whatever sweets she brought back were made to last for two days and her mother had some too. This year however Sejabou [their neighbour] had said to her mother, 'It isn't right for a girl of a good family to wander round from house to house collecting sweets as if she were a peasant girl. It doesn't look nice.' So from then on she was not allowed to go.

As Ray put the problem in his 1982 lecture:

> You had to find out for yourself how to catch the hushed stillness of dusk in a Bengali village, when the wind drops and turns the ponds into sheets of glass, dappled by the leaves of *saluk* and *sapla*, and the smoke from ovens settles in wispy trails over the landscape, and the plaintive blows on conchshells from homes far and near are joined by the chorus of crickets, which rises as the light falls, until all one sees are the stars in the sky, and the stars that blink and swirl in the thickets.

Pather Panchali never had a proper script. Unlike every other Ray film, there is no red shooting notebook for it. Instead, he had a treatment which he had started on board ship from London and, from early 1952, a sheaf of sketches of the most important shots in black ink which he deposited, years later, at the Cinémathèque in Paris. Most of the film's dialogue, three-quarters of which came from Banerjee, he kept in his head. By showing producers these sketches, which were of course unheard of in Bengali films, and telling them the story, he hoped to raise interest in a film with him as its director.

First, though, he took his work to Banerjee's widow – whose husband had died just after Satyajit's return from London – to persuade her to part with the rights to the novel. She received him warmly, being an admirer of both Upendrakisore's and Sukumar's work, and of Satyajit's cover designs. She said that her husband had always believed his writing had film potential but that no one had seemed interested. She gave her agreement in principle, but no financial arrangements were discussed. When the news was announced in the papers, she received letters from friends rebuking her for her faith in an unknown; but, fortunately for Ray, she stuck by him throughout the long and painful gestation of his film.

Like Renoir, who touted the script of *La Grande Illusion* round French producers for three years (often with Jean Gabin, his chief draw, rather than a famous story, in tow), Ray spent nearly two years trying to sell his idea on the back of the novel's fame. Most of those who half-listened to him could not see beyond the fact that he offered neither songs nor dances; a few who had more imagination nonetheless insisted on a co-director. 'They were stupid people,' says Ray. 'They believed only in a certain kind of commercial cinema. But one kept hoping that presented with something fresh and original and affecting, they would change.'

One of them, who undoubtedly perceived commercial possibilities in the story if conventionally done, played a trick on Ray. This man met him, heard him out, and suggested a further meeting a week later to draw up a contract. In the meantime he paid a visit to Mrs Banerjee with a proposal that the successful director Debaki Bose do the film, and made a large offer for the rights. She turned him down.

Ray got only one genuine offer, and that fell through when the producer's then-current film opened and failed. But the man who had arranged this meeting, Anil Chowdhury, joined the small group around Ray (including Subrata Mitra and Bansi Chandragupta) which would make *Pather Panchali* possible. He became production controller of that and all subsequent films by Ray.

In mid-1952 Chowdhury recalls Satyajit declaring to him in his office at D.J. Keymer that he could live in limbo no longer. Four years before, he had written to Norman Clare, 'It looks as if I'll have to rot and be exploited in Keymer's for some time [yet].' He now decided to borrow around seven thousand rupees from his insurance company and another two thousand or so from his relatives, to shoot enough footage to persuade a producer to back the whole film. If no one would, he said to Chowdhury, he would have to remain a commercial artist forever.

Ray was determined to prove the industry's professionals wrong in their conviction that outdoors shooting with amateur actors was unworkable. He and Subrata Mitra hired an old 16mm camera and set off one weekend for Gopalnagar, the village on which Banerjee had based his fictional one. It was the rainy season and they had to squelch through knee-deep mud to get there. They filmed in 'the dim light of a mango grove, in pouring rain and in the falling light of dusk.' Every shot came out.

But the village itself Ray considered to be insufficiently photogenic. So his next problem was to find a location suitable for the daytime scenes in the film (the night-time ones were to be shot in the studio from the beginning). Besides a house of the right general layout and decay to fit Harihar Ray's, the story demanded a pond nearby, a river, fields and a railway line. In the event, Ray settled for two locations: the ruined house and pond in the village of Boral only six miles from the centre of Calcutta, and the fields (where Apu and Durga run together) and the railway line about a hundred miles away. The river he decided to drop. After negotiations with the owner of the house, 'a nasty old man' bedridden in Calcutta to whom they had to pay fifty rupees every month for the next two and a half years, Chandragupta set to work on an extensive conversion.

They began shooting on 27 October 1952, in the fields. Ray felt that the scene in which Apu chases Durga through a field of white *kash* (similar to pampas grass) and sees a train for the first time, would make a fine come-on for a producer. But he did not appreciate just how tough a target he had set himself as a director. Some of the lessons it taught him he has recorded in various articles in *Our Films Their Films*; they concern, mostly, the correct use of camera and lenses, but one involved the direction of Apu. He was expected to walk haltingly through the *kash* as if on the lookout for Durga. 'Little did I know then that it was twice as hard to achieve impeccability in a shot like that than in a shot of, say, charging cavalry.' It did not help that Subir Banerjee was a decidedly unresponsive actor. Ray's solution in the end was to lay small obstacles in the boy's path for him to measure his progress by, and to have various assistants hiding in the *kash* on either side who would call him at prearranged moments. Ray's perception of the way that De Sica handled the father in *Bicycle Thieves* (rather than the boy) helped to give him the confidence to direct his child actor as a puppet too.

In his first film Ray confesses he felt 'safer with non-actors', but it would be wrong to assume, as many have done, that all the actors in *Pather Panchali* had no prior experience. When Ray attended a seminar in the US in 1958, organised by Robert Flaherty's widow who greatly admired *Pather Panchali*, he had to use a lot of persuasion to convince her he had been right to use non-villagers in the film. In fact, of the main characters, Indir Thakrun, Harihar, the two women neighbours and the grocer-teacher were all played by professionals, while Karuna Banerjee (Sarbajaya) and Uma Das Gupta (Durga) had had experience on the stage; only the smaller roles were played by the villagers of Boral.

To find Apu, Ray had advertised in newspapers asking five- to seven-year-old boys to come and see him. Hundreds turned up – even a girl,

whose parents had had a salon cut her hair and powder her shoulders –
but the choice eventually fell on a boy whom Bijoya spotted playing on
the roof next to the flat they were now renting in south Calcutta. Durga
was discovered by a friend of Ray's who knew the headmistress of a girls'
school in Calcutta. When Uma Das Gupta met Ray she thought she was
auditioning for a stage play. She put on a pearl necklace of which she was
proud. 'The first remark Manikda made was that I would have to take it
off.' Karuna Banerjee (who is the mother in real life of the young Durga
in the early part of the film) was suggested to Ray by her husband Subrata,
his friend and colleague in Keymer's. She was not enthusiastic and wrote to
Satyajit saying so, suggesting another actress. Although she had acted a good
deal in the Indian People's Theatre Association (IPTA) – the federation of
groups formed all over India in the early 1940s to which creative people
of all kinds were drawn – she was fairly conventional in her view of the
cinema as unsuitable for respectable women. Family pressure persuaded
her otherwise. As Sarbajaya, she never felt any difficulty in identifying
herself with a village housewife living in poverty. Although her life had
been spent in cities, she had been born in a large family in East Bengal
and, like the Ray family of Sukumar's generation, she used to return to
the ancestral village at festival time when she was growing up.

But of all Ray's casting in *Pather Panchali*, his most inspired choices
must be Tulsi Chakravarti as the grocer-teacher, and Chunibala Devi as
Indir Thakrun. Chakravarti, at the time Ray cast him, was very well known
in Bengal for a kind of broad comic acting which Ray did not much care for.
He had run away from home when he was fifteen or sixteen and joined a
circus party where he became a trapeze artist. Later, after acting in silent
films, he joined the payroll of New Theatres (where Satyajit's uncle Nitin
Bose was a director), and played bit-parts like landlords, money-lenders
and grocers. Ray had felt a marvellous expressiveness in his face, and sensed
that he was being wasted. He was delighted when Chakravarti agreed to
play in *Pather Panchali*; 'I was a nobody at that time – in the film business
anyway,' he says. At the end of the first day's shooting, Chakravarti told him,
'I've never had so much interesting business.' A few years later, not long
before his death, he gave one of the best performances ever delivered in
a Ray film, as the humble clerk who finds the philosopher's stone in the
film of that name.

The early shots of *Pather Panchali* had already been taken before
Ray located an old woman capable of playing Indir Thakrun; it still
surprises him to think that he could have been so heedless of the risk
he was running. During the shooting he often found himself thinking that
Pather Panchali could not have happened without Chunibala. Banerjee's
description of the old woman was a tall order to fulfil: 'seventy-five, sunken
cheeks, slightly crooked at the waist and hunched forward – she cannot see
things at a distance as she once could.' Not that Calcutta lacked for such
old women, but the part also required acting ability, stamina and a good

memory. Ray's chances were not improved by the fact that he intended using no make-up, as his newspaper advertisements made clear; he was always against making up a younger actress for the part.

He heard about Chunibala Devi from the professional actress Reba Devi (no relation – 'Devi' simply indicates a married woman), who played the part of the shrewish neighbour in *Pather Panchali*. It turned out that Chunibala was the mother of a well-known actress, though unmarried. She was about eighty and had been on the stage in the first decades of this century, when she also acted in silent films. Since then she had been more or less retired.

Satyajit paid a visit to Chunibala's house in a red light district of north Calcutta. He was soon satisfied. When asked if she could recite a rhyme Chunibala recalled many more lines of a particular lullaby than Satyajit himself knew. And when asked if she were capable of rising at six, travelling fifteen miles to the location, standing up to a day's shooting followed by the journey back, she was quite certain she was. The only condition she made, apart from a small salary, was that she should be provided with her daily dose of opium. The one day she did not get it, she fainted.

From the beginning, Chunibala grasped Ray's intention that the film should display no artifice. 'She was constantly aware that authenticity was the touchstone of her performance', he has written. She was careful to wear her widow's sari with its torn portions knotted, as a poor woman in her position would do. After a while the garment became really ragged and barely covered her decently. When word of her feelings reached Satyajit he asked for a new piece of cloth to be provided for her with fewer holes in it. This was done, but when Chunibala next appeared on set she was still wearing the old sari. Her memory for continuity was formidable. Ray remembers that she often picked up details he had missed, with comments like, 'That time it was my right hand which was wet', 'Wait, there was no sweat on my face before', 'In this shot my shawl wouldn't be covering me', 'Was my bundle in my right hand? No, it was in my left. My brass pot was in my right.'

The village of Boral provided most of the remaining actors. Although Ray had an introduction to someone in the village, the initial reaction to him and his team was not very friendly, at least among the older villagers. This quite soon improved though, as the conversion of the ruined house progressed and shooting began using some of the locals. Anil Chowdhury recalls that one incident was particularly effective in thawing the atmosphere. Ray had seen someone in the village whom he wanted to play the bald-headed villager woken by the first drop of monsoon rain on his pate, but he did not know his name. So he scribbled a quick sketch of the man, who was promptly fetched by his excited neighbours.

The enthusiasm that comes from breaking new ground pervaded the production. In the words of Subrata Banerjee, who watched some of the shooting, 'Satyajit seemed a different person. He was rarely withdrawn. There was an abandon about him. The warmth in his relations with others that was rarely evident came out clearly ... He could easily set the mood for an occasion by his own behaviour. He seemed to live through the experiences of the characters he was creating for his film and so did the individuals who portrayed the parts.' Banerjee's wife Karuna agrees, as do the great majority of those who act with Ray; their most frequent observation is that they 'never felt they were acting'.

There was one person in Boral who intrigued Ray more than any other, though he does not appear in *Pather Panchali*. He was the first to greet them the day they arrived to shoot. He called out loudly, 'The film people are 'ere! Watch out! Reach for your spears, reach for your spears!' He believed that the villagers were equally untrustworthy, as he confided when he came to know Ray and his team a bit better. They had cheated him of land, he said, and he had ancient deeds to prove it. He believed that deceit was in the very marrow of Boral. Once, he told Ray, 'Imagine ten men walking along a village path in single file on a totally moonless night. Not one of them has brought a lamp – they're that mean. The leading man falls into a hole, and as he does so, he keeps himself to himself – he doesn't warn the others. And so every one of them falls into the hole and none of them lets out a peep for fear of benefitting the others. That's what they're like here in Boral.' He had names for many of them too, reckoning Churchill and Hitler among his neighbours. He would see a certain man cycling by and say, quite seriously, 'That's Roosevelt. He hasn't forgotten his tricks. What a devilish fellow!' Subodhda, as this crackpot was called, must have helped Ray create the memorable madman in *The Postmaster*. About five years after he had left Boral, Ray had occasion to return there. He felt disappointed to find Subodhda sane. Gone were his ancient land deeds and his accusations. His only vaguely interesting remark was, 'I wish you'd come in the mango season. They were good this year.'

The shooting in Boral did not begin until early 1953. There had been a gap of some months after those first shots in the field of *kash* while Ray made a fresh effort to interest producers in his footage. In the meantime there came encouragement of a different sort – the first international film festival to be held in India. He and his friends rushed from cinema to cinema, seeing about four films a day for a fortnight. 'Mercifully,' says Ray, 'there were no jurors, no prizes, no seminars, few parties, and only a handful of visiting celebrities.' The director Mrinal Sen, who was then a medical representative, noted in his diary:

10 a.m.–12 noon   Visiting doctors: 4 will do.
3 p.m.   At Purna Theatre: *Rome, Open City* by Roberto Rossellini
6 p.m.   At Menoka: *Jour de Fête* by Jacques Tati
9 p.m.   At Light House: *Miracle in Milan* by Vittorio De Sica.

The film that made the biggest impression on Ray and his friends was *Rashomon*. They knew of its rave reviews at Venice the previous year. Ray saw it three times on consecutive days 'and wondered each time if there was another film anywhere which gave such sustained and dazzling proof of a director's command over every aspect of film-making.' He was thrilled by the camerawork in the woodcutter's journey through the forest, 'cut with axe-edge precision'. Only the sharp-tongued Kamal Majumdar disagreed: when asked, he said that 'the scene by the river where the policeman brandished his stick was good.'

The success of the unknown Akira Kurosawa in the West gave further impetus to Ray's fledgling ambitions, and suggested that *Pather Panchali* might one day find a western audience too. A film made in India at that time, which Ray later described as a 'landmark', also encouraged him, since it was made partly on location, concerned a peasant family, and involved few songs and no dances. This was Bimal Roy's *Do Bigha Zamin* (*Two Acres of Land*) which won the Prix International at the 1954 Cannes Festival.

Seeing Ray's footage, a producer called Rana Dutta eventually came forward, and advanced enough money for Ray to shoot some scenes in Boral. No one involved could be paid, bar one assistant, Santi Chatterjee (who remained with Ray until his death), and, among the cast, Chunibala Devi. Things were run on such a slender shoestring that Anil Chowdhury took to sleeping in taxis for lack of an alarm clock; the taxi-driver simply parked his vehicle on a tramway and woke up as soon as the first tram of the day appeared!

Shooting was in progress when some of Rana Dutta's films opened and failed. There was no money now even to buy lunch. Chowdhury turned, in desperation, to Bijoya, who agreed to pawn some of her jewellery. It realised Rs 1300. They had to get it back later, in exchange for some belonging to Chowdhury's sister, so that Bijoya could wear it at a ceremony just before the birth of her son Sandip; neither she nor Satyajit wanted his mother to discover what they had done for the sake of the film (they later found out she already knew but had kept the secret to herself).

The nadir of Ray's hopes was reached in the latter part of 1953 and early 1954. He had shown his four thousand feet of edited footage to just about every producer in Bengal and they had been 'completely apathetic'. In several attempts to find producers he had paid middle men with money raised by selling his art books and records, without telling even his wife, and been cheated. The only bright spot was his absolute conviction that he was doing something important, certainly in Indian films, and perhaps internationally too. 'The rushes told us that. The rushes told us that the children were behaving marvellously and the old woman was an absolute stunner. Nobody had ever seen such an old woman in an Indian film before.'

Ray's friends at the coffee house, and the British Managers at Keymer's, also helped to maintain his confidence. He had been showing them stills as the work progressed; R.P. Gupta remembers his feeling of excitement on first seeing these. One – a three-shot of Sarbajaya and Durga getting Apu ready for school – was selected for Edward Steichen's exhibition 'The Family of Man'. Ray was also showing rushes to some of his friends. He remembers Chanchal Chatterjee telling him that 'this is India's first adult film.'

The Managers permitted Maneck Roy, who was the jewel in their crown, to take time off to shoot his film as he saw fit. This leave was both paid and unpaid. The Manager of the Bombay branch, Robert Hardcastle, recalls visiting Calcutta on business some time in 1953/54 and seeing Ray's sketches at the insistence of the Calcutta Manager. He was very struck by 'their power and atmosphere'. Shooting was at that time suspended and Ray told Hardcastle one of his main anxieties was that his elderly actress would die.

The gap in the shooting lasted almost a year. In the early months of 1954 two sources of help appeared, one foreign, the other indigenous. Monroe Wheeler, of New York's Museum of Modern Art, turned up in Calcutta in April in pursuit of work for an exhibition of Indian textiles and ornaments. He got to hear of the film and visited Ray at his office. The stills he saw there excited him. 'He felt it was very high quality lighting, composition, faces, textures and so on,' says Ray. 'That gave him the notion it would be a film worth showing at his festival.' Together with Pritwish Neogy they paid a visit to Santiniketan, which has a strong craft tradition that interested Wheeler. He came to know Ray quite well, and 'I think he got the impression I would come up with something exciting. "Do you think you could let us have this film for our exhibition?" he asked. "That's a year from now."' Ray could hardly believe his ears.

The second source was the Government of West Bengal, whose Chief Minister was then an energetic figure with a Brahmo background and Gandhian sympathies, Dr B.C. Roy. He had helped Uday Shankar fund his film *Kalpana*. Satyajit's mother had a friend who knew him. Though doubtful about film-making as a way of life, she never doubted her son's talent, and was distressed by the failure of his hopes; so she arranged for her friend to see the edited footage. The friend then persuaded Dr Roy to see it too. He was sympathetic but, from the beginning, misunderstood the film's nature, seeing it as a documentary promoting rural uplift. Clearly, he did not know the novel. But he directed his officials in the Home Publicity Department to examine the costs of backing *Pather Panchali*.

They cared little for the novel either and still less about the film. Ray's experience with them was one of pure frustration, but even today, he restrains his criticism. One of the officials, watching the magical scene in which the procession of sweet-seller, Durga, Apu and a village dog is reflected in a pond, shouted out that the film was running backwards!

Contracts were drawn up, in which Mrs Banerjee was paid for the film rights to the novel, Rana Dutta for the money he had already spent, and Satyajit Ray nothing. Nothing was put in writing about foreign rights

either, but Ray made a verbal agreement with the head of the Publicity
Department that he would share in these, should the film be sold abroad, as
Ray suspected might happen. This was later overlooked by the Government
– which meant that Satyajit Ray received no income whatsoever from *Pather
Panchali.* 'They get the money but I got the fame,' he told Marie Seton a
few years later.

The most tiresome aspect of this relationship was that Ray and his team
had to render accounts for each stage of the shooting, before the officials
would release the next instalment of money. 'It was very unpleasant,' says
Ray today. 'It meant, for one thing, that we missed the rainy season, and
we had to shoot the rain scenes in October. Throughout the rainy season
we had no money. It meant going to the location every day with the entire
crew and cast and just waiting. There were days and days of waiting and
doing nothing . . . it was a kind of picnic, but not a very pleasant picnic.
We would keep looking at the sky and at little patches of cloud which
wouldn't produce any rain.'

If it is amazing that they were able to make such an authentic film
under these conditions, it is a miracle that they did not fall foul of other,
more intransigent obstacles. Three miracles to be precise, according to
Satyajit: 'One, Apu's voice did not break. Two, Durga did not grow up.
Three, Indir Thakrun did not die.'

Ray even sees advantages in the delays. First, he learnt to assess the
length of a scene in scenario form, and secondly, to edit a film in sections,
thus saving time later. This way of editing soon became a habit with him,
even when it was no longer a necessity. More important, he learnt a lot
about technique from a severe scrutiny of the material he had shot before
being forced to stop, which was about half the film, and he applied this in
shooting the second half. Today he feels the first half needs cutting, because
'the pace sometimes falters . . . And there are certain things we couldn't
do anything about, like camera placements. I don't think the relationship
of the three little cottages is very clear in the film. You have to choose a
master-angle which you keep repeating so that people get their bearings.
If you keep changing the camera angle, it becomes very confusing. In your
mind the plan is very clear but to make it clear on the screen you have to
use certain devices which we didn't know at that time.'

The shooting of *Pather Panchali* was a mixture of the premeditated
and the improvised. It is quite clear from Ray's initial sheaf of sketches
how much he improved his scenario by his long exposure to the locations
themselves. All the elements in the opening sequence of the film – Durga
picking up fruit and skipping home to Indir Thakrun, Sarbajaya drawing
water wearily from the well with the suspicious neighbour watching her
and then ticking off Durga for stealing – are there in Ray's sheaf of initial
sketches, but in the film the inter-relationships are made more graphic
because the neighbour actually sees Durga take a fruit and Sarbajaya is
forced to overhear her caustic comments.

One of the premeditated sequences was the passing away of Indir Thakrun. Her solitary death, followed by the children discovering her corpse, was entirely Ray's invention; as Durga playfully shakes her squatting form, it crashes over and her head hits the ground with a sickening thud. This is the only scene at which Chunibala demurred – not because of the potential injury but because she felt Indir's death at the village shrine, as it is in the novel, to be more appropriate. Ray persuaded her both to do the scene his way and not to worry about hurting herself. He will always remember the mixture of elation and exhaustion on her face after taking that shot.

For her funeral, which is not described in the novel, Ray again decided to be unconventional by avoiding the usual chant; in his experience there were always some people in an Indian audience who would feel obliged to join in. His aim was to invest the scene with beauty as well as sadness, rather than just making it grim. So he decided to have Indir Thakrun's body carried out on a bier at sunrise down a village path, to the accompaniment of her familiar mournful song.

At five o'clock they were standing ready to shoot. When Chunibala arrived by taxi Ray plucked up his courage and broke the news to the old lady, 'Today we will carry you out on a bier.' She was not in the least put out. So they spread a mat on a bamboo bier, covered her with the shawl that in the story she begs from a neighbour, and fastened everything securely with rope. There was a rehearsal and the funeral procession began. The shot complete, the bier was put down and the ropes untied. But Chunibala Devi did not stir. The team looked at each other. What could have happened? They were in a cold sweat. Suddenly they heard Chunibala's voice – 'Is the shot over? Why didn't anyone tell me? I'm still lying here dead'!

Another scene involving death was handled with less certainty by Ray. This is the return of Harihar to find his house ruined and his daughter dead, followed by Sarbajaya's breakdown. Her grief-stricken wail is expressed not by her own voice but by the *tarshehnai* playing a passage of high notes; the effect is to intensify Sarbajaya's pain and to transform it into something nobler and universal.

This substitution was not in Ray's mind at the time of shooting. The day before he had written Karuna Banerjee a note about the situation, and on the day itself she remembers that he told her, 'Don't be afraid to distort your face. If it gets distorted, don't worry, just be normal, as it comes.' But in the editing-room he came to feel that the scene required a 'special, heightened quality' not accessible to the naked voice. After adding the music he considered keeping the crying sound too, but he decided they were ineffective in combination. He did not tell Karuna, though; when she first saw the film, she jerked forward in surprise at that point. Although it disappointed her then, she now feels Ray's notion was a wonderful one.

A tiny detail from that same sequence gives a good idea of how definite Ray's intentions in his first film normally were. When Sarbajaya first hears Harihar calling out for his children, she is vacantly squatting, with her arm and a white bangle pressed against her cheek. Involuntarily, she reacts to her husband's voice and moves her arm; the bangle slips down slightly. The indifference of her gesture suggests just how indifferent to the world she has become. It took Ray seven takes to get it to move exactly as he wanted it to.

He was also determined to get a typical village dog to trot along behind Durga and Apu as they follow the sweet-seller. The dog he chose was fine in rehearsal but wholly uninterested under the camera's gaze. This time it took twelve takes, about a thousand feet of film and a *sandesh* invisibly held out behind Durga's back to make the dog perform properly.

Of the scenes that were wholly improvised, three are outstanding. First, there are the water-skaters and dragonflies exploring the twigs and plants in the pond like Apu exploring his village; along with Ravi Shankar's sitar music, they herald the coming of the monsoon. The scene only occurred to Ray after the music had been composed. Secondly, there is the train rumbling away from Apu and Durga into the distance leaving a swathe of black smoke against the white *kash* flowers. Five trains were used in shooting the scene. After the last had departed, Ray noticed the unusual spectacle produced by the smoke: 'Within seconds, the camera was set up and the shot taken in fast-fading sunlight. But I think that this last-minute improvisation added a lot of beauty to the sequence', says Ray. Lastly, there is Apu's concealment of the necklace once stolen by his sister; he throws it into the pond near the house, and the weeds slowly blink and close over the place where it falls. This is a delicate visual rendering of the same event described in the novel, where Apu hurls the necklace into a bamboo grove; along with the snake that crawls into the deserted house – which is not in the novel at all – these two touches are Ray's masterly solution to the problem of how to hold his audience's interest after they know that Harihar and his family are leaving the village. The idea of using the pond weeds in this way struck Ray one day at the location when he and the others were 'picnicking' during a patch of wrong weather. He was idly throwing pebbles into the pond. 'Suddenly I noticed this phenomenon happening.' Instead of pebbles, why not the necklace? He almost jumped up in excitement.

About six months after Monroe Wheeler's visit to Calcutta, he sent an emissary to check out Ray's progress on the film. John Huston had actually come to India in search of locations for *The Man Who Would Be King*. The first Bengali he met as he stepped off the Pan Am flight at Dum Dum airport was R.P. Gupta, who had learned of Huston's visit through his employment at J. Walter Thompson which handled the Pan Am account. Amazed to find that Gupta had read a piece of his in the *New Yorker*, Huston expansively invited him to his hotel. Over large whiskies Gupta mentioned Ray's film. A screening of some silent rough-cut of *Pather Panchali* was soon arranged.

Ray selected fifteen or twenty minutes, including Apu and Durga's first sight of the train. According to Ray, Huston thought it 'a fine, sincere piece of film-making', but he also warned him against showing too much wandering. 'The audience gets restive. They don't like to be kept waiting too long before something *happens*.' Just before his death in 1987, Huston recalled that 'I recognised the footage as the work of a great film-maker. I liked Ray enormously on first encounter. Everything he did and said supported my feelings on viewing the film.'

Ray was now up against a very tight deadline; the film had to be finished for screening in New York in April 1955. In six months he had to complete shooting and editing it, add the sound-track – including the music, which was yet to be composed – get approval from the Government as the film's producer, and arrange for it to go to New York. In one respect at least, he was fortunate; he was able to use most of the sound recorded on location. Since he and his actors were relatively unknown, they had managed to work in Boral and other locations in conditions of quiet. Never again – or, only very rarely – would this occur.

The West Bengal Government officials, meanwhile, persisted in their obstructive attitude to the project. Early in 1955, a screening was arranged for Dr B.C. Roy in the presence of Ray and others. He and his advisors felt that the film's ending was insufficiently positive for the spirit of the times, and that it should be altered. Ray wisely said nothing and allowed others to defend his creation for him. Ironically, the argument that won the day was that one could not tamper with the story of a classic novel without incurring public disapproval; the very same point has often been used by Ray's Indian critics since as a stick to beat him with, particularly in his adaptations of Tagore which make significant departures from the original.

The most important passages of music in *Pather Panchali* were composed by Ravi Shankar in an all-night session lasting about eleven hours until 4 a.m., because of Shankar's touring commitments. Although he was able to see only about half the film in a roughly edited version, he was deeply moved by it. He already knew the novel and, when Ray met him in Calcutta, he 'sort of hummed' for him a line of melody with the feeling of a folk-tune about it but which also had a certain sophistication. It became the main theme of the film, usually heard on a bamboo flute, and is 'certainly a stroke of inspiration' according to Ray. During the recording itself, Ray would say 'Now let's do a piece for such and such a portion' and Shankar and Aloke Dey, who is still Ray's flautist, would 'go into a huddle and work out a score right then and there.' The whole recording session was 'hectic', according to Ray, 'with Ravi Shankar humming, strumming, improvising and instructing at a feverish pace, and the indefatigable Aloke Dey transcribing the composer's ideas into Indian notation and dealing out the foolscap sheets to the tense handful who had to keep plucking and bowing and thumping with scarcely a breathing space.' Shankar also composed two solo sitar pieces – a life-affirming one in raga *Desh* which is conventionally associated with the rains, and a sombre piece in raga *Todi* to follow Durga's death in the storm.

The high notes of the *tarshehnai* played when Sarbajaya bursts out in grief were played by Daksinaranjan Tagore in raga *Patdeep*, chosen by Ravi Shankar. 'When we started recording,' remembers Ray, 'I kept signalling to Daksinaranjan to stay with high notes. When I got the length I wanted, I signalled to him to stop.' One or two other pieces had to be chosen by Ray after Shankar had departed. The comic twanging that so perfectly accompanies the stocky sweet-seller and his yoked sweet-pots, the hopeful children and the dog, is made by an *ektara* played by a refugee from East Bengal; the composition was by the cameraman Subrata Mitra, who also plays the sitar elsewhere on the sound-track.

'The effort to catch the Museum's deadline took on epic proportions, and my editor and I were done up to a frazzle by the end', says Ray. In fact, his editor Dulal Dutta at one point clasped Satyajit's feet and said that he could not bear the strain any longer. Anil Chowdhury recalls that they were *living* in the Bengal Film Laboratories then – not bathing, shaving, or sleeping for six or seven days. At one point, Satyajit's legs simply gave way beneath him as he stood up. The owner of the laboratory stayed up all night too to help them.

On the day of despatch, Ray had to go out to find a suitable trunk and make official arrangements for it. While waiting he fell asleep in a chair, so that people thought he must be ill. When the trunk was packed and finally ready to go, the team gathered round as if it were a bride about to go away forever to her husband's home. Ray's relative and coffee house companion Subhash Ghosal had persuaded his employer J. Walter Thompson to send the film free to New York via Pan Am. Ray was afraid he would fall asleep at their office too, in front of all the sahibs, but he managed not to and the film departed safely for Monroe Wheeler.

It had no subtitles, and Ray had not had a chance to view what he had despatched, even once. Sitting in Calcutta, going through the motions of his job at Keymer's, he nervously awaited news from the Museum where the film was to be screened in front of a hand-picked audience. Billed as *The Story of Apu and Durja*, it was one of six evening performances, including the first appearances in the US of the *sarod* player Ali Akbar Khan and the dancer Shanta Rao. Ray's apprehensions were proved wrong. 'Although the first cable from Monroe Wheeler saying "a triumph of sensitive photography" only confirmed my doubts, a letter – not from Wheeler – which soon followed assured me at length that the film had gone down well at the Museum.'

The story of *Pather Panchali*'s release in Calcutta is more complicated. As a result, a myth has become established that the film was a failure in India until its success at the Cannes Festival in 1956.

The fact is that the West Bengal Government was in no hurry to release the film. It turned down one offer of distribution before eventually placing *Pather Panchali* in the hands of Aurora Films, which would later part-finance *Aparajito*. August 26, 1955 was agreed on, with a booking until the end of September. In the meantime, Satyajit decided to design some large advertisements, and have them printed and pasted up entirely on credit. They made a big impact. He also designed a neon sign showing Apu and Durga running together, which was mounted above K.C. Das, the most famous sweet-seller in Calcutta.

Less happily, Ray allowed himself to be persuaded to give the film its Calcutta première at the annual meet of the Advertising Club of Calcutta in the ballroom of the Ordnance Club. As Chidananda Das Gupta, one of its organisers later observed, 'the audience was more interested in drinking whisky than in seeing stark reality on the screen.' Ray says he was 'extremely discouraged' by the reaction. 'There were lots of Englishmen in the crowd – men and women – and they came forward to say how much they liked it. Only English people came forward; nobody else did. There was a little buffet afterwards and people just talked of other things.' In the coffee house afterwards, Subhash Ghosal repeated to him various comments, such as why was the sequence with the water-skaters so long?

All the criticisms were being related to me in the hope that I would probably make some changes. But I didn't. I just listened to them. My feeling was that the circumstances of the showing were so dismal. The projector was right in the middle of the room and it made a terrific noise and the place had wooden floors, so if people moved their chairs there was a creaking noise. They were not the right circumstances for the first screening of a film that demanded attention. It needs ideal projection conditions and a quiet audience and rapt attention.

When *Pather Panchali* opened a little later at a proper cinema, it ran poorly to begin with; but within a week or two word got round, and by the end of its booking it was filling the house and people were seeing it three times in a day. If it had not been for the next booking – a south Indian spectacular – the cinema house would have kept *Pather Panchali*. In due course it opened again at another cinema, where it ran for a further seven weeks. As R.P. Gupta says today, 'All middle-aged and older men and women know the furore, the sensation that followed its first release in Calcutta.'

At 6 a.m. the morning after *Pather Panchali* was taken off at the first cinema, there was a ring at Ray's door. It was the producer of the south Indian film. He had seen *Pather Panchali* and loved it. With tears in his eyes he informed Ray that if he had known about the film in advance, he would have agreed to postpone his own opening. Another producer, boss of one of the large Calcutta studios, came up with an offer that Ray should direct five films for him. Ray was tempted, but they were unable to come to an agreement on rates for his production team that Ray felt were acceptable, and so the deal fell through.

It seemed that only one person remained unwilling to fall under *Pather Panchali*'s spell – Kamal Majumdar, Ray's sparring partner in the coffee house. He held out a long time against seeing the film. When finally he did so, he stopped seeing Satyajit. Eventually word reached him that Kamal Babu liked only the scene with the sweet-seller, the children and the dog. Although he had also been alone in his cool response to *Rashomon*, that was not much consolation. Many years later, however, when the criticism had ceased to hurt, Ray wrote in his affectionate obituary of Majumdar, that he now accepted he was not capable of making a film on village life which could please such a connoisseur.

6

The Apu Trilogy:
Pather Panchali 1955
Aparajito (The Unvanquished) 1956
The World of Apu (Apur Sansar) 1959

＊＊[⚘]＊＊

ABOUT twenty years after the release of *Pather Panchali*, Akira Kurosawa said of it:

> I can never forget the excitement in my mind after seeing it. I have had several more opportunities to see the film since then and each time I feel more overwhelmed. It is the kind of cinema that flows with the serenity and nobility of a big river.
>
> People are born, live out their lives, and then accept their deaths. Without the least effort and without any sudden jerks, Ray paints his picture, but its effect on the audience is to stir up deep passions. How does he achieve this? There is nothing irrelevant or haphazard in his cinematographic technique. In that lies the secret of its excellence.

Ray's is the art that conceals art; by the greatest economy of means he creates films that are among the most life-like in the history of the cinema. This means that they resist thoroughgoing analysis, as the critic Robin Wood acknowledges in his sensitive study of the Apu Trilogy and Satyajit's father encapsulated in his essay on Tagore: 'Where poetry is coextensive with life itself, where art ceases to be the mere expression of imaginative impulse, it is futile to attempt a comprehensive analysis.' By the standards of most directors not very much happens in most of Ray's films, and yet each (with a few obvious exceptions like *The Chess Players*) seems to embody a section of Bengali society; together, like Kurosawa's films, they describe a culture.

The three films of the Trilogy, *Pather Panchali*, *Aparajito* and *The World of Apu*, are very different in their dominant moods and in the rewards they offer the viewer. They reflect the consciousness of Apu as it evolves from innocence, and this gives them a coherence which it is tempting to call musical; as a whole the Trilogy is reminiscent of the development of a raga, the basic melodic form of Indian classical music, as it meanders through the prescribed phases towards its emotional catharsis – Apu's reunion with his small abandoned son.

At the beginning of *Pather Panchali*, Apu does not of course exist.
We first see him as a baby, rocked by his auntie Indir, but we first
meet him as an eye. He is by then about six. On Sarbajaya's instruction,
Durga wakes up Apu for his first day at school by gently prising open his
reluctant eyelids. He is a skinny, shy little boy with a ravenous curiosity,
and frequently a hunger for food too – but his mother can seldom provide
what she would like to give him. No matter – he and his sister live in their
own worlds, sometimes separate, sometimes together. Secretly they share
a delicacy made with oil stolen from their mother, trail behind the itinerant
sweet-seller whose wares they cannot afford, listen to auntie telling them
ghost stories at night, marvel at the peep-show of the 'bioscopewallah', and
huddle together in a monsoon downpour, as the village seasons change. One
day, cross with each other, they run across the fields around the village and
out of their familiar world. There, in the unknown, they become friends
again and have their first tingling encounter with a railway train belching
black smoke. On their way back home through the forest, leading the family
cow and giggling and tickling each other, they meet something even more
incomprehensible – Death. Their 'auntie', rejected by Sarbajaya, has come
into the forest to die. Sometime later Durga too dies, from a fever brought
on by the monsoon, during a savage thunderstorm. Without being told, Apu
begins to understand death for himself. Harihar is away at the time, trying
to make some money; on his return he has to confront his full failure as a
husband and as a man. He decides to take Sarbajaya and Apu to Benares,
where he will earn a living by reading aloud the scriptures. The last image
of the film is of the three of them trundling slowly away in an ox cart.

While *Pather Panchali* never leaves the village and its environs,
Aparajito is constantly on the move as Apu grows up and becomes
restless for new experience. It opens in Benares in 1920 with Apu
freely wandering the ghats, lanes and temples of the sacred city. A welter
of impressions play upon his receptive young mind: the daily rhythm of
ablutions in the Ganges at the different ghats, the contrasting styles of the
various priests who sit there reciting – some earthy, others spiritual like his
father, a muscleman swinging a club who offers him a go, pigeons, cows
and monkeys everywhere, festival firework displays and sparklers to hold.
He also encounters their upstairs neighbour Nanda Babu, a sluggardly
bachelor who feels obliged to tell the angelic Apu that the bottles in his
room are medicine prescribed by his doctor. A little later, as Harihar lies
dying, Nanda Babu will make a pass at Sarbajaya.

Harihar's death from an unspecified fever leaves Sarbajaya with no
choice but to take a job. She works as a cook for a rich Bengali family,
while Apu plucks the grey hairs (not lice, as *Time* magazine's review would
have it!) of the head of the household, and does other odd jobs in exchange
for a few *paise*. It is a dead end for both of them and she knows it. When
an older relative, Bhabataran, invites her and Apu to settle with him in his
village in Bengal, she soon accepts.

Apu spends the next five or six years of his life there. His elders expect him to follow tradition and become a priest. But it is the crowd of boys from the local school who really appeal to Apu. He wins over his mother by agreeing to carry out his religious duties too, and proves himself a star pupil. Years pass, and we see an older Apu with a small moustache standing bashfully before the headmaster again, accepting a scholarship to study science in distant Calcutta. Only his mother stands in the way; her health is beginning to fail and, anyway, she feels Apu should be a priest. They quarrel and she slaps him; then, consumed with remorse, she agrees to let him go and to pay his way in the city.

The rest of *Aparajito* is a deeply experienced clash between mother and son, and between incompatible beliefs. Studying during the day and earning his keep at night in a printing press, Apu grows away from Sarbajaya while she, as inexorably, declines into morbid depression. On a night sparkling with evanescent fireflies, her life leaves her. Apu gets to the village too late. After weeping bitterly, he finds the strength of mind to reject the shade of his father's life and retrace his steps to make a new life in Calcutta.

As the third film opens, Apu is a graduate without either a job or much desire to get one. He has written a novel about his struggle to live and hopes to become a writer. Living alone in a very dingy garret room above a railway station in the heart of Calcutta, with only his books and his flute for company, he is a figure ripe for romance – something of which he has not an iota of practical experience, as his old college friend Pulu bluntly points out. He has tracked Apu down, determined to drag him off to his cousin Aparna's wedding in a village in East Bengal. Over food, Apu gives in and in the boat on the way there, Pulu reads his manuscript and excitedly proclaims its quality.

To his complete surprise, Apu goes to the village a bachelor and returns a married man; it turns out the bridegroom is mad and Apu, again giving in to his friend, agrees to take his place lest Aparna be cursed to remain unmarried for life. For a brief, sweet spell, Apu and Aparna live in his primitive rooms in Calcutta. He works as clerk, she keeps house. They are utterly absorbed in one another. When she leaves him to have their child in the village, he drifts blissfully through his dreary routine awaiting the moment of togetherness again. Instead, Aparna dies, leaving a baby son. Apu is laid waste by grief, contemplates suicide, and leaves Calcutta.

Wandering by the coast, in the forest and on the mountains, he renounces his former life, his novel, and Kajal, the son he has not seen. For five years he disappears until Pulu again tracks him down – this time, in an isolated industrial settlement. The sight of Pulu stirs up old memories. Apu feels driven to contact Kajal. Though the boy has grown up wild and withdrawn and at first distrusts the strange bearded man who woos him, a tentative bond eventually forms between them. In a searing finale, Apu sweeps the little boy into his arms and, united, they set off for Calcutta.

Aparajito is based on the last fifth of the novel *Pather Panchali* and about the first third of the novel *Aparajita*. *The World of Apu* draws on the rest. The relationship of the second film to its sources is close. Bibhutibhusan's depiction of the mother-son conflict took a strong hold on Ray's imagination from the start: 'their relationship had some echoes on a purely psychological plane' for Ray, as we know. Although he would not lose his mother until 1960, Satyajit was gripped by Bibhutibhusan's 'daring and profound revelation' that: 'For some time after Sarbajaya's death Apu became familiar with a strange sensation . . . his immediate reaction had been one of pleasure, like a surge of release . . . a delight in the breaking of bonds . . . There was no doubt he loved his mother, but the news of her death had at first brought him pleasure – he couldn't avoid that truth.' The latter portion of the film consists, says Ray, 'of improvisations on that extraordinarily revealing statement.'

The Apu of the third film follows the author's Apu less closely. Ray's Apu is here a nobler creation. He has dispensed with some of Apu's contradictions, attenuated his narcissism and drawn him as someone of heightened sensitivity and refined emotion. In the novel, Apu leaves Aparna in the village for about a year after their marriage, and when she dies in childbirth, he reacts to the news with a calmness that surprises even himself. Ray, on the other hand, was 'very touched by the fact that although it's an arranged marriage they fall in love', and decided to emphasise that in the film.

The author's Apu does in fact have a much wider contact with other girls before he meets Aparna than does Ray's. While still a boy in Benares, he forms an attachment to Leela, granddaughter of the rich man he and his mother work for. He continues to visit her occasionally from then on, and after Aparna's death he comes close to her again. Early on, she is part of the influence of Calcutta in alienating Apu from his mother.

Ray failed to find a suitable girl to play Leela in *Aparajito*; after two failures, his third actress was abducted from him on the first day of shooting by her irate fiancé. Reluctantly, Ray wrote Leela out of the script, which meant, of course, that she was out of the third film too. 'I'm, never sure whether Apu's attachment to the city without the element of the girlfriend is strong enough,' Ray says today; 'the pull that the city exerts is a bit abstract I think, and yet . . . watching *Aparajito* recently I didn't feel the absence of Leela at all.' His own experience in his formative years may have influenced him here; the only girls he knew well were his various cousins, including Bijoya, whom he early on decided to marry.

I would like now to consider some of the striking sequences from the Trilogy to get a clearer picture of Ray's *mise en scène*. They have been chosen to reveal, I hope, how Ray builds up Apu's world and allows us to enter his thoughts as they grow in maturity with age and experience.

Early in *Pather Panchali* Apu returns home with his father from his first day at school. Sarbajaya is cooking. Durga is out of sight but she calls Apu. Conspiratorially she tells him to fetch her secret stock of mustard oil from the top of some shelves inside the house. Meanwhile, Indir Thakrun, by showing off her tattered shawl to Harihar, induces him to promise her a new one. He is overheard by a resentful Sarbajaya. When Harihar then asks for coals for his pipe, she gives them reluctantly and launches into a list of all the things he is failing to do for his immediate family, without mentioning the shawl directly. 'Have you taken a look at the state of the house, what the children are eating, what clothes they are wearing?' she asks.

Apu can no doubt hear all this but he is intent on reaching the high shelf. His parents' preoccupation will help him to do this unnoticed. As Sarbajaya carries on, we see Apu approach the shelf and then, in an interesting shot from *behind* the shelf, pick up the coconut shell of oil. Exactly the same pair of shots will be repeated at the end of the film to powerful effect, as Apu clears the shelf and discovers the necklace his dead sister once stole from the neighbours.

In their corner, the children now share the tamarind paste Durga has made. Apu is tasting its strong sourness for the first time. He lets slip a sound. Durga slaps him lightly: 'Idiot! Mother will hear you.' After this brother and sister share their delicious secret in silence, in several shining close-ups. But suddenly Durga is on to something new; her alert hearing has caught the faint tinkle of bells belonging to the sweet-seller. Obviously she knows him from past visits. Tamarind paste and parents forgotten, the two children jump up and go to a gap in the wall of their house. Outside, the jovial sweet-seller pauses enquiringly. Durga sends Apu running off to beg money from their father who is an easier touch than their mother. But Sarbajaya, still in the kitchen, knows what is going on and tells Harihar not to agree.

Disappointed, the children run out after the sweet-seller; they know he is heading for Sejabou's house nearby. A village dog trots out after them, sensing food. Then, as the procession passes along, it is reflected upside down in the waters of a pond lightly ruffled by a breeze. The plonking, rustic sound of the one-stringed *ektara*, accompanied by sitar, imparts a perfect rhythm to the odd little group: the tripping sweet-seller yoked to his swaying, bobbing pots, pursued with eager innocence by the children and their canine accomplice. This brief wordless interlude of lyrical happiness belongs uniquely to the cinema; it is the kind of peak in Ray's work that prompted Kurosawa to say: 'Not to have seen the cinema of Ray means existing in the world without seeing the sun or the moon.'

In these few scenes, Ray conveys to us the inter-relationships of Harihar's family members with pinpoint clarity. Simultaneously, we come to feel how each parent sees Apu and Durga, how each child sees their mother and father and each other, and how Ray sees them all. *Pather Panchali* is a film about unsophisticated people shot through with great sophistication, and without a trace of condescension or inflated sentiment.

Towards the end, the morning after Durga's death, there is another sequence that epitomises the many-stranded texture of the film – this time with overt emotion. It begins with Apu silently cleaning his teeth near the pond, an unfamiliar faraway look in his eyes. Sarbajaya, her hair dishevelled and her sari crumpled, draws water from the well. Apu goes into the devastated house, roughly combs his hair and wraps his shawl around him – actions that a doting sister and mother once performed. He picks up an empty oil bottle and is about to set off for the local store when he looks up at the sky and decides to fetch an umbrella; now he has to think of that too.

The verandah where the long-deceased Indir Thakrun used to cook, has somehow escaped the storm. Sarbajaya finds herself cooking there. She is dead to the world, and when a neighbour comes bringing food, she does not even notice her presence. It takes the sound of her husband calling for his children to make her stir. We know that Harihar has returned, oblivious of the disaster to his family. Characteristically, both for him and for Ray's sense of drama, he is in good spirits, despite the damage to his house that he cannot avoid seeing around him. As Sarbajaya mutely fetches him a seat, towel and water from inside and turns to go, Harihar stops her. He wants to show her the presents he has managed to bring. The third item, a sari for Durga which he presses her to admire, is too much for Sarbajaya. To Harihar's great surprise she breaks out in unstoppable weeping, expressed by the high notes of the *tarshehnai*. When Harihar at last grasps that he has lost his daughter, he collapses over his wife's body.

Another director might have chosen to end the scene there. Ray returns to Apu, a sad little figure standing behind the house holding the bottle of oil, which is now full. Without expression he absorbs the sound of his father's agonised cries. This wordless shot, repeated, creates a satisfying sense of Apu's emerging knowledge of the world, and is a subtle pointer to the growing dominance of Apu as the Trilogy progresses.

In *Aparajito*, the sequence of scenes that describe the illness and death of Harihar demonstrate Ray's unobtrusive use of contrasts of all kinds to enrich a film and make it mysterious and poetic. First, we see Sarbajaya and Apu visiting the chief shrine of that temple-ridden city Benares, the Viswanath Temple, where they gaze at the evening ritual of chanting and bell-ringing through a haze of incense. It mesmerises Sarbajaya, but not her son. Back in their ground-floor rooms, she decorates them with a hundred little points of light, the burning wicks that a pious Hindu lights to celebrate the festival of *Dusserah* (or *Diwali*, as it is also known).

Into this luminous setting comes Harihar carrying some shopping, and obviously in a weak condition. He has to lie down. Outside the window next to him, a series of fireworks explode in a burst of light and noise that is slightly menacing. Then in bursts Apu holding a large sparkler, eager to show it to his mother. His face falls. Sarbajaya tells him to sit with his father. A little hesitantly Apu answers his father's friendly questioning. Harihar's mind has taken a nostalgic turn; he asks Apu if the Benares fireworks are as good as the ones in their village. Probably to please his father Apu says they are not. But what he really wants is to get back to his friends outside. His father gently releases him. Instead, he discusses with Sarbajaya a house that he may have found for them. Outside, as the night is filled with sparks and bangs, Apu is humming his own version of the tune he has picked up earlier from their upstairs neighbour Nanda Babu. The original is a *thumri* with a slightly disreputable air about it; Apu, with the ingenuousness of a child, has drained it of its erotic quality. Nothing is spelt out here, but in this little detail lingers the faint suggestion that we have not heard the last of Nanda Babu.

The following morning, despite Sarbajaya's protest, Harihar goes out to the ghats to earn money by recitation. The steep climb up the steps on the way back is too much for him; he collapses dramatically, and has to be helped home. He is clearly dying. As the doctor, Sarbajaya and neighbours gather round him, the bulky figure of Nanda Babu loiters outside behind the bars of a window. 'I hope he hasn't hurt himself,' he says. Immediately after this sombre picture we see Apu gazing fascinated at a bulging leather bag as it is drawn from a well by bullocks. Pressure forces water to come spurting out through numerous small ruptures. One thinks, without being asked to, of the life that is leaking out of Apu's father. We see him lying motionless.

The shot that follows this is one of the most expressive of the many examples in Ray's work of the 'dewdrop that reflects the universe around it'. It begins with a close-up of two pathetic kittens (like those Durga used to look after) playing with a wooden toy typical of Benares beside the steps leading upstairs from Harihar's rooms. From the top of the frame now appear two feet clad in shiny new pumps – obviously Nanda Babu's. One of the pumps prods one of the skinny little creatures, not so much because it is in the way, but out of a casual cruelty typical of its owner. That is all. In one sense nothing of any significance has happened, and yet Sarbajaya's defencelessness has been crystallised; we now expect the worst. Again Nanda Babu appears behind the barred window but this time no one is there, except for the prone motionless figure of Harihar.

Ray's handling of what happens next – Nanda Babu's pass at Sarbajaya – is charged with meaning for an Indian. She is in the kitchen where outsiders do not normally go and where contact with others while cooking is taboo. As she hears the sound of the pumps approaching she draws her sari over her head in a timeless gesture of Indian womanhood. His face unseen, Nanda Babu slips off his pumps, crosses the threshold, and takes a few steps, his fingers splayed out and trembling with excitement. '*Bouthan,*' he says in a low voice, 'are you making *pan*?' – the spicy preparation whose connotations range from the devotional to the frankly disreputable, but which are always associated with intimacy. 'It is a nucleus for hospitality,' wrote E.M. Forster in his celebration 'Pan', 'and much furtive intercourse takes place under its little shield.' Sarbajaya, with blind instinct, threatens Nanda Babu with a kitchen blade, and he beats a hasty retreat.

From here on the sequence is unrelievedly bleak. At dawn Harihar just manages to get the words 'Ganges water' past his lips, and his wife knows he is almost gone. Apu goes to the river to fetch it and returns in the nick of time. As Harihar's soul departs his body, a huge flock of pigeons takes flight and wheels dramatically against the dawn sky, accompanied by the falling notes of a flute playing a melody based on raga *Jog*. This will reappear when Sarbajaya herself begins to die, and in *The World of Apu* when Apu is mentally dead. Ray recalls that at the Venice Festival in 1957, this moment in *Aparajito* brought forth 'a spontaneous burst of applause' from the capacity audience.

Aparajito after the Benares scenes becomes a slightly less concentrated experience. It acquires a firm narrative thread which links Apu's entire adolescence. At that time, Ray comments, he was still under the influence of Hollywood to some extent and 'didn't mind lapses of time so much'. Up to a point he agrees with the American critic Arlene Croce who wrote of his 'smooth, page-turning professionalism' in *Aparajito*. 'That is a very shrewd comment. It's a kind of novelistic problem – because I had to tell Apu's story as told in the book. It's a kind of chronicle. I never really went back to that form any more.'

Then there was Apu's changing physical appearance to contend with. 'It is always a problem with that kind of film. I kept thinking of *Great Expectations* and Pip growing up. We got very fond of the boy Pip, and when at a certain point you suddenly have John Mills appearing as a grown-up Pip, you know it's a different actor and therefore it's a different person altogether. You get a shock, and then you accept it after a certain point.'

Ray is probably being over-critical of his second film in the Trilogy – the most admired of the three, incidentally, by his fellow Bengali directors Ritwik Ghatak and Mrinal Sen. Certainly, it is not as lyrical as the first, nor as moving as the third, but its characterisation is the richest of the three. Its portrayal of a mother and her growing son is perhaps the finest yet created in the cinema. Banerjee's novel and Ray's own experience fused seamlessly with the total conviction of Karuna Banerjee and Smaran Ghosal. 'I was absolutely overwhelmed by her personality,' Karuna says. 'It all came so naturally to me. Every word, every look, every small movement, the deep attachment towards the alienated son, they all developed within me, as leaves grow outwards on the branch of a tree. Sounds poetic? But believe me, that is exactly how I felt whenever I had a chance to work with Manik. Not a single turn of the character that I portrayed was forced, illogical, artificial.'

The most poignant sequence in Sarbajaya's relationship with Apu occurs when he returns to the village for the first time since starting college in Calcutta. Sarbajaya is sitting listlessly sewing beneath a tree. As the train from Calcutta comes beetling across the near horizon, she busies herself to receive her son. A solo *sarangi*, the most piercing of the Indian string instruments, expresses her loneliness with heart-wrenching pathos. She is still drawing water when Apu arrives. Instead of pulling the bucket up, she simply lets the rope snap back in her joy; no embrace could have been more eloquent, especially given the calm way in which we have earlier seen her drawing water.

Apu is genuinely pleased to see his mother, but the gap between them is evident from the moment he arrives. He has barely exchanged a few sentences with her before he is off for a dip in the village pond. That night as she sits fanning Apu at his evening meal, as once she fanned Harihar, Sarbajaya longs for him to open up and tell her all that he has been through in Calcutta. They grope for common ground. Apu reassures her that he still prefers her cooking. Later, he reads, she sews. With some asperity she tells him to put his book away and talk to her about what he has seen. He recites a list of Calcutta place names quite meaningless to her and adds, with a yawn, 'Keoratala'. 'What's there at Keoratala?' enquires Sarbajaya. 'Burning ghat,' says Apu, in English. This makes his mother pensive. She wonders out loud what has obviously been on her mind in Apu's absence: what will happen to her if she falls ill? Will Apu look after her? she asks. Of course he will, Apu says, without thinking. Sarbajaya presses him: 'You're not going to come to me and leave your studies, are you? Will you arrange for my treatment with the money you earn? Will you, Apu?' But Apu has gone to sleep. Immediately we remember another such moment, in *Pather Panchali*, when Harihar drifted off to sleep while Sarbajaya delivered herself of her worries. We know instinctively that Sarbajaya has not got long to live; and the music reinforces this – it is the first time since Harihar's death that we hear the flute playing this melody, here in a gentler variation.

The World of Apu was not conceived until *Aparajito* had been completed and released, and not shot until 1958/9, with two other films intervening.

It is a film one virtually cannot avoid being moved by. It introduces two actors who were to become regulars for Ray. When Soumitra Chatterjee came to play Apu, having initially approached Ray for the role in *Aparajito* and been found too old, he identified with almost every aspect of Apu's character, like most of his friends in Calcutta. 'We were to a great extent Apus of our time,' he says today. Sarmila Tagore, who plays Aparna, was only fourteen and still at school. She is related to Abanindranath and Gaganendranath Tagore, the painters, and the more orthodox side of the Tagore family. She had no acting experience, but she was already a dancer. Ray met her for the first time when her parents brought her to him and his wife in a frock. 'We made her wear a sari, did her hair differently, and put the sari over her head to suggest a married woman', he says. 'I took a photograph of her and she looked exactly like Aparna.' Though she learnt very quickly, her performance was 'heavily directed'. Ray literally talked her through each shot: 'Now turn your head, now look this way, now look that way, now look down, now come with your lines, pause pause here, and now come with your lines again.' As Sarmila puts it today, 'Manikda is a tremendous actor.'

No trace of these efforts appears on the screen. We first see Aparna as a young, bashful bride being decorated for her wedding by the other women of the family. Apu is outside all of this, but the way in which he is included in the editing of the sequence implies that he will be drawn into the wedding. First, the band arrives, escorting the marriage party along the bank of the river. Above them, along the top of the bank, lies Apu dozing beneath a tree with his head on a collection of Tagore's poetry and his flute in his hand, like the god Krishna on the banks of the Kalindi. The band plays their own raucous version of 'For He's a Jolly Good Fellow' – which sounds quite familiar to Bengali ears used to hearing it at the annual immersion of the Durga image in Calcutta, though the words are long since lost. This juxtaposition of Apu and the band is enriched by our earlier memory of Apu listening to a marriage band play 'Tipperary' in *Pather Panchali*; but then he was thrilled by it, whereas now he is blasé, Calcutta-returned.

The bridegroom, of course, turns out to be touched; he is tearing to pieces his marriage head-dress of pith. There is tremendous consternation, and the bride's mother locks herself away with the bride. When Pulu, desperate to help his young cousin, approaches his friend Apu on the river bank and asks him to wed Aparna instead, Apu sharply rejects him with the words 'Are you still living in the Dark Ages?' But in fact, upon reflection in the day's fast-fading light, Apu does agree; he puts it to Pulu 'in a very oblique way' typical of Ray – by asking if Pulu can really get him the job he had earlier promised and which Apu had rejected as too routine – 'because any direct statement like "OK, I agree to marry your cousin" would have sounded terrible,' says Ray. 'A western viewer ignorant of orthodox Hindu customs must find the episode highly bizarre', he commented further in an article. 'But since Apu himself finds it so, and since his action is prompted by compassion, the viewer accepts it on moral grounds, though given no opportunity to weigh the pros and cons of a seemingly irrational practice.'

That this is true is mainly because Ray, with his Brahmo background and rejection of Hindu beliefs, could not accept Bibhutibhusan's version of Apu's marriage. In the novel, Apu sleeps upstairs and is woken up by Pulu in the middle of the night with the news about the bridegroom; he agrees to fall in with Pulu's plans immediately – which really *would* have left a western viewer bemused. Banerjee and his novels are Hindu to the

core, and both Soumitra Chatterjee and Sarmila Tagore responded to this
instinctively in a way that Ray could not. In fact even today neither of
them regards this marriage as at all 'bizarre' or even more than a little
dated. 'What is after all so extraordinary about it?' asks Chatterjee. 'It's
nothing but an extension of a normally negotiated marriage, except that
that takes a little more time. Apu had to give his consent on the spur of
the moment.' He knows a well-known actor in Calcutta who went through
a similar experience. 'He was also very educated and very romantic like
Apu.' To Chatterjee, *The World of Apu* does not seem like a film about
a past period at all; unlike, say, *The Music Room*, whose period is only
marginally earlier. 'In the first place, the hope of getting married earlier
has come back again, just as it came back in America. A lot of young
people, who are not as romantic as Apu, find it convenient to get married
early and on the spur of the moment, even today. *Apur Sansar* is at root
about a young man trying to struggle for a living.'

Sarmila's understanding of Apu's behaviour is somewhat closer to
Ray's than to Chatterjee's. 'He doesn't think. He's a romantic. He gets
somehow honour-bound – what will happen to the girl? He gets carried
away with the moment, being what he is, half living in his imaginary world.
Then there's his friendship and loyalty to Pulu. Apu doesn't have that very
clear I'm-sorry-I-can't-do-it capacity. He's not the kind of person to let his
friend and his friend's family down. He hasn't got that whatever you might
call it to say no.'

In fact, Ray was realistic enough to appreciate that there would be
another factor propelling Apu to agree; he would be sexually attracted
to Aparna. The erotic quality of their relationship does not receive full
play until they return to Calcutta, but Ray made it clear to Chatterjee in
a long résumé of Apu's character that sexual curiosity would be in Apu's
mind. It barely surfaces though when Apu and Aparna are seen together
for the first time, immediately after the wedding, standing in a flower-strewn
bedroom. This is one of the most touching scenes in the film. A western
viewer naturally assumes that it follows on the various prayers and vows,
but in fact a traditional Hindu couple must await the third night of their
wedding; in between, they sleep separately, the bride surrounded by her
female the groom by his male relations.

When the third night comes, custom lays down that the groom
be alone with the bride in his house. Apu is too poor to do this. As
he tells Aparna: 'Have you ever heard of a bride and groom spending
their *phulsajya* ['bed of flowers'] in the bride's home?' Not surprisingly,
he feels that he is there on false pretences – does Aparna know anything
about the man she has married? His mood is self-lacerating as plangent
boatmen's songs come drifting through the window from the dark river
outside, but he lightens up with a joke about his neighbours: 'I told
them I was going to a wedding, and now I'm returning with the bride!'
At the point where Aparna softly tells him that she can accept poverty,

her transparent devotion winning him over, the poignant *esraj* expressing their love (in raga *Lachari Todi*) changes into the fast rhythm of the sitar first used to express Apu's carefree nature as he walked back to his garret room along the railway tracks at the beginning of the film.

This dingy place above the railway line to which Apu brings his bride, still decked out in her finery, is pure Ray and not from the novel at all. The sights and sounds of railway trains are the woof of the Trilogy, drawing it together into an epic work; in fact a small book could be written on that subject alone. 'As soon as I decided to do *Aparajito*,' says Ray, 'I decided to bring back the train; and when I decided to do *Apur Sansar* I had this inspiration. I thought I would take away the lyrical element of the train and have the couple living right on the railway track and being bothered by all the whistle and steam and this and that. And then the idea came to my head that after Aparna's death Apu would try to throw himself on the tracks and take his own life. But all that came later.' For Ray, it is essential that his screenplays evolve; he hardly ever begins with a framework and fits his characters into it.

The series of scenes in Calcutta lasting about twenty minutes that show the two lovers together are, in Robin Wood's phrase, 'one of the cinema's classic affirmative depictions of married life.' Part of their pathos derives from their taking place in the very same conditions in which we came to know Apu the bachelor. Almost unconsciously, we compare the two. As Apu emerges from inside playing his flute (a well-known melody of Tagore's later used in a hit Hindi film), and watches every action of Aparna preparing to cook on her brazier, we think of Apu lying alone on a crumpled bed, closing the window against the stare of the girl next door with the tip of his flute on which he plays a quite different melody, just before Pulu bursts in on his life.

Each of these little scenes dissolves effortlessly into the next. Finally, after husband and wife have been to see a hammy mythological film, the cinema screen blends into the back window of a horse-drawn carriage, and they are alone again in their lovers' world. The intimacy and the precise shifts of mood in their conversation inside the cab can only partially be conveyed by subtitles, but the scene nevertheless remains one of the high points of the film, accompanied by the same musical transition as after the wedding – from the *esraj* playing Apu and Aparna's theme to the sitar in carefree mood. As Aparna strikes a match to light the cigarette that Apu has unthinkingly put in his mouth (forgetting his promise to his wife to smoke only after meals), he notices the flame has brought a strange and wonderful glow to her face. 'What is there in your eyes?' he asks with great tenderness. 'Mascara,' she answers mischievously, according to the subtitle. But in Bengali she says 'Kajal', which is the word for kohl or mascara. It is also the name of the son she will soon bear Apu and who will cause her death. A vital link of feeling and meaning in the film is thereby lost on the western viewer, for whom the word 'mascara' conjures a totally inappropriate image. Satyajit Ray is among the most natural writers of dialogue the cinema has produced, but unfortunately only Bengalis can appreciate this fully.

The long sequence at the end of the film in which Apu finally returns to Khulna to see Kajal for the first time is equally marvellous in its employment of the total resources of cinema. It comprises the most emotionally saturated scenes in Ray's oeuvre, bearing the full history of Apu's life and struggle up to that point. As he sits upstairs in his father-in-law's house watching the little boy who does not know him sleeping, the boatmen's songs again drift in off the river and we cannot help but think of another occasion in that same house. Can Kajal ever replace the image of his mother that Apu keeps in his heart?

The boy's rejection of this stranger is at first total; Apu's attempts at friendliness are rebuffed. Only when, without thinking, he goes to Kajal's rescue when his father-in-law is about to strike him with his stick, is a spark of trust ignited for a moment. And then, as Apu sets off alone leaving Kajal behind, it becomes a flame. Like his friend Pulu who requested him in more or less the same spot to marry Aparna and was at first refused outright, Apu has given up on Kajal. But Kajal, with a child's instinct, has decided to trust Apu. Watched by his grandfather in the distance, he runs to Apu and is swept up in his arms to the piercing sound of a high *tarshehnai*, heard only once before in the Trilogy, when Harihar and Sarbajaya wept over the death of Durga. It is as if the love that was destroyed then has, after many years, been rekindled. Through Kajal Apu has transcended his grief at last, and is a better, more whole person. The music which plays out *The World of Apu*, as Apu carries off his son on his shoulders to a new life together, expresses this complex of emotions: the basic notes are recognisable as those of the Apu-Aparna theme last heard in the carriage, but they have a nobility and serenity of emotion more reminiscent of a hymn.

The reception of the Trilogy at the time of its release, both in Bengal and abroad, makes an interesting and revealing story. *Pather Panchali* was sufficiently well received at the Museum of Modern Art in New York, even without subtitles, to attract an offer from the film distributor Edward Harrison. He subsequently became a complete devotee of Ray, visiting his shooting in 1961 and releasing all his work in the US until his death in 1967. ('I think Ed was one of those rare human beings who must be classed under the category of Essentially Good Men in spite of being rabid reactionaries,' Ray wrote at the time in a letter to Seton.)

Despite sustained opposition in both the West Bengal Government and in the Government of India in Delhi because of its depiction of poverty, *Pather Panchali* was sent to Cannes in 1956 with the personal approval of Jawaharlal Nehru, after important efforts on its behalf by Marie Seton (who had gone to Calcutta in late 1955 and met Ray, after seeing *Pather*

Panchali in Delhi). By a quirk of fate, its screening there clashed with a party given by the Japanese delegation for a film by Kurosawa. Those who did see it – like André Bazin, Gene Moskowitz and, privately, Luis Buñuel – or who knew of its merits independently – like Lindsay Anderson – were incensed. A rescreening was arranged and the British member of the jury James Quinn, with two others, put forward *Pather Panchali* as worthy of a prize. 'The initial reaction was one of shock if not of horror by most of those present,' says Quinn, 'especially the French scriptwriter Henri Jaenson [*Un Carnet de Bal*] who referred to *Pather Panchali* as "*cette ordure*" – as I vividly remember.' But *Pather Panchali* was too good for French hubris to kill it off; it was awarded a special prize, for 'Best Human Document'. As Anderson remarked in his Cannes review for the *Observer*: 'Cannes 1956 has discovered a new masterpiece of poetic cinema . . . You cannot make films like this in a studio, nor for money. Satyajit Ray has worked with humility and complete dedication; he has gone down on his knees in the dust. And his picture has the quality of intimate, unforgettable experience.'

Nevertheless, Ray did not feel he had truly arrived in the international cinema until *Aparajito* won the Golden Lion at Venice the following year. This was all the more welcome for being wholly unexpected; the film had not enjoyed anything like the same success in Bengal as its predecessor, probably because its portrait of the mother-son relationship was so unsparing and lacking in conventional pieties. By and large *Aparajito* upset the Bengali middle class: the people Ray had grown up with. He himself felt the film had some technical failings – in the sound-track in particular. He recalls 'squirming' in his seat in the six-thousand-seater Grande Salle. 'It was a formal occasion and in the balcony sat Henry Fonda, Maria Callas, Toshiro Mifune and a host of celebrities.' But the audience reaction, usherettes included, was good. Still Satyajit says he had 'not the slightest hope of winning any prizes'. Three days before the award ceremony a journalist gave Ray a hint, but on the afternoon of the day itself 'a young girl of pronounced good looks came to our hotel, sought us out and started briefing me on what I had to do on the stage that evening. "On the stage?" I asked. "Yes," she said, "your name will be called out and you come up to take the prize." "What prize?" "Lione d'Oro."' According to Ray, he kept his cool with some effort, but his Bengali companion sprang up and kissed the girl smack on the lips. Ray was so excited that he rushed off a cable to Bijoya, addressing it with her pet name Monku. His mother felt so proud that she started a scrap-book of cuttings about her son.

Again, it had been a British member of the jury, Penelope Houston, who wanted Ray to win. After much argument, the chairman René Clair acquiesced with good grace; but on the boat back from their meeting place to the awards ceremony, Houston recalls Clair saying to her – without a trace of malice towards Ray: 'But now I hope Ray will go away and learn how to make films'!

Because of delays in subtitling, *Pather Panchali* did not open in Britain until Christmas 1957. It ran well and its reviews were almost uniformly outstanding. But it was in the US, the following autumn, that it had its biggest success of all – on a scale no other film by Ray has ever again approached there. It ran for eight months at the Fifth Avenue Playhouse in New York. Ray, who had been invited to the US by Robert Flaherty's widow for the film seminar in Vermont, was present in the lobby for the US première. In 1982 he wrote:

I watched the audience surge out of the theatre blear-eyed and visibly shaken. An hour or so later, in the small hours, came the morning edition of the *New York Times*. It carried Bosley Crowther's review of my film. Crowther was the doyen of New York critics, with power to make or mar a film's prospects as a saleable commodity. Crowther was unmoved by *Pather Panchali*. In fact, he said the film was so amateurish that 'it would barely pass for a rough cut in Hollywood.'

About a week later Crowther was compelled to recant, at least to some extent, such was the public response to the film. But he could never quite accept the fact that *Pather Panchali* owed little or nothing to Hollywood and so could not be judged by Hollywood's criteria. Several other critics felt rather similarly, but the majority verdict was that the film had, in Ray's words, 'irresistible human appeal', whatever its opacities for the West and its technical roughness. *Time* magazine called it 'perhaps the finest piece of filmed folklore since Robert Flaherty's *Nanook of the North*', the *New Yorker* spoke of 'a demonstration of what a man can do with a camera and an idea if he really puts his mind to it', while Arlene Croce in *Film Culture* observed that 'I don't know anyone who hasn't seen *Pather Panchali*.' But the most perceptive US response to Ray came from Paul Beckley writing in the *New York Herald Tribune*, not about *Pather Panchali* but about *The World of Apu*: 'The connoisseur must feel a kind of glow of surprised enthusiasm at the endless rightness of Ray's effects. If they seem in the beginning merely happy, the endless aptness soon makes clear that chance could have little place in the making of a work so beautifully controlled. Yet it is not entirely adequate to speak of control, rather a sort of constancy of inspiration.'

On his first visit to the US, Ray met a number of American directors and writers. In New York he had long chats with Elia Kazan, Paddy Chayevsky and Sidney Lumet, and in Hollywood talked to Stanley Kubrick, George Stevens and Billy Wilder who was then shooting *Some Like It Hot*. 'You won a prize at Cannes?' were his first words to Ray. 'Well, I guess you're an artist. But I'm not. I'm just a commercial man, and I like it that way.' Ray visited all the major studios, becoming 'absolutely terrified by the plethora of equipment and personnel', despite the forewarning impression he had received from Renoir in 1949. Two aspects of his trip particularly lodged in his mind: there were no 'poets' among those he met, and virtually no

one had more than 'the vaguest notions about India'. An MGM executive
he lunched with in the studio's basement cafeteria had proudly confided
to him his casting for a film about the Buddha – Robert Taylor! As Ray
remarked in a letter to the Sri Lankan director Lester James Peries in
December 1958, after he got back home to Calcutta: 'One realises what the
Indian film-maker is up against – a colossal ignorance and only a moderate
inquisitiveness. It is a miracle that *Pather Panchali* is doing so well at the
Box Office. The notions about Japan are equally nebulous, and this airing
of ideas about *Kabuki* etc., is just sheer pretence. The East is still as far
away from the West as it has ever been . . .'

7

Comedies:
The Philosopher's Stone
(Parash Pathar) 1958
Mahapurush (The Holy Man) 1964

···❈[◖ ⚙ ◗]❈···

R AY'S gift for comedy is perhaps the least known of his cinematic talents outside Bengal. Although there is little of it in the Apu Trilogy, there are strong hints in some of his serious films, such as *Days and Nights in the Forest* and *The Chess Players*. Its clearest display, however, is in two films based on stories by the same Bengali humourist: *The Philosopher's Stone*, shot after *Aparajito* in late 1957, and a one-hour film *Mahapurush*, shot in 1964.

The first of these is considerably the better; in fact it would belong among Ray's best work, were it not for some rough edges which betray the speed at which it was shot. Ray was making use of a break in the shooting of *The Music Room* enforced by Chhabi Biswas's absence abroad (collecting a prize in Berlin). Unfortunately, its humour only partly transplants to the West; though some non-Bengalis have liked it very much, the general reaction is summarised by Eric Rhode's comment in *Sight and Sound*: 'mannered facetiousness', which makes the film sound like a second-class Ealing comedy. Some of the problem lies in western ignorance of the nuances of Bengali social life, which can make the posturings of a brown sahib, for instance, seem merely hammy instead of the clever caricature they in fact are – like the British characters in, say, the television series *Dad's Army*. To appreciate *The Philosopher's Stone*, requires some feeling for the vacuousness and pretentiousness of the Calcutta rich and *nouveau riche*, for the Indian obsession with gold, as well as for the struggling Bengali clerk – the down side of the Bengali Renaissance – those thousands upon thousands of Bengalis who have Apu's dreaminess and frustrations but not his talents, and who must get by through deference to office superiors like Sukumar Ray's mustachioed *babu*.

The original creator of the story Rajsekhar Bose, writing under the pseudonym Parasuram, has been a household name in Bengal since the 1920s. The Bose family, gifted in the sciences as well as the arts, were old friends of the Rays; Rajsekhar's younger brother, who studied under Freud, was the Ray family physician while they were at Garpar Road. Rajsekhar himself was a chemist, 'the force behind Bengal

Pharmaceuticals,' says Ray. 'He gave wonderful names to toothpastes and lotions and this and that – all based on Sanskrit words. He also wrote a Bengali dictionary which is constantly referred to, and his summaries of the *Ramayana* and the *Mahabharata* are the best one can think of. He was a fabulous person.' But Rajsekhar rarely laughed when the two of them sat together discussing Ray's script; he seems to have been a bit like the melancholy Edward Lear to talk to, and like Lear was a fine comic illustrator. 'It was difficult to see the underlying vein of humour. It was all concealed. It came out in his writings. One didn't believe this was the person who was writing all these extremely funny stories.'

The humour of *The Philosopher's Stone* is somewhat reminiscent of the Goons. As Ray put it in a letter to Seton at the time of release, '[it is a] sort of combination of comedy, fantasy, satire, farce and a touch of pathos.' These are all somehow present in the performance of Tulsi Chakravarti who plays Paresh Chandra Dutta, the humble middle-aged clerk both blessed and cursed by picking up 'the stone that turneth all to gold' in a monsoon shower on his way home from work. Chakravarti recalls Chaplin at his best. Instead of a moustache, he has a pair of eyes as bulbous as a frog's which he opens wide with every emotion known to Man.

Dutta is an essentially good man, but weak and timid. His better instincts tell him to throw the stone away after transforming a few household items, like a spectacles case and a pair of nutcrackers, into a little something for his and Mrs Dutta's old age; but greed and his craving for the limelight soon take precedence. Sitting in a garishly appointed taxi – something he could not have afforded before – and cruising past the imposing statues of British rulers, Dutta gets his first delusion of grandeur: a memorial with the inscription

TO THE MEMORY OF
SRI PARESH CHANDRA DUTTA
A GREAT SON OF INDIA

He looks up, and there he is – a smiling, nodding head perched on top of a massive black body covered in garlands.

He will get there not by climbing on other men's shoulders, but by the simple expedient of giving away endless gold medals at endless functions. Soon he acquires a fine new house, servants and a car, a secretary with the sonorous name of Priyatosh Henry Biswas and a burgeoning love affair, and an expensively dressed wife whose main occupations are now devotional singing and admiring her growing pile of jewellery. When an invitation arrives to attend his first cocktail party, Dutta gleefully agrees. But alcohol will be his downfall. Incensed by the snooty disdain of the brown sahibs at the party, Dutta tears off the formal jacket he is unaccustomed to wearing and brandishes the small object that has made possible his presence in this élite assembly. Ping! He has transformed a naked figurine (imitation-Italian classical, of course) into shining gold. Even this blasé group is stunned; a

16 Woodcut illustrations for abridged edition of *Pather Panchali* by Ray, 1944

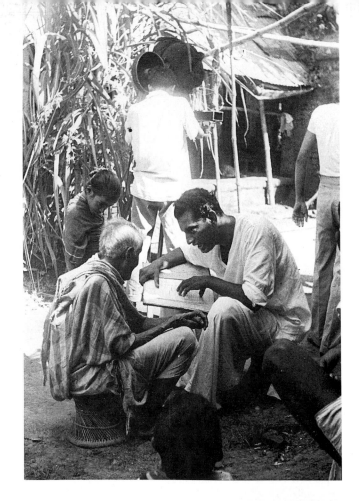

17 The making of *Pather Panchali* (*Bansi Chandragupta*)

18 *Pather Panchali*: one of many sketches by Ray showing conception of film, 1952

19 *Pather Panchali*: Indir
Thakrun, Durga (*Teknica*)

20 *Pather Panchali*: 'The
Family of Man' – Sarbajaya,
Durga, Apu (*Teknica*)

21 *Pather Panchali*: Apu
(*Teknica*)

22 *Pather Panchali*:
Harihar, Sarbajaya (*Teknica*)

23 *Aparajito*: Apu (*Teknica*)

24 *Aparajito*: Apu, Nanda
Babu (*Teknica*)

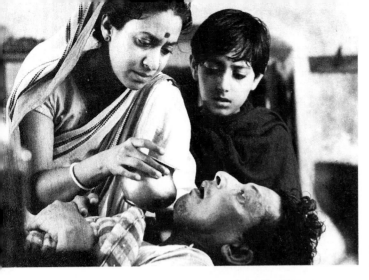

25 *Aparajito*: Sarbajaya,
Apu, Harihar (*Teknica*)

26 *Aparajito*: Apu,
Sarbajaya (*Teknica*)

27 *Aparajito*: Headmaster,
Apu (*Teknica*)

28 *Aparajito*: sketch of headmaster by Ray

29 *The World of Apu*: sketch of Apu's room by Ray

30 *The World of Apu*: Apu (Teknica)

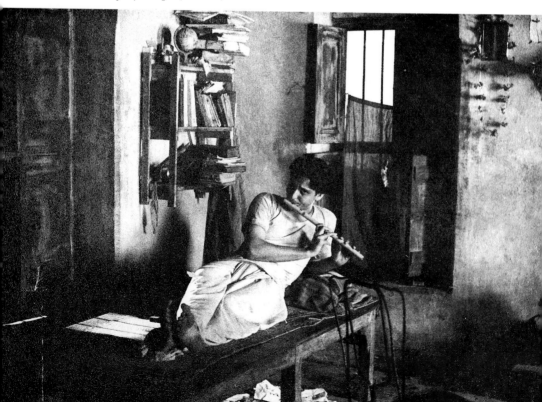

31   *The World of Apu*: Apu, Aparna (*Teknica*)

32   *The World of Apu*: Apu, Aparna (*Teknica*)

33 *The World of Apu*: Pulu, Apu (*Teknica*)

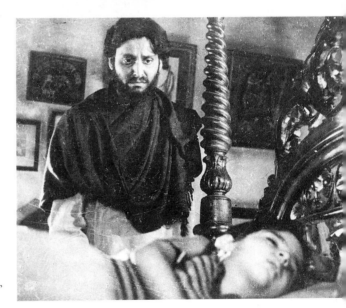

34 *The World of Apu*: Apu, Kajal (*Teknica*)

35 *The World of Apu*: Apu, Kajal (*Teknica*)

36 *The Philosopher's Stone:* Paresh Chandra Dutta (*Teknica*)

37 *The Philosopher's Stone:*
poster by Ray

38 *Mahapurush*: Birinchi
Baba (*Teknica*)

39 *Mahapurush*: *adda*
(*Teknica*)

40 *The Music Room*:
Mahamaya, Biswambhar Roy
(*Teknica*)

41   *The Music Room*: Biswambhar Roy (*Teknica*)

42   *The Music Room*: Taraprasanna, Biswambhar Roy (*Teknica*)

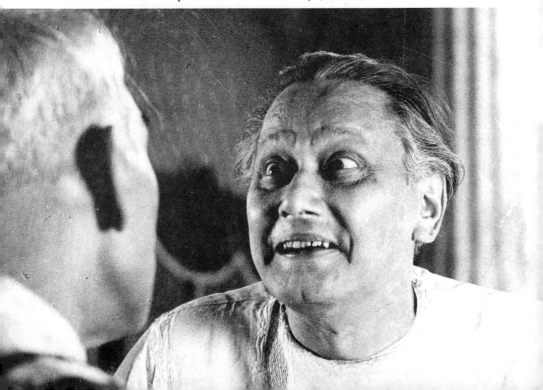

43   *The Goddess*: Kalikinkar Roy, Doyamoyee (*Teknica*)

44   *The Goddess*: Umaprasad, Doyamoyee (*Teknica*)

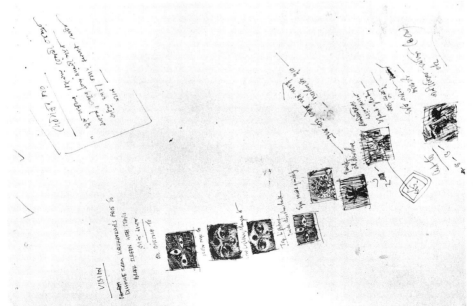

45 *The Goddess*: sketches by Ray of Kalikinkar's vision and of Doyamoyee after she loses her mind

সত্যজিৎ রায় প্রোডাকসন্স্-এর

মূল কাহিনী
প্রভাতকুমার মুখোপাধ্যায়

শ্রেষ্ঠাংশে
ছবি বিশ্বাস। মৌমিত্র চট্টোপাধ্যায়
শর্মিলা ঠাকুর। করুণা বন্দ্যোপাধ্যায়

সংগীত
আলি আকবর খাঁ

পরিবেশক
জনতা পিকচার্স
এণ্ড থিয়েটার্স
লিমিটেড

46   *The Goddess*: poster by Ray

particularly unappealing lady, heavily laden with gold of her own, falls to the ground in a swoon.

The next morning, thoroughly hung over, Dutta realises his mistake: gilt has exposed guilt. His host of the previous night has come calling; either Dutta must reveal his secret, or the newspapers will have the story. Playing for time, Dutta fobs the man off with the 'Sanskrit' formula – a piece of nonsense by Sukumar Ray (see p. 25) – and prepares to leave Calcutta in a hurry. But before he goes he reveals all to his secretary and, at his request, gives him the stone. As Dutta and his wife set off at dawn, the day's newspapers have already hit the streets: 'IRON TURNS INTO GOLD – AMAZING OCCURRENCE AT COCKTAIL PARTY'. Their car breaks down near the Victoria Memorial, and they are arrested and taken away for interrogation.

Meanwhile, the stone has been swallowed by the terrified secretary as the police rap on the door. Elsewhere in the city there is total panic at the prospect of a slump in gold prices. The police want to operate to remove the stone, but X-rays show it is being digested in the secretary's colon. As Dutta and his wife sit helpless and pathetic in front of a severe senior police officer (who, it is hinted, was present at the notorious party), all the golden objects touched by the stone, wherever they may now be, suddenly revert: the secretary's gastric juices have done their work, and the crisis is over.

Though the dominant mood of the film is Dutta's innocent delight in being important, Ray's satire is often biting; he gives rein to some of the contempt he feels for the rich and powerful in Indian society, a contempt which was latent too in some of his father's verses. This is epitomised by Satyajit's treatment of the cocktail party. In his draft of the screenplay Ray notes that 'the drawing room is chock-full of the so-called cream of society – male and female', and nearby is a little sketch of Groucho Marx, looking a bit like Paresh Chandra Dutta.

Ray feels a deep distaste for those who pursue money and power as ends in themselves. He has given little thought over the years to increasing his own income, sometimes to the distress of his wife. In fact as we know, he thinks of himself as 'pretty rich' just as he is. As for the personality cult that surrounds most big film directors, Ray does not encourage it: an attitude that his critics regularly label as 'remote', 'arrogant' or 'Brahminical'. Ironically, it is these very aspects of Indian society he is recoiling from. 'I hate the public figure syndrome. I absolutely hate that. Opening exhibitions and that sort of thing I really detest, because you say all the clichés. You have to make a speech. It's the speech that worries me. Nowadays what I have to do is write out a few lines of good wishes. It doesn't affect me at all. I know exactly what to write in the circumstances. I don't mean what I say, but this is one hypocrisy I have to do.'

These aversions did not prevent him from enjoying some fun at the expense of politicians, businessmen and the *nouveaux riches* in general in *The Philosopher's Stone*. At the cocktail party, where everyone present bar the ladies gets steadily drunker while Dutta capers around causing absolute chaos, Ray assembled 'practically everyone from the Calcutta industry' to put in a guest appearance just for one day. 'About ninety per cent of them are now dead: all the character actors,' he says today. 'It was a great experience shooting that scene. Everyone had to be given something to do at that point, so that everyone would be happy. It was all equally apportioned – the various businesses – except for Chhabi Biswas. I told him "You have just done something very important for me [*The Music Room*], so I'll neglect you. So don't mind." His very presence was enough.'

Opinion is divided about whether the scene comes off or not, partly depending on how much one has noticed of brown sahibs under the influence. In the case of Ray, who has never liked alcohol, the answer is quite a bit, as an advertising man in a British-owned firm. But even Chandragupta was critical of the scene: 'I think Satyajit has preconceived notions about the rich – their propensity to drinking, gambling etc. They appear as caricatures and types rather than people. In *Parash Pathar* he has an unusual disgust for alcohol and drunkards. It is this prejudice against drink that has influenced this scene.'

According to Seton, this was the scene that provoked the need for a disclaimer at the beginning of the film saying that all the characters are fictitious, but Ray does not remember. The witty and devastating portrait of a typical public figure created by Ray and Chakravarti is a more likely cause. Ray was actually asked by the Board of Censors to make black the white 'Gandhi cap' worn by Dutta after he gets rich, because this cap was – and is – integral to the image of Congress politicians (even though Gandhi himself did not wear one). By insisting that Dutta is wearing the cap to hide his baldness, Ray got permission to leave it as it was.

Although *Mahapurush* is near to straight farce, it still has a rich script carried off with much aplomb and relish by its cast. Unfortunately for non-Bengalis, this film is much wordier than *The Philosopher's Stone* – packed with puns, different accents and literary and other allusions which are virtually untranslatable. Nevertheless, it was highly praised by Kenneth Tynan in the *Observer*. Many Bengalis, by contrast, disliked it; some because it was not farcical enough in the manner of Rajsekhar's original, others because they found the humour too broad; Chidananda Das Gupta even claimed to find it 'intolerable' for this reason.

In some ways there is more of a barrier for non-Bengalis in the plot too, as well as in the language, than in the plot of *The Philosopher's Stone*. It revolves around a north Calcutta *adda* and around a fake guru (or sannyasi or *baba*) and his credulous followers. The film's *adda*, like the one Ray shared in the coffee house with Majumdar and others (and like Sukumar Ray's Monday Club before that), is carried on by a small group of like-minded friends who take pleasure in gossip and games. Its atmosphere is at once indolent and sharply alert. In catching it on film, Ray drew on Rajsekhar Bose's book, but also on his own memories of the vivacious house of his grand-uncle H. Bose, the perfumer, which he visited as a boy in the 1920s and 30s. 'Today,' he says, 'you don't have *addas* of that type any more. Life has become too complex and difficult. Too many problems. People don't relax to the same extent. We have a few exceptions, hangovers from the old days like R. P. Gupta, but in the 1930s and 40s things were much more like what is described in the story.'

Ray's early intimacy with his ascetic uncle Subimal (Chotokaka) perhaps helped him get the fake guru Birinchi Baba correct. Chotokaka regularly visited *babas* whom he admired, when they came to Calcutta, and reported his experiences of them. But according to Ray today, 'all the *babas* my uncle knew were genuine. None of them was exposed. They were fairly humble people, not show-offs like the Maharishi [Mahesh Yogi]. There were quite a few of them, still regarded as very genuine people.'

Even if a *baba* is not genuine, Ray has more sympathy for him – provided he is not simply a criminal like the other *baba* he has created in his detective film *Joi Baba Felunath* – than for his followers, especially if they happen to be lawyers. Their capacity for emotional self-indulgence and for swallowing all kinds of irrational nonsense, which seems to have multiplied severalfold all over the world in the years since *Mahapurush*, is repellent to Ray. 'Birinchi Baba at least has some imagination. He's exploiting some very gullible useless people – religious people, useless people. I felt he was deserving of more sympathy than his disciples in most cases. If you have such foolish people, why not exploit them?' Or as one of the cynical procurers for Birinchi Baba puts it – it is not *young* followers he wants to attract, but old ones, who are 'blinded by faith or by cataract'.

The other early influence at work in *Mahapurush* was Ray's love of games and magic. He felt the need to invent something for Birinchi Baba to do which would convince his public he had supernatural powers. Apart from the laying on of hands, in which Birinchi Baba is adept, Ray devised, as a supposed symbol of Time Future and Time Past, the revolving of hands: the index finger of the right hand must rotate clockwise (Time Future), while that of the left hand rotates anticlockwise (Time Past). Anyone who cares to try this will see how difficult it is to do. 'I was very good at it from my early childhood; it's one of the things I learnt pretty early on in life,' says Ray with a laugh. 'So we had a session of teaching Birinchi Baba and the other character. They practised at home for hours on end. They were told about it long before the film was shooting.'

The basic situation on which all this chicanery hangs is simple enough, even if the dialogues and details of behaviour are not. Birinchi Baba and his disciple get a grip over a foolish widower, along with many other middle-aged well-to-do people. His daughter is supposed to be getting married to Satya, one of the members of the *adda*. Satya is in despair because she is now to take vows to follow the *baba*, along with her father. Having satisfied themselves by direct observation that the *baba* really is a fake, the members of the *adda* hatch a plot to expose him by setting what appears to be a fire outside his prayer room and starting a panic. The *baba* and his disciple, still dressed up as a many-armed god, are last seen making off into the night with ladies' handbags snatched from the deserted prayer room swinging from the disciple's 'arms'. These contain their 'future', as the disciple wisely points out, earning an approving smile from a temporarily disconcerted Birinchi Baba. And so, Satya will get his girl, the *adda* will go back to its natural indolence, and the followers will feel foolish and somewhat the poorer and, maybe, learn a lesson.

Birinchi Baba himself, who is played by Charuprakash Ghosh (Nanda Babu of *Aparajito*), is richly convincing as the fleshy, theatrical merchant of yarns as long as a sacred thread. Not only was he around in Babylon when Nebuchadnezzar was a mere lad, where he happened upon his disciple in a fruit market, but he once had 'such a row with Plato' about Time, taught Einstein $E = mc^2$, and was on first name terms with Gautama and Jesu. 'You knew Jesus Christ?' asks a lawyer follower excitedly. 'People call it Crucifiction,' intones Birinchi Baba. 'I call it Crucifact. Because I have seen it with my own eyes.' He also has a nice line in holy chants with which to conclude evening prayers: 'O Mores! OMnific! OMniscience! OMnibus! OMnivorous!' 'Is he a Tantric?' enquires Satya in genuine innocence. 'No,' says the cynical procurer, 'but he's certainly a *dhantantric*' – which is to say in Bengali, a capitalist.

8

The Music Room
(Jalsaghar) 1958

···✄[◦✦❀✦◦]✄···

The Music Room is a deeply felt, extremely tedious film. On the one hand its western derivations are patent (the Greek-revival mansion no more than the Chekhovian theme). On the other hand its chief indigenous element, the Indian music, is simply uncongenial and tiresome to our ears. No doubt these are excellent musical performances for those who understand them, but they make us start counting the bulbs in the theater chandelier.

S O WROTE the American critic Stanley Kauffman, when the film was released in the US in 1963. At the same time, his colleague on the *New York Times* – none other than Bosley Crowther who dismissed *Pather Panchali* – wrote 'I wish I had space to be more voluble about the special felicities of this film – about the delicacy of the direction, about the performance that Chabi [sic] Biswas gives as the decaying landowner, about the pathos of Padma Devi as his wife, about the eloquence of the Indian music and the aura of the *mise en scène*.'

To Ray's surprise, *The Music Room* is a film that excites passions abroad, and enjoys a minor cult status. Its showing in Paris in 1981 was largely responsible for opening French eyes to Ray's films after years of indifference. The anonymous London *Times* critic in 1962 felt that it 'offered pleasures of unique delicacy and refinement', and British critic Derek Malcolm, writing in 1975, described it as Ray's 'most perfect film'. But when he made it in 1958, says Ray today, 'I didn't think it would export at all.'

The Music Room is his only film, with the possible exception of *The Goddess*, in which the central character has no capacity for change. It shows a man living in his past, finally destroyed by his own inflexibility. The opening scene sets the tone. The ageing zamindar Biswambhar Roy is reclining motionless in a chair on the roof of his palace at dawn, watching the stars go out. His servant, also no longer young, brings him his beaker of sherbet and settles it beside his hookah. 'What month is it?' asks Roy, after a pause. Then, when the servant is gone, the peace that Roy is obviously used to is disturbed by the notes of a festive *shehnai* drifting over the roof.

His neighbour, the money-lender and businessman Ganguli, is holding a celebration of his son's *upanayan* – where he will be invested with the sacred thread.

Memories of Roy's own son receiving his thread come flooding back. We are transported to the time when Roy was at the height of his powers. After the ceremony and a lavish firework display, there is a grand musical soirée (*jalsa*) in Roy's imposing, pillared music room. As Roy and his guests (including a younger Ganguli) look on, well supplied with drink, a female singer performs Lucknow *thumris* bursting with emotion, which describe a gathering storm. Later that night, we gather from Roy's slurred conversation with his wife in their bedroom that he is willing to spend his last gold coin to hear such singing. Music totally obsesses him; he even has dreams of the musicians and dancing girls at the royal courts glowingly described in the great epics.

The next *jalsa* takes place on the night of a real thunderstorm. His wife and son have meanwhile gone away to her family, but Roy has sent word that they should return for the *jalsa*, which he has announced to celebrate the (Bengali) New Year – also, to spite his *nouveau riche* neighbour Ganguli. The atmosphere in the music room is charged, as a bearded Muslim singer gives a pyrotechnic display of *kheyal* with complex ornamentation and filigrees, while lightning flashes outside. Roy's wife and son have not arrived. As a winged insect trapped in his glass struggles helplessly to escape, Roy senses the worst.

The drowning of his family on their way home at his behest parallels the steady drowning of Roy's zamindari estate by the mighty river Padma that flows by it, which has eaten up so much of East Bengal's history. He feels his life to be finished and, as the years pass, falls further and further into torpor. Only his decaying palace, a few faithful servants, and Toofan the stallion and Moti the elephant remain; he cannot bring himself to part with these last two. On the morning that he hears Ganguli's *shehnai*, he decides to pay a visit downstairs to see them after his long retreat from the world. Toofan is pleased to hear his voice again, but when Roy turns his gaze on to Moti who is grazing in the distance, to his disgust the picture is obscured with dust thrown up by some intrusive lorries.

They belong, of course, to Ganguli, and to the modern world. When the man himself, oozing self-made prosperity, then comes personally to invite the zamindar to his new music room for a performance by the up-and-coming dancer Krishna Bai, Roy naturally refuses the upstart. But the invitation, and the music he hears drifting across from Ganguli's house that night, sting him into action. There and then he lays plans for one final *jalsa*, with Krishna Bai, to demonstrate to Ganguli the élan of the real connoisseur and aristocrat.

After all the guests are gone, lurching around the deserted music room with only alcohol, his servant and his memories to keep him company, Roy begins to lose his mind. Besotted by his aristocratic past framed in the portraits of his ancestors all around him, he convinces himself, as the candles in the chandeliers start to go out with the coming of morning, that he is the last of his line. He must extinguish himself with a grand gesture; and so, mounting Toofan, he gallops off across the sands at a terrible pace. As the horse encounters the half-buried hull of a boat – perhaps the very one in which Roy's family drowned years before – it shies, throwing its drunken rider, whose life finally ebbs out of him while his two servants look tearfully on.

The film is based on a very well-known Bengali short story by Tarasankar Banerjee. It drew Ray for several reasons: partly because the audience would know the story, partly because the main character interested him, but mostly because it offered legitimate scope for music and dancing, the ingredients that Bengali producers have always sought from a director. At a time when concerts of Indian classical music were full to overflowing, this would be the first film to employ such music and dancing as an integral part.

The fact was that in late 1956, after the failure of *Aparajito* at the box office, Satyajit Ray knew that he needed a winner. As he put it then, in a letter, 'I am more or less back where I started from. Bank balance is low and the future looks none too rosy . . . One thing is certain – I have to make money on [my next film] if I am to continue as a film-maker and not revert to advertising.'

His intention had been that the film should be more frivolous than it turned out to be, using music of a lighter, less austere nature. But his true feelings towards the character and the music, combined with those of Vilayat Khan, the composer, ended by modifying the original idea. 'In the process of writing the screenplay,' remarks Ray today, 'it became a fairly serious study of feudalism and also the music became very high-classical stuff.' In May 1957, as shooting began, he wrote to Seton that the film was 'a rather showy piece about a decadent music-loving zamindar and his fantastic efforts to uphold family prestige'; but in a letter of February 1958 it had become a 'brooding drama'.

The discovery of the palace was a story in itself. Ray and his team had just inspected their thirtieth nobleman's palace and rejected it, when an old man in a tea shop overheard them talking and suggested they visit the palace of the Chowdhurys at Nimtita on the border with East Pakistan (as it then was). Without much hope, they agreed to go. 'Nimtita turned out to be everything that the old man claimed – and more. No one could have described in words the feeling of utter desolation that surrounded the palace', wrote Ray in his gem of an article 'Winding route to a music room'. The owner was a seventy-year-old zamindar who knew one of Ray's grand-uncles and who was the antithesis of Biswambhar Roy: he neither drank alcohol nor listened to music. But he had experience of that kind of behaviour through his late uncle Upendra Narayan Chowdhury, builder of the palace music room. (This last was the only disappointment for Ray; it was too small, so the film used a music room lovingly created by Chandragupta.) By an amazing coincidence, Upendra Narayan was the very zamindar on whom the writer Banerjee had based his character, as Ray later discovered back in Calcutta when he told him about finding the palace at Nimtita.

The film's composer, Vilayat Khan, like all the great Indian musicians until recent times, had grown up in the service of a rich patron and was wholly in sympathy with Biswambhar Roy; where Ray would have favoured 'an ironic edge' to the music, Vilayat Khan sought to convey only 'sweetness and greatness'. 'He wrote a lovely theme for Biswambhar Roy, which I was rather worried about,' says Ray. 'I wanted a more neutral kind of approach to the music to go with the zamindar, not suggesting that I was full of sympathy for him, but a kind of ambivalent attitude. But I liked Vilayat's theme as a piece of music and I felt the story would tell what I wanted to tell and the music would not interfere with my general attitude to feudalism.'

Ray had already experienced serious difficulties in working with a classical musician as film composer, in *Aparajito*; and the making of *The Music Room* only reinforced his growing reservations. None of the great musicians with whom he has worked – Ravi Shankar, Vilayat Khan and Ali Akbar Khan – could entirely mould their talents to the demands of a film, and none of them could begin to approach Ray's understanding of western music. Fortunately for *The Music Room*, Vilayat Khan's younger brother Imrat was able to act as a kind of interpreter and mediator; he had an intelligent appreciation of film music, having seen a lot of foreign films.

While much of the music in the film is pure classical, including of course all the performances in the three *jalsas*, some of it is an unorthodox combination of instruments and eastern and western elements – the beginning of experiments by Ray that he would continue to develop with beauty and subtlety as his own composer from 1961 onwards. As the film's opening titles roll, for instance, 'a rather bleak, rather austere morning raga' *Todi* is heard against a string background. 'We had decided to use violins,' recalls Ray, 'not necessarily for melodic purposes, but to give a body, a background texture, instead of using a *tanpura*, which is a drone. I felt that would make it sound too much like a concert performance. So we decided on using strings as a drone, holding the tonic, even doing rhythmic things, instead of using the *tabla* or the *mridangam*, which would again make it sound like a concert performance. And Vilayat agreed to that.' Another example of mixing occurs near the end when Roy is gripped by fear of his own doom at the sight of the silently darkening chandeliers. Ray felt that Indian music alone could not convey Roy's terror, which has an element of the macabre in it too. In the editing room he added to Vilayat's playing some Sibelius, amongst other things, in a key that did not clash. 'This combination gives you a sound texture that is more than just a music-track,' he comments.

In the middle of the film, by contrast, when the zamindar is in high spirits, a pure raga is used at several points to express Biswambhar's sense of his tradition. As the dusty, shrouded music room is opened up once more and made ready for the last time, Vilayat and Imrat Khan play a duet – a south Indian raga now used in north Indian music, which Ray very aptly describes as 'wonderfully bright-sounding'. 'That was the high point of the film, where music comes into the foreground almost.'

Not that it is ever quite allowed to take over. Even during the three *jalsas*, Ray keeps the balance between the music and the characters listening to it – otherwise the unexpected enthusiasm from foreign audiences would have turned into a more predictable reaction. He also took the precaution of casting only the best performers: Akhtari Bai from Lucknow to sing the *thumri*, Salamat Ali Khan to sing the *kheyal*, and the exquisite Roshan Kumari as the *Kathak* dancer. They are able to hold the attention of the uninformed by the sheer emotional charge and technical virtuosity of their performances. One of the rainy season ragas was chosen for the *kheyal*, which was particularly meaningful in conjunction with the storm and with Roy's emotional turmoil; and this was repeated for the astonishing dance performance too.

Though it has quite often been said that Ray shows his sympathy for the feudal order in his portrayal of Biswambhar Roy, there is not much evidence of this on the screen, other than by extrapolation from his clear contempt for the moneyed class personified by Ganguli, which has risen and risen in India since the period depicted in the film. The zamindar, according to Eric Rhode for instance, 'is shown as the last representative of a civilization Ray admires'. But according to Ray the film 'tries to show the inevitability of the old order being replaced by a new – but not necessarily – better system.' Certainly, there are aspects of the feudal world Ray does admire, but they are not the Evelyn Waughish ones many western admirers of the film adumbrate, that belong to a world of caste orthodoxy. 'The fact that the man doesn't know what is happening really, doesn't know the process of history, makes him a figure of pathos. He's pathetic, like a dinosaur that doesn't realise why it's being wiped out,' Ray says. 'But there is no doubt that the zamindars were real connoisseurs of music, and sponsors of music and that musicians owed a great deal to them. Without the feudal lords music wouldn't have flourished the way it did, for long periods, starting from the Mughals.'

This brings to mind another character from a film Ray made twenty years later, Wajid Ali Shah, King of Oudh, in *The Chess Players*. Both are irresponsible men whose faults typify their class, but both are redeemed by a genuine love of music and dancing. The comparison is a revealing one; where Ray, through many small touches, convinces us of Wajid Ali's refinement and imagination, he does not entirely do so in Biswambhar's case. Despite a series of scenes in which his musicality is implied or displayed, Chhabi Biswas never quite satisfies us that he is a connoisseur. The effect of this doubt is to bring him closer in character

to the boorish Ganguli; one seems sophisticated, the other crude, to be
sure, but the feeling is aroused that the difference may be one of breeding
rather than sensibility. Once this impression lodges in the mind, it naturally
follows that Ray himself must share Biswambhar's unthinking acceptance
of his profligate hubristic existence, in which love of money and prestige
seems sometimes to override love of music.

The true rationale is not far to seek: like von Stroheim, who played
the Prussian officer in *La Grande Illusion* with no more than a smattering
of German in real life, Biswas was virtually tone-deaf. 'I discovered this
rather late,' says Ray with a rueful laugh. Biswas told him he would try
to act a connoisseur by producing the right facial expressions at certain
points, saying 'wah-wah', shaking his head, 'looking dreamy-eyed' and so
on. 'I would have used more of that, had he been musical, had it come
spontaneously. But I avoided it as much as possible, because I could see
his acting wasn't up to the real thing.' He did insist, though, that Biswas learn
how to fake the playing of an *esraj* so that he could be seen accompanying his
son's singing of scales. 'He did a very convincing job – I don't know how –
through sheer grit, I think.' He also asked Biswas to do something much
simpler: to lift one finger of his right hand while he was listening to the
strains of dancing coming from Ganguli's house. Biswas had no idea why
he was doing this, but in fact, to musical connoisseurs, this makes it clear
that Roy knows the rhythmic cycle of the dance music. Later, during the
mixing, it gave Ray real satisfaction to coincide the lifting of that finger
with the precise beat of the music on the sound-track.

Biswas's musical failings definitely do detract from the film and prevent
it from taking a place in the first rank of Ray's oeuvre. A vital link seems to
be missing. There are also a few melodramatic and perfunctory passages
in the film, such as Biswambhar's discovery of his son's death, and his ride
to his own death (not helped by Biswas's inability to ride and the lack of a
good stuntman in Bengal). That said, *The Music Room* still has the power
to mesmerise us through its music, its expressionistic lighting, its utterly
convincing sets (so much so that they at first fooled the *thumri*-singer
Akhtari Bai!), and Chhabi Biswas's monumental performance. Whether
strutting around in sparkling white with a cockade and a riding crop,
glancing in private at his meagre 'purse' for the dancer with disdainful
resignation, subduing the vulgar Ganguli with a flick of his ivory cane, or
staggering in drunken elation and depression around the music room, he
is a formidable presence. 'He was keyed up to play that last scene right
up to the hilt,' says Ray. 'The idea of the candles going out one by one
was devised on location while we were shooting. I was working like I
usually do; every evening I was sitting with the script and thinking in
case any fresh ideas might come for the next day's shooting. And this
suddenly came to me in a flash and I described it to him. He was terribly
excited; he said "I have never come across such a brilliant and fresh and
expressive idea." '

At that time he and Ray were staying at either end of a vast verandah in the palace at Nimtita. In the morning and afternoon there was shooting, and in the evening Ray would retreat to his room – where a famous writer of the previous century had worked – to study his screenplay by hurricane lamp while Biswas sat in his, steadily drinking, supplied with bottles by one of Ray's assistants. Though Ray disliked his habit, they were on very good terms, taking dinner together regularly. 'He was almost an alcoholic,' says Ray. 'He was absolutely fresh in the morning but in the evening he was insufferable – absolutely.'

One evening, a band-party had come from Murshidabad and was practising below the verandah for its performance the following day in the film (after the *upanayan* ceremony). Ray was occasionally instructing it to play this or that piece. Suddenly he heard a loud roar from the opposite end of the verandah – 'Mister Ray!' Hurrying out he saw Chhabi Biswas gesturing distractedly at the band. 'What on earth is all this?' he said scornfully. Ray told him.

'You call this a band? It possesses neither rhythm nor spirit – huh!'

'But a village wouldn't really have a good band,' Ray said with some embarrassment.

'Ugh! They can't play a thing – nothing!' – Then, suddenly: 'Why don't you conduct?'

When Ray declined, Biswas himself took up the challenge. In a precise reversal of his film character, a purist who claps his hands over his ears at the sound of 'Colonel Bogey' from Ganguli's residence, he clambered on to the balustrade and began conducting with his hands above his head. 'Everything – ' says Ray, 'the band, the jackals, and the crickets – was drowned out by his fortissimo "One, two, three – One, two, three – ".'

9

The Goddess
(Devi) 1960

·····{ ⊙ }·····

DESPITE being set in the 1860s, *The Goddess*, which Ray made in 1959/60, is a film with strong resonances in today's India, and even further afield, wherever religious fanaticism exists. It is Ray's most 'Hindu' film, and one whose impact depends greatly on atmosphere and suggestive details – which can make it difficult of access to those unfamiliar with Hindu rituals and practices.

Its pivot is a religious belief with ancient roots: the notion that a woman can become an incarnation of a goddess. In this case she is a young and defenceless village bride, Doyamoyee, living in a rich orthodox zamindari household; and the goddess is Kali, the Mother, who is worshipped in shrines all over Bengal. Her father-in-law Kalikinkar Roy, an ageing pious zamindar who lost his wife some years previously, is responsible for perceiving her divine status; he has a compelling vision of it one night, and falls at her feet. Her husband Umaprasad, Roy's younger son, is away from home at the time – studying in Calcutta, absorbing English ideas and literature (as Ray's great-grandfather Dwarkanath Ganguli did at this time). A letter sent by his sceptical sister-in-law, who is married to Roy's older son – an ineffectual figure who obeys his father in all matters, including his deification of Doyamoyee – brings Umaprasad back to the village. The stage is set for a confrontation between father and younger son, between opposing philosophies. Umaprasad, deeply repelled by his father's irrationality, has the courage to tell him he is mad. His father quotes Sanskrit verses from memory at length to prove he is not; but much more telling is Doyamoyee's apparent power to cure a sick child from the village. As word of this spreads, devotees gather from all over the area, just as they would today, in Catholic Europe as much as in India. Umaprasad remains unconvinced, but his impressionable young wife begins to believe in her incarnation. A hidden power appears to prevent her from following her husband out of the village by night, and he is too uncertain of himself to defy his father outright and compel her. By the time he has made up his mind to do so, after consulting his professor in Calcutta, it is too late; the sister-in-law's only child, on whom Doyamoyee used to lavish her affection, has died for lack of medical treatment in her arms, placed there by their father-in-law in his blind faith – and Doyamoyee has lost her mind.

Satyajit Ray wrote in 1982:

> The western critic who hopes to do full justice to *Devi* must be prepared to do a great deal of homework before he confronts the film. He must read up on the cult of the Mother Goddess; on the 19th century Renaissance in Bengal and how it affected the values of orthodox Hindu society; on the position of the Hindu bride in an upper-class family, and on the relationship between father and son in the same family. All the turns and twists of the plot grow out of one or more of these factors. The western critic who hasn't done his homework will pin his faith on the rational son to save him from the swirls and eddies of an alien value system; but even here the son's ultimate helplessness will convince him only if he is aware of the stranglehold of Hindu orthodoxy in 19th century Bengal.

By the same token, says Ray, some of Buñuel's films, and even a film like *The Seventh Seal*, can be unsatisfying to him since he does not know that much about Catholicism and surrealism. 'Buñuel can be very obscure because he adds the surrealist element'; *The Milky Way*, for instance, left Ray 'completely cold', whereas he liked *The Discreet Charm of the Bourgeoisie*.

The vast majority of western criticism of *The Goddess* lends weight to Ray's contention, though Pauline Kael admired the film tremendously. One British reviewer wrote that 'the story itself is dauntingly alien', another that the film 'is an exquisite bore – the action is as remote as one of those endless temple friezes depicting the gods about their bloody business.' For the London *Times* the film was 'more a matter of uncluttered story-telling than of atmosphere and the loving accumulation of detail – always Mr. Ray's strong points', while Eric Rhode, writing in *Sight and Sound*, found himself asking, 'Would an intelligent girl like Doyamoyee – and in Sharmila [sic] Tagore's performance she comes over sharp as a pin – allow herself to be deified, even a hundred years ago? And would a husband as shrewd as Soumitra Chatterjee makes Umapada [Umaprasad] allow himself to be so easily checked?' These are honest doubts, but they betray a near-total misreading of the character of both Umaprasad and his wife.

There are perhaps two outstanding misconceptions among non-Indians that seriously hinder appreciation of the film. The first is the idea that God is male, which is integral to western religious thinking. In India the female nature of God is celebrated too. Tagore, who gifted the theme of *Devi* to the writer Prabhat Kumar Mukherjee (who published it as a brief short story in 1899), expresses this beautifully in *Creative Unity*:

What I have felt in the women of India is the consciousness of an ideal – their simple faith in the sanctity of devotion lighted by love which is held to be divine. True womanliness is regarded in our country as the saintliness of love. It is not merely praised there, but literally worshipped; and she who is gifted with it is called *Devi*, as one revealing in herself Woman, the Divine. That this has not been a mere metaphor to us is because, in India, our mind is familiar with the idea of God in an eternal feminine aspect.

The second misconception is that the Mother is a force for creation but not for destruction too. In the case of Kali this is implied by her appearance. She wears a girdle of severed arms and a necklace of skulls. Her tongue is sticking out – some say in a coy gesture familiar in Bengali girls, others so that she can lick up blood. She has four arms. In her two left hands she holds a decapitated head and bloody sword, while her two right hands confer blessings on her devotees and make a gesture similar to that seen in statues of the Buddha, signifying 'be without fear'.

The symbolism here is shockingly explicit, and it is certain to repel those who have embraced that curious western heresy which declares that the pretty and the pleasant are more 'real' than the ugly and the unpleasant. Hindu philosophy, on the other hand, declares that the unpleasant and the pleasant are equally real (or unreal) and that both these strands of experience are woven by the same power . . . So Kali is shown as the Mother and the Destroyer, giver of life and death, blessings and misfortunes, pleasures and pains. To her devotees, the fortunes and misfortunes of life are simply to be regarded as 'Mother's play'. And, surely, any other view of the human situation is mere sentimentalism. So we must learn to love Kali, whether we want to or not. When we have done so, we shall be able to accept our experience in its entirety. And thus we shall have conquered fear and aversion as well as desire.

This passage was written by Christopher Isherwood in *Ramakrishna and his Disciples*. It describes the state of mind to which Kalikinkar Roy aspires through his lifetime of devotion to Kali and, subsequently, to Doyamoyee. Ramakrishna, the extraordinary Bengali mystic who experienced multiple visions from about 1856 until his death thirty years later, worshipped his wife as Kali. His life, including the many miracles attributed to him, allows us an insight into the psychology of *The Goddess*. It was minutely documented by one of his disciples, known as M, whom Ray describes as Ramakrishna's Boswell. Although Ray finds Ramakrishna's miracles extremely hard to accept, he admires the streak of humanism in him and in his conversation. 'It was really scintillating, with puns, allusions and metaphors. I think he was a very remarkable man and his Boswell was a phenomenon. He reproduced the words exactly – as if he was doing a tape-recording job – and everything rings true.'

One anecdote in M's account bears directly on a scene in which

Doyamoyee gently massages her father-in-law's feet as he reclines in a chair with his hookah, his head resting on a leopard skin. To the non-Indian eye at least, this seems an erotic act. Ray denies this intent, but accepts the scene's 'Freudian connotations': 'I had not a shred of that element in my mind. *Padaseba* [foot-massage] is a conventional Hindu conception and *swasur padaseba* [foot-massage of a father-in-law] would be considered a very admirable thing for a daughter-in-law to do. You can read a sexual element there if you want to, but it wasn't in my mind. Otherwise why does he [Roy] install her as a goddess? That immediately removes that element from his life.' Roy's state of mind, by Ray's reckoning, would be much closer to that of Ramakrishna when his wife was massaging his feet one day. She asked him, 'How do you think of me?' And he answered, 'The Mother who's in the temple [i.e. the image of the goddess Kali] and the Mother who gave birth to me . . . that same Mother is rubbing my feet. That's the truth: I always see you as a form of the blissful Divine Mother.' This is the ideal behind the honorific 'Devi' added to the first name of all married women in Bengal.

The reaction of Ramakrishna's disciples to his fatal illness in 1886 is especially interesting when compared to the response of the various characters in *The Goddess* to the illness of the little boy – who eventually dies at the hands, so to speak, of the Goddess-incarnate. His mother, Doyamoyee's sister-in-law, lacks faith and would prefer him to receive medical treatment but is not totally opposed to supernatural treatment, his grandfather has blind faith, while Umaprasad (though not present) makes clear that only medical treatment has any value. When he finally dies, his mother believes Doyamoyee is a demon, his grandfather is distraught, believing that he has somehow offended Kali, while Umaprasad bluntly informs the old man that he is responsible for killing his own grandson.

When Ramakrishna lay dying, his disciples formed three groups around their Master. The first reasoned that, as a divine incarnation he could not be subject to illness. His sickness must therefore be 'a kind of play-acting', in Isherwood's phrase, which he would abandon when he thought fit. The second believed that the Master's illness was the Divine Mother's doing, whose instrument Ramakrishna was. She had made him sick, for the good of humanity, and she would make him better in her own time. The last group, while believing firmly in the divinity of the Master 'drew a clear distinction between his divine nature and the physical nature of his body.' If human science could heal that, then it should be invited to do so. One member of this last group was Narendranath Datta, who, as Swami Vivekananda, founded the Ramakrishna Mission and began to spread Ramakrishna's thought to the West in the 1890s, while fervently preaching the scientific attitude to Indians.

How does Ray attempt to capture this powerful brew of emotions without alienating a secular modern audience? The answer is, by weaving into the main story of obsession universally recognisable human touches, and infiltrating a richly sensuous texture: elaborate settings, exquisite shawls and saris, oppressive rituals, glowing lamps and lights of all kinds, and lingering camerawork (at least up to the beginning of Umaprasad's first confrontation with his father), all of which create an atmosphere charged with dark feelings.

Ray chose to make the confrontation more powerful, too, than in the original story. There, the clash is only latent. 'The son's character is very much developed in this film according to *my* feelings,' says Ray, 'for dramatic reasons. I was full of sympathy for him. I believed his arguments were much stronger than the father's arguments, because of the irrationality involved.' And at the end, rather than follow Mukherjee's merciless conclusion in which Doyamoyee hangs herself with a sari, Ray softened it to make her fate 'a little more lyrical and mysterious.' As Umaprasad desperately calls 'Doya, Doya', she is seen darting away across the field next to their house and vanishing into the mist, decked out in her entire wealth of jewellery and gold ornaments.

Hers is the most absorbing personality in the story. While the other characters are never less than convincing, they are relatively straightforward. Doya throughout is only half-perceived; although she is very sensitive and alert, we can only guess at the true thoughts behind her sloe-like eyes – she seems composed mainly of instinct. According to the teenage Sarmila Tagore speaking a few years afterwards, '*Devi* was what a genius got out of me, not something I did myself.' Ray gives her more credit than that. He did not direct her to nearly the same extent as in *The World of Apu*. 'She once said to me, "But Manikda, you're not directing me so much." I had to tell her I felt she was doing it all right. "Why should I direct you when you don't require any direction of that kind?"'

By a series of suggestive glimpses of Doyamoyee's routine as a young daughter-in-law in a wealthy orthodox Hindu household, Ray builds up a feeling for the many admirable qualities in her that are subsumed in Tagore's conception of a *devi* combined with some naïve attitudes that help to persuade us why she should obediently accept her father-in-law's wishes after his vision, instead of following her own instincts.

From the beginning we discern her devotion to the little son of her sister-in-law, and to her husband Umaprasad, in Ray's light sketch of the two of them lying on their bed bantering about his studies and his future; and yet it is clear from her questions that she cannot comprehend why he wants a life different from that of his elder brother, away from the family home. With her father-in-law, her devotion is almost palpable; not only in the way she ministers to his comfort by bringing him medicine and sherbet and massaging his feet, but by her careful readying of the family shrine for his worship of the goddess.

The little sequence that shows her doing this while he approaches is one of the finest in the film, a visualisation of Kalikinkar's feelings towards Doyamoyee which perfectly prepares the way for his vision to come. It begins with the image of Kali and a devotional song on the sound-track in the manner of Ramprasad, a famous eighteenth-century devotee of Kali. We cannot see who is singing. Then we see Doyamoyee from the back, sitting before Kali, her sari draped round her head. There is a cut to her seen from the front, as the passionate song continues. She lovingly arranges the various accoutrements of worship. 'Why have you turned your face away?' the song asks of Kali, and we notice Doyamoyee turn her head slightly at the percussive sound of her father-in-law's wooden sandals above her. The old man is slowly making his way down some stairs to perform his puja, his mind filled with the reverential yearnings described by the song. We first catch sight of him from below, pausing at the bars of a window overlooking the shrine. Then, as we hear the slow clack of his sandals descending, the camera moves languidly across to catch him emerging downstairs; and, as it does so, a single pigeon – sacred symbol of fertility – flutters inconsequentially in and out of the frame. It means nothing – and yet, hardly perceptibly, it thickens the emotional atmosphere.

We now see Kalikinkar clearly, wrapped in a beautiful old shawl, wearing on his shoulder the appropriate ritual garment, and at the same time it at last becomes clear who is singing the song: a villager at the steps of Roy's house, crying his heart out for Kali. Roy looks at him, then at the shrouded figure of Doyamoyee at the shrine, and then utters the single syllable that is both a blessing and a curse: 'Ma!' It is the conventional mode of address for both goddess and human – Kali and Doyamoyee; to Roy they are both Mother, and as the film progresses, they are less and less to be distinguished in his mind.

He appears behind her as she completes her preparations. As a young and respectful daughter-in-law, she does not speak to him, but he feels obliged to express his gratitude to her and to say that he hopes she does not mind taking on such duties for him. Significantly, we do not see her reaction to this; Kalikinkar does not expect one. He takes his position in front of the shrine and begins to pray.

Although this closes the scene between them, the shot that follows it is worth mentioning, as an example of Ray's technique in *The Goddess*. He dissolves from a close-up of Roy's head in prayer to a parrot in a cage. The irony is obvious but not at all heavy-handed on the screen. Suddenly, from one side, appears Doyamoyee's fresh, radiant face. She talks affectionately to the bird, ticking it off for being so demanding. In reply it too utters the doomed syllable 'Ma! Ma!' Like the human characters in the house it responds to her loving touch. Towards the end of the film, after Doyamoyee has been deified but before she goes mad, exactly the same shot is repeated; but this time there is a note of poignancy in her action. She is just as human as ever, but others will no longer permit her to express it.

A brief passage of music, raga *Bhairavi* associated always with delight in renunciation, underlines Doya's mood on the second occasion. It is played by Ali Akbar Khan. Much of what he composed for the film is haunting, especially an unorthodox piece changing ragas several times and then returning to the original one, which Ray used to establish Doyamoyee's shifting moods. But in general, his working relationship with Ray was not happy. 'It was rather an unpleasant experience,' says Ray. 'There were no fights; it was all in my mind – all the anguish.' He was not convinced, for instance, by Ali Akbar's choice of his basic raga, *Chandranandan*, which he happened to have composed at the time; Ray felt that for a story of the period of *The Goddess* 'an old, established raga' should be used.

Ray himself chose the western elements in the film's music, such as a loop consisting of the ninth to twelfth bars of Schubert's *Unfinished Symphony* which he used to create the tension in Doyamoyee's abortive night-time flight with her husband. He also composed two songs, his first for a film. 'I explored the whole of Ramprasad, but I didn't find a song which fitted the situation so well. Many songs using that same melodic structure in the style of Ramprasad had been composed later by other composers. So I had no qualms about writing another one,' he says with a laugh. The second of them, sung by the same villager as before, following the miraculous recovery of his sick grandson as the devotees pour in to see the Goddess, happened to be sung by a Kali devotee who had been one class senior to Satyajit at school. 'As soon as he came to the studio I immediately recognised him. "Weren't you at Ballygunj School?" He didn't recognise me. Then he sang these songs very well. After that I heard he was a police officer of the most ruthless kind, known for beating and kicking prisoners.'

Upon its release in India, *Devi* ran into a lot of trouble; one has only to recall the fierce ideological clash in 1987 over a case of apparent *sati* in a village in Rajasthan to know why. Even supposing the young bride there died voluntarily, is there any place for such devotion in a modern society? Ray's film was widely seen as an attack on Hinduism, and there was a determined attempt to prevent its screening abroad, though it was eventually given the President's Gold Medal by the Government. Ray found himself in the same position as Tagore half a century before, defending his work as an attack on extreme orthodoxy but not on Hinduism itself. But, as with Tagore, his critics could see that the two were not easily to be separated. As Ray puts it today, with a smile, 'Well you see that was one way of defending myself. It's a fine distinction, a thin line.' While he finds organised religion antipathetic, his own beliefs remain fundamentally private and unarticulated. He keeps an open mind about reincarnation – witness his later film *The Golden Fortress* – but about *The Goddess* he says, 'at no point am I convinced that Doyamoyee is an incarnation. There's no question of that.' Perhaps his attitude is clearest in the ultimate, enigmatic shot of the film which replaced his original idea of having Doyamoyee die in the arms of her husband saying 'no' to her divinity. It shows an unfinished clay model of Kali waiting to be dressed and decorated for worship; it is humans who create and recreate gods, Ray seems to imply, and the human mind that decides whether they are used for the benefit of Man or not.

10

Three Daughters
(Teen Kanya) 1961

···✦❨ ◦❋◦ ❩✦···

R AY conceived the trilogy of films known as *Three Daughters*, made after *The Goddess*, as a tribute to Tagore in the centenary of his birth, 1961, along with the documentary film *Rabindranath Tagore*, commissioned by the Government in Delhi. He chose to adapt three of Tagore's shorter stories rather than one novel or another longer work, partly because of his long-standing affection for them but mainly because he felt the necessity of expressing the diversity of the man. It is hard to think of another film-maker who has made three films simultaneously of such variety and consistent quality. If I were forced to pick only one work by Ray to show to someone unfamiliar with him, it would have to be *Three Daughters*.

The films are linked by having a female character at their centre: a village waif in *The Postmaster*, the childless wife of a rich business-man in *Monihara* (*The Lost Jewels*), and a village tomboy in *Samapti* (*The Conclusion*). In most other respects they differ. The predominant note of the first is poignant, underscored by some delicious humour, the second is a sophisticated ghost story, while the third one is principally a comedy. In Bengal they were shown in the above order, while abroad *Monihara* was dropped, leaving only *Two Daughters* (*Dui Kanya*); this was because *Monihara*'s subtitles could not be completed in time. Ray recalls working through the night to get the films ready for the centenary in May 1961. As he commented to Lester Peries about a year later, '*Teen Kanya* has turned out to be *nearly* as much work as three full length features.'

He believes – and I would agree – that *The Postmaster* is the best of the three films. In fact, it ranks as one of Ray's best films altogether. It feels faultless in every department of film-making. When Ray met Renoir again in 1967, he found that he loved the film too. It fits with Renoir's own best work: however wrong-headed the characters in *The Postmaster* are, including the village madman, they radiate charm and give fresh meaning to Renoir's well-worn dictum that 'everyone has his reasons'. *The Postmaster* is humanist cinema of the highest sort, without a trace of the sentimentality or banality that mars *The River*.

Much of its appeal derives from Tagore himself. *The Postmaster* was one of his first short stories, written in 1891 soon after he took over the management of the Tagore estate in East Bengal, and it is very loosely inspired by a postmaster he knew there – who also figures in his lyrical letters to his niece, *Glimpses of Bengal*. In Tagore's story the postmaster is a fish out of water: a poetising Calcutta boy from an impoverished middle-class background posted to a village in what he regards as the back of beyond. His salary is as meagre as the company he has to keep. He lives in very basic rooms set aside for the holder of the job, and these come with a servant attached: Ratan, a wispy little girl not yet a woman, without either father or mother. She cooks and cleans for the postmaster, fetches his water for him (which he persists in storing in pitchers for his bath as people do in Calcutta, rather than taking a dip in the village pond), stokes his hookah, and nurses him when malaria strikes. She is vital to his survival in the village.

Without much to do, the postmaster feels forlorn and bored. As Tagore puts it:

> The shimmer of freshly washed leaves, and the banked-up remnants of the retreating rain-clouds were sights to see; and the postmaster was watching them and thinking to himself: 'Oh, if only some kindred soul were near – just one loving human being whom I could hold near my heart!' This was exactly, he went on to think, what that bird was trying to say, and it was the same feeling which the murmuring leaves were trying to express. But no one knows, or would believe, that such an idea might also take possession of an ill-paid village postmaster in the deep silent midday interval in his work.

On an impulse he begins teaching Ratan to read and write and she responds very eagerly. Soon she lives for his call. To him, however, she is a pastime.

The attack of malaria is what finally drives him to leave. Ratan asks if she may come with him. 'What an idea!' he says, without realising for a moment the depth of her feelings. When, out of pity, he later offers her a substantial portion of his final month's salary, she falls at his feet, begs him not to give her anything, and runs away to hide her tears. He is very taken aback. As he is borne away from the village on the monsoon-swollen river, leaving Ratan to his replacement, the postmaster 'consoles himself with philosophical reflections on the numberless meetings and partings in the world, and on death, the great parting, from which there is no return. 'But Ratan', Tagore reminds us, 'had no philosophy.'

Tagore's interpreter Ray altered Ratan's pleading with the postmaster to create a much more restrained ending, on the grounds that the original was 'sentimental'. He also introduced some new characters: the harmless madman who terrifies the postmaster into trying to read his book upside down, and the village elders who gather round him in his battered office for a ruminative *adda.* They resemble the creatures who gather round Alice to run the Caucus Race; instead there is an excruciating musical evening at the home of one of their number, which the postmaster must do his best to endure politely.

These wonderful old characters were recruited from among the villagers at Boral, some of whom had already appeared in the Apu Trilogy. One had selected a song for the occasion and intended to accompany himself on a harmonium. When Ray listened to it he realised that it was the wrong raga for an evening *adda.* The old man was not in the least put out when Ray mentioned this: 'within ten minutes he had wrestled the song into the form of *Purabi.*' His subsequent performance for the camera, with his own ideas of facial and hand gestures, impressed Ray as worthy of the most professional actor.

The discovery of the film was Chandana Banerjee as Ratan. Her miraculously natural acting, combined with 'the squirrel-like character of her face', in Seton's phrase, defines her vividly as an individual; and yet she can also seem to represent all the world's struggling children. Many years later Ray wanted to make a documentary on child labour. It would have consisted simply of shots of boys and girls working, without commentary or narration. The Government refused him permission on the grounds that child labour is illegal in India.

He spotted Chandana in a dancing school. He was told that 'this was a school where you could go and watch a lot of girls in action. There would be dancing and you could pick one if you liked,' he says with a laugh. 'So I picked her. She turned out to be an absolutely fantastic actress: ready, no tension at all, and intelligent and observant and obedient – perfect to work with. Anil [Chatterjee], who played the postmaster, was constantly worried that no one would look at his performance with her there on the screen.'

The scene of their parting, which is almost wordless, makes a fitting conclusion to this charged little duet. Besides the acting, the camerawork and editing show Ray at his most imperceptible, and the trembling, hesitant plucking of the rustic *dotara* and *sarinda* with which it opens (played by two refugees from East Bengal who were so good that Ray scrapped his own music on hearing them) is as suggestive as the zither in *The Third Man.* All we actually see is Ratan, lugging a pail of water from the well for the new postmaster, passing by the old postmaster as he makes his way down the village path towards the boat. To one side – a dark outline beneath the trees – crouches the madman, unmoved by normal human passions. Ratan has been crying, but she is too proud and hurt to accept the coin that the postmaster is ready to offer her; in fact she does not even stop or look at him until she has gone well beyond him, when she needs to relieve the weight on her arm. She disappears, and a few moments later the postmaster overhears her familiar voice saying, 'I have brought your water, Sir.' But she is talking, of course, to his replacement. Emotion overwhelms

him then, as he gazes at the useless rupee in his hand. Replacing it in
his pocket he very slowly walks off down the path, his figure gradually
receding, leaving forever Ratan, the madman, and his life in the village.
The little drama 'is expressive and touching beyond words', wrote Bosley
Crowther. 'It says almost all that can be managed about the loneliness of
the human heart.'

Loneliness is the theme of *Monihara* too, but its effect on Manimalika,
the isolated wife of a rich man, is instead to make her avaricious and
cruel: traits that are unique to her among Ray's women characters. She is
utterly obsessed with jewels and ornaments – quite a common condition
in zamindari households, according to Ray – which she accumulates by
nagging her husband Phanibhusan, who imagines that they will help to
buy her love. Though they have been married ten years, she is still cold to
him and they have no children. Her consuming fear is that one day he may
ask for the jewellery back. When a fire destroys his business, she decides
to test him and suggests the idea of selling the jewellery. But when he
shows interest she withdraws in hysterical panic. Her husband goes away
then to Calcutta to raise money in other ways, leaving her behind in their
vast, silent palace cluttered with Victorian furniture and bric-a-brac like
stuffed birds and animals; Manimalika acts swiftly. In secret she calls a
'cousin' Madhusudhan who lives nearby, and demands that he escort her
to her parents' house some distance off. Madhusudhan eventually agrees,
but he clearly has his own plans for the jewel box which Manimalika shows
him with a crazed glint in her eye; we already know him as a dubious
character, since he has attempted to blackmail Manimalika about their
past life together. That same night, while the servant is away in the village,
the two of them slip out of the palace together, Manimalika wearing her
entire precious collection around her neck and arms and feet.

   She will not be seen again, in human form. The following morning,
her husband returns to the palace and is alarmed to find first his wife
and then her jewels gone. No one knows how she disappeared. He has
even bought her a new piece of jewellery in Calcutta, as he had promised.
That night strange things begin to happen: as Phanibhusan opens the new
box of jewels there is a peal of manic laughter, and later, when he is
in bed, he hears the jingle of jewellery as someone passes along the
corridor and pauses outside his bedroom, followed by two knocks. Half
believing his wife has returned, he gets up, opens the door – and sees
only the empty corridor and his old servant. Later still, in the dead of
night, the sounds repeat themselves, but this time Phanibhusan does not
get up. Instead he stares, fascinated, at the bedroom door. As it creaks
open a silhouette appears, floats towards the bed and stops not far from
him. He calls softly, 'Mani, have you returned?' The black figure slowly
shakes its head. Afraid now, he intuitively grasps what his spectral wife
has really come for: the jewel box at his bedside. Hesitantly, he reaches

out to stop her and a skeletal arm, still wearing its gold bangles, shoots forward to grab the box, accompanied by horrible unearthly laughter.

Ray's story is considerably different from Tagore's, more so than his other adaptations in *Three Daughters*. He has intensified both the mystery and the horror in the original. Nevertheless, he retains a device of Tagore's which some may feel weakens the film: an on-screen narrator, actually a local schoolmaster with a penchant for writing stories and for hashish, who is seen a number of times during the film. He is telling this particular story to a hooded figure with a peculiar, hollow voice whom he has come across one evening sitting on the river ghat opposite the palace of the story. At the end this figure tells the schoolmaster that he has enjoyed listening to the story but that much of it is false. He reveals himself to be Phanibhusan Saha, and promptly evaporates.

Such a story-teller is certainly in the Indian tradition – in fact there are shades in him of Satyajit's eccentric schoolmaster uncle Chotokaka who used to tell Satyajit ghost stories – but his interjections defuse the creepy atmosphere that the film is working to create. To Ray that is not a weakness but of a piece with the style, though he does feel that the poor dubbing by the actor playing the schoolmaster spoils (for a Bengali at least) what is otherwise a polished film. It would have been a weakness, he implies, if he had been aiming for the suspense of Hitchcock, whose *Psycho*, which Ray saw shortly before making *Monihara*, had suggested to him how stuffed birds might be used in a film; but Ray's drama is mainly psychological, flesh-tingling rather than nail-biting. Even in a ghost story, he takes great pains over his characters; it is as if he is determined to render the dividing line between the explicable and the supernatural as fine as possible. Strange happenings may simply be the products of overwrought minds. He is critical of Hitchcock, whose characters, 'are supposed to exist on a level of everyday reality, and yet have no existence beyond the needs of a melodramatic plot designed solely to generate maximum suspense.' Ray cites Hitchcock himself, who, in Truffaut's book about him, regrets his own 'thin characterisations' and says that it is not simple to correct them, 'because when you work with strong characters, they seem to take you where they want to go.'

In *Monihara*, the forbidding power of Manimalika is enhanced both by Ray's music and by the brooding presence of the palace – a magnificent studio set created by Chandragupta, apart from a few exteriors shot by the Ganges. Ray selected for Manimalika one of Tagore's most haunting songs, based, unusually for Tagore, on a south Indian song and famous for its difficulty. Sung by Ray's relative Ruma Guha Thakurta, it becomes in effect Manimalika's theme, first heard when she first enters the palace – as just the introductory notes, a dying fall that catches her sense of insecurity with sharp clarity. 'It is a very ornate, very lonely song,' says Ray 'that absolutely suited the mood. It's not that the words actually reflect her situation – they are not important here – it's the tune.'

*

Although *Samapti*, the last of the *Three Daughters*, is a comedy bordering on farce, its characters are again full and rounded. The humour derives essentially from the institution of marriage – arranged and otherwise. Given the permutations of marriage thrown up by the Indian scene, there is nothing inherently improbable in the story, even if much of it is likely to seem so to the western mind. Both Tagore's original and Ray's adaptation abound in the kind of acute social commentary in which Sukumar Ray specialised in his satirical verses.

Where Aparna, Apu's bride in *The World of Apu*, was meek and submissive, Mrinmoyee, bride of the young graduate Amulya in *Samapti* – Soumitra Chatterjee again – is a wild, rebellious creature. She and her future husband set eyes on each other for the first time when he is floundering around in mud, having just jumped over-confidently from the boat that has brought him back to his village from Calcutta after an exam triumph. She bursts into girlish giggles and runs away.

Amulya is received with affection bordering on suffocation by his widowed mother, who soon announces she has plans for him – a nice, dull girl from a neighbouring village. Amulya already knows of her and is appalled at the prospect. How can he, with his degree, his bust of Napoleon and his love of devotional songs which he plays on his hand-cranked gramophone, marry a pudding called Pooty, whose only accomplishments are in the household arts? He first refuses his mother outright; and then relents, to the extent of agreeing to see the girl.

Amulya's visit to her is a disaster from beginning to end. His carefully polished shoes – an important symbol of his status as a gentleman – arrive at the next village in total disarray, after he has picked his way along a very muddy path. The girl is utterly conventional, and while he is being forced to admire her needlework and singing, pandemonium breaks loose, in the shape of Mrinmoyee, whose pet squirrel Chorky invades the room. Then he finds his shoes have vanished and has to set off home through the mud again in a borrowed pair of the wrong size. One of his own shoes soon reappears as mysteriously as it disappeared, chucked on to the path, and Amulya stealthily captures its abductor Mrinmoyee. This time it is she who makes off floundering in the mud, watched by an excited Amulya.

Amulya is now hooked on her and, despite his mother's tearful objections, he marries Mrinmoyee. We soon discover why her nickname is Paglee ('Madcap'). On their wedding night – the *phulsajya* so unforgettably portrayed in *The World of Apu* – she climbs out of their room, shins down a tree and spends the night on a favourite swing on the river-bank. The following morning, much to Amulya's humiliation and the wrath of his mother, she has to be locked back into the marriage room alone, in front of the villagers. In a childish tantrum she hurls Amulya's belongings around, including his cherished books. When he finally enters the room to put a stop to her behaviour, he quietly insists that she pick up everything and announces that he will return to Calcutta and leave her at her mother's home until such time as she wants to see him again. Silently moving about the room, still dressed in her bridal ornaments (including the traditional womb-shaped ear decorations, like Paisley patterns, that symbolise fertility), she still casts a strong spell over Amulya. 'I suppose you are used to sleeping on a swing', he says softly with a smile – a line that creates a fine tremor of eroticism in a Bengali listener. When they finally come together it is in the same room in a tender scene of much charm deliberately divested of its comic possibilities. Although Amulya has been lured back from Calcutta by his mother on a false pretext, he still goes in search of Mrinmoyee in the rain. Her heart has grown fond of him in his absence and his eagerness to find her dissolves the remaining barrier between them. Just when he has finally given up hope of discovering her in the forest nearby and goes back to his room, she mysteriously reappears there. Surprised, he asks her how she managed it? By climbing the tree again of course, she says, and adds, 'But I won't do it again.'

If *Samapti* seems slightly less satisfying than *The Postmaster*, it is because the acting of Aparna Das Gupta as Mrinmoyee does not have quite the authenticity of Chandana Banerjee as Ratan. She is delightful as Mrinmoyee but she has one flaw that jars occasionally, even a little on the non-Bengali ear. As Ray puts it, 'The only trouble was her accent in Bengali, which was rather sophisticated. I was still at that point not dictatorial enough to mould that.' The effect is slightly to blur Mrinmoyee's appeal to Amulya; it is her freshness and lack of guile that should draw him, but Aparna Das Gupta can make her sound more like an affected city-bred girl.

That was one of the reasons why Ray had earlier decided against casting Aparna, the daughter of Chidananda Das Gupta, as her namesake in *The World of Apu*. She remembers that when she was about eleven Ray came to their house, ostensibly for some other reason but in fact to give her the once-over. 'I was very self-conscious. He kept looking at me and talked to me a little. And every time I went out with my parents to see a film society show, he would look at me and discuss me with his wife.' She fitted into the part of Mrinmoyee from the first, as Ray had sensed from these periods of observation. 'I didn't *act* in *Samapti* at all,' she says. 'I was told what to do from beginning to end. I remember Soumitra telling me that I should try to live the part, and believe that I was Mrinmoyee. I had already started behaving like her without being told to do so, maybe because I just liked doing so.' Several things that she did in the film – falling off a tree while trying to climb it, releasing her pet squirrel into the 'girl-viewing session' – were not pre-planned; Ray simply liked the way she did them and kept them in. In the scenes involving more complex emotions to do with her awakening love for Amulya, Ray avoided discussion of her feelings and limited himself to direction of what she should do. When she first confronts Amulya face to face, for instance, as he grabs his second shoe back from her, Aparna recalls that Ray told her, 'You're uncomfortable'. 'I was completely confused as to what I should do and all I kept hearing from the other end of the camera was "Frown! Frown!" very loudly. I kept frowning for all I was worth,' she says. The effect on the screen is a marvellous combination of pleasure and discomfort.

Much later in the film, after Amulya has gone to Calcutta, we see Mrinmoyee in a big close-up lying down quietly for a long time; Ray dubbed this 'the growth of love' in his shooting notebook, writing it in English. In three dissolves, her little brother appears with a fruit he has picked for her which she rejects; her mother appears, abuses her and then tearfully hugs her while Mrinmoyee cries; and finally, her little brother reappears and tells her that Chorky is dead and dangles the pathetic corpse of the squirrel in front of her face. The catharsis is now complete and she can bear the sight of her dead pet; as she lies there wearing a fresh sari and kohl on her eyes she begins to smile to herself, thinking of her husband. 'Just put your thumb in your mouth and think of lovely wonderful things,' was all Ray told Aparna. Although she was only twelve or thirteen at the time, she guessed what he was trying to convey to her.

One revealing moment in the shooting of *Samapti* neither Ray nor his actors were responsible for. It happened in the studio. Satyajit was up on a trolley and Sandip – then about seven years old – was standing behind him watching, as he likes to do whenever his father is shooting. 'In the middle of the shot something went wrong, and before I said "Cut" he said "Cut" – and ran away. He just couldn't help it,' remembers Satyajit today with visible affection.

11

Kanchenjungha

1962

❊❊❊

R AY'S first original screenplay and his first film in colour,
Kanchenjungha, which is backed by the first full-length score of his
own composition, is one of his most complex films. It also contains some
penetrating criticism of the richer sections of Bengali society, which has
lost none of its bite in the years since the film was released in 1962.

These are reasons enough for the film's virtual disappearance at
the time; the Calcuttan reaction could almost bear comparison to the
ferocious Parisian reaction to Renoir's *La Règle du Jeu* on the eve of the
Second World War. While most Indian critics and viewers dismissed it as
incomprehensible – or, according to Chidananda Das Gupta, 'lightweight'
– there were two who reviewed it at length, producing a pair of reviews
which are probably the most contrasting that a Ray film has ever received
in India. P. Lal, whose non-Bengali extraction must have hampered his
appreciation of the dialogue, dubbed *Kanchenjungha* an 'anti-film' and
accused Ray of avoiding displays of emotion as vulgar, of being confused,
amoral and blasé, and of having created 'picture-postcard artificial relations'.
The Bengali Jyotirmoy Datta, was laudatory and concluded that the film 'is
a disquieting and unflattering mirror held up before the viewer. And the
easiest way of escape is to refuse to see one's image in it.'

Kanchenjungha's distribution abroad suffered from its difficulties
at home. In the US Edward Harrison released it in 1966 to mixed
reviews. In Europe it went unseen, bar one festival, because, it appears,
its producers failed to make available a subtitled print. Those critics who
did manage to see it plus subtitles, felt it would have run well in Britain; it
shares much of the appeal of the later *Days and Nights in the Forest*. That
view was confirmed by the appreciative response to its British television
première in 1988. Perhaps *Kanchenjungha* will eventually be released in
Britain and enjoy the same belated success as Ray's films have in Paris.

The plot is both as simple to summarise and as difficult to define
as that of *Days and Nights*. Set around 1961, it shows a hundred-odd
minutes in the life of a group of Calcutta Bengalis on the last day of their
holiday in the hill station of Darjeeling, during which they have failed to

catch a glimpse of the great peak Kanchenjungha. They are the family of a rich industrialist, the director of five companies, who holds a title given him in British days of which he is still very proud. As the film begins, he is preparing to leave his hotel, along with his wife and younger daughter, to take a walk after lunch. He has arranged to meet a man whom he wants to be her future husband, and hopes that he will propose to her if they are left alone together. Her feelings about this, and the unfavourable reactions to the idea of her mother, uncle, elder sister and brother-in-law, form the substance of the film, along with her feelings towards an outsider, a boy from Calcutta who meets her almost by accident. Although nothing definite develops between them, his very presence, combined with the inspiring mountain setting, decides the girl to reject her suitor. She is helped too by her knowledge of her mother's unhappiness and of the obvious failure of her elder sister's marriage. By the time the walk is over and the industrialist arrives at a pre-arranged rendezvous, expecting to find his family gathered there with the successful suitor, certain decisions have been taken and accommodations reached without his knowledge by each member of the group; and none of them is there to greet him – only Kanchenjungha. As the mists at last roll away from the awesome summit, the industrialist is so preoccupied he no longer cares to admire it.

The underlying psychology of the film derives in large part from the setting. In order to understand the effect of that on the characters we have to appreciate what Darjeeling means to Bengalis. In 1912 Sukumar Ray compared it to Bournemouth in a letter from Britain, mainly because of the steep roads they share, but the analogy could be taken just a little further: people visit both places to escape the big city, and they behave differently in them from the way they do at home. 'Darjeeling is something very special for Bengalis,' says Ray, 'because you have the sea at one end of Bengal and the snow-peaks at the other. In that narrow waist of India you get the full range of landscapes.' Tagore wrote a poetic novel, *Seser Kabita* (*Farewell, My Friend*), about a love affair set in a hill station like Darjeeling, which *Kanchenjungha* is likely to evoke in the mind of any educated Bengali.

From the middle of the last century onwards, both the English in Bengal and the Bengalis used to flock up to the hill stations to escape the worst heat of Calcutta. A thoroughly anglicised atmosphere was created there, which influenced both Sukumar and Satyajit Ray who stayed as children in Darjeeling with relatives – some of whom were undoubtedly brown sahibs, at least in their outward appearance. On his first trip there in the late 1920s, Satyajit recalls that the bandstand still stood in the Mall and the band would play in it, as it does in the film though in a different place. He mixed with no English children then, but in later years an older cousin of his (who is in the film) settled there; he knew everyone, and via him Ray was able to persuade an English tea-planter to appear in his film. *Kanchenjungha* is therefore a 'very personal film' for Ray: first, because it involves characters and a place he knows well; secondly, because its cinematic form is original.

Ray sketched out his ensemble in a letter to Lester Peries during editing of the film in early 1962: 'a domineering British title-holding father, resigned once-talented mother, bird-watching philosophical brother-in-law, brink-of-divorce elder daughter and husband, playboy son, sensitive younger daughter, eligible prosaic bachelor suitor, and young unemployed intellectual stranger.' The father Indranath Roy Chowdhury, played to a tee by Chhabi Biswas, is a bully of a type that no longer quite exists in Bengal with the passing of the generation that served the British Raj, but his general outline is only too familiar today. Ray has very little sympathy with him – not because he assisted the Raj and made himself rich, but because he is a philistine who has suppressed his wife and regards his own daughter as a marketable commodity. This is clear from a dialogue near the start of the film in which he is irritated by his wife's brother Jagadish, who takes no interest in his plan to 'catch' the suitor, being much more interested in watching birds; according to Indranath, birds are only of interest if they can be caught and roasted.

His wife Labanya has given up fighting her husband years before and habitually wears a long-suffering lonely expression, except alone when she releases her pent-up feelings by singing one of Tagore's more anguished songs; like many Bengali women of her status, she has a singing voice which has gone unused since her marriage. She is played with great conviction by Karuna Banerjee, who comments today that 'being the wife of a most "undominating" husband [Ray's friend Subrata Banerjee] in real life, it was really an entirely new experience to feel crushed yet rebellious under a dominating husband.' One of the most touching moments in the film occurs when Jagadish steals up behind her while she is sitting singing on a bench overlooking the mountains and places his hand on her shoulder; she looks up, smiles, and calls him 'dada' (elder brother), and he tells her it is a long time since he heard her sing like that.

Her three children, growing up in the shadow of 'his lordship', have reacted in different ways. Anima, the elder daughter, has a lover whom she first knew before her arranged marriage; but her deceptions have not fooled her husband, who has taken increasingly to drink and horses. Their loveless marriage is held together only by the existence of their young, rather frail daughter, and by the stigma divorce would entail. Anil, the son, played by Anil Chatterjee (of The Postmaster), is still a bachelor and a rather absurd figure, interested mainly in photographing attractive girls in the cafés of Darjeeling in order to flirt with them, somewhat to his father's disgust. He can be of no more help to his younger sister Manisa in her dilemma than Anima. Manisa is the intellectual of the family, sensitive to and knowledgeable about literature and studying for her BA; she clearly takes after her mother. She is also beautiful.

Her suitor Mr Banerjee, as she carefully calls him in reply to his 'Manisa', is an excellent match by conventional standards – an engineer ten or fifteen years older than her with very good prospects. He is also thoroughly uncongenial to her, ignorant of Nature, of Bengali literature (he knows Browning but not Tagore), and of her feelings, though he is genuinely kind and unwilling to force her into marriage. As he eventually chooses to put it, in an unfinished sentence that encapsulates the theme of the film. 'If you ever feel that security is more important than love or that love can grow out of security . . .'

Asok, the young graduate from Calcutta Manisa meets, represents insecurity – no doubt about that. His only income is from ill-paid tuitions, but he has too much pride to be able to accept a job offer from Indranath, a family connection; being in Darjeeling gives him the courage actually to say no. On the other hand, he has all the interests in common with Manisa that Banerjee so signally lacks.

Apart from a number of excellent small roles which include Anil's sophisticated girlfriends, Asok's grasping uncle (a past tutor of Anil), an English resident of Darjeeling, other local people (and Sandip Ray as a boy on a swing), there is one other character of importance: a snotty-nosed little Nepalese boy who tags on to the various characters at different stages in their shifting relationships, in the hope of baksheesh. He receives from Banerjee at the end a bar of chocolate originally intended for Manisa and sings an artless little song under the puzzled gaze of Indranath as he munches it. He was an addition to the script whom Ray spotted while shooting. 'He symbolised Darjeeling for me because he was the only rooted character.'

The language of communication (or, more usually, of lack of communication) of all the outsiders to Darjeeling – excepting only Asok – is Bengali but liberally sprinkled with English phrases. As Banerjee proffers a flower to Manisa, he informs her in his best Oxford tones, 'I made extensive trips to locate it' – and then feels bound to admit this is not actually true. Indranath, walking alone with his wife, makes a pun on Manisa's BA – as less important than her *biye*, the Bengali word for marriage – and draws a wan smile by telling her in English, 'You know I'm an optimist and I don't like glum faces.' These English intrusions can be quite disconcerting for a non-Bengali, particularly if he is embarrassed by the colonial past, and even for a Bengali, though for different reasons as Ray was aware: 'The amount of English the characters use was very much against the norm of the Bengali film and the Bengali attitude to the cinema.' Or as Jyotirmoy Datta puts it in his review:

The good Bengali feels irritated and humiliated by the dialogue. Like too many raisins in a cake, or rather, flies in milk, the Bengali dialogue teems with English words and gives one a sickening feeling. One blushes at the thought that this is the *khichry* language each language-proud Bengali uses even while in love. The absurd aping of British manners is not as irritating, not as deflating to one's ego, as the inability of apparently civilised human beings to express quite simple thoughts without recourse to English.

And yet, it is a faithful reflection of one type of Bengali who used to holiday in Darjeeling. Ray recalls:

There was a seminar at the Max Mueller Bhavan [a cultural institute in Calcutta], and there was an American woman who said 'Who are these characters? I don't like them at all.' She was only interested in the poor Indians, the lower-class Indians, the Indians who suffer and who are really rooted. These very hybrid sort of characters disturbed her greatly. I think they're just as valid. Remember the two-hundred-year colonial rule and you will understand that these characters are very valid, very true to India; there's nothing wrong with them as such. You may object to the fact that I have made a film about them. That's a different matter altogether. But they *are* Indians. You meet thousands of Indians like that.

Ray's initial conception of a film using such characters was a family picnic stretching over a day in an amazing old house he knew belonging to a branch of the Tagores. When permission to shoot there was not forthcoming, he decided to shift the setting to Darjeeling. He wrote the first draft of the screenplay there, sitting in the Windermere Hotel as its sole guest. He soon felt the change to be a great improvement, with more scope for his impulse to create a new kind of story – one more concentrated in time. 'It could be said of each of my first four or five films that they are simple stories straightforwardly told. All of them have filmic qualities, but none of them has much variety of technique. The first exception to this undoubtedly comes with *Kanchenjungha*.'

He aimed consciously for a screenplay with a musical structure, which is what he means when he describes *Kanchenjungha* as 'western in feeling'. He attributes much of its failure in Bengal in 1962 to the audience's lack of sensitivity to this structure. 'In a sense *Kanchenjungha* is a very artificial kind of creation. It's a manufactured situation where everything takes place according to a certain preconceived pattern. It's a very deliberately contrived screenplay – very decorative. Yet the total effect is natural – but that's another thing. Underneath, there's extremely conscious planning of words, gestures, movements, transitions – that's why I say it's musical. It's a very composed film.'

That is also true of Ray's use of colour in it. There were two reasons why he chose to move into colour. The first, and more important, was the opportunity it offered to reflect the personality of each character through clothes, since none of them changes his clothes during the course of the afternoon. They are identified as much by the clothes they wear (which is 'so very true of the upper class', says Ray) as by their behaviour, making colour a 'unifying poetic element in the film' through the patterns it creates over time. Thus Manisa dresses for her encounter in a gorgeous ochre sari and wears a white coat over it. Ochre being the colour of renunciation, she is giving an unambiguous signal that she does not welcome her father's choice of husband for her (if she did, she would probably have chosen red), and, to the sensitive Bengali viewer, the colour, the situation and the autumnal season together may well remind him of some famous lines of a Tagore song which reinforce the message of the ochre sari.

The second reason for using colour was, naturally enough, to capture fully the moods of Darjeeling that are integral to the film. Ray had been initiated into these early on while watching the sunrise over Kanchenjungha as a child. His screenplay was planned in such a way that Nature and his characters are matched in mood throughout, by contrast with his next colour film *Distant Thunder* where nature smiles while men starve and do terrible things to each other. Ray says:

> The idea was to have the film starting with sunlight. Then clouds coming, then mist rising, and then the mist disappearing, the cloud disappearing, and then the sun shining on the snow-peaks. There is an independent progression to Nature itself, and the story reflects this. When it becomes misty, the mother breaks into a Tagore song; and the young daughter and the suitor part at that point; and Indranath meets Asok for the first time; and the elder daughter Anima and her husband experience the bitterest moment between them. And then when the sun comes out again, the young girl [Anima's daughter] finishes her ride and comes back to her parents; and they accept her and the misunderstanding is cleared up; and the younger daughter and the young man from Calcutta have a very pleasant sort of relationship with a future in it.

What grows imperceptibly in the viewer is an awareness of the inter-relatedness of things; we come to share in Jagadish's fears for the fate of his beloved birds whose path of migration seems to have been disturbed by atomic tests, as he muses to Asok. Ray is gently stating, following Tagore, a deep-noted Indian perception: that unless men and women can learn to respect each other, they can never achieve harmony with their surroundings, and vice versa.

The matching of screenplay with weather made for certain practical problems in the shooting, as well as some advantages. Ray changed his usual practice and asked the actors to learn all their lines properly in advance, so that they would be ready for any scene as the weather dictated. It made shooting much quicker overall since, whatever the conditions, there was usually a scene to match them waiting to be shot – though that could mean a dash for the right location while conditions held. Film team and actors were constantly on the move around Darjeeling. In twenty-six days during October and November 1961, shooting on a ratio as low as three to one, Ray finished *Kanchenjungha*. He noticed that a Bombay director shooting in Darjeeling at the same time was unable to complete even one scene – so keen was he to show his stars in sunshine!

Most of Ray's actors coped admirably with these unorthodox conditions, managing to be both word-perfect and spontaneous in their delivery. The exception was N. Viswanathan, the south Indian actor playing Banerjee, who had felt obliged to learn his lines rigidly because his Bengali was not fluent. 'I wanted to make some small changes during shooting, but he couldn't do anything with them. All the original dialogue kept coming,' recalls Ray with amusement. 'I think I ticked him off slightly.'

The person most affected by this was of course the actress playing Manisa. Alaknanda Roy was then at Presidency College. Ray had discovered her through friends who had seen her in a college play. She knew absolutely nothing about film-making as a process and was surprised how easy she found it. She did not feel at all heavily directed by Ray. 'He'd act a little, but not very much. He wouldn't walk into a scene, say the lines, do the business and then walk out and say I want you to do it like that. He would say – look this is the situation. The girl is naturally very much shaken, she wants to run away and she should have a little frown on her forehead and she should start walking a bit faster. If he liked the way I did it, he'd say "Fine, let's take it."'

In the case of her invitation to Asok to meet her in Calcutta near the end of the film, Ray's directions were quite clear. 'He told me that it was not a romantic ending – I should forget about what I'd seen in the film so far. He said, "You are not in love with this boy. So I don't want you to look at him with stars in your eyes. It's just a very casual invitation to a person you liked and whom you would like to know a bit more about." Manikda did not really want me to feel involved with this character.' In fact she felt at the time that she was not being sincere to her own feelings at this point in the film. 'In Manisa's situation I would definitely have opted for the engineer and married him, maybe to my later regret. But in those days we used to think a lot about well-established eligible bachelors. We did not really have those romantic notions about having our own choice and choosing a mate who wouldn't really know what we would do in later life.' In Alaknanda's view this accounts for much of the antipathy of the Bengali audience to the film; they must have regarded Manisa's rejection of Banerjee as perverse, especially as the film offered no balancing romantic interest, no boy-meets-girl. Instead, she says, 'The film ends where they were expecting it to begin.'

As for Ray's own attitude to such marriages, he stresses that no conclusions can be drawn from this film or from his many other films about unsuccessful arranged marriages. '*Apur Sansar* has an arranged marriage,' he points out. 'I've seen both kinds of marriage working *so* well among orthodox Hindu families, apparently, looking from the outside; one never knows what goes on within the four walls of the house. We use the problematic marriage in films because of its dramatic possibilities. A conventional marriage has few dramatic things happening to it. It's when the marriage is on the brink that it's cinema.'

He prefers to attribute the original lack of success of *Kanchenjungha* with his home áudience – it is better liked in Bengal now – to lack of film sense rather than dislike of its content. 'This is a film that could not have been a novel, could not have been a play. It's conceived right from the start as a screenplay. This is one special quality about *Kanchenjungha*.' Ray certainly has a good point, but I suspect that Jyotirmoy Datta was nearer the mark when he wrote: 'Ambiguity, innuendo, paradox, irony – how different are these from the high stuff of romantic drama! What a shock it must be for the Bengali audience to be confronted with something as different from the Apu Trilogy as *Kanchenjungha*!' To Alaknanda Roy the problem is more straightforward still: 'just plain simple limited vision. They didn't want to try to see beyond what they usually heard.' They didn't like to see themselves as others see them? 'Exactly. That was what I meant.'

12

Abhijan
(The Expedition) 1962

···✦✧[۱ ☾◯☽ ۱]✦✧···

T H E film following *Kanchenjungha*, shot in the first half of 1962, is proof of Ray's capacity to communicate with a mass audience when he wants. *Abhijan* was among his most popular films in Bengal, even though it is little known elsewhere. It represents, like *The Music Room*, Ray's conscious response to box-office failure which had made him 'anxious to reach out to a wider audience' by taking a story with certain strong popular elements in it and seeing 'how well one could do it without making it too melodramatic.' Its very dissimilarity from his other films was a kind of challenge that interested him.

The route by which he came to direct it was rather a curious one. A producer friend, Bijoy Chatterjee, with ambitions to direct, came to him in August 1961 and persuaded him to write the script for a film of *Abhijan*, a story by Tarasankar Banerjee (author of *The Music Room*), which Chatterjee was to direct with the help of others and with backing which was already in place. Ray duly did so and, in the meantime, got on with the writing and shooting of *Kanchenjungha*.

When that was over and the film released, Ray found himself at something of a loose end for ideas and got lured into helping Chatterjee and friends with their preparations to shoot. He went with them to Dubrajpur, a small town not far from Santiniketan, where they showed him a wilderness of rocks somewhat like those at the Marabar Caves in *A Passage to India*. Ray was soon set on using them in the script of *Abhijan*; egged on by Chatterjee, he rewrote it, and in doing so his interest in the film grew. But even then he did not think of himself directing it. He attended the first day's shooting as a friendly gesture and found himself agreeing to direct the first scene. By the end of the day the original directing cooperative had persuaded him to take over. 'They lost their nerve,' says Ray today, chuckling. 'It was a kind of distress call – SOS!'

As it happened, the location and the characters had got a grip on his imagination; these, coupled with his lack of other commitments and a desire to help his friends, were what persuaded Ray to agree. This would occur only once more in Ray's film career, when he took over the detective story *Chiriakhana* from his assistants five years later.

The characters in *Abhijan* 'by their very nature act more than they talk', as Ray puts it. They are drawn from areas of Bengali society of which he had little first-hand experience, unlike the milieu of *Kanchenjungha*. There are five who figure most. The first is Narsingh – hero of the film. He is a proud, hot-tempered taxi-driver with a passion for the vehicle he runs and owns, a Chrysler of 1930 vintage. With his height, his refined features and his imposing beard, he carries about him something of the Rajput warrior stock that is in his blood. He is respected for this, and for his bold driving, by his assistant Rama, a smallish, monkey-like man, who acts as Narsingh's side-kick and comic foil.

The third main character is Sukhanram, a chubby, prosperous merchant, the piety of whose religious observance is in direct proportion to the shadiness of his business practices. In this he is typical of the community to which he belongs: he is a Marwari, member of that shrewd diaspora of businessmen that originated in Marwar in the desert of Rajasthan and has gradually taken over more and more of the trade of eastern India, especially in Calcutta – often to the resentment of the Bengalis. (Most film producers in Bengal are Marwaris now.)

The other two main characters are female and make a strong dramatic contrast. Neeli is a Catholic schoolmistress, 'a quiet reserved girl', according to Ray's shooting notebook, 'who has completely outgrown – through education and her own strength of will – the traces of her low-caste origin. She has pride, dignity and intelligence . . . While in the beginning the element of reserve in her might appear a little abnormal, prudish and schoolmistressish, it is illuminated and justified the moment we discover that Neeli has been long and deeply in love'. Gulabi, on the other hand, is warm, demonstrative, and of dubious morals. Like so many in India she has been forced into prostitution by personal tragedy and is being 'kept' by Sukhanram. She nevertheless retains a purity of heart that responds instinctively to Narsingh.

The setting of these people is a small town on the borders of Bengal and Bihar. Narsingh has driven there with Rama on the rebound from a humiliating experience at the hands of a bureaucrat, whose car he unwisely overtook. Although the local taxi-drivers as a group do not welcome him, there is one who does – Joseph, who also introduces him to Neeli, his sister. Unaware that she has already committed herself to another man, a cripple, Narsingh makes tentative overtures and begins to turn himself into a reformed character; he even takes an interest in Christianity, leading to the only explicit conversation about theology in Ray's oeuvre, with the exception of *An Enemy of the People*.

But paradoxically, Narsingh also falls in with Sukhanram and his drug-running business. Their first encounter is in the middle of the night when the merchant flags down Narsingh's car and talks him into giving a lift to himself and his 'maidservant' – in exchange for a fee. He now becomes a courier for Sukhanram, carrying tins of opium to a contact address in a neighbouring town, and begins to make money. He does not regard himself as tainted though, despite the hints dropped by Gulabi – the 'maidservant' – whom he has taken under his chivalrous protection.

When Neeli then asks for his help in a mysterious night-time assignation, he willingly agrees, imagining that it will bring him closer to her. His illusions are rudely shattered: he finds himself obliged to drive her and her crippled lover away from the town so they can elope. When he returns later, sozzled, he orders Rama to get Gulabi instead, to satisfy his wounded pride. He also allows himself to be seduced into a partnership with Sukhanram and a lawyer friend of his; they convince him that his contribution must be to part with his beloved car. Both Rama and Gulabi are aghast at this idea; but Narsingh angrily affects not to care what they think.

It is Joseph who turns the tide, confronting Narsingh over his opium-running, shaming him into an attempt at returning the latest tin Sukhanram has given him to transport. But Narsingh finds the house is deserted; the merchant has decamped, taking Gulabi with him. 'The light of chivalry – a heritage of the [Rajput] past, dormant so long but kindled at this moment by the warmth of love' now shines within Narsingh (shooting notebook again). Instead of riding to Gulabi's rescue on a stallion he and Rama chase Sukhanram in the car and, in a dramatic finale, Narsingh seizes the woman he truly loves and drives away into the night.

The elements of melodrama are obvious. According to Chidananda Das Gupta *Abhijan* was a 'total failure', mainly as a result of Ray's miscasting of Narsingh. He selected Soumitra Chatterjee, whose flair for different kinds of Bengali gave Ray confidence that he would be able to speak the kind of slang a taxi-driver would use. Chatterjee's rather refined look was acceptable, Ray felt, given Narsingh's supposed Rajput ancestry and provided that it was suitably coarsened by make-up. He was fitted with a wig and beard, and the red dust of Dubrajpur was rubbed into them.

The weakness in his performance, such as there is, is not a matter of miscasting – the discrepancy between Narsingh's honourable features and his dishonourable work for the Marwari is always interesting and pertinent to the story – but of a more subtle problem. The fact that Ray himself does not drive, means that he was probably unable to enrich Narsingh's love for his vehicle with telling details, as he normally would. Somehow, Narsingh never convinces us that he is capable of tuning his own carburettor or adjusting his points, say; his love for the car seems always a bit artificial, like that of another man-car relationship, in the 1958 comedy *Ajantrik* by Ray's contemporary Ritwik Ghatak, a film which is sometimes compared with *Abhijan*. This is a consequence, perhaps, of Ray's own distance from machines, in which he is closer to Tagore and the average Bengali than to his inventor grandfather and process-engraver father. 'Man is man, machine is machine, /And never the twain shall wed', wrote Tagore, in reply to Kipling's famous lines.

It is Rama who constantly cleans and polishes the car, whose feelings for it seem most genuine. Rabi Ghosh's funny performance – his first for Ray – had much to do with *Abhijan*'s success and is the best in the film. He based it on days of careful observation of taxi-cleaners at a taxi-stand near his home in Calcutta: he imitated their mannerisms and their ways of talking, which often leave words indistinct. Ray was delighted. One day he mentioned to Ghosh that the cleaners have a habit of wolf-whistling and told him he would dub it in the film. Ghosh asked, 'Manikda, do you want it directly?'

'It's very difficult.'

'I can do it. Shall I do it now?'

'Do it.'

So Ghosh did it. 'That, a gentleman should not do!' he comments today with his usual exuberance – but Ray was very pleased and used it several times in the film.

Ghosh's only worry was that the audience would not accept him when, at the end of the film, he turns serious and begs Narsingh not to sell the car. Ray remembers it to have 'worked very well', however. 'There was no titter from the audience; the hall was absolutely in the grip of the film at that point. Rabi was so happy; he said "All right, I have passed the test."'

In fact all the performances, apart from Chatterjee's, are of a high standard. Charu Ghosh as Sukhanram (and before that Nanda Babu in *Aparajito*), a non-professional actor, is superb in his mixing of the comic and the sinister; he is a 'nasty piece of work', but with a human dimension. His real-life business activities – he sells radiograms and electronic goods – certainly helped. And Ruma Guha Thakurta, as Neeli, manages perfectly that combination of reserve and sincerity that Ray originally conceived for her.

Waheeda Rehman, who plays Gulabi, was the first star of the Bombay cinema to work with Ray. Though her normal fee equalled the entire budget of a Ray film, she willingly agreed to appear for much less in what is a comparatively small part. She speaks 'a kind of part Hindi, part Bengali that she could quite easily learn', says Ray. 'She never really learnt Bengali, so there was no question of casting her in a [pure] Bengali film.' Her performance is one of considerable charm and subtlety, though it does not belong in the same class as those of Sarmila Tagore, and Madhabi Mukherjee in *Mahanagar* and *Charulata*. There is a little too much coyness about it that seems to owe something to the Bombay cinema, as well as – quite properly – to the part she is playing. But her account of her sad life and her devotion to Narsingh, are certainly affecting. Ray treats their relationship with his customary restraint; we see her appear in Narsingh's room at night at his drunken call, immediately followed by a shot of the two of them the following morning, Narsingh smoking, she with her bangles off. 'Obviously the bangles would get in the way of an intimate scene, actual physical contact,' says Ray. If he had tried to show this more explicitly he thinks Narsingh would have lost the audience's sympathy, 'because after all he has a soft corner for Neeli also. It's a difficult question of balancing relationships . . . I never had it in mind to show the relationship more intimately. The fact that he sends for her – he tells Rama to get that girl and Rama whistles and the girl comes – I think was all that was needed. At that point of course a very open, frank treatment of sex was not even so common in western films. It came in the 1970s really. The first film that showed physical relationships so frankly was Louis Malle's *Les Amants*. Even the French were not used to treating scenes of love-making so frankly.'

Besides its Bombay star, *Abhijan* was also a first for Ray in showing a fight – between Narsingh and Rama and the other taxi-drivers. It was a last in this respect too – there has never been another fight in a Ray film – but not because it was a comparative failure; simply because no natural opportunity for a fight has subsequently presented itself (with the exception of some fisticuffs in *The Adversary*). 'The fight in *Abhijan* wasn't staged very well,' Ray admits. 'We were shooting in the height of summer. The temperature was 114 degrees in the shade and it was supposed to be winter, so they were all wearing warm clothes. It was physically an excruciatingly difficult scene to shoot. And after a point one just had to give up. I would have wanted more shots, more close-ups, more of the business of the fight. But Narsingh was wearing a false beard and moustache, so there couldn't be too much grappling.' So he definitely wanted there to be more violence in it? 'Oh yes, there's no question of that. I'd have very much liked a John Ford-type rough-and-tumble.'

13

Mahanagar
(The Big City) 1963

❈❨◖◗❩❈

'NOT for a moment did I feel that I was acting. The character was so real. I seemed to know her. She was like someone I had seen,' says Madhabi Mukherjee of her wonderfully expressive performance as Arati in *Mahanagar*, which Ray shot in the first half of 1963.

This is his first examination of more or less contemporary Calcutta, concentrating on the struggles of the poorer section of the middle class – a very particular world, whose characters are nonetheless made to feel intimately known to viewers far removed from such struggles. As *Time*'s review put it, 'Ray's camera merely eavesdrops on everyday life.' This is an illusion of the critic, however; the emotional ethos of the 'joint' family, which permeates every cranny of the film, can never truly export from Bengal, and those who have lived within it will respond very differently to the film from those who have not. I myself saw it a number of times, before I fully understood who was related to whom; to a Bengali that is usually obvious, not only from modes of address used, which are untranslatable, but also from the quality of each relationship. All this adds layers of meaning to the film which give it a texture lost on the non-Bengali viewer.

At its simplest, *Mahanagar* is a story of clashing values: those of an older generation that would keep women at home, set against those of a younger generation that see the necessity for change, whether for economic or social reasons, or both. But the film is also a scathing critique of social conventions in Bengali society in general, made all the more pointed by Ray's characteristic presenting of the characters so that each enjoys our sympathy to some extent. He and the story-writer Narendranath Mitra (who thoroughly approved of Ray's script), leave us in no doubt of where they stand – in favour of freedom of choice for both women and men – but neither do they minimise the responsibilities and risks of change. Without it, however, they are clear there can be only stagnation.

At the heart of the film is the plight of a young woman of pronounced talents being wasted in the name of a false standard of behaviour. Everyone, herself included, cooperates in this hypocrisy. Each is playing a role, concerned about what 'they' – Bengalis in general – will think. The effect is to paralyse their own independence of mind. Once the former housewife has established herself as a working woman, through sheer grit, those around her quite quickly accept the idea and relish the things she brings. In Ray's view, this hypocritical, herd-like tendency is one of the pernicious facts of Bengali life; it is why, for instance, so many Bengali actors have been laughably bad – they are acting only because their families expect it, not because they have a natural talent. Ray tries consciously to expose this tendency in his films, in a spirit of 'social service' which he regards as similar to that which inspired his father to devote his energies to the reform of the Brahmo Samaj.

Mahanagar is set in about 1955 and there have been major shifts in Bengali society since then. Ray's own move away from his joint family in 1948 was a forerunner of these. Many more middle-class women are now working, and the joint family, as depicted in *Mahanagar*, has become the exception rather than the rule. Widespread resistance to respectable women taking jobs other than in teaching (which they had been doing since the early years of this century), is a thing of the past. If this diminishes the topicality of *Mahanagar*, it does not make it seem dated; and that is because the real tension within Arati is a perennial one: not whether she should work, but whether she should try to please everyone – husband, child and in-laws – or please mainly herself. For the Indian woman the conflict can be particularly acute, because those around her expect more than is expected of women in the West. As Arati's husband puts it to her, with an affectionate but definitely not ironic smile, 'A woman's place is in the home.' Expressed in English as it is in the film, the proverb gives the western viewer a small jolt, but it is an authentic sample of a Victorian value system that still roosts in more orthodox circles in Bengal. 'You cannot translate it,' says Ray, 'it's so pithy.' Significantly, he wanted the English title of the film to be *A Woman's Place* instead of *The Big City*, but the idea did not catch on.

In his view, and that of Madhabi Mukherjee, the situation shown in the film may still apply in Calcutta, though he is cautious of being definite about it. In his own family women have long held jobs, beginning with Upendrakisore's mother-in-law Dr Kadambini Ganguli – who, as we have seen, was attacked by the orthodox press for her daring – followed by Satyajit's mother, and his wife, who worked in the Supply Department of the West Bengal Government during the war before their marriage, and as a teacher. 'Orthodoxy is something which dies hard you know,' says Satyajit. 'Of course we don't feel it because we don't mix with that crowd. That is not my milieu. But talking to people – some of whom belong to orthodox families – I hear things that suggest that such problems still exist.'

Hearsay, along with the deep familiarity of the story-writer

Mitra with what was his milieu, and the painstaking research of
Bansi Chandragupta, all contributed to the conviction of Ray's recreation
of lower-middle-class life. The claustrophobic atmosphere of the family
house – 'a dingy first floor affair with three small rooms, a small courtyard
and a makeshift kitchen' – derives from one of the best sets Ray has used.
'The smallest rooms ever built!' he wrote excitedly to Seton at the time of
shooting in January 1963. They had four walls, none of them removable
on wheels. 'In those days I don't think anyone built four-walled rooms,'
says Ray today. 'It gave us very little room to move about, so there are
no long shots at all.' Once, he and Subrata Mitra were squeezed on to
a bed with a heavy blimped camera when it collapsed. Luckily a trunk
was underneath; otherwise one or both of them could have been injured,
especially as Mitra is as wellbuilt as Ray is tall. This general appearance of
cramped, and sometimes forced intimacy, is supplemented with music and
other noises from the neighbours, who believe that radios were invented
to be played from the moment they start relaying to the time the station
goes off the air. There is a neat list in Ray's shooting notebook of the
songs and programmes the family would be overhearing. 'And when the
radio stops,' he points out, 'the ensuing silence, which is soothing, gives
way to very intimate scenes between the couple.'

Into this small space are crowded husband and wife, small son
Pintu, husband's fourteen-year-old sister Bani and husband's parents,
getting on in years and unable to support themselves. Everyone depends
totally on Subrata, a minor official in a bank. He is a mild-mannered man
of average intelligence, talents and goodness, with a basically conservative
disposition, married to a woman of charm, sensitivity and beauty. As
the film progresses she increasingly reveals strength of purpose and
character too.

Madhabi Mukherjee, who plays Arati, was not Ray's discovery,
though her best work has definitely been for him, first in *Mahanagar*,
then in *Charulata*, and finally in *Kapurush* (*The Coward*). After difficult,
impoverished early years as a refugee from East Bengal appearing on the
stage, she was cast around 1959/60, in Mrinal Sen's *Baisey Sravan* where
she gave an appealing performance. Ray approached her on the strength of
that; he had been looking for the right actress for *Mahanagar* since 1959.
As her husband he selected Anil Chatterjee, last seen in *The Postmaster*.
To play his father he approached Sisirkumar Bhaduri, then the doyen of
stage actors (and Soumitra Chatterjee's guru), but he turned Ray down
with the words, 'In films the actor doesn't act – only the director does.
What's the point of taking me?' After considering Kanu Banerjee (Harihar
in *Pather Panchali*), Ray finally settled on a lesser-known actor to bring to
life the cantankerous retired schoolmaster.

The film begins with a typical moment in the family's daily
routine: Subrata's return from the office. The very first shots,
under the titles, establish the workaday mood of the story. They show

something that is part of the fabric of Calcutta existence – the intermittent flashing and popping of an overhead connector on a moving tram, the kind in which Subrata must travel every day to get to his bank and back. The last shot of the film will show a different, equally engrained detail of the city – a half-broken streetlamp – giving *Mahanagar* a satisfying, unemphatic cohesion, appropriate to its name.

Subrata's financial worries harass him the moment he steps into the flat: his father wants to know what news he has of the pair of glasses he has been requesting. Privately he hopes that one of his many ex-pupils in Calcutta, who has made good as an optician, may provide a pair gratis, since Subrata apparently will not buy them. A moment later we see Bani, doing her homework in another room, wearing glasses – a subtle indication of the conflict between young and old and the resentment building up in Subrata's father. His son too seems to doubt the value of Bani studying, because he tells her playfully that she will only end up in the kitchen like Arati.

When Arati comes into the room a moment later, radiating femininity, she is, as we expect, wrapped up in her household duties: giving medicine to her father-in-law, feeding and putting to bed their petted son, helping her mother-in-law cook or doing it herself, making tea for her husband, and a hundred other little things. One would perhaps describe her putative western counterpart as 'bustling around', but in Arati's actions there is no display, no ego; she is the family's anchor, not its figurehead, the very personification of the hoary proverb in which her husband believes.

Yet it is he who first disturbs her mental composure by mentioning a couple they know whose wife had gone out to work. He does it quite unthinkingly, but the seed is planted. It grows amazingly quickly – his placid-seeming wife can be highly impulsive when she feels like it, as she will demonstrate again and again – and that night she urgently informs her husband's sleepy form that she wants to go out to work. The series of little scenes in which she makes up her mind, show Ray and his finest actress at the height of their form, psychologically speaking. It is as if, momentarily, we can pass through Arati's outer form and feel as she does. 'Ray has an unmatched feeling for the moments when a situation catches people unawares and minds perceptibly expand or contract when confronted with some infinitesimal stress', Penelope Houston has written of this film.

Again, it is the husband who finds the potential job in the small ads section of the newspaper, and he who makes the necessary arrangements for his wife to apply – in the course of which she has to sign her married name 'Arati Mazumdar' in English, that language of the world of applications which she barely speaks. 'Is it a "z" or a "j"?' she asks Subrata hesitantly. ' "z",' her husband replies, 'as in "zoo" ' – except he uses the Bengali word for zoo, *chiriakhana*. At this, a small voice pipes up twice: 'Who's going to the zoo?' It is Pintu, who does not want anyone to leave him out. A richly suggestive little exchange on screen in which Arati's domestic world, and the conflicts to come, are all implied to a remarkable degree.

Of course Arati gets the job – as a salesgirl selling a new knitting machine to the rich homes of Calcutta. We do not see the interview, of which she is nervous, but her husband makes light of it beforehand. If they ask 'Who killed Cock Robin?' he tells her, she must answer 'Sparrow' – which is Satyajit's 'translation' of a Bengali dialogue based on one of his father's fantasy creatures. Her boss is a jowly, somewhat patronising Bengali called Mukherjee who quickly sees her potential. There are four other girls too, three of whom are giggly, fashion-conscious Bengalis, the other is an Anglo-Indian called Edith who speaks mainly English to Arati but also understands Bengali. She is forthright, even a little brash, in a way that Arati could never be, but they become friends. Mukherjee, on the other hand, dislikes Edith and makes this plain; he is decidedly prejudiced against the offspring of 'our ex-rulers'.

As Arati settles in and begins to earn a commission too, the atmosphere at home changes. Her decision to take a job had already provoked a 'cold war', as Subrata terms it, between her husband and his father. Now, too, her husband's pride is badly hurt by all the things she brings home and the new confidence she has acquired. After tense scenes between them he bluntly asks her to resign; he will take part-time work on top of his regular job. Though for his sake she agrees, fortunately for both of them she cannot quite bring herself to do it immediately, as she sits in front of Mukherjee. His phone rings. It is Subrata. He has just lost his job at the bank after a crash there, and tells her desperately to hang on to hers.

She continues to work, now as the sole breadwinner, efficient and loyal as ever, while at home her husband sinks into unemployed gloom, and becomes distant from her. Physically they rub shoulders, but they are not on each other's wavelength any more. As so often, things finally come to a head by accident, rather than design. The catalyst is Edith. She has been ill, off work, but Mukherjee does not believe her, accuses her of loose living instead, and sacks her on the spot. This is too much for Arati who overhears him shouting at Edith and listens to her sobbing story in the Ladies'. On the spur of the moment she confronts Mukherjee and asks him to apologise to Edith. Baffled and even somewhat hurt he tries to explain that he did it for Arati's own good – so that she could be put in charge of the sales-force – why is she fighting for this Anglo-Indian? But Arati is resolute; without losing her temper for a moment, a determined gleam has entered her eye. Mukherjee warns her she is putting her own job at risk but she persists. Suddenly, on an impulse, she produces the old resignation letter from her bag, drops it on his desk and coolly walks out, followed by Mukherjee's startled cry 'Mrs Mazumdar!'

This powerful scene, which works only because Madhabi Mukherjee has earlier built up Arati so convincingly, is prompted by the same attitude that made Asok refuse to beg a job from Indranath in *Kanchenjungha*, and is the first of many crises of conscience in Ray's films about modern Calcuttans. In this case, it is impossible not to see Satyajit himself in Arati's reaction; that, one imagines, is very much how he must have confronted his dishonest boss in the London office of D.J. Keymer in 1950 – with forthright disgust blind to the consequences.

On the way out, rushing down the stairs, Arati's anger begins to evaporate, giving way to panic: neither she nor her husband now has a job – how will the family survive? She falters, and just then hears her name called. It is Subrata, about to go up to see Mukherjee to talk about a job he had earlier promised him. He senses her distress but not its cause, and she is at a loss for words. Eventually they come bursting out of her, in the desperate hope that he, at least, will understand what she has done. After an initial shock he does, and they come close again, her head upon his chest, weeping with suppressed feeling. Then, slowly, wonderingly, she looks up at the tall buildings that surround their private world of anguish. 'What a big city! Full of jobs,' she says softly. 'There must be something somewhere for one of us.' And on that note of cautious optimism husband and wife walk off into the early evening office crowd around Dalhousie Square and become indistinguishable, as a serener, maturer version of the original theme music of the film rises and the camera tilts up and pulls back – revealing the luminous bulb of a streetlamp, and beside it an empty holder where the second bulb is missing. Finally, the camera closes on this and the film ends. Ray comments:

> It so happened that I needed a long shot of the two merging into the crowd after office hours. And I saw, as I tilted up the camera as they were walking away, a lovely shot of these two lamps in the foreground. My God! – the amount of interpretation that has taken place because of that one missing bulb is incredible. I had nothing in mind. I didn't want to suggest anything at all, except that it was typical of Calcutta for the streetlights not to be working properly . . . It makes the shot more interesting, because it adds another layer of meaning to it which I'm afraid was not intended. As I discovered it, I was quite happy. I felt it was better than both lights working.

Few people would disagree that this shot has a mysterious ambiguity which matches the mood of the two people whose story we have followed as their intimacy waxes and wanes. But the behaviour of Arati just prior to this last shot is less satisfactory; in fact critics, at least in the West, almost universally decried it as the one false move in an otherwise deeply sincere work. Would Arati really recover her optimism so quickly after such a disaster? In Mitra's book, according to Ray, 'the wife comes home and the in-laws say, "What a foolish thing to do. Why did you give up your job?" They'd probably say the same thing, even in my film, but we don't see them.' His ending he regards as 'semi-optimistic'. 'They're optimistic because they've come together emotionally, after a long period of separation that's psychological. It's the kind of optimism where they know it will be very difficult to find jobs, but at least for the time being they are again husband and wife. So this optimism is permissible in the context I think.'

This seems true, but I nevertheless share the widespread queasiness about the ending. It would have worked perfectly had husband and wife simply embraced and then walked off together; the artifice arises from Arati's sudden, unnatural response to Calcutta in the abstract – a mode of thought that is foreign to her. It is people who arouse her feelings, not so much ideas, as she has just courageously shown in Mukherjee's office. When she takes Edith's side there, he asks her if she knows what 'these Anglo-Indian girls' are really like? Perhaps not, asserts Arati in reply, but she knows what *Edith* is like. One feels that Ray felt the urge to emphasise the city as an entity in the dialogue so as to round off a film called *The Big City*, but it was really not necessary; his visual flair alone would have been fine.

Although the film was generally highly appreciated in India, as it would later be all over the world, it suffered from political difficulties, as *The Goddess* had. An Anglo-Indian MP who had not seen it, accused Ray of prejudice against that community, and Mrs Gandhi, then in charge of information and broadcasting in Delhi, was deputed to investigate the charge – though she felt it was extremely unlikely to have any substance. Even so, the charge to some extent stuck and prevented *Mahanagar* from winning the Indian Government's highest award. It also complicated Ray's life when he was invited to show the film at the Berlin Film Festival in 1964. 'We really cannot afford to stay longer than 10 days in Berlin,' he wrote to Seton before leaving Calcutta, 'in view of the absurdly small amount of foreign exchange sanctioned in Delhi – Rs 7000 for a party of 6! . . . And this in spite of all my personal efforts and repeated dinning into the ears of the powers that be over the last six or seven years. I'm disgusted.' Happily *Mahanagar* was awarded the festival prize for Best Direction – a worthy accolade for one of Ray's most unassuming and life-like creations.

··∗⫸{[14]}⫷∗··

Charulata
(The Lonely Wife) 1964

··∗⫸{ ⟨⟨◉⟩⟩ }⫷∗··

In a film like *Charulata*, which has a 19th century liberal upper-class
background, the relationship between the characters, the web of con-
flicting emotions, the development of the plot and its denouement,
all fall into a pattern familiar to the western viewer. The setting is
a western-style mansion, the decor is Victorian, the dialogue strewn
with references to western literature and politics. But beneath the
veneer of familiarity the film is chock-a-block with details to which he
has no access. Snatches of song, literary allusions, domestic details, an
entire scene where Charu and her beloved Amal talk in alliterations
(thereby setting a hopeless task for the subtitler) – all give the film a
density missed by the western viewer in his preoccupation with plot,
character, the moral and philosophical aspects of the story, and the
apparent meaning of the images.

To give an example. Early on in the film, Charulata is shown
picking out a volume from a bookshelf. As she walks away idly turning
its pages, she is heard to sing softly. Only a Bengali will know that she
has turned the name of the author – the most popular Bengali novelist
of the period – into a musical motif. Later, her brother-in-law Amal
makes a dramatic entrance during a storm reciting a well-known line
from the same author. There is no way that subtitles can convey this
fact of affinity between the two characters so crucial to what happens
later. *Charulata* has been much admired in the West ... but this
admiration has been based on aspects to which response has been
possible; the other aspects being left out of the reckoning.

(Satyajit Ray, *Sight and Sound*, 1982)

I N FACT *Charulata* is today one of Ray's most popular films. Its
reviews in the West when it was released in 1965, include perhaps the
most perceptive Ray has yet received there, from Penelope Houston writing
in *Sight and Sound*. Admitting her fascination and unfamiliarity with the
period and with India, she commented that 'the interplay of sophistication
and simplicity is extraordinary.' They also include a grotesque error, by
Penelope Gilliatt writing in the *New Yorker* also in glowing terms, who

managed to confuse the two male members of the triangle in the film's freeze-frame finale.

The chorus of praise was by no means universal. The Cannes Film Festival rejected the film (which subsequently won the prize for Best Direction at Berlin – the second year running for Ray), and there was a persistent undertow of criticism of the film as 'slow'. To the *New York Times* reviewer (not Bosley Crowther), *Charulata* 'moved like a majestic snail, as do all Ray films', while Kenneth Tynan, writing in the *Observer*, put it most bluntly when he wrote: 'It's a sensitive movie but sluggish, full of unpregnant pauses and stained now and then with sentimentality. We must beware of overpraising films like this simply because they are understated.'

Tynan notwithstanding, it is a fair bet that *Charulata* will, in the longer term, find its niche in a list of the twenty best films ever made. It has the most complete fusion of eastern and western sensibility in the cinema – which is exactly why difficulties arise. The film conceals almost as much from the Bengali who is unfamiliar with western civilisation, as it does, in other ways, from the westerner who does not know Bengal. To the London *Times* reviewer in 1965, 'this stratum of Indian life' seemed 'oddly, more English than England itself.' But to the cultured Bengali it presents a quite different, quintessentially Bengali face. He could never find it slow; rather, he requires three or four viewings to absorb it to the full. It is Ray's most allusive, fully realised film; the one which, if pressed, he chooses as his best.

Consider, for instance, the way in which Bankim Chandra Chatterjee, 'the most popular Bengali novelist of the period', is woven into the film. He is the bond that helps to draw the lonely and childless Charu, wife of a somewhat earnest newspaper owner and editor, towards her insouciant 'brother-in-law' Amal (her husband Bhupati's cousin in English terms). After dropping her embroidery at the beginning of the film to wander bored through the house, she embroiders Bankim's name in the air by humming it while she is taking one of his novels from a bookshelf. Later, as Amal arrives during a sudden violent storm of the kind that all Bengalis know during the month of *Baisakh* (mid-April to mid-May), he shouts out, in theatrical manner, a line from Bankim and asks his pleased sister-in-law: 'Have you read Bankim's latest?'

Some time later, Amal is debating with Bhupati the relative value of literature and politics. With some disgust, Bhupati tells him that his friend and assistant on the newspaper lost three nights' sleep after reading one of Bankim's books, and comments that he finds this absurd; when one has real issues and people to address, why read novels? Bhupati's view is as unacceptable to Amal as Amal's to him, but that is not to mean that Amal and Charu at least are agreed; though he admires Bankim, Amal feels that his own taste has moved beyond him, as he somewhat patronisingly informs Charu during a languid afternoon discussion in her bedroom. She is unmoved by this boasting, just as she is unmoved by politics; she has read the new writers admired by Amal and finds them spurious.

Like her husband, Charu thinks that Amal should get married, and it is when the three of them come to talk this over that Bankim is invoked again. When Bhupati tries to entice Amal with visions of a trip to England promised by his prospective father-in-law, Amal finally rejects his overture with some well-known words from *Anandamath*, 'Bankim's latest' – from 'Bande Mataram', a rousing patriotic song in the novel that later became the anthem of Bengal and the rallying-cry of Bengali nationalists (as Ray shows in *The Home and the World*).

The final reference to Bankim in the film occurs at another crucial psychological moment, when Charu tries to persuade Amal to stay, ostensibly to help her husband run his newspaper. This is the alliterative conversation Ray refers to above, in the course of which Amal mentions Bankim as one of the main reasons why he must return to Bengal, if and when he does go to England.

What is the significance of all these references? At the moment in modern Bengali history in which *Charulata* is set, 1880, Bankim Chandra Chatterjee was at the height of his fame, a leading light of the Bengal Renaissance of the generation preceding Rabindranath Tagore. Born in 1838, he joined government service in Bengal in 1858 and remained in it until his retirement in 1891. While serving as a magistrate and revenue official he pursued a parallel career as a novelist, essayist and editor, and by 1880 had written nine novels in Bengali; a further five were to follow before his death in 1894. He was known, in the fashion of the day, as the 'Scott of Bengal', and some of his novels were translated into English. 'In respect of love of the Romantic variety, he was the pioneer' in Bengal, according to Nirad Chaudhuri. 'His depictions of love rivalled the dithyrambs of the great Romantic exponents of love in Europe. This seemed so strange to traditional Bengalis, and yet took such a strong hold on the young, that Chatterjee was accused of corrupting the youth of Bengal.'

That, of course, is how Bhupati views Bankim, and Amal's callow attempts at literature. (Bhupati would be of the same generation as Bankim, since he is thirty-five in the film.) But he is likely to have had more sympathy for Bankim's social criticism, which could be as biting as Tagore's later was, despite an attachment to traditional Hinduism not shared by Tagore. Unlike either of these writers, though, Bhupati is in thrall to western political and social concepts. He sincerely believes that India's salvation lies in these, and in the victory of the Liberal party in Britain. Like thousands of other Bengalis of his time, including the parents of Nirad Chaudhuri (and later, Chaudhuri himself), Bhupati has 'imbibed the notion that European history was a series of struggles for freedom, as a result of which the ambit of a beneficent and fertilising freedom had been enlarged in ever widening circles in the course of modern history.'

Bankim exerted both a literary and a personal influence over Tagore in his formative years; he was one of the first to recognise Tagore as a new poetic voice and proclaim its potential genius. The journal he edited made an overwhelming impression on the teenage Rabindranath and no doubt, too, on his beloved sister-in-law, the literary Kadambari Devi, who in 1884 committed suicide for reasons unknown. Her death was the first tragedy in Tagore's life. There seems hardly any doubt that it was she who inspired Tagore to write in 1901 *Nastanirh* (*The Broken Nest*), the novella on which Ray based *Charulata*. She in some ways resembled Charu, he Amal, while his elder brother had much of the unworldliness and naïvety of Bhupati. 'Tagore had known the pains, the tensions and the anguish that eat into a man's soul, the real nature of the emotional crisis one has to go through – all this Tagore knew very well,' according to Ray. He has seen a very early manuscript of *Nastanirh* with marginalia which refer many times to Hecate – Rabindranath's name for Kadambari. There is even a profile portrait sketch – 'the sort that one would do when one is groping for ideas and not actually writing' – which is obviously of Kadambari. 'She was at the back of his mind – there's no doubt of that,' says Ray. 'And that I thought was significant.' In fact Tagore even admitted to the artist Nandalal Bose when he was in his late seventies that it was Kadambari's eyes which lay behind the hundreds of haunting portraits of women he painted in old age.

Like so much that Tagore did, *Nastanirh* attracted adverse criticism from Bengalis at the time. The story gave the foundations of family life a shake, which many people resented. Ray had read their comments before setting to work on his adaptation; the general tenor was – why can't Tagore write about a straightforward marriage instead of introducing extramarital relations? He found people still sensitive to the issue sixty years later, when he discussed with them what he had in mind. 'It's a sort of hypocrisy,' he says today. 'A lot of people seemed to think it was a very risky subject because of this illicit relationship. I never had any such doubts at all. I made the film and it was proved that I was right, because it was very widely accepted.' Nevertheless, there remains in Bengal, as Ray is perfectly aware, a reluctance to accept the full implications of Charu's behaviour reminiscent of the attitude that insists Indian erotic sculpture depicts only divine love-making. Although there is definitely not 'a powerful sexual bond' between Amal and Charu, as Penelope Gilliatt would have it, there is amorousness and barely controlled passion in Charu. It will inevitably mature if Amal stays – which is exactly why he doesn't.

The main reason for Bengali unwillingness to see the relationship for what it is, is peculiar to Bengal. Ray comments:

There is a Bengali convention about the relations between a wife and her *debar*, her younger brother-in-law. It's always a very affectionate relationship, and she is free to come out before him, not before other men. The brother-in-law might well be studying in college, with lots of free time, making demands on her to cook certain foods. In fact it goes

even closer than that. It always verges on a kind of intimacy which is
exactly as shown in *Charulata*, where the younger brother is attracted
to the sister-in-law but is afraid of going beyond a certain point. He
realises that the danger is there. So it creates a situation that is rather
tense, and also pleasing for both the characters. The pleasure is very
much there, because he has the sanction of the convention that he can
mix with her. So there is always the possibility that a relationship of a
rather deep nature might develop. Even now, in comparatively orthodox
Hindu households, the *debar* is a very special figure from the wife's
point of view.

Besides this convention, Charu is also embroiled, as Kadambari herself
was, in the conflicts surrounding the role of Bengali women in the later
nineteenth century, which are still being fought through in *Mahanagar*
three-quarters of a century later. Should she be *Prachina* (Conservative
Woman), concerned only with housework and having children, or *Nabina*
(Modern Woman) who, traditionalists fear, is more interested in reading
novels and even getting employment outside the home? Manda, the earthy
wife of Charu's brother (whom Bhupati invites to stay so as to give Charu
company), is naturally *Prachina*, while Charu tends towards *Nabina*. An
important part of her feels differently however; it is not so much the
outside world she craves, but love.

The husband who does not give this to her until it is too late,
is an archetypal figure of the Bengal Renaissance, a decent dreamer
and spinner of half-understood words and ideas, not a doer, like the
majority of those who embraced western political ideas and social values
at that time. And so, in his own way, is his cousin Amal, though he shows
more signs of practicality than Bhupati. Together, they are an indictment
of the Renaissance to which both Tagore and Ray subscribe. Although Ray
treats both characters with great sympathy, it is clear that he is critical of
them. It is wrong to think of Ray as the 'Last Bengali Renaissance Man',
as many have liked to do; though he has imbibed much from the literature
and music of that period, he has rejected its typical attitudes as superficial,
rhetorical and uncreative, and has made his own commitment to science,
technology and a thoroughly twentieth-century art form, the cinema.

In order to mould Tagore's story into a film, Ray had to solve
some knotty problems. First, there was the right balance to be struck
between western and Bengali elements. 'Nastanirh is a story which may
not be deeply rooted in Bengali tradition,' Ray explains. 'It has a western
quality to it and the film obviously shares that quality. That's why I can
speak of Mozart in connection with *Charulata* quite validly, I think. But
the whole idea, of the *debar* character and the wife's relationship is very
Bengali, deeply rooted in convention. But what happens, the dénouement,
is more western than Indian, I think. There's a strong western element in
the telling of the story.'

Secondly, Ray had to settle on a date for the story. Tagore is vague about this but various clues, not least its probable autobiographical origin, led Ray to the early 1880s rather than to 1901, the date preferred by the translators of the English edition, for instance. He fixes it as April/May 1880 in the film by the date on Bhupati's newspaper and by various references to the British election in which Gladstone was returned to power. Other references, to the war in Afghanistan, to the Press Act and to various taxes, reinforce this. Ray enjoyed the background research in the National Library in Calcutta and elsewhere and felt that the film gained considerably from the addition of details such as Disraeli's nickname (which Bhupati relishes using on Amal, to his utter confusion).

Thirdly, there were psychological weaknesses in the story, with which Ray had to wrestle. He explained his solutions at length in a remarkable article in Bengali written in reply to a critic who had queried, 'What is the difficulty in incorporating in the script the story from beginning to end without any change?' 'I don't think an article like that has been written by any other director ever,' he says today. There were two principal faults he identified: the lack of build-up to the treachery of Bhupati's manager Umapada, Charu's brother, who embezzles a large amount of money from the newspaper; and the 'prolonged marathon incomprehension' on the part of Bhupati of Charu's love for Amal. Ray's solutions are elegant, economical and subtle, depending on a much fuller rounding-out of the character of Umapada than Tagore allowed, an intensification of Charu's loneliness, and the portrayal of Bhupati as a somewhat more sensitive figure. The story was also compressed in time, into about a month's span – something Ray has more and more liked to do with his screenplays. And where Tagore's story makes reference to the early years of Bhupati's newspaper and his marriage to Charu, in *Charulata* all is implied, either in words or in actions.

In transferring his screenplay to film, Ray for once allowed himself as much time as he needed. For the first time he worked without a deadline. 'I said that I will hand over the film when it is ready and then you make arrangements for releasing it.' He has no doubt that this has much to do with its final quality.

To begin with, he was fortunate in his cast: probably the best he has worked with. Madhabi Mukherjee, in *Mahanagar* all natural grace and intelligence, in *Charulata* is so finely-tuned that we can enter her every thought and feeling. That, far more than her physical appearance, which can look quite ordinary, is what makes her profoundly beautiful. 'Is Charu the archetypal Ray woman?' someone once asked Ray. 'Yes, she is,' he replied without qualification. According to Rabi Ghosh, who has acted with her in many films, 'Madhabi is basically an instinctive actress. In Ray she found a director who could explain to her everything about a character; and that not only amused Madhabi, it made her happy. And once an instinctive actress is happy, she's always tremendous. She knows her weapons, and how to throw them. That's why you get the inner feeling in her face in *Charulata*.' Ray echoes this when he says quietly that, 'I would always indicate the psychological implication of a particular action, because I would anticipate that there would be a question in her mind about why she was being asked to do this, and not something else. I would always explain. But this didn't take very long; it was not like a classroom lecture. It was a pleasant kind of conversation.'

She presented one major problem though, the solution to which was out of his control. Madhabi had bad teeth, and she was also addicted to eating *pan* (just as Charu is), which destroys the gums over a long enough period as well as staining the teeth black. 'I had to photograph her very carefully not to show that side of her,' recalls Ray. 'It's the lower set that are bad – I had to put the camera at a lowish angle, so that even when she spoke, the lower set of teeth wouldn't show. I suggested taking out her teeth but the mother objected it was too early for that.' Was it a severe problem in shooting? 'Oh my God! In fact my wife had serious objections to using Madhabi at all for her teeth, but I knew the camera could manage that. Madhabi accepted that.'

As Amal Soumitra Chatterjee fits his role brilliantly too, and gives his finest performance in the fourteen films by Ray in which he appears, full of verve and wit. Bhupati was played by a stage actor, Sailen Mukherjee. He came to Ray and said, 'Manikda, I know nothing about film-acting. I'll be your pupil, you teach me,' Ray remembers. 'His performance was a directed one right from the start, every gesture, every word, every inflection – he followed me implicitly. Of course he's actually a much better actor than he claimed to be.'

Charulata's sets are as convincing as its performances: not a single interior was shot on location. This is a tremendous achievement by Chandragupta and Ray, when one considers that almost the entire film takes place indoors. They visited a lot of Calcutta houses built in the Victorian period. When Ray went into retreat at a hotel by the sea to finish the script, as he sometimes likes to do, he sent Bansi detailed notes about the set as it was forming in his mind. They illustrate Chandragupta's dictum that 'a set should exist only in relation to the script'. 'For instance in *Charulata*, the bedroom scenes were dominated by a huge Victorian bed. We arranged the whole set around this feature, piece by piece, detail by detail. This is putting it very badly but it is the only way I can describe my method,' he said in an interview in 1965. Where necessary – but *only* where necessary – Ray demanded of him a fanatical attention to detail. The wallpaper in Charu's drawing-room, for instance, a specially printed pattern similar to a William Morris design, came in sheets of 30 × 40 inches which had to be pasted on to plywood. One of the patterns required extraordinary care in alignment. 'It took a whole day and a night just to stick the paper,' Chandragupta remarked.

The atmosphere in Bhupati's printing-press was another product of painstaking research. The premises of U. Ray and Sons at 100 Garpar Road were at the back of Ray's mind. He borrowed the downstairs layout for the house in *Charulata*. 'The difference was that this was only a printing-press producing a newspaper, whereas ours was much larger: it had block-making, processing, everything, and the printing-press was much more primitive in the film than the kind of press that we had. Ours was already twentieth century,' says Ray. With his interest in typography he was particularly concerned to capture the correct look for Bhupati's newspaper. Its title, the *Sentinel*, its motto, 'Truth Survives' (which acquires a heavy irony as the film progresses), and its masthead design, were all Ray's creation, but otherwise it was virtually a facsimile of the *Bengalee*, the newspaper started by one of the earliest Bengali nationalist politicians, whose speeches get Bhupati very excited. Even its advertising rates – the subject of discussion between Bhupati and Umapada – were the same.

Getting the correct street sounds for 1880 was trickier, for obvious reasons, and Ray devoted much attention to it; he felt unable to complete the script without them. Some still existed, some he could recollect from childhood, some could be culled from literary sources, and others came from the memory of older people. Apart from the first sequence in the film showing Charu's wandering, where these sounds are very prominent and attract her attention, their contribution to the shuttered authenticity of the house is registered almost sub-consciously. In a letter to Seton of December 1963, Ray wrote: 'Splendid work so far, and not being saddled with too much content or plot can concentrate on *style*. Much fascinating cutting, camera movement, lovely 1880 period reconstruction by Bansi, excellent acting by all concerned . . . [sic] A true *chamber* film.'

By now he had plenty of experience at getting the effects he wanted with background music too, having composed full scores for *Kanchenjungha, Abhijan* and *Mahanagar*. The score for *Charulata* excels these, and may be Ray's best ever, if we discount his musicals. 'The possibilities of fusing Indian and western music began to interest me from *Charulata* on. I began to realise that, at some point, music is one,' he said in 1980. The score he composed after *Charulata*, for James Ivory's film *Shakespeare Wallah*, showed the direction his thoughts were taking. It includes some lovely pieces of indefinable origin.

At one point he considered using baroque music alone for *Charulata*, but fortunately dropped the idea. Two of Tagore's songs provide a basis for much of the music in the film, either in their original form or in snatches and phrases embroidered by Ray. The first of them, '*Mama Citte, Niti Nritye*', opens the film as Charu is seen embroidering 'B' for Bhupati on a handkerchief. It is a very simple, catchy tune with a spring in it, used to teach young girls dance-steps and to train beginners in Tagore-singing. Its predominant emotion is wistful delight: the words articulate the duality of life – as Amul does to Charu when he moodily tells her that there is a pattern: 'birth and death, happiness and sadness, meetings and partings, day and night – you can't have one without the other.' This melody and Ray's barely detectable variations on it, might be said to express the Indian elements in the characters and story.

The second song, 'Phule Phule' (from an early dance drama), is based on a Scottish tune which Tagore heard as a young man on his first visit to England, and it naturally complements the western elements. This relationship refers more to the melody than to the words Tagore set to it. Amal sings it first, to himself when he is unpacking his belongings, and then teases Charu with it when she enters the room and begins fussing over him. Later Charu herself sings it while she swings back and forth in the garden observing the handsome figure of Amal lying on the ground thinking about his writing. Later still, in the longest single piece of music in the film, the tune provides the magical atmosphere into which Amal dreamily dips at Bhupati's behest while he considers whether to take up the marriage offer and go to 'the land of Shakespeare, the Isles of Greece, and the Mediterranean' – a name which Amal feels is 'like running one's fingers over the strings of a *tanpura*.' Ray's treatment of 'Phule Phule' here manages to conjure up just this kind of association.

Besides these songs, there is a melody by Jyotirindranath Tagore (Kadambari's husband) with words by Rabindranath which Amal sings for Charu with full instrumental backing – the first such treatment of a song by Ray and the only slightly jarring note in the film – and a number of original compositions too. One that works strikingly well and differs from all the other music in the film, accompanies Charu's daydream as jumbled scenes from her village childhood flit across her mind: the boats of East Bengal with their vast decorated sails, an elderly relative spinning, Catherine-wheels throwing off showers of sparks, and the grotesque Fellini-like faces of sadhus and *jatra* (folk-theatre) performers. Beginning on a very high, echoed flute, the music has a folk edge that cuts straight through the rest of the film's music and the sophistication of Charu's surroundings as the wife of a Calcutta intellectual. Immediately after it ends, she gets up and begins composing her first piece, entitled 'My Village', which Amal later recognises as the work of a completely fresh voice.

Having considered the significant aspects of *Charulata* in general terms, I want to conclude with a discussion of five scenes that highlight the film's sophistication. The first is bound to be the beginning of the film, which in Ray's words 'attempts to use a language entirely free from literary and theatrical influences. Except for one line of dialogue in its seven minutes, the scene says what it has to say in terms that speak to the eye and the ear.'

It introduces a number of motifs that will help to give the film its rich texture and resonance. The first is the letter 'B' which Charu is embroidering. She will later give the handkerchief to Bhupati, provoking him to wonder how she has time to do things like that – a question which produces his first dim apprehension of her loneliness. At the end, as he drives alone in his carriage, trying to come to terms with his failed marriage, he again encounters that 'B', while wiping his face of tears. It seems to hint at the possibility of a reconciliation.

Charu lays down her embroidery, as the grandfather clock strikes four. This is the second motif in the film: as in *The Home and the World*, the striking of clocks is several times used for dramatic purposes. In *Charulata* the hour has a particular meaning: it is when tea must be taken to Bhupati in his office. Charu calls to the servant to remind him of this. Clearly, Bhupati's office is in the house itself. 'Her duty done,' comments Ray, 'Charu comes back to the bedroom. For a few moments she is undecided what to do. This, of course, is an inevitable aspect of boredom. One has time on one's hands, but is frequently at a loss how to use it. Charu briefly admires her handiwork, then picks up a book from the bed, riffles through the pages and puts it down.' She now comes out of the bedroom and walks towards the outer apartments and the drawing-room where the books are kept. She is restless and Ray's mobile, probing, sometimes playful camerawork conveys this marvellously throughout. It also performs the useful function of showing us the various rooms in the house and their layout. 'The setting itself is a character,' says Ray, 'and must be established as carefully in all its details as any human participant in the story.'

At this point, enter Bankim – the film's third motif – as Charu picks out his early novel *Kapalkundala* only to put it down again almost immediately, her attention diverted to the world outside. She can hear the insistent drumming of a monkeyman beyond the shutters. Going to her husband's study she opens them and peers out. There he is, with his monkeys. Suddenly, Charu has an idea. She walks quickly back to the bedroom, opens a drawer and takes out a lorgnette – fourth motif, (and one which took a lot of finding; it was eventually tracked down in a Calcutta bazaar). As she hurries back to the study, the camera follows the swinging lorgnette in her hand behind the stair-railings – an odd visual clash of two movements with the vertical – to be repeated later when she hurries to Amal carrying in her hand the magazine which has published her piece. Through the lorgnette Charu now observes the monkeyman, followed by a *palki* (palanquin) with chanting bearers, then the passage of a fat, oiled-looking man in a dhoti carrying a furled umbrella on his shoulder and a pot of sweets dangling from his hand. 'It was important to stress this playful aspect of Charu,' observes Ray, 'because this is where she is farthest from her staid husband and closest to the youthful, exuberant Amal.'

As the man disappears from view, Charu once more is at a loose end. The first musical motif, the opening of '*Mama Citte, Niti Nritye*' referred to earlier, is now heard as Charu wanders pensively towards the piano. She strikes a note but then her attention is again diverted – this time by a sound of footsteps within the house. It is her husband, we guess, in his booted feet and shirt-sleeves, walking purposefully towards the bedroom. Charu watches as he disappears inside, and soon after reappears, carrying a fat book and studying it intently. Although he walks right past her, he is not aware of her presence, even though he stops next to her to turn a page. As he recedes down the verandah Charu gazes after him. Then, unable to resist the temptation, she raises her lorgnette to take a closer look at him just before he vanishes down some stairs to his office. A moment later she lowers it and pauses, her face as outwardly expressionless as ever in this first scene, for a few more seconds. Finally, she lets the lorgnette flop down and the camera follows with a sharp pull-back, described by Ray as 'like a flourish with a pen at the end of an essay . . . We know that Charu is resigned to her state of loneliness. And this brings the scene to a close.'

The second scene is probably the best known in the film and again has relatively few words in it. It takes place in the sunlit garden as Amal lounges on the ground while Charu sits on a swing under the trees, still with her lorgnette. Placed apart from him like this, she feels the first disturbing stirrings of love for her brother-in-law. Her state of mind is revealed by the song she sings, rocking back and forth and watching Amal below her. A prose translation of 'Phule Phule' gives some idea of its restless yearning: 'What a sweet swaying breeze blows gently over the flowers! For whom do the ripples of the murmuring stream yearn? How the groves do echo with the cuckoo's call! Cuckoo! Cuckoo! Cuckoo! it sings. Whom it is calling, I know not. But my whole being calls too.'

She gets up and returns with Amal's notebook which she has embroidered with his name. After she has been fulsomely thanked in his finest vein of poetic fancy, she again sits quietly on the swing, holding the lorgnette, and dreamily absorbs her surroundings. Humming the little phrase she had first devoted to the name of Bankim, she now transfers it to the English words 'thank you' which Amal has just uttered. Then, through the lorgnette, her gaze roves lazily over the leaves of the nearby grove until, through a gap, it is brought up close to a baby not far off being cuddled in the arms of its mother. This has an immediate impact on the childless Charu, reminding her, no doubt, of her husband and her distance from him. She lowers the lorgnette, her head turns almost inevitably towards Amal as the first musical motif returns, and she raises the lorgnette again, just as she did with Bhupati. For a long moment she absorbs his equally intent expression, but her emotions are totally different from those aroused by Bhupati's absorbed look. It is transparently clear from the tiny ripples that flit across her face that her feelings are in turmoil: one of the most memorable moments in all Ray's films.

Her mood is abruptly interrupted by Amal, who has just reached the end of the notebook, and is carried away by the urge to read his new composition. The rest of the scene is a kind of tiff between the two of them, which culminates in a piece of gross insensitivity by Amal. He reveals, as he was supposed not to do, that it is Bhupati who has asked him to encourage Charu to write. 'Oh!' she reacts, quietly but emphatically and, before Amal knows it, the spell is broken and Charu is on her way indoors, saying she must order tea. 'I'll send my piece to a publisher,' he calls out, expecting to get a rise out of her since Charu earlier made him promise not to. 'Please do,' comes the huffy reply.

He takes her at her word. The third scene occurs when Amal announces triumphantly to the household that a magazine has published his piece. Ray is particularly proud of this scene and feels it may justifiably be termed 'Mozartian', involving as it does four 'voices' like the ensemble-singing in Mozart's operas. In his own words:

> Amal's unexpected duplicity has stung Charu to the quick, and she runs through a whole gamut of feelings – shock, disbelief, smouldering anger, heart-wrenching agony – assuming with supreme effort a normal façade when her unsuspecting husband butts in, spouting politics, while a self-centred Amal, flushed by his first literary success, rubs salt in Charu's wound by his unfeeling ebullience – the entire goings-on observed with pensive detachment by Manda, Charu's earthy, uncomplicated sister-in-law. This is the scene where the note of tragedy is struck for the first time, and it is this note which, like a pedal-point, holds the scene together.

The dialogues here are seamlessly integrated with the actions. But Ray is equally gifted at writing dialogue that draws attention to itself – his version of the 'smart' dialogue he dislikes in Bengali films. The fourth scene, in which Amal and Charu hold their witty alliterative conversation in order to keep their deeper emotions in check, is a showcase for this. Bhupati's musical soirée celebrating the victory of Gladstone (of all unlikely things) can be heard in the background, a mournful song by Raja Rammohun Roy turning Amal's thoughts to the tragedy of Roy's death in exile, in Bristol fifty years previously, and to the promise of a trip to Britain made him by his prospective father-in-law, a lawyer in neighbouring Burdwan. Amal and Charu try to begin each word, Bengali or English, with a 'b' – which is also, of course, the letter on the handkerchief:

Charu: *Jabe age Bardhaman, tarpar Bilet, tarpar* barrister –
        (First it's off to Burdwan, then Britain, then barrister –)
Amal: *Uhuh! age Bardhaman, tarpar biye, tarpar Bilet, tarpar* –
        (Not quite! first Burdwan, then marriage, then Britain, then –)
Charu: *Tarpar?*
        (Then?)
Amal: *Tarpar Bristol.*
        (Then Bristol.)
He laughs.
Charu: *Tarpar barrister. Tarpar?*
        (Then barrister. Then?)

Amal: *Tarpar, back to Bengal – Black Native, bap bap bole – Keman?*
               (Then, back to Bengal – Black Native, tail between my
               legs – isn't that so?)
Charu: *Bengal? Byas?*
               (Bengal? Nothing else?)
Amal: *And Bankim – Babu Bankim Chandra.*
He picks up Bankim's novel *Bisabriksa.*   ·
Amal: (softly) *Bisabriksa.*
Charu: *Ar Bouthan?*
               (And what about sister-in-law?)
Amal reads a line from *Bisabriksa,* but he has subtly altered it to
suggest that Charu may be a disturbing influence. Charu immediately
senses the tease.
Charu: *Bouthan baje? Biri? Beha—?*
               (Is she no good? A bad girl? Shame—?)
She stops herself from saying 'shameless'. Their eyes meet and
it is obvious that the playful conversation is finished.

From here on, the film becomes decidely sombre in tone. Umapada's
treachery is discovered by Bhupati, Amal goes away in fear that he too
will betray him, Bhupati tries to make amends for neglecting Charu, and
eventually the bitter secret gets out, leaving Bhupati devastated. The very
last sequence of the film – my fifth and final scene – is one of Ray's most
thought-provoking endings, which he admits was influenced in style by the
ending of Truffaut's *Les Quatre Cents Coups.* It consists of a freeze and
a series of still photographs, as if from an album. Bhupati has been out
in his carriage driving round Calcutta trying to come to terms with his
colossal insensitivity to what was happening under his own roof. Charu
is inside the house, facing the damage done to her marriage with a calm
sharply contrasting with her storm of grief over Amal's departure. Calling
the servant to bring a lamp, she goes to the door of the house and opens
it. Bhupati is standing on the other side as if rooted to the spot. Gently
but gingerly she bids him enter and, after hesitating, he does so, reaching
forward for her hand. It is on this gesture that Ray freezes the action, before
cutting in succession to her half-lit face, his half-lit face, the servant holding
the glowing globe-shaped lamp, a mid-shot of Charu and Bhupati and, as
the very last image of the film, a long shot of them both, frozen in time at
the end of the verandah. As dissonant music rises to a crescendo, recalling
the end of *The Music Room,* the printed word '*Nastanirh*' appears boldly
on the screen in Bengali script – 'The Broken Nest'.
   'One thing is certain,' says Madhabi Mukherjee. 'A gap will always
remain between husband and wife.' She was kept unaware of the ending
throughout the shooting. 'We used to guess at it all the time. But he said,
"No, I won't give it away." We didn't have the courage to probe him too
much. I found that it was much better, more beautiful and effective in the

film than in the story.' That ends with a single word. Bhupati is about to go to Mysore and Charu suddenly tells him 'Take me with you.' He hesitates and so Charu says *'Thak'*, which means 'Let it be.' Ray explains:

That was a kind of very abrupt, logical conclusion, and I wanted a visual equivalent of *Thak*; instead of the word, an image, which would suggest that the two are about to be reconciled and then are prevented from doing so. I couldn't end with a word because I have a feeling that the really crucial moments in a film should be wordless. It's very difficult to express what was precisely meant to be achieved with that series of still shots, but it was something that told me instinctively it would be the right conclusion for the film. I can't explain beyond that.

···➤[15]➤···

Kapurush
(The Coward) 1965

···➤[◖◗]➤···

RAY followed *Charulata* with a double-bill of films very different
in period, milieu and mood. Unable to find a story suitable for a
full-length feature film, he picked one he had known from his schooldays,
Mahapurush (already discussed), and another by Premendra Mitra, a
modern Bengali writer, which he thoroughly adapted to make *Kapurush*
(*The Coward*).

In this film, according to Soumitra Chatterjee whose role forms
part of another triangle, 'much is left to the imagination of the
audience.' This is true, and the film is like *Kanchenjungha* in so far as the
plot is perfunctory and the surface of the film simple, almost to the point
of dullness – but probe beneath it, and a whole complex of emotions can
be felt. It may be, however, that exposure to Bengali middle-class mores
is necessary for a proper appreciation of these undercurrents. Certainly
Kapurush failed to make the impression Ray hoped for when it was shown
at the Venice Festival in 1965, its first and last showing outside India.
Within India it ran as a double bill, both in Bengal and, a first for a Ray
film, in a dubbed Hindi version elsewhere with such extra ingredients as
snatches of Hindi film songs (to replace those by Tagore) and a feeble,
done-up ending. Ray has not really discovered what the reaction to that
version was like, but hopes for revival of his own version in due course.
'These are twin films I have considerable affection for,' he says. 'I have
a pretty high opinion of *Kapurush* myself and I was disappointed by
the response.'

His affection is understandable because there is a good deal of
him in the film; again like *Kanchenjungha*, though not to the same
extent, it is a notably personal work. It develops the theme of conflict
of conscience among city-bred people seen in *Mahanagar*, which is so
evident in later films like *The Adversary*, *Company Limited*, and *The
Middle Man*. In *Kapurush* it haunts two members of the triangle and
robs them of their peace of mind. The film is a penetrating insight into 'a
certain type of cowardice,' as Ray puts it, 'and a certain selfishness, which
seem to be concomitants of modern middle-class sophistication. The stress

of modern living, and the uncertainty of getting a foothold and retaining it, are important causes of these complexes.'

The setting is crucial. It is a tea-plantation, somewhere on the borders of Assam and Bengal, probably not very far from Darjeeling. The atmosphere is therefore one of remoteness, physical labour and boredom, relieved – for the males – by heavy drinking. It is also very anglicised: not only is the Bengali spoken littered with English phrases and expletives, but there still operates a 'rigid caste system' (in the words of Gupta, the planter member of the triangle), evolved over 150 years by the British, whereby a planter can mix only with another socially acceptable planter. 'How can I suddenly make a one man revolution?' asks Gupta. 'How can I uproot the system? At first, I didn't follow it; it got on my nerves. Later, I realised that by following it, life becomes easier, smoother' – Ray's commentary on the collaborative mentality of Indians under the Raj, underscored by Gupta's use of the phrases 'rigid caste system', 'one man revolution' and 'life becomes easier, smoother' in English. A hermetic existence with hints of violence and oppression, disliked by Ray (following his great-grandfather Dwarkanath Ganguli) – but in Gupta he gives it a human dimension very far from that of a cardboard cut-out.

Ray's excellent background score adds to the feeling of isolation throughout. And it is his only one to feature a saxophone, for which he composed a sort of blues to capture the 'very special kind of mood in a tea-plantation – the languor and the life of the planters, very western. I don't know how I got hold of it, but I loved that piece of music.' Though it reminds one a little of the music in Wajda's *Ashes and Diamonds*, Ray acknowledges no debt. Its impact is increased by contrast with his very simple use of a sitar to suggest the more Bengali elements in the story, especially the feelings of the planter's wife, and by the snatches of Tagore songs that are hummed or heard on the radio.

This saxophone music is heard under the film's opening titles, which appear over a garage interior, indicating from the very first shot that this is to be Ray in a new mood and milieu. The owner of the car being serviced is more as we expect though – a gentle-faced svelte young man without much idea of what happens beneath the bonnet. He is Amitava Roy, a tyro screen-writer for Bengali films from Calcutta visiting the area in search of local 'colour'. His taxi has broken down and he is stranded for the night. A corpulent, round-faced, balding man wearing baggy shorts, who happens to be filling his jeep, comes to the rescue. He offers to put Roy up for the night at his bungalow nearby. He introduces himself as Bimal Gupta (Haradhan Banerjee, Arati's boss in *Mahanagar*), 'a lonely planter'; with his loud bonhomie and frank talk, he hardly seems ideal company for his introverted guest. His idea of film-writing is, as he puts it, that 'boy meets girl, boy gets girl, boy loses girl' – a motif that will return several times in the film, catching the more sophisticated Roy unawares.

As the jeep pulls up at a large bungalow, the sound of a radio can be heard; it is Tagore's dance drama *Chitrangada,* imperfectly received because of distance and the hills. Gupta's wife Karuna (Madhabi Mukherjee) is trying to improve the reception as her husband and his unexpected guest enter. He introduces her in a manner which is so casual that he fails to catch the look of startled recognition that passes between them. Though it soon vanishes, it makes obvious they were once lovers. This, of course, is the concealed tension that gives the story its drive. Amitava, the screen-writer, met his girl some years before, got her, and then lost her, while Gupta never even tried, ending up with a beautiful and sensitive wife whom he cannot understand, after an arranged marriage. With comic pathos the three are now forced together as a trio. Sometimes, however, the husband is absent and the erstwhile lovers are free to confront the changes in themselves, made poignant by three scenes from their past together in flash-back. The alternation of threesomes and twosomes gives the story a very satisfying rhythmic structure.

Gupta is genuinely delighted to have somebody to talk to, on whom he can unload his preoccupations and his troubled conscience, once his tongue has been loosened by alcohol. His wife, who sits quietly by, saying little, (as she is obviously used to doing), does not touch alcohol, and neither, to his disappointment, does their guest. For the rest of their time together Gupta does his best to break this embargo, using the argument that as a writer Roy must have the experience of drinking. To be polite, Roy consents to take sherry, but he hardly touches it. Like his namesake Satyajit, he avoids alcohol; having accepted the sherry, 'he makes valiant efforts to suppress his intense dislike of the taste of the liquid', to quote Ray's shooting notebook.

Gupta's pre-supper monologue addressed to Roy is that of a man who, though crude in many ways, is intelligent enough to realise that he is missing life's finer aspects and honest enough to dislike the compromises of his existence as a manager. He is curious about his companion's work, wants to know whether he enjoys it and whether he intends to use him as a character in it. 'Just don't make me a villain,' he tells him affably, 'because my wife would be really hurt.' He is pleased to discover that he and Roy share a dislike of the same college subject – Economics (another autobiographical touch by Satyajit). 'So we have a lot in common,' he guffaws. 'Except that you're writing film scripts and I'm working all day in this blasted tea-plantation, and at night drowning in this,' and he lifts his glass. His wife looks on, embarrassed, but doing her best not to show it.

That night, after Amitava has tried unsuccessfully to regain a little of his old intimacy with Karuna when she brings him a glass of water, he falls into a restless doze and dreams of the moment when he last saw her. She arrived, uninvited and clearly agitated, at his bachelor flat, which she had never visited before. Ray selected this room for its odd

47 *Three Daughters* (*The Postmaster*): Nandalal and villagers (*Teknica*)

48 *Three Daughters* (*The Postmaster*): Ratan, Nandalal (*Teknica*)

49 *Three Daughters* (*Monihara*): Manimalika (*Teknica*)

50 *Three Daughters*
(*Monihara*): Phanibhusan
(*Teknica*)

51 *Three Daughters*
(*Samapti*): Jogmaya,
Mrinmoyee (*Teknica*)

52 *Three Daughters*
(*Samapti*): Mrinmoyee,
Amulya (*Teknica*)

53 *Kanchenjungha*: Asok, Manisa (*Teknica*)

54 *Kanchenjungha*: Jagadish, Asok (*Teknica*)

55 *Kanchenjungha*: Manisa, Sankar (*Teknica*)

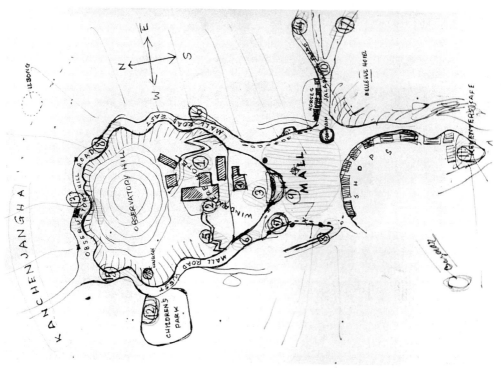

56   *Kanchenjungha:* sketch map of locations in Darjeeling by Ray   57   *Abhijan:* Ray, Soumendu Roy, Subrata Mitra (*Ram Panjabi*)

58   *Abhijan*: Narsingh, Rama (*Teknica*)

59   *Abhijan*: Gulabi, Narsingh (*Teknica*)

60 *Mahanagar*: Subrata, Bani, Arati (*Teknica*)

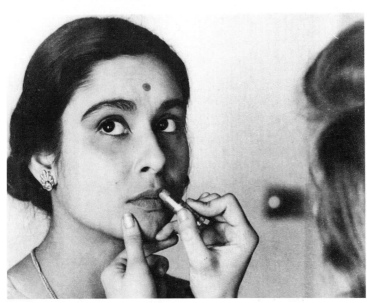

61 *Mahanagar*: Arati, Edi (*Teknica*)

62 *Mahanagar*: Priyagopal Arati's father, Subrata (*Teknica*)

63 *Charulata*: Charu, Bhupati (*Teknica*)

64 *Charulata*: Umapada, Amal, Bhupati (*Teknica*)

65 *Charulata*: Amal, Manda, Charu (*Teknica*)

66 *Charulata*: Amal, Charu
(*Teknica*)

67 *Charulata*: Charu
(*Teknica*)

68 *Charulata*: Amal, Charu
(*Teknica*)

69 K. Kawakita, Ray, Bijoya Ray, Soumitra Chatterjee, Bansi Chandragupta. Calcutta, 1965 (*Lindsay Anderson*)

70 David McCutchion with Ray (*Ray family*)

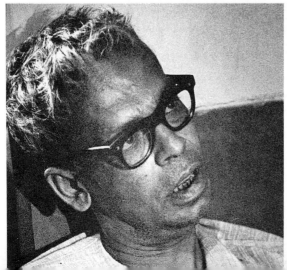

71 Ritwik Ghatak (*Nemai Ghosh*)

72 *Kapurush*: Karuna (*Teknica*)

73 *Kapurush*: Karuna, Amitava (*Teknica*)

74 *Nayak*: Aditi, Arindam (*Teknica*)

75 *Nayak*: Biresh, Arindam (*Teknica*)

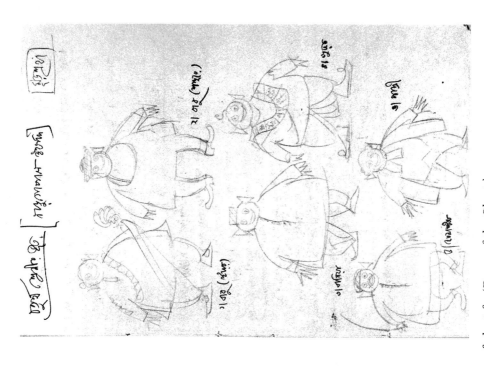

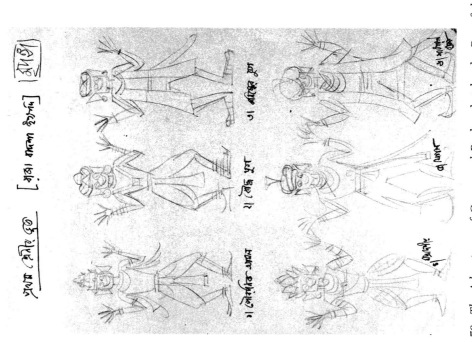

76 *The Adventures of Goopy and Bagha*: sketches by Ray of three classes of ghost for 'Dance of the Ghosts'

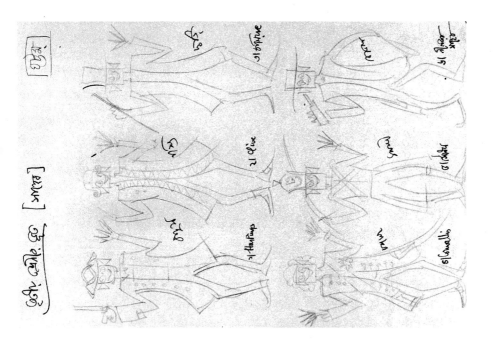

77   *The Adventures of Goopy and Bagha:* sketches of scientist-magician by Ray

78 *The Adventures of Goopy and Bagha*: Bagha, Prime Minister of Halla, Goopy (*Nemai Ghosh*)

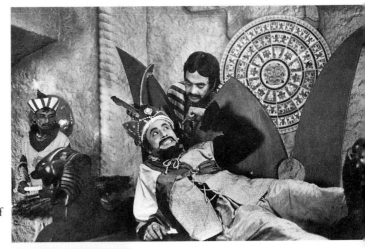

79 *The Adventures of Goopy and Bagha*: King of Halla, Prime Minister (*Nemai Ghosh*)

80 *The Adventures of Goopy and Bagha*: poster by Ray

81 *The Kingdom of Diamonds*: Goopy, Bagha (*Nemai Ghosh*)

82 *The Kingdom of Diamonds*: King Hirak, courtier, Goopy (*Nemai Ghosh*)

83 *Days and Nights in the Forest* (*Nemai Ghosh*)

84 *Days and Nights in the Forest*: Sekhar, Duli (*Nemai Ghosh*)

85 *Days and Nights in the Forest*: Asim, Hari, Sekhar, Jaya, Aparna, Sanjoy (*Nemai Ghosh*)

86 *Days and Nights in the Forest*: Aparna, Sekhar, Asim (*Nemai Ghosh*)

appearance, which is very characteristic of a certain part of north Calcutta. He knew such rooms from his childhood; one of his mother's aunts used to live in one. 'A road branches off from the main road at an acute angle, and there's a house which narrows down and a verandah in front which is triangular, and the room behind it also has a funny kind of a rhombus shape,' he observes.

'So this is the famous triangular room,' says Karuna to Amitava, who stands watching her, somewhat uncomfortably, his face unshaven. On the wall hangs a kind of hat which was popularised by the students of Santiniketan – perhaps a subtle hint by Ray of the weakness that Amitava will betray. 'Just right for one person,' Karuna adds. She has come to him in desperation to say that she must very soon leave Calcutta for good. Her uncle, who is determined to scotch her relationship with the penniless Amitava is sending her away – unless . . . they marry immediately and run away from him together. There is no other option; it is now or never. She knows it will be difficult for them both, but she thinks they will manage and be happy. Trustingly, she looks to him for confirmation, certain that he must feel the same.

But Amitava is thrown very much off-balance by this world-shattering proposition. He falters, 'a typical example of the thinking male, too busy weighing the pros and cons of a given predicament to act on an impulse,' comments Ray. 'It's a big ruthless city, Karuna,' says Amitava uncertainly. But she has been swept away by her emotions. She breaks down, while he tries ineffectually to comfort her. Then, as she sits more composedly and looks at him standing by the window, turned away from her in confusion, the truth dawns: his feelings for her do not extend to running away together. The camera closes in on her distress, as a series of fire-bells pass in the street outside; barely controlling herself, she presses her handkerchief to her mouth. As Ray said of *Charulata*, 'I have a feeling that the really crucial moments in a film should be wordless.' The power of this particular one is magnified by Karuna's 'theme' played on the sitar.

It is now Amitava's turn to explain himself to Karuna, and he appeals to her, perfectly reasonably, to understand the difficulty of his taking on a partner without having either money or position himself. He believes that she has grown up used to comfort and fears that he cannot match her expectations, though she denies this. He appeals for a day to think. But she, for better or for worse, has made up her mind: 'What you lack is not time but something else,' she tells him bluntly; in other words, he is a coward. She leaves him. Years later, unable to sleep with these painful recollections, Amitava gets up, washes his face, and goes into the sitting-room for some night air. Karuna too has been upset by his unexpected arrival and, hearing a noise, suddenly appears from her bedroom. He pleads with her, 'Are you happy in your marriage?' and confesses that he was unable to consider marriage at all after they broke up. She listens enigmatically, refusing to get involved. Their whispered dialogue ends on a prosaic note with him begging for sleeping pills. 'Don't take more than two,' she says softly. 'What if I do?' he asks, with some self-pity. 'I don't think you will,' she replies, knowing him of old.

At breakfast the following morning on the shady verandah – a virtuoso combination of set (the bungalow) and location (the verandah with the plantation behind) – the threesome resumes its uneasy colloquy, loaded with ironies. Gupta is now sober, and the three of them drink only tea, brewed from the local product. He talks openly of the social taboos which he, as a manager, must observe and then, seeing Roy hesitate, guesses what is in his mind. 'Conscience?' he says in Bengali. 'Mr Roy, it's very simple,' – in English – 'if you have a conscience you suffer' – in Bengali – 'you drown it in alcohol' – in English. And he laughs loudly at his own joke, while Amitava looks disconcerted. 'How's the tea?' asks Gupta, reverting to Bengali. 'It's excellent,' Amitava says. 'I'll give you a packet to take back,' replies Gupta with another laugh, 'but your conscience won't drown in it. It always floats to the surface.' Karuna too now smiles.

Thoughts of the past pursue Amitava as relentlessly as they did in the night while Gupta's jeep makes its way down the mountain road to a favourite picnic spot. Gupta sings his own painful rendering of 'Isle of Capri': 'Beneath the shade of a walnut tree, I found her.' What is Karuna thinking? There is no way that Amitava can tell, but he finds himself transported back, this time to their very first meeting as college students on a tram, where he got her out of a tight corner by buying her ticket. She was then girlish, spontaneous and warm, so different from the Karuna he is now sitting behind. Or is she? As the jeep grinds onwards (to the accompaniment of patchy back-projection), she softly sings a Tagore song with words that suggest she has forgotten nothing of their happiness together. But at a sharp bend in the road she suddenly puts her hand on her husband's shoulder. Once more, Amitava finds himself daydreaming: he is in a dingy tea-shop sitting across from a radiant Karuna reading her palm as an excuse to hold her hand. Tenderly they talk of their future together and he asks her for her hand in marriage.

By the time they reach the picnic spot Amitava feels urgently that he is allowing an important chance to slip away once more. When Gupta goes off for a moment and again while he dozes after food, muttering 'boy meets girl, boy gets girl, boy loses girl', he snatches his chance to persuade the woman he still loves to leave her husband and come with him. 'Forget the past, please, Karuna. Then I lacked courage.' She, wrapped in a bold striped sari, headscarf and dark glasses, seems unmoved by his appeals. 'You don't know him,' she says. 'You can't know a man in a day.' Nevertheless, he writes her a little note on a scrap of napkin, requesting her to meet him at the station that night if she changes her mind.

They drop him off there, after the picnic. Disconsolately, dully, he buys a ticket, settles down to wait, and dozes off on a station bench. Sitting there in the darkness, he does not see the figure that slowly approaches him. It is Karuna. At the same time the headlight of the train appears. The noise of its approach wakes him. Looking up he is startled to see her and begins to smile, but her grave demeanour suggests that she has not come to stay. In a choked voice she says, 'Have you got the sleeping pills? Please give them to me. The shop is shut.' Seeing him hesitate, she appeals to him again, 'Please, darling.' He hands the bottle over and, without even saying goodbye, she walks slowly away to the sound of the simple phrase repeated on the sitar that was heard when she left him years before. As the train comes clanking in, our last sight of Amitava is a close-up of his face turned towards the camera in anguish.

This description of the screenplay can only hint at its true distinction, unfortunately, or at the finesse of all three actors, especially Madhabi Mukherjee, whose contrast between repressed passion as a married woman and generous emotional abandon as a lover, is wonderful, even if it seems slightly limited after the gamut of feeling she compresses into a single scene in *Charulata*. *Kapurush* reveals Ray at his very sharpest as a psychologist; every scene is a model of supple, life-like dialogue and probing, telling camerawork. It is even possible to interpret the film in two wholly different ways and still make sense of it: Gupta may or may not have known what was going on between his wife and their guest. 'While making the film, I had in mind this double aspect,' says Ray. 'As to which is true, I have left this as a permanent question.' If Gupta did know, he avoided acting on this knowledge because he was confident of his wife's loyalty; some of his comments to Amitava, such as his remarks about 'conscience', then acquire a rather different ironic edge. Whatever the possibilities this ambiguity might have afforded the actor, Ray chose not to suggest it to Haradhan Banerjee during shooting, preferring he should not consciously alter his performance to allow for it.

What I hope does come across from the above description is an idea of the areas of the film that are not so accessible to a western viewer, who will likely find *Kapurush* 'slight but agreeable' (in the words of critic John Russell Taylor). Tynan, for instance, rated it not much higher than a typical British television play of the time, and Dilys Powell felt it was overacted, according to Ray. 'You may say that about the planter. He talks a lot but that's a different thing from overacting. He's talking a lot because at last he's found a man to make conversation with,' Ray observes.

There is the unique ethos of the tea-plantation, for instance, and its language with a high proportion of English words mixed with Bengali; these can be discomforting and sometimes risible for the westerner. Unfamiliar too, though to a lesser extent, is the typical atmosphere of the Calcutta student milieu hinted at but not developed in *Aparajito*. What is daring and genuinely courageous there, may seem rather tame to an outsider, and what is romantic may seem mawkish. A non-Bengali may miss the starkness of the dilemma facing Amitava when asked to marry Karuna, or the trauma she will have to endure if she disobeys her uncle. Paradoxically, it may be that the closer Ray's characters and settings get to those of western films, the less universal they seem to a western viewer. *Kapurush*, in this respect, is like its placid setting; there is much below the surface that does not strike the casual gaze.

16

Nayak
(The Hero) 1966

❖[◦◦◦◦◦◦]❖

DURING the second half of 1965, Ray made a film from his second original screenplay. He broke new ground in it by casting in the main role Uttam Kumar, *the* star of the commercial cinema in Bengal at that time. As he had shown in *Abhijan* in 1962, when he cast Waheeda Rehman in a smallish role, and has subsequently proved in *The Chess Players* and in the work he has done with his son for television from 1985, Ray admires the talent of some of the stars of big-budget films. He has not felt able to use it more often, simply because he has usually required actors fluent in Bengali, not because of his aversion to the crude films in which these actors normally appear. Here, though, a star was doubly appropriate since he was being asked to play a matinée idol and, according to Ray, he had read somewhere that 'if you are showing a matinée idol, then you have to cast a star. Nobody else would do; people wouldn't accept the fact. So I thought that I was doing the only possible thing.' On the other hand, he 'always believed Uttam had it in him to give good performances.' Nevertheless, Ray had to face some criticism for 'selling out' after his relative lack of success with *Kapurush-o-Mahapurush* – notably from Mrinal Sen. 'Mrinal said – now he has sunk to the level of using a matinée idol!' recalls Ray with a slightly wry chuckle.

Although Uttam Kumar was in Ray's mind when he set off for Darjeeling off-season in May to write *Nayak (The Hero)*, he was thinking of him more as a phenomenon than as an individual. Uttam had no hand in the formation of the character he was to play, and Ray to this day is surprisingly ignorant of Uttam's life. 'He was a clerk at the customs or port commissioners I think and his autograph was very much the signature of a clerk. That's about all I know. There's an autobiography – ghost-written – which I haven't read,' says Ray with a fairly disdainful laugh. Like Arindam, the film hero he plays, Uttam had done a lot of stage-work before entering films. 'Success gave him a personality,' recalls Ray. 'In his early days' – that is, when Satyajit was building up the Film Society – 'he was very bad.' After that he worked with some good directors, and by 1965 he was at the top, where he stayed until his death in 1980. For twenty-five years he ruled the roost in Bengal. When Ray shot a scene at Howrah Station in Calcutta, thousands and thousands of people turned out to watch. 'I don't know how we took that shot,' he says. 'It was not very well done. The police were around but they were watching him.'

By then, Soumitra Chatterjee was established as the other romantic lead in Bengali cinema, but his appeal was much more limited than Uttam Kumar's. 'Certainly the intelligent section of the crowd, particularly the girls, the Presidency College girls, would prefer Soumitra to Uttam. But they were in a minority, I'm afraid,' says Ray. Uttam could produce acceptable acting even from bad material, just by playing himself. 'Whereas with Soumitra, who's much more intelligent, given bad material, he turns out a bad performance, because his distaste for the material shows.'

In writing his screenplay, Ray was driven by a desire first to investigate the psychology of such a star, secondly the psychology of his adulators and detractors, and lastly, to make a film about a train journey. The central thread of the story, around which several subplots interweave, is the relationship between the star – who is travelling to Delhi from Calcutta officially to collect a prize, but really to get away from it all for a few days – and Aditi (Sarmila Tagore), a young journalist who edits a serious women's magazine, and whose heavy black glasses and pen clipped to her blouse do little to conceal her feminine charm. She regards Bengali commercial cinema and its chief star Arindam with mild contempt, but her two travelling companions egg her on to get an interview with Arindam for her magazine. One of them admits to enjoying Arindam's pictures, and her husband jokes that Arindam is 'a modern Krishna' surrounded by his wife and all the ladies like her, who are 'his secret *gopis*'.

Aditi walks over to Arindam's table in the dining-car, introduces herself as an autograph-hunter, and then quickly adds that she wants his for her cousin, not herself. They strike an immediate rapport based on Arindam's relieved realisation that he does not have to play the star with her. It soon leads to him pouring out his life story, prompted by her initial question, 'In the midst of having so much, don't you feel there's something missing in your life? Some emptiness somewhere?' and a nightmarish daydream in his compartment in which he drowns in an ocean of bank-notes. In a series of conversations with Aditi, interspersed with alarming dreams and painful memories of his past, he reveals his guilt – about leaving the theatre for films against the express wishes of his old teacher (who told him that in films he would only be a puppet, just as Sisirkumar Bhaduri once did to Satyajit Ray); about taking to alcohol to steady his nerves; about his rejection of an ageing actor desperate for work in revenge for an old insult; and about his refusal to help an old friend in union politics. Finally, blind-drunk on whisky and half-contemplating suicide falling from the train, he orders the conductor to fetch him Aditi. He begins to confess to an affair with a married woman who wanted a part in one of his films and a brawl he had with her husband, but Aditi stops him, moved to pity by his condition, and watches him stagger back to his compartment. 'You know the voice of Conscience in the village dramas? That's the part for you,' he had told her earlier on in the dining-car. 'Is that a bad part?' she had asked. 'No – ' he replied, 'but a terrible nuisance. I wish I could sweep it away like all the rest.' 'Conscience? But isn't that what makes you human?' Aditi had retorted with naïve conviction.

The other passengers in the train who interact with Arindam all help to explain his state of mind, without one feeling for a moment that they have been put there by Ray for the purpose. Their various reactions to him each show them to be star-struck, unable to be indifferent about his presence among them. In Arindam's own compartment is a family of three: senior businessman, wife and young daughter. His womenfolk are admirers, while the paterfamilias looks down on film people as scandalous types; his interest lies in getting to know better the attractive young wife of the advertising man down the corridor who is wooing him for business. To clinch the deal, her husband encourages her to butter the businessman up, but she is repelled by this; her heart lies in getting into films, and her proximity to a film star seems like a golden opportunity too good to miss. When she tells her husband what she intends, it is his turn to be appalled; flirting is good for business, but film-acting – never!

Two other passengers complete this microcosm of Bengali middle-class sanctimoniousness. In the advertising man's compartment sits a saffron-clad swami, who remains studiously silent until near the end of their journey, when the deal with the businessman has fallen through. Then he offers his own deal, a modest budget to advertise his organisation, the World Wide Will Workers: 'Where there's a will, there's a way to prognosticate and prevent all catastrophes and calamities' is its creed. And in another compartment, all on his own, travels a wizened old journalist, a sort of provincial Nirad Chaudhuri, famous for his newspaper articles and letters inveighing against the depravity of the age. He 'never goes to the cinema on principle', and bluntly informs Arindam that he stands for all that is most detestable in modern Indian life.

Nayak undoubtedly invites comparison with *Kanchenjungha*, Ray's first original screenplay. It lifts a group of prosperous contemporary characters out of their usual setting and thrusts them together for a brief period of time; it sets up a situation tailor-made for romance and then stalls it; its emotions are, generally speaking, very restrained; and it has a woman for its conscience-keeper. Most important though is the way it dramatises the trivial courses of a handful of lives by weaving them together in a carefully calculated manner. This was expressed very well by Ray's friend David McCutchion (who worked closely with Satyajit on subtitling his films in English, from *Three Daughters* until his premature death in 1972), when he reviewed *Nayak*:

How can the normal be made interesting? What is the point of a work of art that tells us what one already knows? I would say the delight of this film lies in its structure – the way the themes are patterned – and in the pleasure of recognising the familiar pinpointed by art. These are both features of classicism. *Nayak* is like *Kanchenjungha* in its commonplace undramatic material arranged in counter-pointing themes, especially as presented through contrasting groups of characters. But this patterning is not merely formal – it also has moral depth, it investigates the central moral issue from a variety of angles.

Kanchenjungha is, however, the better film. Apart from the disadvantage of being shot in a studio, *Nayak* suffers from two significant weaknesses: a sense of artifice in some of the patterning, and an incompleteness in the two central characters.

To understand the first of these criticisms, consider the chief difference in technique between the two films: *Nayak* is full of flash-backs and dream sequences, *Kanchenjungha* has none at all. These definitely interrupt the flow, however reasonable they may be in principle with an insecure, haunted character like Arindam telling his story. They also, which is the more serious criticism, encapsulate and concentrate Arindam's worries too neatly to preserve the illusion of life as it is lived, even by a star. His hang-ups are too clear-cut: riches versus friendship, cinema versus theatre, make-believe versus politics, drunkenness versus sobriety. It is significant that the best scenes in *Nayak* all take place when Arindam is interacting with other passengers, and that of the flash-backs and dreams the most powerful is the most jumbled one. 'Planning the story of *Nayak*,' wrote Ray in 1966, 'I dismissed quite early the notion of an orderly, step-by-step account of the making of a matinée idol. That seemed to belong to the cinema of the thirties and forties. In the film, the hero's past is revealed in flash-backs and dreams which make inroads into a very tight time-space pattern (twenty-four hours in a train).' Ray was certainly right to reject the conventional approach he mentions, but his own solution can unfortunately seem something of a contrivance on the screen too.

The problem of the central performances is harder to pin down and may not strike the Bengali viewer so much as the westerner; though it should be said that *Nayak* won the Critics' Prize at Berlin in 1966 (where Pasolini, one of the jurors, admired it), and received decent reviews in the USA, where it was released in 1974. (In Britain it had no release.) In comparison with the by no means dissimilar couple at the centre of *Kapurush*, there seems to be a missing ingredient in Arindam and Aditi. At root, Uttam Kumar does not project the real star quality that would make him so admired and disliked. He may well be a modern Krishna, but where is his flute? He lacks elan and seems insufficiently masculine for a matinée idol; one looks in vain for a bit more Burton and a little less Bogarde. With his penchant for self-pity and alcohol, Arindam seems to inherit something of the personality of Bengali screen heroes of an earlier period, whom Ray has always disliked. Some of that feeling in Ray, coupled with his comparative lack of empathy with Uttam himself, may have prevented him from seeing the role of Arindam as consistently from the inside as he normally does. Although he admired Uttam's talents in many ways, large and small – including the ability to sign his autograph by dipping his pen in water while continuing to talk – Uttam's intellect was not among them.

> I never bothered to explain the character to him. So I never discovered whether he really understood the implications of the part. And it doesn't really matter whether he did or did not. There were a lot of things he did understand because they probably corresponded to his own life and his own experience. He was not very articulate as a person, actually. Perhaps he was conscious of the fact that he would not be able to talk at the same level as us, so he kept quiet. Some people who are stupid would come out with all sorts of stupid things. So I didn't discuss the psychology of the part at all. I merely told him that this is what you have to do. Trust me and it should be all right.

Of course, it *is* all right, in fact it is first-rate by ordinary standards of cinema – it just is not Ray at his best.

17

Musicals:
The Adventures of Goopy and Bagha (Goopy Gyne Bagha Byne) 1969 The Kingdom of Diamonds (Hirak Rajar Dese) 1980

➤◄[◈◈◈◈]►◄

NOTHING demonstrates the gap between Ray's Bengali audience and his foreign audience more clearly than the two musical comedies he has made – *The Adventures of Goopy and Bagha*, in 1968/69, and its sequel *The Kingdom of Diamonds*, in 1979/80. In Bengal, both had long runs, the longest ever for a Bengali film in the case of *Goopy and Bagha*. As Ray wrote to Seton about six months after the first film opened: 'It is extraordinary how quickly it has become part of popular culture. Really there isn't a single child in the city who doesn't know and sing the songs.' Whereas abroad, the first film was barely released, and the second one not at all. When it was screened in London's West End as part of the London Film Festival in 1980, the audience was ninety per cent Bengalis, Ray recalls. 'The English were all watching *Napoléon* across the street. And I was making trips to that theatre, watching *Napoléon* and then coming back to watch my film.'

At a special private screening of *Goopy and Bagha* in London, Ray remembers feeling a 'not very exciting reaction. Lindsay [Anderson] said it had got lovely things in it but it went on for too long.' When it was released in Britain in 1972 (minus a couple of songs Ray had cut in response to such criticism) the critics mostly felt that the film dragged and that the trick effects were weak, despite many felicitous touches. 'Satyajit Ray at his least convincing', wrote the *Guardian* critic. 'Perhaps it would appeal to singularly unfidgety children', wrote the *Observer* critic. A third summed up for them all, in the *Times*: 'Ray is a true poet of the cinema, but he finds his poetry in everyday reality; in all-out fantasy he seems somehow prosaic.'

There is, at bottom, no mystery in these opposed responses to the two films, though the contrast does have its less analysable aspects, which relate to the West's historic disinterest in the legends of India. Both films boast dialogue and lyrics of singular poetry and wit which can be only palely reflected in their English subtitles – even when Ray is the translator – along with songs and music that display a delightful capacity for parody

and transmutation of styles from the folk, devotional and classical music of
Bengal and other parts of India. 'They are my songs if you come to think
of it,' says Ray. 'I have definitely set a style of singing which doesn't come
from Tagore, doesn't come from western music, but which is essentially
me.' Unlikely though the comparison may seem at first sight, the total
effect reminds me of the lyrics and music of Tom Lehrer, the brilliant
American satirist; he has the acute moral sensibility found in Ray, and the
razor-sharp humour, coupled with a marvellous melodic gift. And none of
Lehrer's work could possibly make the same impact on an Indian audience
as it does on an American or, to a lesser extent, a European audience.

Goopy and Bagha released the pent-up love of fantasy in Satyajit
Ray that is given free rein in his grandfather's and father's work,
and the love of singing and song-composing which was so strong in his
grandfather. Its inspiration comes from Upendrakisore, while that of *The
Kingdom of Diamonds* derives more from Sukumar – its word play and
juggling of ideas is much akin to his plays.

Goopy and Bagha first made their appearance in *Sandesh* in
1914, with illustrations too by Upendrakisore. Satyajit first read the
story when he was about eight, after he had left Garpar Road. It was very
enjoyable, 'but in those days one didn't think in film terms you know,' he
says with a laugh. It was not until the early to mid-1960s, after the revival
of *Sandesh* in 1961, that Ray reread the story. He decided to republish,
and at the same time began to contemplate filming it.

A constellation of reasons eventually compelled him to take his idea
seriously. His son Sandip, then about the age when Satyajit first read
the story, had been nagging him to make a film which was less 'grim
and adult' (in Satyajit's words). This chimed with Satyajit's own desire
to reach out to children by giving them something vital, original and
Bengali, which he felt did not necessarily mean having a child actor.
That this would also allow him to include songs in substantial numbers
greatly appealed. He had recently composed a charming love song for his
detective film *Chiriakhana*, and had developed a taste for song-writing.
He also relished the chance to shoot in Rajasthan, the desert state of
western India which he had known by its old name of Rajputana when he
was a boy reading about it in the tales of Rajput princely adventure, *Raj
Kahini*, by Abanindranath Tagore. 'The tales were about real kings and
real princes,' Ray wrote in a foreword to Raghubir Singh's outstanding
book of photographs of 'India's enchanted land', 'but so filled were they
with the stuff of romance and chivalry that they didn't seem real. We read
of a land of desert and forest and mountain fortresses; of marble palaces
rising out of lakes like gem-studded lotuses; of brave Hindu warriors on
faithful, fearless steeds charging into battle against invaders; and of their
womenfolk who threw themselves into the flames rather than be snatched
away as prizes by alien conquerors.'

Not least of his reasons was Ray's perception of an audience for such a film – and of a size which might recover a position at the box-office that was not especially healthy after *Kapurush-o-Mahapurush* and *Nayak*. His production controller Anil Chowdhury was less sanguine. 'He threw up his hands and said "It's going to cost a lot of money",' remembers Ray. 'I said it's also true that nothing like this has ever been made here. It might be very popular. It would reach every stratum of the audience. My films are generally aimed at the literate, the educated people; there's a large section of the public left out of consideration. He was finally convinced and we drew up a budget.'

As Ray was well aware, this was a time of great turbulence in the film industry in Bengal, brought about by general social and political unrest and the increasing reluctance of producers and distributors to invest in Bengali films whose market was so much smaller than that for Hindi films. Both the financing and distribution of *Goopy and Bagha* were to be badly hit by this. R.D. Bansal, who had produced *Mahanagar, Charulata, Kapurush-o-Mahapurush* and *Nayak*, 'had a sudden loss of confidence' in *Goopy and Bagha*, according to Ray. He had already made an initial reconnaissance trip to Rajasthan when Bansal decided that the film would cost too much. For the rest of 1967, during which he also worked on the screenplay and production of his science fiction project *The Alien*, Ray found himself casting around for finance in both Calcutta and Bombay, seeing his hopes alternately raised and then dashed. When Seton called on him in December, he told her that he was almost back to his position in the days before *Pather Panchali*, except that 'I haven't had to pawn my books and records!'

Just before Christmas the money unexpectedly appeared, from the producer-distributors Nepal and Asim Dutta, but sadly, not enough to shoot in colour. That had to wait for the sequel. In *Goopy and Bagha* Ray makes a virtue of necessity by switching into colour for the last scene in the film, when the two characters finally get what they wish for: two gorgeous princesses. It is a tribute to Ray, and to Chandragupta in particular, that really it is not until that scene that the viewer realises what he has been missing; one Bengali I know even thought the entire film was in colour!

In the opening scene we meet only Goopy, a young farmer's son with a passion to be a singer and a marked absence of talent; 'He doesn't know *Sa* from *Ga* and yet he has a mad urge to sing at the slightest provocation', Ray noted in his shooting notebook. Some crafty Brahmins sitting under a tree playing dice flatter him and send him off to try his luck at court. As the sun rises he sits on a wall below the King's bedroom, strumming his *tanpura* and filling the air with unmusical sounds. Sure enough, a palace guard soon appears and invites him into the royal presence. But instead of saluting him, the King, in front of his fawning courtiers, smashes Goopy's instrument and orders him banished from the kingdom.

Riding an ass, a crestfallen Goopy eventually arrives at a forest.

He can hear an odd sound which, after some searching, turns out to be water dripping on to a drum. The drum belongs to a monkey-like man dozing at the foot of a tree. He is of course Bagha, and his passion is for drumming; he too has been banished on an ass from a neighbouring kingdom for lack of talent. Their friendship is cemented by the appearance of a tiger in the forest nearby. Fortunately for them, it has other things on its mind than eating people, and soon wanders away.

A little later, as the dynamic duo are dancing jubilantly in a clearing, the forest ghosts materialise and begin their own bizarre, dazzling dance. Their King, a sprightly, spangled apparition with a vibrant, high-pitched voice fascinating to listen to, offers the two incompetent musicians three boons. They choose instant food and clothing, instant travel, and musical talents so marvellous that those who hear them are transfixed. The key to all this magic is two pairs of exotic slippers: all they have to do is wear them, clap their hands together and wish.

Thus equipped, they sally forth to correct some of the world's injustices, as naïve as before, but now with infinite scope for impish exploits. Ray knew that Tapen Chatterjee and Rabi Ghosh were ideally cast as Goopy and Bagha; certainly the film was great fun to make. They 'infected the entire unit', he says. Rabi he settled on at an early stage, but Tapen was harder to discover; Ray resolutely refused the part to Soumitra Chatterjee, while initial tests with a young Left journalist were not very promising. Ray had known Tapen Chatterjee for years – as the nephew of his friend Chanchal Chatterjee, who used to open the door to Satyajit when he went to Chanchal's house to listen to music. 'He was also working for *Sandesh* part time getting advertisements,' Ray remembers. 'Then one day he dropped in and said very confidently: "Give me that part and I will do it. I know I can do it." So I took a test with him and Rabi and it turned out to be very good.'

The first public performance by the duo, at a music contest held by the Good King of Shundi far away from their native Bengal, provides the occasion for an open-hearted statement of human fraternity that is moving without being sentimental. 'We are coming from the land of Bengal,' sings Goopy, accompanied by Bagha (and full orchestration), 'but although we know only Bengali we know another language that is beyond nation and situation – the language of music.' Naturally, with their ghost-given magic, Goopy and Bagha are the winners; they can entrance even the hard-bitten practitioners of classical styles sitting in a circle at the edge of the royal concert chamber. The duo are immediately given positions as court musicians.

Meanwhile, in neighbouring Halla, a war against Shundi is being hatched by the Bad King, who is not really bad but drugged with a potion prepared by the court magician, a mad professor in wizard's garb. He works for the power behind the throne, the wicked, greedy and flabby Prime Minister – the best villain Ray has created. A declaration is sent to

Shundi and the underfed Halla army is put on alert. Spurred on by the
King of Shundi's promise of a princess in marriage, Goopy and Bagha
become embroiled in trying to prevent the conflict.

They find themselves among a cowed group of tax-defaulting
peasants being glared at by the Bad King, who promptly orders
their heads to be removed. As the grinning executioner arrives, the duo
breaks into song, freezing the court stock-still. Here Ray chose to parody
a south Indian style, using a *vina* and percussion as accompaniment. It
has a lugubrious air that matches the comic villainy of the King and his
henchmen; and Ray is able to round it off to perfection by having his
heroes escape sideways making the jerky neck movements typical of south
Indian (*Bharata Natyam*) dancing. Eventually they are captured, thrown
in a palace dungeon, and gloated over by the Prime Minister, who forces
them to eat the horrible fare eaten by the people of Halla. Although they
left behind two of the slippers when they were caught, they can still summon
up a banquet in their cell with the remaining two when the Prime Minister
has gone. This so entrances the famished guard that he opens the gate and
they escape again.

Famished too, the royal army of Halla now refuses to respond
to its general's (punning) command '*Ut, utho!*' – 'Camels, rise!' In
desperation the Prime Minister begs for his magician's help, and the army
begins to march. But Goopy and Bagha exert their spell too, with a stirring
song delivered from among the graves of real Rajput warriors on a hillside
near Jaisalmer, which they then cap by calling up great pots full of sweets
to descend from the sky; as these land, they are set upon by the ravenous
soldiers. The Prime Minister, realising that the game is up, tries to claim
his share too, but a passing boot smashes his pot.

The King, meanwhile, has reverted to his normal state of
mildness. Goopy and Bagha bring him sweets to try, and then
spirit him away to Shundi, where, after an unseemly tiff over who
should get the princess, a second princess – only daughter of the King
of Halla – is quickly produced. A whispered consultation, a clap of the
hands, and Goopy and Bagha suddenly spring into resplendent costumes
fit for a wedding. The film ends with a close-up of the *prajapati* (butterfly)
design on the floor of the King's concert chamber, which, as every Indian
knows, symbolises marriage.

The trick effects are not all they might be, especially as compared
with technical developments since 1968/69 in the West. Ray is the
first to agree to this. But they seem of marginal significance in assessing
the film's imaginative vitality. This is at its most intense in the Dance of
the Ghosts, a 6½-minute sequence which Ray described in two letters
at the time of shooting as 'a most abstract, avant-garde affair which I haven't
the faintest idea how people are going to react to' – 'It is surely the most
striking thing ever done in cinematic choreography.' Given a knowledge of

the history of Bengal and of south Indian percussion-playing, as well as a fine appreciation of human and camera movement, Ray is probably right.

From early on he decided to dispense with certain conventions about Bengali ghosts: that their ears are like those of an elephant, their teeth like long radishes and so on. He felt that these, and the conventional ghost-dance, would lack the right impact on the screen. Since Upendrakisore's story gave no clues he decided to invent a completely fresh dance. He settled on four classes of ghost because 'since we have so many class divisions the ghosts would have the same.' These came to be kings and warriors, sahibs, fat people (like pundits, padres and lawyers), and the common people – no doubt a significant number to choose, given the four basic castes in Hinduism. As for the music, he felt it should have 'some order, form and precision' and not be just 'a woolly formless kind of thing'. With the idea of four classes in mind, he now happened to remember a south Indian classical form he had once heard live at the Delhi Film Festival. It uses only percussion instruments – twelve in all, of which Ray selected four. He deliberately avoided melody 'because melody suggests a kind of sophistication'; he wanted only rhythm. The kings and warriors got the *mridangam*, a drum like a *tabla*, because this is regarded as a classical instrument. The sahibs got the *ghattom*, a kind of rice-pot which makes a sort of stiff clatter suited to their buttoned-up appearance. The fat people got the *mursring*, a comical folk-instrument rather like the sweet-seller's accompaniment in *Pather Panchali*. Finally, the common people got the *ganjira*, a drum similar to that played by Bagha.

Each class, except for the sahibs, is played by actors dressed and made-up according to their social position. The sahibs are shadow-puppets which were undercranked at sixteen frames per second for a wooden, mechanical effect. The dance begins with each class introducing itself, to the sound of its characteristic instrument, while making its characteristic movement. Negative printing and an effect that makes the image shimmer are sometimes applied. Thereafter, through a long series of mesmerising visual and aural cuts, the classes oscillate to a faster and faster tempo as their percussive accompaniment speeds up. It is clear that a conflict is in the offing, which appears to be mainly internal, rather than between classes – a corpulent padre gesticulates at a pundit with a book, obviously the Bible or some tract; a sahib rudely dismisses a hookah brought by his servant – the kind of behaviour increasingly prevalent among the British in Bengal following the initial phase of 'Indianisation'. Eventually, as the percussion reaches a frenzy, swords are brandished and each quarrelsome class does itself in. But in the final scene – a sort of coda – the four classes are again seen dancing, this time in four layers one above the other, a bit like the remarkable rhythmic layers of figures sculpted on the outside of the great Sun Temple at Konarak that Ray sketched just after leaving Santiniketan. Music is able to restore the harmony of ghosts, even if humans will insist on fighting, killing and dying.

All this, and the indescribable camerawork and cutting, was the outcome of much solitary pondering. Satyajit would have discussed it with his son, as he does such matters now, but in 1968 Sandip was only fourteen. Once he was clear in his own mind, Satyajit set about looking for a choreographer. 'He and I sat down and worked it out and he got hold of his own group of dancers, the same group that performed each time with different make-up and costumes,' explains Ray. He admits that there can be few children able to grasp the total concept of the dance, but he feels that this does not matter. The majority will respond as he did as a child when his grand-uncle used to read to him from the *Mahabharata*. 'The story it tells is definitely an adult story,' Ray says of the dance, 'but children enjoy it for the dancing and all the things that happen. A child might ask, "Why four ghosts?" and parents may then explain – I don't know how.'

The Kingdom of Diamonds, made about ten years after *Goopy and Bagha*, contains nothing quite as visually striking as the Dance of the Ghosts. Although the second film too required magnificent sets and costumes, allowing Ray scope to apply colour as he wished, its ingenuity and originality lie more in its dialogues and songs than in its appearance. It is a more serious-minded, sombre film than its predecessor, as Ray agrees. 'I was definitely using more ideas in it than in *Goopy Gyne*. That was more a straightforward narrative of very funny and exciting things happening to those two characters. Whereas in *Hirak Rajar Dese* the King becomes very important, and so do the courtiers and the scientist, and there are definite ideas expressed through their actions and words: adult ideas, perhaps, but still comprehensible to a child. Brainwashing for instance: this is a contemporary idea incorporated into their heads.'

Most Indians sensed the political content of the film behind the fantasy; to Utpal Dutta, the Marxist producer, playwright and actor who played the King, the film was 'out-and-out political'. For once, despite his aversion for labels and politics, Ray himself does not demur at the notion. He is willing to associate the scene in the film in which the King's soldiers drive away all the poor people so that visitors will not see them, with the bulldozing of the slums in Delhi and other cities during Indira Gandhi's 1975–7 Emergency. 'In a fantasy one can be forthright,' he observes, 'but if you're dealing with contemporary characters, you can be articulate only up to a point because of censorship. You simply cannot attack the party in power.' When Bangladesh television showed *The Kingdom of Diamonds* in 1981, the words of its main songs appeared all over the walls of Dhaka.

Goopy and Bagha still have their *joie de vivre* but, like their creator, they are older and less carefree. After a lively duet as the titles roll, in which they introduce themselves through song to those who have not yet met them, they are discovered reclining in the lap of luxury

in the palace as favoured sons-in-law. It is apparent that they have not
done much since they sorted out the little problem at Halla ten years
previously. Suddenly Bagha can take it no more.

Bagha: Ten years spent in slothful bliss – we can't go on like this.
Goopy: How true! There must be something we can do.
Bagha: Time takes its toll and spares none.
Goopy: And what it does can never be undone.
Bagha: Today's sapling is tomorrow's withered oak.
Goopy: Tiny tadpoles turn to frogs that croak.
Bagha: Tots who crawl about today,
          Grow bent with time's decay.
Goopy: The hand that holds a walking-stick,
          Once held a lollipop to lick.
Bagha: Those who slick and comb their hair,
          Will one day be in despair.
Goopy: Because the hair won't stay!
Bagha: The few that's left will all turn grey.
          And how ruthless!
          That age should make one toothless.
Goopy: And what a blight, to be robbed of your sight!
Bagha: No Goopy, this won't do.
          It's most remiss.
          To waste one's time like this.

'The dialogue in this film is almost untranslatable; for one thing it's got
end rhymes,' comments Ray. 'I've done the songs in rhymed translations,
but I couldn't manage to translate the dialogues. The problem is that
there are two different kinds of dialogue in the film: one in which the
King and his ministers speak – very formal, rhymed kind of speech, very
artificial; and another kind of speech that ordinary people like the miners
or the peasants use, which, is naturalistic . . . Now, I couldn't differentiate
between the two in translation: it was impossible.' As an example of Ray's
difficulties, take 'And how ruthless!/that age should make one toothless.'
The original reads '*Datgulo sab haowa!/Kyamane habe mangsa khaowa?*',
which literally translated is 'Teeth all gone with the wind!/How will meat
be eaten?' Other dialogues refer to habits, proverbs, animals and so on with
no equivalents in English, quite apart from including literary, religious and
other allusions to Bengali life.

Ray constructs an important plot motif out of rhymes. The evil
King of the land where diamonds are mined, to which Goopy and Bagha
find themselves invited to give a concert performance, keeps a tame Poet
Laureate (dressed in the garb of the Santiniketan degree – Ray's sly dig
at his alma mater). When the King's scientist-wizard informs him that he
has invented a method of brainwashing the royal subjects, the King orders

the Poet Laureate to produce rhyming verses that can be implanted in his subjects' minds, such as,

> To keep my taxes pending,
> Means trouble never-ending.

and

> Miners must be underfed.
> Miners fat are miners dead.

These loyal sayings have a habit of popping up and embarrassing the King at the wrong moment, such as when a brainwashed peasant wanders into a concert gathering and has to be hustled out by palace guards.

Goopy and Bagha are of course soon involved with the opposition to the King, led by the school-teacher (played by Soumitra Chatterjee) whose school has been closed down by the Minister of Education because it encourages questioning minds – a scene with quite as much bite in it as anything in Orwell's *1984*. He has gone underground, so to speak, into the mountains and forests, and the diamond mines, from where he arranges attacks on the King's position. One of his former pupils knocks the nose off a huge statue of the King with a catapult, for instance, under the King's own nose – just as the statue is being unveiled. Eventually it falls to Goopy and Bagha to raid the royal treasury for diamonds to bribe the King's soldiers. Using the slippers, they get past the guard but are confronted by a tigress in charge of the key. In order to reach it, Bagha has to stretch over her, while an equally terrified Goopy has to keep her enchanted with a song sung in an ornate, completely classical style to 'enhance the comedy' (Ray's words) in which Goopy begs Bagha to get a move on. 'If I die it'll be for a Satyajit Ray film!' was Rabi Ghosh's thought at the point of bending over, he says. The tigress had its mouth sewn up, but there were its claws to consider and the sedative was unpredictable in effect. While Ray was in darkness just behind the cage shooting over the tigress's shoulder towards Goopy and Bagha in bright light, she suddenly turned round and smacked at the cage wall. 'We stopped shooting for a while,' says Ray. 'But then we went on and took every shot we'd planned. That's why the scene cut so well.'

The last few scenes of the film – in which Goopy and Bagha give a musical reprimand to the King for his evil-doings and he and his ministers are put into the scientist-wizard's brainwashing machine and come out keen to join the people in pulling down the King's statue – are not entirely successful. The solution is too pat. Perhaps its real weakness can be traced to Ray's affection for baroque machines that owes more to an earlier generation of science fantasy like Jules Verne, than, say, Arthur C. Clarke. The brainwashing machine and the scientist-wizard are, despite some amusing and interesting touches, a bit of a bore. All is redeemed though by the last scene of all. Goopy and Bagha stride along, heading out of the now-happy kingdom, their voices joyously raised in a kind of reprise of their opening song.

Would Ray like to make a third film, completing a Goopy and Bagha trilogy? He constantly gets letters from children asking for more of them. 'Well, at the end of the last song in *Hirak Rajar Dese* they say "We'll come back." All you have to do is to let us know at Shundi where we'll be staying. And children loved that. These are very difficult films to make. Whether I'll be up to it physically I don't know. With the help of my son and if I get another idea . . .' says Satyajit reflectively. 'It would use the elements of science fiction and children being made to work. Child labour, and these two chaps rescuing, and love interest – a prince and a princess.'

18

Days and Nights in the Forest
(Aranyer Din Ratri) 1969

D AYS *and Nights in the Forest* was a complete change after Goopy and Bagha. It follows four young men away from Calcutta on a spree. This is how Ray conceived their characters in his shooting notebook, before writing the script of the film:

Asim: the wealthiest of the four. Had once had a conscience about his affluence and even done some politics – but is now part of the establishment – with a safe job. Has a way with girls – is confident about them – and has had some conquests to his credit. But remains a bachelor. Is a bit of an intellectual with leanings towards poetry. Likes to dress well – is conscious of it. Has no time for anything except light magazines now. Smokes good cigarettes. For him the reasons for the journey are: 1. to try out his new car, 2. to be irresponsible in the company of his friends (security means he feels the effects of the rat race).

Sanjoy: had once the same political leanings as Asim. Retains more of his values than Asim, but is essentially timid and therefore prone to compromise. Is shy with girls. Has a scholarly turn of mind. Is knowledgeable about many things. Aspires to an easy life, and has an eye for pretty girls but is not adventurous about sex. Probably will eventually have an arranged marriage. His reasons for the journey: 1. he is a true lover of places, 2. he needs relaxation from the cares of his work.

Hari: essentially a sportsman. Not intellectual. Has an easy boyish charm which some girls might find irresistible. With the right girl of his class he might even make a good and lasting match – because he is essentially good. He has a feeling of inferiority which he hides beneath a glum exterior. Reason for the journey: the girl he wants to forget about.

Sekhar: a hedonist, happy-go-lucky, witty, more frustrated [sic] (although he will very easily strike a pose of frustration), a dabbler in many things, apparently adventurous but really a bit of a conservative. With six more inches to his height he could be a ladies' man. As it is, he can make quick friendships with them, advise them on their affairs, and hold their hands (which he does frequently) on the pretext of a handshake. He is apparently content with the role he plays and we needn't concern ourselves with what goes on beneath the surface. Reasons for the journey: his friends want him for the tonic effects of his company.

The place that the four of them are heading for in Asim's car, is ideally suited to the adventure they want. Palamau, a forest area of Bihar several hundred miles from Calcutta, has an untamed wildness about it. They know it from a classic account entitled *Palamau*, published around 1880. Its author is Bankim Chandra Chatterjee's elder brother, Sanjiv Chatterjee, who was a sort of forest officer there and came to know its tribal inhabitants, the independent-minded Santhals, very well. As the place of first encounter with tribal India by a modern Bengali in Bengali literature, it made a deep impression on the Bengali imagination – something like the effect of the Wild West in north America.

The member of the group most aware of this is Sanjoy. As the car speeds along in the opening shots of the film he reads passages from *Palamau* to his friends: 'Bengalis are so accustomed to the plains that even a mere hillock delights them.' 'Men and women drink together in Palamau, but I've never seen a local woman drunk, although the men are often completely intoxicated.' 'The woman are dark-skinned, and all young. They are scantily dressed and naked from the waist up.' The interest of the car's occupants is decidedly aroused.

Setting the whole film in Palamau – and indeed shooting it there (in the early and middle months of 1969) – was typical of Ray's approach to *Aranyer Din Ratri*, a novel by Sunil Ganguli whose film rights he bought simply on the strength of an outline in a Bengali magazine advertisement. Neither Chatterjee's book nor the place plays any part in the original novel. 'I discovered the parallels while reading Sanjiv Chatterjee and thought it would go very well,' says Ray. He also altered Ganguli's foursome; instead of being unemployed and travelling ticketless by train, three of them have jobs and one a car. Their hangups are basically those of the established middle-class in Calcutta, not of rowdy vagabonds. Out of this group Ray went on to create what was virtually an original screenplay, but *en route* to it he had several sessions with Ganguli, who was touched to see that Ray had almost the whole novel by heart. 'He was asking me the background of those boys and details like where did they meet in Howrah Station? At that time he was thinking of a railway station, not a car. And which part of Calcutta they're from? Did they travel by taxi or tram-car? And what was the season in the forest?'

When Ganguli saw the finished film he was rather taken aback. He had not expected such enormous changes. 'I felt that I didn't know these characters.' But he liked the film even so. Ray well understands his feelings about it: 'Days and Nights was based on his personal experiences,' he points out. 'Sunil didn't resent the film's changes – but he was sad about them.' Others are more critical. Dhritiman Chatterjee, who played a character somewhat comparable to Asim and Sanjoy in Ray's next film, The Adversary, thinks that the relationships in the novel are 'far more complex' than in the film. 'They're cruder people in the novel, more confused. That confusion doesn't come through.' Ray has chosen to refine them, to bring them closer to people he himself knows – with the exception of the Santhal girl to whom Hari, the sportsman, makes love.

Soumitra Chatterjee, who plays Asim, admits to a certain distaste for the film's content, while retaining great admiration for its style. Ray is 'making an attempt to understand this new generation who live in nothingness, who drift in a vacuum,' according to Chatterjee, 'who could spend endless film time asking the question whether to shave or not in the morning. They are nowhere people.' His sympathies lie more with Ganguli's characters, who he feels retain some idealism – or with a character like Asok, the penniless graduate in Kanchenjungha. 'He's a better person, and he's so recognisable,' says Chatterjee. 'He's a very typical general middle-class young man. But these characters [in Days and Nights] are not so much – they are just drifting.' This is, in a sense, Apu talking, the voice of many Bengalis who dislike the increasing individualism and materialism of modern Bengal, the concomitants of 'westernisation', as they see it. For them, the characters of this film have slipped from some hypothetical standard of Bengaliness; they are not true Bengalis. 'People who read Tagore and believe in Tagore's culture don't want to accept these values,' explains Ganguli.

For Ray's western audience this aversion is not a stumbling-block. The young man who has everything but lacks something in his life, is as thoroughly familiar as the idea of a few days in the country to get away from it all. To western critics the film seemed almost European in attitude and they reacted accordingly. David Robinson wrote that 'every word and gesture is recognisable, comprehensible, true . . . Ray's work at its best, like this, has an extraordinary rightness in every aspect of its selection and presentation – the timing, performance, cutting, music – which seem to place it beyond discussion.' While Penelope Houston thought the film 'lucid, ironic and superlatively graceful . . . On the surface, we're watching the casual, unstressed flow of life; actually there isn't an incident or a character . . . whose role isn't functional.'

On the other side of the Atlantic, the New York Times described the film as a 'rare, wistful movie that somehow proves it's good to be alive', and Pauline Kael felt that 'Satyajit Ray's films can give rise to a more complex feeling of happiness in me than the work of any other director . . . No artist has done more than Ray to make us reevaluate [sic] the commonplace.' But the critic of the Village Voice, William Paul, had a completely opposite response; every frame of Ray's analysis of Calcutta mores seemed to grate upon the nerves of this member of the Manhattan intelligentsia. 'Days and Nights', he wrote, 'seems anachronistically the ideal art-house film of the 50s: vaguely humanistic without any feeling for the complexities of human life, pretentious, short on plot but striving to be long on character, stylistically awkward as a sign of sincere emotions, and all of it held together by a title that is more poetic than anything in the movie itself.'

Both the admirers and the detractors in the West were convinced that the film was transparent to them. They seemed unaware that many of its 'words and gestures' might conceal an unfamiliar world. If Ray sometimes seems half-baked, it is because he is only half-perceived. 'I think Days and Nights is really a Bengali film,' he says. 'I wasn't so conscious of the fact [when I was making it] that westerners would fairly easily identify with it. I thought it was a very Bengali film.'

A persistent belief of western critics, for instance, is that the film's characters speak English with their Bengali because their minds have been culturally colonised. To one British critic they are 'victims of the departed Raj', and to Pauline Kael, Sekhar is 'a joke the British left behind . . . who drops pidgin-English phrases into the conversation as if they were golden wit.' A third critic (British) imagined that the characters are like 'snobbish late Victorian Englishmen peppering their talk with French words.' Such comments do not grasp the subtlety of the interaction between Bengali and English, which is as complex and irreducible to stereotypes as the influence of the West as a whole on Bengal. The fact that Ray can speak and write Bengali and English better than most Bengalis and Englishmen does not prevent him from employing an English phrase or sentence in the middle of a Bengali conversation if it expresses his meaning or tone more precisely. With him, and other genuinely cultured Bengalis, access to English means an extension of communication, not the emasculation of their mother-tongue. Often English offers the only way to capture a social nuance that has arisen from the impact of western mores on Bengali society. Why is Asim overheard saying in English 'Thank God for corruption', as he bribes the caretaker (chowkidar) of the bungalow on arrival? 'In Bengali it wouldn't sound so clipped and precise,' says Ray. 'Somehow it works better in English.' Then he reflects for a moment. 'Oh, of course he had to say it in English so that the chowkidar wouldn't know what he was saying.' I am not suggesting here that the idea of corruption is a western import, only that it acquired a special flavour with the arrival of the British. If the viewer is conscious of the East India Company's dirty doings, Asim's remark acquires an extra layer of meaning, with echoes that are magnified by the setting in which it is spoken – the compound of a forest rest-house, of the kind once used by supposedly incorruptible British officials on their tours of duty. The reverberation it sets up at the beginning lasts right through to the end of the film.

An overall quality of composedness is an aspect of Days and Nights that immediately strikes a western viewer and does not mislead him, unlike its English dialogue. It is not so marked as in *Kanchenjungha*, but still very considerable. Again, there is an ensemble at its centre and an intricate pattern of relationships, and once more this seemed to confuse the Bengali audience on release of the film. 'I think they [Bengalis] liked to identify with one single character, and follow his development and his relationships with the girl or whatever,' remarks Ray. *Days and Nights* has a structure and mood that can only be described as musical, and, once again, Mozart springs to mind. With its unobtrusive patterning of motifs, its wonderful range of voices and, most of all, its capacity to be serious by being humorous, the film defies total analysis. 'The first half has the appearance of light comedy,' wrote Ray to Seton while tackling the screenplay, 'but there's a steady modulation to a serious key.' What started as a spree ends up changing the lives of three out of four of the group – all except Sekhar.

The agent of this change is of course female – in the shape of two Calcutta ladies, Aparna and Jaya, on holiday at their Palamau cottage, and a Santhal girl from the village nearby. But first, Ray brilliantly sets the scene among the males, with an eye for insignificant details which acquire significance later that strongly recalls his comments to Chandragupta nearly twenty years before:

> the conventional approach tells you that the best way to tell a story is to leave out all except those elements which are directly related to the story, while the master's work clearly indicates that if your theme is strong and simple, then you can include a hundred apparently irrelevant details which, instead of obscuring the theme, only help to intensify it by contrast, and in addition create the illusion of actuality better.

The theme of *Days and Nights* might be said to be the way in which urban living cuts us off from each other and from our true environment and blunts our moral sense, though it is never stated as openly as that. Everything, from the young men's lack of interest in the sick wife of the *chowkidar* and their inability to appreciate the forest and the sunset except in terms of *Tarzan* and old Burt Lancaster movies, to their excruciating embarrassment at being caught bathing in their shorts by the ladies, serves to develop this theme, even though very little of it is 'plot' in the conventional sense. The constant intercutting of scenes of Santhal women walking gracefully along, dancing and singing, are a rhythmic counterpoint to further intensify our awareness of the city people's artificial behaviour. They are like the young Santhal girls who once stood watching Satyajit's art teacher Binode Bihari Mukherjee at Santiniketan and pointed out the missing element in his painting of buffaloes.

The way that the relationship develops between the men and the two 'Brahmo' ladies from Calcutta is masterfully managed. The men spend their first night getting drunk at the local liquor shop, where Rabi first sets eyes on the Santhal girl he fancies. The following morning, while they are considering whether to shave or not and how to get hold of eggs for breakfast, Sekhar spots 'sari and slacks' through the bungalow window, and the search is on. By asking in the bazaar they locate the house of the Calcutta people and pluck up the courage to introduce themselves to the family. Asim is immediately interested in Aparna (Sarmila Tagore), a cool, reticent girl whose widowed father jokes that he never knows what she is thinking. Sanjoy is attracted to Jaya (Kaveri Bose), Aparna's sister-in-law, a young and vivacious widow with a small son. Hari has already fallen for the Santhal girl they met at the liquor shop. Only Sekhar has no particular ambitions to pair off.

At this first meeting Asim is fairly patronising. He insists that Aparna show him her retreat near the house, examines her record collection and furnishings, asks her some personal questions and declares that he 'can't quite make her out.' He is not used to women with minds of their own, and she begins to intrigue him. This makes it all the more mortifying when, the next time he meets her, he is half-naked and covered in soap by the well at the rest-house. She is in the family car which has appeared unexpectedly to return the wallet that Hari dropped at their house earlier on. 'So *kind* of you,' says Sekhar in his very best English, grinning idiotically, and adds, 'Have a nice trip!' When the car has gone he tells his friends triumphantly in Bengali, 'I handled that with English aplomb.' ('*Dekhli kirakham par par correct ingreji ballam,*' or literally – 'Look at the way I spoke all that correct English.') But Asim knows better; he feels that he has blown his chances with Aparna for good.

His third encounter with her, were he but aware of it, would have made him squirm even more. That night they get drunk again and, staggering back, do 'Tribal Twist' on the dark forest road, refusing to budge when a car comes along and honks its horn. 'Do you know who we are?' shouts Asim, lurching into its headlights. 'VIPs – Ve-ry Impor-tant Pee-pul!' Inside the car of course are Aparna and Jaya, highly amused at the sight of these four clowns. In the novel they were all naked, but Ray baulked at this. 'Ray asked me several times how he could handle that scene,' says Ganguli with a laugh. 'I told him "Why don't you? What is the harm? Censor won't object because they're male." He gave it thought . . . but it's not in accordance with his style.' If he had been asked to go nude, Soumitra Chatterjee says he would probably have refused anyway.

The following day, when the group arrives to apologise for oversleeping and missing breakfast, Aparna does not let on about what she saw in the headlights; she saves that up for the end. After they have thanked Jaya for leaving some eggs outside the bungalow, Aparna contents herself with a mischievous joke about the forgotten wallet. She hopes that Hari remembered to check its contents after it was returned the previous day? He did, mumbles Hari politely without thinking, and then they all laugh together as the implications sink in. It is obvious that Aparna has very much the upper hand over the group when she wants it. That afternoon her hand is further strengthened with the arrival of the two ladies at the rest-house for a picnic. They come in the nick of time: the visiting official in charge of the rest-house is about to eject the four for staying there without a booking, but plainly he cannot do so if they are friends of the ladies, whom he knows. From being incorruptible, he quickly descends to being cooperative. 'Thank God for corruption,' the four men no doubt reflect, but this time to themselves.

The game that the six of them now play, sitting in a circle under the trees by the rest-house, is a scene of which Ray is rightly proud. It makes use of the fullest scale of possibilities for psychological probing through acting, dialogue and editing. Nothing much happens on the surface, but underneath are turbulent emotions. Each person present has to add the name of someone famous to a chain of such names, after rehearsing the chain so far. If he forgets a name, he is out. Their choices reflect their personalities: Jaya chooses Rabindranath, Aparna Cleopatra, Sekhar Atulya Ghosh (a well-known party boss in the Bengal Congress), Hari Helen of Troy, Sanjoy Mao Tse-tung, Asim Shakespeare. The mixture is cosmopolitan and can be fully appreciated only by a Bengali as it develops. Soon, Asim and Aparna are the only ones playing; but after a little while she simply gives up and lets him win.

They decide to get up and visit a local fair, and the mood changes from playful to pensive, rather as it does in *Charulata* after Amal admits to Charu that his encouragement of her writing stems from Bhupati. The ensemble divides up: Hari to the forest with the Santhal girl, Sekhar to gamble at the fair, Sanjoy to walk with Jaya, and Asim to walk with Aparna. Each of the men, Sekhar excepted, now experiences a moment of epiphany, rather like the characters in *Kanchenjungha*. Hari makes love to Duli, the Santhal girl, and promises to help her come to Calcutta. As a prank she takes his wallet – which he had earlier dropped and accused a servant of stealing – but gives it back to him. On the way out of the forest he loses it once more, this time for good, after being badly clubbed by the same resentful servant who has followed him. Sanjoy is invited into the cottage by Jaya for a cup of coffee. He sits waiting for her while her coffee gets cold. Suddenly she reappears, dressed in startling Santhal jewellery she has bought at the fair. She has decked herself out as seductively as she can. 'Are you nervous?' she asks him softly. 'No,' he replies, his face shining with sweat. 'I am' – and she places his hand over her heart to show him how much. He lacks the courage to make the next move. 'It's meant to come as a surprise,' says Ray, 'but the kind of surprise that one feels is justified and logical,' he continues, laughing. 'There you have the middle-class behaviour of the boy. Typical values – timid – whereas she was very bold and forthright.' Kaveri Bose here is extraordinarily compelling and entirely in keeping with the frankness of her character in the film until this point and with the hints she has given of her loneliness. In fact, she, and Rabi Ghosh as Sekhar, give the two best performances in the film.

Asim's conversation with Aparna does not carry quite the same conviction. In it his humiliation is complete, when she reveals that she has even seen him doing 'Tribal Twist' in the forest. 'I still cannot make you out,' he tells her, and this finally prompts her own confession: her brother, Jaya's husband, committed suicide while in Britain, and her mother was burnt to death when Aparna was only twelve. 'You've never faced any great sorrow in your life, have you?' she tells Asim quietly. Whereas Jaya's wild outburst of passion was indeed 'justified and logical', Aparna's revelation comes with a jolt, like the optimistic ending of *Mahanagar*. The problem lies not with the screenplay but with Sarmila Tagore's portrayal of Aparna: her one-upmanship, her fashionable hairdo and clothes and her manner of speaking, which owes something to Bombay-coy, just are not psychologically consistent with a girl who nurses these twin sources of grief. In a film less finely tuned than *Days and Nights in the Forest*, this would hardly interfere, but it is definitely a weakness by Ray's standards, particularly as he regards Aparna as the character 'you are supposed to sympathise with.'

Here, the critic in the *Village Voice* quoted above may even have a point when he complains that 'Ray's women in *Days and Nights* are creatures of superior moral sensibility and his men all helpless children', and requires 'some critical distance from this disastrous spiritual inequality of the sexes.' As Ray would readily agree, he does take that view of women overall (though not of men), based on his experience of them, especially perhaps his mother. He feels that 'some balancing element was needed' – given women's comparative weakness physically – 'so Nature made them that way.' But in Aparna, unlike Charu (or Aditi of *Nayak*, for that matter), Ray goes a little too far; as well as appearing sensitive and mature, Aparna seems slightly supercilious and vain about her superiority.

The conclusion of the film is perfect however. The foursome depart as they arrived three days earlier, in Asim's car, and yet they are different, less jaunty. Asim's self-confidence has been undermined, but the future holds the promise of love. Sanjoy too has lost confidence and will probably now marry his boss's daughter, in recognition of his failure to take the initiative with Jaya. Hari, heavily bandaged, has found his casual attitude to women that made him come on the trip in the first place, given rather a shaking. Only Sekhar – 'the little India-rubber man of the party' (in Penelope Houston's amusing phrase) – is unfazed. As usual, he is more interested in the present than the past or the future. The *chowkidar* has just handed him a box that was left for them by the ever-practical Jaya early that morning; untying it and opening it, he cries out gleefully 'Eggs!' He holds one up – a suitably ambiguous symbol of their relationship with Palamau – the car moves out of the rest-house, and the anxious, tainted *chowkidar* quickly moves to shut the gate behind them.

19

The Calcutta Trilogy:
The Adversary (Pratidwandi) 1970
Company Limited (Seemabaddha) 1971
The Middle Man (Jana Aranya) 1975

··➤➤[◎░◎]◀··

THE three films that Ray made in the 1970s about contemporary Calcutta life were not intended by him as a trilogy, but they cohere well when seen together. They all depict, through the world of work, the stress of Calcutta living on young educated men at a time when this had never been more intense: the rise of revolutionary terrorism and massive government repression, followed by the Bangladesh war and refugee crisis, corruption and nationwide Emergency, leading eventually to the emergence of the Communist government that ruled Bengal in the 1980s. In *The Adversary* (1970) Siddhartha desperately searches for a job without success; in *Company Limited* (1971) Syamalendu has a safe job and wants promotion; and in *The Middle Man* (1975) Somnath creates his own business. From each one of them Calcutta exacts its toll.

By the mid-1960s the city had changed very substantially from the one in which Satyajit grew up. First there had been the effects of the war and the Famine, then riots, the loss of East Bengal to Pakistan at Partition and an influx of refugees, followed by the gradual rundown of the city as a port and industrial base, and as a centre of political power in relation to New Delhi, which was accelerated by the death of the Congress Chief Minister B.C. Roy (*Pather Panchali*'s backer) in 1962. By 1966 an economic crisis was ready to boil over. In March a food movement led to raids on grain shops and many deaths through police firings, followed by widespread strikes and student unrest. The Communists had already captured the students' union at Presidency College (where three generations of Rays had studied), and the college was soon drawn into the conflict; on 8 December Calcutta University had to close for the first time in its 110 years of existence.

The following February, a United Front government came to power in Bengal, the first non-Congress government in the state since Independence. It was dominated by India's two Communist parties, the pro-Moscow CPI and the CPI (Marxist), in coalition with a breakaway group from the Congress. Expectations of reform were aroused both in the rural areas and in the towns and cities. Two and a half months later, the first clash between peasants and the Government took place, when a policeman was killed, followed by the shooting of nine villagers by the police. It occurred in Naxalbari, the district connecting the northern tip of West Bengal (which includes Darjeeling) with the rest of the State; bounded on the west by Nepal and on the east by East Pakistan (as it then was), Naxalbari provided a perfect base for an insurrectionary movement, especially as it was close to China. It was to give its name to a new word in the vocabulary of revolution – 'Naxalite'.

The main leader of the movement was Charu Majumdar, the educated son of a landlord from the same region of Bengal as Naxalbari, who had been a member of the CPI since 1938. During the 1960s he identified himself with the Chinese and left the pro-Moscow CPI when it split in 1964, joining the CPI(M). At the end of 1967 he was expelled and became the effective leader of an attempt to overthrow the Government by armed struggle, which fast became known as the Naxalite movement. His slogans – including the notorious 'China's Chairman is Our Chairman' – littered the walls of Calcutta from 1967 onwards, forming a threatening backdrop to *The Adversary*.

The United Front had imprisoned some of the Naxalite leaders (though not Majumdar) in 1967, but in February 1969, on being re-elected to office, they released them. On 22 April, the anniversary of Lenin's birth, the Naxalite leaders set up the CPI (Marxist-Leninist) with Charu Majumdar as General Secretary, in opposition to the CPI(M), whose main leader was Jyoti Basu (Chief Minister of West Bengal in the late 1970s and 1980s). Its formation was announced on May Day 1969 at one of the vast political meetings on the Maidan (Calcutta's equivalent of London's Hyde Park) in which the city specialises. (In *The Adversary*, Ray conveys the atmosphere unforgettably from the top of the tallest building in Calcutta.)

Throughout the rest of 1969 the movement gained strength and unrest spread in the rural areas. It did not seriously impinge on Calcutta itself until early 1970. 'In the posh areas of Park Street and Chowringhee,' writes Sumanta Banerjee (younger brother of Ray's ex-advertising colleague Subrata) in his study of the Naxalites:

> gathered all the gaiety and frivolity of the city. Swanky business executives and thriving journalists, film stars and art critics, smugglers and touts, chic society dames and jet-set teenagers thronged the bars and discotheques. All mention of the rural uprising in these crowds was considered in distinctly bad taste, although the term 'Naxalite' had assumed an aura of the exotic and was being used to dramatise all sorts of sensationalism in these circles – ranging from good-natured Bohemianism to Hippy-style pot sessions.

Many of those who became Naxalites at this time – like the younger brother of the protagonist in *The Adversary* – were from Calcutta and came from well-educated, comparatively prosperous families. They were generally students in their late teens and early twenties, without experience of politics. Mostly, they were driven by ideology, like others of their age all over the world then, rather than by their failure to find employment; they were too young to have experienced much of that.

In the early months of 1970 – as Ray got ready to shoot – at Majumdar's call Naxalites began killing policemen and police informers in broad daylight in the city streets. By October, twenty-five police employees had died and 350 been injured. The police were caught off their guard, particularly as the sympathy of the public was often with the attackers, such was the accumulated hostility towards the police. But by September, when an anti-terrorism law enacted by the British was invoked, the police were ready to take reprisals. For the next year or so Calcutta became an urban guerrilla battleground, between the police and the Naxalites, the Naxalites and the CPI(M), one Naxalite faction and another, and criminal elements in all groups. In addition, the Naxalites broadened their target to include small businessmen, government officials and college teachers (including a vice-chancellor); but such obvious targets as private schools, clubs, bars and restaurants were, somewhat surprisingly, left alone.

The police retaliation was truly fearful. Localities in the city were cordoned off by the Army for 'combing operations', often for twenty-four hours at a time. CPI(M-L) members, or suspected members, were simply shot dead on being caught, or beaten to death in prison vans. In February 1971, five boys were shot dead in front of their parents. On 12 August, a hundred young people from one locality were dragged out by police with the help of hired hoodlums, and slaughtered; their bodies were later thrown into a nearby canal. Police sources give the number of CPI(M-L) members and supporters killed between March 1970 and August 1971 as 1783, which according to unofficial sources should be at least doubled, writes Sumanta Banerjee. And this does not include the numbers killed inside jails by police firing on unarmed prisoners. For the rest of Calcutta, whose citizens learnt to raise their arms when crossing the street almost by reflex, 'those months of 1971 were to remain scalded on the memory', says Banerjee.

> Clumps of heavy, brutish-faced men, whose hips bulged with hidden revolvers or daggers, and whose little eyes looked mingled with ferocity and servility like bulldogs, prowled the street corners. Police informers, scabs, professional assassins, and various other sorts of bodyguard of private property stalked around bullying the citizens. Streets were littered with bodies of young men riddled with bullets.

By the end of the year the movement had spent itself, and Calcutta had received a further influx of refugees fleeing from even more terrible massacres by the soldiers of West Pakistan, as the new country of Bangladesh was born. Politically, the initiative lay with the Congress

Party again because the CPI(M) had forfeited much of its support in its bloody internecine struggles with the CPI(M-L). The Government began handing out sops to erstwhile Naxalites in the form of temporary jobs and financial inducements, and it resuscitated the battered educational system, which the Naxalites had wanted swept away. But instead of using the opportunity for reform, the politicians actively encouraged mass-copying in examinations to recruit new supporters; invigilators who tried to intervene were assaulted. The Calcutta University authorities consequently cancelled a large proportion of the examinations. 'Corruption of the youth appeared to be the corner-stone of the Congress urban strategy', comments Banerjee. 'An entire generation of young people was thus gradually depraved, made susceptible to bribery and other forms of corruption, and denuded of all idealism, reduced to prematurely old cynics irresponsibly pursuing their own selfish ends. They raised the spectre of an ignorant uninformed group of drop-outs, incompetent to deal with society's real evils, and with too many stakes in the corrupt social system to rebel against it.'

This situation and its causes are the territory explored by Ray in the Calcutta Trilogy. His general perspective is one of sympathy for those trying to change post-Independence Bengali society, but not for their violent methods. Politically he has always leaned to the Left but never joined a party. 'Manik's far too much of an individualist to be a Communist,' says his cousin Nini. In 1962, for instance, during India's war with China, he refused to join in the chorus of condemnation of the Chinese, despite his admiration for Nehru as a man; 'the last few weeks have been fraught with all manner of doubts, despondency etc.', he wrote to Seton, and the novelist V.S. Naipaul, who visited at this time, remembers him as virtually incommunicado. (Invited to make an anti-Chinese documentary, Ray apparently remarked to someone with grim humour that he would consider it, *if* a Chinese dead body could be produced for him.)

Ray rarely mounts a public platform in support of a cause but in 1966 he agreed to lead a huge silent procession in protest at the Government's imprisonment of demonstrators without trial during the food movement, when many others were afraid to speak out. 'At every such moment you can rely on him to do the right thing, without rhetoric. This is something I find admirable. He needn't do it', says Utpal Dutta, who owes his own release from prison around that time to Ray's reluctant intervention with Mrs Gandhi. (This was so that Dutta could take up his role in James Ivory's *The Guru* as planned.) The effect was 'electric', says Dutta; the next day the Communists set up huge hoardings with Ray's name and appeal printed on them. 'One may say that the ruling party lost a lot of its support because Ray had decided to hit', says Dutta. Around this time he also agreed to take part in a rally against the Vietnam War and to read out an international appeal. Ray says he would not have gone along, given the choice. 'I would probably have stayed at home, because I'm built differently. But there were so many of my friends involved, I said "All right. I'll come." I believed in what was being done. I wasn't merely assuming an attitude. It's not that. But it is just not me. I don't like taking part in public rallies. I'm very much a private person.'

Like many thoughtful Bengalis, he welcomed the election of the United Front in February 1967, believing that whatever they did was sure to be better than the rule of the Congress Government which had provoked the food riots. But by July he was writing to Seton: 'The political situation is getting so rough here that I'm beginning to worry about any Calcutta [film] project.' This concern contributed to his decision to shoot his next two films – *Goopy and Bagha* and *Days and Nights* – away from Calcutta or in the studio. But two years later the political situation had become so compelling that he felt it was the only possible subject for a film. 'You felt certain changes taking place, almost in day-to-day existence. You felt that without reflecting those changes, you couldn't make a film,' he says today. Sunil Ganguli's new novel *Pratidwandi* was the opportunity he had been waiting for. He read it in October 1969 and by February he was in production, just about the time the Naxalite shooting campaign was getting going. By May, with the film in the can, he was writing to Seton of 'the present EXPLOSIVE atmosphere here – anarchy and revolution and violent anti-American feeling. I'm pretty tense about the possible reaction to my new film – certainly the first truly contemporary film made here – and *basically* though not blatantly – pro-revolution – because I feel nothing else can set the country up on its feet.'

Ray remembers Calcutta as 'a nightmare city' in 1970–1 and, according to his letters to Seton, he considered leaving it, though today he says that the thought was never a serious one. 'For me Calcutta is the place to work, the place to live, so you take what comes – you accept the fact of change.' He found the degree of violence by the young incomprehensible, and very upsetting. He knew a boy, for instance, who became a violent Naxalite at the age of about twenty and bashed one of his college professors on the head, killing him. Ray knew his father too, a heart specialist who as a student of chemistry had helped the terrorists make bombs during the Raj. 'The son had obviously imbibed some of this – even at the age of fourteen or fifteen he was anxious to do away with the Marwaris completely,' Ray comments.

He felt isolated. 'I might have understood more the young peoples' minds if my son had taken to that movement. But he was a victim of that,' Satyajit says. Sandip was surrounded and threatened with a dagger when he turned up for his BA exams. They told him, 'You are the son of Satyajit Ray. We'll see how you can pass this examination.' Luckily a friend of his was passing in a car and Sandip was able to jump in and escape. 'But it was really a very frightening experience,' his father says.

Nothing quite so unpleasant happened to him, but he was mercilessly

The Adversary:
dhartha and other
erviewees (*Nemai Ghosh*)

88   *The Adversary*:
Siddhartha, Sutapa (*Nemai
Ghosh*)

89   *The Adversary*: Keya,
Siddhartha (*Nemai Ghosh*)

90 *Company Limited*: Tutul, Syamal (*Nemai Ghosh*)

91 *Company Limited*:
Syamal's wife, Tutul (*Nemai Ghosh*)

92 *Company Limited*:
Syamal (*Nemai Ghosh*)

93　*Company Limited*: Ray rehearses Harindranath Chatterjee as Sir Baren Roy, watched by Barun Chanda (*Nemai Ghosh*)

94　*The Middle Man*: Ray rehearses Utpal Dutta as Bisu (*Nemai Ghosh*)

95　*The Middle Man*: Bisu, Adok, Somnath (*Nemai Ghosh*)

96 *The Middle Man*:
Somnath, Sukumar (*Nemai Ghosh*)

97 *The Middle Man*:
Somnath, Mr Mitter (*Nemai Ghosh*)

98 *The Middle Man*: Kauna,
Juthika, Somnath (*Nemai Ghosh*)

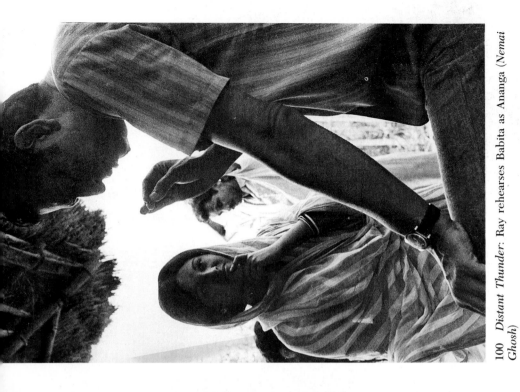

100 *Distant Thunder*: Ray rehearses Babita as Ananga (*Nemai Ghosh*)

99 *The Middle Man*: Ray paints wall-poster (*Nemai Ghosh*)

101 *Distant Thunder*:
Ananga (*Nemai Ghosh*)

102 *Distant Thunder*:
Gangacharan, Ananga (*Nemai
Ghosh*)

103 *Distant Thunder*:
'Scarface' Jadu, Chutki
(*Nemai Ghosh*)

104 *Chiriakhana*:
Byomkesh Baksi and assistant
(*left*) (*Teknica*)

105 *The Golden Fortress*:
Amiyanath Burman, Mandar
Bose (*Nemai Ghosh*)

106 *The Golden Fortress*:
Feluda and Rajasthani
peasants (*Nemai Ghosh*)

107 *The Elephant God*: Ambika Ghosal and grandson Ruku (*Nemai Ghosh*)

108 *The Elephant God*: Jotayu Topse,(*Nemai Ghosh*)

109 *The Elephant God*: Ray rehearses Santosh Dutta as Jotayu, Soumitra Chatterjee as Felu, Siddhartha Chatterjee as Topse and Jit Bose as Ruku (*Nemai Ghosh*)

110 *The Chess Players*: Mir
Roshan Ali, Mirza Sajjad Ali
(*Nemai Ghosh*)

111 *The Chess Players*:
Captain Weston, General
Outram (*Nemai Ghosh*)

112 *The Chess Players*:
Khurshid (*Nemai Ghosh*)

113 *The Chess Players*
Wajid Ali Shah, Ali Na[d]
Khan (*Nemai Ghosh*)

114 *The Chess Players*:
Mirza Sajjad Ali, Mir Roshan
Ali (*Nemai Ghosh*)

115 *The Chess Players*
rehearses Amjad Khan [a]
Wajid Ali Shah (*Nemai
Ghosh*)

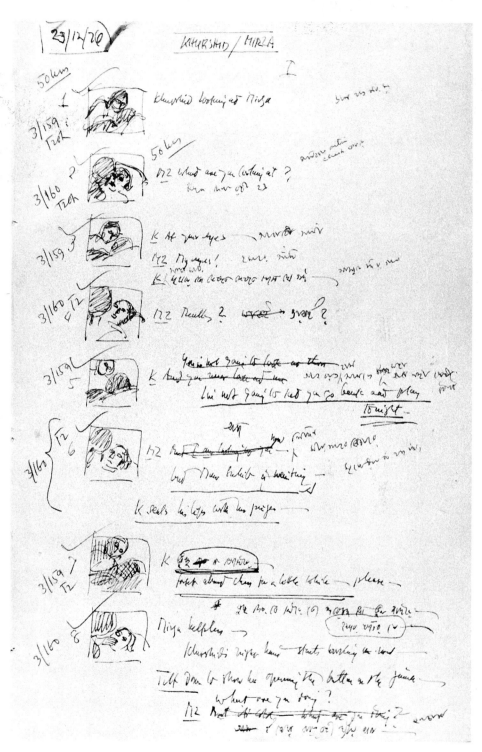

116 *The Chess Players*: page from shooting script

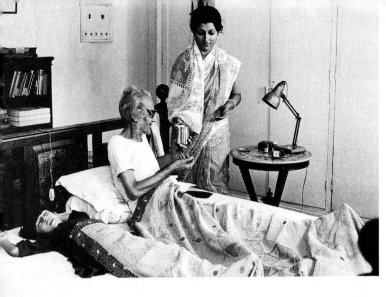

117 *Pikoo*: Pikoo, Grandfather, Seema (*Nemai Ghosh*)

118 *Pikoo*: Pikoo (*Nemai Ghosh*)

119 *Deliverance*: Jhuria, Dukhi (*Nemai Ghosh*)

120 *Deliverance*: Ghashiram, Dukhi (*Nemai Ghosh*)

121 *Deliverance*: Jhuria (Nemai Ghosh)

122　*The Home and the World*: Bimala, Nikhil (*Nemai Ghosh*)

123　*The Home and the World*: Bimala (*Nemai Ghosh*)

124　*The Home and the World*: Sandip, Bimala, Nikhil (*Nemai Ghosh*)

125 *The Home and the World*: Bimala (*Nemai Ghosh*)

126 *The Home and the World*: Bimala, Sandip (*Nemai Ghosh*)

127 *The Home and the World*: Ray composing on synthesiser (*Nemai Ghosh*)

128 *The Home and the World*
set sketch by Ray

129 *The Home and the World*:
Sandip Ray, watched by
Soumitra Chatterjee (*Nemai Ghosh*)

attacked in speech and print, along with some other artists, in one issue of the Presidency College magazine especially. 'The same set of arguments are always applied when you are attacked as a bourgeois film-maker,' he says with a wry chuckle. Two or three years later Presidency College students of both sexes came to him asking if he would design the cover of the next magazine. Characteristically, he agreed. 'I being an ex-student, they had a claim on me,' he says. He was also persuaded by their attitude that there had been a real change of heart, that 'they were having qualms of conscience.'

Much more worrying than some agitprop was the effect of the economic and political unrest on his work. Film-making in Calcutta is always a technical battle; in 1969/70 it had become a kind of siege. In an article he published in India at the time, entitled 'The Confronting Question', Ray finally gave full rein to his feelings about this:

Here, while a shot is being taken, one holds one's breath for fear the lights might go down in the middle of the shot, either of their own accord, or through a drop in the voltage; one holds one's breath while the camera rolls on the trolley, lest the wheels encounter a pothole on the studio floor and wobble – thus ruining the shot; one holds one's breath on location in fear of a crowd emerging out of the blue . . ., come to watch the film (how can shooting ever be *work*?); one holds one's breath while the film is processed for fear of it being spoiled through sheer carelessness; one holds one's breath too, while the film is being edited, because one never knows when the ravaged Moviola might turn back on the editor in revenge and rip the previous film to ribbons. No wonder film-makers become prone to heart diseases.

The Adversary was almost finished when Ray wrote to Seton in August describing it as 'the most provocative film I have made yet.' At the end of October, as police suppression of the Naxalites was getting into full gear, the film was released. 'I could feel the impact on the audience last night,' Ray told Seton. 'All of which surprises and pleases me a great deal, because the film is deadly serious, and much of the style is elliptical and modern.' It soon became an issue. 'People either loved the film or hated it,' recalls Dhritiman Chatterjee, who played its protagonist Siddhartha. Students demonstrated and shouted slogans for and against it. When it was shown at Calcutta's most radical university (whose vice-chancellor it was that met a violent death at this time), friends of Chatterjee, 'who have obviously mellowed since', shouted Ray down. 'Oh, it raised a whole lot of emotions,' Chatterjee says.

By the time Ray came to shoot *Company Limited*, between March and May 1971, bombings and shootings had become part of the fabric of daily life. His mind turned away from them towards the tragedy in East Pakistan. 'Incredible brutality and barbarism on the part of the W. Pak. solders, and incredible feats of heroism by the poorly armed Bengalis', he wrote to Seton. 'I'm dumbfounded by the apparent apathy of the outside world – and even of the Afro-Asian nations. China has openly supported W. Pak. which for me makes them the most inhuman and coldly calculating power in the world.' Over the previous few days he had been meeting and talking to refugees, among them two leading film actors from Dhaka who had walked seventy-five miles to reach the border. 'It turns out that the main targets of the soldiers have been intellectuals and young people. Most of the best minds (college professors – both men and women) have had to face the firing squad. We are helping as much as possible with arms and medicines, but it sounds from all accounts like an unequal struggle. Perhaps the rains may help the Bengalis . . .'

By October, Ray's attention had returned once more to the local political situation which was 'as grim as ever.' As in the Bengal Famine of 1943, he had decided that the tragedy in Bangladesh was really too vast for individuals to do anything about it, although he was considering making a documentary about the refugees in the camps in Calcutta. 'But what really fascinates me', he observed, 'is the way the normal rhythm of life is slowly but surely being restored. I doubt if a film on this would make the right kind of propaganda impact.'

Parts of south Calcutta had been turned into a 'liberated zone' by the Naxalites; they were living in some of the studios there, and using make-up rooms and editing-rooms for storing ammunition. This meant constant police raids, followed by arrests, gunfights and beatings-up, until two of the biggest studios, including the New Theatres, had to close down. 'The whole thing has taken on a nightmare quality – more so because people seem to be getting used to killings of the most macabre sort', wrote Ray to Seton. 'And it's becoming increasingly difficult to make out the political murders from the non-political ones. Unless the situation improves, I may have to move to Bombay or Madras, and you know how much I'd hate to do that . . . I'm hoping that the situation will improve.'

Within a few months it did – at least the killing stopped. For the next three years or so Ray chose to turn away his attention from contemporary themes in his work. During 1972 and 1973 he made *Distant Thunder*, his long-cherished film about the Bengal Famine, the first of two detective films for children *The Golden Fortress (Sonar Kella)*, and the short documentary about his teacher at Santiniketan, Binode Bihari Mukherjee, *The Inner Eye*. The quality of life in the city meanwhile continued to deteriorate under the control once more of a Congress government, headed by S.S. Ray, a school-friend of Satyajit. 'Life here's getting to be more and more chaotic everyday,' he noted in a letter of May 1974. 'We are going to have TV in Calcutta in October – right in the middle of the most acute power shortage. And of course they had to have a nuclear test in the middle of the biggest and longest railway strike ever!' Six months later, when he had already begun work on the script of *The Chess Players*, he added, 'I find the contemporary scene doesn't lend itself to crystallisation. And since the really important truths cannot be told for obvious reasons – it's best to leave it alone.'

The publication of the novel *Jana Aranya (The Middle Man)* by Moni Sankar Mukherjee (known as Sankar), at the end of 1974, changed his mind. It chimed with his mood of bleak cynicism at the time: 'I felt corruption, rampant corruption all around, and I didn't think there was any solution,' he says today. 'I was only waiting, perhaps subconsciously, for a story that would give me an opportunity to show this. I felt that what I was doing in the film was right and necessary and that it was valid to the Calcutta of those days.' Its shooting was completed just as India was consigned to yet another period of trauma, the Emergency declared by Mrs Gandhi in late June of 1975, that lasted until the surprise elections called by her in early 1977. Ray thus found himself in a peculiar position; he had created what is his most scathing film about politicians at the moment when it was likely to be most controversial to screen it.

Like almost every other film director, he was soon telephoned by Central Government officials in New Delhi asking him to make films. Most directors did, but Ray refused, saying that he was a very bad propagandist. He never made a direct public statement to the effect that the Emergency was wrong, although he criticised it freely to his friends and co-workers, as Soumitra Chatterjee noticed to his surprise. Instead, he made himself clear through *The Middle Man*. 'You see they were very very powerful,' he says today:

He [Sanjay Gandhi, Mrs Gandhi's younger son] was really being a dictator at that point. He had his henchmen and the police were under his thumb. They were doing reckless things in Delhi. Delhi was a nightmare city at that point. I had occasion to go there and I heard some stories of what Sanjay Gandhi was doing. It was pretty horrifying. Obviously in a situation like that an artist can hope to do things at a very great risk, and I thought that instead of direct attack I should indicate by some means that I was not in favour of the Emergency and I was not going to help them in any way. That would be better.

The film incorporates a somewhat sinister caricature of Mrs Gandhi drawn on a wall, which Ray had done himself, and a scene with a Congress politician which he regards as 'the most explicit criticism of Congress ever put into a film.' When it was first shown, Ray had one of a number of Congress politicians sitting beside him. 'This man said, "My God, where is this going to end? How long is it to go on?" He was nervous and ill at ease but he didn't mind it. He liked the film, and so did Siddhartha [S.S. Ray – then Chief Minister of West Bengal] – very much.' He must have done, because the West Bengal Government awarded *Jana Aranya* prizes for Best Film, Director and Screenplay in 1975. Even in Delhi it won the prize for Best Direction (though not the President's Gold Medal usual for Ray). Someone, unknown to Ray, saw fit to excise one of the film's most provocative exchanges, however. As Ray told an interviewer from the *New York Times* in April the following year, after declining to comment on the Emergency, 'One can perhaps get away with this kind of thing once, maybe not again.'

The Adversary has at its centre a character to whom Ray feels closer than almost any other that he has created, including Apu. Siddhartha is twenty-five, educated and jobless; he is also intelligent, sensitive and frustrated. The first two qualities have led to the third in a society where it is often better not to think too much. He feels trapped, obliged to support a widowed mother and family but unable to find any job deserving of his talents; he is too honest at job interviews, and too much the individual to submerge himself in politics, let alone revolution. He is Ray's archetypal man of conscience, in many ways a projection of his own feelings and attitudes. 'I felt very strongly for the character,' he says. 'He was very close to my heart.'

He moulded him out of Sunil Ganguli's Siddhartha, who had been based on the author's own experience of joblessness in 1964/5. As Ray writes, in a foreword to an English edition of the novel:

> I should put Sunil Ganguli high among present-day writers whom film-makers could read with profit. For one thing, he is a very visual writer. Characters, incidents, relationships are all largely built up by means of sensitively observed external details – a fundamentally cinematic device. The dialogue is sparse and life-like, with not a trace of high-falutin didacticism. If the surface appears simple, there is depth and density underneath; and there is lyricism too – for Sunil is a poet – to set beside the sudden, bold, wrenching scenes which strike one as much by their unexpectedness as by their conviction.
>
> In *Pratidwandi* one finds all these qualities, given point and cohesion by the central character of Siddhartha, so endearing and believable in his contradictions, set by turns against his family, his friends, the girl he takes a fancy to, and the society which ultimately drives him to take refuge in a small job in a small town. If I were asked to give just one good reason for choosing *this* literary work, I would say it was Siddhartha.

In the film Ray makes him older, maturer and more intellectual than in the novel, where he is only nineteen; and he was lucky to find a superb fit for the character in Dhritiman Chatterjee, who had just finished a degree at Presidency College (where he had been friends with some of those who became Naxalites) and was at a loose end – circumstances resembling Siddhartha's. He was recommended to Ray by the son of one of Ray's cousins, and Satyajit remembers chatting to him about the part while sitting together on a sheet in the middle of his empty flat at Lake Temple Road; this was in January 1970 and Ray and his family were about to move to the mansion flat in Bishop Lefroy Road in central Calcutta, where they live today. At first he thought that Dhritiman's Bengali was not good enough because he spoke mainly in English, but it soon became clear that he was bilingual – a fact that Ray used to advantage in the film.

Siddhartha's younger brother Tunu, a bomb-making student who models himself on Che Guevara, is an altogether less complex character, though no less convincing. Ray's attitude towards him is summed up in a comment by George Steiner that he carefully noted in his shooting book for *Company Limited*: 'The evil of politics lies precisely in the separation of the human person from the abstract cause or the strategic necessity.' Ray definitely admires the courage – which he says he does not possess – that enables the revolutionary to face bullets, but that is as far as his sympathy with their methods goes. In a flash-back to Tunu and Siddhartha's childhood, instead of showing Tunu nauseated by the decapitation of a chicken by a servant – as in the novel – Tunu is seen to be fascinated. Ganguli demurs, saying that some Naxalites whom he knows *were* scared to look at blood as children. Perhaps, if circumstances had permitted Ray to make what he calls his 'Eisensteinian' film about the 'controlling characters' behind the Naxalite movement, he would then have adopted Ganguli's psychology – to show a revolutionary leader, rather than a follower.

In-between Tunu and Siddhartha in age is their sister Sutapa, another vividly realised character, who is as certain about the merits of the capitalist system as Tunu is about the Marxist. Without inhibition she has used her charm to become personal assistant to a businessman, whom the rest of the family – Siddhartha, his mother and the uncle who lives with them – are convinced is taking advantage of her. They disapprove of her unconcern about the whole matter; to them the family prestige at least is at stake, even if she is careless of her own reputation. But Sutapa feels that she can look after herself; besides, she is more interested in clothes, make-up, modelling and having a good time than in family prestige. Criticised at home, despite the money she is making that helps the family to survive, she withdraws into self-centred silence.

These are the three characters around whom the rest revolve; the tensions between them are a microcosm of life in modern Calcutta. This film, more than any other by Ray about contemporary life in the city, speaks best to those who know that peculiar place – and this may account for its initial lukewarm reception in the West, where critics found it hard to throw off preconceptions about Calcutta's awfulness. A British critic in the *Listener* spoke of the film being 'painstakingly schematic in pigeon-holing members of a modern Calcutta family', having missed the warmth beneath the grim surface. And at least two major critics in New York, a city often loosely compared with Calcutta, found the film to be a moving comedy. I can understand that kind of reaction to *The Middle Man*, though I do not share it, but applied to *The Adversary*, it suggests a near-absence of empathy with the idealistic spirit and disinterest in materialism that has kept the battered city alive and given Ray his eminent place in it as a serious artist with a popular following.

The film touched a nerve in Calcutta. Its first long sequence, as the titles roll over a relentless series of shots of a fearfully overcrowded bus carrying Siddhartha to a job interview, articulated the daily experience of thousands of Calcuttans at the time. When Siddhartha without rhetoric replies to the interviewers that in his opinion the most significant world event of the last ten years is the 'plain human courage' shown by the Vietnamese people, rather than the moon landing (as they suggest), Ray is speaking through him about his own values, and those of his giant predecessor Tagore. 'You see, no one knew they had it in them,' Siddhartha tells the stolid bureaucrats, who then pointedly enquire 'Are you a Communist?' He loses the job there and then. Moral victories don't pay, he begins to realise, even if they make one feel good for a while.

A series of inconsequential incidents now drive him into the clutches of his friends, two medical students sharing a room in a noisy hostel; Siddhartha had been studying medicine too but had to abandon it when his father died, which is where the film began. The seemingly desultory nature of these incidents tells us much about Siddhartha's character and his relationship to the city in which he wanders: little is said in words or facial expressions, but much is revealed. Siddhartha sits alone in a tea house after the interview, and tells the waiter that his cup is cracked. A man whose face we never see now comes up and lectures him in a deep, trustworthy voice (actually Ray's own) about not wasting his life in interviews; why doesn't he return to the party work he used to do at college so well? Although Siddhartha does not say much or smoke in front of this man as a customary sign of respect, he indicates his lack of interest; what he needs is a job to support the family. Sensing this, the party-leader mentions a possible opening as a medical representative (the job once held by Mrinal Sen). Siddhartha leaves and enters a local pharmacy to get some relief from his aching head. While he waits, a weak, shifty-looking man comes in and whispers to the attendant – clearly after contraceptives. Procreation is beginning to take second place to survival in the city.

Feeling hot and tired Siddhartha heads for a cinema-hall to cool down in air-conditioned comfort and have a doze. The film being shown is ideally suited: a government newsreel about Mrs Gandhi's forthcoming budget. This will mean 'a greater sense of security for the lower income groups,' a Films Division commentator intones in his best BBC-style English; Siddhartha closes his eyes. But almost the next second there is a big flash: everybody out of the cinema – a bomb has gone off. Walking away Siddhartha drops his watch and breaks it. He alters course for a watch-repairer in a nearby market; but the wizened old man who squints at it asks more than he can afford, small amount though it is. Again, Siddhartha moves on. Waiting to cross a main road he spots a well-built, sexy girl coming the other way between the traffic. Suddenly we are inside his head in a flash-back: a lecturer is explaining the anatomy of the female breast to a lecture hall crowded with male and female medical students. 'There are lots of things going on in Siddhartha's head,' says Ray, 'and he has no one to communicate his thoughts to.' Flash-backs and dreams occur throughout *The Adversary*; they are mostly successful, if occasionally over-schematised.

Siddhartha now crosses the road and sits down inside a small decaying pavilion at the edge of the Maidan. It is quiet at last. Gratefully he smokes and watches a ragged beggar, while the sun gleams on a stagnant pond nearby. Its mesmerising effect takes him back to his childhood for a moment: he sees three children running together in slow-motion towards him, archetypally carefree – himself, and his brother and sister. American accents jerk him back to the present. Hippies have invaded his pavilion. 'Oh what a be-yoo-tiful place! This is where the world started. This is where the magic is . . . Look at the cow! Dee-lightful!' Siddhartha, who is loitering for quite other reasons, finds these flower people hard to take; he shortly decides to quit the pavilion and go in search of his friends.

These particular hippies were picked up in a once-favourite hippy haunt in central Calcutta and invited to do whatever they felt like. One of them was from San Francisco and knew Ray's work because his films were often shown there. 'It turned out she was very rich,' Ray remarks. 'Probably they were using her money, I don't know.' 'They were using cough-syrup as their main high,' says Dhritiman Chatterjee, who felt that out of Ray's unit only he and one other were at all sympathetic to them. 'Everyone else was very mad at them, including Manikda, except he didn't show it – not at all. He kept a very low kind of a profile – just trying to get his job done.' Ray does not remember feeling angry, but he certainly found it chaotic working with the hippies. 'There was a shot in a hotel where they were doing things to an Indian sadhu. They'd got hold of him in the street and taken him to their room. Extraordinary things were going on,' he says, half-smiling at the memory rather mysteriously. In the film this shot is silent; and, disappointingly, it does not reveal just what these 'extraordinary things' consisted of.

With Siddhartha's milieu now established, the plot, such as it is, begins to develop. In the hostel Siddhartha is disgusted to find one of his friends removing coins from a Red Cross box with a knife. After a tussle with him he goes out with the other friend to see what is cracked up to be a hot movie at a local film society. It isn't; everyone remains fully clothed. 'I wanted more porn,' says Ray, 'but Marie [Seton – who had procured it in London] thought this was adequate.' 'However', he wrote to her at the time, 'I had a brain wave.' He reshot the boys' reactions to show Siddhartha looking thoroughly bored and his friend looking embarrassed – at the let-down, rather than at the film itself.

Unfulfilled sexual desire is a constant theme of *The Adversary*. As Siddhartha reaches home after his fruitless day, he interrupts the wife of his sister's boss who has come to their house unannounced to vent her suspicions to Sutapa's mother. When she has gone tempers rise. Siddhartha tries to remonstrate with his sister but she fends off his concern with affectionate irony. Suddenly he feels as if *he* is the younger of them, that she is no longer the little sister he once knew. His mind jumps back once more to the two of them playing as children far away from the city, having a picnic near a river. She cries out, hearing a piercing birdcall. He listens too; but no one seems to know what kind of bird it is. Stirred up by the intensity of the memory, Siddhartha sits brooding. The enigmatic birdcall will haunt him for the rest of the film. He feels unable to share the feeling with a living soul; his sister has grown too far away from him, and his brother has no idea what he is talking about – such questions are about as relevant to the armed struggle as brotherly affection.

Driven by a mad urge, Siddhartha decides to visit Sutapa's boss and teach him a severe lesson. But once there in front of the man, sitting in his big house, he crumples, and actually asks him for a job. Then, in despair at his own pusillanimity, he runs away before the boss can return from making a telephone call. His steps lead him inexorably back to the medical students' hostel, via the scene of a car accident (where Siddhartha half-heartedly joins in the fray as passers-by belabour the driver) and a chat with the party-leader's doctor friend, who offers him a post outside Calcutta: as a mere medical salesman, not a representative. This time it is the unscrupulous Adinath, the rifler of the Red Cross box, who goes out with him – for a meal. Initiating him into alcohol – such is Siddhartha's pent-up state that he agrees – he leads him up some shabby stairs nearby, into the room of a beautiful prostitute. She also works as a nurse (which provoked a very strong objection from the city's Nurses' Association) and, as she slowly removes her uniform, gleefully observed by Adinath, Siddhartha becomes more and more agitated. This calculated encounter is totally at odds with his own imaginings about sex. As he reluctantly lights her cigarette, the picture goes into negative, accompanied by some chords on an organ – an effective dramatisation of his revulsion. Pursued by Adinath, he runs away once again.

There is no evidence of Ray's so-called puritanism in the way he handles this scene, but it is true that for background research he was unwilling to visit prostitutes himself; Art Director Bansi Chandragupta required considerable persuasion too, Dhritiman remembers. 'That's the problem with these guys. When Mrinal [Sen] and I were at Berlin together for the Festival there was a sex shop opposite the Palace. Mrinal wanted to go there very much but he said, "No no, there's so many people walking around!" '

While making his escape Siddhartha now encounters the erotic in a new form, which will soon grow into attachment. A girl calls him from out of the shadows of a house across the street. Can he mend a fuse? His relationship with Keya, a direct, innocent girl with a core of sadness due to the death of her mother when she was still a child, is what keeps Siddhartha sane, as his home relationships disintegrate and no job appears. Neither of them is happy and neither is in a position to make a commitment to the other, but they do enjoy a meeting of minds that Ray gently establishes in various scenes together, of which two are especially fine. In a restaurant that Siddhartha can ill afford, they examine the diners to see if Siddhartha (playing the medical student) is right when he says that people are 'basically the same'; and from the top of the tallest building in Calcutta, they look down upon ant-like political supporters at a meeting, while waves of unintelligible sound from the loudspeakers filter up to them through the sultry air. There they make a kind of vow to keep in touch, whatever may happen to either of them.

For Siddhartha will have to leave Calcutta, the city he both hates and loves. This follows from a final job interview he attends at which all the candidates are kept waiting for hours in the heat without enough seating or ventilation. Siddhartha, perspiring in silence against a wall, has a sudden shocking vision of the entire corridor of interviewees just as they are, sitting or standing, but stripped to the skeleton. As he had told Keya only days before, referring to the corpses that he used to dissect, 'They're all basically the same, except for abnormalities.' The waiting drags on. When the interviewers announce a lunch-break, Siddhartha's patience snaps. In a burst of fury of the kind that was occurring en masse all over Calcutta in 1970/1 to far more terrible effect, Siddhartha barges into the interviewers' room, yells at them and smashes whatever he can lay hands on, before striding off in righteous anger.

With a strikingly modern transition from slogan-ridden walls blurred by movement to the blurred landscape outside the window of a moving train, Ray lets us know that Siddhartha has given in. He is on his way to take up the salesman's job in a dreary, squalid small town many miles from the big city. His illusions are shattered but, as he tells Keya in a letter he is writing to her in voice-over, he still cherishes their relationship. He is settled temporarily in a hotel, though it barely deserves the name. He won't write any more just now because he is feeling very tired – except to mention one small thing. He has heard that birdcall again, and this time it is not in his mind, but for real. He walks out on to the small balcony of his unprepossessing room. The bird calls again, and below him, Siddhartha hears the monotonous chant of a funeral procession 'Ram Nam Satya. Ram Nam Satya . . .' ('The Name of God is Truth . . .') As Siddhartha starts turning back towards the camera he is frozen in time and the two words 'iti – Siddhartha' appear on the screen – the conventional words with which a Bengali would close a letter.

This is one of Ray's most profound endings, open to many interpretations, none of which he will endorse. It is essentially cinematic, irreducible to words. Perhaps Sunil Ganguli, whose own ending has Siddhartha stalking the streets of the small town at night cursing the world in impotent rage (like in a Mrinal Sen film), gets closest when he says: 'It's a great ending, when I detach myself. The dead man and the sound of the bird carry a sense of eternal life. It is elevated to another level. Siddhartha becomes immaterial at that moment. The director shifts away from him and says: "Now we can leave Siddhartha here and life goes on. And in life and death the world moves. And Siddhartha is just . . . a dot." '

Nothing in the second film of the trilogy quite rises to the artistic level of the ending of *The Adversary*. Nor, in a sense, is it appropriate that it should, because its central character, Syamalendu (Barun Chanda), a rising young executive, is incapable of Siddhartha's flights of imagination. He is, as the London *Monthly Film Bulletin* reviewer nicely pointed out, what Siddhartha might have become had he prevaricated over his answer about the significance of the Vietnam War and the moon landing.

In Ray's words to Seton in October 1971, *Company Limited* is 'a definitive film about the boxwallahs' – that is, the western-oriented commercial community in Calcutta, especially those that work in large companies. Their life style revolves around the office, cocktail parties, clubs and race-tracks, and they are generally very anglicised or, nowadays, Americanised. Ray's attitude to them is summed up in his answer to a question I once put to him: 'Do you think that to be in business is to be slightly immoral?' Without hesitating he said, 'Yes – like I feel about lawyers.' His experience with the British-owned D.J. Keymer confirmed this, although he never went through any executive-training process himself and, anyway, Keymer's was a small firm. Also, in the years after he left it, he watched his friends in other companies, particularly in advertising, who had been on the Left in the 1940s and early 1950s, rise up the tree and 'try to rationalise their positions'.

But despite his proximity to that world, Ray needed to do a lot of research for *Company Limited*, especially as Chandragupta had temporarily left him to work in Bombay. A typical extract from the shooting notebook of the time reads:

> *Arrange to see:*
> 1) A labour canteen (Try Britannia or Usha)
> 2) GEC Office
> 3) Sample Trade Agreement (Usha and Calcutta Fan)
> 4) Another Fan Factory

and he makes a very detailed list of the objects in Syamalendu's room in his company flat, as well as sketching over and over again possible designs for the company logo – one example of his fascination with typography out of many dotted through his notebooks. He also took the advice of Sankar, the novelist, who recalls that Ray once phoned him to enquire precisely where in a batch of fans the defects were located which nearly wreck Syamalendu's career – in the armatures, or in the blades?

As a result, the film wears an air of effortless conviction, and feels like one of Ray's most fluent works. Although our sympathies are inevitably (and quite deliberately) drawn towards Syamalendu's beautiful sister-in-law Tutul (Sarmila Tagore), Syamalendu is not without charisma, even if it does wear thinner as the film progresses. He is an essentially decent fellow, still willing to heed the advice of the woman who had been the girl next-door in Patna ten years before; but his ambition to be a company director gets the better of him. 'I am slightly sympathetic to him,' says Ray, 'while I do not admire what he's doing. He's not *quite* the boxwallah; but inevitably in future he will become a boxwallah,' he adds with a laugh.

Tutul, who is visiting him in Calcutta after a gap of many years (in which Syamalendu has not returned to Patna because of pressure of work), is the conscience of the piece. 'Is that good or bad?' she asks her brother-in-law, with ingenuous charm, when he tells her that Indians like themselves can now be part of clubs that were once open only to whites. But Ray is too subtle a moralist to give her all the cards. 'Is that good or bad?' Syamalendu throws back at her a day or two later, after she has told him that he has still a lot of his home-town in him. Tutul refuses to answer directly; she is still making up her mind. When she finally does so, in the closing scene of the film, she does not need to say a word; Syamalendu knows only too well what she has decided.

Through telling dialogue and acute characterisation of almost all the smaller parts in the film (bettered only by *The Middle Man* to follow), Ray manages the feat of holding our interest in office politics. With skill and humour he interweaves the home and office lives of Syamalendu, which, as every ambitious executive knows, have a tendency to merge for the good of the company. Increasingly, we can see that Syamalendu is living in a hermetic, affluent world, into which Tutul's visit can only be an intrusion, however much his old self might welcome it. Where Siddhartha is out on the streets and in the buses, the nearest the city comes to Syamalendu is through the elevated windows of his company flat: the distant boom of explosions – bombs? gunfire? who knows? Not the tenants or their party-guests, none of whom regards it as his business which persons are responsible, or what they stand for.

Everything goes swimmingly for Syamalendu until out of the blue there comes a phone-call from the fan factory informing him that a whole consignment of fans destined for abroad, is faulty. It is 8 March; if the company does not despatch the fans by 15 March, they will lose a lot of money because of a penalty clause, and he, as Marketing Manager, will be held partly to blame. Hurriedly he goes to consult the Managing Director, a Balliol-educated Englishman. There appears to be no solution. Feeling depressed, Syamalendu takes the papers home to brood, assisted by whisky. He takes Tutul into his confidence, though not his wife, but she is not much help. That night, after the two women have gone to bed, he hesitantly calls the company labour officer over from a nearby flat; there is a close-up of the coiled black telephone wire as they speak – an image with an enigmatic power comparable to that of Nanda Babu's shiny pumps nudging the kittens on the stairs in *Aparajito*. Together, they hatch a plan.

Within a day or two trouble breaks out in the factory, the company declares a lock-out, and the contract is saved. No matter that the factory watchman has been badly injured by a bomb thrown by one of the workers. He is lying in hospital at the company's expense. 'Aren't people dying in Calcutta all the time?' the labour officer tells a conscience-stricken Syamalendu. If the man had proved so inconvenient as to die, the company would simply have sent even more flowers, along with a personal condolence note from Syamalendu Chatterjee; it's been done before, the labour officer implies. And they both laugh at his sick joke.

Not long afterwards, the expected occurs; Syamalendu becomes a director. Congratulations all round. His wife is thrilled, his rival desolate, but Tutul, the only one whose praise he really wants, keeps quiet. In another charged ending, Ray has a triumphant Syamalendu return to his quarters to find the lift out of order. Gaily he starts to climb the stairs, but as he ascends he gets slower and slower, and near the top all we can hear are his shoes rubbing on the steps. By the time he reaches the top – both literally and metaphorically – his mood is half-spent; but his wife notices nothing. Exhausted, but still pleased, he sits and calls for his sister-in-law. When after a pause she appears, she walks slowly towards the window with her back to him, then takes a seat too. They exchange glances and, without uttering a sound, she removes the watch he had earlier lent her for the duration of her stay in Calcutta, and quietly places it on the table. From a point near the revolving fan on the ceiling – agent of his crisis – we silently observe as Syamalendu bows his head in his hands and Tutul fades from the picture, echoing the fate of Syamalendu's better instincts and leaving him utterly alone.

In *The Middle Man*, last of the Calcutta Trilogy, corruption has infected the very marrow of the city. Everyone is implicated, with the exception of two characters, and they are self-deluded. The whole of society is decaying. That was what was new in the early 1970s: not the fact of corruption, but its extent. In this quotation from the second volume of his autobiography, Nirad Chaudhuri describes the typical moral climate of Calcutta in the early 1920s, when he was the same age as Somnath, the central character of Ray's film: 'a shallow top soil of dry-as-dust prudery, but one [could] easily hear the squelching of the soggy layer of weak vice underneath. The moral weather of Hindu society is regulated by the high and low pressure of the winds of opinion prevailing in it, and not by absolute moral judgments. No one can become tolerant of this kind of commonness without becoming deadened in moral sensibility.' This, of course, is what *The Middle Man* is about: the deadening by society of the moral sensibility of a young man in whom it was never very strong.

'The story *demanded* black and white,' says Ray emphatically – and, by extension, all the shades of grey in-between. Its milieu is the small business premises, restaurants, hotels and demi-monde of a Calcutta that is suffering from constant power cuts, even though the Naxalites have been crushed and the politicians are back in power. Some of its most compelling scenes take place in near-darkness; the blackness of its humour is amply reflected in the film's crepuscular lighting.

All of which atmosphere demanded much background research. One of the film's delights is its '19th century thoroughness', as Penelope Houston has pointed out – the Dickensian relish with which Ray dwells upon the details of the petty world into which Somnath naïvely launches himself. Once again, it was necessary to create the ambience of prostitution. Sankar, the author, came to Ray's rescue. 'Are all these details in it authentic?' Ray asked him. He said they were; he had been to such places and spoken to such women. He even mentioned some details not in the novel, 'such as a woman who has to go out on an assignment with a client. Just before leaving she says she must fortify herself and takes a glass of green coconut juice,' comments an amused Ray.

Another of the film's rewards – in fact one deserving the highest praise – is the standard of acting by *everyone* in it; 'few of Ray's films have offered so wide a range of quick, exact characterisations', comments Houston. The members of each world in which Somnath moves are exquisitely real: his family circle (father, elder brother and wife); his college friend Sukumar whose family live in poverty and whose attractive sister Somnath meets so unexpectedly near the end; the disreputable denizens of the office in which he keeps a desk; the senior businessman for whom he acts as pimp; the dapper PRO Mitter (Rabi Ghosh) with a conscience as spotless as his handkerchief who acts as procurer for Somnath; the repellent preening Congress politician; a housewife-turned-whore; and a sentimental madam who is an outrageous concoction of the genteel and the louche. They are all unfailingly interesting, funny and piquant, and one can only watch and marvel at Ray's uncanny capacity to extract extraordinary performances from ordinary actors, and in roles with which he himself could not possibly have more than a passing acquaintance in real life. As the exuberant Rabi Ghosh says, whose performance in this film is his best for Ray, 'Manikda's one of the finest actors. He gave me expression, delivery, timing, pace, gaps, everything when I played Mitter. He can make a cow act!'

With some actors, this can occasionally prove a problem. Utpal Dutta, who plays Somnath's streetwise mentor in business, admits frankly that he could not take full advantage of Ray's direction 'because I hadn't even found out that he *was* directing, you see. He would never tell you what to do. He would come around and suggest little changes here and there: maybe that would be better. Then, after a while, you'd find you were doing something quite different from what you started out with. It's an unobtrusive direction which I like very much, but I could only take advantage of it later,' – that is, in *Joi Baba Felunath* and *Hirak Rajar Dese*. Such skill cannot really be analysed or encapsulated in theories. It is just that Ray has developed the acutest ability to observe people – beginning from his solitary childhood, coupled to a very active curiosity and a versatile, overflowing imagination. A friend recalls Satyajit meeting a Congress minister, for instance, in 1973 and afterwards imitating 'his table-thumping, his head-shaking, his mispronunciations and his tedious references to "the Leader" ' – the nucleus of Ray's unflattering portrayal of a politican two years later, no doubt.

The Middle Man is unusual for Ray in having a lot of plot, as well as much of the sort of psychology in which *The Adversary* excels. The story begins with rampant cheating in an exam-hall where the honest Somnath narrowly misses honours in his college finals, very probably because of an overworked, underpaid examiner's irritation at his small handwriting. His father, an old-fashioned, upright man who has just retired, wants to get his son's scores checked, but his elder son persuades him that this is quite pointless, given the prevailing chaos. Reluctantly, Somnath begins the search for employment in a market flooded with applicants, along with his friend Sukumar, who has a somewhat more realistic assessment of their chances than Somnath: zero. At an interview we see Somnath asked the usual inane questions that drove Siddhartha to distraction in *The Adversary*, culminating in one that really stumps him: 'What is the weight of the moon?' After this he abandons the effort.

Strolling along a little later he slips on a banana skin and, as he is being helped to his feet, finds himself face to face with Bisuda (Utpal Dutta), an older man whom he used to meet at football matches. Soon, despite his father's lack of enthusiasm for business, Somnath is set to make money as an 'order-supplier' – someone who uses his contacts to buy cheap and sell dear – a middle man or, in Bengali, a *dalal*, which has the secondary meaning 'pimp', as Somnath is uncomfortably aware. *What* he buys and sells is entirely up to him, says the paternal Bisuda whose office space Somnath hires as a base. It could be anything 'from *alpin* [pins] to elephants', he adds, relishing his own alliteration – or women, as Somnath will discover. With a little cunning and some luck, Bisuda tells Somnath that he will take off . . . 'and reach the moon [*chad*]?' asks Somnath naïvely. 'Almost,' says Bisuda playfully, but with a touch of menace, 'at least some silver [*chadi*].'

With an innocent look and a clear conscience Somnath plunges into action and fairly quickly finds himself earning real money. Sukumar meanwhile has gone downhill under the pressure of joblessness and poverty; he has accepted a job as taxi-driver from the politician he knows who had earlier preached to him and Somnath that their path to fulfilment lay in self-sacrifice for the good of the country. Somnath prefers to emulate the politician's worldly success. He has amibitions: all his orders are for small amounts and he wants a bigger deal. It looks as if a businessman whom he has met will oblige him with a contract. Somehow though, the man seems to be in no hurry to sign. A puzzled Somnath now calls in Mitter, to whom he had earlier been introduced by one of Bisuda's many business cronies. He is the sort of man who thinks nothing of bathing early in the morning in the holy Ganges to get to know a pious client better; his days and his nights are dedicated to identifying and playing on the weak spots of the rich and influential. He diagnoses Somnath's difficulty and recommends a remedy at a price: if it is agreeable, he will arrange a girl for Somnath's client and Somnath will deliver her to him. Somnath's hesitation leaves him unmoved. In a superbly crafted encounter across a table in one of Calcutta's expensive cafés, Mitter ruthlessly dissects the aspiring contractor:

Mitter: Are you prepared to die for a cause?
Somnath: I doubt it.
Mitter: Could you work as a labourer? You'd earn a lot more
             than you do now.
Somnath: I know.
Mitter: But you can't. Have you the guts to be a factory worker?
Somnath takes off his glasses and rubs his eyes.
Mitter: You admit you're a weakling in mind and body.

Somnath gives in. But there is worse to come. On the evening of the assignation Mitter and Somnath visit the chosen lady, but her husband returns at the wrong moment blind-drunk and sees them off. Desperately they dash to another establishment, where Mitter is greeted by a very large and friendly Alsatian and then has to perch on a sofa below a cheap print of some saccharine doggies while he chats up Madam. Yes, she says, one of her daughters will be available, but she cannot travel to meet the client. Now reduced to real panic at the approaching deadline Mitter drags Somnath off to a third, less salubrious place. This time the girl is available, but, by a fateful coincidence, it turns out Somnath knows her already – she is Sukumar's sister, working under a pseudonym. Trapped, he asks her to take the money and go. But she is a professional; she will go through with what she is being paid to do. Somnath, his conscience salved, goes along with her decision and delivers her to the hotel as arranged. He gets the contract, but like Syamalendu in *Company Limited*, he no longer desires it as once he did. When he steps softly through the darkened door of his family's flat, he is no more the innocent boy, but a tainted adult who will always feel the urge to hide in his own shadow.

It is hard to regard such a film essentially as a comedy, but that was the view of many western critics when it was released in 1976/7 to some highly appreciative reviews. Though it is soaked in irony, and Ray does indeed have a 'zest' for his crooks, its predominant note – especially during the final desperate hunt for a willing whore – is grim, and even shocking. Ray calls the last scene 'tragic', and it can bear that weight. The *Sunday Times* critic was nearest the mark in writing that the film is a 'sour, witty, tough, individual comedy' which shows 'a reality . . . that must be more disturbing than funny for those who have to live there.' Shyly smiling Somnath never did find out the weight of the moon, let alone reach it – though we may be sure that from now on he will merchandise it if he gets the chance – but he has received and accepted his equivalent of thirty pieces of silver.

20

Distant Thunder
(Asani Sanket) 1973

··➤►[◖◗]◄◄··

DURING 1972, after completing first *The Adversary* and then *Company Limited*, Ray turned towards village Bengal once more, where he had not set an entire film since making *Three Daughters* over ten years before. As always he wanted to keep experimenting. The source he chose for his new film was the novel *Asani Sanket* (*Distant Thunder*) by Bibhutibhusan Banerjee, that he had first read on publication in 1946. He had been taken then, both by its pathos and by its cinematic descriptions. The possibility of filming it had been in his mind since the mid-1960s.

Its subject-matter, the Bengal Famine of 1943–4, held a strong fascination for him. As we know, the event left him comparatively indifferent at the time – his first year of employment at Keymer's – and he had come to feel somewhat guilty about this. Guilt is certainly one of the emotions in his approach to the story, along with a desire to educate younger Bengalis; many have only a dim notion of when the Famine occurred and no accurate idea of its causes. Ray had also been impressed by Mrinal Sen's early film on the same subject, *Baisey Sravan*, and may perhaps have wanted to show his mettle.

By settling on Banerjee's novel he was choosing to avoid his own experience of the Famine in the big city and focus on its impact on rural Bengal. He could very easily have constructed a story in which a middle-class city-dweller with a safe supply of food wrestles with his conscience in the hunger-struck streets of Calcutta. It might well have been compelling and would definitely have satisfied those Indian critics who found *Distant Thunder* insufficiently 'angry' or direct in its statement. That Ray did not do this probably has something to do with how disturbing and raw he still felt the event to be, but more to do with his sense of propriety. He could never indulge in the emotional rhetoric of, say, Roland Joffé's *The Killing Fields*. If he had felt unable to place himself truthfully in the situation of the famine victims he would not have made a film at all. To have looked at them through the eyes of an outsider would have been obscene, somehow, however interesting a story it might have made.

In *Distant Thunder* there is therefore none of the anguish of

Calcutta's better-off inhabitants described in another novel of the time, Bhabani Bhattacharya's *So Many Hungers*:

> The ceaseless, whining wail, the long, hollow wail threshing out of depths beyond the throat, out of the belly's deep despair: 'Ma! Ma-go-ma! [Mother! Oh, Mother!] A sip of rice water, pray, Ma, Ma-go-o!' You heard it and you heard it, and sickness rose to your throat, and the food you ate stuck like glue. You heard it day in and day out, every hour and every minute, at your own house-door and at your neighbours', till the surfeit of the cry stunned the pain and pity it had first started, till it pierced no longer, and was no more hurtful than the death-rattle of stricken animals. You hated the hideous monotony of the wail. The destitutes became a race apart, insensitive, sub-human. A destitute had been given a bowl of rice-water for the child in her arms. Suddenly she had burst into wailing: 'Ma-go-o! What is this you gave us? my child is dead. Look Ma-go-o, what have I done to you that you have killed my tiny one?' The shamed, bewildered folk of the house had to pay two rupees to quieten the broken-hearted woman. They had not known that the woman had been carrying a dead child from door to door, blackmailing charity. They were like that, the befouled ones.

No Bengali who heard those cries has forgotten them. The Famine was at one and the same time both an elemental and a complex phenomenon; and this makes it difficult to write about. An American historian Paul Greenough, author of the most comprehensive study of the famine *Prosperity and Misery in Modern Bengal*, has compared its impact to that of the Depression on the industrialised world. Its roots went deep into Bengali society. The questions it raises are of the same order as those raised by the Holocaust or the atrocities of Stalin's Russia: how could a disaster on such a scale have happened? how could the privileged have remained so indifferent? why did so many of the famine victims accept their fate passively? why were there so few riots? 'They died in the streets in front of shops bulging with grain,' an English medical officer of the time testified, 'and it was due to [their] passive, fatalistic attitude . . . that there were no riots and they were dying.'

As *Distant Thunder* implies, the catastrophe was primarily a rural one; the very areas that produced the precious rice were those least able to feed themselves. Calcutta's regular population was basically provided for, protected by government purchasing of rice from outside and by relief programmes for those who could not afford the rising prices. But the impact on the agriculture and culture of Bengal as a whole was frightful. The Famine, and then the Partition, destroyed what remained of Bengal as a land of plenty – *Sonar Bangla*, Golden Bengal – to which the boy Apu refers when he recites the poem in *Aparajito*: the land in which Upendrakisore Ray and his ancestors grew up. *Distant Thunder* describes more than just famine; it shows the eclipse of a whole way of life. As a Bengali journalist put it in early 1944, in his conclusion to a hastily assembled study of the Famine:

> Gone are the cultivators, gone are the householders, rice is gone from the houses. There are no longer cows to give milk. The deities are starving, for there is no worshipful service. The cultivators have sold their draft cattle for the sake of mere subsistence and somehow manage to survive, yet even they don't understand how to carry on. The ponds have dried up, turning to mud. Water is scarce and pure water completely lacking. Numerous diseases have broken out, and the former spontaneous joy of the Bengalis is absolutely ruined. Their simple, easy and natural existence has disappeared, and they are now anxious and preoccupied with illnesses. The noose of poverty has entangled their body and soul, and they have become paralysed. Beginning with the world war, the collective existence of Bengal and the Bengalis has been thrown into confusion. Everything has been looted. In every direction there stretch rough, colourless and endless fields without paddy, fruits or grain. The cultivator sings no more, the lamps no longer burn in the huts at sundown. Bengal's former beauty has disappeared into the womb of oblivion.

There is no doubt that it was Man who brought this on himself, even if natural calamities did make some contribution. The Second World War, and in particular the fighting with the Japanese in Burma, was the indirect cause – not so much as a result of the demand for rice by the troops, which was not their staple food, but because the war disrupted the economic system of Bengal and Burma in many ways, including its concentration of a privileged workforce in Calcutta and other cities. A never-strong network of supply and demand soon broke down under the impetus of the profit-motive. Free enterprise, in the form of speculation unchecked by a corrupt state government divided against itself and an overstretched, indifferent British Raj, was the main cause of the Famine; speculation by everyone, from the humblest cultivator to the richest Marwari merchant in Calcutta fattening himself on every kind of business generated by war. In the village, a web of unenforceable obligations binding landlord to peasant, essentially feudal in nature, was cruelly dissolved by the love of money, leaving the peasants nothing to take its place.

This human failure at all levels, rather than the terrible reality of starvation itself, is the backdrop to Ray's theme – the growth of moral awareness through adversity. Just as it was the restoration of order and purpose in the lives of Bangladeshi refugees in Calcutta that interested him as a film-maker in 1971, not the agonies they had passed through on the way, so in *Distant Thunder* it is the attitudes that give rise to mass death that he examines, rather than the stinking corpses. *Distant Thunder* is not really about famine as such, but about its causes.

None of the characters, the residents of a small village in the paddy-fields of East Bengal, has much idea of what is happening to him to begin with. All they know is that mysterious birds drone over them from time to time – their village is in the flight path of aeroplanes heading east to Burma – and that there are increasing shortages of kerosene and rice. The only one who knows more, Gangacharan the priest and schoolmaster, is hardly better informed: 'Our king is fighting the Japanese and the Germans,' he tells the villagers. He also knows that a place called Singapore has fallen to the Japanese, but he hasn't the faintest notion where it is. His learning is on a par with that of the pot-bellied grocer-teacher in *Pather Panchali*, even if he does know some dog-Sanskrit – which greatly impresses the illiterate folk at whom he intones it.

He is shrewd about using what he does know, and not too curious to extend his horizons further. As the only Brahmin in the village – a situation he has quite recently contrived for its freedom from rivals – he receives as of right the deference of the villagers, including the prosperous headman and landowner Biswas, extracting fees from them in kind for tuition and for ceremonies performed. The Brahmin is holier-than-them, as he has always been and shows every sign that he ever shall be. Nevertheless, Gangacharan does not exploit them excessively; he is at bottom an unambitious, mild-mannered man with decent instincts, satisfied with his small but significant economic privileges and his position in society. Soumitra Chatterjee, who plays him, begins by carrying around a nicely judged aura of myopic complacency, mixed with some concern for others; but as the story progresses, the proportions of this mixture alter visibly.

The main focus of his attention, apart from himself, is his luscious young wife Ananga, whose sweetly innocent radiance affects all who meet her in the village. Where Doyamoyee (in *The Goddess*) has a face which personifies the goddess Durga, Ananga's round peach-like features call to mind Lakshmi, the goddess of good fortune, an idea loaded with connotations for any Bengali brought up in an atmosphere of orthodoxy, of a type interwoven with the concept of Golden Bengal. By selecting the actress Babita, who is from Bangladesh, to play Ananga (rather than Sarmila Tagore whom he had earlier considered), Ray was capitalising on all these associations to intensify his story for Bengalis. In the process, he also helped to make her the leading actress of Bangladesh in – as he puts it – 'terrible commercial films'. 'She has not done a single serious film since *Asani Sanket*,' says Satyajit, who often sees her when she visits Calcutta.

Under western eyes, she can seem overripe, not just honeyed but cloying – something like the effect en masse of Indian miniatures of ladies pining for their lovers, especially for Krishna: a surfeit of sensuousness. Pauline Kael, for instance, sensed in Ananga 'an almost pornographic charm'. 'Played by Babita (that should mean Baby Doll), Ananga is the Indian version of a Hollywood darling. She seems to have been created for the pleasure of man; she has been bred to think of nothing but her husband ... She wants to be a tempting morsel so that her husband can take a juicy bite', wrote Kael in the *New Yorker* in 1973. 'She obviously doesn't know how pretty Brahmin's wives can be in the village,' observes Ray matter-of-factly when reminded of this review, and then adds with a laugh, 'The fact that Babita was pretty didn't bother me at all. I had seen much more beautiful and luscious and baby-dollish Brahmin wives in villages. Actually Babita's very responsive and much more intelligent than she looks. She looks kind of soft and luscious, but she's very sharp.' In fact this response of Kael's carries a large baggage of cultural assumptions with it that I shall return to later.

Other associations for a Bengali audience cluster around the natural environment of the village – the ponds, paddy-fields, palm-trees, banyan-trees, butterflies and flowers with which the film makes much play. Ray had hoped to shoot in Bangladesh, but settled for a village just outside Santiniketan. A house was prepared there for Gangacharan and his wife three or four months in advance of shooting by Ray's art director Asok Bose, Chandragupta's assistant, who had taken over from him. 'He had trees growing in it and they had to have a chance to grow,' recalls Ray, 'and the house had to acquire a look of having been lived in.' At one point Chandragupta returned from Bombay and came to the location to take a look. After nodding his general appreciation, he suddenly pointed out that the thatched roof of the house should have contained many more ordinary household articles tucked between it and the bamboo laths. 'The range of his power of observation just left me wonder-struck,' remembers Soumitra Chatterjee. 'And he was not even a Bengali!'

Although the beauty of such villages and their surroundings has been celebrated in countless poems by Tagore and paintings by Ray's art teachers Bose and Mukherjee, amongst others, it is part of his intention in *Distant Thunder* to stress the *lack* of relationship between the moods of Nature and those of Man, in contrast to his first colour film *Kanchenjungha*. Ray says:

> The response to Nature is related to the class to which the characters belong. Village people are not so responsive to Nature. For instance, there's a film of Mrinal Sen's called *The Royal Hunt*, where the villagers go to see the sunrise – which is totally wrong. They never go out to see the sun rise or set because they're so used to it. But a city person would do it because nowadays it's impossible to see the sunrise because of the high-rise. So it's natural for him to feel it is a special experience.

He uses colour in the film so as to point up the contrast between Nature's throbbing vitality and lushness, and the gradual ebbing away of life from Man. People are dying even though there is a good rice-crop. The sun sets behind Gangacharan in a gorgeous riot of colour, but only we, the audience, have eyes to see it. 'Ray has chosen to photograph the film in rich, warm colours,' wrote the *New York Times* reviewer, 'the effect of which is not to soften the focus of the film but to sharpen it. The course of terrible events seems that much more vivid in landscapes of relentless beauty.' In Bengal a section of Ray's audience disagreed, accusing him of glamorising the Famine. He rebutted the charge by pointing out the existence of colour in both poverty and prosperity and explaining its counterpoint in the film; but he recognised that the relentless association of colour with glamour in Indian cinema made it hard for Bengalis to adjust to *Distant Thunder*. Not so long before, Hollywood had considered colour suitable only for certain kinds of lighter picture.

The colours of artefacts in the film, such as clothes, almost always blend with their natural surroundings, as would have been the case in a remote village at this time, where few artificial dyes would have penetrated. When Ray occasionally does create a clash, it is consequently striking, just as the harshness of machine-produced items in India so often jars on the eye because of the beauty of readily available hand-produced goods made from natural materials: the cheaply glazed cracked cup at the railway-station tea-stall beside the little disposable clay beaker, for instance. So when a man in an electric-blue shirt which can only have come from outside the village, confronts one of the village women on a path in the forest and offers her rice in exchange for sex, the way the shirt clashes with her sari and with the surrounding vegetation underlines the shock of the encounter and subtly prepares us for the woman's eventual elopement to the city with this man in a desperate bid for food. 'That blue is very deliberate,' comments Ray, 'and blue was not used in the film before that; nobody wears blue, and even the sky is a very light shade of blue which you're not conscious of.'

Ananga's saris, by contrast, suggest the warmth of her bucolic nature, and her sensitivity to natural rhythms. Even her hand floating freely in the water of the local pond, with which the film opens, has a shape reminiscent of the *sapla*, an archetypal water-flower of Bengal. She is Mother Lakshmi, as some of the villagers like to call her, from whom bounty naturally flows. Her spirit is purely creative, fertile; unlike that of Kali, in whom creation and destruction, compassion and cruelty, are in perpetual tension. The hands of Kali both give and take away, while Lakshmi's can only give.

Hands are a motif of *Distant Thunder*. Some of the most crucial moments in the film are focused on them. It is as if Ray wants to symbolise the disintegration of caste barriers by the degree to which people are willing to touch or help each other. But as well as giving succour, hands are also the agents of violence; Ray gives expression to both aspects in his compositions. He interlinks these images, as so often, at both the conscious and the unconscious levels. They are never overstated – in fact one could view the entire film without becoming aware of the motif – and yet the total impression has done its work in the mind, helping to convince us of the authenticity of Gangacharan's breaking of a caste taboo at the end of the film. Ray handles this rather as he handles the idea of caste in the film: not as something kept isolated like a Catholic dogma, in which some believe and others do not, but as a state of mind shared in different degrees by all the characters, with an effect on their actions that fluctuates with the outside influences on them.

The first appearance of the motif after the opening shot occurs after the first signs of disruption in Gangacharan's comfortable little universe have already appeared, like a symptom warning of the disease to come; a decrepit old Brahmin, who had earlier waylaid Gangacharan for food on his journey back from a ceremony, instals himself in his house while he is out, and obtains a meal from his obliging wife. When Gangacharan returns he wants to eject the guest but Ananga gently insists that they ask him to stay one night. In their bedroom that night, while the old man sleeps on a mat on the verandah, Ananga quietly offers to take up work husking rice, in exchange for one measure of rice per so many husked. Her husband is both shocked and amused at the idea. In the light of the kerosene lamp which will soon run dry, he takes her hand, which is unlined by physical labour, and looks steadily into her eyes. He cannot imagine her as a working woman.

Soon after, he is compelled to alter his view, after he finds himself roughly thrown to the ground while helplessly watching a near-riot over rice at Biswas's rice-store. Returning home, his hand heavily clasps the spikes of the gate he would normally have pushed open in high spirits. His wife asks him how much he had to pay for rice that day. Glumly he says he has got none. But Ananga has; she proffers the precious white grains in the palm of her hand. Without waiting for him to agree she has done the practical thing and gone to work husking with the other village women.

Rice gets steadily scarcer and more expensive. The next occasion on which it is offered in the palm of a hand is rather different; the hand belongs to the man in the blue shirt, whose face is terribly scarred – the result of a firework accident. He attempts to bribe Chutki, one of the village women, to go with him. Although she refuses and nearly assaults him, sheer hunger later drives her to agree. Everyone's behaviour is changing as the pressure to survive increases. Ananga is willing to consider eating even the pond-snails mentioned to her by Chutki. Gangacharan, after silently observing the hunched figures of women collecting the snails from the weeds in the pond, feels compelled to reflect sombrely to his wife that 'The peasants do all the work, and we live off them. That's what's wrong.' His ignorance of their work is certainly telling; he has only just learnt that the rice-crop cannot be eaten immediately after it is harvested. Something he fully understands though, is his wife's next gesture; slowly but quite unhistrionically she removes her bangles and offers them to him in the palm of her outstretched hand. Selling these may keep them from starvation for the time being at least.

While he now sets off to walk a fair distance to a neighbouring village where someone is believed to have rice for sale, she goes into the forest nearby with Chutki and another woman in search of wild potatoes. As the other two dig Ananga stands by, unable to help and somewhat reluctant too, unused as she is to physical labour. She sees a solitary pink flower, which matches the pink of her sari, and picks it; and for a moment, seeing it in her hand, we recall the tranquillity of that first gesture in the film in which her hand loitered in the pond like a lily-flower or a lotus. The feeling is immediately crushed by the two women's triumphant extraction of the potato tuber from the forest earth and a close-up of the hand of a man smoking a cigarette in the shade of a nearby tree. As the three women set off back, carrying their prize, the hand flicks the butt into the water of a stream, and its owner goes into action. A little later we see the stream again, this time discoloured by blood; a man's hand floats loosely in it, but its motion is that of death, not life. Without realising the force of her blows Chutki has beaten Ananga's assailant to death with the bar she had used to extract the potato.

Chutki shares Ananga's gut sense of revulsion at the advances made to her by the man, but unlike her she would rather live in dishonour than perish in chastity. Eventually she slips away to join the scar-faced man, who lives at a ruined brick-kiln near the village. As she approaches it, ready to give in to him, Ray suddenly shows us a chameleon perched with ancient alertness and perfect camouflage on some outcrop of the old kiln – and then reverts to Chutki and the man. It would be pointless to try to pinpoint in words the effect of this little touch; 'What kind of animal is Man?' is perhaps as close as one can get. The richness of its ambiguity, in the context of a hundred other such juxtapositions of Man and Nature during the course of the film, is one of the hallmarks of Satyajit Ray as an artist.

Wishing desperately for her behaviour to be accepted by Ananga, Chutki now hovers at the door of her house and offers her rice in her palm. 'Don't you have a husband?' asks Ananga, when she realises its provenance, simply unable to comprehend how she can sink so low, though she knows that it was Chutki's husband who sold off his rice at a profit when the price first went up.

Finally the first death by starvation occurs. The victim is a young Untouchable girl from Gangacharan's previous village whom we first met at the beginning of the film as a welcome visitor to their house but whom they must not physically touch, by mutual consent. She drags herself back to them for help at the end, her eyes glazed for lack of food, and collapses under a tree. But when Ananga comes offering her food in the shape of arum root, which is all that she has, the girl is unwilling to touch either it or the hand that brings it, though she manages feebly to raise her own hand with four extended fingers to show she has not eaten for four days. In her own mind she remains Untouchable even at the point of death, and the food she desires is equally illusory – not arum root, but fish curry, a symbol of Bengali prosperity, which she could hardly have afforded even in times of plenty.

Just as the girl's wretched condition persuades Ananga that she may touch her, so Gangacharan too abandons taboos and readily picks up the girl's hand to take her pulse. It flops in a dramatic silhouette against the sunset; and we know her life has just left her. But her corpse remains, and Gangacharan, breaking yet another taboo – and this time a strict one – feels obliged to give it a proper cremation rather than leave it for the jackals to consume. The stripping away of his own means of livelihood has stripped him of his illusions and awakened his conscience. He feels some responsibility for the girl in death which he did not feel in life, and even for the greedy old Brahmin whom, even as they speak about the dead girl, he and his wife can see approaching, returning to their house, trailing his family of dependants. 'What shall we do?' asks Ananga. 'Well we'll be ten instead of two,' says Gangacharan simply. 'Eleven,' she adds with a shy pause, and looks at him. And at long last he realises what she has been delicately hinting for weeks: in this atmosphere of death a new life is on its way to them. This is where the film leaves him and his wife, facing a very uncertain future, as the screen fills with silhouettes on the move, an army of famished people, and the following statement appears to grim musical accompaniment: 'Over five million died of starvation and epidemics in Bengal in what has come to be known as the man-made famine of 1943.'

Distant Thunder is one of the films of Ray that has made a big impact on western critics and audiences; but, despite much praise from critics (and the top prize at the Berlin Festival), many of them have also found it to be melodramatic in places, 'forced' (to quote Kael), in a sense too simple, like a 'fable' or 'folk-tale' (*New York Times* and *Time*). They probably felt a little impatient with what they perceived as a lack of subtlety compared with Ray's other work; 'One famine is much like another', is an attitude easy to slip into when viewing Third World disasters from the West. How else to explain the wide variations in the death-toll of the Famine as reported by the critics, and the fact that no less than two major British critics wrote that the Brahmin's wife, rather than her neighbour, eventually sells herself for rice? or the comment of the *Times* reviewer David Robinson, intended as praise, that 'from the first moments of any Ray film the spectator forgets the racial and cultural difference of the characters and sees only human beings.' It is certainly a tribute to Ray's artistry that he can elicit such a reaction, but that does not make it a credible statement, as Ray himself agrees. That it should be applied to his most caste-ridden film (excepting only *Deliverance*), makes it all the odder.

The film's simplicity is deceptive. Ray's theme has been perceived by critics, but not the 'hundred little apparently irrelevant details which, instead of obscuring the theme, only help to intensify it by contrast, and in addition create the illusion of actuality better.' The film's characters are at one level recognisable types; Gangacharan, with his umbrella and his trim moustache, returning home to his wife after a hard day's priestly duty, does have something of a suburban commuter in the West, as one reviewer remarked. He is jealous of his small privileges and relishes his comforts like a large benign fish in a small village pond. But he also has a very Bengali side to him and so has the film. It abounds in specific references: to Lakshmi, to the different saris worn by Ananga, and to the blowing of conches at nightfall, as well as to patterns of behaviour like the old Brahmin's expectation of food and Gangacharan's willingness to oblige him, and the chastity and self-sacrifice of Ananga. These have no easy modern equivalents in the West. The 'almost pornographic charm' of Ananga that Kael sensed, and her very un-American subservience to her husband, make a rather different impression on Bengalis. She may be naïve in one way but she also epitomises some of the good qualities that seem to belong to an older, more graceful age, like Biswambhar Roy in *The Music Room*, and King Wajid Ali Shah in *The Chess Players*.

Satyajit Ray is ambivalent in his feelings for this old world, which was part of the reason for his indifference to the Famine victims in 1943, and why, as Mrinal Sen puts it, 'there was stink in the air but not much anger' in Calcutta at the time – among the enlightened as well as among the hard-hearted. On top of being overwhelmed by the scale of the disaster, as we know he was, Ray also felt a certain lack of sympathy with the world from which the victims came, with their caste mentality, that led both to their emotional blackmail of city-dwellers and to their fatalistic attitudes – their belief, as Greenough aptly puts it, that 'submission to authority is the essence of order, and that men and women, adults and children, patrons and clients, rulers and ruled stand in different relations of necessity to the establishment of prosperity.' Satyajit felt their suffering and their misery, but he also believed that the old, irrational system of values that had helped to create it, must pass. At heart he is a revolutionary; it is vital to him that Gangacharan should, of his own volition, begin to reject caste, despite the terrible crisis required to bring this about, than that the status quo should be maintained in all its benighted sterility. Gangacharan's decision to cremate the girl's corpse is, to Ray, 'a big step forward, an enormously progressive gesture'. That is why *Distant Thunder*, though it ends with one death and the certainty of five million more, is a much less bleak film than *Deliverance*, which ends with only one death and a Brahmin priest disposing of an Untouchable body under cover of darkness like an animal's carcass, before returning to his house, unmoved, to wash away his pollution and resume his centuries-old routine.

21

Detective Films:
Chiriakhana (The Zoo) 1967
The Golden Fortress (Sonar Kella) 1974
The Elephant God
(Joi Baba Felunath) 1978

···❧[◖⊙◗]❧···

R AY has had a penchant for Sherlock Holmes ever since he read
the stories as a boy. He and Holmes resemble each other in certain
respects to a remarkable degree, though Satyajit could never act with the
cold-bloodedness of Holmes. Feluda, the detective Satyajit has described
and illustrated in more than a dozen novels since 1965, along with his
teenage side-kick Topse are Bengali relatives of Holmes and Watson, by
way of Ray. When Soumitra Chatterjee (who plays the detective) met
Ray after he had written his first Feluda novel, he told him: 'Manikda, I
think you have modelled Feluda on yourself? The illustrations look a bit
like you.' To which Satyajit replied laughing, 'But no, many people have
come to me and said it looks like you!' Today he admits the resemblance
quite happily: 'I'm sure there's a lot of me in him but I can't tell you to
what extent.'

'The good life' does not interest Feluda; nor does he drink or
seek out the company of women – in fact, he is unmarried – and he
has a natural ability to communicate with children. We learn that his
upbringing, like Ray's, was somewhat out of the ordinary, because he
lost both parents at an early age, and was raised by Topse's mother and
father, a fairly conventional, decent, middle-class Bengali couple. He has
grown into a reserved, thoughtful man with inexhaustible curiosity and
encyclopedic knowledge, which he now puts to use fighting criminals for
the sake of adventure with a worthwhile goal: not money. Although he has
strong feelings, they are restrained; he never loses his temper, however
irrational or ill-judged the behaviour of those around him, preferring irony
as his method of rebuke. His entire outlook is modern and scientific, but
he preserves a healthy open-mindedness about the supernatural. He is a
sceptic but certainly not a cynic.

But before going further with Feluda, I shall briefly discuss *Chiriakhana*
(*The Zoo*), Ray's very first detective film – shot in 1966/7 – which has not
been seen outside Bengal and which I have been able to see only once.
It is based on a short story by Saradindu Banerjee, Ray's only authentic

predecessor in this genre in Bengal, who created a series of stories around
a detective called Byomkesh Baksi, played in Ray's film by Uttam Kumar
(of *Nayak*).

Chiriakhana takes place mainly in a peculiar colony set up at a
distance from Calcutta for the benefit of misfits and outcasts from
society. Its founder is a retired judge with a conscience about the people
he condemned to death. He comes to Baksi in Calcutta to enlist his help
in obtaining the details of a film which contains a haunting love-song he
heard one night in the colony. It turns out it was sung by an attractive
actress who made only that one film eight years previously and then
disappeared; she was last seen with her lover in a gathering, at which
a murder took place. It appears that she must be in the colony, though
unrecognisable in the photographs of the residents that Baksi snaps while
posing as a Japanese horticulturist (a funny scene in which he slips out of
'Japanese' Bengali into ordinary Bengali when no one is listening). The
mystery deepens when the retired judge himself is murdered, followed by
one of the colony's residents. A rough, bearded Punjabi is apprehended by
the police. It turns out that he is the first husband of the retired judge's
wife. The judge had condemned him to hang some years before, but he
had somehow escaped the noose. He has the motive to be the murderer
but Baksi is not convinced that he is guilty. The clue to the culprit eventually
emerges from Baksi's tape-recorded interviews with the colony's residents;
one of them, a young woman who claims to be from Hooghly near Calcutta,
lets slip a dialect word that identifies her as someone from East Bengal. She
is lying to cover for herself and one of the other residents, her erstwhile lover,
a shady doctor who committed the murders. He will not admit to them until,
in front of everyone, Baksi plays the old film song on his tape-recorder.
This is too much for the young woman, who now picks a bitter row with
her partner. She was the actress who sang in the film and it was he who
was responsible for cutting short her career: he arranged plastic surgery
for her, so that she would not be recognised after they eloped. The police
now arrest him, as Baksi blithely terrifies his associates with a pet snake
that he keeps about his person. He could solve the mystery because he
trusts no one absolutely, he tells them; not even them – no one, that is,
except his snake.

Apart from demonstrating that Ray, the composer of the song that
causes all the trouble and then unravels it, could have made his fortune as a
songwriter in the mainstream Indian cinema (as could Tagore), *Chiriakhana*
shows Ray's command over the idiom of the American thriller of an earlier
time. It is an idiom that suits Uttam Kumar, who here has something of the
sexuality of Bogart or Mitchum. But instead of simply imitating that style,
Ray creates something fresh with 'a total avoidance of occidental thriller
clichés', as he wrote to Seton; 'it's certainly not one for the Bond addicts!'
His aim was to retain a whodunit structure which would 'manage to remain
thoroughly Bengali, to invest a western genre with an indigenous character,

scrupulously avoiding pandering and forcing alert participation on the part of the audience.'

He had in fact agreed to the film only to save his assistants from dire straits. They had bought the story and persuaded Uttam Kumar to star in it, and then lost confidence in themselves. Since Ray, in the absence of finance for *Goopy and Bagha*, was at a loose end, he agreed to take over. 'I accepted willy-nilly,' he says. 'Whodunits don't make very good films, because of the very long explanation at the end, where the film becomes very static. This particular story needed that scene; it was obligatory. But, as against that, I must say that it had a whole lot of interesting characters, and I could make an interesting casting using very skilled professionals in these parts: people I hadn't used before. That was rather an attractive aspect.' Nevertheless, he does not regard *Chiriakhana* as a true Ray film. 'There seems to be a great dearth of prizeworthy directors in India!' he wrote to Seton at the end of 1968. 'You'll be tickled to know that I won the State Award as the best director – for *Chiriakhana*!!'

The first film about his own detective, *The Golden Fortress* (*Sonar Kella*), was shot from December 1973 with finance obtained from the West Bengal Government (where Ray's old school friend S.S. Ray was again Chief Minister), after three producers had turned it down. Ray got right away from a conventional whodunit, even though he had used this structure in his own novel *Sonar Kella*, the third of his stories to feature Feluda. He felt it would be more interesting to let the audience know who the villains were at an early stage, but keep the *detective* guessing – 'so it becomes more or less like a Hitchcock story where you know who the killer is.' Character therefore takes precedence over plot, although there is plenty happening to hold one's attention, and – more to the point – the attention of a child.

Feluda holds centre-stage, assisted always by Topse (who tells the story, Watson-like, in the novel but not in the film). Topse is about fourteen, bright and cheerful, and hero-worships Feluda; and like his hero he shows no interest in girls. To western tastes, he is perhaps slightly colourless, a bit of a goody-goody, but he makes an excellent foil for Felu and friend to Jotayu, the third member of the problem-solving trio. Jotayu's real name is Lalmohan Ganguli, but as nom de plume he has taken the name of the courageous mythical bird who attacks Ravana in the *Ramayana* while he is abducting Sita. He writes spine-tingling tales of adventure, with titles like *Sahara Shivers* and *Fearless Foe*, that Topse has read. He insists on joining Feluda and Topse when he encounters them on a train to Rajasthan, having discovered to his great excitement that Feluda is a real detective; he himself is on a tour of India collecting experiences for his fictional detective Rudra and the encounter is providential, he feels. Feluda is not so sure, but in time he becomes very fond of this foolish, voluble enthusiast, whose daring dreams bear no relation to this abilities or his physique, but who is completely good-hearted and uncomplicated. 'Whatever I have failed to become, I have implanted in my heroes', he tells Feluda happily.

'I needed a third character,' says Ray, 'and I thought of a writer of cheap thrillers who would never have had the experience of an actual thrill. He relishes life. He enjoys everything. He's not terribly bright but he thinks he's bright . . . But he's the first one to suspect one of the villains of being a fake. He's a very Bengali character. You have writers of thrillers like that. I have not ever met any but I can imagine them being like him more or less.' As with Topse, the western audience is likely to feel less drawn to him than the Bengali one. The idea that successful thriller-writers are hard-boiled and cynical is so engrained in the West that Jotayu can seem merely silly, instead of comic – an impression reinforced by the fact that his jokes do not translate well. His nearest equivalent is perhaps the bumbling duo Thomson and Thompson in the *Tintin* books, which Ray feels may have been at the back of his mind when making *The Golden Fortress*. Both he and his son have been fans of them ever since Satyajit was presented with a French edition for Sandip in Brussels in 1958. He thinks *Tintin* has 'a very very filmic approach'.

The other main characters in the film consist of two villains, a young boy, and his guardian, a parapsychologist who is taking the boy round Rajasthan to see if he can identify the 'golden fortress' which he claims to have known in a previous life. The villains are after them, believing that the boy will lead them to hidden treasure, and Felu, Topse and Jotayu are in pursuit of them all. One of the villains – a plump, goateed man with fierce black spectacles and a large bald patch – is the brains; the other, a heavily built man, also balding, with long sideburns and a penchant for blaring shirts, carries out his orders. Between them they manage to push the parapsychologist off a hillside and make off with the boy, but after that most of their plans go awry. They both give splendid performances, full of wit and invention.

In casting the boy Mukul, Ray was exceptionally fortunate. Kusal Chakravarti's performance, and that of Chandana Banerjee as Ratan in *The Postmaster*, are the two highest points in Ray's illustrious career as a director of children. Kusal was brought to Ray by his father when it was announced that *Sonar Kella* was to be filmed. Satyajit says:

His father had close associations with the stage and the boy was in the habit of going to watch adult theatre performances. He was able to mimic some of our well-known stage actors. He was exceedingly gifted. And he seemed quite unaware of the camera, completely stage-free and unselfconscious. A very rare kind of boy. I don't think I have come across any other boy so free from nervousness. When he was told that he would have to be away from his mother for more than a month, he said 'Well that's all right, because I'll be working.'

He and Satyajit struck up a fine rapport, as happens with the majority
of children he directs. 'Most of us talking to children assume a different
sort of posture, as if they are inferior or unequal, but Manikda treats
them as equals, as people in their own right, not as half-grown human
beings,' says Soumitra Chatterjee, who remembers a touching example
from *Sonar Kella*:

> One night we were coming back from location to our camp in Jaisalmer
> fifty miles or so, 2½ hours' drive. We had been shooting from the
> early morning until late in the evening and all of us were absolutely
> falling dead. We were so tired. Manikda as usual was sitting by the side
> of the driver where he gets more leg-space. Three of us were in the
> back. Mukul was at the front with Manikda. He was at that time at that
> peculiar age when children start asking questions about everything. No
> one was in a mood to talk. He was asking me questions too – 'Soumitra
> Kaka, what do you think is the reason for all the stars?' and I would just
> give a very small answer without hurting the boy. But Manikda, who
> is basically so grave and reserved, not babbling or talking, was sitting
> and looking at the sky and saying to Mukul 'because of this, because
> of that' in exactly the same mood as he had been talking throughout
> the day with me – with patience and that attitude he was talking to
> another individual, not to a child.

'Do you think about what will interest children when you write
a screenplay like *Sonar Kella*?' I once asked Ray. 'Yes I suppose
subconsciously one does. But also what interests me,' he replied with a
chuckle, rather as his grandfather Upendrakisore, whose explanations to
children appealed equally to adults, might once have done.

In this case, it was the research into reincarnation conducted by
a certain Dr Banerjee, a parapsychologist at Rajasthan University in
Jodhpur, that sparked off Ray's story. He came to Ray's house at Bishop
Lefroy Road and told him about a young boy who had vivid recollections
of a place that he had never visited. Dr Banerjee was able to guess where
it was, take the boy there, and find that his descriptions tallied with the
reality. Ray does not know whether he believes in reincarnation, but he
says 'There are so many examples of cases I think one should keep an
open mind.'

The idea of setting the film in Rajasthan and of associating
Jaisalmer with a golden fortress, had been planted in Ray a few
years before, while shooting *Goopy and Bagha* there. He had seen
'fortresses perched on hilltops, fortresses rising out of barren plains,
fortresses in forests, fortresses in the middle of cities, and fortresses
nestling in the lap of mountains.' Jaisalmer was perhaps the most striking
of them all. There, as he describes with understated relish in 'Meetings
with a Maharaja', he was shown objects made out of the local stone that

quite astonished him:

> A bearer came in with a tray with an assortment of stone objects on it: a tumbler, a teacup, a spoon, a necklace, some cuff-links. The gleaming purity of the saffron Jaisalmer marble made us hold our breath. It was as if gold had renounced its lustre and turned ascetic.
>
> 'Bring a bowl of water,' ordered the Maharaja, and the bearer obliged by bringing a blue plastic bowl half filled with water. The teacup and the tumbler were now gently placed in the water. They stayed on the surface, floating. It was like magic, and we all but applauded.
>
> 'They were made by a Muslim craftsman who is now dead. These were his last gifts to me. The only other craftsman who can carve them so thin and with such perfect balance has gone to Pakistan.'

In *The Golden Fortress*, it is Felu's first encounter with some objects like these in a shop in Jodhpur that enables him to guess that Mukul's recollection probably refers to Jaisalmer, the city far out in the desert built of this golden stone.

Some of the best scenes in the film are, as ever with Ray, the wordless ones, sometimes accompanied by his fine background score. There is the trio chasing a train on camel-back, for instance: a major achievement with only one camera. 'Kurosawa would be using nine!' jokes Satyajit. Some American critics felt this scene was like an elaborate Hollywood production. As *Variety* commented: 'It's the kind of film that points out the glaring weaknesses in films being turned out recently [1975] by some major studios.' Or an intimate scene perhaps, like the one at night where an unmoving camera positioned outside the perimeter of the Circuit House in Jodhpur watches its lighted windows and passages as the small silhouette of Mukul is seen affectionately pulling the taller, rounder figure of the brainy villain off to supper, while from somewhere not far-off a plaintive song floats through the cool evening air of the surrounding desert. Or again, there are the scenes around a tiny railway-station in the middle of nowhere, as the trio settle down to a long wait for the train that is due in the small hours. Jotayu, his back still suffering from the camel-ride, exercises it by strutting along the platform and back again and the camera follows him, passing behind several figures sitting motionlessly wrapped in red shawls; one of them, we realise, is the brawny villain disguised as a Rajasthani peasant. Behind them all, the sun rapidly sets over the desert, filling the sky with a glorious flush of red. This scene and the next one, where Feluda watches some plangent desert musicians at night and spots the villain through his disguise, demonstrate not only the use of dramatic film language in a dramatic context, but also a powerful feeling for natural colours which is evident throughout the film. 'We avoided as much as possible the use of yellow before Jaisalmer,' says Ray. 'Nobody wears yellow, none of the walls is painted yellow, no dress is yellow except in the far background. There's no emphasis on yellow.

The first yellow you come across is when Mukul sees the fortress through the train window.'

Most of the qualities evident in *The Golden Fortress* also appear in Ray's second Feluda film *The Elephant God* (*Joi Baba Felunath*), in suitably modified form. Instead of Rajasthan, its setting is Benares, where the trio have come on holiday and got tangled up in solving the theft of a priceless image of Ganesh, the elephant-headed god. The possibility of shooting Benares in colour, twenty years or so after *Aparajito* – during the first half of 1978 – appealed to Ray, as did the opportunity to depict the ethos of Bengalitola, the area of the city where a large population of Bengalis live, some of them in extraordinary mansions tucked away between narrrow alleys. One particular family in Bengalitola, for instance, live in a complex of interconnecting annexes that gives away nothing from the lane outside. They have been in Benares for almost four hundred years, since the Mughal time, and theirs is the city's oldest *Durga Puja* ceremony, in which their clay images of Durga, Lakshmi, Saraswati, Kartik, and Ganesh are taken through the lanes on separate palanquins to the ghats for immersion. It is from such a family – grandfather, son, and small grandson in the film – that the gem-studded gold Ganesh is taken, and the process of putting the finishing touches to just such a many-armed Durga image, forms the striking, faintly sinister opening scene of the film. (Ray even discovered a potter called Feluda in Bengalitola while shooting, who complained of the teasing he had to put up with because of his name.)

Other elements in the story that appealed to Ray were a knife-throwing sequence and the villainous Marwari dealer in stolen antiques, Maganlal Meghraj (played by Utpal Dutta) who arranges it, in order to give poor Jotayu the fright of his life and to warn Felu against meddling in his affairs. 'He's a very polished and ruthless kind of baddie,' says Satyajit. 'He's certainly the most ferocious character that I have created. I wanted a really colourful and cruel villain – a strong adversary for Felu.'

Compared with *The Golden Fortress*, *The Elephant God* is a rather sombre film – not really a children's film at all, as Utpal Dutta agrees. Corruption is integral to it in a way that is not true of the first film, and Felu shows signs of a harder heart. Ray, who wrote the script in the aftermath of the Emergency period, was possibly influenced by the same pessimistic mood that produced *The Middle Man*. 'It could have happened,' he says, 'but whether that feeling crept into the film I don't know, because much of the material comes from the book itself which was written some time before.'

The second film also differs in being a whodunit, and it is somewhat less interesting for that reason. Its style is not at all similar to *The Golden Fortress* because the story is so different, as Ray observes. 'There isn't that element of moving from place to place. It goes to Benares and settles down there. It is a film which meditates, while Felu attempts to cogitate his way to

a solution of the problem of who has taken the Ganesh. The action is studded
with interludes, such as the doings of a muscleman who is staying in the same
hotel as the trio, that are usually absorbing but not always so well integrated in
the story as they might be. Possibly this is because the form of the whodunit
demands a faster pace than Ray allows it. 'Once the various elements of the
story which are supposed to interact are established,' according to Ray, 'you
can introduce little things like that [i.e. the muscleman] because the mind
is attuned to a certain kind of structure and expectations arise. So you play
about. You have the stem of the tree and these are the little branches. One
is conscious of the stem and you also have the branches and the leaves and
the flowers and the fruits.'

The film is still a rich and engrossing one, with 'well-knitted
characterisations and inventive incidents', to quote Gene Moscowitz in
Variety, and it is a pity that neither it nor *The Golden Fortress* has
been seen outside festivals (except in Bengal). The ghats on which Apu
gazed in wide-eyed curiosity in *Aparajito*, have become the shop-window
of thieves and swindlers in *The Elephant God*, though they are no less
fascinating for that. One such is Machli Baba, a much more sinister fake
than the benign conman Birinchi Baba in *Mahapurush*. He is in league
with Meghraj, a 'fence' for stolen antiques, which are presented to him,
carefully concealed, as gifts, while all around the air is filled with the
devotional songs to Krishna known as *bhajans*. The Graham Greene-like
contrast between appearances and reality in this scene – as if smugglers
had spiked communion-wafers with cocaine – excites Ray, particularly as
the *bhajans* are so well sung. It is comparable to the blackly comic scene in
The Middle Man where the PRO Mitter takes Somnath to a similar religious
gathering in Calcutta, points out a client and whispers to him that this man
will always be sure to shed a tear when a certain point in the song is reached.
Ray has never been able to take organised religion seriously; it brings back
memories of sitting for hours in Brahmo meetings as a child. One of the
things he cherishes most about making *The Elephant God* was the sight
of the actors playing Topse and Jotayu, dressed as sadhus, making their
way to a certain point on the ghats for filming and having to stop every
ten seconds or so 'because people were falling at their feet'! He noticed
that Santosh Dutta (Jotayu) even half closed his eyes and gave blessings
with his head and hands.

Another vivid memory concerns the difficulty of shooting in the
lanes of Bengalitola. Ray wanted to get shots of the trio ambling along at
night gossiping in the half-light, which they are doing so that Jotayu can
gather atmosphere for his next novel. When he turned up with the actors
and crew at eight in the evening, about a thousand people had gathered
to watch the shooting. Although this had been tolerable on the ghats, in
the lanes there was absolutely no question of shooting in such a crowd.
Somehow his assistants managed to shout loud enough to get this fact
across, but the people did not disperse. So Ray ordered everyone back to

the hotel, expecting to have to finish the scene in the studio in Calcutta.

After supper that night there was a knock at the door of his room. Two young men were standing outside. They came from the area where he had been trying to shoot. Holding his feet with their hands they implored him, 'Dada, come again tomorrow, come a little later – we guarantee no crowd. If you come to Benares and leave our area without getting what you want, we won't be able to show our faces here. It will be a stain on the face of Benares for all time . . .' Satyajit agreed to try again the following night at eleven. When they returned as promised, they found no crowd at all. But there was a new problem. During the day a man from a local Bengali shop Rinku Silk House, had plastered the area with posters, hoping to advertise his wares in the film. He had turned up for the shooting too. Patiently it was explained to him that with so many posters around there was a danger that the audience wouldn't be able to see Felu for Rinku. Could he therefore please remove them? The man looked rather downcast, but had to agree. In half an hour members of Ray's unit had removed all but a few of the offending slogans, and Ray was able to shoot. They worked until three in the morning, with less interruption than if they had been shooting in a studio.

22

The Chess Players
(Shatranj ke Khilari) 1977

···❊❂{ ❀❂❀ }❂❊···

'THE most significant fact of modern days is this,' wrote Tagore in 1922, 'that the West has met the East. Such a momentous meeting of humanity, in order to be fruitful, must have at its heart some great emotional idea, generous and creative.' Whereas in fact, Tagore noted sadly, the interaction of the two reminded him of the ravaged battlefields in France he had just visited: 'Something of the same sense of oppression in a different degree, is produced in my mind when I realise the effect of the West upon Eastern life – the West which, in its relation to us, is all plan and purpose incarnate, without any superfluous humanity.' Or, as Lord Curzon said in 1905 in his last speech as Viceroy, his ideal for the Englishman in India was that he should

> fight for the right, abhor the imperfect or the mean, swerve neither to the right hand nor the left, . . . care nothing for flattery or applause or odium or abuse – it is so easy to have any of them in India – never let [his] enthusiasm be soured or [his] courage grow dim, . . . [in order to] feel that somewhere among these millions [he] has left a little justice or happiness or prosperity, a sense of manliness or moral dignity, a spring of patriotism, a dawn of intellectual enlightenment, or a stirring of duty, where it did not before exist – that is enough, that is the Englishman's justification in India.

'It's a very, very complex mixed kind of thing, the entire British heritage in India', says Ray. 'I think many of us owe a great deal to it. I'm thankful for the fact that at least I'm familiar with both cultures and it gives me a very much stronger footing as a film-maker, but I'm also aware of all the dirty things that were being done. I really don't know how I feel about it.'

The opportunity to probe some of these deep equivocations in himself drew Ray, in 1974/5, to tackle a film about the British Raj that differs in certain important respects from all his films until then. *The Chess Players* remains by far his most expensive film, drawing as it does on stars of the Bombay cinema – and even of western cinema – and large period sets. Its most fundamental difference, however, is that it is Ray's first and only fictional film venture into a culture and a language not those of Bengal (if we discount his later short film for television, *Deliverance*). Writing and directing a screenplay in a language other than Bengali was something Ray had once declared he would never attempt. *The Chess Players* is in Urdu and Ray would have to get round the language problem by finding first-class Urdu-speaking collaborators and actors with a higher degree of professionalism than most of those in Bengal.

His love of chess, of Lucknow as a setting and of its high culture, especially its music and its dance, and of Prem Chand's short story about the annexation of Lucknow in 1856, were the reasons he changed his mind. Chess had been an addiction with him in the 1940s and the first part of the 1950s; as we know, it faded away only with the onset of a greater passion, *Pather Panchali*, when Satyajit sold his collection of books on chess as part of his drive to raise funds. His visits to Lucknow as a boy, when he was taken to all the famous places in the city, had left an indelible impression on him, though he knew no nawabs as such, only the guests in the house of his famous composer uncle Atulprasad Sen, whom he remembers indulging in 'a great display of Urdu good manners'. He experienced that atmosphere once again as an adult when he returned to Lucknow to arrange for the singer Akhtari Bai to appear in *The Music Room*; her barrister husband was 'absolute perfection in his behaviour and courtliness,' Satyajit recalls.

Even now, more than a century after the eclipse of the nawabi power at Lucknow, the city occupies a special place in the life of India. In the latter part of the eighteenth century and the first half of the nineteenth, it and Oudh, the rich state of which it was capital were the repository of Mughal culture after the erosion of Mughal power in Delhi. The British recognised this and created the rulers of Oudh kings in 1814, while steadily undermining their sovereignty and revenues from 1765 onwards. They, and the city they embellished with palaces and mosques, gradually became bywords for decadent refinement in every department of life, whether it was dress, banquets, the hookah, pigeon-breeding, music and poetry, or love-making; Lucknow in its heyday was the 'Paris of the East', the 'Babylon of India'.

The best guide to this culture is a wonderful book that appeared in an English translation published in London, just as Ray was beginning his research on his film: *Lucknow: The Last Phase of an Oriental Culture*, by Abdul Halim Sharar. It is, in the words of its two British and Indian translators, 'a primary source of great value, a unique document, both alive and authentic in every detail, of an important Indian culture at its zenith', as Ray himself gratefully acknowledges. One of the most pleasing responses he had to *The Chess Players* was a letter from one of Sharar's translators, Fakhir Hussain, who observed that every detail of the film was correct.

Sharar's credentials were both impeccable and unique. Born in 1860 he spent the first nine years of his life in Lucknow and the next ten in Calcutta at the court of the exiled King of Oudh, Wajid Ali Shah, whose forced abdication is of course the central event of *The Chess Players*. Most of the rest of Sharar's life was spent in Lucknow, and in due course he became a pioneer of the modern Urdu novel, a historian 'of refreshingly wide horizons', and an essayist 'equipped with a profound knowledge of Arabic, Urdu and Persian literatures and Islamic theology', to quote Hussain. He was also, like most thinking Indians of his time, deeply affected by the West, and this included paying a visit to Britain. Western influence makes his book fascinatingly schizophrenic: loving, minutely documented detail is accompanied by indictments of Lucknow's moral laxity worthy of the most self-confident Victorian imperialist, sometimes appearing within a few pages of each other. Perhaps without his fully realising it, Sharar's life dramatised vividly the conflict and the creative possibilities at the heart of India's response to the West.

These are at their most stark in relation to the King himself, whose character, wrote Sharar, 'appears to be one of the most dubious in all the records of history' and yet who is also 'extremely devout, abstinent and a strict observer of Muslim religious law'. Sharar was disgusted by Wajid Ali Shah's versification of his love-affairs and amorous escapades in his youth with servants, courtesans and other women – 'he even had no hesitation in showing shamefully low taste and in using obscene language' – but he delights in the King's mastery of classical music, both as a connoisseur and as a composer. 'I have heard from reliable court singers,' wrote Sharar, 'who were his companions, that even when asleep the King's big toes used to move rhythmically.' Still, he could not avoid condemning Wajid for prostituting his talents by adding to an existing style of 'light, simple and attractive tunes which could be appreciated by everyone' – *thumris*, several of which find their way into Ray's film.

Very early on in his extensive research for *The Chess Players* (which took him as far afield as London), Ray ran into his own antipathy for the King, which was mixed with admiration. At several points he felt like giving up altogether and wrote to say so in a number of letters jointly addressed to his Urdu collaborator Shama Zaidi and to Bansi Chandragupta, who was then in Bombay too. On one occasion Shama had written to Ray offering to translate Wajid Ali's autobiography for him, in which the King describes his sex life from the age of eight. 'Manikda said – don't tell me all this because then I'll dislike him even more,' Shama recalls with a laugh. Satyajit says now:

> I think there were two aspects to Wajid Ali Shah's character, one which you could admire and one which you couldn't. At one point I wrote to Shama that I just could not feel any sympathy for this stupid character. And unless I feel some sympathy I cannot make a film. But then finally, after long months of study, of the nawabs, of Lucknow, and of everything, I saw the King as an artist, a composer who made

some contributions to the form of singing that developed in Lucknow. The fact that he was a great patron of music – that was one redeeming feature about this King.

From the earliest scenes of the film, Ray emphasises Wajid Ali Shah's musicality. We see him dressed as Krishna in an opera he had himself composed, or beating a drum at the festival of Muharram, or watching an entrancing *Kathak* dance performance. 'Nothing but poetry and music should bring tears to a man's eyes,' he tells his Prime Minister with a hint of sternness, on seeing him weep after an interview with the British Resident. Later, at the moment when he decides to give up his throne without a fight, he delivers himself of the *thumri* that entered common currency in India – rather as Richard III's cry at the Battle of Bosworth Field has done among English-speakers:

> *Jab chhorh chaley Lakhnau nagari,*
> *Kaho haal adam par kya guzeri . . .*

which means roughly (though such *thumris* cannot really be translated),

> When we left our beloved Lucknow,
> See what befell us . . .

Satyajit knew its tune as a boy, because a Brahmo song had been based on it. Later he learnt that it had been composed by Wajid Ali Shah. Later still he came to know the style of *Kathak* dancing developed under Wajid Ali, and liked it very much, while continuing to admire *Bharata Natyam* most among the Indian dance forms. 'Good *Kathak* dancing is more acrobatic than *Bharata Natyam*,' he says. 'I can enjoy it very much, but not to the same extent as *Bharata Natyam*. Those two are complementary and they represent for me the entire gamut of Indian dancing, leaving aside *Kathakali*.'

This side of Lucknow culture is not much mentioned in the short story 'Shatranj ke Khilari' which Ray adapted to make *The Chess Players*. Prem Chand is instead full of condemnation for Lucknow's degeneracy. 'It was the time of Wajid Ali Shah', the story begins. 'Lucknow was plunged in pleasures. The young and the old, the poor and the rich – all were pleasure-bent. To kill time, some held dancing parties, others smoked or sipped opium in company with great gusto. Apathy was writ large across every aspect of life: administration, art, literature, industry and social conduct.' The censorious tone is not surprising, given Prem Chand's background and the date of the story, the mid-1920s, when Indian nationalist feeling dictated outright disgust for India's recent past. Prem Chand's instinctive milieu was the life of the small town and village rather than the big city, seen from the point of view of the less privileged. Many of his best stories are biting attacks on the exploitation of the poor; 'Sadgati' ('Deliverance'), which Ray filmed, is typical of these.

The main characters in *Shatranj ke Khilari* are the two chess-playing nawabs, Mirza Sajjad Ali and Mir Roshan Ali; Wajid Ali Shah is hardly mentioned, and the Resident, General Outram, not at all. Although Prem Chand, in a tone of irony, does make explicit the analogy between the chess-king and the real King – who falls to the British while his loyal subjects are trying to save their chess-kings – his chief concern is to make the two nawabs believable. He presents them as apathetic towards public affairs but not inherently cowards; though they run away to avoid being called on to fight for their King and to continue their games undisturbed, they show courage when roused to passion by each other's behaviour. In fact, they duel together with swords and kill each other, which is how Prem Chand's story ends.

Ray, who had first read it in translation at Santiniketan some thirty-five years before, altered much of its approach in his film. He abandoned the fight to the death, for instance, in the first place because it is difficult to make such a situation – where both combatants die – convincing on the screen; secondly because he felt that such an ending would be taken as symbolising the end of nawabi values in 1856, which was historically not true at all. He also introduced, unlike in *Distant Thunder* (and *The Home and the World*), a prologue giving the brief history of the rulers of Oudh and their relationship with the British, through paintings, documents, cartoons and 'live' vignettes of life in Lucknow and of Wajid Ali Shah. 'People just didn't know anything about the history of Lucknow and its nawabs,' says Ray. 'The present generation knows absolutely nothing about this and it applies to most people. They know vaguely about the annexation of Oudh but nothing about what preceded it and the British-nawab relationship. I was trying to think of a way to do it, and I felt it had to take a documentary approach.' His discovery of the letters of Lord Dalhousie, then Governor-General, clinched the matter; they suggested both the sardonic tone of Ray's prologue and its use of animation: 'The wretch at Lucknow who has sent his crown to the [1851] Exhibition would have done his people and us a good service if he had sent his head in it – and he would never have missed it. That is a cherry which will drop into our mouths one day,' declares a fruity voice, quoting Dalhousie's letter; and just after that, following a shot of the crown sitting on Wajid Ali's head, we see a hand plucking crowned cherries in quick succession: the states annexed by the East India Company in the 1840s and 50s – leaving only the cherry of Oudh.

This idea of Ray's is perfect in principle but shows a slight lapse in taste in its execution. The cartoons are too brash in style; they interfere with one's feelings for Dalhousie. As Zaidi nicely observes: 'Manikda should have done the sketches himself. They should have looked like Victorian cartoons of the period.'

Apart from the British characters and the courtiers of Wajid Ali Shah, Ray introduced two other characters into Prem Chand's story. The first is Munshi Nandlal, the Hindu friend of the chess players, who shows the amity between the two communities in Lucknow and who teaches the nawabs the rudiments of chess played in the British fashion. The second is the peasant boy Kalloo, who emerged in the following way, according to Ray:

> Prem Chand has Mir and Mirza playing chess in a dilapidated mosque towards the end of the story. I tried to picture the scene and found myself thinking of all the dirt and rubble the friends would have to contend with (not to speak of bats and rats and cockroaches and scorpions), before they could settle down to a quiet game. So I decided to drop the mosque and replace it with a new locale – a placid rural setting in contrast to the claustrophobic nawabi interiors. Some more pondering and I realised that the noblemen would feel utterly at a loss without someone to take the place of a servant, someone to run errands for them, prepare their hookahs, bring them food and so forth. Thus emerged Kalloo, who not only serves Mir and Mirza but also serves as the only representative in the film of the common man and the only person who displays patriotic feeling.

The most awkward problem remained, however: how to make cinematically interesting the act of chess-playing and the relationship of the nawabs' game to the larger political one. For months Ray wrestled with this and with his dislike of the King's character. 'You see, the problem was to interweave the main story with Wajid and the British and the whole business of annexation', he wrote to Saeed Jaffrey (Mir) in May 1976, seven months before shooting began. 'Also, to establish the idea of obsession – which is basic to the development of the story – with a game which is basically abstract and intellectual. If it had been *gambling*, there'd be no problem. But the beauty of the story lies in the parallel that Prem Chand draws between the game and the moves of the crafty Raj leading to the "capture" of the King.'

Ray knew he was taking a risk in inventing such a complex structure; would the audience, at the end of the film, perceive a harmony in the two stories, or would they be tempted to shrug off the idea as a conceit that did not quite come off? As Mir says to Mirza rather pathetically in the final scene beneath the trees, after he has nearly shot him by mistake in outraged pride: 'We can't even cope with our wives, so how we can cope with the Company's army?' In this remark, the two stories in a sense become one – or fail to do so, depending on the point of view. One has to catch the film's tone of voice correctly; neither sombre like *The Middle Man* nor farcical like *The Philosopher's Stone*, nor elegiac – even tragic – like *The Music Room*, it most closely resembles that of *Days and Nights in the Forest*. 'I saw the story as a fairly light-hearted one which would nevertheless comment on certain aspects of nawabi decadence as well as make a timeless comment on non-involvement', says Ray.

Some of this feeling derives from Prem Chand, some of it from the historical attitude of the British in India (so precisely evoked, for instance, by the 'bridge party' in Forster's *A Passage to India*, where the Collector pleasantly does the rounds of his guests, nearly all of whom 'he knew something to the discredit of '); mostly though, it comes from Ray's own cultivated ambivalence to the colonial experience. He is a pastmaster of the oblique comment, who likes to keep his audience pleasurably alert, rather than resting comfortably in their prejudices and stereotypes – and *The Chess Players* is one of his most oblique films, delighting in nuance and refined emotion as the culture it depicts once did. An example of this is the moment when Mir cheats at chess while Mirza is out of the room with his wife. Instead of catching Mir move the piece in flagrante, the camera spies his hand through a gap in the curtains: Mirza may not have caught him at it (though he has long since guessed that Mir cheats), but the all-seeing eye has. The sins and frailties of Lucknow, however carefully concealed behind etiquette, will eventually catch up with each citizen including their King. Not that the British are any better; it is just that they have the self-confidence, or rather the arrogance, to cheat openly, rather than in secret.

V.S. Naipaul is not exaggerating when he says of *The Chess Players* that 'it's like a Shakespeare scene. Only three hundred words are spoken but goodness! – terrific things happen.' For the first time in Ray's work non-Bengalis had an opportunity to judge him properly as a dialogue-writer. In the conversation between General Outram (Richard Attenborough), who speaks with a soft Aberdonian accent, and his ADC Captain Weston (Tom Alter) who – unlike Outram – speaks Persian and Urdu, Ray demonstrates his precise instinct for plasticity and nuance in film dialogue (which he does not quite equal, it has to be said, in several later scenes with Outram):

Outram: Tell me, Weston, you know the language, you know the people here – I mean, what kind of a poet is the King? Is he any good, or is it simply because he's the King they say he's good?

Weston: I think he's rather good, Sir.

Outram: You do, eh?

Weston: Yes, Sir.

Outram: D'you know any of his stuff?

Weston: I know some, Sir.

Outram: Well, can you recite it? Do you know it by heart?

Weston   (taken aback): Recite it, Sir?

Outram: Yes, I'm not a poetry man. Many soldiers are. But I'm curious to know what it sounds like. I rather like the sound of Hindustanee.

Weston remains silent, slightly ill-at-ease.

Outram: Are they long, these poems?

Weston: Not the ones I know, Sir.

Outram: Well, go on man, out with it!

Weston recites a four-line poem.

Outram: Is that all?

Weston: That's all, Sir.

Outram: Well, it certainly has the virtue of brevity. What the
           hell does it mean, if anything?

Weston: He's speaking about himself, Sir.

Outram: Well what's he saying? It's nothing obscene, I hope?

Weston: No, Sir.

Outram: Well, what's he saying?

Weston   (coughing lightly):
           Wound not my bleeding body.
           Throw flowers gently on my grave.
           Though mingled with the earth, I rose up to the skies.
           People mistook my rising dust for the heavens.

           That's all, Sir.

Outram: H'm. Doesn't strike me as a great flight of fancy, I'm afraid.

Outram rises from his chair slowly.

Weston: It doesn't translate very well, Sir.

Outram: And what about his songs? He's something of a composer,
           I understand? Are they any good, these songs?

Weston: They keep running in your head, Sir. I find them quite
           attractive. Some of them.

Outram: I see.

Weston: He's really quite gifted, Sir.

Outram glances briefly at Weston and begins to pace the room
thoughtfully.

Weston: He's also fond of dancing, Sir.

Outram: Yes, so I understand. With bells on his feet, like nautch
           girls. Also dresses up as a Hindu god, I'm told.

Weston: You're right, Sir. He also composes his own operas.

Outram: Doesn't leave him much time for his concubines, not
           to speak of the affairs of state. Does he really have 400
           concubines?

Weston: I believe that's the count, Sir.

Outram: And 29 'muta' wives. What the hell are muta wives?

Weston: *Muta* wives, Sir. They're temporary wives.

Outram: *Temporary* wives?

Weston: Yes, Sir. A muta marriage can last for three days, or
           three months, or three years. Muta is an Arabic word.

Outram: And it means temporary?

Weston: No, Sir.

Outram raises his eyebrows.

Outram: No?

Weston: It means – er, enjoyment.

Outram: Oh. Oh yes I see. Most instructive. And what kind of a
            king do you think all this makes him, Weston? All these
            various accomplishments?

Weston   (smiling): Rather a special kind, Sir, I should think.

Outram stops pacing, stiffens, turns sharply to Weston.

Outram: *Special*? I would've used a much stronger word than that,

Weston: I'd have said a *bad* king. A frivolous, effeminate,
            irresponsible, worthless king.

Weston: He's not the first eccentric in the line—

Outram   (interrupting): Oh I know he's not the first, but he certainly
            deserves to be the last. We've put up with this nonsense long
            enough. Eunuchs, fiddlers, nautch-girls and 'muta' wives and
            God knows what else. He can't rule, he has no wish to rule,
            and therefore he has no business to rule.

Weston: There I would agree with you, Sir.

Outram: Good. I am glad to hear that. I have it in mind to
            recommend you for a higher position when we take over—

Weston: Take over, Sir?

Outram: Take over, Weston. And any suspicion that you hold a brief
            for the King would ruin your chances. You remember that.

Richard Attenborough gives one of the best performances of his
career as Outram, and even manages to look quite like 'the little
General'. Ray, who had considered several other British actors for the
part, was completely satisfied with him from the moment he came on to
the sets in Calcutta in May 1977 (in heat and humidity so trying that his
acting must command still more respect). In fact the casting of the film
was one of the few difficulties Ray did not have to face in making *The
Chess Players*. For once, he could take Bombay actors without hesitation,
provided they spoke good Urdu. He chose Amjad Khan to play the King
after seeing him as a bad hat in the blockbuster *Sholay*. Sanjeev Kumar
(who plays Mirza), he had seen in several films and noted his 'wonderful
flair for comedy'; they had also met at a party in Bombay. Shabana Azmi,
the daughter of an Urdu poet and writer, Ray took to play Mirza's neglected
beauty of a wife, on the strength of her playing in Shyam Benegal's first
feature film *Ankur* (*The Seedling*). In it, Ray had written in 1974, there
are 'two high-pitched scenes [where] she pulls out all the stops and firmly
establishes herself as one of our finest dramatic actresses.'

Ray had also had his eye on Saeed Jaffrey for some years, though he did
not actually meet him until late 1972, and then in curious circumstances.
'We were on the same Air India plane,' recalls Saeed.

I met him at Beirut Airport. I had long hair then and was much
thinner. There, standing quite close to me, was this tall, majestic figure

of Satyajit Ray, a man I'd admired ever since I saw *Pather Panchali* in Delhi on the eve of my departure for the West. I felt that he sensed that I wanted to speak to him. So he eased the way and he said 'You must be Saeed. You are Saeed Jaffrey, aren't you?' and I said 'Yes, Mr Ray, I've been a great admirer of yours.' He said, 'I know quite a lot about you. You used to be married to Madhur. And you worked with James Ivory and Ismail Merchant and I saw you in *The Guru* and you were by far the best thing in it.' This beautiful basso profundo voice complimenting me in the middle of the night at Beirut Airport was too much for me. So I said 'Is there any possibility of us working together?' And he said 'You're a very patient man. I know a lot about you. You've become good at waiting for the right opportunities. So could you wait a little longer? It'll happen but I don't know when.' And then I said, 'Shall we have a drink when we get back on the plane?' And he said 'Well I only drink Coca-Cola'; which suggested perhaps he had also heard that I liked my whisky.

When the two of them finally did collaborate, their relationship was exceptionally fruitful and produced the finest performance in the film (as well as Jaffrey's personal best). This was partly because Jaffrey was steeped in Urdu culture, including a knowledge of and affection for Wajid Ali Shah and his compositions, and partly because of his fondness and respect for Ray. Saeed remembers that Bijoya Ray used to tell him that Manik came back from the studio singing and skipping with pleasure at the day's work. Saeed had earlier worked with John Huston (on *The Man Who Would Be King*) and been impressed by the way he 'challenged' him as an actor. Ray was quite different. 'With Manikda there's an antenna-tuning,' says Saeed, 'and then total trust. And because of that trust you don't waste immediacy and energy in over-rehearsing anything. We had one rehearsal, one take, one rehearsal, one take. At one point I remember I said "Manikda, that was fine, but do you think we could have one more take?" "My dear Saeed, have two, have three" he said, and laughed loudly. And I said, "Well you did say you're used to the three-to-one ratio." It was a very happy time.'

Sometimes he gave Jaffrey 'little notes' to improve his performance. Saeed remembers one in the final scene, when Mir returns falteringly to Mirza after disappearing to hide his shame at having nearly killed his friend with his pistol. 'When you come back, don't look at him at all,' Saeed was told by Ray. 'That was marvellous; it made the whole thing so much more poignant and funny,' Saeed says now. Late that night in a hotel room in Lucknow he had to dub his voice on to the scene, because he was required back in Britain and there was simply not time to post-synch the voice properly in a studio. The sound recordist just played the scene back and the actors immediately rerecorded it. 'I said to Manikda,' Saeed remembers, ' "Without a picture, how will it all fit?" He said, "Well, trust

me. I've had to do it many times. You have a musical ear. That helps. But
I'm listening to it and I can tell exactly how close it is to the master copy."
That obviously inspired the young boy playing Kalloo who also dubbed his
performance like this.'

That final scene was shot in a village outside the city. To shoot
scenes set in Lucknow in the city itself presented such formidable
difficulties that Ray restricted them to a bare minimum and depended
instead on Chandragupta's skills in a Calcutta studio. Not only did the
usual gallery of spectators turn out to watch, but the city's appearance
had changed drastically in the century or so since Wajid's day. The dawn
shot of the two nawabs climbing a slope on their way out of the city with
the minarets and dome of the great mosque, the Bara Imambara, behind
them and the strains of one of Lucknow's famous *Bhairon* ragas playing on
shehnai, is the most striking example of location-shooting; it is regrettable
more was not possible.

The arrival of the British army in the city – seen in the near-distance
as a long imposing column of Indian and British infantry, cavalry, camels
and elephants – had to be shot in Rajasthan, near Jaipur, because only
there could Ray get the animals he needed. The Europeans were obtained through a brain-wave of the producer Suresh Jindal. He wrote
to foreign embassies, High Commissions and foreign correspondents in
Delhi offering them a weekend in Jaipur in exchange for their 'acting'
in the film. The twenty-four selected made the journey in blistering June
heat, either by car, or (theoretically) air-conditioned bus. At the location
chaos took over and a scene that should have taken half a day to shoot,
took three. Eventually, when the shooting was over, recalled Seton who
was present, Ray lost his temper out of sheer exhaustion. 'But after the
row had subsided, Satyajit said to me that no matter what happened, he
would finish the film.'

By September he had done so and the film could be seen by
distributors all over India. That was when it hit a snag Ray had
not really encountered before, having always depended on the Bengal
market alone in India: on seeing the film, some of the major distributors
backed out, leaving the producer with substantial laboratory debts. Their
verdict, according to Ray, was that 'Mr Ray has made the film for a foreign
audience'; they were expecting some songs and dances and were disturbed
by the use of high-flown Urdu and English. Nevertheless, when the film
was given a private screening in Bombay in late October, the response was
tremendous. In time the rumour became established that some big guns in
the Bombay industry, nervous at Ray's use of stars and the film's potential
all-India appeal, put pressure on distributors not to support *Shatranj ke
Khilari*. Whatever his suspicions may be, Ray refuses to be drawn on the
point and has avoided wasting his time trying to find out the truth; but
Shama Zaidi, who knows Bombay's film world well, thinks the existence of
a conspiracy against the film is 'quite probable'. Certainly it is true that in

Bangalore the film ran for fifteen weeks, whereas in Bombay it was taken off after only two, while running to good houses.

If the Indian reaction was somewhat disappointing, abroad the film was well received, after its memorable première at the London Film Festival in December 1977 without subtitles, which I have described in my introduction. The very qualities that distinguished it from Ray's other films – its direct portrayal of the Raj and its use of a well-known English actor, its exotic settings, and its big production values (at least by Ray's standards) – helped to make Ray known to a wider audience than before. But the general critical reaction was one of somewhat muted praise (with the exception of the *Guardian* critic Tim Radford: 'Satyajit Ray seems to be able to achieve more and more with less and less.') 'I have never enjoyed a film more which – because we expect continual miracles from Satyajit Ray – disappointed me so much', wrote the *Evening News* critic in London. And the *New York Times* noted that 'Ray's not outraged. Sometimes he's amused; most often he's meditative, and unless you respond to this mood, the movie is so overly polite that you may want to shout a rude word.'

Neither East nor West seemed quite satisfied with *The Chess Players*, despite laudatory individual reactions. It seemed to possess neither enough of the 'plan and purpose incarnate' that Tagore identified in the West and which might have pleased audiences geared to the terse cinema of plot and action favoured by Hollywood, nor enough of the 'superfluous humanity' that grabbed audiences in, say, *Pather Panchali*. It deliberately lacks the kind of easy emotional gratification that the subject could have lent itself to, by oversimplifying the British (as in *Gandhi* or *A Passage to India*) or by portraying Wajid Ali Shah as Outram saw him – 'frivolous, effeminate, irresponsible, worthless'. That, according to one Indian critic in the *Illustrated Weekly* to whom may Ray responded at length, is more or less how Ray's Wajid appears to be. Whereas according to a western writer, who is also a literary critic, 'Prem Chand judges, he condemns, but he can also praise. Ray does neither.' 'Easy targets don't interest me very much', Ray said in 1978.

The condemnation *is* there, ultimately, but the process of arriving at it is different. I was portraying two negative forces, feudalism and colonialism. You had to condemn both Wajid and Dalhousie. This was the challenge. I wanted to make this condemnation interesting by bringing in certain plus points of both the sides . . . by investing their representatives with certain human traits. These traits are not invented but backed by historical evidence. I knew this might result in a certain ambivalence of attitude, but I didn't see *Shatranj* as a story where one would openly take sides and take a stand. I saw it more as a contemplative, though unsparing view of the clash of two cultures – one effete and ineffectual and the other vigorous and malignant. I also took into account the many half-shades that lie in between these two extremes of the spectrum . . . You have to read this film between the lines.

23

Two 1964
Pikoo 1980

··•⊷[Ⅰⓒ⵩ⓞⓞ⟡⵩ⓘ]⊶•··

R AY'S two shortest films, leaving aside his documentaries, the fifteen-minute *Two* and the twenty-six minute *Pikoo*, have much in common. Both were prompted by offers from foreign television producers, both are based on original screenplays by Ray (*Pikoo* being adapted from his own short story 'Pikoo's Diary') and, most significantly, both are about young children. Together they beautifully express the quite unsentimental, clear-eyed innocence of Ray's gaze.

Two was made in 1964 as part of a trilogy of short films from India, commissioned by the US public television service under the banner 'Esso World Theater'. The other two featured Ravi Shankar and the Little Ballet Troupe of Bombay. Ray's contribution is wordless. He was asked to make a film in English that would be set in Bengal – an idea that did not really appeal to him – and thought of wordlessness as the best solution. As someone who reveres the best of silent cinema he felt excited by the challenge. He had already played with an idea – just one of the many that never got made into films – in which an office boss and a petty clerk are trapped in a lift for half an hour, with 'business' predominating over words. In *Two* he takes the encounter of a rich boy in Calcutta and a slum boy (from a real slum) he can see below his window. The first has all the goodies he could want, the second almost nothing, but the first is absolutely determined to prove his superiority. When the slum boy brings out a plaintive flute, the rich boy brandishes a raucous toy trumpet and drowns him; when the slum boy switches – Apu-like – to a warrior's mask and spear, the rich boy becomes a cowboy with a revolver; and when the slum boy decides to fly a humble kite, his rival shoots it down with an air rifle. Finally, the slum boy gives up the attempt to be friends and the rich boy retires satisfied to play with his vile toy robots alone. But not for long – their mechanical racket cannot entirely obliterate the notes of the flute that now float maddeningly through his window once more. The little episode ends with him pondering his unspoken defeat, as first one and then another of the soulless robots trips over itself and crashes to the floor.

Ray's story shows a remarkable convergence of spirit with an anecdote of Tagore's, who tells of the moment in his childhood in the 1870s when one of his friends was given a toy 'bought from an English shop' which was 'perfect, big and wonderfully life-like'. It soon killed off the fun of their games together. Tagore is certain, he says, that if his friend could have used 'the modern language of history', he would have said that 'he was more civilised than ourselves to the extent of his owning that ridiculously perfect toy.'

Slight as it is, *Two* is able to provoke this kind of reflection too – much enhanced by a mysterious ditty (without words) all Ray's own that is repeated again and again to haunting effect. The film 'packs quite a punch in its ten [sic] minutes', Ray wrote to Seton at the time of making it. Without the least effort, it says more about war and peace than yards of political analysis. As Siddhartha told his interviewers in *The Adversary*, the 'plain human courage' of the people of Vietnam is a much more remarkable matter than the landing of a man on the moon.

Where *Two* is like a fairy-tale, *Pikoo* recalls the dew-drop Tagore wrote his poem about in the young Satyajit's autograph book. It has, in the words of *Newsweek*, 'a master's crystalline simplicity' – which makes it particularly difficult to analyse. '*Pikoo* is a very complex film,' Ray comments. 'It is a poetic statement which cannot be reduced to concrete terms.'

He made it for French television at the behest of a free-lance producer Henri Fraise, whose brief to him, according to Ray, was simple: 'He said you make a film for us. Doesn't matter what kind of film: you can place your camera at your window and shoot the house next-door – we will accept that. That sort of instruction,' says Ray with a laugh. The offer came while he was making *The Kingdom of Diamonds*. By the time he took it up, in August 1980, he was in a state of some depression. As he wrote to Seton in October, '*Diamonds* was finished four months ago, but hasn't opened yet. No theatres. They've all been closed for over a month – labour trouble. Even if and when they do reopen, the power shortage, lack of maintenance and general callousness of the exhibitors (apparently owning theatres to play Bengali films is no longer paying) have brought them to a state where watching a film has become a pitiful exercise. If things go on like this the film industry will collapse.' His son was then considering his first film *Fatikchand*, based on a novella by his father. 'He is certainly ready technically', wrote Satyajit. 'The only pity is that he can't enjoy the fruits of technology, but must face all the hardships I did in my early stages ... I know – and he knows – that he is handicapped by being my son, but he has enough equanimity not to be bothered.' A large and very well-attended exhibition to celebrate Ray's twenty-fifth anniversary as a film-maker was then running in Calcutta. 'How ironical that I have now to think – for the first time – of moving to Bombay – a prospect that doesn't please me at all', he wrote, apparently forgetting the strength of his feelings about the state of the city ten years previously.

His mental state may have had some influence on the film. His original story is a childish diary written by a young boy in a prosperous south Calcutta household who writes about the behaviour of his mother, father, grandfather, elder brother and servants without understanding it. The house is obviously full of tension – the mother has a lover (known to Pikoo as Uncle Hitesh) and her husband has guessed it, grandfather is frail with heart disease, elder brother is mixed up in politics. Pikoo senses the tension but does not grasp its causes fully. He is not sure why but Uncle Hitesh and Mummy have started giving him nice presents, like an air rifle, which he tries to shoot sparrows with. This is how he writes about it in his diary:

> When Father came back from the office he said Why have yet more guns? Mummy said Why not? and Father said Isnt there enough bang-banging without bringing a gun into the house? and Mummy said Whats wrong with it? Then Father said You have no sense and Mummy said Why do you start shouting at me when you get back? and Father said I dont and then they both talked a lot in English. Mummy was talking very fast like at the cinema. Ive seen Jerry Lewis and Clint Eastwood and those Hindi films with lots of crying and no fighting now my pens running out.

The film is more explicit than this, of necessity; it includes a bedroom scene between the mother and her lover, for instance. It still belongs mainly to Pikoo but the perspective is no longer entirely his own; the dying grandfather's and, especially, the mother's, also become important. 'One statement the film tries to make is that, if a woman is to be unfaithful, if she is to have an extramarital affair, she can't afford to have soft emotions towards her children, or, in this case, her son,' says Ray. 'The two just don't go together. You have to be ruthless. Maybe she's not ruthless to that extent. She's being very Bengali. A European in the same circumstances would not behave in the same way.' He is referring to the fact that, having packed Pikoo off to the garden with a new set of felt pens bought by Uncle Hitesh to draw all the flowers he can see, the mother retires to the bedroom with her lover, but cannot restrain her tears when she looks out of the window before closing the curtains and catches sight of the little figure in the garden bent over his drawing-pad.

Aparna Sen, who plays her (and who has made something of a reputation in India as a champion of women through her film *Paroma* that shows an adulterous liaison), does not accept Ray's morality on this point. 'What I find perfectly understandable and also realistic and something I've seen, is a mother's love, and a very genuine mother's love, in combination with adultery. I don't think the feelings are at all exclusive. In our country it's still very difficult to convince people that women may have sexual choice, as men do. A double standard exists here – and everywhere else.' Ray's reaction to this is interesting. 'It doesn't matter,' he says, after a moment's pause for thought: 'as long as it rings true [on the screen].' When directing that particular scene, he said little to Aparna. 'I just told her that you see your son and you have lied to him and you suddenly have a feeling of guilt and a feeling of tenderness for the boy who's taken your word for it and is excited.' But he admits that she did not find the scene easy to play. 'She's probably not very adept at crying on the screen. There are certain actresses who have this difficulty. It called for about three or four takes before she could really weep.'

Aparna's performance in the film as a whole, good though it is, is flawed by her inner uncertainty. But Pikoo himself is wonderfully right. Ray brings to his portrayal of the boy all the insight of his own experience as a similarly solitary child in a household of adults. They have certain experiences in common, such as the glass marbles that roll across the marble floor tiles sounding different notes, and the air-gun (which is in the story only, not in the film). 'I had an air-gun; in fact I was pretty cruel,' Satyajit recalls. 'I used to aim at birds constantly, sparrows and so on. I managed to kill a *salik* when I was about nine or ten. Cruelty is a trait that most children share, though possibly girls are less cruel. I mean, you're satisfied that your aim is so good that you're able to hit a bird.'

Maybe because it has a child at its centre, the film is remarkably rich in those enigmatic moments in Ray's work that resonate in the mind and make *Pikoo* one of his most intense films. Near the beginning, as Pikoo wanders the house at a loose end, one of the games he plays with himself is to try to silence the loud barking of the neighbour's dog by shouting out 'Hush!' Delightedly, he finds that it works. Then, a little later in the day, he finds an occasion to try his power again. He can hear Ma and Uncle Hitesh arguing behind her bedroom door and he doesn't like it. 'Hush!' he cries – and immediately they stop.

Just before this comes the film's most beautifully judged scene; it carries in it Ray's quintessence as a film artist. Accompanied by bright snatches of music that match the innocence of his face and movements, Pikoo has been intently moving from flower to flower in the garden, making coloured sketches of those he likes. Suddenly, he is brought up short: before him stand some inviting white blooms – but he has no white-coloured felt pen to draw them. 'Ma!' he calls up towards the curtained window behind the balcony, 'I'm drawing the white flowers in black, Ma – there's no white colour.' No answer – but inside the bedroom his mother interrupts her love-making – to the irritation of Hitesh. Pikoo calls again. Still no answer, and now a large drop of rain has fallen on his drawing and made an ugly smudge. He decides to go inside, where he immediately discovers that his grandpa is no longer alive.

This short scene is, as Ray has said of the film itself, 'a poetic statement which cannot be reduced to concrete terms.' Gorgeous Nature and its indifference to Man, Pikoo's innocence – the way he sees the world in blacks and whites – and his mother's inability to do that, Hitesh's harshness and hypocrisy, and Death – all these fuse together here through the alchemy of Ray's implacable instinct for truth. For a few moments he lets us pierce the surface of things and obtain a glimpse of Reality beyond.

24

Deliverance
(Sadgati) 1981

•••{ ◦ ⦾ ◦ }•••

*D*ELIVERANCE *(Sadgati),* the fifty-minute film Ray made in late
1981 for Indian television, moved a Bengali who knows India's villages
well to tell me that 'Satyajit has travelled a long way from the poetry of *Pather
Panchali* to the terrifying prose of *Sadgati*.' Sunil Ganguli has described it
as Ray's 'cruellest' film. It is certainly his starkest, his most naked work.
As he himself puts it, '*Deliverance* is a deeply angry film, but it is not the
anger of an exploding bomb, but of a bow stretched taut and quivering.'

The plot, taken from a short story by Prem Chand, is distilled
simplicity itself, in keeping with its ancient theme: the harsh exploitation
of one class by another, with society's sanction. In this case it is the lowest
castes under the control of Brahmins in a village in central India (not in
Bengal, where this century caste rigidity has not been as severe – witness
Distant Thunder). Dukhi is a *chamar*, someone who works with hides and
skins and who is therefore particularly objectionable to a Brahmin. His
name means 'sorrowful', an attempt at averting the envy of the gods. He
belongs in the last of the four main castes – Brahmin, Ksatriya, Vaisya, and
Sudra – the name of which 'symbolises a man who has no margin around
him beyond his bare utility', as Tagore puts it in *Creative Unity*. 'The
word denotes a classification which includes all naked machines that have
lost their completeness of humanity, be their work manual or intellectual.
They are like walking stomachs or brains, and we feel, in pity, urged to
call on God and cry, "Cover them up, for mercy's sake with some veil of
beauty and life!" '

When the film opens, Dukhi is cutting grass in a field near his hut.
He needs it as part of a gift to Ghashiram, the local Brahmin priest, so
that he will come to his hut and bless his only child, an elfin daughter
whose marriage he is already planning. Without the priest to perform
his auspicious acts, her marriage is inconceivable, and if that means that
Dukhi must suffer at the priest's hands, then so be it; that is how it has
always been in the village.

But today the situation is worse than usual; Dukhi is feeling weak,
suffering from some undefined malaise. His wife Jhuria almost begs him

not to pay a visit on the priest, but Dukhi feels he must, for the sake of his daughter; he has put off going there for too long already. As Jhuria watches him, he sets off on foot for the Brahmin quarter of the village, with the pathetic bundle of grass on his head, and merges with a herd of cows passing along the path by their hut, their bells making a melancholy jangle that matches the short, restrained snatch of flute used by Ray at a number of points in *Deliverance* – the only music he permits himself during the film.

In casting Om Puri as Dukhi and Smita Patil as Jhuria, Ray selected the finest actor and actress of the post-Independence generation. In *Deliverance*, both of them are able to convey with searing truth the struggle of poor people to remain human under inhuman pressures; there can be no higher praise than to say that their performances are on a par with Chunibala Devi's in Ray's first film. Neither of them has a conventionally attractive face – in fact Om Puri's has led him to be cast mainly as a man of violence – but both have the rare capacity of transforming their appearance according to mood. Smita Patil's sudden death at the end of 1986 was a tragedy: 'there is really no one to replace her', Satyajit wrote to me.

Their excellence also helped to give him confidence while directing what was his first film in Hindi. As with *The Chess Players*, he wrote the script of *Deliverance* in English; it was then translated by Prem Chand's son. 'I can write Hindi now,' says Ray, 'because we learnt Sanskrit at school and so we learnt the alphabet, but I have not yet come to the position where I can judge whether a line of dialogue which has been translated from my original English is the best possible dialogue in the circumstances.' That is where the actors come in; they suggest alternatives, which the translator accepts or rejects. 'This would never happen with my Bengali films,' Ray comments; 'There nobody questions the rightness of the dialogue.'

The Brahmin Ghashiram, for whom Dukhi now labours without payment in money or kind, is a figure who could easily have been overstated. Instead, Ray relieves Ghashiram's callousness with just enough humanity to make his condemnation of him all the more devastating. The priest tries to persuade his wife to feed Dukhi but gives up in the face of her truculence; and even that slight effort is mainly self-serving – a way of squeezing more work out of Dukhi's unhealthy body. He has hardly more regard for the *chamar* than the SS guards had for the Jews labouring in the concentration camps. In the terms of Nirad Chaudhuri writing in *Hinduism*, Ghashiram is a 'typical traditional Hindu', which he amplifies with a quote from a Bengali article of 1884 written by Bankim Chandra Chatterjee:

We know of a landowner who is a Brahmin and a very strict Hindu. In winter as in summer he gets up very early in the morning and takes his bath. After that he performs his daily worship for many hours with the utmost scrupulousness. He feels as if he is stunned by a blow on the head if there is even a slight interruption of it. He takes only one vegetarian meal during the day and that in the afternoon. Then he attends to the business of his properties. At that time his mind becomes wholly intent on the problem of ruining one or other of his tenants, depriving an unprotected widow of all her possessions, cheating his creditors, securing false witnesses to send some innocent person to jail, or concocting evidence to win his cases, and his efforts in all these directions are successful. Yet we also know for certain that he is wholly sincere in his devotion to the gods and Brahmins and that there is no hypocrisy whatever in that. Even when faking a document he utters the name of Hari [i.e. Vishnu, the Preserver], and he believes that this will make the fraud effectual.

Dukhi's first task for Ghashiram is to sweep his verandah – an act that Ray follows with the kind of rapt observation that gives fresh meaning to the phrase 'dignity of labour'. Then Ghashiram gets him to lug heavy sacks of rice husks from one shed to another, and Ray, in a few deft shots, makes us feel Dukhi's growing stress. Finally, while Ghashiram delivers a religious homily to console a young villager whose wife has just died, he puts Dukhi to work on the task that will eventually kill him. Using a blunt axe he is expected to split a hunk of wood as solid as a boulder. Manifestly, it cannot be done; but, such are the mental accretions of centuries, it does not even occur to Dukhi to refuse, even though he has not eaten that day.

A succession of individuals now watch his futile task from their various angles. First, an older man of a slightly higher caste (a Gond) from a hut nearby, advises him that he must demand food from the Brahmin as a bare minimum, but Dukhi cannot bring himself to do this. Even the coals to light his tobacco that he begs from the Brahmin's wife, are literally tossed in his direction in a gesture of total disdain, burning his ankle. He fears an even worse humiliation from a request for food. 'If we weren't so ignorant,' he calls out in abject apology to her for crossing her threshold, 'why would we suffer as we do?'

After a smoke, Dukhi begins to whack the log again with renewed vigour. But it yields barely a splinter. Its pitiless mass is beginning to drive him crazy. In a moment of madness he flings the axe away and nearly decapitates a passing Brahmin. Aghast, Dukhi runs to retrieve the axe and apologises with profuse humility. When the appalled Brahmin departs to warn others, Dukhi subsides against the banyan whose branches overlook the recalcitrant log, and dissolves into a fit of weary tears, lacerating to observe. Propped up by the tree's gnarled trunk, he dozes in the midday heat, like everyone else.

A little later, well rested after his meal and siesta, Ghashiram slips into his sandals and, clutching his sacred thread, comes out to see if the wood has been chopped. Finding Dukhi asleep he stands at a distance and abuses him. He soon rouses him to a Herculean effort to split the log and waddles off into the house before Dukhi reaches his climax. But Ghashiram's son, a little boy with a permanently frightened look, stays to watch, and it is he who witnesses Dukhi's dreadful death. Silently he edges up to the body where it lies splayed beside the log – the axe-head bitten home at last – then rushes inside to tell his father what has happened to the *chamar*.

Ghashiram is now in a quandary. Though he and his wife may quarrel about who is to blame, they are both instantly aware of their responsibility for driving the *chamar* to his death. They have to find a way to dispose of the body and hush up the incident. But caste rules forbid the least contact between Ghashiram and Dukhi – alive or dead. The *chamar* community in the village, briefed by the Gond not to remove the corpse, refuse the shifty appeal that Ghashiram now makes to them, while his fellow-Brahmins insist that until the corpse is removed, they can draw no water from the well nearby. Meanwhile Dukhi's wife Jhuria has grasped the terrible truth – a scene all the more powerful for the herd of cows that are ambling home behind her tortured face, their bells clanking metallically as ever. She comes in search of her husband's body beside the log, and breaks down.

Monsoon rain, which begins as she cradles his lifeless form, now comes to Ghashiram's rescue. That night, as a thunder-storm gathers force, and having ignored an anguished wail of despair from Jhuria who collapses at his door and feebly beats upon it, Ghashiram decides that he must manage his own corpse-removal before police can arrive with awkward questions. As dawn breaks, we see the rain-soaked corpse on the ground. A hooked stick appears, followed by the bottom of a dhoti, a sacred thread and a hand, which manipulates the stick around one of Dukhi's legs and raises it up. The other hand now slips a noose around the raised ankle and pulls it tight. At no point does either hand break the taboo against actually touching the corpse. Ghashiram sets off, hauling and yanking Dukhi along with all his strength, huffing and puffing at the unaccustomed exertion. He is clearly determined to drag his load a fair distance from the village. The last resting-place of Dukhi's mortal remains is a dumping ground for animal carcasses; there his tormentor at last abandons him among skulls, delivered from earthly cares in a way he could never have dreamt of – by a Brahmin, no less.

But Ray does not let us off the hook quite yet. Dukhi is gone and already Ghashiram is on the way to convincing himself that the Untouchable never existed. He walks around the log with the axe stuck in it and, as he does so, fastidiously sprinkles water on it from a small brass pot in his hand and chants Sanskrit *slokas*; these he is completely confident will purify him and his little world.

Such benighted social attitudes are reminiscent of the village India conjured up by V. S. Naipaul in his 1964 book *An Area of Darkness*. The most shocking aspect of *Deliverance* is its demonstration of how little really changes in certain of these rural areas – particularly Bihar and Madhya Pradesh, where Ray shot the film. Prem Chand's short story appeared in 1931, but Ghashiram and Dukhi could easily belong to today's India, half a century later, or to Bankim Chatterjee's, half a century before it was published. Ray has changed rather little in adapting the story; *Deliverance* is among the most faithful to its source of his films.

He had several reasons for picking the story. First, it has 'strong cinematic elements which can be told as a gripping narrative.' It also struck him that it would fill a gap in his work by dealing with a 'stratum of society that I hadn't treated at all in my films.' And he felt a duty too to make Indians aware of what was going on in their own country. 'These all came simultaneously,' says Ray; 'one is not more important than another. Had the story been less gripping or less cinematic, I wouldn't have considered it, although it might have been telling about poor people.'

The anger inherent in his treatment is really the culmination of Ray's human commitment first expressed so sympathetically in the Apu Trilogy. Lindsay Anderson puts it well when he says that 'the kind of intensity of humanism present in that work has in our time to express itself finally in anger.' Things came to a head at the time *Deliverance* was shown. Ray deliberately embroiled himself in controversy with the Minister of Information and Broadcasting in the Central Government, who was then attempting to curb the showing of poverty in films, including Ray's own plan for a documentary on child labour. So annoyed did he feel at this diktat that he openly stated he was all in favour of as many films about poverty as possible.

Unlike the majority of his educated fellow-countrymen he is unequivocal in condemning caste and religious orthodoxy, as one might expect. 'I'm firmly against the kind of orthodoxy which is based purely on religion because I don't consider religion to be that important,' he says. 'What can you say in favour of orthodoxy which creates division between people, between castes, and puts up a wall which is so artificial?' He distrusts any notion that it was caste that prevented India from losing its identity under the impact of foreign invasions.

Some people defend caste in the early stages of Indian history because it made for a certain degree of order in society; people were expected to do certain things, because they belonged to a certain caste. I feel that certainly doesn't apply to life today. It was what happened in the early stages of Indian history, Aryan history – it was the Aryans who brought this caste with them. Whatever rationalisation you can think of for the caste system, there's no question that eventually, in time, it proved very wrong and certainly created barriers which were very unpleasant. So I have nothing to defend in caste at all – nothing at all – or in orthodoxy.

To Ray, these are attitudes that destroy conscience and create people like Ghashiram in *Deliverance*. 'That is what happens when you have 2000 years of orthodoxy,' says Ray. 'You're not conscious . . . you think you're doing the right thing. You think this is what is expected of you. You think that this will lead you to heaven, and not pollute you. And so you have justification for everything you do: spiritual justification.'

The screening of *Sadgati* in 1982 on Doordarshan, the government-run television service, provoked a strong reaction from audiences and critics. Many people seemed unable to accept the film; it was said to be both too shocking and not shocking enough, even by the same critic. Ray feels that part of this response derives from poor conditions of viewing on black-and-white television sets: 'I have seen *Sadgati* like this,' he says, 'and it loses three quarters of its strength and appeal. The shot at the end – with the skulls – was completely lost.' But when the film was shown again, in 1984 – by which time television sets in India had improved and moved into colour – the reaction was basically similar. As one confused critic put it: 'Delicate nuances don't work.' But he then added: 'One wonders at the incredible turmoil this slick sort of "art" cinema can cause in the not so discerning mind.' He recommended that, for a mass audience at least, 'morality themes should replace the stark cold-bloodedness of *Sadgati*.'

> In matters of caste India is still not ready for the bitter truth per se. It must be sugar-coated for easy consumption with the dosage increasing gradually or the reaction could be negative. And the good must breast the tape first even if they fall on their faces right through the race . . . We are still a nation where a cinematic murder is shown by a killer deliberately unsheathing a knife, windows slamming, wind howling, thunder and lightning tearing the sky, knife-blade glinting, blade falling, shrieks, crescendo music, rivulets of red, birds flying off trees and the candle going out

– the very rhetoric of which *Deliverance* (and *Pather Panchali* for that matter) is so singularly free and which may well have been responsible for dulling the tastes and consciences of millions of cinema-goers in India since films began there. That Ray is right to shun it, both as an artist and as a moralist, and that such critics are deceiving themselves, like those government officials who think that a 'positive' image of India is best projected by uncontroversial subject-matter, is suggested by Utpal Dutta's experience with *Sadgati*. He and his acting troupe were playing in a working-class area of eastern Calcutta on the day the film was transmitted. They were due to begin at five o'clock but the workers said they wanted the meeting at six instead, after seeing *Sadgati*. They and the troupe sat in the community hall together and watched it. 'They were stunned,' Dutta says. 'After the film had finished the silence continued. A crowd like this is usually very noisy – but that silence you could have touched.'

25

The Home and the World
(Ghare Baire) 1984

·····◄[◦◦◦◦◦◦◦]►·····

I N H I S classic *The Autobiography of an Unknown Indian* Nirad
Chaudhuri wrote that as an adult he was unable to read the words, far
less whistle the tunes of the songs written by Tagore around the time of the
1905 Partition of Bengal when he was a boy 'without instantly bringing back
to my ears and eyes all the sounds from the soft rumble of the rain on our
corrugated-iron roofs to the bamboo pipe of the cowherds, and the sights
from the sails of the boats on our great rivers to the spreading banyan tree
– the sounds and sights which embody for me the idea of Bengal.'

Such is the emotional atmosphere on which Ray's 1984 film
The Home and the World draws and which makes it his most
demanding work for a non-Bengali viewer, with the possible exception
of *The Goddess*. Like *The Chess Players*, it shows the interaction of
India with the West in microcosm, but, unlike that film, Ray provides
no key to unlock its background. Westerners have therefore tended to
stumble badly over both the film and its original, the novel by Tagore
that Ray first considered for film dramatisation back in 1947/8. Bertolt
Brecht thought it a 'fine, powerful piece of work' but his contemporary,
the Marxist critic Georg Lukács wrote that Tagore had put himself 'at the
intellectual service of the British police' in his 'libellous pamphlet', 'a petit
bourgeois yarn of the shoddiest kind' containing, in his portrait of Sandip,
a patriotic leader, 'a contemptible caricature of Gandhi'. This profound
misunderstanding of the novel would be merely funny today, were it not
that it appears to persist. The *New York Times*, reviewing the film, noted
that it dramatised the political differences between Tagore and Gandhi in
the persons of Nikhil and Sandip, while the *New York Review of Books*
felt that these two were respectively 'the radical and the humanist, the
two faces of modern Bengali culture'. Probably Pauline Kael of all the
critics in the West came nearest to the truth with her comment that the
film has 'a large theme ... presented in a formal style that owes almost
nothing to the conventions of American or western European films.'

A small book, written by a Bengali with Ray's breadth of sympathy,
would be needed to elucidate the immediate political, social and cultural

setting of the film. The English viewer might like to imagine himself as a Bengali might feel watching a film about the impact of the First World War on British upper-class society – *Oh! What a Lovely War*, say – except he will probably know rather less than the Bengali about its background. Since the Bengal British of 1905 failed to grasp the emotions they had stirred up, it is hardly surprising that today's western audience has difficulty with the story. 'Look, we were not born in Bengal,' a Bengali satirist has the British say in an anti-Partition play of the time, 'we have not learned Bengali, we do not practise Bengali traditions or customs, we will not settle down or establish landed property in Bengal; but we still understand what is good for Bengalis better than they can themselves. Their lack of understanding is the cause of our sorrow.'

To Lord Curzon, the Viceroy of India at the turn of the century, Partition was a cause célèbre. It began as an administrative convenience in the minds of certain of his officials in Bengal, who felt that the province was too big. But in 1903 Curzon took it up, recognising its potential to 'divide and rule' the troublesome Bengalis: the Hindus would become a majority in the west of the province, and the Muslims in the east. What was more, the Hindu agitators in Calcutta would lose their easy contact with those in East Bengal.

From late 1903, when the proposal was first published, until the formal division of the province on 16 October 1905 (a month before Curzon left India), there was continual agitation against the plan, in the form of petitions, speeches, newspaper articles, plays, songs and mass-meetings. After Partition, a boycott of foreign-made (*bideshi*) goods in favour of Indian-made (*swadeshi*) substitutes, quickly gathered force. So did tensions between Bengalis, especially between Hindus who could generally afford the boycott, and Muslims who generally could not. Violence soon followed, in April 1906, and relations between the two communities rapidly deteriorated – to the satisfaction of British officialdom. In due course, around the time at which Tagore's novel is set (1907/8), the violence was turned against them too, in a series of bombings and shootings which inaugurated the tradition of Bengali terrorism that expressed itself again in the Naxalite movement of the late 1960s and 70s.

None of Ray's immediate family was involved in terrorism but most of them felt sympathy for the aims of the young idealists, if not for their methods. Sukumar Ray, as we know, composed patriotic songs and a playlet at this time and took a famous photograph of Tagore in *swadeshi* clothes. He also used *swadeshi* goods, though not without poking fun at their poor quality. While Satyajit was growing up, he was exposed to *swadeshi* ideals too, but in a different form – the Swadeshi Mela set up in a field not far from his uncle's house in south Calcutta, and the craze for spinning started by Gandhi that affected Satyajit's whole household.

As in the early 1930s, so in the 1905 period, the *swadeshi* fad soon palled, leaving behind it a residue of crushed aspirations. 'The *swadeshi* movement of 1903–08', writes the author of a classic study Ray consulted, 'leaves on the observer of the present day two major impressions, contradictory and yet perhaps equally valid – a sense of richness and promise, of national energies bursting out in diverse streams of political activity, intellectual debate and cultural efflorescence, and a feeling of disappointment, even anticlimax, at the blighting of so many hopes.'

Its most enduring positive legacy is, by general agreement, the body of stirring and beautiful songs composed by Rabindranath Tagore as a *swadeshi* leader, one of which is sung by Sandip in the film. Besides, it helped to produce the new movement in art known as the Bengal School, led by Abanindranath Tagore and Nandalal Bose (which Upendrakisore, Sukumar and later Satyajit all disliked), and it encouraged the research into folk-tales that gave rise to several collections including Upendrakisore's still-popular retellings.

Women too were affected by the movement, which indirectly initiated their liberation – carried on by Gandhi on a much greater scale. The concept of *swadeshi* goods had gradually made its appearance in women's magazines in the decade before the Partition. During the movement itself some women actually canvassed from house to house collecting subscriptions for the Cause. It ceased to be unheard-of that orthodox women should emerge from seclusion, as Bimala does in *The Home and the World*.

The darker side of the movement continues to haunt Bengal and the rest of India to this day. The wealthy middle-class Hindus who led it achieved little contact with the masses they hoped to lead, particularly as these were mainly Muslims. Their indifference to them stemmed partly from their material circumstances, which were utterly incompatible (as they are today), but also 'from a long tradition of contempt or at best condescension for men who worked with their hands', coupled to 'a sense of alienation' through having been educated in a foreign language, English – in the words of Sumit Sarkar, Ray's source quoted above. Instead of promoting friendship between communities, the movement actually accentuated the Hindu-Muslim split and helped to create the conditions for the terrible 1947 Partition. Nikhil – the liberal zamindar in Ray's film, whom Ray says 'is really Tagore' – recognises this. On hearing that a riot is about to break out on his estate, he says, 'Think how we ourselves have treated the Muslims. Have we ever given them their dues as human beings?'

The Ray family were untypical among Bengalis in their open-minded attitude to the Muslim heritage of India. Upendrakisore's father was so fine a scholar in Persian that he was better known as Munshi Syamsundar, as we know, and several of his descendants were knowledgeable too, down to Satyajit, with his love for Lucknow. But in general, educated Bengali Hindus in the last century and a half have ignored the culture of the majority population of Bengal. 'I do not know of one great Bengali writer, religious reformer, or political leader after Rammohun Roy,' Nirad Chaudhuri has observed, 'who had any first-hand knowledge of Islam as a whole or of any of its aspects. After the end of Muslim rule Hindu society had broken completely with Islam' – and that really has to include Tagore too.

The dominant influence in nineteenth-century Bengal had of course become British, rather than Mughal. By 1905 the houses of prosperous Bengalis were crammed with goods from Europe bought in the big stores of Calcutta like Whiteaway Laidlaw (where Satyajit would pay thrilling pre-Christmas visits a quarter of a century later), while their minds nurtured impossible dreams of political power seeded by their reading of western political thinkers. The trouble was that there was hardly any economic foundation for these hopes to build on. Successful Bengali businesses like U. Ray and Sons were very much the exception; *swadeshi* in practice was a sham. 'It is the weakness of our national movement,' wrote the pioneering art historian Ananda Coomaraswamy at the time, 'that we do not love India; we love suburban England, we love the comfortable bourgeois prosperity that is to be some day established when we have learned enough science and forgotten enough art to successfully compete with Europe in a commercial war.' How up-to-date that remark still sounds.

Rabindranath and other members of the Tagore family had been among the earliest Bengalis to experiment with *swadeshi* businesses. His elder brother, the unworldly Jyotirindranath (the model for Bhupati in *Charulata*) had gone as far as to establish a steamer service and been forced into bankruptcy by fierce competition from a British line. When Nikhil refers wryly to his abortive efforts to make soap and other items on his estate, we may be sure that Tagore was thinking of himself. His whole attitude to the national movement in due course came to be that Bengalis must learn to help themselves. He had no use for the mendicancy practised on the British power by many politically minded Bengalis, nor did he favour focusing the movement's energies on throwing the British out. He believed instead in trying to set up parallel institutions in Bengali society, ignoring the Raj but extracting from the West as much expertise and intellectual nourishment as possible. Unlike Gandhi, Tagore believed passionately that India neither should nor could shut out western influences.

It took him until 1906–7 to arrive at this position, however. In the earliest years of the century, the period of his founding the school at Santiniketan, he had a decided bent away from the West, towards the fashionable glorification of India's past that for a while even led him to justify caste and some other orthodox Hindu practices. The high-water mark of his enthusiasm for such politics came in late 1905 with a magnificent symbolic gesture that caught the imagination of all Calcutta on the day of proclamation of the Partition – Rakhibandhan: the mass-linking by ceremonial thread (*rakhi*) of complete strangers, bound arm to arm as in the Hindu marriage ritual, in protest against the attempted severance of

Bengalis by their British overlords. *In Rabindranath Tagore*, Ray recreates the moment, to the sound of crowds singing Tagore's songs.

When the movement turned violent in 1906, Tagore withdrew from its leadership, attracting severe censure from other leaders in the process. There followed a gap of about nine months between 1906 and 1907 when he produced no essays on political subjects. He then wrote a whole series, of great importance and eloquence, in which he returned firmly to his original modernist position of the 1890s. Unfortunately for the movement though, Tagore was no Gandhi. His plea was for constructive work, rather than boycotts and speeches, but he lacked a concrete social or economic programme with imaginative appeal for the masses. His ideas seemed instead timid and anaemic. He was a creative individual, not a political leader, and from 1907 onwards he took no more part in the rough and tumble of active politics.

Ghare Baire (*The Home and the World*) grew out of his experiences during those years. He did not actually write it until 1912, after the publication of his best-known novel *Gora*, and it was published only in 1915, followed by an English translation by his nephew in 1919, the year in which Rabindranath returned his knighthood after the massacre at Amritsar. Nikhil in the novel is literally Tagore's spokesman, as Ray points out:

> Tagore's essays on the terrorist movement and some of the other things that he wrote are actually put in the mouth of Nikhil – exact sentences even. He represents Tagore's attitude to the terrorist movement and its ultimate futility. It's a very valid viewpoint, very rational. It was really a middle-class movement with no connection with the lower strata of society at all. So ultimately it just fizzled out, and in other cases it turned into very violent riots between Hindus and Muslims. It was a failure and Tagore could see it was going to be a failure, although the political leaders didn't see it his way.

Each of the three main characters – Nikhil, his wife Bimala and his friend Sandip, the political leader – is given portions of the novel told from his or her point of view in the form of a kind of diary. The novel thus consists of a series of diaries which interlock and tell the story, beginning and ending with Bimala's. Each member of the fateful triangle by turns reveals his or her inner thoughts and motivations. The language, even in English, is florid, and in the original Bengali still more so. It bears little relation to real speech and can be quite off-putting. E.M. Forster, in a rather lordly review, wrote that Tagore had tried an 'experiment' that had not quite come off; 'throughout the book one is puzzled by bad tastes that verge on bad taste', he remarked. And yet, as he admitted, much of the novel is beautiful and compelling; it is just that the characters have to be accepted as vehicles for Tagore's always interesting philosophy and not be required to function as individuals with a life of their own, which they are not. 'In spite of the predominance and suffocating weight of so much polemic,' Anita Desai candidly wrote, in her introduction to the 1985 reissue of the novel, 'there are extraordinary flashes of light and colour, as if created by the striking of flints, as well as touches of tenderness and childishness which lighten the lowering clouds of the prevalent mood of disaster and give the novel variation and vivacity . . . It is a dramatic tale, yet not particularly dramatic in the telling.'

Its central situation is a true one, but peculiar to Tagore. Nikhil, as a modern man, wishes to bring his wife out of purdah and into the outside world to meet Sandip; only when she has been given a chance to lose herself there, will he feel that he can accept her love for him as genuine. He knows that this entails a risk – which is of course what gives the story its tension – but that is the duty he owes to his radical belief in female emancipation.

The Tagores went in for such behaviour, according to Ray. 'There is a story that Satyendranath Tagore [Rabindranath's eldest brother] took a friend and introduced him to his wife while she was in bed under a mosquito net. He pushed his friend under the net and left them to get acquainted,' he says with a laugh. Even so, it seems to weaken *The Home and the World*. One cannot help to some extent sharing Sandip's incredulity at his old friend's determination to ruin himself for an ideal. At least one British critic of the film, John Coleman (who is usually very sympathetic to Ray's films), wrote that Nikhil seems to expose his wife to 'some weird fidelity-test'; while a critic for a women's magazine in London remarked, not without reason, that the film 'tells us all about relationships and love. And tells us virtually nothing.'

If the novel, and to an extent the film, are not entirely convincing about love, they are both triumphantly successful in their depiction of the link between individual and national selfishness. They are powerful meditations on 'the roots of what is perhaps modern India's greatest tragedy' – in Sarkar's view – 'the failure to intermingle the currents of national and social discontent into a single anticolonial and antifeudal revolution.' But they are more than that: the conflict between Nikhil and Sandip, who dresses up his private belief that 'greed is natural' in high-sounding political language, has reverberations around the world, not just in India – as a writer in the *New York Times* recognised in 1985:

The Soviet Union stands as an exemplar of a secular ideology carried to its bitter end, while Iran is in the throes of an upsurge of fundamentalist fervour that condemns moderation as a crime. Such movements despise the Enlightenment ideal, still prized in the West which takes the individual as the measure of things and resists abstractions that claim to go beyond the dimensions of man, the justification of cruelties to individuals for the sake of a faith or an ideology, the justification of pain in the present for the sake of a Utopian future or a paradisical hereafter. That central battle of our era may be glimpsed in *The Home and the World*.

Ray, by his own admission, sees the novel more as a love-story than as a struggle between opposed values; the dramatic irony inherent in Nikhil's decision to free his wife 'from her moorings', as his disapproving widowed sister-in-law puts it, is what principally drew him to it – and this may be responsible for the weakness in the film as well as in the novel. Some critics have imagined that Ray could not bring himself to adapt Tagore's novel ruthlessly enough, but there is not much evidence of that. For a start, there is barely one line of dialogue in the film taken from the novel. Secondly, Ray has altered the plot substantially, while preserving its separate voices in four sections: Bimala's, then Sandip's, then Nikhil's, and then finally Ray's own. By beginning the film at the end, so to speak, with Bimala's 'epitaph' for Nikhil, Ray has intensified the sense of predestination in the events that follow: an example of what Kael meant when she wrote that the film obeys its own non-western canons. From its outset we know that Nikhil and the woman he loves are doomed. Thirdly, Ray has made concrete all the elements of the palace and the characters which Tagore, in his preoccupation with their thoughts, hardly bothers to describe.

Lastly, Ray has done away with most of the high-falutin miasma that surrounds Sandip and, to some extent Bimala. Sandip has become a much more ordinary person and been given a ration of decent instincts to mitigate his unscrupulous manipulation of those around him. He still has some courage and great ability as an orator, but he is weaker and more sentimental than Tagore's Sandip. Like many clever Bengalis he lacks application, or, as Nikhil puts it to his schoolmaster friend, he suffers from 'a deep sense of frustration. With all his gifts he couldn't really accomplish anything.' In other words he is a typical Bengali Congress politician of an earlier generation, somewhat reminiscent of Subhash Chandra Bose, who joined the Japanese in the Second World War. (At one point in the novel, but not in the film, Sandip even brazenly declares that 'When I was attached to the Congress party I never hesitated to dilute ten per cent of truth with ninety per cent of untruth'!)

He is definitely no revolutionary (though his teenage disciple Amulya may be, in Ray's much-improved version of him), any more than Nikhil is the conservative he appears at first sight. Sandip's chief goal is a sinecure with some power attached, to be gained by whatever means available, but preferably not by disrupting the status quo too much. Nikhil's is nothing less than government by love. As the *Sunday Telegraph* reviewer observed: 'The film catches the conservative element in some revolutionaries and the revolutionary element in some conservatives as well as any film I know.'

It is with Ray's conception of Nikhil rather than Sandip that the real difficulty seems to lie. 'I felt very close to him when I read the book,' says Ray. As portrayed in the screenplay, Nikhil is apparently meant to come across as wholly admirable, his every action motivated by unselfish instincts, down to his last ride out into the night and his death attempting to quell a riot on his estate (his fate is left open in the novel). But this interpretation is a significant, and in my view mistaken, departure from Tagore's more complex Nikhil, who comes gradually to feel that he may have committed an error in insisting on his wife's liberation against her will. In several beautiful passages he contemplates his failure to inspire those he loves and his lack of creative spark:

I am not a flame, only a black coal, which has gone out. I can light no lamp. That is what the story of my life shows, – my row of lamps has remained unlit ... Those to whom I have surrendered my all have taken my all, but not myself with it ... I have begun to suspect that there has all along been a vein of tyranny in me. There was a despotism in my desire to mould my relations with Bimala in a hard, clear-cut, perfect form. But man's life was not meant to be cast in a mould. And if we try to shape the good, as so much mere material, it takes a terrible revenge by losing its life.

These are the thoughts that make Nikhil a human, not a saint, and their absence from Ray's screenplay makes him slightly unreal. Ray's conception of Nikhil recalls the way Tagore himself struck Satyajit when he was a student at Santiniketan. He felt uncomfortable in the great man's presence. 'He never used a wrong word. I mean if you recorded his normal conversation it would sound like a prepared speech. Everything was so incredibly perfect.' That is true too of the dialogue and thoughts Tagore wrote for Nikhil, but he did not set him up on quite so high a pedestal as Ray has done. It is particularly odd that Ray should have chosen to do this here, with his lifetime's immersion in Tagore and his works.

His casting for all three main parts, as well as the five subsidiary ones (including Jennifer Kendal as Bimala's English governess), is inspired. Victor Banerjee as Nikhil, Swatilekha Chatterjee as Bimala, and Soumitra Chatterjee as Sandip (though he is occasionally a little lacking in élan) all give outstanding performances. During the 1960s Ray had earmarked Soumitra to play Nikhil – the obvious choice given his good looks and the romantic screen image he had acquired after playing Apu – but when Victor appeared on the scene in the late 1970s, Ray decided to reverse the roles. To play Bimala he had earlier considered Madhabi Mukherjee and also the heart-throb of Bengal, Uttam Kumar's screen-partner and wife, Suchitra Sen. Both actresses he found, in a sense, too attractive for the part; Bimala is a woman of character, but she is not, according to Tagore, a beauty, notwithstanding the idea of her held by many Bengalis. Ray preferred to have a new face for the part, one which did not fit the stereotype, and in Swatilekha, a stage actress he saw in 1981, he found someone who had both personality, command of Bengali, and 'the intellect to understand what she was doing.'

He had planned to begin shooting in early 1982, with finance from a private producer; but the producer withdrew and he was unable to start until December. The backer by then was India's National Film Development Corporation, which was feeling guilty, according to Ray, over the large sums it had invested in a foreign production, Attenborough's *Gandhi* – an amusing irony, given Lukács's description of *The Home and the World* back in 1922 as 'Tagore's Gandhi Novel'.

Everything went well until October of the following year, when Ray suffered his first heart attack, brought about by a combination of the high blood pressure he had long suffered from and persistent over-work. For nearly a year he would be in and out of hospital in Calcutta and in Houston, where he underwent bypass surgery in mid-1984. In the meantime he supervised his son Sandip's completion of the film in time for the Cannes Festival in May 1984.

Its reception at the Festival, where it failed to carry off the Grand Prix, and in Britain, where it was released in September, have tended to foster the impression that Ray's illness affected its quality. Nearly all the critics showed it much respect and some, such as Pauline Kael and Peter Ackroyd (writing in the *Spectator*), real enthusiasm; but they did not, on the whole, class it with Ray's best work like *Charulata*, which it somewhat resembles (and which, it is worth remembering, Cannes managed to reject altogether twenty years before).

It is true that there are some flaws in the sound-track and dubbing of the film (including the mismatch of Soumitra Chatterjee's voice with that of the singer of the songs Sandip declaims) – some of which Ray removed after his recovery, before the release of the film in Calcutta – but these are minor. The lighting and colour too is not always as subtle as one might expect from the maker of *Distant Thunder*, *The Chess Players* and *Deliverance*; the night scenes cry out for the shifting lights and shadows of real candles made possible by the fast film stock not then available in Calcutta. As it is, the prettiness of the colours sometimes distracts the eye.

But the real awkwardness in the film lies, as already suggested, in Ray's (and Tagore's) conception of the characters, which the performances cannot quite overcome, and which is responsible for the common criticism that the film is too 'talkative'. It is as if 'intuition', a modern English word for a very old sensation, to which Sandip, Nikhil and Bimala all pay tribute and which none of them truly possesses, has also, for once, eluded Ray too. They none of them seem to come alive quite in the way that Amal, Bhupati and Charu do in the earlier film. Nikhil bears most blame for this, in my opinion; and yet it is fascinating to read the film's reviews and find that each of the three characters has been singled out for conviction, including Bimala, who was widely criticised in India for her lack of glamour and supposedly inferior acting by Swatilekha Chatterjee.

Some comparison with *Charulata* does seem fair. Both films are based on Tagore, both are set inside an unorthodox zamindar's palace, and both deal with a triangle in which a childless woman emerges from traditional constraints into unfulfilled sadness. Yet the two films differ fundamentally in tone, key and texture. *Charulata* is at root a simple tale of unrequited love. *The Home and the World* is high tragedy: its ambit is of much greater complexity, shorn of easy romance, its characters forced to confront the wider effects of their own deficiencies. The vision is deeper, maturer and darker. 'There's a kind of tension in the film; you know everything is going to fall apart,' says Ray. 'That probably prevents people from enjoying it in the way they enjoy *Charulata*, which perhaps has more lyricism in it.'

Charu is a creative woman and Bimala is not; that is the basic difference between them, which affects each frame of the two films. Bimala is a much more conventional woman, who concludes that God will punish her for her affair with Sandip; Charu feels no guilt at her feelings for Amal, only a pragmatic awareness of her situation as a respectable married woman. All her emotions are more intense and finely tuned than Bimala's, and this fact (through Madhabi's wonderful performance) fills the film with a grace that is denied its successor by design.

The music Ray composed for both films reflects this; taken together, it is among the best he has done. For each, he imaginatively adapted the lovely tune of a Tagore song (not the same one) in various ways; but whereas in *Charulata* one tune dominates the film (being first heard under the titles), in *The Home and the World* the Tagore tune takes second place to the sombre main theme and is heard properly only when Nikhil and Bimala slowly emerge together from the inner apartments to meet Sandip for the first time.

Each film has a different musicality too. Whereas *Charulata* recalls Mozart's operas, *The Home and the World* might bring to mind late Beethoven. 'It is the movement and growth of character and relationships that's more important than what's happening on the surface. But even so there's a kind of musical structure and development,' comments Ray.

Take the third meeting between Sandip and Bimala, when she meets Amulya for the first time. Amulya leaves and then she is concerned because Amulya has suggested there is danger in the kind of work they are doing. Then she starts walking and the camera also starts moving, with Sandip in the foreground, keeping the relationship between him and Bimala the same throughout. Although Bimala walks the camera moves in the opposite direction. Then she wanders around the room. She now has freedom to explore the room for the first time, because she is freer now in the presence of Sandip. During the first encounter she was all the time seated. In the second one she was nervous in his company and she left as soon as possible with an excuse. The third time she has all the time in the world, therefore she doesn't sit down. She walks, first to the window, sings, sits down at the piano, and then walks again, takes her time in front of the mirror and then there's a conversation there.

And then there comes a point where she's offended by something Sandip suggests and she wants to leave and then they really come together. It was necessary to have a point for them to come together and here was a perfectly logical reason because Sandip naturally wants to prevent her from leaving, and he comes as close as possible to an embrace; but it's not yet time for an embrace because the relationship hasn't got to that point yet. Anyway he holds her hand and she has to say, 'Please let me go.' And there's a slight suggestion that he's holding her hand so tight it's actually hurting her. And then she goes . . . Psychology dictates her movement and therefore the movement of the camera and therefore the musicality of the scene is dependent on the relationship between the two characters.

If the film as a whole does not allow us inside the heads of the trio quite as much as in *Charulata*, it still includes many startling moments of insight – flashes of light in the encircling gloom, so to speak. Towards the end Nikhil, brooding on the dreadful strain he has brought upon himself by tolerating Sandip too long, heavily climbs the stairs to his bedroom and goes to stand alone beside the window. As he reflects on his oppressive sense of failure, we see him distanced, reflected in a bedroom mirror – one of many in the film – a mere shadow of himself against the window-frame and the luminous blue rectangle of light from the night sky outside, with one of his exquisite red cushions glowing richly in the radiance of a lamp inside the room. Despite the aura of foreboding hanging over him and over his home, one gets a momentary feeling of absorption into his mind, of a harmony behind the *maya* of physical appearances – the exact cinematic apprehension of Nikhil's words in the novel: 'All at once my heart was full with the thought that my Eternal Love is steadfastly waiting for me through the ages, below a veil of material things. Through many a life, in many a mirror, have I seen her image, – broken mirrors, crooked mirrors, dusty mirrors. Whenever I have sought to make the mirror my very own, and shut it up within my box, I have lost sight of the image. But what of that? What have I to do with the mirror, or even the image?'

26

Documentaries:

Sikkim 1971 Sukumar Ray 1987
Bala 1976 Rabindranath Tagore 1961
The Inner Eye 1972

··➤❴ ❨❨❨❩❨❩❩ ❵◀··

R AY'S documentary films about people have two characteristics in
common that reflect his own personality. First, they are informed by
deep admiration of the subject; secondly, they are remarkably self-effacing.
Although the commentary is usually spoken by Ray himself, he hardly ever
intrudes into the film as an individual, even in the film about his father, and
he certainly never appears on screen. As he once put it to Chidananda Das
Gupta, who had asked him for advice on a film about the scholar Ananda
Coomaraswamy that he was making, 'What *you* think is unimportant; you
must show what *he* thought and did. He was a writer. Where is the shot
of him writing?'

If such a shot is not available Ray may sometimes decide to
create it for himself. He has no taboo against using reconstructions
in his documentaries, which come off particularly well in *Rabindranath
Tagore* for instance. Cinéma vérité strikes him as being just as risky as
using actors. 'There is a slightly false element to it,' he says. 'I've seen quite
a few, including one about a pop-singer. He's shown doing everything, even
changing his dress. They go backstage and to his home – everywhere. Now
the performances are interesting and the adulation of the fans – all that
is fascinating. But the other scenes, where he's shown at home, all seem
a bit phony, because he's obviously acting for the camera. I would rather
have it all staged, rather than attempting an appearance of spontaneity,
since nobody can be spontaneous before the camera – except actors,' he
adds with a laugh.

The main impetus behind Ray's wish to make documentaries – an unusual
one for a successful feature film director – has always been the appeal to
him of a particular personality, rather than any cinematic considerations;
in fact, in the case of Tagore, only his overwhelming importance to Ray
could have maintained his interest in what turned out to be a very difficult
film to make. Balasaraswati, the *Bharata Natyam* dancer (in *Bala*), Binode
Bihari Mukherjee (in *The Inner Eye*), Sukumar Ray and Tagore, were all
people to whom Ray was very strongly drawn: similarly Beethoven – and

to a lesser extent Nehru – both of whom he considered as documentary subjects. He met Nehru for the last time at Santiniketan in December 1962 with the intention of making a film to help him in his hour of crisis, following the Indo-China war. But he found him so depressed that he did not even broach the subject. The idea went the way of the documentary about the Bangladesh refugees he had contemplated making in 1971, and probably for the same underlying reason: Ray's unwillingness to propagandise.

Although he has seriously considered making several films about people in a particular setting – a dance performance at Ellora and the picaresque musicians of western Rajasthan who had entranced him when he was making *Goopy Gyne* and *The Golden Fortress*, for instance – he has actually made only one. *Sikkim*, about the small Himalayan princely state north of Darjeeling, which I have not seen, was commissioned by the Chogyal (ruler) of Sikkim and his then wife, an American called Hope Cook. Ray's cousin living in Darjeeling, who appears briefly in *Kanchenjungha*, knew the couple well and persuaded Satyajit that he would get a well-paid holiday with complete editorial freedom. Ironically, first Ray's sponsors and later the Indian Government would have their say in the film – the only instance of this in his career – and Ray is not satisfied with the film as it stands now. (Only one print officially exists incidentally, in a US university where it was deposited by Hope Cook.) He was compelled to make about forty per cent of the film into something 'bureaucratic with statistical information' and a disproportionate emphasis on the Sikkimese population instead of on the Nepalese, as would have been appropriate given the latter's actual preponderance in the state. He remembers one scene in particular that got cut out when he showed his original version to the Chogyal and his wife. It showed a party with a senior bureaucrat shot in a 'not very flattering way – he was eating noodles, I think.' Hope Cook kept saying 'That's wicked! That's wicked!' and Ray knew that this was one part of his film that would never make it to the finished version.

But he did manage to preserve his own seven-minute opening – a wordless evocation of the atmosphere of Sikkim – along with his ending. The opening includes a shot of a parallel ropeway with two carriages advancing towards each other. 'While they're reaching this point,' says Ray, 'I cut to a shot of a piece of telegraph wire. It's raining and there are two drops of rain approaching on a downward curve . . . It's a very poetic seven minutes. And the end is also very lively, very optimistic, with children, happy, laughing, smoking, singing. The whole thing builds up into a paean of praise for the place.'

Unfortunately the Indian Government, when it took over Sikkim in 1975, did not see the film in this way. It suppressed it, as certain officials would like to have done twenty years before to prevent *Pather Panchali* being shown abroad – and would have done, but for Nehru's intervention. The film showed Sikkim as a monarchy, with shots of people prostrating themselves before the Chogyal. 'And that's now democratic

Indian territory,' chuckles Ray. 'It's not a very logical reason for banning the film because after all it shows Sikkim at a certain point in history. It doesn't claim to show Sikkim of today.'

Sukumar Ray was made for the West Bengal Government in mid-1987 in time for transmission on Calcutta television on 30 October, the centenary of his birth. It was not an easy film to make, because Satyajit had to depend entirely on photographs of his father and family and on his illustrations and writings, plus dramatisations of his work; there was no footage of him at all, since he died in 1923. Ray rejected the idea of actors to play Sukumar on the grounds that he himself 'wouldn't be convinced' by it. This dependence is one reason – combined with the untranslatability of humour – why *Sukumar Ray* will always remain inaccessible to non-Bengali audiences. Ray has not attempted an English version, because he believes it would miss the essence of the subject.

Characteristically, he opens his tribute with a wordless sequence – a technique he used in *Rabindranath Tagore* and *The Inner Eye*, as well as in *Sikkim* – in this case a series of shots of his father's comic drawings, accompanied by the equivalent of a jew's-harp and the comment (by Soumitra Chatterjee, who reads Ray's commentary): 'There can be few Bengalis who do not know these characters.'

Ray's skilful use of such drawings throughout the film never allows it to seem slow, despite the slightly excessive use of mournful music based on Tagore – perhaps Satyajit's expression of his sense of loss at not knowing his father – but it is his dramatisations of Sukumar's work that bring it, and its subject's sense of humour, properly alive. The first of these is simply Utpal Dutta dressed as a pundit delivering a comic monologue from *Jhalapala* with panache. The second is a scene from Sukumar's spoof *Ramayana*, and the third is taken from his 'most famous Bengali composition', *Ha-Ja-Ba-Ra-La*, which was inspired by *Alice's Adventures in Wonderland*. The scene is reminiscent of the Mad Hatter's Tea Party, where Time stands still at teatime (and it also perhaps reminded Ray of the adult relatives who surrounded him as a child and seemed like children themselves). There are three characters: an innocent boy, a quarrelsome balding old man, and a bossy crow perched in a tree, all of whom appear in the film in black silhouette against a bright purple backlight:

Old Man: How much do you weigh?
Boy: I don't know.
Old Man prods him with his fingers a few times.
Old Man: Two and a half seers [a seer is about two pounds].
Boy: Certainly not – Patla weights twenty-one seers and he's a year and a half younger than me.
The Crow butts in.
Crow: You calculate in the wrong way.

Old Man: Now write this down – Weight 2½ seers, Age 37.

Boy: No! I'm eight years and three months old, not 37 like you said.

Old Man thinks for a moment and then says:

Old Man: Is your age rising or falling?

Boy: How can age get less?

Old Man: Why not? Why should it only increase? That would be terrible! I never want to see my age rise to 60 or 70 or 80 years. By then I would be old and then I would die!

Boy: Don't be stupid! When a man is 80 years old, he *is* old.

Old Man: *You* are stupid! Why should someone's age ever reach 80? When it reaches 40 we turn it round again. So it never reaches 41 or 42 – it goes down again – 39, 38, 37. When it reaches ten again, it starts rising once more. My age has risen, fallen and risen again – just now I'm thirteen.

Ray's one-hour tribute in English to his father's close friend Rabindranath Tagore 'is not a film which on first viewing reveals what has gone into its creating', as Marie Seton remarks. To Ray, writing to Lester Peries a year after finishing the film, it was a 'back-breaking chore' which took two or three times as long as a feature film. It was fortunate that he began discussing it with the Central Government as early as the beginning of 1958, giving him time to complete it for the centenary of Tagore's birth in May 1961.

Efforts were made at the time to establish a committee to monitor his progress. Fortunately, Nehru's good sense prevailed; 'we need a film-maker, not a historian', he is reported to have said. Even so, Ray was conscious that he was making an official portrait of India's National Poet and that his warts should be omitted from it. 'I felt it had to be a film which really praised him, showed the best side of him. I avoided the controversial aspects,' he says frankly. It therefore contains no mention of his sister-in-law, Kadambari Devi's suicide, nothing about the fraught relationship between Tagore and the Bengali public, no mention of his ill-advised praise for Mussolini's Italy, hardly any of his criticism of Gandhi, and nothing about the waning of his reputation in the West in his own lifetime.

On the other hand it is very far from being propaganda of the type churned out by the Indian Government's Films Division or a film like Shyam Benegal's lengthy portrait of Nehru. One of the reasons for avoiding some of Tagore's aspects was simply a severe lack of visual material to illustrate them. 'I started by writing out as a screenplay what information had to be conveyed verbally, hoping to support it with images,' says Ray. 'And then started looking for photographs and other materials. I was *very* disappointed with the lack of live footage. We looked through the catalogue of Pathé, Gaumont, and another company and there was nothing. There was masses of footage on Gandhi and Nehru, but nothing at all on Tagore.'

Two further restrictions existed too: both major and both self-imposed. First, Ray decided to dispense with interviews: an extraordinarily bold move given how easy it would have been to rely on them. There is not one in the entire film. Secondly, notwithstanding Tagore's primary fame as a poet, Ray included no recitation of his poetry. 'It was difficult to know how to use one,' he says. 'I was not very happy with the English translations, frankly speaking. I had the feeling they wouldn't make the right impression if recited. People would wonder – well if this is the stuff then he couldn't have been a very great poet – that sort of idea,' he remarks with a mildly embarrassed laugh. In his view, Tagore never wrote idiomatic English. 'To me it seemed he was always translating from Bengali.' Then he adds, 'Actually he was a poet and one would expect more poetry in the film. This was a comment made by some of my friends also when they first saw the film.'

What one does get are some passages of singing and music which are both charming and in places extremely moving. The *Times* review in 1961 singled out certain portions of the film 'in which it is plain that Mr. Ray is one of the most poetic of modern young film-makers.' One of these is the sequence in which a young boy plays Rabi around the age of ten or twelve, hating school, receiving an education at home, and travelling with his grave father the Maharsi to the hill station of Dalhousie in the Himalayas. There, as the stars begin to come out, and the distant peaks glisten with snow, Rabi sings devotional songs of great purity and beauty to his silent father. The whole sequence is wonderfully elating; it shows clearly to the most sceptical western mind that Rabindranath's response to life was direct and uncluttered – something which is also transparent in his best poems (but only when read in Bengali).

Another of these vivid passages comes with his move to the Tagore estate in East Bengal in his twenties, where he wrote some of his finest poetry and short stories, sitting aboard his house-boat. Here, by simply showing us a succession of ordinary riverside scenes, such as those described in his letters, supported by music that swings rhythmically along like the dipping oars of a boat, Ray conveys the relaxed flow of riparian life and reminds us at the same time of Apu and Pulu passing slowly up-river to that fateful wedding. The dramatic impact of the monsoon on these rivers, which Ray shows us next, is then all the more striking, reinforced as it is by one of Rabindranath's exultant rainy season songs. We really feel – to quote one of the letters – 'the storm [droning] like a giant snake-charmer's pipe, and to its rhythm [swaying] hundreds and thousands of crested waves, like so many hooded snakes.'

A third passage of fine distinction involves Rabindranath's paintings. Naturally Ray eschewed commentary here. He created instead an intriguing score to accompany a series of works which begins with snatches of flute and drum sounding like a tropical aviary on some planet not quite our own, and then merges into the poignant strain of the violin-like *esraj*, as the works change from fantasy creatures to landscapes and figures and portraits that are recognisably human. 'Humans, birds, fish and animals in his paintings inhabit a world which belonged uniquely to Rabindranath,' Ray has written in the foreword to a collection of the work. 'But his special field remained the study of women. These women are recognisably Bengali, portrayed in an infinity of moods and expressions. The lack of anatomical accuracy does not matter since, in the best examples, the total effect is haunting.'

The total effect of his film, despite its limitations, is certainly a moving one. When it was shown with an exhibition of Tagore's paintings that toured Britain in 1986–7, it consistently held the attention of visitors. 'The final impression left by the film, even on me, was good,' says Ray. 'Ten or twelve minutes of it are among the most moving and powerful things that I have produced.' It has not really dated, but still succeeds in giving a sense of the impact Tagore had on those who had the good fortune to know him. Alex Aronson, Satyajit's Jewish refugee friend, for instance:

> To me who was present when his ashes were brought back to Santiniketan – to me his death seemed more than merely physical dissolution. I felt, together with all those who had lived within the orbit of this unique personality, that what had passed away was indeed a way of life, a way of dreaming, the like of which no age like ours could possibly reproduce again.
>
> And it is no exaggeration to say that we then were filled with a sense of awe and veneration which has never left us since. For I know that no one who has ever been near him, whether Hindu or Moslem, Christian or Jew, Black or White or Yellow, could ever again escape into irony and sarcasm when either his common sense or his imagination failed him.

Satyajit first saw Balasaraswati, 'the greatest *Bharata Natyam* dancer ever' according to him, in Calcutta in 1935. He was fourteen – just falling under the sway of western classical music – and she was about seventeen. He immediately fell for her. 'The memory is still absolutely fresh in my mind,' says Ray. 'This is one dance form that brings out the best in a woman; I mean her feminine qualities.' Unlike the classical ballet of the West, it uses every possible human attribute, all codified in a system with roots 1500 years old and then interpreted afresh by every great exponent of the art. 'An Englishman once told me he didn't like *Bharata Natyam* because the women tend to smile too much, show their teeth too much: he thought that classical dancing should be cool and detached,' says Ray. 'I think that *Bharata Natyam* brings out the femininity of a woman because there's a lot involved in the facial expressions which ballet doesn't use, certainly to that extent. Ballet is more form, [performed] more through gestures than through facial expressions.'

Ray was originally to have made his film in 1966, when Bala was forty-eight. Something went wrong and he could not get started until 1976. He felt a twinge of regret at having missed recording her in her prime but consoled himself 'with the thought that Bala filmed at 58 was better than Bala not being filmed at all.' When he finally met her at home in Madras her 'regal presence' took his breath away. Though she had lost weight – from diabetes – 'she had lost none of her poise and vitality', Ray later wrote. 'Face to face with her, I felt a fresh surge of enthusiasm for the film.'

It turned out to be a fairly conventional piece by Ray's standards, with the exception of the last scene, which is one sustained performance: a lyrical *varnam* to reveal the full range of her dancing. He himself feels that the film's main value is archival; he has put on film a rare performer for future generations to marvel at. What it somewhat lacks, apart from the whole-hearted cooperation of Balasaraswati herself (who was shy of speaking in English and unwilling to be drawn about her early life, when dancing was considered by polite society to be virtually synonymous with prostitution), is the total grasp of its subject that Ray brings to, say, Indian and western classical music. He admits that he did not seriously study *Bharata Natyam* until he came to make *Bala*. That is probably why, despite the many pleasures the film affords the sympathetic spectator, it also seems a little slack.

The Inner Eye, by contrast, is a small masterpiece. It is quite simply the finest short documentary about a creative artist I have seen, and it is not difficult to see why this should be so. Binode Bihari Mukherjee, its subject, was Satyajit's inspiration at Santiniketan. Besides being 'by far the finest living Indian painter', as Ray described him to Seton in 1973, he had a 'total lack of flamboyance' which Ray found strongly appealing – as is evident from the various absorbing conversations they had together during the making of the film in 1971–2 which Ray later recorded in one of his best Bengali articles. He was pleased when Mrs Gandhi, who had always been responsive to good painting, created Mukherjee Professor Emeritus on the strength of Ray's film.

Mukherjee's eyesight had been poor from birth. In 1957, after an unsuccessful cataract operation, he went totally blind. He was then fifty-four and had produced a fine body of work – much of it in the form of murals on the walls of the various buildings at Santiniketan. For an artist at the height of his powers this was obviously the greatest tragedy he could experience. 'But he took it with his usual stoicism', comments one of his pupils K.G. Subramanyan. 'There was not a trace of self-pity in his attitude; he took it as easily as if it were a passage from one room to another.' Much later he dictated a unique piece of writing about his blindness that helped to inspire Ray, who read it in manuscript and regards it as 'a very fine piece of literature'. It portrays a character, sometimes in a surrealist vein, called

Kattamosai (meaning 'master of the household') who is clearly the sightless
Mukherjee himself. Here is part of Subramanyan's translation:

One evening [Kattamosai] is sitting alone in his room running his
fingers over a large lump of wax. He sees vividly that a cat has got
into that lump. But he is not able to lay hands on it. His tussle with
the lump makes him distraught. Then, all at once, he gets a grip on
the cat's tail. It can't escape now. With great satisfaction he pulls out
the cat's limbs, head, shoulders and so on. Then he starts looking for
its ears. At that moment his attention is disturbed. He feels there is
somebody there by his side and asks 'Who is that?' He gets the answer,
'Your [friend] Chaturjay. Sadhuji has come to see how you make your
figures. He is sitting just in front of you.'
  'How is it that all this escaped my notice?' asks Kattamosai. 'We
came and sat when you were locked in your struggle with the lump
of wax. Now, let me introduce you to Sadhu Baba.'

Ray absorbed these insights and combined them with his own
observation of Binodeda creating, and their private conversations in
Mukherjee's room, with the master sitting in his wicker chair, wearing his
dark glasses and keeping his cigarettes, matches and ashtray on a wicker
table in front of him, along with a wastepaper-basket between his legs with
a flask of tea kept upright in it. Satyajit was determined to penetrate Binode
Bihari's blindness and reach his 'inner eye, an inner vision born of long
experience and deep devotion which the artist could call upon to come
to his aid and to guide his fingers' as Ray puts it in his simple, heartfelt
English commentary. 'Blindness is very complex,' Binodeda told him one
day after enquiring of him how it had been shown in the cinema:

I couldn't have understood it before. It involves a new awareness of
space. Space becomes a substance with density which I have to clear
away as I move forward. Unless I can touch something it has no real
existence for me. As soon as you see a chair you know it exists; I don't
until I sit down in it. I can't know whether it has arms until I touch
them. And whether those arms are of wood or wicker, thick or thin,
polished or rough, curved or right-angled, I can only get to know by
running my hands over them. If I touch something unexpected with
my hand, I feel surprised. This chair I'm sitting in – I know there's a
stick lying cross-wise on its arms in front of me – but if I forget about
it and then come into contact with it, I feel shocked.

Another day Binodeda asked Satyajit: 'Will you show the Khoyai in
your film?' – that is, the desolate and beautiful ravine around Santiniketan
where Ray's mother once took him, aged seven, and sang Tagore songs in
the moonlight. 'I want to – but it all seems to have disappeared,' Satyajit
replied. 'It's still there in one place,' said Binodeda. 'Taltor, towards Prantik
Station. Near Chip Sahib Kuthi. Don't leave the Khoyai out. The Khoyai,

and within it a solitary palm-tree – they're vital. They contain my spirit. If my roots lie anywhere, it's there. You can say – that's me.'

These remarks, and many others, informed Ray's film and helped to make every shot in it tell. Without us being aware of it he mixes past and present and manages to distil Binode Bihari's essence, to make comprehensible the extraordinary fact of his continuing to create art without sight. There is no trace of didacticism in the way we learn of his early, Brahmo-oriented life among artistic brothers, his bad eyesight, his coming to Santiniketan to work with Nandalal Bose, his lack of interest in mythological subjects and his responsiveness to his surroundings despite his handicap. When, in 1937, he went to Japan, he was able truly to assimilate the approach of their painters: a fact that Ray conveys with the most sensitive and exquisite use of details from certain Japanese works that Binode Bihari had shown Satyajit the student thirty years before. They, and Mukherjee's awareness of western art, were influential in the subsequent murals he created at Santiniketan that are the peak of his achievement as an artist. Says Ray:

> Twentieth-century Indian painting is very derivative, with the exception of certain very gifted painters like Subramanyan. I have grown less and less interested in painting over the years somehow. But Binodeda was very deeply rooted. He perfectly synthesised what he picked up in Japan and in the West and what is already there in Indian painting. The synthesis makes it a perfectly satisfying unity. You never feel that 'Oh, now he's copying so-and-so's composition or now he's doing this or that.' You feel he's being himself – very much so. It's a reflection of his own personality and his ability to get the best out of all the elements and make a whole.

These are words that could equally apply to Ray himself. He has given the whole of himself to *The Inner Eye*, including his marvellous feeling for music. This really comes to the fore at the end, with a stirring, radiant composition on sitar by Nikhil Banerjee accompanying images of Binode Bihari drawing and making wax creatures with a remarkable resemblance to those found at Mohenjo-daro, the birthplace of Indian civilisation. 'The raga that comes after the blindness is *Asavari*,' says Ray. 'A morning raga. Very few morning ragas are optimistic in character because there is something wistful about dawn. This suggests that mood.' And as the music flows on, the image freezes on a profile of Binode Bihari's face wearing his dark glasses, and the following words appear:

> 'Blindness is
> a new feeling,
> a new experience,
> a new state of being.'

> Binode Bihari Mukherjee

27

Unmade Films:
Sakha Prasakha The Mahabharata
A Passage to India The Alien

······

THERE can be few film-makers nearing the end of their careers who cannot think of a number of film projects they never got off the ground. In nearly forty years of cinematic activity Satyajit Ray has abandoned many ideas, usually because he found them uncastable, long before undertaking any serious work on them. The four discussed in this chapter are his most important exceptions, and their disparity is an indication of Ray's unique range as a film-maker.

The first of them exists in the form of the preamble and opening scenes of an original screenplay, which he began to write in 1966. Its title, *Sakha Prasakha*, means literally *Branches and Twigs*, while Ray has contemplated calling it *Reunion*. Its theme is the growing apart of a family, the fact that 'you can feel much closer to a person who's not related to you, than to your own brother, your own flesh and blood,' as Ray puts it. Its focus is a successful self-made industrialist who has founded a town some hours' drive from Calcutta (modelled partly on a man Ray met when shooting those scenes in *The World of Apu* during Apu's exile). As he is getting to his feet to give a speech at a function organised by his grateful employees to celebrate his seventieth birthday, he suffers a heart attack. His family gathers round his bedside, having rushed to get there from Calcutta, where three out of his four sons are living, to find the old man unconscious. Four generations suddenly find themselves thrust together – the industrialist has a father still living (who is quite senile) and one of his sons has children – and nobody has anything specific to do. Everything seems fine to begin with when the industrialist regains consciousness – the point at which Ray stopped writing – but 'then comes a period where he has no further attacks and it becomes a big question how long he's going to survive, and then boredom sets in,' observes Ray. 'They want something to happen: either the doctor to declare that he's out of danger completely and you can go home now back to your work, or that the danger is still there. That is a very interesting situation.'

Ray's planned development, if he ever puts his mind to it, will include a picnic at a place the brothers used to visit as children which will be a total failure, 'because they can't bring back their own childhood' – leading to a quarrel. A relationship between the industrialist and his young grandson will also develop. 'The industrialist is under the impression that his children are all very well placed in life, all very happy, that he's succeeded in bringing them up as he hoped to. Whereas the grandson will come and tell stories to his grandfather which suggest that everything is not as he hoped.'

This last idea recalls a similar relationship in *The Elephant God*. There are echoes from his other films too: from the earlier *Kanchenjungha* (which Ray originally saw as a picnic story) and *Mahanagar*, and from the later films *Days and Nights in the Forest*, *The Adversary*, *Company Limited* and *Pikoo*. (And the idea of a reunion in itself calls to mind Bergman's *Fanny and Alexander*.) Does Ray at all feel the territory has already been covered? 'I hope not to repeat myself,' he says. 'I hope it'll be a fresh kind of treatment of a fresh theme.'

The *Mahabharata*, the later of India's two great epics, got a grip on Satyajit when he was as young as six or seven; his grand-uncle Kuladaranjan (Dhondadu) read the whole work to him in Bengali as we know. Ray's fascination with filming it began in the late 1950s and persists to this day. In late 1958 he wrote to Lester Peries that he had been reading and rereading the epic and 'never ceasing to marvel at it. The concentration [in a film] has to be on the personal relationship – so profound and so timeless, and the reflections on war and peace, with their eternal verities.' But six years later, after giving it much thought he told an interviewer that he was still stumped by the problem of how to introduce even the main characters to a non-Indian audience, whom he assumed would have to see it to make a film financially viable. (The producers he spoke to in India insisted on 'a battery of advisors'.) He felt that this problem could only be solved by recourse to uncinematic devices.

It still defeats him. As he says today: 'I gave up for the very good reason that I couldn't establish the relationships for a foreign audience. In a film you have to address somebody as an uncle three times at least to establish that he is an uncle.' He was also bothered by the choice of language, especially as he had in mind an international cast, including Toshiro Mifune. 'Bengali wouldn't do,' he says, 'and Hindi doesn't sound right when spoken by *Mahabharata* characters. Perhaps English would have been better.' Sanskrit he didn't even consider; his aim, like that of Peter Brook in his stage production, was to create 'very modern human beings with modern psychological feelings.' That, and its particular cinematic possibilities, explains Ray's attraction to filming just the dice game episode of the epic. 'It shows all the characters, and all their aspects,' he says. 'I don't think I could have tackled the War at all. You see Peter Brook can suggest a whole chariot with just a wheel. In cinema you can't do that kind of thing.'

Having seen Brook's stage version of the whole story in English, which Ray has not yet been able to do, I think Ray has been correct not to take the plunge into a film version. Brook's writer Jean-Claude Carrière is wrong to put this down to 'lack of funds'. The real reason is Ray's unique sensitivity to the work, which allows him to view it through both western and Indian eyes, separately or together at will: to comprehend as one its profound themes and the proliferation of character and incident that illuminates them, like the structure of his own films. Viewed in this way, he knew he could never do the work justice – a perception that Brook's splendid, ingenious but ultimately unmoving cavalcade amply confirms, in a manner curiously reminiscent of Renoir's failure to make sense of Hinduism in *The River*, despite some wonderful moments – even down to Renoir's uncomfortable use of English, a language in which he was no more at home than were many of Brook's actors.

Ray's failure to film *A Passage to India* is one of the saddest lost opportunities in cinema. The novel's setting, and its qualities of intimacy, atmosphere and psychological refinement, including stretches of outstanding dialogue, would have been a marvellous match for Ray's talents.

He had been nurturing the idea (and a dog-eared copy of the novel) since the early 1960s, and had received encouragement from many quarters, but not, alas, from E.M. Forster himself, who resolutely refused offers to film any of his books. In 1966, about three years before Forster's death, a meeting was at last arranged between them in Forster's rooms in Cambridge. Forster's friend Richard Marquand introduced Ray and tried to impress the old man with Ray's credentials in case he had not seen any of his films. 'He probably hadn't,' says Ray, 'but he knew my name.' The meeting was not a success. 'He kept shaking his head much of the time which meant he didn't want the book to be filmed. That was the drone – no! – in words, gestures, looks, everything. He was adamant. And I felt there was no point in asking why.' Since Forster had already had a heart attack, Ray was even less willing than he might have been to press his case.

After that, he gradually lost interest in the idea. When Forster's trustees at King's College wrote to him in 1980, he wrote back saying he was not interested. He was 'a little bothered by the logistics', he comments today, having passed through the trauma of making *The Chess Players* in the intervening period, and he felt unwilling to ignore Forster's veto. 'The moment I found out that he was not interested I said I'd better not pursue this any more. I felt it would be wrong. I remembered how the old man had reacted.' He also had some doubts about the novel itself, or, as he put it in a letter to Seton in late 1978, 'The trouble is I find I can identify more easily with Fielding than with Aziz, which somehow seems unsatisfactory.'

Ray's *Passage*, had it happened, would surely have given Dr Aziz some of the dignity and polish of the two nawabs in *The Chess Players*, without losing his immaturity, as well as filling out some of the Hindu characters. 'I think I could improve the book by doing away with its Muslim bias,' Ray told an interviewer in 1967. 'I would also make the Muslim characters speak Urdu among themselves – in the book they speak "Indian English"; it falsifies the tone.' In his view, too, Forster overdid the mysteriousness of India – he finds the incident in the Caves somehow spurious (and Forster himself seems to have had second thoughts about it). 'This is because India's seen from the English point of view. For instance, there's a Bengali couple who promise to send their carriage for the two ladies but then the carriage never comes. It's supposed to be very strange . . . The incident has the kind of plausibility that suggests Forster himself may have had the same experience and felt just as nonplussed as Mrs Moore and Miss Quested. And yet for an Indian there is no mystery here', Ray points out. The Bengalis suddenly panicked at having to converse in their fractured English. They had agreed to Mrs Moore's idea of visiting them, simply to avoid seeming discourteous and having to fumble for explanations. This, at bottom, is the chief limitation of Forster's novel, according to Ray; he spoke 'no Indian language and thus had no 'access to large areas of the Indian mind'. That is why, while his English characters, and especially Fielding, are so thoroughly convincing and engaging, his Indians – even Aziz – seem slightly insubstantial.

By the time David Lean took up the novel as a film project in 1981, Ray had become wholly detached from the idea of filming it himself. Though somewhat taken aback by Lean's claim at the time in the London *Times*, that 'I don't think anyone has really captured India on the screen, with the possible exception of parts of Renoir's *The River*', Ray assisted him, when approached by his producers, by suggesting for the part of Aziz Victor Banerjee, whom he already had in mind to play Nikhil in *The Home and the World*. He was the only Indian actor Ray felt could speak English well enough and look like a doctor and a Muslim (which of course he is not), having directed him as Wajid Ali Shah's Prime Minister in *The Chess Players*.

Ray's comments on Lean's *Passage* give us the clearest picture we are likely to get of the film of Forster's novel that he decided not to make. After viewing excerpts from it in a video-recording of the Royal Première in London, he wrote to me in March 1985 that he was

> horrified to see Aziz's house shown as a sort of log cabin – unthinkable in the plains. If this is an example of the kind of research that has gone into the film . . . I am happy for Peggy Ashcroft [who had keenly hoped to play Mrs Moore for Ray] and have no doubt that she deserved the Oscar. I feel both Adela [Quested] and Fielding have been miscast. Susan Wooldridge [of *Jewel in the Crown* fame] would,

of course, have been the ideal Adela, and for Fielding I had someone like a young Cyril Cusack in mind. [James] Fox is unconvincing both as a schoolmaster and as someone with a sense of humour.

Some months later he saw the entire film. 'Some professional competence but not Forster at all', he wrote. 'The whole thing is too picturesque and spick and span – the trains, the bazaars, the costumes, the mosque, the club . . . One longs for quiet moments. For me none of the characters comes alive – not even Mrs Moore – Peggy Ashcroft's performance notwithstanding . . . Victor is inconsistent – though the fault may be Lean's. The film is watchable though, but for reasons which actually reduce its stature. It had a poor run in Calcutta.'

The *Alien* project has to be the most bizarre episode in Ray's career, reinforcing the impression left by his first visit to the US (in 1958) that 'The East is still as far away from the West as it has ever been' – at least, in the cinema.

It all began in 1964 with a letter from Ray to Arthur C. Clarke in Sri Lanka asking him for his good wishes for a science-fiction film club he and others had started up in Calcutta. Clarke replied expressing admiration for Ray's films and a correspondence developed, which led to a meeting in London on the way back from a studio with Clarke where they had been watching Stanley Kubrick shooting *2001*. Ray outlined an idea he hoped to film. Clarke liked it and when he went home to Colombo spoke about it to Lester Peries and also to his close friend Mike Wilson, a fast-talking American, originally from New Zealand, then living in Sri Lanka too. Wilson had already written, produced and directed a film set in the island starring a Sri Lankan secret service agent James Banda and – to quote Ray – 'had rounded up virtually the entire European community of Colombo to play sinister bit-roles in the film.' He was also a highly professional skin-diver who had stumbled on a seventeenth-century Mughal galleon off the east coast of Sri Lanka and retrieved from it, with Clarke's help, a chestful of silver coins. 'When a man like that writes and tells you that he is ready to set up a co-production deal for you [with Clarke's financial backing], you are inclined to take his word on trust', wrote Ray many years later in a long, witty newspaper account of the project's history entitled 'Ordeals of the Alien', that appeared in the Calcutta *Statesman* in 1980.

At the time, the tail-end of 1966, Ray had no more than the bare bones of a story and some striking ideas. A few years before he had written and illustrated a story for *Sandesh* – one of his earliest stories in fact – entitled '*Bankubabur Bandhu*' ('Banku Babu's Friend'), in which a benign alien creature descended on a forest near an insignificant village in Bengal and made contact with one of its humblest residents, Banku Babu. Neither the alien's character nor that of his friend was much developed; the bulk of the story consisted of amusing dialogues between other residents of the village about strange lights seen in the sky, and their taunting of Banku Babu.

Apart from this story, Ray's oeuvre then included two ideas which he agrees are also precursors of *The Alien*, although he was unconscious of the links when writing the film's script. The first is from *The Philosopher's Stone*, – the stone itself which falls from the skies in a shower of rain (Ray's idea incidentally; the story-writer has it found lying on the ground), plays havoc with society, and vanishes. The second is the singing Nepalese beggar-child in *Kanchenjungha* who trails along behind the visitors from Calcutta. 'The Alien and the child in *Kanchenjungha* could be very close,' says Ray, 'because the child is the only one who belongs to Darjeeling but is unaware of the fact. He's the only one who's free, who has no problems.'

The Alien is a small humanoid creature whose spaceship splashes down in a pond in a Bengali village far from the metropolis. There it is promptly taken to be a submerged temple which has risen up, because a golden spire can be seen sticking out of the lotus-covered surface of the pond, and most of the locals begin to worship it. Those who do not include Haba, a poor village boy who survives – like Durga in *Pather Panchali* – off stolen fruit and beggary and who forms a rapport with the creature after it has entered his dreams at night and played with him; Mohan, a sceptical journalist from Calcutta; and Joe Devlin, a 'can-do' American engineer from Montana, who distrusts anything he has not personally experienced. He is in this backwoods area to drill tube-wells on behalf of a rich Marwari industrialist called Bajoria. Like many of his community – notably, the Birla family whose best-known member G. D. Birla funded Gandhi – Bajoria wishes to improve his image by good works. If these can be combined with religion as well, so much the better. (The Birlas were responsible, to the disgust of Ray and especially of his friend David McCutchion, for renovating and pinkwashing many old ruined temples in Bengal at this time, and they influenced Ray's characterisation of Bajoria.) On seeing the golden spire, Bajoria instantly perceives its possibilities as 'the holiest place in India'. He wants Devlin – for a consideration of course – to pump out the pond, so that he can 'cover the floor of that pond with marble, and build marble steps leading down from all four sides, and arches and pillars, and a little marble plaque to say: Salvaged and restored by Gaganlal Laxmikant Bajoria'!

The Alien has other ideas. Consumed with playful curiosity about the world in which it has just landed, it gets up to all sorts of mischief: ripening a villager's corn overnight, making a mango tree belonging to the meanest man in the village fruit at the wrong time of year, causing an old man's corpse on its pyre to open its eyes in front of his grandson, and other pranks. Ray's description of the Alien's first exploratory expedition on Earth gives a fine sense of the creature's magical powers and of the whimsical charm of Ray's screenplay, which distinctly recalls the mixture of fantasy and human frailty in the imaginary world of his father Sukumar, and the multi-coloured diary of his eccentric uncle Chotokaka:

In a series of fantastically quick, short steps over the lotus leaves, the Alien reaches the shore of the pond.

He looks down at the grass, examines a blade, and is off hopping into the bamboo grove.

BAMBOO GROVE – NIGHT

There the Alien sees a small plant. His eyes light up with a *yellow* light. He passes his hand over the plant, and flowers come out. A thin, soft, high-pitched laugh shows the Alien is pleased. He plucks a flower, puts it in his mouth, and hops on all fours to an ant-hill.

He pokes the ant-hill with his fingers, and causes agitated ants to swarm out of their holes. The Alien's eyes turn *blue*.

MICRO-DETAIL OF ANTS

The Alien observes the ants microscopically, and attunes his ears to make audible the sounds made by the insects.

Looking up, the Alien laughs to see a swarm of fireflies dancing round a mango tree.

He leaps up, catches hold of a mango branch and keeps swinging, while the fireflies dance around him.

Poised in mid-air, the Alien sees Haba's shack. He goes flitting through the air to reach the door of the shack. He peers inside.

INTERIOR OF HABA'S SHACK – NIGHT

The Alien sees Haba huddled in sleep on a mat. The Alien's eyes now turn glowing *red*.

PROCESS SHOT

This enables him to see Haba's respiratory system, and to listen to his regular heart-beats.

PROCESS SHOT

The red in the Alien's eyes turns *violet*, enabling him to look into Haba's brain, and sink into his subconscious.

HABA'S DREAM

Haba is dreaming, and the Alien becomes part of his dream. We see Haba and the Alien happy, playing hide-and-seek in a strange black-and-white world of geometrical forms.

INTERIOR OF HABA'S SHACK – NIGHT

The light in the Alien's eyes now dims, and with another high-pitched laugh, he is gone from the bamboo grove.

PADDY FIELD – NIGHT

The Alien now arrives at the paddy-field. The wide open spaces seem to delight him, and he dances around for a while.

Then he notices the withering crop and examines a paddy plant.

His eyes turn *yellow*, and he goes whirling about in the field

while all the paddy around him ripens and stands aspiring in the
moonlight.

Standing on the tip of a ripe paddy plant, the Alien looks up at the sky.

NIGHT SKY WITH MOON

He sees the nearly full moon in the sky, and seems fascinated by it.

PADDY FIELD – NIGHT

The Alien turns on his telescopic *green* eyelights.

NIGHT SKY WITH MOON

The moon is brought up close for inspection, so that its gigantic orb
marked with craters and mountains and valleys now fills a good half
of the sky.

Inspection over, the Alien pushes the moon back into place.

PADDY FIELD – NIGHT

The Alien now jumps off the plant, and flits back laughing
to the spaceship.

FADE OUT

Ray wrote the first draft of this screenplay in Calcutta in ten days
during February 1967. Mike Wilson was present in the flat much of the
time at his own request, but Ray says he took up just one of his many
suggestions: that the spaceship should be golden in colour. Later, when
the draft was finished, Wilson made some small changes to the dialogue
of Devlin, the American driller (and specified the songs he sings). That
was the extent of his contribution to the writing of *The Alien*, though
Wilson later claimed co-authorship of it.

Their conversation now turned to casting and Ray suggested that Peter
Sellers would fill the role of Bajoria well. He felt that no Indian actor was
quite right for it, and of course he knew he needed a name or two in the
film to raise money. He had seen and admired Sellers in *Dr Strangelove*
and knew that he had already played an Indian in *The Millionairess*. So far
as accent was concerned, Ray had two LPs of Sellers doing 'things with his
voice and tongue which bordered on the miraculous.'

A couple of months later, the two of them met, in Paris, over lunch
arranged by Wilson. 'Sellers knew no French, but spoke "Franglais"
which had the waiters in stitches', wrote Satyajit in his article. 'Half
a dozen of them had thronged around our table, some with autograph
albums. Inspector Clouseau had gone over big in Paris.' At some point
he managed to ask Sellers if he knew Ray's work at all. He didn't, but he
said 'Jonathan Miller swears by you, and his word is good enough for me.'
Ray, however, felt this alone was insufficient. He asked Wilson to arrange
a screening of *Charulata* for Sellers in Paris. The print was a poor one,
but at the end of it Sellers turned to Ray red-eyed and said 'Why do you
need me? I'm not better than your actors, you know.' But he agreed in
principle to play the part, as outlined to him there by Ray.

The next stop on Ray's *Alien* tour was now Hollywood. He arrived there on 1 June, after receiving a cable from Wilson that Columbia wanted to back *The Alien*, and that Sellers was there too, playing another Indian in a comedy (*The Party*), and was keen to talk again. Wilson checked Ray into the chic Château Marmont, into 'an elegant, self-contained two-storied cottage with all mod cons' (in Ray's words) and reassured him, 'Don't worry, Maestro, Columbia has made an advance against expenses. You can't afford anything but the best, you know; you made the Apu Trilogy!'

Ray met Sellers again at Ravi Shankar's place, where Sellers sat cross-legged on the carpet watching Shankar play, in order to imitate his fingering later in *The Party*. On the way back Sellers talked enthusiastically about his role in that film and said he did not mind at all that his part in *The Alien* would be smaller. He also added that an Indian astrologer in London had told him he would be working with an Indian director. 'So this is as much an act of volition as a decree of fate', he said. They never met again, and today Ray is still unsure to what extent Sellers really wanted the part. 'At times he seemed very keen, very excited – he laughed and we discussed the script and he enjoyed listening to his part and was already beginning to devise little bits of business . . . I think he was dependent to a certain extent on some kind of a holy man prophet.'

Having observed, at Sellers' insistence, some shooting on *The Party*, Ray had begun to have his doubts about Sellers' judgment. When he finally caught up with that film in Sydney, about a year later, just before Sellers withdrew from *The Alien*, these suspicions were fully confirmed. 'He plays an Indian in a Hollywood setting,' Ray wrote to Seton soon after – 'quite the most tasteless, heavy-handed caricature of an Indian ever put on the screen. I was so disgusted that I would in any case have found it most difficult to work with him.' He also noted, not without amusement, a sly reference in the film to himself. 'I'm sorry,' says the hero to a girl who has invited him into her flat. 'I'm sorry, but I must go back to my monkey.' 'Monkey?' 'Yes. My pet monkey. Apu.'

Whatever doubts Ray may already have had about Wilson, were reinforced by his stay in Hollywood. Although Ray had been warned against teaming up with Wilson by Seton at a very early stage, he accepted the idea would help him in procuring foreign finance on terms acceptable to him: that the story should be shot entirely in India (with effects done in Hollywood), in Bengali and English together, and that he would have final festival cut (though not final cut for the release of the film). An ability to wheel and deal is not one of Ray's skills, but he has some respect for it in others. Nevertheless, he was taken aback to discover mimeographed copies of his screenplay in the cottage in Hollywood bearing the legend 'copyright Mike Wilson and Satyajit Ray' (and in that order too!) 'Two heads are better than one, Maestro,' Wilson assured him when questioned; the double copyright line was for Ray's own better protection, Wilson said.

Satyajit was then whisked off to a series of parties – Wilson was making the most of the Summer of '67 – one of which was held in the vast mansion once owned by Greta Garbo, by then belonging to Jennifer Jones, who had recently visited India. She told him she wanted to work under him, while her husband producer David Selznick began to get visions of an Indian version of *Anna Karenina* in which Ray would play Vronsky opposite his wife. Ray felt he had strayed into 'Carrollian Wonderland'. He met stars and actors of the 1940s – Olivia de Havilland, Rita Hayworth, William Wyler, King Vidor – who had filled his mind in wartime Calcutta and after, and whom 'one scarcely believed existed in the flesh.' He also met an old friend, Jean Renoir, and finally saw *The River*, sixteen years after it was completed. When the screening was over, the two of them were brought on stage together and introduced with the comment, 'Ray owes a lot to Renoir.' But Renoir told the audience, 'I don't think Ray owes anything to me. I think he had it in his blood. Though he's very young still, he's the Father of Indian Cinema.' Nevertheless (or perhaps because he remembered Renoir's unhappy experience in Hollywood), Satyajit left there 'firmly convinced that *The Alien* was doomed.'

Back in Calcutta again, his thoughts turned once more to getting finance for *Goopy Gyne Bagha Byne*, but then a letter arrived from Sellers – in verse. He had promised to introduce Satyajit to the writings of William McGonagall, 'the greatest Bad Verse writer of all time'. Having just seen *Pather Panchali* he wrote to Ray in McGonagallese:

> *In the year of 1967 and in the month of December*
> *An auspicious month coming as it does at the end of the year*
> *And not the slightest alike to November*
> *Is a month I will long remember.*
> *I received one day*
> *From Satyajit Ray*
> *Information I required without delay*
> *So that I could say to my friends the evening of that day.*
> *The film you are about to see*
> *Is the film of a Trilogy*
> *And is called* Pather Panchali
> *In which there is a scene of two children in a field of barley*
> *Watching a train go by*
> *Under an azure sky*
> *So beautiful you want to die . . .*

The Alien had life in it yet. In October Ray went to London expecting to meet Sellers again, James Coburn (as a possible Devlin) and Columbia UK, who had taken over the project. Wilson had already been there a week and had fixed himself a suite at the Hilton, with a separate one for Ray. On the one evening Ray ventured to Wilson's suite, 'the scene that met my eye through the pall of [pot] smoke could have been a set piece out of Petronius. The carpet was strewn with bodies, male and female, and Subbulakshmi [the south Indian vocalist] sang above the whirr of a movie projector and the Bengali dialogue of what turned out to be a 16 mm print of my own film *Devi*, flickering fitfully on a bare wall of the room, a son et lumiere to end all son et lumieres.'

When the Columbia executive in charge of the project eventually managed to get Ray alone, he asked him if Wilson had passed on the ten thousand dollar advance made to Ray for the screenplay. Ray had received not a cent of it. 'By now I had begun to feel like a full-fledged Kafka hero,' he wrote later. 'Mike was supposed to be associate producer, but there was as yet no agreement between us.' Wilson was now anxious to settle this small point, though. On their way to the airport, in a Rolls-Royce with built-in cocktail cabinet commissioned by Wilson for the occasion, he slapped a sheaf of papers down on Ray's knee and told him, 'If you would just sign here, Maestro.'

I said: 'I'm sorry. I can't even read what I'm supposed to sign.'

Mike zipped out a pocket torch and flashed it on the top page of the bunch.

'It's just to say you and I are partners.'

'I can't sign anything in the car, Mike,' I said. 'Not even in a Rolls-Royce. Send the papers over to me in Calcutta.'

Back home again Ray found that no papers arrived. Instead, there arrived the Columbia executive a few months later. He wanted Ray to write to Wilson and ask him to pull out. He did so and received a 'sizzling reply'. But what shocked Ray was not that but a letter which then arrived from Sellers, in July 1968. Sellers wrote: 'I should tell you straightaway that though the part may appear more or less complete to you, it does not seem so to me and I don't see how I could contemplate playing it as it is.' Ray replied in verse:

> *Dear Peter, if you had wanted a bigger part*
> *Why, you should have told me so right at the start.*
> *By declaring it at this juncture*
> *You have simply punctured*
> *The Alien balloon*
> *Which I daresay will now be grounded soon*
> *Causing a great deal of dismay*
> *To Satyajit Ray.*

There was no answer to this from Sellers. Three weeks later Ray wrote to Seton prosaically that the project had 'begun to assume an aura which I found both distasteful and disconcerting' and that he had more or less decided to call it off, since it was obvious that Columbia would follow Sellers and withdraw from it too.

But in fact Columbia remained interested, subject to the withdrawal of Mike Wilson. Ray felt that Arthur C. Clarke was the only person who might bring this about. A letter he wrote to Sri Lanka in mid-August outlined the impasse as he saw it and gave a rare glimpse of himself. His Hollywood experience, he said, was 'the beginning of a period of profound uneasiness. I didn't reveal this to Mike because it is not in my nature to have done so. For one thing, I was too *deeply* disturbed, and for another – I was in a strange sort of way *fascinated* by the sinister turn of events and waited to see which way and how far it would go.' He concluded with a plea: 'I am depending a great deal on you, Arthur . . . I know the whole thing must sound terribly sordid to you – but that's how it is. I'm sure your wise counsel would help enormously towards a satisfactory and sensible solution.'

Clarke's reply reached him in October – a brief letter saying that Mike Wilson had shaved his head and gone off to meditate in the jungles of south India. (He took the name Swami Siva Kalki, and later went to live in a remote part of southern Sri Lanka). A letter from the 'shaven-headed monk' himself now followed. As Ray wrote, 'He was relinquishing his rights to the screenplay, although obviously too close to sainthood to spell it out in mundane terms. This is the way he chose to put it [referring to the battle between evil and good in the *Ramayana*]: "Dear Ravana You may keep Seetha. She's yours. Keep her, and make her and the world happy." '

For the next ten years and more Ray was variously encouraged to revive the project – by Ismail Merchant, by Sellers' ex-agent, by Columbia and others (including Wilson!) – and he continued to treat it as possible. It was not until the appearance of Spielberg's two films *Close Encounters of the Third Kind* and *E.T.* (as well as another film with the same title as Ray's) that he gave up hope. *E.T.* in particular, which began life as a Columbia project, has much in common with Ray's concept of the Alien: the benign nature of the creature, and the fact that it is 'small and acceptable to children and possessed of certain superhuman powers – not physical strength but other kinds of powers, particular types of vision, and that it takes an interest in earthly things,' says Ray today. 'The appearance of my Alien was much more interesting though. Mine didn't have any eyes. It had sockets so the human resemblance was already destroyed to some extent. And mine was almost weightless and the gait was different. Not a heavy-footed gait but more like a hopping gait. And it had a sense of humour, a sense of fun, a mischievous quality. I think mine was a whimsy.' Ray can understand the success of Spielberg's alien though he found *E.T.* 'a bit corny at times'. But he did not care for the extent to which the alien had been humanised. 'It ought to be more subtle than that,' he says. 'But the children are marvellous. Spielberg has talent in handling children; I'm not sure about otherwise.'

Someone else who had obviously spotted the similarities was Arthur C. Clarke, who has described them as 'striking parallels'. He telephoned Ray from Colombo in January 1983 and suggested that he write politely to Spielberg and point out the resemblances. 'Don't take it lying down' he said, according to Ray. But although Ray is firmly of the view that

E.T. 'would not have been possible without my script of *The Alien* being available throughout America in mimeographed copies', he is not interested in pursuing the matter further. He agrees with Clarke that 'artists have better things to do with their time'; and he knows that Spielberg's view, according to a letter Clarke wrote to the London *Times* in 1984, is that he was too young to have been influenced by *The Alien* screenplay. 'Tell Satyajit I was a kid in high school when his script was circulating in Hollywood', he told Clarke on a visit to Sri Lanka 'rather indignantly' – which does not really resolve the doubts.

Naturally, Ray regrets that his film never got made. His only consolation is that if it had been, the delicate effects in his screenplay might well have been crushed by the crassness of the kind of Hollywood production values that determined David Lean's film about India would not receive an Oscar. (The Academy gave one to the film's music instead, which was the worst part of the film!) If even a man as intelligent as Clarke could conclude his letter by describing Ray and Spielberg as 'two of the greatest geniuses the movies have ever produced', one can just imagine the fate of Ray's Bengali 'whimsy' in Hollywood hands. Perhaps it was really for the best that Ray's project vanished like the Alien's spaceship, before the Bajorias of Wardour Street and Beverly Hills could pump the water out and get a real grip on it.

28

Ray as Designer,
Illustrator and Writer

···❬◦❮❅❯◦❭···

EVEN if one had no knowledge of Ray's first incarnation as a commercial artist before he took to film-making, his film credit sequences would soon make one aware of his talent as a typographer, calligrapher and illustrator. They range from the archaic priestly script of *Pather Panchali*, through the exquisite 'postcards' of Darjeeling life printed in 'Tibetanised' Bengali in *Kanchenjungha* and the delightful drawings of kings, courtiers and peasants in *Goopy Gyne*, to the modern type-faces of the titles in *Days and Nights in the Forest* and *The Home and the World*, behind which can be seen the blurred motion of the forest and the flickering conflagration of Nikhil's funeral pyre. Nearly every one of Ray's films has titles that subtly and elegantly contribute to the mood of the film.

As we know, Ray's cover designs for books were famous in Calcutta in the 1940s and 50s. After he became a film-maker, his typographic energies were diverted from book jackets, but he has never entirely given up designing them. His covers for *Eksan*, a Bengali quarterly, are striking examples of his capacity to produce variations on a single idea – in this case the three Bengali letters of its title 'Now'. Ray has created its cover ever since it was founded in 1961 by Soumitra Chatterjee and Nirmalya Acharya, who now edits it alone and publishes in it Ray's film scripts in Bengali. Ray uses the cover to experiment with bold juxtapositions of colours and with lettering of all kinds, from calligraphy like that of *Pather Panchali* and scribbles reminiscent of Picasso to styles entirely of his own invention, and from shapes torn out of paper reminiscent of Matisse and Binode Bihari Mukherjee to clean lines made from the kind of sticky papers cut into geometrical shapes used by children. Some of the covers are also like certain traditional sari designs, and a few have carried drawings by Ray: of Dante in 1965 (for the seven-hundredth anniversary of his birth), of Marx in 1968, and of the writer Manik Banerjee – one of the series of author's portraits Satyajit drew for Signet Press in the 1940s which included Bibhutibhusan Banerjee.

At exactly the same time as the first issue of *Eksan* was published,

Ray and a poet friend of his, Subhash Mukherjee, brought out the first issue of the revived *Sandesh*, the magazine Upendrakisore Ray had founded in 1913 and which had collapsed in 1926/7. It appeared in May 1961 on Ray's fortieth birthday. In it were reprints of two of the best early stories and illustrations of Upendrakisore and Sukumar, a piece by Tagore, as well as new work by Ray's aunts Lila Majumdar and Sukhalata Rao, by then successful children's authors, and pieces by his uncle Subimal Ray (Chotokaka) and others. Satyajit himself contributed only a translation of Edward Lear's poem about the Jumblies (to be followed later by his translations of 'Jabberwocky' and the poems in *Alice's Adventures in Wonderland*). Soon, however, he felt the need to 'feed' the new monthly, and he began to write stories and to illustrate them and the stories by other contributors on a regular basis. The cost of production came out of his own pocket and he quickly came to realise that the 'lavish' standard he and his co-editor had enthusiastically set themselves was quite impractical to maintain. He had no notion then that within about fifteen years his writing would become so popular in Bengal it would provide his main financial support as a film-maker, rather than the other way around. At the beginning though, it seemed necessary to put the venture on a more business-like basis. His cousin Nalini Das (Nini), by then a well-known teacher and also a writer, took over the management of *Sandesh*, and Lila Majumdar joined the two of them as the third editor. Although she and Satyajit do not always see eye to eye on the choice of stories, the three of them make a good team, in the family tradition of the old magazine. It is clear from the way Ray's two co-editors talk about him that they regard Manik primarily as a writer and illustrator for children, rather than as a film-maker. Satyajit himself certainly loves *Sandesh*; his only real regret is that they cannot afford to make it look like the superb magazine he fondled as a child; a circulation of five thousand copies or so does not permit it. But, as his cousin affectionately points out, he has partly himself to blame; though she begs him to write letters to advertisers and others on behalf of *Sandesh*, he usually refuses. 'Manik's not the type to go to someone else,' she says firmly; 'someone else has to come to him.'

Sera Sandesh, the *Best of* Sandesh, a large hard-cover book issued by the publishers of Ray's Bengali books in 1986 to celebrate the twenty-fifth anniversary of the magazine, gives a fine sense of Satyajit's skills as an illustrator. His styles range almost as widely as his films; he can handle a brush or pen as exquisitely as some of the Far Eastern artists he copied at Santiniketan under Nandalal Bose, or as audaciously as the brashest comic-strip draughtsman. There are other gifted illustrators in *Sandesh* and elsewhere in Bengali magazines, but Ray's work is usually distinguished from them by its vitality, humour and freedom from cliché. This is particularly true of his caricatures and fantasy drawings, as one might expect, but some of his 'realistic' illustrations are fine too – those for the memoir of his childhood, *Jakhan Choto Chilam* (*When I Was Small*) first published in *Sandesh*, and for his aunt Punyalata's memoir *Chelebelar Dinguli (Those Childhood Days)*, being especially delightful.

Nothing he has produced achieves the heights of Upendrakisore's and Sukumar's best work, however, as Satyajit himself acknowledges; his own talent seems instead to be more widely spread, embracing both Upendrakisore's feeling for people and Sukumar's comic eye. 'My grandfather had a wonderful feeling for faces and types', he says. 'He could do a Brahmin so marvellously. He could do kings, crafty people and simple village folk, and ghosts, demons and goblins. He even illustrated one Chinese folk-tale; there he used a Chinese technique. Whereas my father had an incomparable talent for comic drawings, which grandfather probably wouldn't have been able to do so well. There's no one like him in India.'

As a writer, too, he feels that he must consciously avoid repeating what his grandfather and father did with such élan in their very different ways. Only in the last few years has he tried his hand at writing for really young children as his grandfather did. He has produced a number of distinctive modern fairy tales, including a magical story of a young boy whose skill as a *harbola* – a person who can perfectly imitate bird and animal sounds – enables him to slay a monster and marry a princess. 'For the first time I feel how my grandfather must have felt writing those stories [like *Goopy Gyne Bagha Byne*]. But this is the first time. It's happening now, but never before,' says Satyajit.

In general, he thinks of his own writings as 'essentially "entertainment" – in the Graham Greene sense' and he intends most of them for older children, without wishing to draw hard and fast distinctions about who will enjoy them. (His translations of eleven of them, which appeared in Britain, France and the US in 1987, were sold as a book for adults.) They are written 'for fun', he says, and because 'there is such a dearth of good writing here for young people'; but they outsell every other Bengali writer bar Tagore. He does not have (and never did have) any ambition to write a full-scale novel for adults. 'When I think in terms of adults,' he comments, 'I prefer to think in terms of a screenplay.' As we know, at no point in his life has he much cared for literary language per se; when he left Santiniketan in 1942 he had 'no literary bent at all', he remarks in his introduction to his *Stories*. Sadly, this means he may never write an account of his adult life – also because he feels it would be too big an undertaking, and he is unsure which language, English or Bengali, to use.

On first acquaintance Ray's stories seem slight. 'Plot is the thing here rather than character or the overtones one has come to expect from the contemporary short story', wrote a reviewer in the *Boston Globe* in 1987, even if, as the London *Times* put it, the reader is being offered 'sheer entertainment and pleasure'. But beneath the surface Ray's best stories have much more in common with his films than is obvious – in their rationality, open-mindedness and sense of wonder, in their restraint, gentleness and humour, in their sympathy for children and their receptiveness to western life and ideas, and in the total absence of stylistic gimmickry. There are horror and suspense stories that recall *Monihara*, comedies reminiscent of *The Philosopher's Stone*, a story about a lonely child who makes friends with ants that calls to mind *Pikoo*, tales about people haunted by the past like Biswambhar Roy in *The Music Room*, about the prickings of bad conscience shown in *The Middle Man*, as well as the fairy-tales like *Goopy and Bagha*, and of course the detective novellas featuring Feluda and Topse, now numbering over a dozen, which are Ray's most popular writings. The latter appear first in magazines, and then in book form, earning Ray substantial sums. He has of course filmed two of them in Bengali, and a third has been shot in Hindi by his son Sandip with the Bombay actor Shashi Kapoor in the role of Feluda.

What his stories undoubtedly lack, in comparison with his films, are strong women characters; so do the writings of his father and grandfather, as Satyajit observes. The central character tends to be a lone male, a possible reflection of Ray's own introversion throughout his life but perhaps especially in his later years, following the death of several of his close friends, among them David McCutchion and Bansi Chandragupta (in 1981). 'I've received so many letters complaining about the lack of girls and women in my stories that it's in my head that I must try to do something about it,' Satyajit says with a smile.

He has written a great many stories, on the other hand, with an aspect not found in many of his films: science and science fiction, both of which caught Satyajit's imagination at an early age, beginning with Conan Doyle, Jules Verne and H.G. Wells. In these stories Ray speculates freely about the origins of the human condition dramatised so sympathetically in his films, and his thoughts are as uninhibited by convention and his lack of higher scientific knowledge as were Tagore's. Back in the 1940s an artist working alongside Satyajit at Keymer's remembers him remarking one day 'What if there was no gravity and we all just floated out?' While a few years ago he told an Indian interviewer he had a feeling:

> that this universe, and its incessant music, may not be entirely accidental. Maybe there is a cosmic design somewhere which we don't know. Take for instance the apparent sizes of the moon and the sun. They're exactly the same. At the time of total eclipse, the moon covers the sun edge to edge. The whole business of propagation of the species – of sexual intercourse – has been possible because of the delight that goes with it. Who made coitus so intensely pleasurable? Is that a coincidence too? Watch the protective colourations of birds and insects. The grasshopper acquires the exact shade of green that helps it merge in its surroundings. The marine life and the shore birds put on the exact camouflage. Could it all be coincidence? I wonder. I don't

mystify it either. I think some day the human mind will explore all the mysteries of life and creation the way the mysteries of the atom have been explored.

Such perceptions seem to have coloured the thinking of Upendrakisore and Sukumar (and Tagore) before Satyajit, but with one significant difference: the two older Rays, had more of a scientific training, which was both theoretical and practical. One cannot easily imagine Satyajit writing the kind of lucid exposition of half-tone theory that they wrote; he is much more typical of the average artistically minded Bengali in his attitude to technology (as we know from *Abhijan*), with the result that most of his science fantasies have an air of contrivance. It is most obvious, perhaps, in Professor Shonku, next to Feluda his most important fictional character and a brilliant scientist-inventor of gentlemanly mien whose adventures have taken him all over the world since his first appearance in print in 1961. Ray describes him as a 'mild-mannered Professor Challenger', Conan Doyle's scientist. But John Gross in the *New York Times* felt that he was 'not only less assertive but also less amusing and less fully realized a character than his bulky Edwardian predecessor. Still, he infuses the stories with an agreeable flavor of an old-fashioned pseudo-scientific yarn.'

That seems about right. Where Ray's detective duo Feluda and Topse truly belongs to modern Calcutta and not to the Victorian age of Holmes and Watson, Shonku is a wilful anachronism. Charming and readable though some of his exploits are, his vision of scientific research bears about as much relation to contemporary reality as the magical weapons in the *Mahabharata* do to today's military space research.

The most successful Shonku adventures are probably those where the constraints of physical reality are entirely suspended, such as 'The Unicorn Expedition', or alternatively those where Shonku has no artificial aids to understanding like 'Tellus', where Shonku is called in to investigate the strange, childlike behaviour of an electronic brain. In 'The Unicorn Expedition' Shonku leads an expedition to Tibet to discover the truth behind the mysterious diary of an English explorer who died a year previously of wounds inflicted by a band of robbers; his last entry contains the claim that he has just seen a herd of unicorns. Shonku is intrigued and notes that:

> like the dragon of the east and west, the unicorn has been known as a product of human imagination. But I have some hesitation in using the word imagination. I have a book open before me on my desk which is about the ancient civilisation of Mohenjo-daro. Apart from pottery, toys, figurines and ornaments, diggings at Mohenjo-daro have revealed a large number of rectangular clay and ivory seals bearing the carvings of, amongst other things, animals such as elephants, tigers, bulls and rhinoceroses. In addition to these familiar animals, there are representations of a beast unknown to us. It is shown as a bull-like creature

with a single curved horn growing out of its forehead. Archaeologists have taken it to be a creature of fantasy, although I see no point in depicting an imaginary creature when all the others are real.

After many trials and strange experiences, Shonku and friends succeed in flying into a magical region in the far Himalayas with the help of gem-studded boots belonging to a dead lama that they discover in his lamasery. There they see not only unicorns but a phoenix, a gryphon and other legendary creatures brought to life by the 'sheer force' of enough people believing in them. Attempts to take them back to the familiar world of the plains are fruitless, however; they simply vanish.

There is not a single Shonku story that lacks an interesting idea to sustain attention, but the character of Shonku himself, unlike Feluda, seems always to hang in a kind of limbo. Ray's best stories overall are generally those rooted in Calcutta or at least centred on typical Bengali behaviour, often but not always containing a supernatural element, and which involve no technological gimmicks: equivalents, so to speak, of his two films *The Philosopher's Stone* and *Monihara* in their strongly contrasting ways.

In 'Ashamanja Babu's Dog', for instance, we are in the world of small clerks like Paresh Chandra Dutta, content with 'two Hindi films, a dozen packets of cigarettes a month, and fish twice a week'. But instead of finding the philosopher's stone, Ashamanja Babu buys himself a dog from a Bhutanese in the market, fondly believing that he will be able to make it obey commands in English; but he discovers instead that it has the capacity to laugh and thereby make him a fortune – or not, as he characteristically decides.

'Patol Babu, Film Star' belongs to a roughly similar milieu but involves nothing supernatural. Besides being one of Ray's own favourites, it is also one of his very few stories about film-making: not about his own kind of films, however, but about the kind he has always refused to make. Its central character could easily be one of his own gifted non-actors though; he has the same quiet pride of the old men from Boral who play the villagers in *Pather Panchali* and in *The Postmaster*.

Patol Babu is an ex-clerk, 'fiftyish, short, bald-headed', struggling to get by after losing his secure job with a British company fifteen years previously. One day a neighbour tells him he has recommended him to his youngest brother-in-law who is scouting for an actor for a film. He needs someone to play an 'absent-minded, short-tempered pedestrian'. As soon as the scout meets the diffident Patol Babu, who last acted in the dim past on the amateur stage, he offers him the part. 'I hope it calls for some dialogue', says Patol Babu. 'Certainly,' says the young man. 'It's a speaking part.'

The following morning, a Sunday, Patol Babu turns up promptly at the appointed place in the street where the shooting is to take place. There is the usual crowd and the usual wait for his turn to come. Patol Babu finally summons up courage and asks for his lines. An assistant scrawls something on a page from his notebook. When Patol Babu glances at it, he feels weak; how could they be so cruel as to make fun of him by asking him there just to say 'Oh'? But the assistant strongly disagrees: 'What are you saying, Grandpa? You think that's nothing? Why, this is a regular speaking part in a Baren Mullick film – do you realise what that means?' Another assistant now comes up, puts his hand on Patol Babu's shoulder and explains his role: to collide with a rising young executive played by the rising young star Chanchal Kumar, who is dashing from his car into his office without looking, and to cry out 'Oh!' at the moment of impact. 'Just think how crucial the shot is', adds the assistant encouragingly.

After much reflection, sweetened by the memory of the advice of his old teacher on the stage ('each word spoken in a play is like a fruit in a tree'), Patol Babu feels reconciled to his role. He begins to see its possibilities. Here is Ray's self-deprecating comment on his own fastidious attention to detail as a director, a sort of quizzical artistic testament:

> Oh, oh, oh, oh, oh – Patol Babu began giving the exclamation a different inflection each time he uttered it. After doing it a number of times he made an astonishing discovery. The same exclamation, when spoken in different ways, carried different shades of meaning. A man when hurt said 'Oh' in quite a different way. Despair brought forth one kind of 'Oh', while sorrow provoked yet another kind. In fact, there were so many kinds of Oh's – the short Oh, the long-drawn Oh, Oh shouted and Oh whispered, the high-pitched Oh and the Oh starting low and ending high, and the Oh starting high and ending low . . . Strange! Patol Babu suddenly felt that he could write a whole thesis on that one monosyllabic exclamation. Why had he felt so disheartened when this single word contained a gold-mine of meaning? The true actor could make a mark with this one single syllable.

By the time the director is ready to roll with him, Patol Babu is really excited. He even makes the suggestion that he be reading a newspaper for added verisimilitude, and the director agrees. Then the director has an idea. 'Just a minute, Kesto,' he calls to yet another assistant, 'I think if we give the pedestrian a moustache, it would be more interesting.' 'What kind, sir? Walrus, Ronald Colman or Butterfly? I have them all ready.' 'Butterfly, butterfly – and make it snappy!'

And so Patol Babu has his moment of fame. He times the collision so well that he almost knocks out both himself and the star, but he pulls himself together just in time and, 'mixing fifty parts of anguish with twenty-five of surprise and twenty-five of irritation', cries 'Oh!' He has performed his part to his own standard of excellence, he feels. 'All these years of struggle hadn't blunted his sensibility.'

When the assistant comes to find him ten minutes later at the *pan* shop where he had asked him to wait, Patol Babu is not there. He cannot simply accept money for his labours – ten, fifteen, twenty rupees. 'It is true that he needed it very badly,' Ray concludes, 'but what was twenty rupees when measured against the intense satisfaction of a small job done with perfection and dedication?'

Insensitivity to Nature, and hence to Man, is another common theme in Ray's stories, reminiscent of such films as *Kanchenjungha* and *Days and Nights in the Forest*. A recent untranslated example is the delightful 'Katum Kutum' – the nonsense name Abanindranath Tagore gave to the interesting shapes one finds outdoors, such as a piece of wood that looks like an animal. In Ray's story, a man called Dilip finds one of these, takes it home and gets disturbed by a kind of wailing sound it makes at night. He tells a friend, who agrees to stay the night with him and hear the sound for himself. The following morning, without saying why, the friend insists that Dilip take him to the place where he found the piece of wood. There they find another piece that looks almost the same, except that it lacks a tail. When they put it beside the first piece the wailing ceases. 'There are more things in heaven and earth, Dilip, than are dreamt of in your philosophy', says his friend. 'But what do we call them?' asks Dilip. 'Katum and Kutum', says his friend.

The theme becomes malevolent in one of Ray's best stories, the creepy 'Khagam', a full-blown example of the genre with 'a marvellous flavour of sinister understatement', as the American cartoonist Gahan Wilson wrote in a review. It shows that Ray's supernatural effects come off best when 'buttressed with prosaic detail' (in John Gross's words), and also when he conjures an atmosphere that he knows at first-hand, like the gloomy, isolated palace in *Monihara* (or *The Music Room*). In 'Khagam', it is a forest rest-house and the resting-place of a sadhu below a huge tamarind tree not far away. The reader gets the authentic sensation of being in the land where 'cows are still holy ... and God is still a phallus', as Ray described the West's impression of India with amused irony in *Sight and Sound* some years ago.

'This is the land of tall stories', says the sceptical Dhurjati Babu to the open-minded narrator:

You'll hear of strange happenings all the time, but never see one yourself. Look at our *Ramayana* and *Mahabharata*. It is said they're history, but actually they're no more than a bundle of nonsense. The ten-headed Ravana, the Monkey-God Hanumana with a flame at the end of his tail setting fire to a whole city, Bhima's appetite, Ghatotkacha, Hidimba, the flying chariot Pushpaka, Kumbhakarna – can you imagine anything more absurd than these? And the epics are full of fake holy men. That's where it all started. Yet everyone – even the educated – swallows them whole.

Of course, it is Dhurjati Babu who gets swallowed in the end by

the very forces he has scoffed at, deliberately taunted and eventually
unleashed upon himself. A latter-day curse of Khagam, a sage mentioned
in the *Mahabharata*, falls on him. By killing the sadhu's pet king cobra
Balkishen (an epithet of the dark-coloured god-child Krishna) to demonstrate his contempt for all holy men, Dhurjati Babu becomes fated to
fulfil the sadhu's prophecy: 'One Balkishen is gone; another will come to
take his place. Balkishen is deathless . . . ' He will be transformed into a
snake himself, as Khagam did to his friend.

The process of metamorphosis, as reported by the narrator, is dramatised
by Ray with the sure instinct of the story-teller, detail by chilling detail. Very
early on we guess what will happen to Dhurjati Babu. The two companions
eat together at the rest-house in the forest by the light of a hurricane-lamp
and then get ready for bed in neighbouring rooms. But Dhurjati Babu does
not seem to be sleepy. Not only does he make whimsical hissing noises
and recite rhymes about snakes to the narrator, but something is biting
him and making 'greyish, diamond-shaped blotches' on his skin, and he is
having trouble pronouncing the letter 's'. When the narrator looks at his
tongue, a thin red line has appeared down the middle of it. Eventually, he
tries to force him to go to bed and then the penny really drops: the man's
skin is as cold as ice! Dhurjati Babu observes the narrator's shock with a
slight smile and stares at him for a whole minute without blinking. Then
his knees buckle and he drags himself into the darkness under the bed.

The appalled narrator retreats into his own room, bolts the door and
climbs into bed, heart thumping. Soon after there comes a knock at the
foot of the door – once, twice, thrice . . . 'I didn't stir out of bed. I was not
going to open the door. Not again.' Then Dhurjati Babu's verandah door
can be heard opening, and shortly after that, a pair of beady eyes can be
seen behind the room's mosquito netting over the window staring fixedly
at the narrator in the dim light of the room's lantern, before vanishing
into the night.

The following morning Dhurjati Babu's room is empty and, after
spending the day fruitlessly searching for traces of him, the narrator
feels compelled to return to the sadhu to ask for information about his
companion. A gentle smile spreads over the Baba's face, on hearing the
question. 'Your friend has fulfilled my hope', he replies. 'He has brought
back my Balkishen to me.' And, sure enough, near the hole where the
dead cobra lived, the narrator spots the freshly sloughed-off skin of another
snake – or is it?

It was actually the sloughed-off skin of a man. A man who had ceased
to be a man. He was now lying coiled inside that hole. He is a king
cobra with poison fangs.

There, I can hear him hissing. The sun has just gone down.
I can hear the Baba calling – 'Balkishen – Balkishen – Balkishen'.

The whole tale is thoroughly cinematic in its style of telling, and Ray seriously considered it as a film for television to be made by his son. The logistical difficulties of working with and killing a king cobra put him off, as did the existence of a (bad) US film on the same theme, and especially the fact that the story was potentially so horrific for children (just like most traditional Bengali folk-tales, it is true, but then no one films them); he had even felt doubtful about publishing it in *Sandesh* in the first place.

Although he never pursued 'Khagam' as a film, he did write several horror screenplays as part of a series of thirteen half-hours for Indian television directed by Sandip in Hindi in 1985–6. The others in the series were also scripted (and scored) by Satyajit and covered a wide range of moods and milieux; a majority were based on his own stories, several were original screenplays, one was adapted from a story by Sunil Ganguli, and another from Chekhov's story 'A Work of Art'. One of the best, the story of a successful young magician shadowed by an ailing old magician who had once refused to teach him his tricks, draws directly on Ray's childhood passion for magic, which has found only occasional expression in his films for adults. 'The whole idea of the series was contrast,' says Satyajit, articulating his familiar guiding principle. He had Roald Dahl's *Tales of the Unexpected* in mind: 'I was conscious that I was trying to make entertaining films, films which would entertain an all-India market but be at the same time intelligent and sophisticated. Nobody was making that sort of film in India.'

The audience responded as Ray had hoped it would, on the whole. The series, transmitted in 1986 under the title *Satyajit Ray Presents*, was widely felt to be the most imaginative indigenous television of 1986, despite occasional awkwardness in the direction, some triteness of plotting and characterisation and one or two episodes which were definitely medio-cre. In technical terms Ray sees 'hardly any difference' between films for television and for theatrical release, with the exception that on television one needs more close-ups of characters 'to establish their looks', and that it has greater possibilities of carrying off intimate long scenes with words. 'But I don't see any difference between *Jewel in the Crown* as a feature film and as a television film,' he says. The difference lies not with the medium itself so much as with the market, and the implications that has for his choice of language in the future. If he sticks to the language he knows and loves, the available budget is too low to be useful, but if he branches out into Hindi, as he did with *Deliverance*, he tends to lose the very quality and exactness of control he has cherished ever since the beginning of his career. The only solution for screening serious work on television seems to be to make the film in Bengali and then subtitle it in Hindi. 'That hasn't been done yet,' Ray said in 1988, 'but perhaps one could explore that.'

29

'Some Aspects of His Craft':
Ray as Film-maker

··➤❦【❦◦❀◦❦】◄··

'TECHNIQUE. A means to an end. The technique of warfare, of poetry, of automation. The technique of making love, of making soufflés ... of making films', wrote Ray in 1960 at the beginning of an article entitled 'This word "technique"'. 'The best technique is the one that's not noticeable,' he maintains today, just as he did in making his early films in the 1950s. 'For me to point out why certain things are being done means that they haven't worked for that person.'

To achieve his simplicity and immediacy on screen has required of Ray a high degree of discipline. The unobtrusiveness of his technique stands in direct proportion to the power of Ray's concentration on it: 'everything in a film is difficult,' he says with inimitable candour. But it also invites dismissal by those who feel that a film should draw attention to its style. There is a widespread impression, even among some of Ray's admirers, that his technique is somehow 'old-fashioned', in keeping with his moral outlook. They are misled by Ray's constant urge to experiment and his lack of external trademarks. His technique derives from the subject-matter in hand, and so his films are linked together not by their surface but by their essence: the attitude shown to the people in them by their maker.

Ray's principle here is that all departments of film-making must serve the needs of the source material and not vice versa. A film must have organic cohesion growing naturally from its original inspiration. If that inspiration is disjointed then so should be its artistic interpretation, as it is in *The Adversary* or in Godard. 'As *Breathless* and subsequent films proved,' Ray commented in 1971, 'Godard was perfectly justified in applying rough and ready methods to films which dealt basically with unconventional people in an unconventional era. In other words, the Godard form grew out of the Godard content, and the Godard content has always embraced some aspect of contemporary European youth – journalist, soldier, prostitute, working girl, intellectual – caught in the whirl of modern living. The syntax is new, the pace and rhythm are new, the conception of narrative is new.'

Ray's revolution has been a quiet, bloodless one compared with

Godard's, as befits his temperament and feeling for tradition and continuity in life, but the attitude he brings to the selection of material is equally uncompromising and his search for new ways of expression an endless one. He is ruthless with himself, and so it is not surprising that he can be ruthless with his co-workers too at times, despite his normal courtesy and subtlety. 'He can treat incompetence with total contempt,' says Sarmila Tagore, 'and that can be very shattering you know' – and Soumitra Chatterjee says the same. The two most talented members of his production team eventually rebelled against his single-minded vision of film-making – permanently in the case of Subrata Mitra (after *Nayak*) and temporarily in the case of Bansi Chandragupta, who remained a very close friend to the end of his life.

Ray's writings about the practice of film-making – many of which appear in *Our Films Their Films* and *Bisoy Chalachchitra (On Cinema)* – are a faithful reflection of his clarity of mind. Reading them never fails to rejuvenate one's awareness that film is an art. Together they form one of the most articulate bodies of analysis of the subject ever written, Ray's own conviction of the inadequacy of *any* printed description of film-making notwithstanding. 'So complex, so intricate and elusive is the triangular relationship between the maker, the machines and the human material that is deployed, that to describe even a single day's work in all its details of conception, collaboration and execution would call for abilities beyond most film-makers. Even with such gifts, a lot of what goes on in the dark recesses of the film-maker's mind would go unsaid, for the simple reason that it cannot be put into words', Ray comments in the introduction to *Our Films Their Films*. 'The flow of ideas is something which one can never account for nor recapture.'

Nevertheless, in 'Some aspects of my craft', written in 1966, he summarised his approaches to the various elements in the making of a film, which I shall now use as a basis for my own analysis of his technique.

Story and Script
Only five of Ray's screenplays – *Kanchenjungha, Nayak, The Golden Fortress, The Elephant God* and *Pikoo* – have been entirely original, and of these the last three were based on existing stories by himself. 'I don't have enough experience of life,' he says, to tackle all the situations that interest him without borrowing from other people's work. 'My experience is all middle class and that's rather a limited field . . . I can deal with something I do not know at first-hand only with the help of someone who does.'

Bibhutibhusan Banerjee was the first of his sources of course. His *Pather Panchali* and *Aparajita* were on the scale of a saga, which Ray's Apu Trilogy reflects. Since then he has moved steadily away from such lengthy time-spans, towards long short stories concentrated in time and space, in which the emphasis is on change in character. In *The Middle*

Man, for instance, says Ray, 'a totally innocent, honest boy has to move to a point of total corruption – then and only then can he stand on his own feet.' Psychology itself is what really interests him. 'In *Pather Panchali* it wasn't there so much, but from *Aparajito* it came in and developed in *Devi* and after, and now it is of capital importance to me . . . The movement from a certain state of character to another state of character – this total inner change fascinates me most. If you don't have this, with all your action, you don't make a film.'

Obviously, Ray looks for such dynamics when picking a story for adaptation and then develops them in writing his screenplay. After the first few films he treated the originals without inhibition, as Sunil Ganguli discovered when Ray adapted his novel *Aranyer Din Ratri*, but no writer has ever been displeased with what Ray did to his work. The critics in Bengal too keep quiet and reserve their 'main invectives', as Ray put it in 1966, for his adaptations of the safely deceased Tagore. In Ray's view they are like those who attacked Verdi for altering Shakespeare; criticism of an adaptation is legitimate, he feels, only if it is not a work of art in itself, like Lean's *A Passage to India* (as opposed to his *Great Expectations*). In this respect Ray feels like Renoir – who started his career with a determination not to adapt literature for the screen – but wrote in his autobiography when he was eighty that

> We don't admire a painting for its fidelity to the model: all we want is for the model to stimulate the painter's imagination. This summary statement is inadequate [though], because things become complicated if the painter is carried away by a sense of his own importance, in which case the final result is likely to be nothing but a monument to his own vanity. A real artist believes that his function is to follow the model. He is convinced, while he is working, that he is recreating the model, whether it be an object, a human being or a thought.

A strong, developed screenplay before shooting is something Ray regards as a necessity: only *Pather Panchali* did not have it. The reason is partly that it makes his film-making more economic, but chiefly that it suits Ray's outlook and belief in order, his so-called classicism. 'If classical implies an orderly unfolding of events with a beginning, a middle and an end – *in that order*; a firm rein applied to emotion; and an avoidance of disorientation for its own sake, then I will be only too happy with the label', he commented in 1982.

It is not that he distrusts improvisation – far from it – simply that he believes the most fruitful improvisation results from the most thorough preparation, whether it be in the director's head or on paper. 'I do not think spontaneity is incompatible with careful planning and careful film-making,' he has said, 'but I do feel that it is incompatible with lack of imagination and inspiration. A film that gives the impression of spontaneity is in nine cases out of ten the result of a high degree of discipline applied to an imaginative process that is sustained to the last stages of making the film.'

So much thought has gone into a screenplay before Ray starts writing it out in his shooting notebook that he can start doing so at any point – in the middle of the story even. Very likely he will take a key scene and try to write its dialogue, that being the most important element – he does not waste much effort on description. 'Writing a screenplay is not a literary business at all,' he points out.

His ear for dialogue and his ability to write it for film is, as I have said, among the finest in the cinema. Perhaps his exposure to Bengali films in the 1940s and 50s helped to sensitise him and draw out his latent talent. That was an era of 'smart dialogue'. 'One often heard it said that "so-and-so is unsurpassed as a writer of smart dialogue"', Ray observed in the lecture he gave in 1982.

> The implication seemed to be that dialogue was something to be admired for its own sake and not, as it should be, as a concomitant of the characters who speak it . . . The best film dialogue is where one doesn't feel the presence of the writer at all. I am talking here of the kind of film that tries to capture the feel of reality. There are also films which attempt a larger than life style, or an oblique, fractured or expressionist style: I myself wrote dialogue with end rhymes in *Hirak Rajar Dese*, which was a fantasy. But the overwhelming majority of narrative films belong in the tradition of realism, where the dialogue sustains the feeling of lifelikeness that is conveyed through the camera.

The intensity of this 'feeling of lifelikeness' conveyed by Ray's films, at least to a Bengali, is one of his hallmarks. The incompleteness and incoherence of real speech is there, and yet the dialogue is not naturalistic. 'Let's call it "realistic"', he once suggested. 'It's not as if it's off a tape-recorder, because then you would be wasting precious footage. You have to strike a mean between naturalism and a certain thing which is artistic, which is selective. If you get the right balance, then you have this strange feeling of being lifelike. But if you were to photograph candidly a domestic scene it wouldn't be art at all . . . I think the cinema is the only medium that challenges you to be naturalistic, be realistic and yet be artistic at the same time. Because in the cutting is the creation you see.'

Besides the characters who are speaking the dialogue Ray also generally has the actors in mind when he is writing a screenplay. Most parts in his films – Paresh Chandra Dutta in *The Philosopher's Stone*, Indranath in *Kanchenjungha*, Arindam in *Nayak*, Charu in *Charulata*, Outram in *The Chess Players*, for instance – were written for known individuals. 'I write the dialogue with an actor's particular style of delivery in mind and also one thinks of the character itself,' says Ray. 'It's a combination of the two. There is always an alternative way of saying something. You choose the one which you think would suit the actor best.' With the exception of the

Urdu in *The Chess Players* and the Hindi in *Deliverance*, Ray's actors very seldom want to change his dialogue. 'A Satyajit Ray script is so clear and natural that no discussion is necessary,' says Madhabi Mukherjee firmly.

Casting and Handling of Actors

Ray has no taboos about the actors he selects. He has worked with every type of person, from box-office stars like Waheeda Rehman and Uttam Kumar, to people who had never seen a film, like the old relative of Sarbajaya in *Aparajito*, whom Ray spotted on the ghats at Benares. He may occasionally yearn after working with a repertory company like Ingmar Bergman's, but he knows that it is neither economically feasible for professional actors in Bengal (who must accept all kinds of work to earn a living) nor artistically desirable, given the tremendous range of subject-matter that he likes to cover. The best solution has always been to pick someone new to him if the story dictates it and mould his performance by whatever means brings the right result. 'Since it is the ultimate effect on the screen that matters, any method that helps to achieve the desired effect is valid', is Ray's credo. His definition of a star in an article written in 1971 is equally all-embracing and free of Hollywood hang-ups: 'a person on the screen who continues to be expressive and interesting even after he or she has stopped doing anything. This definition does not exclude the rare and lucky breed that gets five or ten lakhs [hundred thousands] of rupees per film; and it includes anyone who keeps his calm before the camera, projects a personality and evokes empathy.'

His methods of identifying such unknowns are as varied as Calcutta society is. Occasionally he selects someone from among the many people who come to his flat in the hope of getting a part, but usually – and especially in the earlier period of his career – he and his assistants and friends have to go out and get people, visiting all sorts of places on the off-chance of seeing the kind of face that Ray, with his skill as an illustrator, had pictured in his mind. He is like his own creation Patol Babu (see pp. 301–3) in the importance he attaches to the insignificant parts in his films – such as the occupants of Somnath's order-supply office in *The Middle Man*. Sometimes he has advertised in the newspapers – for the parts of Apu and Indir Thakrun, for instance – but seldom with any success: 'my own experience is that people with talent suffer from an inhibiting fear of rejection and never answer ads', he once wrote. In the end, 'you are left to scour the streets and scan the faces of pedestrians. Or go to race-meets and cocktails and wedding receptions, all of which you hate from the bottom of your heart.' A candidate once discovered, Ray will normally spend an hour or two talking to him at his house, if the part warrants it, without getting him to perform. He has preferred to avoid the expense of a screen test.

Rehearsals too Ray generally keeps to a minimum, though he has no objection to discussing a part in full if that is what the actor wants. He waits until the set or location is ready for shooting before rehearsing, with the exception of certain technically demanding shots (like the one of Apu and Pulu walking at night along the railway tracks in *The World of Apu*). Prolonged rehearsal he feels is more likely to produce stiffness than perfection on the screen. Instead, he creates an atmosphere on the set of alertness and concentration that is both economical of time and money and a reflection of himself. It is really the devotion he elicits – more than any specific technique of directing he may have developed – that produces the on-screen miracles in his work. As Saeed Jaffrey has remarked: 'With Manikda there's an antenna-tuning, and then total trust.' Or, as Swatilekha Chatterjee put it after the shooting of *The Home and the World*: 'I felt like a bud. He made me blossom like a flower.' Anil Chatterjee, the postmaster in *Three Daughters*, is more explicit:

> There is a great deal of affection ... he employs a peculiar psychological approach which inspires tremendous confidence. His attitude to an actor's performance is never negative. The atmosphere is personal and friendly. It is a lack of this kind of feeling elsewhere that makes an actor often say 'I am at my best with Ray.' He never demonstrates or acts out a scene. He merely describes the setting. This, too, is most unusual in the many directors I have worked for. Ray's attitude draws out the improvisation, technique and *depth* that an actor is capable of giving to his performance.

Utpal Dutta, who is himself a considerable Shakespearian actor, gives a good impression of how Ray manages this without an actor being fully aware of it:

> He will be sitting behind the camera and looking at us through it, apparently unconcerned with what the actors are doing, arranging the lighting, shifting a property from here to there. Suddenly he will stoop to an actor's ear and say 'That line you're saying – how about saying it like this?' and then again back to the lighting – 'I want a little more here' – and then back behind the camera. He will sit behind it for hours and hours, looking through the lens. And then you'll change a sentence and look at him for approval or disapproval, but he will do nothing, not even look at you, but let you develop on your own, make it your own: he doesn't want to *force* you to do anything.

In *The Kingdom of Diamonds*, for instance, Dutta remembers Ray giving him some advice while he was pacing up and down in a royal rage haranguing his courtiers and tearing off their precious necklaces. 'Ray suddenly came and suggested – "When you say that, why don't you kick in the air?" The first rehearsal I didn't do it, didn't pay any attention to it, and he didn't say anything; but then I remembered. The second rehearsal I tried a kick and I think the shot became really funny and really convincing because the King was kicking at shadows.' 'When he directs, the actor should listen intently, for every nuance, for every little

aside; he sometimes even talks to himself – but within your hearing,' says
Dutta with a chuckle, 'so that you're helped by his soliloquies.'

According to Rabi Ghosh, 'Manikda never strains the actors'; and
everyone who has acted for Ray agrees with this. He is radically different
from his emotional contemporary Ritwik Ghatak, who often hugged all
the performers after a successful take. Madhabi Mukherjee describes the
contrast with amusement:

> Satyajit Babu would read a scene out and give his instructions verbally
> – that I must walk from one point to another. While I was doing this he
> would ask me to stop in the middle, take two steps and then start again.
> But Ritwik! – he would say 'Follow me as I walk. Take two steps just
> like me – not three!' Satyajit Babu, if he was not satisfied with my take,
> would usually say: 'Fine, but let's have another one.' He never attacks
> your self-confidence; he always respects it. But Ritwikda would start by
> saying 'Look here. These are the words you have to speak. Will you be
> able to do it? – I rather doubt it.' Two things can then happen: either
> your confidence is totally shattered, or you lose your temper.

Which is not to say that Ghatak's approach never worked, but it
was certainly unpredictable in its results.

Occasionally Ray can be tough with an actor too, as Soumitra
Chatterjee found out in *The Goddess*. By that time he and Ray had
come to an agreement that he would not memorise his lines before
shooting because Soumitra felt this would diminish his spontaneity.
Suddenly, when they were shooting a scene by the river, Ray asked him
if he had his dialogues with him. Chatterjee said he didn't; they were in
the camp, half a mile away over sand. 'I think you should now have your
dialogues memorised,' said Ray. 'Go and get them.' And Chatterjee did,
'shattered' by such unexpected autocracy.

Design

'To the extent that a director knows what he wants, he can impose his
ideas on the designer. The designer is independent only up to the point
the director allows him', wrote Ray in 1966. He had by then been working
with Bansi Chandragupta for about fifteen years, forming a friendship that
lasted until the designer's untimely death in 1981, surviving his move to
Bombay around 1970 (which meant that he designed only one of Ray's
films after *The Adversary* – *The Chess Players*).

Chandragupta accepted his subservient role wholeheartedly in the
films he designed with Ray, even though he had directed documentary
films in his own right and could expect much greater control over design
elsewhere. He believed that 'a set exists only in relation to the script . . . It
is not a replica of what already exists, otherwise there would be no need for
designers. A film set is built for the camera and for the camera-angles only.
Anything that is not effective through the lens is a waste of good money

and effort, however pleasing it might look to the naked eye ... Ray has a keen camera eye and each carefully picked detail helps to build the atmosphere.'

Theirs was a collaboration of perfectionists – as is obvious from the high quality of Chandragupta's work for other directors, in such films as Mrinal Sen's *Baisey Sravan*, Avtar Kaul's *27 Down*, Rabindra Dharmaraj's *Chakra*, and Aparna Sen's *36 Chowringhee Lane* – and they sometimes disagreed over the importance of a particular detail. But Chandragupta was convinced, at bottom, that film is a director's medium and he had too much respect and admiration for Ray, both as a technician and as an artist, to press his point of view. 'Satyajit is in full control of all technical departments and every technician gives his best because in him he recognises a fellow-technician with a superior sensibility', said Chandragupta in 1965, adding that as an artist Ray 'strikes a carefully judged balance between the form and the content. He does not let one part override the other. I have seen him rejecting locations only because he thought they were too spectacular and overpowering. Action photographed there would have upset the balance. Though there are hardly any bravado effects in his films, they are always rich cinematically speaking.'

Camerawork and Lighting

Some of their richness derives from the camerawork and much of their authenticity from the lighting, originally developed by Subrata Mitra, which Ray described in 1966 as 'truthful, unobtrusive and modern'. Mitra was responsible for operating the camera too, until *Charulata* when Ray himself decided to take over. Soon after that Ray and Mitra parted company altogether and Mitra's assistant Soumendu Roy took over the lighting. The last film Mitra photographed for Ray was *Nayak*, before starting to work for other directors (who all know him as the most talented – and demanding – cameraman in India). The trend of Ray's thinking was evident as early as 1957. He wrote excitedly to Chandragupta from the Venice Festival that he had just seen five films by Mizoguchi photographed by five different cameramen, 'but the same style prevails and it is the most masterly I have come across.' About ten years later, in 'Some aspects of my craft', he made a similar observation about Orson Welles and the two different cameramen he used on *Citizen Kane* and *The Magnificent Ambersons*, and went on: 'There is no such thing as good photography *per se*. It is either right for a certain kind of film, and therefore good, or wrong – however lush, well-composed, meticulous – and therefore bad.' We are back with his conviction that every aspect of a film's production exists to serve the needs of the material – which was the original impetus behind the pioneering system of shadowless 'bounce' lighting Mitra used in *Aparajito* to convey the inside of a typical Benares house: the methods of studio lighting then accepted all over the world, would have given Harihar's home a stagey, unlifelike look.

The same applies to camerawork, which Ray describes as 'mainly instinct'. The way the camera moves – or does not move – must 'arise out of the needs of the situation', rather than out of fixed notions of what will look stylish on the screen. That is why the opening of *Charulata* is so satisfying: the mobility of the camera and the use of zooms and close-ups matches the playful, restless, bored behaviour of Charu – and why the relative stillness of the early part of *The Goddess* is equally appropriate, allowing us to absorb the lethargic brooding atmosphere of the zamindar's mansion. In neither case does Ray wish to call attention to the camerawork, but each style acts on the mind as part of an integrated composition of light, movement, sound, speech and music. 'We don't actually see with our eyes – we see with our brains,' an eminent eye-surgeon told Subrata Mitra, whose sight – like Binode Bihari Mukherjee's – was defective. Ray, in his best camerawork and lighting, seems to have taken that remark to heart, so that the viewer feels himself to be in direct touch with Ray's characters and settings through the lens of his sensibility.

Editing

'Editing is the stage when a film really begins to come to life', wrote Ray in 1966, 'and one is never more aware of the uniqueness of the film medium than in watching a well-cut scene pulsate with a life of its own.' He is quite ruthless with his own footage – and with that of others, as James Ivory recalls from watching Ray recut his first film *The Householder*. 'Dulal Dutta, Ray's regular editor, did the actual work, while Ray stood behind the Moviola crying out "Cut!" at the points where material was to go. This took some getting used to – not so much losing sequences, but the explosive force of the command that blew them away.' Even those who do not much admire Ray's films tend to admit his consummate ability as an editor; he shows an economy and poetry matched by only a very few – Akira Kurosawa for one. 'His work can be described as flowing composedly, like a big river', Kurosawa says of Ray today – the same quality that Ray finds in much of Kurosawa. Both directors want to preserve a lifelike sensation in their films, beginning with the screenplay and culminating with the editing. 'I hate conventional time-lapses', said Ray in 1958, before the Apu Trilogy was completed. 'They draw attention to themselves. I like strong modulations from one thing to another. You see, I am always hopefully concerned to get the feeling of the movement of life itself. There are no neat transitions in life. Things make the transition for me. A travelling train, for example. Again, there is no moment of evident transition, say, from childhood to boyhood, or on to youth.'

Over and over again in his films since then he has managed such transitions with surgical skill. Mostly, however, they do not come about at the editing stage but are already present in the screenplay or in the shooting – 'cut in the camera'. This is because Ray is so clear about his intentions before he begins shooting – which has the added advantage of making his shooting ratio astonishingly low. Where there is real scope for alternatives (and where Ray's editor Dulal Dutta comes into his own) is in scenes of dialogue.'These offer endless variations of emphasis, unlimited scope for pointing up shades of feeling. It is not unusual for an important dialogue scene to be cut in half a dozen different ways before a final satisfactory form is achieved', wrote Ray in 1966. It is superfluous to try to describe examples of such scenes in Ray's films. One has only to think of the hesitant conversation between Ratan and the Postmaster about his family in Calcutta, the alliterative tête-à-tête between Charu and Amal, the planter's drunken monologue to Amitava in the presence of his wife in *Kapurush*, the picnic and memory game in *Days and Nights in the Forest*, or Mr Mitter's humiliation of Somnath over a plate of omelette in *The Middle Man*. No wonder Ray's serious interest in cinema began with the taking of scribbled notes in the dark on the cutting of US movies, back in the mid-1940s.

Music Composition

Ray took over composition of his background music from *Three Daughters* onwards, after working with Ravi Shankar on the Apu Trilogy and *The Philosopher's Stone*, Vilayat Khan on *The Music Room*, Ali Akbar Khan on *The Goddess* and Jyotirindra Moitra on *Rabindranath Tagore*. Since then he has evolved his own style and method of composition to suit his peculiar situation and talents. As early on as possible in the production process he records the entire dialogue track with the silences too and uses it at home to begin making notes of the lengths and orchestral colouring of the music-track that will be needed. The actual business of composition and scoring for the musicians takes place last, normally under great pressure of deadlines. That is when he likes to shut himself away for several days with a piano and (after the early 1970s) a synthesiser. He painstakingly writes out scores in both Indian and western notation, depending on the preferences of the musicians involved. He is able to work like this only because he has the entire film in his head, of course; he does not need to see the scenes he is scoring on the screen, as a composer normally would.

There are two main reasons why he prefers to be his own composer. First, he gets clear ideas of what the film needs by way of music while working on the screenplay and the shooting. Secondly, the great instrumentalists he earlier worked with were simply not film-minded; their first loyalty was to their music and its traditions, not to the film.

The conflict exists in Ray's mind too, as to whether background music is really needed at all. 'If I were the only audience, I wouldn't be using music!' he says. 'I have always felt that music is really an extraneous element, that one should be able to do without it, express oneself without it', he said in 1980.

Why do we use it? Because we are not confident? Because we

underestimate the audience? Because we feel that a certain mood must be underlined in case the audience misses it? Sometimes you feel you can do away with music because you feel the average audience has become far more perceptive in the last 20–30 years; and then you see what is going on around you, the kind of films people are accepting and rejecting and you think that the audiences are right where they were in the '50s.

This is a surprisingly austere attitude, considering the high quality of most of Ray's music, in *Charulata* especially. Perhaps it shows that there is in him some of the 'caste mentality' of the great instrumentalists he knows, who believe in preserving the purity of classical music; Satyajit too may instinctively feel that film and music should not sully each other by attempting contact in background scores. If so this is ironic, because his chief principle as a film composer is that film music 'does not have to maintain caste', as he put it in an article on the subject written in 1964 after the release of *Charulata*. By that he does not mean it should descend to the level of most of what is scored for films in Calcutta, Bombay and Madras but that it should not try to shut out western melodies, structures and instruments. Without them Ray would have been stymied, except in those few films he has made where the influence of the West is minimal: *The Music Room, The Goddess* and *Deliverance*.

From early on he was inspired to experiment with mixing western and Indian elements by a somewhat unlikely source: the *jatra* companies which used to tour the villages of Bengal enacting episodes from the Indian epics, other classic plays and folk-tales in a highly theatrical language with heavily stylised gestures and costumes (as watched by a wide-eyed Apu in *Pather Panchali*). Although today's performances have been vitiated by the influence of the commercial cinema, in the 1950s, when Ray attended them, they were risking quite daring musical experiments on both foreign and indigenous instruments. Their composers had long realised that indigenous instruments alone were incapable of creating the kind of full-blooded dramatic music needed to accompany the powerful voices of the performers. (The twanging of the *sarod*, for instance, clashes unpleasantly with consonants, as Ray learnt for himself in making *The Goddess*.) So they had imported violins, clarinets, cornets, piccolos and other instruments from the West. Since these instruments lacked the *srutis* (microtones) and *mirhs* (slides) of Indian instruments, their influence on *jatra* music was radical and the result – at least to Ray's mind – often deserved to be called art.

What he admired about it was its capacity to absorb musical traditions from elsewhere and blend them with what it had inherited. He is generally opposed to straight borrowing for background scores, whether it be Mozart in *Elvira Madigan*, Tagore songs or extended passages of ragas, partly because the effect is almost always to cheapen the music – as in *Amadeus* – but more significantly because the music distracts the audience from the film. He favours, on the other hand, employing elements from well-known ragas and raginis. Some of these – particularly dawn and evening ragas and ragas associated with spring and the rainy season – are 'matchless', he says, at conjuring moods natural and human, for those familiar with the original ragas.

He also favours the shifting from raga to raga not normally allowed in a concert performance, except in what is known as a *ragmala*, 'a garland of ragas': there, for the connoisseur, it creates a powerful sense of drama which can be exploited by the film composer – as Ray did in *The Music Room* and in *The Goddess*. Without such shifts it is not in fact possible to introduce the necessary tension into a background score of Indian classical music. And if the story calls for the dramatic effect of a wrong note, that too is quite acceptable in Ray's view, even though it would be taboo in a concert performance.

His overall aim is to compose background music that belongs to the particular film rather than to any recognisable tradition. As he put it in relation to *The Home and the World*, 'one should not feel like thinking about whether certain of the themes are Indian or western – they're just purely music, which had to be a mixture of the East and the West for that film.' That is why he was very impressed by the music composed by George Fenton for *The Jewel in the Crown*, in which Fenton used a cor anglais, for instance, to express the first stirrings of love between Daphne Manners and Hari Kumar. 'Particularly when it is played higher up,' says Fenton,

> it has a quality that is not quite as familiar, as labelled as an oboe. Oboes are so pastoral and have so many associations. The cor anglais is playing a raga. Although the strings move, basically they are droning. The cor anglais is played by someone who has studied Indian music. I wrote it with a very odd time-signature in western terms, so that it sounds as if it's playing rather freely. It's not *alap* [the introductory phase of a raga] but it has an exploratory sense about it, searching for the melody. I hoped that the specific sound, and certain specific phrases in it, would transmit itself as a melody and become a tune for the audience, without them realising it is a raga.

Ray's goal in the music of *The Home and the World* was comparable: to adapt certain western elements along with certain Indian and specifically Tagorean ones and make music to interest and satisfy viewers with both backgrounds while expressing the inextricable mixture of influences at work in the characters. His contemporary films pose this challenge still more acutely. Ray's solution has been to adopt a kedgeree of instruments and styles, in keeping with Calcutta itself – 'this monstrous, teeming, bewildering city', in which even Ray's practised eye cannot always discern a person's background from his dress, accent or district. Ragas alone cannot work. 'The average educated middle-class Bengali may not be a sahib,' says

Ray, 'but his consciousness is cosmopolitan, influenced by western modes and trends. To reflect that musically you have to blend – to do all kinds of experiments. Mix the sitar with the alto and the trumpet and so on . . . It's a tricky matter, but the challenge cannot be shirked.'

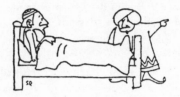

30

The Inner Eye
of Satyajit Ray

'SATYAJIT Ray*er chabi dekhechen?*' – 'Have you seen the latest Ray film?' – the editor of a satirical Calcutta magazine used to ask. '*Mane, apni bolte chan.* Satyajit*er chabi apnake dekheche?* – 'What you really mean is, has Satyajit's film seen you?'

Ray, along with a handful of other film directors, living and dead, conveys through his films a sense of a whole personality, in the same way that great writers, painters, composers and musicians do. Those who like it tend to like all his films; those who do not, tend to depreciate them as one. They are not of a kind to inspire admiration of their separate parts; one either enjoys each as an integrated whole, entering a world perceived by Ray's inner eye – or one fails to see genius in any of his work.

By his own admission, Ray's films are the antithesis of conventional Hollywood films, both in style and content. 'I am aware that they are not of a kind that hits one in the solar plexus.' He consciously eschews glamour, gimmicks and technical polish for its own sake. His characters are generally of average ability and talents (unlike his documentary subjects). Perverted or bizarre behaviour does not appear (except in *Mahapurush* and the two Goopy and Bagha films) – Ray keeps that for his stories – and there is little violence and no explicit sex. His interest lies in characters with roots in their society rather than in those who are deracinated and drifting; a 'road movie' by Ray is unimaginable, for instance. It is the struggle and corruption of the conscience-stricken person that fascinate him, not the machinations of the ruthless or criminal. He feels actual injustices so keenly and sincerely that he cannot parade them on the screen; sometimes, as in *The Adversary* or *The Middle Man*, this depth of response emerges as humour, which the unwary viewer may miss or alternatively mistake for mockery. 'Life itself is full of funny things,' Ray told me when we first met, and so are his films (with the exception of *Deliverance*), but they do not advertise themselves as jokes. Above all, Ray's is a cinema of thought and feeling, in which the feeling is deliberately restrained because it is so intense. Like his old teacher Binodeda, Satyajit indulges neither in emotional rhetoric – nor in any other kind of rhetoric. That is why, when the outburst finally comes – from Sarbajaya in *Pather Panchali*, or Apu in *The World of Apu*, or Charu at the end of *Charulata*, or Siddhartha in *The Adversary*, or Mir in *The Chess Players*, or Dukhi in *Deliverance* – it cuts to the quick as few films can do.

These characteristics all contribute to the conviction of those who are indifferent to Ray's work that he is hopelessly out of touch with the modern idiom and the impact of the cynical materialism that masquerades as liberation all over the world today, and perhaps especially in 1980s India. They miss the sophistication of Ray, because they share western civilisation's historic indifference to Bengali culture and Indian culture in general. He is fortunate in being equipped to respond with confidence to most western art forms; very few westerners can repay the compliment. Here he is reviewing *The Gold Rush*, for instance, in 1964:

> Part of the delight and wonder derives, of course, from Chaplin himself. Watching him, you realise that he must be one of the very few artists of the twentieth century who is able to completely disarm a critic at one moment and, at the next, challenge his sharpest faculties and come out unscathed. If one thinks of Mozart and *The Magic Flute* and the knockabout foolery of Papageno merging into the sublimity of Sarastro, it is because the comparison is a valid one. Here is the same distilled simplicity, the same purity of style, the same impeccable craftsmanship. And the slight tinge of disappointment at the happy ending – the sudden veering towards a bright key after the subtle chromaticism of all that has gone before – isn't that rather like the cheery epilogue to *Don Giovanni*?

or writing to me about *The Jewel in the Crown* in 1984:

> I can say unhesitatingly that it's by far the best film about Anglo-India I have seen. Its strongest points are its casting and the performances. The only flaw is Mrs Sen Gupta (Shalini). One presumes she is a Bengali (although she wears her sari wrongly) and middle class. A woman of her class would never grovel at the feet of a sahib – and that too in public! One can imagine a peasant woman doing so. A pity – because otherwise the film hardly puts a foot wrong. Merrick, Daphne Manners, the three old ladies, Bronowsky, Sarah, are all superb. Hari Kumar is very good too, although the name is wrong – assuming he's a Bengali too. Lady Chatterjee doesn't look right but acts very well. I don't much care for Saeed [Jaffrey]; it's difficult to know what's going on in his mind much of the time. I was a little perturbed by the use of well-known locations (Udaipur, Simla) for supposedly fictitious places, but this won't be noticed in the West so much. The music is splendid – particularly the use of a lovely Indian raga on bass flute and sitar for one of the main themes.

There is no obstacle for Ray in making such judgments, whether he is discussing Chaplin and Mozart or Sukumar Ray and Tagore, and when there is one – such as when he looks at the Japanese film-makers – he readily admits his ignorance of the cultural background. Few of his western critics have been honest enough to do as much; if, that is, they have been aware that they are missing something. Ray has derived much satisfaction from their collective appreciation of his work over the years and freely acknowledges that it has been more perceptive than that of his Indian reviewers, but he remains uneasy about much of it, disturbed by the acclaim that has quite frequently been heaped upon him for the wrong reasons. In 1982, he took the opportunity offered him by *Sight and Sound* of commenting on this for the first time, thereby upsetting a number of foreign critics, especially in Britain, with his condemnation of their slack standards of criticism. He was provoked by their lavish plaudits for a south Indian mythological film *Sita's Wedding* (*Sita Kalyanam*), which he knew to be in the worst possible taste. 'For that film to be praised to the skies is something I can't take,' he remarked at the time.

> It's kitsch. The 'wonderful Carnatic music' that one critic talks of, I found to be seventy per cent Bombay film music. The story was supposed to be the *Ramayana* and it had Muslim decor, Kashmiri and Persian carpets, and stupid colour that was chocolate-boxy and unbelievable ... From that point onwards I view the critics with a great deal of suspicion when they write about Indian films. If they like my films, fine, I'm happy, but if they like something which is unlikable, where is the standard?

To have taken this film as seriously as Ray's work (and that of many other Indian directors) was a little like reviewing *Dallas* in the same breath as, say, Scorsese. The mistake is only possible where a critic lacks basic knowledge of a culture.

Sometimes this is obvious in his writing – as in Bosley Crowther's (favourable) review of *The Big City* in the *New York Times*, which managed to set it in New Delhi – but usually it is concealed, whether consciously or not. In the main, the western critic allows the astonishing accessibility of Ray's films to persuade him that he is almost a western director – rather as British (and sometimes even American) writers have sometimes tried to annex Ray himself as one of the last true Englishmen from the imperial mould. John Russell Taylor's remarks about *Charulata* in *Cinema: A Critical Dictionary*, are a good example of this:

> *Charulata*, it is tempting to say, is Ray's most western film – in discussing it one thinks at once of Ibsen or Strindberg (more in this case than of Chekhov who so often seems to offer close parallels to Ray's dramatic practice). But that is begging the question of whether most of Ray is not western. Obviously there are things about his films, like their frequently very measured tempo (slowness, unsympathetic critics would

say), which it is easiest to discuss as part of his Indianness. But apart from
his subject-matter it is hard to be sure that there is anything in his films
which derives specifically from his Oriental background and heritage: he
is very much a world film-maker, influenced more by Renoir, Donskoi,
Welles (the swinging scene in *Charulata*, and the film's whole loving
re-creation of its period milieu, has more than a hint of *The Magnificent
Ambersons* about it) and even by the theories of Pudovkin, which were
among his early reading, than by Indian cinema and its circumstances.
There is nothing in his films which has to be related to anything but
his own artistic development and taste as an individual; like any artist
he is finally independent of his background, and whatever use he may
make of it is ultimately self-determined.

Or, as Jean Renoir said in 1974, 'He is quite alone, of course.'

Actually Ray is not, as we know. He has not taken much from
Indian cinema, true, but his debt to Bengali and Indian culture – as
well as to the West – is prodigious, and *Charulata* is one of the films
that demonstrates this most fully – if one approaches it knowing what
to look for. He can fairly be described as an exemplar of Tagore's belief
that 'A sign of greatness in great geniuses is their enormous capacity for
borrowing, very often without their knowing it; they have unlimited credit
in the world market of cultures.' This may make knowledgeable criticism of
his work a tough proposition, as I am the first to admit, but it is also why his
films will last when those of some other admired directors are forgotten.

The problem has no instant solution, of course, as Ray frankly
recognised in an article in 1963 when he asked 'But why should the
West care?' and again when he told me in 1982 that: 'the cultural gap
between East and West is too wide for a handful of films to reduce it. It
can happen only when critics back it up with study on other levels as well.
But where is the time, with so many other films from other countries to
contend with? And where is the compulsion?'

Rather than rely on the loyalty of his foreign audience Ray has
preferred to follow his instinct and make films primarily for Bengalis.
He has never been able to predict which of his films would do well
abroad anyway – the success of *The Music Room* came as a real surprise
to him, for instance – and so he has generally aimed to make his films
pay their way in Bengal alone (with the exception of *The Chess Players*).
'It is better not to spend too much rather than to find ways to be sure of
the return,' as he explains. In the majority of cases the sums have worked
out and foreign sales have simply added to the profit in Bengal. 'Whatever
comes from abroad is extra,' Ray says.

It is an interesting question whether Ray would have been able
to survive had he been obliged to operate in a western environment
from the beginning, though as with most such hypotheses the premise is
false: Ray abstracted from Bengal could not have been the individual he

is. Lindsay Anderson considers that probably he would not have lasted very long, if one is thinking of 'someone who sets himself the standards of quality and refinement and seriousness and artistry Satyajit does, and who lives by them and wouldn't think of giving them up, and does not make films according to any popular conception of entertainment.' Anderson maintains that Ray's position compared with western directors is both very much tougher – technically speaking – and also easier – economically speaking – because it costs so much less to make a film in Calcutta than it does in the West.

He may be right, although he perhaps underestimates the perquisites of genius in any setting. There seems no reason in principle why a western Ray should not be able to gather round him the loyal actors and co-workers that Bergman, or even Woody Allen, have done. But certainly one cannot imagine Ray working as part of any large organisation. He has been courted many times, by David Selznick at one extreme to the BBC at the other – whom he eventually declined, in 1978, for the revealing reason that he 'found himself temperamentally unsuited to working for a sponsor – however liberal.'

Perhaps he had his brush with Selznick in mind when he made that remark. It took place at Berlin in 1964 after Ray had won the Selznick Golden Laurel three times at the Festival (for *Pather Panchali*, *Aparajito* and *Two Daughters*). This time Ray had agreed to present the award to Bergman for *Winter Light*. On the day itself he and Selznick had lunch together and Selznick asked him to make a film for him. Ray told him he knew about his famous memos to directors and said he doubted if he could put up with them. Selznick protested 'No! With you it'll be different, because, you know, John Huston used to come drunk on the set, so I had to be careful with him, I had to control him, so I sent memos.' Ray said he would think about it. That evening, before the award ceremony, he found a little envelope waiting for him at his hotel. 'In it was a memo from Mr Selznick,' recalls Ray, 'outlining the speech that I was supposed to make, saying would I memorise the six- or seven-line speech that he had written. Well, I made a different speech. It virtually amounted to the same thing because all you had to do was lead up to the name, which was a *great* secret. There are a hundred different ways of doing that, so I chose my way of doing it – not Mr Selznick's way. After that, of course, he didn't write to me again.'

The other important aspect of Ray that Lindsay Anderson leaves out of his reckoning in imagining him transplanted to foreign soil, is his popularity with his home audience. He is as successful as Bergman is in Sweden, or Kurosawa in Japan, perhaps more so. He hit an all-time high with *Goopy Gyne Bagha Byne*, but there is barely a film he has made that has not had an appeal beyond the confines of a highbrow audience. Without artifice he packs his films with layers of meaning that please everyone in different ways, from university professors who normally despise Indian cinema to sentimental housewives brought up on songs and dances in movies and even the better-educated members of Calcutta's vast working class. No one else in Indian cinema has been able to pull off this feat with more than the occasional film, although the fact is not widely appreciated outside Ray's linguistic area of Bengal. The Bombay film-maker's view of him is summarised by Ramesh Sippy, the maker of the blockbuster *Sholay*, who in 1983 said: 'I always regard Ray as the first moderniser of the Indian cinema and its first artist. The level to which he goes in probing his characters is beyond the reach of an ordinary viewer . . . Ray will never be able to make a film for the masses. His attitude to cinema is different. In our country nobody, not even Ray, has tried to bridge the gulf between art and entertainment.'

While it is true that the television series *Satyajit Ray Presents* has since then helped to make Ray's work better known in India outside Bengal, he is still essentially 'only a name' there – by his own admission. Apart from Bangalore, which turns out a good audience for Ray because of its high proportion of professional residents, his films are generally shown in India's major cities in Bengali only – at most, with English subtitles – and at special screenings, usually on Sunday mornings. They are never released nationwide and, apart from *Kapurush*, have not been dubbed into Hindi. (Subtitles would not do since many Hindi-speakers are illiterate.)

In Bengal Ray sits on the 'Olympian heights', as he once ironically put it – at least by comparison with Bombay. The release of a new film by Ray in Calcutta has long been an event, which triggers a torrent of reviews and comments in the Bengali and English-language press. While intellectuals – self-styled and otherwise – like to view a Satyajit Ray film 'with a Satyajit Ray mind' (to quote Ray's actress relative Ruma Guha Thakurta), other people pass whispered remarks in the auditorium about his more daring challenges to middle-class convention. Sometimes he loses his audience – as in *Kanchenjungha* and *Days and Nights in the Forest* – and occasionally he offends them – as with Apu's harsh treatment of his mother in *Aparajito* – but usually he strongly engages them in the best traditions of popular art. As he once said, 'Popular taste has produced Greek Drama, Shakespeare, *The Magic Flute*, Chaplin and the Western . . . I do not know of a single film-maker who has been dismayed by a wide acceptance of his work.'

But he has never been under any illusions about the difficulties he faces. When he began, in the early 1950s, his audience knew 'tame, torpid versions of popular Bengali novels'; they had been 'reduced to a state of unredeemable vacuity by years of cinematic spoon-feeding'. Today not much has changed. 'You'll find directors here so backward, so stupid, and so trashy that you'll find it difficult to believe their works exist alongside my films,' says Ray. Very often he and they are shooting in adjacent studios; it is eye-opening to leave his set and sample the typical Bengali cinematic fare. From time to time Ray has bouts of cynicism about his audience – he knows too well that what most of them really want is 'a good cry' (which *Pather Panchali* never ceases to deliver them) – but he continues to believe that he can educate them and that there has been a slow improvement in their capacity to appreciate good work. This belief, together with the appreciation of foreign audiences, is what sustained him in his early years, and what he chose to pass on in a tough convocation address to the Class of 1975 about to leave the Film and Television Institute at Pune: 'No matter how you make your film, if you are truly gifted, you will sooner or later create your own market. If not, and you still want to stay in business, then the only rules you would be obliged to follow would be the rules of compromise.'

He is less sanguine about educating the critics in India, 'which, in films, means anybody with access to print'. When he was starting out, 'what passed for film criticism in India usually consisted of a tortuous recounting of a film's plot, followed by a random dispersal of praise or blame on the people concerned in its making. Neither the film-makers nor the public took much heed of it', he wrote in 1982. Although he accepts that it has improved, partly as a result of the film society movement and its writings, Ray maintains that his critics – at least in Bengal – have not affected his work in any way. Since most of them still believe *Pather Panchali* to be his best film, he points out with some irony, how can they claim to have improved him?

In general, he recognises the role of film critic as connoisseur – someone who can interpret original work for the benefit of an audience who may otherwise dismiss it. He values critiques of his own work when they coincide with his own estimation of its strengths and weaknesses, but he feels that few who write about films – whether Indians or westerners – are properly equipped to do it; when they are, he suspects they would prefer to become film-makers themselves, as the *Cahiers du Cinéma* critics, Lindsay Anderson, and he himself did. Reading the total volume of critical writing about him since 1955, one can understand his scepticism. Laudatory though much of it is – often amounting to a 'rave' – it seldom rises to the demands of its subject. 'What is attempted in most films of mine is, of course, a synthesis', wrote Ray in 1982. 'But it can be seen as such only by someone who has his feet in both cultures. Someone who will bring to bear on the films involvement and detachment in equal measure. Someone who will see both the wood and the trees.'

In areas of controversy, such as the showing of sexual behaviour, or violence, or poverty, or political corruption on the screen, Indians – and especially the Indian Government – show a persistent tendency to see only Ray's warts and not his all. While he agrees that the absence of overt sex or violence from his work is a reflection of his own preference for the 'oblique', he would ideally like complete freedom to show what a story demands, and he disagrees with any notion of such overtness being somehow un-Indian. 'Generally speaking, in a love scene, even if it were

between lovers who had no restrictions, I would go to a very frank depiction only if there was something very special involved, some point that
I wished to make in the process of love-making itself, such as the man
being incapable, for instance,' says Ray. 'It's very well done in [Pakula's]
Klute, wonderfully done, when they are having intercourse and the girl
glances at her watch at the same time,' he continues laughing. 'That's the
kind of thing that pleases me. That's valid; that was needed. Without that
the story would lose something. Otherwise I don't think nudity as such
interests me very much, unless one could introduce elements into the
process of love-making that would make it rise above the conventional.'
Ray knows, however, that neither the censors nor his actors and actresses
would accept such a request, and it does not concern him overmuch; in
fact he takes it as a challenge to his imagination.

In nearly every film where a frank treatment might have been
appropriate, a natural barrier to intimacy has existed. In *The Goddess* it
was Doyamoyee's reluctance, in *Charulata* Amal's, in *Kapurush* Amitava's,
in *Days and Nights in the Forest* Sanjoy's (although intercourse between
Hari and the tribal girl is of course suggested), in *The Chess Players*
Mirza's, and in *Pikoo* the mother's (though semi-nakedness is shown
because the film was being made for French television). 'The only
time I wanted [greater frankness] was in *Ghare Baire*: Sandip-Bimala,'
says Ray. 'But they're never in a bedroom, so there's no question of a
bedroom scene. They're always in a drawing-room, where there's a certain
physical disadvantage in being too intimate.' The other two exceptions are
Narsingh-Gulabi in *Abhijan*, which Ray commented on earlier, and the
honeymoon scenes between Apu and Aparna in *The World of Apu*. 'Yes,
but with Bibhutibhusan in mind and his way of doing things . . . ' muses
Ray when asked about this today. 'He's one writer who wouldn't depict a
physical intimacy very openly. He would do it by innuendo.' Here is the
real Ray speaking, the man who told Bombay's premier fan-magazine in
1960 that 'Love between a man and a woman is an elevating experience.
It should be treated as such on the screen. Why use it to lend interest to
a mediocre story?' Even if there had been no holds barred in making *The
World of Apu*, it is doubtful whether Ray would have constructed those
wonderful scenes between the newly married couple any differently, and
whether, if he had, they could have lingered in the mind as touchingly as
they do now, thirty years after the film was made.

Ray's position in the political debate over his films is much clearer
cut, involving no such delicate scruples. But others have been chewing it
over ever since the time when the West Bengal Government demanded
changes in the ending of *Pather Panchali* to make it more positive. It was, as
we know, only through Nehru's personal intervention that *Pather Panchali*
reached the Cannes Festival in 1956. About twenty-five years later, the
very same objections to it were raised in the Indian Parliament, this time
by the late Nargis Dutt MP, heroine of the 1957 blockbuster *Mother India*

(Bombay's answer to *Pather Panchali*) and one of the biggest box-office stars of her time. She accused Ray of distorting India's image abroad during a parliamentary debate and later in an interview symptomatic of Ray's long-running difficulties with his audience outside Bengal:

Int: What does Ray portray in the Apu Trilogy and why do you object to it?

Nargis: He portrays a region of West Bengal which is so poor that it does not represent India's poverty in its true form. Tell me something. Which part of India are you from?

Int: UP [Uttar Pradesh].

Nargis: Now, tell me, would you leave your eighty-year-old grandmother to die in a cremation ground, unattended?

Int: No.

Nargis: Well, people in West Bengal do. And that is what he portrays in these films. It is not a correct image of India.

Int: Do people in West Bengal do such a thing?

Nargis: I don't know. But when I go abroad, foreigners ask me embarrassing questions like 'Do you have schools in India?' 'Do you have cars in India?' I feel so ashamed, my eyes are lowered before them. If a foreigner asks me, 'What kind of houses do you live in?' I feel like answering, 'We live on treetops.' Why do you think films like *Pather Panchali* become so popular abroad?

Int: You tell me.

Nargis: Because people there want to see India in an abject condition. That is the image they have of our country and a film that confirms that image seems to them authentic.

Int: But why should a renowned director like Ray do such a thing?

Nargis: To win awards. His films are not commercially successful. They only win awards.

Int: What do you expect Ray to do?

Nargis: What I want is that if Mr Ray projects Indian poverty abroad, he should also show 'Modern India'.

Int: But if the theme and plot of *Pather Panchali* are complete within the realm of a poor village, how can he deliberately fit 'Modern India' in it?

Nargis: But Mr Ray can make separate films on 'Modern India'.

Int: What is 'Modern India'?

Nargis: Dams . . .

Int: Can you give me one example of a film that portrays 'Modern India'?

Nargis: Well . . . I can't give you an example offhand . . .

Ray did not bother to refute such stuff, but others jumped to his defence including Utpal Dutta, who joked that 'this holy cow should have stuck to her *Mother India* role', and the Forum for Better Cinema – a group of respected film-makers and writers – who wrote to Nargis Dutt:

> The Modern India you speak of is the India of dams, of scientists, steel plants and agricultural reforms. Do you honestly believe that it is this India ,that is portrayed in the so-called commercial films of Bombay? In fact, the world of commercial Hindi films is peopled by thugs, smugglers, dacoits, voyeurs, murderers, cabaret dancers, sexual perverts, degenerates, delinquents and rapists, which can hardly be called representative of Modern India.

It was soon after this exchange that the Government informed Ray it could not grant him permission to make a film about child labour since this did not constitutionally exist in India. So instead, as a deliberate protest against both the ban and the minister concerned (whom he openly described as 'a very dangerous, vicious type of person'), Ray decided to produce *Deliverance* – a film as bluntly prosaic about the human condition as *Pather Panchali* is poetically hopeful.

Ray's love for the land of his birth is powerfully evident in both these films, absolute contrasts though they are: watching them it is plain to see why he has never felt the need to leave India for his film subjects. He has the inner assurance of the true patriot that permits him to move in other cultures on a footing of equality without feeling obliged to do so, combined with a humility to anticipate the pitfalls that springs from his deep knowledge of his own country. That is why his sympathies were for once with the Government when, in 1970, they objected to Louis Malle's mammoth documentary film *Phantom India*. 'The whole Malle affair is deplorable', he wrote to Seton. 'Personally I don't think any director has any right to go to a foreign country and make a documentary film about it unless a) he is absolutely thorough in his groundwork on all aspects of the country – historical, social, religious etc, and b) he does it with genuine love. Working in a dazed state – whether of admiration or disgust – can produce nothing of any value.'

These are the conditions he has imposed on himself of course. Ray's roots grow deep, but he reminds one of a banyan tree more than any English oak. The main trunk is fed by the sights and sounds of Bengal and its literature, art, music and dance, along with those of the rest of the subcontinent stretching right back to the *Mahabharata*, but the aerial roots have spread far and wide, sucking up nourishment from all over the world and thickly shrouding the trunk so that it can no longer be distinguished.

As Satyajit observes, when asked if he feels he is Indian enough, 'I can be – if the need arises.' Foreigners, and especially English people who meet him, often like to call him a 'Brahmin' – aloof, patrician, somewhat cold – while many Bengalis, receiving the same impression of him, regard it as quintessentially British! In fact, of course, his family is not Brahmin; before Upendrakisore's conversion to casteless Brahmoism around 1880, they were Kayasthas. While he and his son Sukumar regarded themselves as Brahmos, Satyajit 'has never been conscious of belonging to any caste at all at any time', and says that he regards it as 'rather stupid to raise a wall around you', as he is sometimes supposed to have done. It amuses and slightly irritates him to see himself described as a Brahmin in the West. If he sees himself as part of any group or tradition, it is that of liberal humanists, of whom Tagore, Upendrakisore Ray and Sukumar Ray were leading lights.

There is more substance in the Bengali belief that Ray is an anglophile. This probably grew out of his early reading of Sherlock Holmes, P.G. Wodehouse, the *Boy's Own Paper* and so on, and was reinforced by the generosity of the British managers at Keymer's in his advertising days and his friendship with the anglophilic Alex Aronson and with Norman Clare. But it does not in any way preclude him from being deeply immersed in Bengali culture too, with the exception of certain of its more irrational and sentimental manifestations, such as Kali worship or the eternally popular writings of Sarat Chandra Chatterjee, on which so many lachrymose films have been based. 'I think both in English and in Bengali, but mostly in Bengali really,' he says. The people he likes best are generally those who share both his orientations, whether they be foreigners, Bengalis or other Indians.

David McCutchion was one of these. A tall, lean, bespectacled Englishman with a distinguished career at Cambridge as a linguist, he came to teach English at Santiniketan in 1957 in his late twenties. A few years later he moved to Calcutta where he taught until his shockingly sudden death from polio in January 1972 – when Ray wrote an intimate obituary of him in the Calcutta *Statesman* under the title 'The lure of terracotta' (subsequently reprinted in a volume of pieces about McCutchion as 'Dozens of scuttling peacocks'). They had first met at Santiniketan in 1960 but it was when McCutchion came to Calcutta that they became friends, beginning with a shared love of western music. Soon they began to collaborate on the English subtitles for Ray's films, starting with *Three Daughters*. 'He insisted on translating every word and getting all the nuances right,' Satyajit remembered, 'while I worried about all that reading matter getting in the way of the images.' It took them half-a-dozen films and almost as many years 'to come to a satisfactory compromise.'

It was during the shooting of *Abhijan* in 1962 in the countryside not very far from Santiniketan, that McCutchion first stumbled on the brick temples that became his passion and began his remorseless documentation and photography of their fascinating carvings for the definitive study that was eventually published years after he died. Ray at first helped to direct his enthusiasm but within a few months McCutchion had become the real expert. 'It was now David who talked while I listened', wrote Satyajit.

His research took him into remote parts of Bengal and Orissa (and later to Madhya Pradesh and Rajasthan), travelling and living under very difficult conditions. On his return to the big city he would immediately look up Satyajit at Lake Temple Road for gossip:

'Was it a good trip?' I asked. David hesitated, and I immediately regretted the casual way I had put my question. I should have known that David would scarcely bring himself to answer with a simple 'yes' or 'no', thereby laying himself open to the charge of imprecision. David was a stickler for exactitude. He was also extremely sensitive to people and places. For him, every journey into temple country was a bundle of experiences ranging from the ridiculous to the sublime. How could he describe in one word, or even in a few words, what it was like?

One particular foray was responsible for the second title of Ray's piece about his friend. He had come across a temple in the desert in the middle of nowhere which looked utterly deserted. But as he approached it, he suddenly heard a great flutter of wings, and 'dozens of peacocks came charging out and went scuttling over the sand.'

McCutchion was absolutely determined that such temples be protected from vandals and he went round Calcutta on his bike collecting signatures from well-known people for a letter of protest. The depredations were being caused, in many cases, by those intent on 'restoring' the temples, as we know from *The Alien*. In other cases parts were being removed for sale to foreign collectors. It saddened and disgusted both McCutchion and Ray but it also had its funny side, as Satyajit recalled, thinking of David's account of a lecture he had given on his researches, arranged by 'X, a veritable bastion of Bengali culture': 'Pelting rain had flooded the streets, and hardly a dozen people turned up. But David started his talk nevertheless. X sat in the front row and kept smiling and nodding her head. "Why, I'm making an impression! I thought," said David. "Then, at one point, I felt thirsty and turned to X and asked for a glass of water. She just kept smiling and nodding her head . . ."!'

Satyajit, whom David had once described to someone as looking 'a bit like Alexander the Great', was stunned by his death for several days. '"Nothing exasperates me more than irrationality"' David used to say', he wrote in the concluding paragraph of his obituary, speaking for himself as well:

And what with his frequent encounters with museum officials, railway booking clerks, customs personnel, keepers of holy temples, self-styled patrons of the arts, and zealous members of the police (a rich story here about being hauled up as a Chinese spy), David surely had far more legitimate reasons to wax eloquent over irrationality than most other people. But what, one wonders – thinking of the circumstances

– could be more irrational in the scheme of things than the death of David McCutchion himself?

Their relaxed rapport, somewhat reminiscent of Satyajit's relationship with the more gifted members of his family, epitomises the way influences of all kinds have had free play in his life and work. There is no sense of strain in his devotion to western culture (as there is in, say, Nirad Chaudhuri's); he never felt he was 'grappling' with something alien – to use his own word – whether he was dealing with western literature, painting or music. He draws upon these arts in the same way as he feels about Binode Bihari Mukherjee's art: '[Looking at it] you never feel that "Oh, now he's copying so-and-so's composition or now he's doing this or that." You feel that he's being himself – very much so.'

When Ray is asked outright, as he frequently has been over the years, what influences there have been on him, he has got used to trotting out everything from Tagore, Kalidasa and the *Mahabharata* to Mozart, Italian neo-realism and the US directors of the 1940s, depending on his mood at the time of questioning. None of these answers is inaccurate, and none excludes the others; they have all played a part, often unconsciously, along with his grandfather's and father's work and very many other sources of inspiration, which Ray has made his own. That is why statements by critics to the effect that the influence of Renoir or Chekhov or Welles or whoever is evident in this or that scene of a Ray film, never quite ring true. For Ray is too original an artist. Some people have thought that Donskoi's trilogy influenced Ray's, for example, but, as he points out, Bengalis once said that Romain Rolland's *Jean Christophe* had influenced *Pather Panchali* – and Bibhutibhusan Banerjee had apparently not even heard of the novel.

The innovatory aspect of Banerjee's novel was of a kind that came from the inside. There is also the kind that is external, and here Ray readily grants a direct influence. Godard, for instance, helped him largely to dispense with fades and dissolves, while Truffaut gave him confidence to use the freeze. These were imitable ideas; not so Renoir's ideas in, say, *La Règle du Jeu* remarks Ray: 'There is a subtle, almost imperceptible kind of innovation that can be felt in the very texture and sinews of a film. A film that doesn't wear its innovations on its sleeve. A film like *La Règle du Jeu*. Humanist? Classical? Avant-Garde? Contemporary? I defy anyone to give it a label. This is the kind of innovation that appeals to me.'

He also finds it in the films of the best Japanese directors – Kurosawa, Ozu, Mizoguchi – which reinforces his conviction that labels will not stick to the greatest works. The 'enormous reserves of power and feeling which never spill over into emotional displays' suggested by Mizoguchi's and Ozu's work, naturally appeal to Ray, but overall he is much closer to Kurosawa than to his two predecessors who 'seem almost anachronistic in their apparent unawareness of western conventions.' It is they rather than Kurosawa who embody Ray's 'preconception of the true Japanese film-maker' – just as Ritwik Ghatak early on struck Satyajit as an artist rooted only in the soil of Bengal, which he has never felt himself to be.

In my view Ray can be said to be both western and oriental as an artist – alert to the physical world *and* to the essence behind appearances – and also unique. In this respect he resembles Tagore, whom Ray has long regarded as unclassifiable. Tagore once identified himself strongly with the idea that 'Asia is One' – in the opening words of an influential Japanese book of the turn of the century – but later came to reject this as too simple when Japan became militaristic in the 1930s. Ray rejects it too, though not the concept of the oriental artist in its entirety. 'I may be wrong,' he wrote in 1963, 'but a phrase of my dear old professor [Nandalal Bose] sticks in my mind: "Consider the Fujiyama," he would say, "fire within and calm without. There is the symbol of the true Oriental artist.' Nevertheless, Ray admitted, 'the Far East is content with only five notes in music while we in India have to have the full chromatic scale, with some quarter tones thrown in (and I, personally, have to have my Bach and Mozart too). And if I love Chinese painting and Japanese woodcuts, it is not at the expense of my admiration for Cézanne and Piero della Francesca. And consider eating habits; the Chinese do not round off their meals with dessert, while we follow a Sanskrit proverb which says "All meals must end with sweets".'

There his eclecticism is apparent – taking 'what you think is good and what you think you can use', as he puts it. He has faith in the idea of East-West synthesis inaugurated in the early nineteenth century by Rammohun Roy, which Tagore too believed in. Like them, he is in direct touch with the art and ideas of Indian and western civilisation (and some of those belonging to the Far East too); there is no mediating influence in his contact with India's past, as there is with the majority of the Indian élite, who usually encounter and laud their own classical culture through English and, until the twentieth century, through the writings of foreign scholars, not Indians. Their 'synthesis', unlike Ray's, is not a genuine one, because the living contact of their ancestors with the culture of ancient Hindu India shrivelled up subsequently in the desiccating atmosphere of caste, producing types such as Harikisore Ray Chaudhuri in Ray's own family or Indranath, the industrialist of *Kanchenjungha*. 'In other words, they were being as imitative when copying ancient Indian ways as they were in copying the Western', wrote Nirad Chaudhuri in *The Autobiography of an Unknown Indian*: 'On the whole it would not be wrong to say that the orientalism of modern Indians was only a product of the wider movement in favour of oriental civilisations which had sprung up in the West, or to put the matter more incisively, it was a reflection of occidental orientalism.'

This is the worm in the core of the Bengal Renaissance, and the reason why Ray is reluctant to affiliate himself to it. Like his father and grandfather he abhors the imitative cast of mind of most 'Renaissance Bengalis': that 'sterility of our intellectual and moral life' – to quote Chaudhuri again – 'dominated by imported phrases on the one hand and archaistic models on the other.' And it is also why, at a less elevated level, Indian Government officials could not grasp the life-affirming qualities of *Pather Panchali* in their insidious obsession with presenting India as a second-class version of a western industrialised nation – Gandhi notwithstanding.

Indian cinema too, from its inception, has suffered the same fatal flaw. As Ray puts it in the introduction to *Our Films Their Films*, India 'took one of the greatest inventions of the West with the most far-reaching artistic potential, and promptly cut it down to size', generating images that range from the absurd to the unspeakable (by way of some wonderful songs, it is true). With very few exceptions Indian film-makers were in thrall to Hollywood, like Ray's friend Harisadhan Das Gupta who in the 1980s still believed that *The Home and the World* would have been a better film if shot from Ray's original 'Hollywoodish' script.

Admittedly, since the 1970s there has been a notable improvement in quality, as a 'new' cinema has grown up in many regions of India, led by film-makers like Shyam Benegal, Adoor Gopalakrishnan and G. Aravindan. 'What sets these film-makers apart from the commercial "All-India" ones is a preoccupation with serious, rooted subjects put across with an imaginative use of modest resources', Ray has remarked. But while this is true, generally speaking, it is hard to avoid an overall impression of these films as lacking commitment to their subject-matter. One is not missing political or social criticism in them – of that there is more than enough – but commitment 'to life, to human beings – anything that interests me deeply', as Ray says of himself. There is a superficiality and dullness in most of the work of the 'new' cinema that seems to derive from the fake urban culture of modern India, and which arises ultimately from the failure of imagination in the Indian 'synthesis' of the last century. No one – perhaps least of all Satyajit – would wish film-makers in India simply to imitate Ray's films, but until they come to observe the life around them with at least some of his richness of mind, inventiveness and emotional involvement, most of their work will continue to be flavourless and parochial.

'If I were asked what has been my main preoccupation as a film-maker,' Ray wrote in an article entitled 'The new cinema and I', 'I should say it has been to find out ways of investing a story with organic cohesion, and filling it with detailed and truthful observation of human behaviour and relationships in a given milieu and a given set of events, avoiding stereotypes and stock situations, and sustaining interest visually, aurally and emotionally by a judicious use of the human and technical resources at one's disposal. I know this sounds pompous, but I can't think of any other way to put it.' This is about the closest he comes in his writings to a theory of art, and it is one he has applied to almost all his films. Its emphasis on discipline and order reminds one of Tagore's view of beauty – that 'it is absurd to suggest that beauty may be created out of weakness or instability of character, out of a lack of restraint.'

To some this will seem passé, to others 'classical' – a favourite criti-

cal adjective for Ray's work. Ray has never been fashionable, in the
way that Godard or Fassbinder (or even Kurosawa) have, because his
work lies beyond fashion. But much of it will still be watched in the
next century. It aspires to the only label that Ray really covets – 'timeless'.
'Bach is timeless', he has written. 'So is Masaccio. So is Buster Keaton. So
are Indian and Egyptian sculpture, the murals of Ajanta, Chinese painting,
Japanese woodcuts, Etruscan vases, Benin bronzes, the horse of Lascaux
and the bison of Altamira . . .' These works all display the mysterious quality
of rhythm, which Tagore called 'the movement generated and regulated
by harmonious restriction', and, despite being products of their place and
time, they are all universal in their appeal. So are Ray's best films – while
those of his Bengali polar opposite Ghatak (now becoming known in the
West) are not. Their differences shed an interesting light on Ray's identity
as an artist and as a man of Bengal.

In a collection of Ghatak's writings in English entitled *Cinema and I*,
compiled by Ghatak's son, Ray and others and published in Calcutta in
1987 some ten years after his death (with a cover design of bold simplicity
by Ray), Satyajit had this to say of Ritwik:

> He was one of the few truly original talents in the cinema this country
> has produced. Nearly all his films are marked by an intensity of feeling
> coupled with an imaginative grasp of the technique of film-making. As a
> creator of powerful images in an epic style he was virtually unsurpassed
> in Indian cinema. He also had full command over the all-important aspect
> of editing: long passages abound in his films which are strikingly original
> in the way they are put together. This is all the more original when one
> doesn't notice any influence of other schools of film-making on his work.
> For him Hollywood might not have existed at all. The occasional echo of
> classical Soviet cinema is there, but this doesn't prevent him from being
> in a class by himself.

The key to understanding Ghatak and his work for both the theatre and
the cinema is his lifelong obsession with East Bengal, where he was born
and spent his childhood and youth. He was just short of twenty-two when
his whole past was torn away from him by the Partition of 1947. His sense
of betrayal and his disgust for those who ignored this terrible consequence
of their demands for political freedom never left him; in fact it gained in
intensity with the passing of the years, the decline of the Bengal he had
once known, and the bloody birth of Bangladesh. He had to put behind
him the kind of close-knit life among the rivers of East Bengal which Satyajit
never knew and which inspired Tagore at the turn of the century to some
of his greatest poetry, short stories, songs and letters. Ritwik's description
of it which follows, has some of the lyricism and emotional charge of his
films (and of Ray's film *The Postmaster*):

> My days were spent on the banks of the Padma – the days of an

unruly and wild child. The people on the passenger boats looked like
dwellers of some distant planet. The large merchant ships coming from
Patna, Bankipore, Monghyr, carried sailors speaking a strange tongue,
with a mixture of dialect in it. I saw the fishermen. In the drizzling rain
a joyful tune would float in the village air pulling at one's heart-strings
with the sudden gusts of wind. I have rocked in the steamer on the
turbulent river after dark, and listened to the rhythmic sound of the
engines, the bell of the *sareng*, the cry of the boatmen measuring the
depths. In the autumn, once I sailed off on a boat and lost my way
among tall grasses where snakes hide. The pollen of the grass flowers
choked me as I tried to pull the boat away. I got hired to act in a play
once, missed my train, and landed up in a remote village at nightfall. It
was the night before the full moon. In front of me was a haunted lake.
I punted down the lake with a friend in the gathering darkness.

Against the horizon a village would appear from time to time, like an
island. In the wet mist we were shaking with cold. Finally, we realised
that the spirits of the lake had got us. We spent the whole night trying
to cover a distance of two hours. Desperate and bewildered, we gave
up trying and waited for dawn.

Like very many young men and women who came of age in the
years of the war, the Famine and the Partition – but not Ray – Ghatak
became a Marxist. He also joined the Indian People's Theatre Association
and wrote and produced a number of plays (including Sukumar Ray's
Ha-Ja-Ba-Ra-La). In 1952 he wrote and directed his first film, the year
Ray began shooting *Pather Panchali*, but it was not released during his
lifetime. This would be the fate of all his eight finished feature films bar
one; he had, comments Ray, 'the misfortune to be largely ignored by the
Bengali film public in his lifetime.'
Viewing his films in the West today it is not difficult to see why.
Though they have the passion of Lindsay Anderson they lack Anderson's
feeling for character and his satirical sense, and while they resemble Buñuel
in their use of private allusions, they lack his inventiveness and wit. Ghatak's
obsessions, like Bergman's, are not Ray's own, but that would not matter
to Ray if Ghatak had the superb dramatic skills of Bergman (who moves
Ray 'not necessarily because of his emotion, but sometimes because of
his sheer excellence. Even a very light-hearted Mozart piece can move
you by being so inventive.') But Ghatak's screenplays, which are always
by him (often from stories by others though), are particularly weak; and
his films often fail to communicate their meanings cinematically, leaving
Ghatak attempting to do so afterwards in print. He lacked, in the final
analysis, the detachment from his material essential for great art, and, as
Ray pointedly notes, his work has '*no* sense of humour – and what little
there is is horseplay.'
As a man he showed the kind of extreme impulsiveness and

temperamental behaviour that Ray famously does not, sometimes with
Satyajit himself. Although they were never close, he did much to help
Ghatak, including getting him a job at the Film and Television Institute
in Pune in 1965–6, where he made a big impact as a teacher and helped
some of the aspiring film-makers. Ray also helped Ghatak get money that
was owing to him and gave him money himself, particularly towards the end
of his life when he had become an alcoholic. His total failure to acknowledge
this assistance hurt Satyajit. Probably, like others in Bengal, Ghatak could
not avoid feeling jealous of Ray, although he did pay him tribute in print.
('*Ekmatra* Satyajit Ray' – 'The one and only Satyajit Ray'). He was a man
with substantial talents driven by frustrated love of his native land but without
the discipline to connect the two successfully except in brilliant flashes: an
archetypally Bengali flaw. 'Ritwik was a Bengali director in heart and soul,
a Bengali artist – much more of a Bengali than I am myself', said Ray in
a memorial lecture. 'For me that is the last word about him, and this is
the most valuable and distinctive characteristic.'

Ghatak could never have been happy outside Bengal – and in fact never
went abroad – just as Ray could never be satisfied by Bengal alone. As with
Tagore, the appreciation of the world is necessary to him as an artist because
of 'an indefinable universality in his outlook', as Seton realised at their first
encounter in Calcutta in 1955. *Pather Panchali* had overwhelmed her but
she knew nothing about its creator. When he made a passing mention of
Venice to the effect that it resembled Benares, she sensed his uniqueness.
There was something in the way he spoke, she felt, that did not evoke the
automatic rejoinder, 'Oh, when were you there?' One of my own strongest
first impressions of him, in London in 1982, was of the ease with which he
fitted into a British context while remaining himself, and of the harmony
between his manner and conversation, and his films. He had the same effect
on John Huston in Calcutta in 1954 and on Akira Kurosawa in Tokyo in 1967
(though Kurosawa struck Ray as unexpectedly gentle compared with the
image created in his mind by *The Seven Samurai*). As Kurosawa later put
it: 'I well recall the indescribable feeling his appearance aroused in me –
with his great height, his candid manner, and his piercing gaze. It came to
me spontaneously that such sublime creations could only be the work of
such a man. Unconsciously, I came to feel great respect for him ... He
is a 'giant' of the movie industry.'

Longer acquaintance with Ray generally reinforces such feelings. He
has the supreme self-assurance of genius but not its arrogance. Glamour,
great wealth and arbitrary power never excited him before and still do
not. Inside he is still the quiet, private teenager who would break into
a fever at the thought of going up to the front to collect a prize. An
appetite for publicity in an artist is a feature of modern western life Ray
has not acquired; he remains as open to new experiences and encounters
as he ever was, even if his health no longer allows him to move around as

freely as he used to do. 'I feel one pronounces fewer judgments as one grows older', he says. 'The important thing is to keep one's senses alert and keep working.'

In the words of his wife Bijoya, who says she is his 'greatest critic': 'What I admire most about Manik is his simplicity, his honesty, his generosity, his kindness and above all, his ability to mix with people from all walks of life. He is at home with everybody. This, I think, is the hallmark of all great men.'

It is true, as some people regret, that there has been a diminution in the lyricism of his works with age, but there has certainly not been any falling-off in their sheer humanity. Who, after seeing *Deliverance*, can doubt that? 'Nothing human is alien to them. They are works of love', wrote *Time* magazine's critic in 1963. 'Will Ray redeem his prodigious promise and become the Shakespeare of the screen?' I would say he has. Throughout his career Ray has continued to experiment with subject-matter and style – surely more than any other director in cinema – but he has always held true to his original conviction that the finest cinema uses 'strong and simple' themes embroidered with 'a hundred little apparently irrelevant details which, instead of obscuring the theme, only help to intensify it by contrast and in addition create the illusion of actuality better.' These themes cannot come from the passing fashions of the period; they must be drawn from the 'permanent values' Ray believes in. 'That's my whole mental attitude,' he says, 'and I have to be true to myself.'

Like the ageing Tagore, contemplating the rise of intolerance all over the globe in the late 1920s, Ray finds it harder now to hold on to his old faith in human beings. Much that he cherished in both Bengal and elsewhere has irreversibly altered for the worse, including the atmosphere of intellectual enquiry and artistic creativity in which his family flourished. But Satyajit himself continues to create, unclouded by cynicism – always hoping, as he once remarked to me, that 'the right people will do the right things'. In a century of unparalleled human self-destruction and ravaging of our natural environment, of which Bengal has had much more than its fair share, Satyajit Ray and his works remind us of the wholeness and sanctity of the individual, and offer us intimations, if we will tune ourselves to him, of a mysterious unity behind the visible world.

31

Postscript:
An Enemy of the People
(Ganasatru) 1989

*****[◦◦ ◦◦◦◦ ◦◦]*****

R AY began shooting his twenty-fourth full-length feature film (and his thirty-seventh film), his own adaptation of Henrik Ibsen's *An Enemy of the People*, on 1 December 1988 – some six years after he began work on *The Home and the World*.

I flew to Calcutta in late November and recorded an interview with him, extracts from which appear below. I also watched about a fortnight's shooting – in the same studio in which I had watched him shooting *The Home and the World*. It was still just as dilapidated but now more or less pigeon-free, as Ray optimistically observed. This time I was able to read Ray's script in the original and to follow the dialogue and much of the direction on set.

There were several differences from the earlier shooting. First, Ray's son Sandip was no longer simply an alert observer; he was behind the camera throughout, operating it confidently after his father had checked a shot and discussed what he wanted. ('Thank God for Babu. He knows exactly what I want,' Satyajit remarked to me.) Secondly, Ray himself now spent most of his time sitting down, watching and listening, getting up only to look through the camera or, occasionally, to demonstrate a point to an actor. Often, he seemed still less in evidence than he had on the sets of *The Home and the World*.

Yet nothing could be clearer than his total absorption in his film, pruning and honing its dialogue each night before shooting – and sometimes making significant alterations – and affectionately guiding his experienced cast towards the precise nuances of pronunciation and expression in his mind. His voice was as supple and as forceful as ever – never more so than when crying 'Cut!' at the end of a take. As ever, it reminded me of something musical: the deft movements of a conductor's baton.

Ibsen's play has been transformed by Ray, unlike its treatment by Arthur Miller. The setting is now totally contemporary: 1989, a small town in Bengal with a reputation as a health resort, some way from

Calcutta. Ibsen's Dr Stockman, that obstinate whistle-blower who destroys
a comfortable life for the sake of a principle, has become Dr Asok Gupta
(Soumitra Chatterjee in his fourteenth role for Ray), the head of a hospital
run by a trust established by a local Marwari industrialist, Bhargava. Gupta's
brother Nisith is a bigwig, as in Ibsen, but younger than Asok (a change
Ibsen himself wanted to make on seeing the première, according to Ray).
He is the head of the hospital committee, and therefore technically his
brother's boss, *and* the head of the committee running the town's very
successful Hindu temple – built at his suggestion with money given by
Bhargava, who is both shrewd and pious.

The introduction of the temple into the story is Ray's masterstroke.
It enabled him to turn Ibsen into Ray – via Chekhov: to make what
'generally ranks as one of the thinnest of Ibsen's mature works', in the
words of an Ibsen scholar, into a rich screenplay, highly topical and truly
Bengali in ethos.

Instead of spa waters, it is the temple's water supply that is
contaminated – the result of shoddy pipe-laying when the temple
was built ten years previously. Dr Gupta is the first to suspect it: there is
an outbreak of jaundice among his patients, most of whom happen to live
near the temple or regularly visit it. Laboratory tests in Calcutta confirm
his suspicions, and the local newspaper editor is at first keen to warn
the town; but neither Bhargava nor Nisith will accept what Asok says.
Bhargava, like many Hindus, believes that holy water – *charanamrita* – in
temples by definition cannot be impure, because it contains Ganges water
and *tulsipata* – sacred basil leaves – afloat in it. Nisith is more sceptical
but he cannot afford to believe his brother: too much is at stake. 'Do you
call yourself a Hindu?' he mischievously calls out to his brother at a public
meeting the doctor has called – as in Ibsen's play – to broadcast the fact
of an epidemic threatening the resort. Ray takes up the story:

> 'Of course I do,' says the doctor, 'but there are certain Hindu religious
> customs that I do not follow because of my scientific training. But I
> definitely call myself a Hindu.' The younger brother says, 'Do you go
> to the temple? Have you ever been to the temple?' Asok says, 'No I
> haven't , for the same reason – because I don't feel the necessity to go
> there. But I'm not saying that you should never drink the holy water.
> You should wait until it is decontaminated. It will take a little time.'
> And then the younger brother asks, 'Have you any idea how many
> drink the holy water every day?' Asok says, 'I don't have a definite
> idea but I should imagine about seven or eight thousand.' Then his
> brother asks 'How many patients have you had so far?' Asok says 'I'm
> not the only doctor, but I myself have received in my hospital and in
> my private capacity about 200, 250 patients.'

At this point, of course, the meeting swings against Dr Gupta,
before he has a chance to try to explain the concept of immunity. For

the time being, at least, irrationality and the majority have won the day, and Dr Gupta, like Dr Stockman, looks set for ostracism as an 'Enemy of the People' – though actually the ending is more hopeful than Ibsen's, as one might expect from Ray.

Once again, he has accurately sensed the mood of the times in selecting *An Enemy of the People* – not just in India, where the scientific attitude has a tenuous hold and religious fanaticism is just below the surface of democratic debate, but all over the world. It is, after all, no more irrational for Hindus to believe that *charanamrita* – holy water – is always free from germs than it is to believe that AIDS is God's curse on Man.

Q: How long have you been interested in *An Enemy of the People* as a potential film subject?
A: Not for many years actually. When I had to decide on a subject for the present film, I was told that I couldn't work on location, everything had to be done in the studio. So that suggested a play rather than a novel. And I couldn't think of a Bengali play which I was interested in. I thought of reading Ibsen's *An Enemy of the People* again. I'd last read it ten or fifteen years ago.
Q: Do you remember when you read it the first time?
A: Well I had a volume of Modern Library Giants. I've read a lot of Ibsen. I've had this particular book since 1946. It was in 1946 or 1947 that I read some of the plays, including *An Enemy of the People*. I liked it as a play very much and I admired the character of Dr Stockman. But I didn't think of it as a film at that time. Then a well-known Bengali theatre troupe – Sambhu Mitra's Bohurupee – produced a version which was more or less a translation rather than an adaptation. It contained practically everything that the original play contained. I don't know how they placed it in a Bengali setting. I never saw the play. I never read it either. So I don't know what they actually did – except that Sambhu Mitra gave a very fine performance as Dr Stockman, according to everybody.
Q: Why didn't you go?
A: I was probably working on a film. They produced it three times – in the 1950s, 1960s and 1970. The first two times the play was not a success, people didn't go; it more or less flopped. But in 1970 it was suddenly a big success. I rather regretted missing it.
Q: Have you seen a foreign production?
A: No, never.
Q: What about foreign productions of other Ibsen plays?
A: No, all the productions I've seen are Bengali ones. Soumitra [Chatterjee] did *Ghosts*, Sambhu Mitra did *A Doll's House*.
Q: I sometimes wonder why you seldom refer to the theatre in your writings and conversation?
A: It's not my field actually. So many gifted people are working in

the theatre that I feel that there is no need for me to participate in any way.

Q: What kind of plays have you seen in London? Shakespeare?

A: Shakespeare I don't remember. I remember *Streetcar Named Desire*, *Venus Observed*, *The Cocktail Party* and Agatha Christie – the unending one.

Q: *The Mousetrap*?

A: Yes.

Q: But why is [classical] theatre unimportant to you?

A: It's not unimportant to me. It's just that I have no function in the theatre. I feel that my material lies in a different direction actually. In the case of *An Enemy of the People* I have taken somebody else's play and turned it into a film. That's all I have done.

Q: But for instance Bergman, Lindsay Anderson and even Kurosawa, who owes quite a lot to the Noh tradition . . .

A: But I have not to that extent been interested in the theatre. I mean I've enjoyed watching lots of things which are produced here – like Utpal Dutta's plays, which are very well produced, very entertaining.

Q: You just said to me there was no Bengali play that interested you?

A: There was no Bengali play that interested me as film material for a contemporary story. I wanted to make a contemporary story – as against *Ghare Baire* which was period. This time I wanted to make a story which would apply to today.

Q: You don't think your feelings about theatre and film could be anything to do with the theatricality of 1930s Bengali films? A kind of reaction to that?

A: It could possibly be that. Actually much of the acting in the Bengali cinema is theatrical – even now, even today. That's a regrettable fact. There's nothing I can do about it.

Q: Do you recall a questionnaire to film directors in the 1950s which you answered by saying that your aim as a film director was to 'banish the last trace of theatricality' from your work?

A: Yes. I'm not doing that in the present case (*laughs*). Those are youthful remarks.

Q: So how did it differ – adapting your first play, instead of a short story or a novel?

A: One problem which cropped up again and again was the entry of the characters. For instance, in the first act, five different people enter at five different points. There's a doorbell and somebody goes and opens it, and in comes a character. That is a very theatrical device. It's not a filmic device at all. So I have done something to remove that impression: the sound of the bell comes in the middle of conversation and we have a glimpse of the servant going to open the door. The conversation goes on and at one point it stops because the person has already come in – so that it's not a theatrical entrance.

Q: But did the fact that a play is all dialogue help you or hinder you, or neither?

A: I thought the dialogue was very interesting. It became more and more interesting as I was doing my treatment. I found that for once one could play with human faces and human reactions, rather than landscapes, Nature in its various moods which I have done a lot in my films. Here I think it is the human face, the human character which is predominant.

Q: At what stage did your wife and son read the script?

A: The first person to read it was my wife. She always is. Her comments are often pertinent and sometimes quite ruthless. In this case she had very intelligent suggestions which I incorporated. Then Babu read it.

Q: Did he have suggestions as well?

A: One or two yes.

Q: But definitely your wife's were important there?

A: She always has very instinctive reactions, feminine reactions to certain things, which I find very useful, which I almost always incorporate.

Q: Can you give me an example?

A: Well in this case I had made Dr Stockman an atheist. She said 'Don't make him an atheist, make him an agnostic.' Otherwise people would immediately reject that character and feel that it was because he was an atheist he was doing all these things, campaigning against the temple etc. As an agnostic he would still have a chance to carry conviction with the people.

Q: Which are you?

A: I was an atheist but I'm beginning to be more and more agnostic, as I grow older. When I speak to my doctors I find they are great believers.

Q: So would you say the play was easier to adapt than, say, *Days and Nights* or *Charulata*?

A: It was easier·to start with, because I already had a structure which was a fairly strong one. That's why the film is in five acts, instead of my usual ten sequences – because the structure of the play was so tight. The difficulty came in transplanting it to Bengal. But it became easy the moment I thought of the temple. That helped enormously and gave it a completely new aspect. I felt that I had it.

Q: How did that idea come to you?

A: Just now I can't remember.

Q: You were sitting in your chair and there it was?

A: There it was. You see the Birla Temple which is coming up in Ballygunj Circular Road [not far from Ray's flat] has often been on my mind (*laughs*). I'm waiting for it to open and to see what happens.

Q: Ibsen wrote the play with certain cases of corruption in mind. Did you have any actual examples?

A: Did you read in the papers yesterday about contaminated water? It's exactly the same situation. It's happening in Calcutta. And about three weeks ago there was an item in a magazine here which said that the water at Tirupati, a very famous south Indian temple, is contaminated and that lots of pilgrims have fallen ill. So I was bucked up by such information. This gives the film a more solid basis in truth.

Q: This came after you wrote the screenplay?

A: Yes, it did.

Q: Do you expect the film to be topical?

A: Yes, definitely. I think it's going to be very very topical, full of contemporary allusions.

Q: What is it that makes it so topical?

A: Well for instance the newspaper. The behaviour of the editor is very typical of today, of a Leftist newspaper, suddenly withdrawing its support . . . And the notion that *charanamrita* – holy water – is perfectly pure. I've talked to many people about this. Lots of people believe it: that the *tulsipata* in holy water is something with a mysterious property, which can't be proved by scientific means.

Q: What sort of people believe that?

A: Well, people who go to the temple. I have spoken to all sorts of people who come to my house and they say that there is something about *tulsipata* that purifies water.

Q: Professional people?

A: Doctors generally in my experience believe in God, for instance. They pray. My own doctor, my house-physician, says that if you inspect the human body – the incredible complexity of it – you have to believe in a superior force. It can't just happen by accident. He and his family have regular puja in their house. And my cardiologist – my God! – he's so devout! Incredibly devout. At the nursing home where I was put after my heart attack, downstairs – in what you might call the lobby – there's a section where there's an image of a god and incense and everything. My cardiologist would stand there for *five minutes* praying before going into his other duties: to inspect the patients.

Q: Do your doctors drink *charanamrita*?

A: My house physician doesn't drink *charanamrita*; but he puts it in his hair. The way *charanamrita* comes is floating down a sort of chute . . . Looking at it, you wouldn't want to drink it at all.

Q: I know.

A: Yes – you've been to Benares? (*laughs*) Incredible!

Q: So is your physician having his cake and eating it – so to speak? Would he admit that?

A: He would admit that. He told me 'I never drink it.' After all, being a doctor he knows all about contamination. But he believes in it to the extent of putting it in his hair.

Q: I would say that doctors as a community in Britain are rather a sceptical bunch.

A: Like Dr Stockman?

Q: Yes.

A: He also is an archetype. You have doctors like that. But you have the other kind as well – you have both kinds.

Q: Do you think Stockman resembles any actual Bengali? Ibsen had someone in mind, didn't he?

A: I can't think of any offhand but of course that type of character is very rare these days. They used to be more common in the early part of the century or in the nineteenth century.

Q: Did you have the great Brahmo reformers in mind at all? Your great-grandfather?

A: They were at the back of my mind, yes – definitely.

Q: I feel there is something of Nikhil and Sandip in Stockman and his brother. Do you?

A: Yes.

Q: Do you think this film will resemble any of your other films?

A: It'll be quite different. Quite different from anything I've done before.

Q: No links with *The Middle Man*?

A: Superficial links – about corruption and all that.

Q: Only that?

A: Only that. Structurally, formally, it will be quite quite different. I have a really strong central character with a strong idealistic basis and strong desire to do good which I have not had in any of my other films to that extent.

Q: And a man too.

A: And a man, yes. This time it's a man. It's a man's film actually, as against *Charulata*, *Ghare Baire* and others.

Q: Would I be right in saying you've put some of *The Alien* into this film?

A: *The Alien*? In what way?

Q: The journalist, the temple, the nexus between religion and money, the Bajoria character . . .

A: Probably the temple element . . . and Bajoria – sort of as a version of Bhargava. It hadn't occurred to me at all . . . But now you mention it I can see the point.

Q: Are you likely to run into any censorship problems?

A: I don't anticipate any. Which aspect do you mean?

Q: I mean the fundamentalist one. I mean like the reaction to *The Goddess*—

A: You mean if they say you've got an agnostic as a hero – that sort of thing – that is something which is objectionable. But I have got away with a lot . . .

Q: But what about that line 'Do you call yourself a Hindu?'

A: Yes yes. That is the only point where the censors might sit up and take notice.

Q: How do you feel about the banning of the import into India of Salman Rushdie's book *The Satanic Verses*?

A: I haven't read it so I don't know.

Q: Could you ever support the banning of a book?

A: I don't like banning books, no, I'm against that as a rule. I think an adult should have his own choice – to read whatever he wants to read.

Q: You once told me that you regard yourself as a 'complete democrat' – at least when you're shooting. What do you think of Dr Stockman's view of democracy?

A: A little odd. I think it doesn't apply today. Arthur Miller also has some qualms about that.

Q: I mean Stockman says 'It's the fools that form the overwhelming majority', doesn't he?

A: Yes that's what he says. There's a grain of truth in that actually, I think.

Q: Only a grain?

A: Maybe a little more than a grain (*laughs*). Democracy here is very much like that.

Q: What kind of democracy do you believe in? Do you think one man one vote is the only way?

A: By and large I think I'm an individualist . . . I feel I'm an individualist.

Q: Does that mean that you don't have views on these things?

A: I do have views on these things. I think democracy is an admirable thing in principle but on occasions the situation in *An Enemy of the People* does occur in actual life. And that justifies Stockman's reaction to it.

Q: Was Nehru an individualist in your sense?

A: I think so. I have a suspicion he was. He was a lonely figure towards the end. He was a very very lonely figure. He had few friends and he was isolated and felt cut off – particularly during the China situation.

Q: Finally – the future?

A: No future, no plans, nothing at all planned. I have no idea what I'm going to do after this. Babu will be making his next film – a feature film – in summer.° And the winter after that – winter 1989 – I hope to be doing something again.

Q: But do you expect that you will go on?

A: Well it depends a little on my experience on this film. If I feel I'm fit and strong after I've finished the film . . . The doctors believe that as soon as I start working again I feel better.

Q: They accept that, because you yourself feel that?

A: Yes, I do feel that.

Q: Are you affected at all by Bergman's decision to 'retire'?

A: I don't accept his retirement – because he's been making films for television, which are shown theatrically. So what kind of retirement is that? I will keep on working as long as I am fit enough to work.

°In early 1989, while completing the post-production of *An Enemy of the People*, Ray wrote a script and ten songs for a third adventure of Goopy and Bagha – this time to be directed by his son.

Q: What about *Sakha Prasakha*?

A: *Sakha Prasakha* unfortunately calls for quite a bit of location work and that will set a problem – because it'll have to be a joint venture then with my son. But I would prefer still to work on my own – alone – and find that kind of story.

Q: I was wondering whether you might do what Tagore did and take up a new medium at about the age of seventy?

A: Well I haven't thought of that. I can't think of a new medium after films. Film has been so satisfactory for me.

Q: You can't see yourself becoming a composer?

A: No, my compositions are to serve the purpose of a film. Definitely not.

Q: And you wouldn't go back to painting?

A: No.

Q: Now what about an autobiography?

A: (*laughs*) Well, if I can't make a film – that is a possibility. Purely about the films that I have made and the various kinds of experiences I've had making them: the various kinds of people that I've met, the mistakes that I made, what I learnt through the process of making a film. That kind of book I would very much like to write, because there aren't very many books like that. Renoir said he would write one like that – but he never did. I'm completely self-taught – right from the beginning – so there is a special situation here. And I might put that in a book if I can't make a film. But I would sooner make a film – any day – rather than write.

APPENDIX A

Glossary

Only words mentioned in the book appear in this glossary. Most are taken from Bengali, but some are from other Indian languages.

adda   Leisurely gossip in a group ranging over every conceivable subject; the group itself.

Bharata Natyam   The oldest existing style of dancing in India, which can be traced back to the fifth century AD, performed solo and only by women. Its system of expression is based on the Natyashastra of the sage Bharata. Until the 1920s and 30s it was performed only inside the temples of south India.

Baba/*baba*   e.g. Birinchi Baba. An honorific used by holy men; a holy man.

Babu/*babu*   e.g. Satyajit Babu. An honorific that implies respectful distance from the person addressed – a rough equivalent of 'Mr'. On its own the word means, depending on the context, someone from the leisured class or someone with pretensions to it.

Brahmin   The highest of the traditional divisions of Indian society, considered to be descendants of Brahma, the creator of the universe. All Hindu priests are Brahmins.

chamar   A low caste throughout India whose occupation is tanning skins.

chowkidar   A watchman or caretaker of a building, village or community (*darwan* in Bengali).

dada   Elder brother, but also sometimes used to address strangers.

dadu   e.g. Dhondadu. Grandfather.

Devi   e.g. Chunibala Devi. An honorific used to address a married woman.

dhoti   About six metres of cloth wrapped around the lower half of the body in various styles by males in north India. Gandhi wore a dhoti. Bengalis pleat and wear their dhotis in ways particular to Bengal.

Diwali   The name of the festival of lights held all over India during November, akin to Christmas. An occasion for exchanging presents, visiting friends, and family reunions.

Durga Puja   The most important festival in the Bengali year, lasting five days during October, celebrating Durga's slaying of the buffalo demon Mahisa. Images of Durga are created all over Calcutta and immersed with tremendous éclat in the Ganges on the last day of the festival. During those few days Calcutta is transformed.

Dusserah   The name given to *Diwali* in Benares and other parts of north India.

jatra   Theatre performances that tour the rural areas of Bengal, traditionally based on the Indian epics and folk-tales, now highly commercialised.

kajal   Kohl. Hindu brides are given receptacles for *kajal* made of gold or silver and shaped like pointed leaves; they wear them in their hair until their *phulsajya* (q.v.).

kaka/Kaka   e.g. Chotokaka. Paternal uncle.

kala-azar   A tropical infectious disease caused by a virus in the liver, spleen etc., characterised by fever and weight loss.

Kalidasa   Sanskrit poet and dramatist of the fifth century AD, author of *Sakuntala* and *Meghdut* (*The Cloud Messenger*), some of the earliest works of Indian literature to be translated into English.

Kathak   A north Indian style of dancing, characterised by fast footwork and interplay of rhythms, performed by both men and women. Unlike *Bharata Natyam*, *Kathak* was influenced by both Hindu and Mughal traditions.

Kathakali   A south Indian style of dancing performed only by men, elaborately made-up and costumed. It combines dance and drama and enacts stories from the Indian epics.

Kayastha   A writer caste from which came clerks, government officials and scholars.

khichuri   Kedgeree (*khichry*).

Ksatriya   The second of the traditional divisions of Hindu society, the warriors and rulers.

kurta   A long shirt slipped over the head and buttoned at the front, worn in the cooler regions of north India like Kashmir.

luchi   A thin circular kind of bread prepared from refined flour and water and fried in ghee; this makes it blow up like a balloon. It is a regular part of marriage feasts and festivals.

nawabi   Pertaining to the nawabs, feudal rulers of north India who derived their authority from the Mughal power. The Nawab of Oudh was eventually created King of Oudh by the East India Company.

pan   A mildly addictive preparation of areca-nut, catechu, lime paste, and other condiments, wrapped in a leaf of the betel tree, chewed all over India, especially as a digestive after meals. The combination of ingredients produces a blood-red juice.

panjabi   A looser version of the *kurta* (q.v.), worn in the hotter regions of north India, possibly imported into Bengal from the Punjab.

phulsajya   Literally 'bed of flowers', the third night after the ritual of marriage in a Hindu wedding, when the bridegroom and bride are alone together for the first time, traditionally in a room decorated throughout with flowers.

prasad   Offerings to the Hindu gods, usually in the form of sweets.

Rajputs   The various Hindu clans living in the desert regions of western India known as Rajputana (now Rajasthan), famous for their toughness, feuding and chivalry. Many of India's princes were Rajputs.

rakhi   The thread with which Krishna bound his beloved Radha and which binds the wrists of the bridegroom and bride at the moment of union in a Hindu wedding. It is symbolic of friendship.

saluk   A water-lily with a pinkish-purple flower common in West Bengal (known as *sapla* in East Bengal/Bangladesh).

sandesh   Bengali sweets made of milk solids and sugar, often perfumed.

130 *Bala*: Balasaraswati and daughter with Ray (*Sandip Ray*)

131 *Rabindranath Tagore*: young Rabindranath in Jorasanko (*Teknica*)

132 *Rabindranath Tagore*: young Rabindranath (*Teknica*)

133   *The Inner Eye*: Binode Bihari Mukherjee, watched by Ray (*Nemai Ghosh*)

134 *The Inner Eye*: drawing
and painting by Binode
Bihari Mukherjee

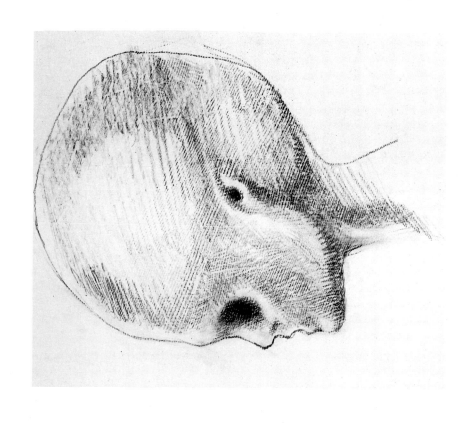

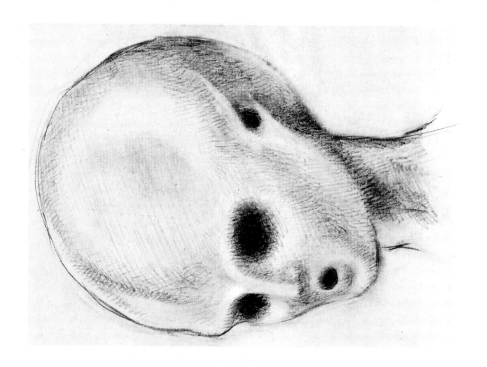

135 *The Alien:* drawings by Ray

136   Nandalal Bose by Ray

137   Rabindranath Tagore by Ray

138 D.W. Griffith by Ray

139 Sergei Eisenstein by Ray

140 Akira Kurosawa by Ray

141 Pablo Picasso by Ray

142 J.B.R. Nicholson, Manager of
D.J. Keymer in Calcutta, by Ray
(dated 6 December 1955)

143 *An Enemy of the People*: Maya, Ranen, Dr Asok Gupta, Indrani, Haridas (*Nemai Ghosh*)

144 *An Enemy of the People*: Nisith (*Nemai Ghosh*)

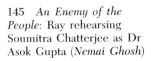

145 *An Enemy of the People*: Ray rehearsing Soumitra Chatterjee as Dr Asok Gupta (*Nemai Ghosh*)

146 *An Enemy of the People*: Ray reads the script to Soumitra Chatterjee, Bijoya Ray and others (*Nemai Ghosh*)

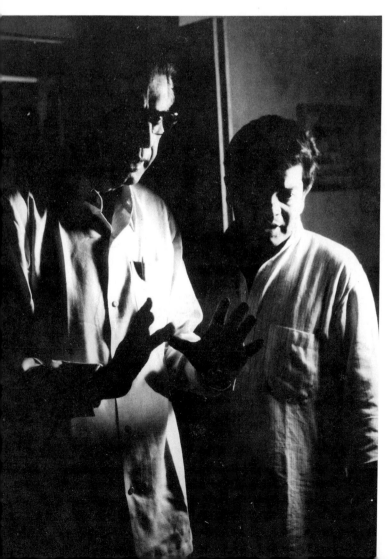

147 *An Enemy of the People*: Ray and son Sandip (*Nemai Ghosh*)

They are ubiquitous as gifts when visiting someone and the commonest way of celebrating the arrival of good news.

Santhals   A tribe scattered all over Bengal, Bihar and Orissa, renowned for the beauty and independence of their women, and the eroticism of their love songs and poetry.

sindur Vermilion powder worn in the parting of the hair by Hindu wives. *Sindur* mixed with glue, known as *kumkum*, is dabbed on the forehead as a beauty spot or religious marking by both married and unmarried women.

Sudra   The lowest of the traditional divisions of Hindu society, those who live by the sweat of their brows.

swadeshi Literally 'of our country', an adjective applied to anything from soap to political movements to denote patriotic intent. The opposite is *bideshi*, i.e. foreign.

Thakrun   e.g. Indir Thakrun. An honorific used to address much older women, such as grand-aunts (but not grandparents).

Vaisya   The third of the traditional divisions of Hindu society, the merchants.

zamindar   A landlord, originally created by the distribution of land revenue rights by the Mughals; later given ownership of land by the British under the terms of the Permanent Settlement of 1793.

MUSICAL TERMS

alap The introductory phase of a raga (q.v.), with no measured rhythm and very slow tempo. It expresses and then unfolds the characteristics of a raga (the phrases, important notes and tone range of its melody).

bhajan A semi-classical Hindu devotional song found all over India and often sung in groups accompanied by instruments like the harmonium.

dotara A two-stringed musical instrument with a gourd sound-box, plucked with a fingernail or plectrum.

ektara A one-stringed version of the *dotara* (q.v.).

esraj A four-stringed instrument with sympathetic strings, played with a bow like the *sarangi* (q.v.), which its lower portion resembles; its upper portion is like a diminutive sitar (q.v.). It produces a softer sound than the *sarangi* and often accompanies *bhajans* (q.v.) and Tagore songs.

ganjira A tambourine with a deeper shell and fewer jingles than its western counterpart, and occasional small clusters of small ankle bells.

ghattom One of India's most ancient time-keeping instruments. It consists of a series of mud-pots with somewhat narrow openings which the player holds against his stomach and strikes in various places with the palm of his hand, fingers and nails, varying the timbre by holding the pot away from his stomach.

kheyal Literally, 'imagination'. It is said to have been the response of Amir Khusru to the rigidity of classical music in the twelfth century. Since then *kheyal* has constantly developed in north India, bringing in elaborate ornaments, particularly ascending and descending vocalisations, trills and grace notes and repeated groups of notes or melodic figures. *Kheyal* is charming and light, often used for love songs. It has been compared to bel canto.

mirh One of the kinds of embellishment characteristic of Indian classical music, in which the player slides from one note to another, connecting the sounds using *srutis* (q.v.).

mridangam The classical drum of south India, as the *tabla* (q.v.) is of the north. It consists of two truncated cones of wood joined together like two flower-pots at their rims, with complex skins stretched across each cone base. The *mridangam* is played with both hands, wrists, fingertips and the base of the thumbs.

mursring A universal folk-instrument. It consists of a thin strip of steel which the player holds between his teeth, plucking the protruding end with his finger. It produces a twangy tone.

pakhwaj A drum used in north India which descends from the *mridangam* (q.v.).

raga (ragini) 'A raga, the sages say, is a particular arrangement of sounds in which notes and melodic movements appear like ornaments to enchant the mind.' Thousands of such combinations exist, but only a few hundred are in regular use. The word derives from the Sanskrit for 'colour'.

ragmala Literally, 'garland of ragas'. The player shifts skilfully from raga to raga or between variants of the same raga from different parts of India, creating a powerful overall impact.

sarangi A three-stringed instrument with as many as eighteen sympathetic strings, played with a bow. No pressure is applied to the strings as such; the stopping is produced by sliding the fingernails against the sides of a string while bowing. The *sarangi* can consequently be both subtle and extremely piercing and very easily lends itself to imitation of the human voice (especially the female voice).

sarinda The rustic predecessor of the *esraj* (q.v.), without frets.

sarod A four-stringed instrument with twelve sympathetic strings, played with a triangular flat wooden or horn piece. Instead of frets the upper portion is covered with a metallic plate. It produces powerful vibrant tones with a high quality of resonance and is one of the most wonderful of all Indian instruments.

shehnai The classical wind instrument of north India. The embouchure consists of double pieces of reed mounted like that of an oboe in a short metal staple fixed into a long cylinder that elongates into a bell. Air blown through these reeds together gives the *shehnai* its incisive sound. It is a favourite instrument in temples and especially in weddings.

sitar The best-known Indian stringed instrument. Originally three-stringed, it became six-stringed in the late eighteenth century. Today it has seven strings and up to twenty sympathetic strings. It also has a second gourd soundbox, like the *vina* (q.v.). A steel plectrum is used to play it.

sruti Microtone. Indian musical theory considers that the ear can perceive sixty-six distinct meaningful intervals within an octave. About twenty-two of those *srutis* are used in practice.

tabla The best-known Indian percussion instrument. Its historical relationship to the *mridangam* (q.v.) and the *pakhwaj* (q.v.) is disputed, but the same playing principles apply to all three. It is the construction that differs: instead of the two skins being part of the same instrument, as in the *mridangam* or *pakhwaj*, they are set up on two separate small drums.

tanpura A four-stringed instrument with sympathetic strings, used as a drone accompaniment for the sitar and other instruments. The player simply plays the same scale over and over again.

tarshehnai An *esraj* (q.v.) equipped with an amplifier.

thumri A style of singing that developed out of *kheyal* (q.v.) at Lucknow and Benares. Its name derives from 'thumuk', the sound of a graceful stamp of the foot. It has always been associated with dance and with arousing the erotic sensation, whereas *kheyal*'s range is much wider. *Thumri* is purely romantic music. One authority has compared it to Mughal miniature paintings, and *kheyal* to the frescoes at Ajanta.

vina The oldest Indian stringed instrument, mentioned in the Indian epics. It has four strings for playing and three for rhythm, and twenty-four movable frets; it also has a second gourd sound-box. In south India it is used both for accompaniment and in its own right. Its sound is not as melodious as the north Indian *vina*, which has a mellow and sweet tone capable of producing a vigorous mood and atmosphere.

APPENDIX B

Filmography

1. Films Directed by Satyajit Ray

The films are listed by date of release in Bengal, or date of completion
if not released. Some minor members of a cast have been omitted.

Note: SR refers to Satyajit Ray.

1955   PATHER PANCHALI (SONG OF THE LITTLE ROAD)

Producer: Government of West Bengal. Screenplay: SR, from
the novel *Pather Panchali* by Bibhutibhusan Banerjee. Photography: Subrata Mitra. Editor: Dulal Dutta. Art director: Bansi
Chandragupta. Music: Ravi Shankar. Sound: Bhupen Ghosh.
115 mins.

Cast: Kanu Banerjee (*Harihar*), Karuna Banerjee (*Sarbajaya*),
Subir Banerjee (*Apu*), Uma Das Gupta (*Durga*), Chunibala Devi
(*Indir Thakrun*), Runki Banerjee (*Child Durga*), Reba Devi
(*Seja Thakrun*), Aparna Devi (*Nilmoni's wife*), Tulsi Chakravarti
(*Prasanna, School-teacher*), Binoy Mukherjee (*Baidyanath Majum-
dar*), Haren Banerjee (*Chinibash, Sweet-seller*), Harimohan Nag
(*Doctor*), Haridhan Nag (*Chakravarti*), Nibhanoni Devi (*Dasi*),
Ksirodh Roy (*Priest*), Roma Ganguli (*Roma*).

1956   APARAJITO (THE UNVANQUISHED)

Producer: Epic Films (SR). Screenplay: SR, from the novel
Aparajita by Bibhutibhusan Banerjee. Photography: Subrata
Mitra. Editor: Dulal Dutta. Art director: Bansi Chandragupta.
Music: Ravi Shankar. Sound: Durgadas Mitra. 113 mins.

Cast: Kanu Banerjee (*Harihar*), Karuna Banerjee (*Sarbajaya*),
Pinaki Sen Gupta (*Boy Apu*), Smaran Ghosal (*Adolescent Apu*),
Santi Gupta (*Lahiri's wife*), Ramani Sen Gupta (*Bhabataran*),
Ranibala (*Teli*), Sudipta Roy (*Nirupama*), Ajay Mitra (*Anil*),
Charuprakash Ghosh (*Nanda*), Subodh Ganguli (*Headmaster*),
Moni Srimani (*Inspector*), Hemanta Chatterjee (*Professor*), Kali
Banerjee (*Kathak*), Kalicharan Roy (*Akhil, press proprietor*),
Kamala Adhikari (*Moksada*), Lalchand Banerjee (*Lahiri*), K. S.
Pandey (*Pandey*), Meenaksi Devi (*Pandey's wife*), Anil Mukherjee
(*Abinash*), Harendrakumar Chakravarti (*Doctor*), Bhaganu Palwan
(*Palwan*).

1958   PARASH PATHAR (THE PHILOSOPHER'S STONE)

Producer: Promod Lahiri. Screenplay: SR, from the short story 'Parash Pathar' by Parasuram. Photography: Subrata Mitra. Editor: Dulal Dutta. Art director: Bansi Chandragupta. Music: Ravi Shankar. Sound: Durgadas Mitra. 111 mins.

Cast: Tulsi Chakravarti (*Paresh Chandra Dutta*), Ranibala (His wife), Kali Banerjee (*Priyatosh Henry Biswas*), Gangapada Bose (*Kachalu*), Haridhan (*Inspector Chatterjee*), Jahar Roy (*Bhajahari*), Bireswar Sen (*Police officer*), Moni Srimani (*Dr Nandi*), Chhabi Biswas, Jahar Ganguli, Pahari Sanyal, Kamal Mitra, Nitish Mukherjee, Subodh Ganguli, Tulsi Lahiri, Amar Mullick (*Male guests at cocktail party*), Chandrabati Devi, Renuka Roy, Bharati Devi (*Female guests at cocktail party*).

1958   JALSAGHAR (THE MUSIC ROOM)

Producer: Satyajit Ray Productions. Screenplay: SR, from the short story '*Jalsaghar*' by Tarasankar Banerjee. Photography: Subrata Mitra. Editor: Dulal Dutta. Art director: Bansi Chandragupta. Music: Vilayat Khan. Music and dance performed by Begum Akhtar, Roshan Kumari, Waheed Khan, Bismillah Khan and company (on screen), and Daksinamohan Thakur, Asish Kumar, Robin Majumdar and Imrat Khan (off screen). Sound: Durgadas Mitra. 100 mins.

Cast: Chhabi Biswas (*Biswambhar Roy*), Padma Devi (*Mahamaya, his wife*), Pinaki Sen Gupta (*Bireswar, his son*), Gangapada Bose (*Mahim Ganguli*), Tulsi Lahiri (*Taraprasanna, bearer*), Kali Sarkar (*Ananta, cook*), Waheed Khan (*Ustad Ujir Khan*), Roshan Kumari (*Krishna Bai*).

1959   APUR SANSAR (THE WORLD OF APU)

Producer: Satyajit Ray Productions. Screenplay: SR, from the novel *Aparajita* by Bibhutibhusan Banerjee. Photography: Subrata Mitra. Editor: Dulal Dutta. Art director: Bansi Chandragupta. Music: Ravi Shankar. Sound: Durgadas Mitra. 106 mins.

Cast: Soumitra Chatterjee (*Apu*), Sarmila Tagore (*Aparna*), Alok Chakravarti (*Kajal*), Swapan Mukherjee (*Pulu*), Dhiresh Majumdar (*Sasinarayan*), Sefalika Devi (*Sasinarayan's wife*), Dhiren Ghosh (*Landlord*).

1960   DEVI (THE GODDESS)

Producer: Satyajit Ray Productions. Screenplay: SR, from the short story 'Devi' by Prabhat Kumar Mukherjee, on a theme by Rabindranath Tagore. Photography: Subrata Mitra. Editor: Dulal Dutta. Art director: Bansi Chandragupta. Music: Ali Akbar Khan. Sound: Durgadas Mitra. 93 mins.

Cast: Chhabi Biswas (*Kalikinkar Roy*), Soumitra Chatterjee (*Umaprasad, younger son*), Sarmila Tagore (*Doyamoyee*), Purnendu Mukherjee (*Taraprasad, elder son*), Karuna Banerjee (*Harasundari, his wife*), Arpan Chowdhury (*Khoka, child*), Anil Chatterjee (*Bhudeb*), Kali Sarkar (*Professor Sarkar*), Mohammed Israil (*Nibaran*), Khagesh Chakravarti (*Kaviraj*), Nagendranath Kabyabyakarantirtha (*Priest*), Santa Devi (*Sarala*).

1961   TEEN KANYA (THREE DAUGHTERS)

Producer: Satyajit Ray Productions. Screenplay: SR, from three stories by Rabindranath Tagore. Photography: Soumendu Roy. Editor: Dulal Dutta. Art director: Bansi Chandragupta. Music: SR. Sound: Durgadas Mitra. *The Postmaster*, 56 mins. *Monihara*, 61 mins. *Samapti*, 56 mins.

Cast: *The Postmaster*. Anil Chatterjee (*Nandalal*), Chandana Banerjee (*Ratan*), Nripati Chatterjee (*Bisay*), Khagen Pathak (*Khagen*), Gopal Roy (*Bilash*). *Monihara* (*The Lost Jewels*). Kali Banerjee (*Phanibhusan Saha*), Kanika Majumdar (*Manimalika*), Kumar Roy (*Madhusudhan*), Gobinda Chakravarti (*Schoolmaster and narrator*). *Samapti* (*The Conclusion*). Soumitra Chatterjee (*Amulya*), Aparna Das Gupta (*Mrinmoyee*), Sita Mukherjee (*Jogmaya*), Gita Dey (*Nistarini*), Santosh Dutta (*Kisori*), Mihir Chakravarti (*Rakhal*), Devi Neogy (*Haripada*).

1961   RABINDRANATH TAGORE

Producer: Films Division, Government of India. Script and commentary: SR. Photography: Soumendu Roy. Editor: Dulal Dutta. Art director: Bansi Chandragupta. Music: Jyotirindra Moitra. Songs and dances performed by Asesh Banerjee (*esraj*) and Gitabitan (both offscreen). 54 mins.

Cast: Raya Chatterjee, Sovanlal Ganguli, Smaran Ghosal, Purnendu Mukherjee, Kallol Bose, Subir Bose, Phani Nan, Norman Ellis.

1962   KANCHENJUNGHA

Producer: N.C.A. Productions. Original screenplay: SR. Photography: Subrata Mitra. Editor: Dulal Dutta. Art director: Bansi

Chandragupta. Music: SR. Sound: Durgadas Mitra. 102 mins.

Cast: Chhabi Biswas (*Indranath Roy*), Anil Chatterjee (*Anil*), Karuna Banerjee (*Labanya*), Anubha Gupta (*Anima*), Subrata Sen (*Sankar*), Sibani Singh (*Tuklu*), Alaknanda Roy (*Manisa*), Arun Mukherjee (*Asok*), N. Viswanathan (*Mr Banerjee*), Pahari Sanyal (*Jagadish*), Nilima Chatterjee, Vidya Sinha (*Girlfriends of Anil*).

1962   ABHIJAN (THE EXPEDITION)

Producer: Abhijatrik. Screenplay: SR, from the novel *Abhijan* by Tarasankar Banerjee. Photography: Soumendu Roy. Editor: Dulal Dutta. Art director: Bansi Chandragupta. Music: SR. Sound: Durgadas Mitra, Nripen Paul, Sujit Sarkar. 150 mins.

Cast: Soumitra Chatterjee (*Narsingh*), Waheeda Rehman (*Gulabi*), Ruma Guha Thakurta (*Neeli*), Ganesh Mukherjee (*Joseph*), Charuprakash Ghosh (*Sukhanram*), Rabi Ghosh (*Rama*), Arun Roy (*Naskar*), Sekhar Chatterjee (*Rameswar*), Ajit Banerjee (*Banerjee*), Reba Devi (*Joseph's mother*), Abani Mukherjee (*Lawyer*).

1963   MAHANAGAR (THE BIG CITY)

Producer: R.D.B. and Co. (R. D. Bansal). Screenplay: SR, from the short story 'Abataranika' by Narendranath Mitra. Photography: Subrata Mitra. Editor: Dulal Dutta. Art director: Bansi Chandragupta. Music: SR. Sound: Debesh Ghosh, Atul Chatterjee, Sujit Sarkar. 131 mins.

Cast: Anil Chatterjee (*Subrata Mazumdar*), Madhabi Mukherjee (*Arati Mazumdar*), Jaya Bhaduri (*Bani*), Haren Chatterjee (*Priyagopal, Subrata's father*), Sefalika Devi (*Sarojini, Subrata's mother*), Prasenjit Sarkar (*Pintu*), Haradhan Banerjee (*Himangsu Mukherjee*), Vicky Redwood (*Edith*).

1964   CHARULATA (THE LONELY WIFE)

Producer: R.D.B. and Co. (R. D. Bansal). Screenplay: SR, from the novella *Nastanirh* by Rabindranath Tagore. Photography: Subrata Mitra. Editor: Dulal Dutta. Art director: Bansi Chandragupta. Music: SR. Sound: Nripen Paul, Atul Chatterjee, Sujit Sarkar. 117 mins.

Cast: Soumitra Chatterjee (*Amal*), Madhabi Mukherjee (*Charu*), Sailen Mukherjee (*Bhupati*), Syamal Ghosal (*Umapada*), Gitali Roy (*Mandakini*), Bholanath Koyal (*Braja*), Suku Mukherjee

(*Nisikanta*), Dilip Bose (*Sasanka*), Subrata Sen Sharma (*Motilal*), Joydeb (*Nilatpal Dey*), Bankim Ghosh (*Jagannath*).

1964   TWO

Producer: Esso World Theater. Original screenplay: SR. Photography: Soumendu Roy. Editor: Dulal Dutta. Art director: Bansi Chandragupta. Music: SR. Sound: Sujit Sarkar. 15 mins.
    Cast: Ravi Kiran.

1965   KAPURUSH-O-MAHAPURUSH (THE COWARD AND THE HOLY MAN)

Producer: R.D.B. and Co. (R. D. Bansal). Screenplays: SR, from the short story '*Janaiko Kapuruser Kahini*' by Premendra Mitra and '*Birinchi Baba*' by Parasuram. Photography: Soumendu Roy. Editor: Dulal Dutta. Art director: Bansi Chandragupta. Music: SR. Sound: Nripen Paul, Atul Chatterjee, Sujit Sarkar. *Kapurush*, 74 mins. *Mahapurush*, 65 mins.
    Cast: *Kapurush*. Soumitra Chatterjee (*Amitava Roy*), Madhabi Mukherjee (*Karuna Gupta*), Haradhan Banerjee (*Bimal Gupta*). *Mahapurush*. Charuprakash Ghosh (*Birinchi Baba*), Rabi Ghosh (*His assistant*), Prasad Mukherjee (*Gurupada Mitter*), Gitali Roy (*Buchki*), Satindra Bhattacharya (*Satya*), Somen Bose (*Nibaran*), Santosh Dutta (*Professor Nani*), Renuka Roy (*Nani's wife*).

1966   NAYAK (THE HERO)

Producer: R.D.B. and Co. (R. D. Bansal). Original screenplay: SR. Photography: Subrata Mitra. Editor: Dulal Dutta. Art director: Bansi Chandragupta. Music: SR. Sound: Nripen Paul, Atul Chatterjee, Sujit Sarkar. 120 mins.
    Cast: Uttam Kumar (*Arindam Mukherjee*), Sarmila Tagore (*Aditi Sen Gupta*), Bireswar Sen (*Mukunda Lahiri*), Somen Bose (*Sankar*), Nirmal Ghosh (*Jyoti*), Premangsu Bose (*Biresh*), Sumita Sanyal (*Promila*), Ranjit Sen (*Mr Bose*), Bharati Devi (*Manorama, his wife*), Lali Chowdhury (*Bulbul, his daughter*), Kamu Mukherjee (*Pritish Sarkar*), Susmita Mukherjee (*Molly, his wife*), Subrata Sen Sharma (*Ajoy*), Jamuna Sinha (*Sefalika, his wife*), Hiralal (*Kamal Misra*), Jogesh Chatterjee (*Aghore, elderly journalist*), Satya Banerjee (*Swamiji*), Gopal Dey (*Conductor*).

1967   CHIRIAKHANA (THE ZOO)

Producer: Star Productions (Harendranath Bhattacharya). Screen-

play: SR, from the novel *Chiriakhana* by Saradindu Banerjee.
Photography: Soumendu Roy. Editor: Dulal Dutta. Art director:
Bansi Chandragupta. Music: SR. Sound: Nripen Paul, Atul
Chatterjee, Sujit Sarkar. 125 mins. approx.

Cast: Uttam Kumar (*Byomkesh Baksi*), Sailen Mukherjee
(*Ajit*), Susil Majumdar (*Nisanath Sen*), Kanika Majumdar
(*Damyanti, his wife*), Subhendu Chatterjee (*Bijoy*), Syamal
Ghosal (*Dr Bhujangadhar Das*), Prasad Mukherjee (*Nepal
Gupta*), Subira Roy (*Mukul, his daughter*), Nripati Chatterjee
(*Muskil Mia*), Subrata Chatterjee (*Nazarbibi, his wife*), Gitali
Roy (*Banalakshmi*), Kalipada Chakravarti (*Rasiklal*), Chinmoy
Roy (*Panugopal*), Ramen Mullick (*Jahar Ganguli*), Brajadas
(*Bankim Ghosh*), Nilatpal Dey (*Inspector*).

1968   GOOPY GYNE BAGHA BYNE (THE ADVENTURES OF GOOPY AND
        BAGHA)

Producer: Purnima Pictures (Nepal Dutta, Asim Dutta). Screen-
play: SR, from the story by Upendrakisore Ray. Photography:
Soumendu Roy. Editor: Dulal Dutta. Art director: Bansi
Chandragupta. Music: SR. Goopy's songs sung by Anup
Kumar Ghosal. Dance director: Sambhunath Bhattacharya.
Sound: Nripen Paul, Atul Chatterjee, Sujit Sarkar. 132 mins.

Cast: Tapen Chatterjee (*Goopy*), Rabi Ghosh (*Bagha*), Santosh
Dutta (*King of Shundi/King of Halla*), Jahar Roy (*Prime Min-
ister of Halla*), Santi Chatterjee (*Commander-in-chief of Halla*),
Harindranath Chatterjee (*Barfi, magician*), Chinmoy Roy (*Spy of
Halla*), Durgadas Banerjee (*King of Amloki*), Gobinda Chakravarti
(*Goopy's father*), Prasad Mukherjee (*King of Ghosts*), Haridhan
Mukherjee, Abani Chatterjee, Khagen Pathak, Binoy Bose, Prasad
Mukherjee (*Village elders*), Joykrishna Sanyal, Tarun Mitra, Ratan
Banerjee, Kartik Chatterjee (*Singers at the court of Shundi*), Gopal
Dey (*Executioner*), Ajoy Banerjee, Sailen Ganguli, Moni Srimani,
Binoy Bose, Kartik Chatterjee (*Visitors to Halla*).

1969   ARANYER DIN RATRI (DAYS AND NIGHTS IN THE FOREST)

Producer: Priya Films (Nepal Dutta, Asim Dutta). Screenplay:
SR, from the novel *Aranyer Din Ratri* by Sunil Ganguli. Photography: Soumendu Roy, Purnendu Bose. Editor: Dulal Dutta.
Art director: Bansi Chandragupta. Music: SR. Sound: Sujit Sarkar.
115 mins.

Cast: Soumitra Chatterjee (*Asim*), Subhendu Chatterjee
(*Sanjoy*), Samit Bhanja (*Harinath*), Rabi Ghosh (*Sekhar*), Pahari
Sanyal (*Sadasiv Tripathi*), Sarmila Tagore (*Aparna*), Kaveri Bose
(*Jaya*), Simi Garewal (*Duli*), Aparna Sen (*Atasi*).

1970   PRATIDWANDI (THE ADVERSARY)

Producer: Priya Films (Nepal Dutta, Asim Dutta). Screenplay:
SR, from the novel *Pratidwandi* by Sunil Ganguli. Photography:
Soumendu Roy, Purnendu Bose. Editor: Dulal Dutta. Art direc-
tor: Bansi Chandragupta. Music: SR. Sound: J.D. Irani, Durgadas
Mitra. 110 mins.

Cast: Dhritiman Chatterjee (*Siddhartha Chowdhury*), Indira
Devi (*Sarojini*), Debraj Roy (*Tunu*), Krishna Bose (*Sutapa*),
Kalyan Chowdhury (*Siben*), Joysree Roy (*Keya*), Sefali (*Lotika*),
Soven Lahiri (*Sanyal*), Pisu Majumdar (*Keya's father*), Dhara Roy
(*Keya's aunt*), Mamata Chatterjee (*Sanyal's wife*).

1971   SEEMABADDHA (COMPANY LIMITED)

Producer: Chitranjali (Bharat Shamsher Jung Bahadur Rana).
Screenplay: SR, from the novel *Seemabaddha* by Sankar. Pho-
tography: Soumendu Roy. Editor: Dulal Dutta. Art director: Asok
Bose. Music: SR. Sound: J.D. Irani, Durgadas Mitra. 112 mins.

Cast: Barun Chanda (*Syamal Chatterjee*), Sarmila Tagore
(*Sudarsana known as Tutul*), Parumita Chowdhury (*Syamal's
wife*), Harindranath Chatterjee (*Sir Baren Roy*), Haradhan
Banerjee (*Talukdar*), Indira Roy (*Syamal's mother*), Promod
(*Syamal's father*).

1971   SIKKIM

Producer: The Chogyal of Sikkim. Script and commentary: SR.
Photography: Soumendu Roy. Editor: Dulal Dutta. Music: SR.
Sound: SR.

1972   THE INNER EYE

Producer: Films Division, Government of India. Script and
commentary: SR. Photography: Soumendu Roy. Editor: Dulal
Dutta. Music: SR. Sound: SR.

1973   ASANI SANKET (DISTANT THUNDER)

Producer: Balaka Movies (Sarbani Bhattacharya). Screenplay:
SR, from the novel *Asani Sanket* by Bibhutibhusan Banerjee.
Photography: Soumendu Roy. Editor: Dulal Dutta. Art direc-

tor: Asok Bose. Music: SR. Sound: J.D. Irani, Durgadas Mitra. 101 mins.

Cast: Soumitra Chatterjee (*Gangacharan Chakravarti*), Babita (*Ananga*, his wife), Ramesh Mukherjee (*Biswas*), Chitra Banerjee (*Moti*), Gobinda Chakravarti (*Dinabandhu*), Sandhya Roy (*Chutki*), Noni Ganguli ('*Scarface*' *Jadu*), Seli Pal (*Moksada*), Suchita Roy (*Khenti*), Anil Ganguli (*Nibaran*), Debatosh Ghosh (*Adhar*).

1974   SONAR KELLA (THE GOLDEN FORTRESS)

Producer: Government of West Bengal. Screenplay: SR, based on his own novel *Sonar Kella*. Photography: Soumendu Roy. Editor: Dulal Dutta. Art director: Asok Bose. Music: SR. Sound: J. D. Irani, Anil Talukdar. 120 mins.

Cast: Soumitra Chatterjee (*Pradosh Mitter known as Felu*), Santosh Dutta (*Lalmohan Ganguli known as Jotayu*), Siddhartha Chatterjee (*Tapesh Mitter known as Topse*), Kusal Chakravarti (*Mukul Dhar*), Sailen Mukherjee (*Dr Hemanga Hajra*), Ajoy Banerjee (*Amiyanath Burman*), Kamu Mukherjee (*Mandar Bose*), Santanu Bagchi (*Mukul 2*), Harindranath Chatterjee (*Uncle Sidhu*), Sunil Sarkar (*Mukul's father*), Siuli Mukherjee (*Mukul's mother*), Haradhan Banerjee (*Tapesh's father*), Rekha Chatterjee (*Tapesh's mother*), Asok Mukherjee (*Journalist*), Bimal Chatterjee (*Advocate*).

1975   JANA ARANYA (THE MIDDLE MAN)

Producer: Indus Films (Subir Guha). Screenplay: SR, from the novel *Jana Aranya* by Sankar. Photography: Soumendu Roy. Editor: Dulal Dutta. Art director: Asok Bose. Music: SR. Sound: J.D. Irani, Anil Talukdar, Adinath Nag, Sujit Ghosh. 131 mins.

Cast: Pradip Mukherjee (*Somnath Banerjee*), Satya Banerjee (*Somnath's father*), Dipankar Dey (*Bhombol*), Lily Chakravarti (*Kamala, his wife*), Aparna Sen (*Somnath's girlfriend*), Gautam Chakravarti (*Sukumar*), Sudesna Das (*Kauna known as Juthika*), Utpal Dutta (*Bisu*), Rabi Ghosh (*Mr Mitter*), Bimal Chatterjee (*Adok*), Arati Bhattacharya (*Mrs Ganguli*), Padma Devi (*Mrs Biswas*), Soven Lahiri (*Goenka*), Santosh Dutta (*Hiralal*), Bimal Deb (*Jagabandhu, MLA/MP*), Ajeya Mukherjee (*Pimp*), Kalyan Sen (*Mr Baksi*), Alokendu Dey (*Fakirchand, office bearer*).

1976   BALA

Producer: National Centre for the Performing Arts, Bombay

and Government of Tamil Nadu. Script and commentary: SR.
Photography: Soumendu Roy. Editor: Dulal Dutta. Music: SR.
Sound: S.P. Ramanathan, Sujit Sarkar, David. 33 mins.

1977   SHATRANJ KE KHILARI (THE CHESS PLAYERS)

Producer: Devki Chitra Productions (Suresh Jindal). Screen-
play: SR, from the short story 'Shatranj ke Khilari' by Prem
Chand. Dialogue: SR, Shama Zaidi, Javed Siddiqi. Editor:
Dulal Dutta. Art director: Bansi Chandragupta. Associate art
director: Asok Bose. Costumes: Shama Zaidi. Music: SR. Songs
sung by Reba Muhuri, Birju Maharaj, Calcutta Youth Choir.
Dance director: Birju Maharaj. Dances performed by Saswati
Sen, Gitanjali, Kathak Ballet Troupe. Sound: Narinder Singh,
Samir Majumdar. 113 mins.

Cast: Sanjeev Kumar (*Mirza Sajjad Ali*), Saeed Jaffrey
(*Mir Roshan Ali*), Amjad Khan (*Wajid Ali Shah*), Richard
Attenborough (*General Outram*), Shabana Azmi (*Khurshid*),
Farida Jalal (*Nafeesa*), Veena (*Aulea Begum, Queen Mother*),
David Abraham (*Munshi Nandlal*), Victor Banerjee (*Ali Naqi
Khan, Prime Minister*), Farooq Shaikh (*Aqil*), Tom Alter (*Captain
Weston*), Leela Mishra (*Hiria*), Barry John (*Dr Joseph Fayrer*),
Samarth Narain (*Kalloo*), Budho Advani (*Imtaiz Hussain*), Kamu
Mukherjee (*Bookie*).

1978   JOI BABA FELUNATH (THE ELEPHANT GOD)

Producer: R.D.B. and Co. (R. D. Bansal). Screenplay: SR, from
his own novel *Joi Baba Felunath*. Photography: Soumendu Roy.
Editor: Dulal Dutta. Art director: Asok Bose. Music: SR. Sound:
Robin Sen Gupta. 112 mins.

Cast: Soumitra Chatterjee (*Pradosh Mitter known as Felu*),
Santosh Dutta (*Lalmohan Ganguli known as Jotayu*), Siddhartha
Chatterjee (*Tapesh Mitter known as Topse*), Utpal Dutta (*Maganlal
Meghraj*), Jit Bose (*Ruku Ghosal*), Haradhan Banerjee (*Umanath
Ghosal*), Bimal Chatterjee (*Ambika Ghosal*), Biplab Chatterjee
(*Bikash Sinha*), Satya Banerjee (*Nibaran Chakravarti*), Moloy Roy
(*Gunomoy Bagchi*), Santosh Sinha (*Sasi Pal*), Manu Mukherjee
(*Machli Baba*), Indubhusan Gujral (*Inspector Tewari*), Kamu
Mukherjee (*Arjun*).

1980   HIRAK RAJAR DESE (THE KINGDOM OF DIAMONDS)

Producer: Government of West Bengal. Original screenplay: SR.

Photography: Soumendu Roy. Editor: Dulal Dutta. Art director: Asok Bose. Music: SR. Goopy's songs sung by Anup Kumar Ghosal. Sound: Robin Sen Gupta, Durgadas Mitra. 118 mins.

Cast: Soumitra Chatterjee (*Udayan, the school-teacher*), Utpal Dutta (*King Hirak*), Tapen Chatterjee (*Goopy*), Rabi Ghosh (*Bagha*), Santosh Dutta (*King of Shundi/ Gabesak, inventor*), Promod Ganguli (*Udayan's father*), Alpana Gupta (*Udayan's mother*), Rabin Majumdar (*Charandas*), Sunil Sarkar (*Fazl Mia*), Nani Ganguli (*Balaram*), Ajoy Banerjee (*Bidusak*), Kartik Chatterjee (*Court Poet*), Haridhan Mukherjee (*Court Astrologer*), Bimal Deb, Tarun Mitra, Gopal Dey, Sailen Ganguli, Samir Mukherjee (*Ministers*).

1980 PIKOO

Producer: Henri Fraise. Screenplay: SR, from his own short story '*Pikur Diary*'. Photography: Soumendu Roy. Editor: Dulal Dutta. Art director: Asok Bose. Music: SR. Sound: Robin Sen Gupta, Sujit Sarkar. 26 mins.

Cast: Arjun Guha Thakurta (*Pikoo*), Aparna Sen (*Seema, his mother*), Soven Lahiri (*Ranjan*), Promod Ganguli (*Grandfather Loknath*), Victor Banerjee (*Uncle Hitesh*).

1981 SADGATI (DELIVERANCE)

Producer: Doordarshan, Government of India. Screenplay: SR, from the short story '*Sadgati*' by Prem Chand. Dialogue by SR and Amrit Rai. Photography: Soumendu Roy. Editor: Dulal Dutta. Art director: Asok Bose. Music: SR. Sound: Amulya Das. 52 mins.

Cast: Om Puri (*Dukhi Chamar*), Smita Patil (*Jhuria, Dukhi's wife*), Richa Mishra (*Dhania, Dukhi's daughter*), Mohan Agashe (*Ghashiram*), Gita Siddharth (*Lakshmi, Ghashiram's wife*), Bhaialal Hedao (*The Gond*).

1984 GHARE BAIRE (THE HOME AND THE WORLD)

Producer: National Film Development Corporation of India. Screenplay: SR, from the novel *Ghare Baire* by Rabindranath Tagore. Photography: Soumendu Roy. Editor: Dulal Dutta. Art director: Asok Bose. Music: SR. Sound: Robin Sen Gupta, Jyoti Chatterjee, Anup Mukherjee. 140 mins.

Cast: Soumitra Chatterjee (*Sandip*), Victor Banerjee (*Nikhilesh*), Swatilekha Chatterjee (*Bimala*), Gopa Aich (*Nikhilesh's sister-in-law*), Jennifer Kapoor (Kendal) (*Miss Gilby, English governess*),

Manoj Mitra (*Headmaster*), Indrapramit Roy (*Amulya*), Bimal Chatterjee (*Kulada*).

1987   SUKUMAR RAY

Producer: Government of West Bengal. Script: SR. Commentary: Soumitra Chatterjee. Photography: Barun Raha. Editor: Dulal Dutta. Music: SR. Sound: Sujit Sarkar. 30 mins.

Cast: Soumitra Chatterji, Utpal Dutta, Santosh Dutta, Tapen Chatterji.

1989   GANASATRU (AN ENEMY OF THE PEOPLE)

Producer: National Film Development Corporation of India. Screenplay: SR, from the play *An Enemy of the People* by Henrik Ibsen. Photography: Barun Raha. Editor: Dulal Dutta. Art director: Asok Bose. Music: SR. Sound: Sujit Sarkar. 100 mins.

Cast: Soumitra Chatterjee (*Dr Asok Gupta*), Ruma Guha Thakurta (*Maya, his wife*), Mamata Shankar (*Indrani, his daughter*), Dhritiman Chatterjee (*Nisith*), Dipankar Dey (*Haridas Bagchi*), Subhendu Chatterjee (*Biresh*), Manoj Mitra (*Adhir*), Viswa Guha Thakurta (*Ranen Haldar*), Rajaram Yagnik (*Bhargava*), Satya Banerjee (*Manmatha*), Gobinda Mukherjee (*Chandan*).

MEMBERS OF SATYAJIT RAY'S FILM UNIT

Assistant directors:	Santi Chatterjee
	Nityananda Dutta
	Sailen Dutta
	Subrata Lahiri
	Ramesh Sen
Make-up:	Ananta Das
	Sakti Sen
Music:	Susanta Banerjee (Recording/mixing)
	Satyen Chatterjee (Recording/mixing)
	Syamsundar Ghosh (Recording/mixing)
	Samir Majumdar (Recording/mixing)
	Aloke Dey (Conducting/coordinating)
	Mangesh Desai (Mixing)
Production controller:	Anil Chowdhury
Production manager:	Bhanu Ghosh
Stills:	Nemai Ghosh
	Naren Roy (Teknica)

2. Films with Contributions by Satyajit Ray

Non-fiction

Script: INDIAN IRON AND STEEL (Director: Harisadhan Das Gupta).
Narrator: MAX MUELLER (Director: John Thiele).
           TIDAL BORE (Director: Vijaya Mulay).
Music: DARJEELING, HIMALAYAN FANTASY (Director: Bansi Chandragupta).
           GANGA SAGAR MELA (Director: Bansi Chandragupta).
           GLIMPSES OF WEST BENGAL (Director: Bansi Chandragupta).
           HOUSE THAT NEVER DIES (Director: Tony Mayer).
           MAX MUELLER (Director: John Thiele).
           QUEST OF HEALTH (Director: Harisadhan Das Gupta).

Fiction

Screenplay and music:
           BAKSA BADAL (Feature) (Director: Nityananda Dutta).
           FATIKCHAND (Feature) (Director: Sandip Ray).
           SATYAJIT RAY PRESENTS (13 short stories for TV) (Director: Sandip Ray).
           SATYAJIT RAY PRESENTS 2 (2 long short stories and a Feluda novel for TV) (Director: Sandip Ray).
Music: SHAKESPEARE WALLAH (Feature) (Director: James Ivory).

3. Radio Talks by Satyajit Ray

MUSIC I LIVE BY, broadcast on All India Radio (Calcutta), 1967.
WHAT BEETHOVEN MEANS TO ME, broadcast on All India Radio (Calcutta), 1970.

4. Films about Satyajit Ray

1963   CREATIVE ARTISTS OF INDIA: SATYAJIT RAY
           B.D. Garga for Films Division, Government of India
           Shows SR at work on *Mahanagar*. Commentary written and spoken by SR.

1968   CREATIVE PERSONS: SATYAJIT RAY
           James Beveridge for W-NET Educational TV
           Shows SR at work in Calcutta and on *Chiriakhana* and location-hunting for *The Alien*.

1969   LATE NIGHT LINE-UP
             BBC Television
             Interview with SR in London at the time of *The Adventures
             of Goopy and Bagha.*

1978   SOUTH BANK SHOW: SATYAJIT RAY
             Melvyn Bragg for London Weekend Television
             Interview with SR in London at the time of *The Chess Players.*

1983   THE MUSIC OF SATYAJIT RAY
             Utpalendu Chakravarti for the National Film Development
             Corporation of India
             Shows SR composing and recording music for *The Home
             and the World.*

1984   SATYAJIT RAY: PORTRAIT OF A DIRECTOR
             Zia Mohyeddin for Central Television
             Interview with SR in London recorded in 1982.

1984   SATYAJIT RAY
             Shyam Benegal for Films Division, Government of India
             Shows SR at work on *The Home and the World.* Extended
             interview.

1988   OMNIBUS: THE CINEMA OF SATYAJIT RAY
             Adam Low for BBC Television (Consultant: Andrew Robinson)
             Interview with SR in Calcutta.

Awards

1. Awards for Films

Abhijan (The Expedition)
President's Silver Medal, New Delhi, 1962

Aparajito (The Unvanquished)
Golden Lion of St Mark, Cinema Nuovo and Critics' Award, Venice, 1957
FIPRESCI Award, London, 1957
Critics' Award for Best Film and Best Direction, San Francisco, 1958
Golden Laurel for Best Foreign Film of 1958–9, USA
Selznick Golden Laurel, Berlin, 1960
Best Non-European Film, Denmark, 1967

Apur Sansar (The World of Apu)
President's Gold Medal, New Delhi, 1959
Sutherland Award for Best Original and Imaginative Film, London Film Festival, 1960
Diploma of Merit, XIV International Film Festival, Edinburgh, 1960
Best Foreign Film of 1960, National Board of Review of Motion Pictures, USA

Aranyer Din Ratri (Days and Nights in the Forest)

Asani Sanket (Distant Thunder)
Award for Music Direction and

President's Gold Medal, New Delhi, 1972
Golden Bear, Berlin, 1973
Golden Hugo, Chicago, 1974

Bala

Charulata (The Lonely Wife)
President's Gold Medal, New Delhi, 1964
Silver Bear for Best Direction, Berlin, 1965
Catholic Award, Berlin, 1965
Best Film, Acapulco, 1965

Chiriakhana (The Zoo)
Best Direction, West Bengal Government, 1968

Devi (The Goddess)
President's Gold Medal, New Delhi, 1961

Ghare Baire (The Home and the World)

Goopy Gyne Bagha Byne (The Adventures of Goopy and Bagha)
President's Gold and Silver Medals, New Delhi, 1970
Silver Cross Award, Best Direction and Originality, Adelaide and Auckland, 1969
Merit Award, Tokyo, 1970
Best Film, Melbourne, 1970

Hirak Rajar Dese (The Kingdom of Diamonds)

The Inner Eye
Prime Minister's Gold Medal, New Delhi, 1974

Jalsaghar (The Music Room)
President's Silver Medal, New Delhi, 1959
Silver Medal for Music, Moscow, 1959

Jana Aranya (The Middle Man)
Best Direction, New Delhi, 1975
Best Film, Direction, Screenplay, West Bengal Government, 1975
Karlovy Vary Prize, 1976

Joi Baba Felunath (The Elephant God)
Best Children's Film, New Delhi, 1978

Kanchenjungha

Kapurush-o-Mahapurush (The Coward and the Holy Man)

Mahanagar (The Big City)
Certificate of Merit, New Delhi, 1964
Silver Bear for Best Direction, Berlin, 1964

Nayak (The Hero)
Best Screenplay and Story, New Delhi, 1967
Critics' Prize and Special Jury Award, Berlin, 1966

Parash Pathar (The Philosopher's Stone)

Pather Panchali (Song of the Little Road)
President's Gold and Silver Medals, New Delhi, 1955
Best Human Document, Cannes, 1956

Diploma of Merit, Edinburgh, 1956
Vatican Award, Rome, 1956
Golden Carbao, Manila, 1956
Best Film and Direction, San Francisco, 1957
Selznick Golden Laurel, Berlin, 1957
Best Film, Vancouver, 1958
Critics' Award, Stafford, 1958
Best Foreign Film of 1959, Afro Arts Theater, New York
Best Foreign Film, Tokyo, 1966
Best Non-European Film, Denmark, 1966

Pikoo

Pratidwandi (The Adversary)
Special Award, New Delhi, 1971
President's Silver Medal, New Delhi, 1971

Rabindranath Tagore
President's Gold Medal, New Delhi, 1961
Golden Seal, Locarno, 1961

Sadgati (Deliverance)

Seemabaddha (Company Limited)
President's Gold Medal, New Delhi, 1972

Shatranj ke Khilari (The Chess Players)
Best Feature Film in Hindi, New Delhi, 1977

Sikkim

Sonar Kella (The Golden Fortress)
President's Silver Medal, New Delhi, 1974
Best Direction and Screenplay, New Delhi, 1974
Best Film, Direction and Screenplay, West Bengal Government, 1974
Best Feature Film for Children and Young Adults, Teheran, 1975

Sukumar Ray

Teen Kanya (Three Daughters)
President's Silver Medal, New Delhi,
1961 (*Samapti*)
Golden Boomerang, Melbourne, 1962
(*Samapti* and *The Postmaster*)
Selznick Golden Laurel Award,
Berlin, 1963

2. Personal Awards

1967   Magsaysay Award, Manila
1971   Star of Yugoslavia
1973   D.Litt., Delhi University
1974   D.Litt., Royal College of Arts, London
1976   Padmabibhusan, India
1978   D.Litt., Oxford University
        Special Award, Berlin Film Festival
1979 \ Special Award, Moscow Film Festival
1982   '*Hommage à* Satyajit Ray', Cannes Film Festival
        Special Golden Lion of St. Mark, Venice Film Festival
1983   Fellowship of British Film Institute
1985   D.Litt., Calcutta University
1985   'Soviet Land' Nehru Award
1987   Légion d'Honneur, France

Notes

As a rule, a source is identified only where directly quoted. To avoid pointless repetition, quotations from oral interviews with Ray between 1982 and 1988 are not identified, nor are comments made by others whom I have interviewed face to face or by correspondence. These include the following:

Lindsay Anderson, Alex Aronson, Peggy Ashcroft, Richard Attenborough, Karuna Banerjee, Victor Banerjee, Henri Cartier-Bresson, Dhritiman Chatterjee, Soumitra Chatterjee, Swatilekha Chatterjee, Nirad Chaudhuri, Anil Chowdhury, Norman Clare, Arthur C. Clarke, Nalini Das, Chidananda Das Gupta, Harisadhan Das Gupta, Utpal Dutta, O. C. Ganguli, Sunil Ganguli, Rabi Ghosh, R.P. Gupta, Robert Hardcastle, Penelope Houston, John Huston, Saeed Jaffrey, Kalyani Karlekar, Imrat Khan, Dinkar Kowshik, Akira Kurosawa, Lila Majumdar, Subrata Mitra, Madhabi Mukherjee, V.S. Naipaul, J.B.R. Nicholson, Lester James Peries, James Quinn, Santha Rama Rau, Bijoya Ray, Sandip Ray, Alaknanda Roy, Amartya Sen, Aparna Sen, Marie Seton, Sarmila Tagore, Monroe Wheeler, Shama Zaidi.

In most cases only brief details of a source are given here; full details generally appear in the Bibliography. Ray's book *Our Films Their Films* is abbreviated to *OFTF*, the unpaginated July 1966 issue of *Montage*, edited by Krupanidhi and Srivastava, to *Montage*.

Introduction

p. 2   'I have long been toying'   Letter, 21 July 1981.
p. 4   'there is something about creating beauty'   OFTF, p. 58.
p. 8   'Important I have to buy'   Letter, 23 September 1983.
p. 9   'the pleasure of recognising' David McCutchion in *Montage*.

1   A Bengali Banyan Tree

p. 14   'would be supremely happy' Rajnarian Bose in David Kopf, *The Brahmo Samaj*, p. 167.
            'The Bengal Renaissance was the child' *British Orientalism and the Bengal Renaissance*, p. 283.
p. 15   'much of the spirit of Christianity'   *Creative Unity*, p. 192.
            'plain living, high principles ...' David Kopf in *The Brahmo Samaj*, p. 114.
p. 17   'There was no hatred'   *Chelebelar Dinguli*, p. 55.

p. 19	'One writer has said' 'Diffraction in Half-Tone', *Penrose Annual*, 1902–3, p. 82.
	'miss an article' *Penrose Annual*, 1904–5, p. 1.
p. 21	'There was no sarcasm in it' *Chelebelar Dinguli*, p. 121.
	'Characters out of the *Ramayana*' Introduction to *The Select Nonsense of Sukumar Ray*.
	'O.C. Ganguly says' '*Bharatiya chitrasilpa*' in *Barnamalatattva o Bibidha Prabandha*, Calcutta, Signet Press, 1957, p. 82.
p. 22	'Where poetry is coextensive' 'The spirit of Rabindranath Tagore' in *Quest*, London, October 1913, pp. 56–7.
p. 23	'an Indian gentleman' *Penrose Annual*, 1920, p. 1.
	'My grandfather was a rare combination' Introduction to *The Select Nonsense of Sukumar Ray*.
pp. 23–4	'A duck once met a porcupine' *Nonsense Rhymes*.
pp. 24–5	'Know this – in the near future' *Nonsense Rhymes*.
p. 25	'A green and gold orang-outang' Introduction to *The Select Nonsense of Sukumar Ray*.
	'I cannot separate Brahmoism' David Kopf, *The Brahmo Samaj*, p. 302.
p. 26	'This book was conceived' Quoted by Satyajit Ray in Introduction to *The Select Nonsense of Sukumar Ray*.
p. 27	'only Sukumar knows about' Introduction to *The Select Nonsense of Sukumar Ray*.
	'On hazy nights' *The Select Nonsense of Sukumar Ray*, p. 44.
	'I do not know of any other humourist' Introduction to *The Select Nonsense of Sukumar Ray*.
	'I have seen a great deal of Death' Final words of the commentary of *Sukumar Ray*.

2 Early Years

p. 28	'You can never tell' *Jakhan Choto Chilam*, p. 5.
p. 29	'Even today, if I catch a whiff' *Jakhan Choto Chilam*, p. 15.
	'I really imagined' *Jakhan Choto Chilam*, p. 13.
p. 30	'Dhondadu threw the hammer' *Jakhan Choto Chilam*, p. 13.
p. 31	'I doubt if there has ever been' *Jakhan Choto Chilam*, p. 40.
p. 32	'When you went to their houses . . . eating it.' *Jakhan Choto Chilam*, p. 18.
p. 34	'Adults treat all children' *Jakhan Choto Chilam*, p. 23.
p. 35	'Once in a blue moon' *Jakhan Choto Chilam*, p. 9.
	'perpetually shrouded' *Sight and Sound*, autumn 1982, p. 270.
p. 36	'Who knows? Perhaps this was' *Jakhan Choto Chilam*, p. 26.
	'weeks of musing' 'My life, my work', *Telegraph*, Calcutta, 27 September 1982.
pp. 36–7	'early example of Indian soft porn' 'I wish I could have shown them to you' in *Cinema Visions*, January 1980, p. 6.
p. 37	'Lillian Gish' *OFTF*, p. 129.

'a forbidden world' 'My life, my work', *Telegraph*, Calcutta, 27 September 1982.

'It opened with a moonlit shot' *OFTF*, p. 131.

p. 38   'We laughed at Jack Hulbert' *OFTF*, p. 143.

'a drop which reflects' *Sight and Sound*, summer 1970, p. 120.

p. 40   'Who would have known that "Front-de-Boeuf"' *Jakhan Choto Chilam*, p. 64.

p. 41   'The fact of the matter' *Jakhan Choto Chilam*, p. 70.

p. 42   'at an age when the Bengali youth' 'My life, my work', *Telegraph*, Calcutta, 27 September 1982.

'immediate and decisive' 'My life, my work', *Telegraph*, Calcutta, 27 September 1982.

'Manik lost his sleep' Anil Gupta in *India Today*, 15 February 1983, p. 56.

p. 43   *A Mole in the Crown*, London, 1985 (privately published).

pp. 43–4   '*Either* 1. Would you rather be damned' 'I Spy With My Little Eye', Calcutta, Bharat Bhavan, October 1937, p. 16.

p. 44   'I do not put my faith' *Creative Unity*, p. 153 (Ray's translation).

'the Bengali's response' *Thy Hand, Great Anarch!*, p. 662.

'Erudition is something' 'My life, my work', *Telegraph*, Calcutta, 27 September 1982.

p. 45   'therapeutic ... place apart' 'My life, my work', *Telegraph*, Calcutta, 28 September 1982.

3   *Santiniketan and Tagore*

p. 46   'long hair' 'My life, my work', *Telegraph*, Calcutta, 28 September 1982.

p. 47   'As a poet, dramatist' Interview with author, 1982, slightly edited to make Foreword to *Rabindranath Tagore: A Celebration of His Life and Work*.

'I cannot speak without Tagore' *Cinema and I*, p. 79.

p. 48   'One stole up to him' 'My life, my work', *Telegraph*, Calcutta, 28 September 1982.

'He never used a wrong word' Radio interview with Julian Crandall Hollick, 1987.

'As I look around I see' 'Crisis in Civilization', Calcutta, Visva Bharati, 1941, p. 17–18.

p. 49   'In front lies the ocean of peace' Quoted in Krishna Kripalani, *Rabindranath Tagore: A Biography*, p. 397.

p. 50   'When are you coming down?' Letter, 19 September 1945.

p. 51   'Film directors can learn' *Bisoy Chalachchitra*, p. 58.

'a great intellect' Letter to Marie Seton, 4 December 1973.

'The entire ceiling was a painting' *Bisoy Chalachchitra*, p. 118.

p. 52   'For a popular medium' *OFTF*, p. 127.

'That's a good outline' 'My life, my work', *Telegraph*, Calcutta, 28 September 1982.

'Under a limitless sky' Dinkar Kowshik, *Nandalal Bose*, Delhi, National Book Trust, 1985, p. 100.

pp. 52–3   'This was basic . . . rhythm' *OFTF*, p. 152.
'Consider the Fujiyama' *OFTF*, p. 157.
'Such was his command of the instrument' 'Ashesh Bandopadhyaya [Banerjee] Plays *Esraj*', sleeve-note on LP, 1978.

p. 55   'My relationship with Santiniketan' 'My life, my work', *Telegraph*, 28 September 1982.

4   *Commercial Artist and Critic*

p. 56   'a nice fellow . . . as I do.' Letter, 22 May 1948.

p. 57   'If a change was required' *Film World*, April–May 1971, p. 33.
'He interpreted the words' *Film World*, April–May 1971, p. 33.

p. 58   'dark and shameful dealings' Letter, 19 September 1945.

p. 59   'Death or suffering . . . fully knew it' *Monsoon Morning*, pp. 169–70.

p. 60   'Thoughtful Britons' *Monsoon Morning*, p. 263.

p. 61   'I propose to have a room' Letter, 19 September 1945.
'not nearly as much comfort' Letter to Norman Clare, 22 May 1948.

p. 62   'Do not look down upon the *addas*' Benoy Kumar Sarkar quoted by R.P. Gupta in *Sunday*, 5–11 January, 1986, p. 25.
'gave vent to his views' *Satyajit Ray Retrospective Souvenir: The First Decade*, pp. 15–16.
'it is beyond me' 'Kamal Babu' in *Samatat*, 41, 1979, p. 4.

p. 63   'That gentleman won't even take' 'Kamal Babu' in *Samatat*, 41, 1979, p. 7.
'The Gothic gloom of the film' *OFTF*, p. 6.
'I am taking the cinema more and more seriously' Letter, 22 May 1948.

p. 64   'I never knew' Letter, 22 May 1948.
'an overbearing English manager . . . "Quit India!" ' *OFTF*, pp. 8–9.

p. 65   'The raw material of cinema' *OFTF*, p. 24.
'We have acquired' Letter, 22 May 1948.
'On one occasion, in the middle of our discussion' *OFTF*, p. 7.
'He was slightly critical' *Sight and Sound*, summer 1970, p. 115.

p. 67   'I was certainly not . . . Hollywoodish' 'My life, my work', *Telegraph*, Calcutta, 29 September 1982.
'Renoir was not only approachable' *OFTF*, p. 111.

p. 68   'fairy-tale element' *My Life and My Films*, p. 161.
'the most important thing I learnt' *My Life and My Films*, p. 250.

p. 69   'Ray is quite alone, of course' Penelope Gilliatt, *Conversations with Renoir*, New York, McGraw-Hill, 1974, p. 31.
'Doubtless the management hoped' *OFTF*, p. 9.

'My mother-in-law gave in' *Illustrated Weekly of India*, 20 November 1988, p. 53.

pp. 69–70　'Would it be possible for you' Letter, 16 January 1950.

p. 70　'I had always thought the English' Marie Seton, *Portrait of a Director*, p. 82.

p. 71　'deification . . . pressures' *OFTF*, p. 211.
'gored' *Sight and Sound*, summer 1970, p. 116.
'I came out of the theatre' 'My life, my work', *Telegraph*, Calcutta, 29 September 1982.

pp. 71–2　'[Zavattini's] greatest assets' *OFTF*, p. 126–7.

p. 72　'unique in its fusion' Foreword to *Henri Cartier-Bresson in India*.
'The entire conventional approach' Marie Seton, *Portrait of a Director*, p. 165.
'the most enchanting' Radio talk, *Music I Live By*, 1967.
'Venice is a fantastic place' Marie Seton, *Portrait of a Director*, p. 119.

5　The Making of Pather Panchali

p. 74　'his hard life had not embittered him' *Thy Hand, Great Anarch!*' p. 90.

p. 75　'The script had to retain' *OFTF*, p. 33.

p. 76　'Durga was a big girl now' *Pather Panchali: Song of the Road*, pp. 156–7.
'You had to find out for yourself' 'My life, my work', *Telegraph*, Calcutta, 30 September 1982.

p. 77　'It looks as if I'll have to rot' Letter, 22 May 1948.

p. 78　'the dim light of a mango grove' 'My life, my work', *Telegraph*, Calcutta, 30 September 1982.
'Little did I know then' *OFTF*, p. 51.
'safer with non-actors' *Film Comment*, summer 1968, p. 10.

p. 79　'The first remark Manikda made' *Montage*.

p. 80　'She was constantly aware' *Bisoy Chalachchitra*, p. 103.
'That time it was' *Bisoy Chalachchitra*, p. 103.

p. 81　'Satyajit seemed a different person' *Film World*, April–May 1971, p. 34.
'The film people are 'ere! . . . good this year' *Bisoy Chalachchitra*, pp. 104–05.
'Mercifully, there were no jurors' 'Our festivals, their festivals', *Statesman*, 3–17 January 1982.
'10 a.m. – 12 noon Visiting doctors' *Views on Cinema*, p. 4.

p. 82　'and wondered each time' *OFTF*, p. 180.
'the scene by the river' 'Kamal Babu' in *Samatat*, 41, 1979, pp. 6–7.
'landmark' Message of appreciation of Bimal Roy on the occasion of a retrospective screening of Roy's films, Calcutta, November 1986.

'completely apathetic' Letter to Seton, 28 November 1955.

p. 83 'Do you think you could let us have' *Sight and Sound*, autumn 1982, p. 269.

p. 84 'They get the money but' Marie Seton, *Portrait of a Director*, p. 96.

p. 85 'Today we will carry you out' *Bisoy Chalachchitra*, p. 103.

p. 86 'Within seconds, the camera was set up' Firoze Rangoonwalla, *Satyajit Ray's Art*, p. 125.

p. 87 'a fine, sincere piece ... happens' '*Sight and Sound*, autumn 1982, p. 269.

'certainly a stroke of inspiration' Foreword to *The Apu Trilogy*.

pp. 87–8 'Now let's do a piece ... stop' *Cinema Visions*, I, 4, 1980, pp. 14–15.

p. 88 'The effort to catch the Museum's deadline' *Sight and Sound*, autumn 1982, p. 269.

'Although the first cable' *Sight and Sound*, autumn 1982, p. 271.

p. 89 'the audience was more interested' *Talking About Films*, p. 18.

'All middle-aged and older men' *Sunday*, 5–11 January 1986, p. 23.

6 *The Apu Trilogy*

p. 91 'I can never forget' *Eksan*, autumn 1987, p. 226 (translation of remarks made in Moscow in 1975, authenticated by Kurosawa in 1988).

'Where poetry is coextensive' 'The spirit of Rabindranath Tagore' in *Quest*, London, October 1913, pp. 56–7.

p. 94 'daring and profound revelation' 'Thoughts on film-making', unfinished article written after the release of *Aparajito* in Calcutta.

'For some time after Sarbajaya's death' Quoted in *Eksan*, autumn 1984, p. 330.

'of improvisations on that' 'Thoughts on film-making'.

p. 95 'Not to have seen the cinema of Ray' *Eksan*, autumn 1987, p. 226 (translation of remarks made in Moscow in 1975, authenticated by Kurosawa in 1988).

p. 98 'It is a nucleus for hospitality' 'Pan' in *Abinger Harvest*, London, Edward Arnold, 1936, p. 311.

'a spontaneous burst of applause' 'Our festivals, their festivals' in *Statesman*, 3–17 January 1982.

'smooth, page-turning professionalism' *Film Culture*, 19, 1959, p. 48.

'I was absolutely overwhelmed' *Montage*.

p. 100 'A western viewer ignorant of' *Sight and Sound*, autumn 1982, p. 272.

p. 102 'one of the cinema's classic affirmative depictions' *The Apu Trilogy*, p. 72.

p. 103   'I think Ed'   Letter, 5 November 1967.
p. 104   'Cannes 1956 has discovered'   *Observer*, 13 May 1956.
                'It was a formal occasion'   'Our festivals, their festivals',
                Statesman, 3–17 January 1982.
p. 105   'I watched the audience surge'   *Sight and Sound*, autumn
                1982, p. 271.
                'irresistible human appeal'   'The new cinema and I' in *Cinema
                Visions*, July 1980, p. 15.
                'perhaps the finest piece'   *Time*, 20 October 1958.
                'a demonstration of what a man'   John McCarten in *New
                Yorker*, 1 November 1958.
                'I don't know anyone who'   *Film Culture*, 19, 1959, p. 46.
                'The connoisseur must feel'   *New York Herald Tribune*, 5
                October 1960.
                'You won a prize at Cannes?'   *OFTF*, p. 139.
pp. 105–6   'absolutely terrified by the . . . as it has ever been'   Letter
                to Lester Peries, 7 December 1958.

7   *Comedies*

p. 107   'mannered facetiousness'   *Sight and Sound*, summer 1961, p. 135.
p. 108   'sort of combination of comedy'   Letter, 10 February 1958.
p. 110   'I think Satyajit has preconceived notions'   *Montage*.
                'intolerable'   *The Cinema of Satyajit Ray*, p. 41.

8   *The Music Room (Jalsaghar)*

p. 113   '*The Music Room* is a deeply felt'   *A World on Film*, New
                York, Harper and Row, 1966, p. 373.
                'I wish I had space'   *New York Times*, 20 October 1963.
                'offered pleasures of unique delicacy'   *Times*, 2 May 1962.
                'most perfect film'   *Guardian*, 19 May 1975.
p. 115   'I am more or less back where'   Letter to Seton, 24 De-
                cember 1956.
                'a rather showy piece'   Letter, 1 May 1957.
                'brooding drama'   Letter, 10 February 1958.
                'Nimtita turned out to be everything'   *OFTF*, p. 45.
p. 116   'This combination gives you'   *Cinema Visions*, I, 4, 1980, p. 16.
p. 117   'is shown as the last representative'   *Sight and Sound*, summer
                1961, p. 133.
                'tries to show the inevitability . . . system'   *Film World*, January
                1980, p. 30.
                'He's pathetic . . . wiped out'   *Cineaste*, XII, 1, 1982, p. 26.
p. 119   'Mister Ray!'   *Bisoy Chalachchitra*, pp. 111–12.

9   *The Goddess (Devi)*

p. 121   'The western critic who hopes'   *Sight and Sound*, autumn
                1982, p. 272.

'the story itself is dauntingly alien' Isobel Quigly, *Spectator*, 4 September 1964.

'is an exquisite bore' Philip Oakes, *Sunday Telegraph*, 30 August 1964.

'more a matter of uncluttered story-telling' *Times*, 27 August 1964.

'Would an intelligent girl' *Sight and Sound*, autumn 1964, p. 195.

pp. 121–2 'What I have felt in the women of India' *Creative Unity*, p. 162.

p. 122 'The symbolism here' *Ramakrishna and his Disciples*, p. 51.

p. 123 ' "How do you think of me?" ' *Ramakrishna and his Disciples*, p. 145.

'a kind of play-acting ... his body' *Ramakrishna and his Disciples*, p. 288.

p. 124 '*Devi* was what a genius got out of me' *Montage*.

p. 126 'an old established raga' *Cinema Visions*, I, 4, 1980, p. 17.

10 Three Daughters (Teen Kanya)

p. 128 '*Teen Kanya* has turned out' Letter, 14 February 1962.

p. 129 'The shimmer of freshly washed leaves' *Collected Stories*, Pocket Edn, Delhi, Macmillan India, 1974, pp. 73–4.

'consoles himself with philosophical reflections' *Collected Stories*, p. 78.

p. 130 'the squirrel-like character' *Portrait of a Director*, pp. 175–6.

p. 131 'is expressive and touching beyond words' *New York Times*, 5 May 1963.

p. 132 'are supposed to exist on a level of' *OFTF*, p. 197.

pp. 134–5 'I was completely confused as to what' *Montage*.

11 Kanchenjungha

p. 136 'lightweight' *Talking About Films*, p. 60.

'anti-film' '*Kanchenjungha*: experiment in "anti-film" ' in *Literary Essays*, Calcutta, Writers Workshop, 1974, pp. 28–34.

'is a disquieting and unflattering mirror' '*Kanchenjungha* – a disquieting mirror' in *Quest*, Bombay, October–December 1962, p. 85.

p. 138 'a domineering British title-holding father' Letter, 14 February 1962.

pp. 139–40 'The good Bengali feels irritated' *Quest*, p. 85.

p. 143 'Ambiguity, innuendo, paradox, irony' *Quest*, p. 86.

12 Abhijan (The Expedition)

p. 146 'total failure' *Talking About Films*, p. 73.

p. 147 'Man is man, machine is machine' *Creative Unity*, p. 109.

13 *Mahanagar (The Big City)*

p. 149   'Not for a moment did I feel'   *Montage.*
            'Ray's camera merely eavesdrops'   *Time*, 25 August 1967.
p. 151   'a dingy first floor affair'   Note by Ray in his shooting note-
            book.
            'The smallest rooms ever built!'   Letter, 15 January 1963.
            'In films the actor doesn't act'   *Sunday Statesman*, 25 August
            1985.
p. 152   'Ray has an unmatched feeling'   *Spectator*, 17 May 1968.

14 *Charulata (The Lonely Wife)*

p. 156   'In a film like *Charulata*'   *Sight and Sound*, autumn 1982,
            pp. 272–3.
            'the interplay of sophistication'   *Sight and Sound*, winter
            1965–6, p. 33.
p. 157   'moved like a majestic snail'   Howard Thompson, *New York
            Times*, 11 September 1965.
            'It's a sensitive movie but sluggish'   *Observer*, 17 October 1965.
            'this stratum of Indian life'   *Times*, 14 October 1965.
p. 158   'In respect of love of the Romantic variety'   *Thy Hand, Great
            Anarch!*, p. 612.
            'imbibed the notion that'   *The Autobiography of an Unknown
            Indian*, p. 108.
p. 159   'Tagore had known the pains'   *Cinewave*, January–March
            1984, p. 13.
            'a powerful sexual bond'   *New Yorker*, 8 July 1974.
p. 161   'prolonged marathon incomprehension'   *Bisoy Chalachchitra*,
            p. 98.
            'Is Charu the archetypal Ray woman?'   *Cineaste*, 1, 1982,
            p. 26.
p. 162   'a set should exist only in relation to the script'   *Montage.*
p. 163   'Splendid work so far'   Letter, 3 December 1963.
            'The possibilities of fusing Indian and western music'   *Cinema
            Visions*, I, 4, 1980, p. 18.
p. 164   'attempts to use a language'   'My life, my work', *Telegraph*,
            Calcutta 1 October 1982
p. 165   'Her duty done ... in the story'   'My life, my work', *Telegraph*,
            Calcutta 1 October 1982.
            'It was important to stress'   'My life, my work', *Telegraph*,
            Calcutta 1 October 1982.
p. 166   'We know that Charu is resigned'   'My life, my work', *Telegraph*,
            Calcutta 1 October 1982.
p. 167   'Amal's unexpected duplicity'   *Sight and Sound*, autumn 1982,
            p. 274.

15 Kapurush (The Coward)

p. 175 'While making the film' Firoze Rangoonwalla, *Satyajit Ray's Art*, p. 111.
'slight but agreeable' *Cinema: A Critical Dictionary*, p. 825.

16 Nayak (The Hero)

pp. 179–80 'How can the normal be made interesting?' *Montage*.
p. 180 'Planning the story of *Nayak*' *OFTF*, pp. 64–5.

17 Musicals

p. 182 'It is extraordinary how quickly' Letter, 15 October 1969.
'Satyajit Ray at his least convincing' Derek Malcolm, *Guardian*, 27 January 1972.
'Perhaps it would appeal' George Melly, *Observer*, 30 January 1972.
'Ray is a true poet of the cinema' John Russell Taylor, *Times*, 28 January 1972.
p. 183 'The tales were about real kings' *Rajasthan: India's enchanted land*, p. 7.
p. 184 'I haven't had to pawn' *Portrait of a Director*, p. 293.
p. 186 'a most abstract, avant-garde affair' Letters to Seton, 4 October and 4 December 1968.
p. 189 'The dialogue in this film is almost untranslatable' *Stills*, autumn 1981, p. 47.

18 Days and Nights in the Forest (Aranyer Din Ratri)

p. 194 'every word and gesture is recognisable' *Financial Times*, 15 October 1971.
'lucid, ironic and' *Monthly Film Bulletin*, December 1971, p. 236.
'rare, wistful movie that' Howard Thompson in *New York Times*, 21 September 1970.
'Satyajit Ray's films can give rise' *New Yorker*, 17 July 1963.
p. 195 '*Days and Nights* seems anachronistically' *Village Voice*, 12 April 1973.
'victims of the departed Raj' George Melly, *Observer*, 17 October 1971.
'snobbish late Victorian Englishmen' Felix Barker, *Evening News*, 14 October 1971.
p. 196 'the conventional approach' Marie Seton, *Portrait of a Director*, p. 165.

19 The Calcutta Trilogy

p. 201 'In the posh areas' *In the Wake of Naxalbari*, pp. 224–5.
p. 202 'Clumps of heavy' *In the Wake of Naxalbari*, pp. 272–3.

p. 203   'Corruption of the youth'   *In the Wake of Naxalbari*, pp. 377–8.
                'the last few weeks have been fraught'   Letter, 10 December 1962.
p. 204   'the political situation is getting so rough'   Letter to Seton,
                25 July 1967.
                'You felt certain changes'   *Gentleman*, December 1984, p. 66.
                'the present EXPLOSIVE atmosphere here'   Letter, 4 May 1970.
p. 205   'Here, while a shot is being taken'   'The confronting question'
                in *Film World*, February 1970, p. 32.
                'the most provocative film'   Letter, 26 August 1970.
                'I could feel the impact'   Letter, 30 October 1970.
pp. 205–6   'Incredible brutality and barbarism'   Letter, 14 April 1971.
p. 206   'as grim as ever . . . will improve'   Letter to Seton, 6 October 1971.
                'Life here's getting to be'   Letter to Seton, 22 May 1974.
pp. 206–7   'I find the contemporary scene'   Letter to Seton, 19 No-
                vember 1974.
p. 208   'One can perhaps get away with'   *New York Times*, 27 April 1976.
                'I should put Sunil Ganguli high'   *Pratidwandi*.
p. 209   'The evil of politics lies'   *The Death of Tragedy*, London,
                1961, Faber and Faber, p. 61.
                'painstakingly schematic'   Gavin Millar, *Listener*, 11 January
                1973.
p. 211   'There are lots of things going on'   *Sight and Sound*, winter
                1972/3, p. 32.
                'I had a brain wave'   Letter, 20 October 1970.
p. 214   'a definitive film about the boxwallahs'   Letter, 6 October 1971.
p. 216   'has a shallow top soil'   *Thy Hand, Great Anarch!*, p. 128.
p. 217   '19th century thoroughness'   *Sight and Sound*, spring 1977,
                p. 121.
p. 218   'his table-thumping'   *India Today*, 15 February 1983, p. 56.
p. 220   'sour, witty, tough, individual'   Alan Brien, *Sunday Times*,
                13 February 1977.

20   *Distant Thunder (Asani Sanket)*

p. 222   'The ceaseless, whining wail'   *So Many Hungers*, reprint,
                Bombay, Jaico, 1964, p. 173.
                'They died in the streets'   Paul Greenough, *Prosperity and
                Misery in Modern Bengal*, p. 266.
p. 223   'Gone are the cultivators'   *Prosperity and Misery in Modern
                Bengal*, p. 3.
pp. 224–5   'an almost pornographic charm'   *New Yorker*, 10 November 1975.
p. 225   'The range of his power of observation'   Interview with
                Chatterjee in *Chitrabhas*, special issue in memory of Bansi
                Chandragupta, p. 37.
pp. 225–6   'Ray has chosen to photograph the film'   Vincent Canby, *New
                York Times*, 12 October 1973.

p. 229 'folk-tale' Jay Cocks, *Time*, 24 November 1975.
'from the first moments of any Ray film' *Times*, 11 April 1975.

pp. 228–9 'hundred little apparently irrelevant details' Ray quoted in Marie Seton, *Portrait of a Director*, p. 165.
'there was stink in the air' *Views on Cinema*, p. 136.
'submission to authority' *Prosperity and Misery in Modern Bengal*, pp. 271–2.

21 Detective Films

p. 232 'a total avoidance of occidental thriller clichés' Letter, 28 September 1967.

pp. 232–3 'manage to remain thoroughly Bengali' Letter to Seton, 5 November 1967.

p. 233 'There seems to be a great dearth' Letter, 4 December 1968.

p. 235 'fortresses perched on hilltops' Foreword to Raghubir Singh, *Rajasthan: India's enchanted land*, p. 8.

p. 236 'A bearer came in with a tray' *OFTF*, p. 79.
'It's the kind of film that points out' *Variety*, 19 November 1975.

p. 238 'well-knitted characterisations' *Variety*, 12 December 1979.

22 The Chess Players (Shatranj ke Khilari)

p. 240 'The most significant fact' *Creative Unity*, p. 97.
'fight for the right' Speech at the Byculla Club, 16 November 1905 in *Speeches, IV (1904–1905)*, Calcutta, Govt of India, 1906 pp. 241–2

p. 241 'a primary source of great value' *Lucknow: The Last Phase of an Oriental Culture*, p. 24.

p. 242 'of refreshingly wide horizons' *Lucknow*, p. 23.
'appears to be one of the most dubious' *Lucknow*, p. 63.
'extremely devout' *Lucknow*, p. 71.
'he even had no hesitation' *Lucknow*, p. 63.
'I have heard from reliable court singers' *Lucknow*, p. 138.
'light, simple and attractive tunes' *Lucknow*, p. 138.

p. 243 'It was the time of Wajid Ali Shah' *The Chess-Players and Other Stories*, Shripat Rai and Gurdial Mallik trans., Delhi, Orient Paperbacks, 1967, p. 133.

p. 245 'Prem Chand has Mir and Mirza' Interview with Iqbal Masud in Swapan Majumdar ed., *Satyajit Ray Retrospective Souvenir: The Second Decade*, p. 25.
'You see, the problem was' Letter, 20 May 1976.
'I saw the story as a fairly light-hearted one' Interview with Iqbal Masud, in Swapan Majumdar ed., *Satyajit Ray Retrospective Souvenir: The Second Decade*, p. 24.

p. 246 'he knew something to the discredit of' *A Passage to India*, Modern Classics edn, London, Penguin 1979, p. 64.

p. 248   'two high-pitched scenes' *OFTF*, p. 103.

p. 250   'But after the row had subsided' *Portrait of a Director*
                (unpaginated).
                'Mr Ray has made the film for a foreign audience' Letter
                to Jaffrey, 30 October 1977.

p. 251   'Satyajit Ray seems to be able to achieve' *Guardian*, 18
                January 1979.
                'I have never enjoyed a film more' Felix Barker, *Evening
                News*, 8 December 1977.
                'Ray's not outraged' Vincent Canby, *New York Times*, 17
                May 1978.
                'Prem Chand judges, he condemns' Frances W. Pritchett,
                'The Chess Players: from Premchand to Satyajit Ray' in *Journal
                of South Asian Literature*, Michigan, summer 1986, p. 77.
                'Easy targets don't interest me very much' Interview with
                Iqbal Masud in Swapan Majumdar ed., *Satyajit Ray Retrospective
                Souvenir: The Second Decade*, pp. 23–4, 26.

23   *Two/ Pikoo*

p. 253   'bought from an English shop' *The Religion of Man*, London,
                George Allen & Unwin, 1931, p. 148.
                'packs quite a punch' Letter, 25 June 1964.
                'a master's crystalline simplicity' David Ansen, *Newsweek*, 20
                July 1981.
                '*Diamonds* was finished . . . at all' Letter, 3 October 1980.

p. 254   'When Father came back from the office' *Pikur Diary o
                Ananya*, p. 10.

24   *Deliverance (Sadgati)*

p. 257   'cruellest' '*Sadgati Dekhar Par*' in *Anandalok*, Calcutta, March
                1982, p. 11.
                'symbolises a man who has no margin' *Creative Unity*, p. 23.

p. 258   'there is really no one to replace her' Letter, 26 December 1986.

pp. 258–9   'We know of a landowner' *Hinduism*, p. 16.

p. 262   'Delicate nuances don't work . . . going out' Bikram Vohra,
                Sunday Observer, Bombay, 7 October 1984.

25   *The Home and the World (Ghare Baire)*

p. 263   'without instantly bringing back' *The Autobiography of an
                Unknown Indian*, p. 225.
                'fine, powerful piece of work' *Tagebücher 1920–1922 Auto-
                biographische Aufzeichnungen 1920–1954*, Herta Ramthun ed.,
                Frankfurt, Suhrkamp, 1975, p. 71 (*Diaries 1920–22*, John Willett
                trans., London, 1979).

'at the intellectual service' *Reviews and Articles*, Peter Palmer trans., London, Merlin Press, 1983, pp. 8–11.

'the radical and the humanist' Ian Buruma in *New York Review of Books*, 19 November 1987, p. 13.

'a large theme ... presented in a formal style' *New Yorker*, 1 July 1985.

p. 264   'Look, we were not born in Bengal' Meredith Borthwick, *The Changing Role of Women in Bengal 1849–1905*, Princeton University Press, 1984, p. 350.

p. 265   'The *swadeshi* movement of 1903–08' Sumit Sarkar, *The Swadeshi Movement in Bengal 1903–08*, p. 493.

'from a long tradition of contempt' *The Swadeshi Movement*, p. 515.

pp. 265–6 'I do not know of one great Bengali writer' *The Autobiography of an Unknown Indian*, p. 196.

p. 266   'It is the weakness of our national movement' Roger Lipsey, *Coomaraswamy: His Life and Work*, 3 vols, Princeton University Press, 1977, III, p. 89.

p. 267   'experiment' 'Two books by Tagore' in *Abinger Harvest*, London, Edward Arnold, 1936, p. 321.

p. 268   'In spite of the predominance' *The Home and the World*, London, Penguin, 1985, p. 12.

'some weird fidelity-test' *New Statesman*, London, 14 September 1984, p. 34.

'tells us all about relationships' Minty Clinch, *Girl About Town*, London, 24 September 1984.

'the roots of what is perhaps' *The Swadeshi Movement*, pp. 515–6.

pp. 268–9 'The Soviet Union' Walter Goodman, *New York Times*, 7 July 1985.

p. 269   'The film catches the conservative element' Neil Sinyard, *Sunday Telegraph*, London, 16 September 1984.

p. 270   'I am not a flame ... its life' *The Home and the World*, London, Penguin, 1985, pp. 194, 197–8.

'He never used a wrong word' Radio interview with Julian Crandall Hollick, 1987.

p. 273   'All at once my heart was full' *The Home and the World*, London, Penguin, 1985, pp. 66–7.

26   *Documentaries*

p. 274   'What *you* think is unimportant' *The Cinema of Satyajit Ray*, p. 65.

pp. 276–7 'Old Man: How much do you weigh?' *The Select Nonsense of Sukumar Ray*, pp. 50–1 (translated by Andrew Robinson).

p. 277   'is not a film which on first viewing' Draft typescript of *Portrait of a Director* from the Seton Collection, p. 205.

'back-breaking chore' Letter, 14 February 1962.

'we need a film-maker, not' Marie Seton, *Portrait of a Director*, p. 169.

p. 278   'in which it is plain that Mr. Ray' *Times*, 29 April 1961.

'the storm [droning] like a giant' *Glimpses of Bengal*, p. 26.

p. 279   'Humans, birds, fish and animals' *The Art of Rabindranath Tagore*.

'Ten or twelve minutes' Henri Micciollo, *Satyajit Ray*, p. 283.

p. 280   'with the thought that Bala ... for the film' 'Working with Bala' in *Journal of the National Centre for the Performing Arts*, December 1976, p. 30.

'by far the finest living Indian painter' Letter, 4 December 1973.

'But he took it with his usual stoicism' 'Translator's Note' in *Nandan*, Santiniketan, Visva Bharati, 1981, p. 38.

p. 281   'One evening [Kattamosai] is sitting alone' 'Kattamosai' in *Nandan*, K.G. Subramanyan trans., Santiniketan, Visva Bharati, 1981, p. 18.

'Blindness is very complex ... that's me' *Bisoy Chalachchitra*, pp. 118–23.

27   Unmade Films

p. 284   'never ceasing to marvel at it' Letter, 7 December 1958.

p. 285   'lack of funds' *The Mahabharata: A play*, Peter Brook trans., London, Methuen, 1988.

'The trouble is I find I can identify' Letter, 2 December 1978.

p. 286   'I think I could improve the book ... very strange' Interview with Andrew Cave, 'Alien in a lotus pond', 1967 (source and date unknown).

'The incident has the kind of plausibility ... Indian mind' *Sight and Sound*, autumn 1982, p. 270.

'I don't think anyone has really captured' *Times*, 9 December 1981.

pp. 286–7   'horrified to see Aziz's house' Letter, 28 March 1985.

p. 287   'Some professional competence' Letter, 24 December 1985.

'The East is still as far away' Letter to Peries, 7 December 1958.

'had rounded up ... trust' 'Ordeals of the Alien' in *Statesman*, 4 and 5 October 1980.

p. 290   'things with his voice ... you know' 'Ordeals of the Alien'.

p. 291   'an elegant, self-contained' 'Ordeals of the Alien'.

'So this is as much an act ... fate' 'Ordeals of the Alien'.

'He plays an Indian in a Hollywood setting' Letter, 25 July 1968.

'Two heads are better ... in the flesh' 'Ordeals of the Alien'.

p. 292   'Ray owes a lot to Renoir ... Indian Cinema' Anon. (but known to be James Ivory), 'Maestro' in *New Yorker*, 22 July 1967, p. 27.

'firmly convinced' 'Ordeals of the Alien'.

'the greatest Bad Verse writer ... to die' 'Ordeals of the Alien'.

pp. 292–3 'the scene that met my eye' 'Ordeals of the Alien.'

p. 293 'By now I had begun to feel ... Calcutta' 'Ordeals of the Alien'.
'sizzling reply ... To Satyajit Ray' 'Ordeals of the Alien'.
'begun to assume an aura' Letter, 25 July 1968.

p. 294 'the beginning of a period ... solution' Letter, 15 August 1968.
'shaven-headed monk ... happy' 'Ordeals of the Alien'.
'striking parallels' Letter to *Times*, 24 August 1984.
'Don't take it lying down' Letter from Ray to author, 11 October 1984.

p. 295 'would not have been possible' *India Today*, 15 February 1983, p. 51.
'Tell Satyajit I was a kid in' Letter from Clarke to *Times*, 24 August 1984.
'two of the greatest geniuses' Letter to *Times*, 24 August 1984.

28 *Ray as Designer, Illustrator and Writer*

p. 298 'essentially "entertainment"' Letter to Alex Aronson, 5 June 1986.
'Plot is the thing here' Robert Taylor, *Boston Globe*, 28 July 1987.
'sheer entertainment and pleasure' Stuart Evans, *Times*, 2 April 1987.

p. 299 'I've received so many letters' *Economic Times*, 9 June 1986.

pp. 299–300 'that this universe' *India Today*, 15 February 1983, p. 51.

p. 300 'mild-mannered Professor Challenger' Introduction to *Stories*.
'not only less assertive but' *New York Times*, 30 June 1987.

pp. 300–1 'like the dragon of the east and west' *Stories*, p. 156.

p. 301 'two Hindi films' *Stories*, p. 47.

pp. 301–3 'fiftyish, short, bald-headed ... perfection and dedication?' *Stories*, pp. 17–30.

p. 303 'There are more things in heaven and earth' *Eker Pithe Dui*, p. 67.
'a marvellous flavour of sinister understatement' *New York Times*, 20 September 1987.
'cows are still holy' *Sight and Sound*, autumn 1982, p. 274.

pp. 303–4 'This is the land of tall stories ... Balkishen–Balkishen – Balkishen', *Stories*, pp. 1–16.

29 *'Some Aspects of his Craft'*

p. 306 'Technique. A means to an end' 'This word "technique"' in *Seminar*, May 1960, p. 21.
'As *Breathless* and subsequent films proved' *OFTF*, p. 87.

p. 307 'So complex, so intricate ... into words' *OFTF*, p. 10.
'The flow of ideas' Firoze Rangoonwalla, *Satyajit Ray's Art*, p. 117.
'I can deal with something' *OFTF*, p. 64.

p. 308 'a totally innocent, honest boy ... you don't make a film' *Cinewave*, January–March 1984, p. 19.

'main invectives' *OFTF*, p. 64.

'We don't admire a painting' *My Life and My Films*, p. 264.

'If classical implies an orderly unfolding' *Sight and Sound*, autumn 1982, p. 273.

pp. 308–9   'I do not think spontaneity' Firoze Rangoonwalla, *Satyajit Ray's Art*, pp. 116–17.

p. 309   'One often heard … the camera' 'My life, my work' in *Telegraph*, Calcutta 30 September 1982.

'Let's call it "realistic"' *Film Comment*, summer 1968, p. 6.

p. 310   'Since it is the ultimate effect' *OFTF*, p. 66.

'a person on the screen who continues to be expressive' *OFTF*, p. 96.

'my own experience is that people with talent' *OFTF*, p. 61.

p. 311   'There is a great deal of affection' *Montage*.

p. 312   'To the extent that a director' *OFTF*, p. 67.

pp. 312–3   'a set exists only in relation to the script' *Montage*.

p. 313   'Satyajit is in full control' *Montage*.

'truthful, unobtrusive and modern' *OFTF*, pp. 69–70.

'but the same style prevails' Marie Seton, *Portrait of a Director*, p. 128.

'There is no such thing as good photography *per se*' *OFTF*, p. 68.

p. 314   'We don't actually see with our eyes' *Montage*.

'Editing is the stage' *OFTF*, p. 70.

'Dulal Dutta, Ray's regular editor' John Pym, *The Wandering Company*, London, British Film Institute, 1983, p. 34.

'I hate conventional time-lapses' *Film Quarterly*, winter 1958, p. 7.

p. 315   'These offer endless variations of emphasis' *OFTF*, p. 70.

pp. 315–6   'I have always felt that music' *Cinema Visions*, I, 4, 1980, pp. 15–16.

p. 316   'does not have to maintain caste' *Bisoy Chalachchitra*, p. 64.

p. 317   'one should not feel like thinking' *Cinewave*, January–March 1984, p. 11.

'Particularly when it is played' *Sight and Sound*, winter 1983/4, p. 50.

'this monstrous, teeming, bewildering city' *OFTF*, p. 161.

pp. 317–8   'The average educated middle-class Bengali' *Cinema Visions*, I, 4, 1980, p. 18.

'but the challenge' *Bisoy Chalachchitra*, p. 67.

30   *The Inner Eye of Satyajit Ray*

p. 319   'Satyajit Rayer *chabi dekhechen*?' Dipten Sanyal, editor of *Achal Patra*.

'I am aware that they are not of a kind' 'The new cinema and I' in *Cinema Visions*, July 1980, p. 16.

p. 320   'Part of the delight and wonder derives'   *OFTF*, pp. 168–9.
          'I can say unhesitatingly that it's'   Letter, 26 November 1984.

pp. 321–2   '*Charulata*, it is tempting to say'   *Cinema: A Critical Dictionary*, p. 825.

p. 322   'He is quite alone, of course'   Penelope Gilliatt, *Conversations with Renoir*, New York, McGraw-Hill, 1974, p. 31.
          'A sign of greatness'   *Rabindranath Tagore on Art and Aesthetics*, p. 59.
          'But why should the West care?'   *OFTF*, p. 161.

p. 323   'found himself temperamentally unsuited'   Letter to Seton, 12 May 1978.
          'No! With you it'll be different'   *Stills*, autumn 1981, p. 46.

p. 324   'I always regard Ray'   *India Today*, 15 February 1983, p. 53.
          'Olympian heights'   Letter to Saeed Jaffrey, 28 August 1976.
          'with a Satyajit Ray mind'   *Montage.*
          'I do not know of a single film-maker'   *OFTF*, p. 98.
          'tame, torpid versions … spoon-feeding'   *Sight and Sound*, autumn 1982, p. 269.
          'You'll find directors here'   *Cineaste*, 1, 1982, p. 29.

p. 325   'which, in films, means anybody'   *OFTF*, p. 12.
          'what passed for film criticism'   *Sight and Sound*, autumn 1982, p. 269.
          'What is attempted in most of my films is'   *Sight and Sound*, autumn 1982, p. 274.

p. 326   'Love between a man and a woman'   *Filmfare*, 1 July 1960, p. 23.

p. 327   'What does Ray portray in the Apu Trilogy?'   *Probe India*, October 1980, p. 14.

pp. 327–8   'this holy cow'   *Probe India*, October 1980, p. 15.

p. 328   'The Modern India you speak of'   *Probe India*, October 1980, p. 16.
          'The whole Malle affair'   Letter, 6 September 1970.

p. 329   'rather stupid to raise a wall around you'   *Sunday Observer*, Bombay, 25 November 1984.
          'I think both in English and in Bengali'   Television interview with Zia Mohyeddin, 1982.

pp. 329–30   'He insisted on translating every word … and nodding her head' in David McCutchion *Shraddhanjali*, pp. 118–25.

p. 330   'a bit like Alexander the Great'   Marie Seton, *Portrait of a Director*, p. 32.

pp. 330–1   'Nothing exasperates me more'   David McCutchion *Shraddhanjali*, pp. 124–5.

p. 331   'There is a subtle, almost imperceptible'   *Sight and Sound*, autumn 1982, p. 274.

pp. 331–2   'enormous reserves … the true Japanese film-maker'   *OFTF*, p. 157.

p. 332   'I may be wrong'   *OFTF*, p. 157.
          'the Far East'   *OFTF*, p. 155.

'In other words, they were being as imitative' *The Autobiography of an Unknown Indian*, p. 456.

pp. 332–3 'sterility of our intellectual and moral life' *Thy Hand, Great Anarch!*, p. 659.

p. 333 'took one of the greatest inventions of the West' *OFTF*, p. 13.
'What sets these film-makers apart' 'The new cinema and I' in *Cinema Visions*, July 1980, p. 14.
'to life, to human beings' Firoze Rangoonwalla, *Satyajit Ray's Art*, p. 105.
'If I were asked what has been my main preoccupation' 'The new cinema and I' in *Cinema Visions*, July 1980, p. 16.
'it is absurd to suggest that beauty' *Rabindranath Tagore on Art and Aesthetics*, p. 3.

p. 334 'Bach is timeless' *Sight and Sound*, autumn 1982, p. 274.
'the movement generated' *Rabindranath Tagore on Art and Aesthetics*, p. 49.
'He was one of the few truly original talents' Foreword to *Cinema and I*.

pp. 334–5 'My days were spent on the banks' *Ritwik Ghatak*, pp. 3–5.
p. 335 'the misfortune to be largely ignored' Foreword to *Cinema and I*.
p. 336 'Ritwik was a Bengali director' *Ritwik Ghatak*, p. 2.
'an indefinable universality' *Portrait of a Director*, p. 33.
'I well recall the indescribable feeling' *Eksan*, autumn 1987, p. 226 (translation of remarks made in Moscow in 1975, authenticated by Kurosawa in 1988).

p. 337 'What I admire most about Manik' *Illustrated Weekly of India*, 20 November 1988, p. 53.
'Nothing human is alien to them. . .' *Time*, 20 September 1963.
'strong and simple . . . illusion of actuality better' Marie Seton, *Portrait of a Director*, p. 165.
'permanent values' *Sight and Sound*, winter 1972/3, p. 33.

31 *Postscript*

p. 339 'generally ranks as one of the thinnest' James McFarlane, Introduction to *An Enemy of the People, The Wild Duck, Rosmersholm*, The World's Classics edn, Oxford University Press, 1960, p. ix.

p. 341 'Do you recall a questionnaire to film directors' Robert Hughes ed., *Film: Book 1, The Audience and the Film-maker*, p. 56.

Bibliography

BOOKS BY SATYAJIT RAY

Non-fiction

Bisoy Chalachchitra (*On Cinema*), 2nd edn, Calcutta, Ananda Pubs., 1983 (collected articles in Bengali)

Ekei Bole Shooting (*We Call It Shooting*), Calcutta, Newscript Pubs., 1979 (describes film-making for children)

Jakhan Choto Chilam (*When I Was Small*), Calcutta, Ananda Pubs., 1982 (memoir of his early life)

Our Films Their Films, Delhi, Orient Longman, 1976 (collected articles in English)

Fiction (Bengali)

Most of Ray's stories and novels first appear either in *Sandesh* or in other Calcutta magazines, especially *Desh* and *Anandamela*. They are then republished in book form by Ananda Publishers, Calcutta, with a few exceptions.

'Feluda' Novels:
Badsahi Angti, 1969
Gangtoke Gandagol, 1971
Sonar Kella (*The Golden Fortress*), 1971
Baksa Rahasya, 1973
Kailase Kelenkari, 1974
Royal Bengal Rahasya, 1975
Joi Baba Felunath (*The Elephant God*), 1976
Feluda and Co., 1977
Gorasthane Sabdhan, 1979
Chinnamastar Abhisap, 1981
Hatyapuri, 1981
Jata Kanda Katmandute, 1982
Tintorettor Jesu, 1983
Feluda One Feluda Two, 1985
Darjeeling Jamjamat, 1987

'Professor Shonku' Novels:
Professor Shonku, Newscript Pubs, 1965
Professor Shonkur Kandokarkhana, 1970
Sabash Professor Shonku, 1974

Mahasankate Shonku, 1977
Swayang Professor Shonku, 1980
Shonku Ekai Akso, 1983

Other Novels, Stories and Screenplays:
Ek Dozen Gappo, 1970
Aro Ek Dozen, 1976
Fatikchand, 1976
Teen Rakam, Kathamala, 1979
Aro Baro, 1981
Ebaro Baro, 1984
Mulla Nasiruddiner Galpa, 1985
Tarini Khuror Kirtikalap, 1985
Pikur Diary o Ananya, 1986
Sujan Harbola, 1987 (fairy-stories)
Eker Pithe Dui, 1988

Miscellaneous:
Sera Sandesh, 1981 (the best of 25 years of *Sandesh*, edited by SR)
Toray Badha Ghorar Dim, 1986 (translations of nonsense verses)
Braziler Kalo Bagh, 1987 (translations of foreign writers such as Conan Doyle, Clarke, Bradbury)

Fiction (in translation)
Podróže Profesora Sanku, Tlumaczyla Elzbieta Walterowa trans., Warsaw, Naaza Ksiegarnia, 1981
Fatik et le Jongleur de Calcutta, France Bhattacharya trans., Paris, Bordas, 1981
Phatikchand, Lila Ray trans., Delhi, Orient Paperbacks, 1983
Fatik y el Juglar de Calcutta, Elena Del Amo trans., Madrid, Espasa-Calpe, 1984
Bravo! Professor Shonku, Kathleen M. O'Connell trans., Calcutta, Rupa, 1986
Stories, Satyajit Ray trans., London, Secker & Warburg, 1987
The Unicorn Expedition and Other Fantastic Tales of India, New York, E.P. Dutton, 1987 (same collection as *Stories*)
La Nuit de l'indigo, Eric Chédaille trans., Paris, Presses de la Renaissance, 1987 (same collection as *Stories*)
The Adventures of Feluda, Chitrita Banerjee trans., Delhi, Penguin India, 1988 (contains *The Golden Fortress*, *The Buccaneer of Bombay*, *Mystery at Golok Lodge* and *Trouble in the Graveyard*)

SCREENPLAYS BY SATYAJIT RAY
Published in Bengali
Place of publication is Calcutta.
'*Aparajito*', *Eksan*, autumn 1984 (with a preface by SR)
'*Aranyer Din Ratri*', *Eksan*, winter 1969

'*Asani Sanket*', *Eksan*, autumn 1973
'*Baksa Badal*', *Eksan*, autumn 1987 (with a preface by SR)
'*Charulata*', *Eksan*, autumn 1982
'*Devi*', *Eksan*, autumn 1981
'*Fatikchand*', *Eksan*, summer 1983
'*Ghare Baire*', *Eksan*, winter-spring 1985
'*Goopy Gyne Bagha Byne*', *Eksan*, autumn 1988 (with a preface by SR)
'*Hirak Rajar Dese*', *Eksan*, winter-spring 1981
'*Jana Aranya*', *Eksan*, autumn 1976
'*Kanchenjungha*', Mitra-Ghosh, 1972 (book)
'*Kapurush*', *Eksan*, autumn 1965
'*Mahanagar*', *Eksan*, autumn 1986 (with a preface by SR)
'*Nayak*', Bengal Pubs, 1972 (book)
'*Parash Pathar*', *Baromash*, autumn 1975
'*Pather Panchali*', *Eksan*, autumn 1983 (with a preface by SR)
'*Pikoo*', *Eksan*, autumn 1980
'The Postmaster', *Chalachchitra*, I, 3, 1961
'*Sakha Prasakha*', *Eksan*, autumn 1966 (reprinted in *Teen Rakam*, 1979
    and *Pikur Diary o Ananya*, 1986)
'Two', *Chitrakalpa*, I, 4, 1964

Published in English
The Apu Trilogy, Shampa Banerjee trans., Calcutta, Seagull Books, 1985
    (with a preface by SR)
'The Chess Players', *Eksan*, Calcutta, summer 1978 (first draft)
The Chess Players and Other Screenplays, London, Faber and Faber, 1989
(contains final screenplays of *The Chess Players* and *Deliverance*, and
    draft screenplay of *The Alien*, with a preface by SR and introductions
    by Andrew Robinson)
'Deliverance', *Eksan*, Calcutta, autumn 1982 (draft)
'The Inner Eye', *Kino*, II, 1, Calcutta, 1973
'*Nayak*', *Montage*, Uma Krupanidhi and Anil Srivastava eds., Bombay,
    Anandam Film Society, July 1966
'*Pather Panchali*', Satish Bahadur ed., Pune, National Film Archive, 1981
'*Pather Panchali*', Lila Ray trans., Calcutta, Cine Central, 1984

FOREWORDS, INTRODUCTIONS, PREFACES BY SATYAJIT RAY

Ray has prefaced/ introduced the following books in English:
Cartier-Bresson, Henri, *Henri Cartier-Bresson in India*, London, Thames
    and Hudson, 1987
Gangopadhyay (Ganguli), Sunil, *Pratidwandi*, Enakshi Chatterjee trans.,
    Delhi, Sangam Books, 1974
Ghatak, Ritwik, *Cinema and I*, Calcutta, Rupa, 1987
Mitra, Narendranath, *Mahanagar*, S.K. Chatterjee and M.F. Franda trans.,
    Bombay, Jaico Publishing House, 1968

Monk, Ray and Robinson, Andrew, eds., *Rabindranath Tagore: A Celebration of His Life and Work*, London, Rabindranath Tagore Festival and Museum of Modern Art, Oxford, 1986

Ray, Satyajit, *Stories*, London, Secker & Warburg, 1987
   The Apu Trilogy, Shampa Banerjee trans., Calcutta, Seagull Books, 1985
   The Chess Players and Other Screenplays, London, Faber and Faber, 1989

Ray, Sukumar, *The Select Nonsense of Sukumar Ray*, Sukanta Chaudhuri trans., Calcutta, Oxford University Press, 1987

Roberge, Gaston, *Chitrabani*, Calcutta, Chitrabani, 1974 (in English and Bengali)

Robinson, Andrew, *The Art of Rabindranath Tagore*, London, André Deutsch, 1989

Singh, Raghubir, *Rajasthan: India's enchanted land*, London, Thames and Hudson, 1981

ARTICLES BY SATYAJIT RAY

There are two collections of articles by Ray: *Our Films Their Films* (Delhi, Orient Longman, 1976), which has been translated by Tony Mayer into French as *Ecrits sur le Cinéma* (Paris, Editions Jean-Claude Lattés, 1982), and *Bisoy Chalachchitra* (*On Cinema*) (2nd edn., Calcutta, Ananda Pubs., 1983). The contents of these two books are listed below, in the order in which they appear, followed by other articles not included in these two collections.

OUR FILMS THEIR FILMS:
(original place of publication given where known)
Introduction
What is wrong with Indian films?   *Statesman*, Calcutta, 1948
Extracts from a Banaras diary   *Indian Film Quarterly*, Calcutta, 1957
A long time on the little road   *Sight and Sound*, London, 1957
Problems of a Bengal Film Maker
Winding Route to a Music Room   *New York Times*, 1963
Film Making
The Odds Against Us
Some Aspects of my Craft   *Montage*, Bombay, July 1966
Those Songs
Meetings with a Maharaja   *Film World*, Bombay, 1968
An Indian New Wave?   *Filmfare*, Bombay, 1971
Four and a Quarter   *Indian Film Culture*, Calcutta, 1974

Renoir in Calcutta   *Sequence*, London, 1950
Some Italian Films I have Seen   *Calcutta Film Society Bulletin*, 1951
Hollywood Then and Now   *Indian Film Culture*, Calcutta, 1963
Thoughts on the British Cinema   *Indian Film Review*, 1963
Calm Without, Fire Within   *Indian Film Culture*, Calcutta, 1964
Moscow Musings   *Kino*, Calcutta 1964
The Gold Rush
Little Man, Big Book

Akira Kurosawa   *Indian Film Culture*, Calcutta, 1966

Tokyo, Kyoto and Kurosawa   'Cinema in Japan': A survey by Federation of Film Societies of India, Calcutta, 1973

New Wave and Old Master

Silent Films

A Tribute to John Ford   Souvenir Publication by USIS on occasion of a John Ford Film Festival, Calcutta, 1974

BISOY CHALACHCHITRA:

Chalachchitrer bhasa: sekal o ekal (Film language: yesterday and to-day)   *Desh*, 1969

Soviet chalachchitra (Soviet cinema)   1967

Atiter bangla chabi (Early Bengali films)   *Anandalok*, 1978

Bangla chalachchitrer arter dik (The artistic aspect of Bengali films)   *Betar Jagat*, 1960

Chalachchitra-rachana: angik, bhasa o bhangi (Film-making: technique, language and style)   *Chalachchitra*, 1959

Diteler samparke duchar katha (A few remarks about details)   *Desh*, 1968

Chalachchitrer sanglap prasange (About dialogue in films)   *Anandabazar Patrika*, 1963

Abahasangit prasange (About background music)   *Desh*, 1964

Duti samasya (Two problems)   *Desh*, 1967

Parichalaker dristite samalochak (The critic as the director sees him) *Desh*, 1965

Apur Sansar prasange (About *Apur Sansar*)   *Desh*, 1959

Charulata prasange (About *Charulata*)   *Parichay*, 1964

Oraphe Indir Thakrun (Alias Indir Thakrun)   *Madhyabitta*, 1955

Dui charitra (Two characters)   *Desh*, 1962

Ekatha sekathe (Some random thoughts)   *Desh*, 1970

Rangin chabi (Colour films)   *Desh*, 1972

Binodeda   *Desh*, 1971

Satabdir siki bhag (A quarter century)   *Anandalok*, 1980

Other articles by Ray:

(in date order)

'Thoughts on film-making', unfinished article written after the release of *Aparajito* in Calcutta in 1956

'This word "technique" ', *Seminar*, Bombay, May 1960, pp. 21–3

Letters to the *Statesman*, Calcutta, 10 Aug., 16 Aug., and 1 Sept. 1965, discussing Mrinal Sen's film *Akash Kusum* (reprinted in Sen, *Views on Cinema*)

'Why not Hindi?', *Filmfare*, Bombay, 24 June 1966, pp. 26–7

'Rabindrasangite bhabbar katha' ('Reflections on Rabindrasangit'), *Eksan*, Calcutta, autumn 1967, pp. 1–21 (analysis of Tagore's songs)

'The changing face of films', *Film World*, Bombay, 1967, p. 101

'Cinemar katha' ('The story of cinema'), *Sandesh*, Calcutta, September–October 1967, pp. 474–7, February 1968, pp. 713–6, September–October 1968, pp. 362–5, September–October 1969, pp. 335–40

'The question of reality', Films Division Souvenir, Delhi, 1969, pp. 85–6
'The art of script-writing', *Film World*, Bombay, April–June 1969, pp. 52–3
'The confronting question', *Film World*, Bombay, February 1970, pp. 31–2
'The art of the cinema', *Sequence*, 3, Dacca, 1970, pp. 11–4 (translation
    from Bengali)
'The lure of terracotta' (obituary of David McCutchion). First published in
    Statesman, Calcutta, republished in a collection of writings about McCutchion
    by those who knew him entitled David McCutchion *Shraddhanjali* (Calcutta,
    Writers Workshop, 1972) under the title 'Dozens of scuttling peacocks'
Letter to *Filmfare*, Bombay, 25 February 1972 (replying to a rejoinder
    to his article 'An Indian new wave?')
Convocation address at the Film and Television Institute of India at Pune, 1975
'Working with Bala', *Journal of the National Centre for the Performing
    Arts*, Bombay, December 1976, pp. 29–32
'Ashesh Bandopadhyaya [Banerjee] Plays *Esraj*', sleeve-note on LP (EMI
    SEMGE 11012), 1978
'Music from Satyajit Ray's Apu Triology', sleeve-note on LP (ECLP 3411), 1978
Letter to *Illustrated Weekly of India*, Bombay, 31 December 1978, pp. 49–51
(replying to an attack on *The Chess Players* by Rajbans Khanna)
'Kamal Babu', *Samatat*, 41, Calcutta, 1979, pp. 4–8
'*Kajer Manush D. K.*', *Bibhab*, Calcutta, winter 1979/80, pp. 19–21 (obituary
    of D. K. Gupta)
'I wish I could have shown them to you', *Cinema Visions*, Bombay,
    January 1980, pp. 6–7
'The new cinema and I', *Cinema Visions*, Bombay, July 1980, pp. 14–16
'Ordeals of the Alien' *Statesman*, Calcutta, 4 and 5 October 1980
'Our festivals, their festivals', *Statesman*, Calcutta, 3–17 January 1982
    (supplement on the occasion of 'filmotsav 82', international film festival
    in Calcutta)
'Under western eyes', *Sight and Sound*, London, autumn 1982, pp. 269–74
    (50th anniversary issue)
'My life, my work', *Telegraph*, Calcutta, 27 September–1 October 1982
    (the Amal Bhattacharji lecture)
'Speaking of *Pather Panchali*', *Pather Panchali*: *a film by Satyajit Ray*,
    Calcutta, Cine Central, 1984, pp. 7–8 (excerpt from a speech)
Message of appreciation of Bimal Roy on the occasion of a retrospective
    screening of Roy's films, Calcutta, November 1986
'Never use animals!', *Ingmar Bergman at 70: A Tribute*, Stockholm, Swedish
    Film Institute, 1988, (*Chaplin* film magazine special issue in English)
'*Amar* Charlie' ('Charlie, the timeless'), *Sandesh*, May 1989, pp. 87–8

SELECT BOOKS ABOUT SATYAJIT RAY

Bengal Association, *Satyajit Ray Retrospective*, Delhi, April 1981 (booklet
    which includes 'The prophet abroad' by Amita Malik, 'Satyajit Ray – the
    seeker of life's truth' by Subrata Banerjee, 'Looking back' by Karuna
    Banerjee, and a message from the Prime Minister Indira Gandhi)

Das Gupta, Chidananda, ed., *Film India: Satyajit Ray*, Delhi, Directorate of Film Festivals, 1981 (an anthology of statements on Ray and by Ray for the New York celebration of Ray in 1981)

Das Gupta, Chidananda, *The Cinema of Satyajit Ray*, Delhi, Vikas, 1980

Datta, Alaknanda and Bandopadhyay (Banerjee), Samik, eds., *Satyajit Ray: a film by Shyam Benegal*, Calcutta, Seagull Books, 1988 (detailed reconstruction of Benegal's film including interview with Ray)

Krupanidhi, Uma and Srivastava, Anil, eds., *Montage*, Bombay, Anandam Film Society, July 1966 (special issue on Satyajit Ray including reviews; articles on aspects of Ray; interviews with Ray, Bansi Chandragupta, Subrata Mitra, Ravi Shankar, Ray's actors; the screenplay of *Nayak* in English; and two pieces by Ray – 'Some Aspects of My Craft' and the commentary of B.D. Garga's film about Ray)

Majumdar, Swapan, ed., *Satyajit Ray Retrospective Souvenir: The First Decade*, Calcutta, 1975 (booklet)

Satyajit Ray Retrospective Souvenir: The Second Decade, Calcutta, 1979 (booklet)

Micciollo, Henri, *Satyajit Ray*, Paris, Editions l'Age D'Homme, 1981

Mukhopadhyay (Mukherjee), Dilip, *Satyajit*, Calcutta, Banisilpa, 1986 (in Bengali)

Nyce, Ben, *Satyajit Ray: a Study of his Films*, New York, Praeger, 1988

Seton, Marie, *Satyajit Ray: Portrait of a Director*, extended edn., London, Dennis Dobson, 1978

Wood, Robin, *The Apu Trilogy*, New York, Praeger, 1971

BOOKS WITH SECTIONS ON SATYAJIT RAY

There are numerous dictionaries and histories of cinema with entries on and references to Satyajit Ray. These have been excluded from the following list unless they are of special significance.

Barnouw, Erik and Krishnaswamy, S., *Indian Film*, 2nd edn., New York, Oxford University Press, 1980 (extended references)

Chattopadhyay (Chatterjee), Amitava, 'Satyajit Ray: A Great Liberal Humanist' in Arun Kumar Ray and Sital Chandra Ghosh eds., *Twelve Indian Directors*, Calcutta, People's Book Pubs., 1981, pp. 1–24

Cowie, Peter, ed., *International Film Guide*, London, Tantivy Press, 1965, pp. 14–18 (critical assessment)

Das Gupta, Chidananda, *Talking About Films*, Delhi, Orient Longman, 1981 (extended references)

Houston, Penelope, *The Contemporary Cinema*, London, Penguin, 1963, pp. 150–3

Kael, Pauline, *I Lost it at the Movies*, New York, Little Brown, 1965, pp. 248–55 (critical assessment of Ray's films up to and including *The Goddess*)

Manvell, Roger, ed., *International Encyclopedia of Film*, London, Michael Joseph, 1972, pp. 412–13 (entry on Ray by Manvell)

Rhode, Eric, *Tower of Babel*, London, Weidenfeld & Nicolson, 1966, pp. 191–205

Russell Taylor, John in *Cinema: A Critical Dictionary*, Richard Roud ed., London, Secker & Warburg, 1980, pp. 813–31

Sen, Mrinal, *Views on Cinema*, Calcutta, Ishan, 1977 (includes 'Satyajit Ray sets the example' and letters exchanged between Ray, Sen and Barman in 1965 concerning Sen's film *Akash Kusum*)

Tyler, Parker, *Classics of the Foreign Film*, New York, Citadel Press, 1962, pp. 205–11

Wright, Basil, *The Long View: An International History of Cinema*, London, Paladin, 1974, pp. 458–70

BOOKS OF RELATED INTEREST

Banerjee, Bibhutibhusan, *Am Atir Bhepu*, Calcutta, Signet Press, 1944, (abridged edn of *Pather Panchali*)
Pather Panchali: Song of the Road, T.W. Clark and Tarapada Mukherjee trans., London, 1968, George Allen & Unwin

Banerjee, Sumanta, *In the Wake of Naxalbari*, Calcutta, Subarnarekha, 1980

Chakravarti, Punyalata, *Chelebelar Dinguli*, Calcutta, Newscript Pubs., 1957

Chaudhuri, Nirad C., *Hinduism*, London, Chatto & Windus, 1977
The Autobiography of an Unknown Indian, Macmillan, London, 1951
Thy Hand, Great Anarch!, Chatto & Windus, London, 1987

Ghatak, Ritwik, *Cinema and I*, Calcutta, Rupa, 1987 (with a foreword by Ray)
Ritwik Ghatak, Shampa Banerjee ed., Delhi, Directorate of Film Festivals, 1982

Greenough, Paul, *Prosperity and Misery in Modern Bengal*, New York, Oxford University Press, 1982

Isherwood, Christopher, *Ramakrishna and His Disciples*, London, Methuen, 1965

Kopf, David, *British Orientalism and the Bengal Renaissance*, Berkeley and Los Angeles, University of California Press, 1969
The Brahmo Samaj, Princeton University Press, 1979

Kripalani, Krishna, *Rabindranath Tagore: A Biography*, London, Oxford University Press, 1962

Ray, Sukumar, *Nonsense Rhymes*, Satyajit Ray trans., Calcutta, Writers Workshop, 1970
The Select Nonsense of Sukumar Ray, Sukanta Chaudhuri trans., Calcutta, Oxford University Press, 1987 (introduction by Satyajit Ray)
Satayu Sukumar, Sisirkumar Das ed., Delhi, Bengal Association, 1988

Raychaudhuri, Upendrakisore, *The Stupid Tiger and other tales*, William Radice trans., London, André Deutsch, 1981

Sarkar, Sumit, *The Swadeshi Movement in Bengal 1903–1908*, Calcutta, People's Publishing House, 1973

Sharar, Abdul Halim, *Lucknow: The Last Phase of an Oriental Culture*, E.S. Harcourt and Fakhir Hussain trans., London, Paul Elek, 1975

Stephens, Ian, *Monsoon Morning*, London, Ernest Benn, 1966

Tagore, Rabindranath, *Creative Unity*, London, Macmillan, 1922
  Glimpses of Bengal, London, Macmillan, 1921
  My Reminiscences, London, Macmillan, 1917
  Rabindranath Tagore on Art and Aesthetics, Pritwish Neogy ed., Delhi,
  Orient Longman, 1961

SELECT INTERVIEWS WITH SATYAJIT RAY

India

Chitrabhas, Calcutta, 1981 (organ of the North Calcutta Film Society;
  . special issue in English in memory of Bansi Chandragupta)
Chitrapat, II, 1, Calcutta, 1964 (with Kiranmoy Raha)
Cine Technique, Calcutta, March 1972 (with Sakti Chatterjee; Satyajit
  Ray special issue)
Cinewave, Calcutta, January–March 1984, pp. 7–20 (with Jayanti Sen)
Cinema Visions, I, 4, Bombay, 1980, pp. 14–21 (with Dhritiman Chatterjee
  and with Bhaskar Chandavarkar on film music)
Economic Times, Calcutta, 9 June 1986 (with Aparna Sen, mainly on
  his writings)
Film World, 'How I make my films', Bombay, October–December 1969,
  pp. 80–3 (with Lindsay Anderson and audience)
'You may call me also a commercial producer', January 1980, pp. 28–31
  (with K.A. Abbas)
Filmaker (sic), II, 4–5, Bombay, 1976–7, pp. 61–9 (transcript of a discussion
  at the Delhi Film Festival between Ray, Antonioni, Kazan and Kurosawa,
  telecast 12 January 1977)
Filmfare, 'Every important director has worked with stars', Bombay, 5
  June 1970, pp. 27–31 (with Suresh Kohli)
Gentleman, Bombay, December 1984, January and February 1985 (transcript
  of Shyam Benegal's interview with Ray for his film *Satyajit Ray*)
India Today, 'I don't live in an ivory tower', Delhi, 15 February 1983, pp. 50–1
Kalkata, Calcutta, 2 May 1970 (with Karuna Shankar Roy; Satyajit Ray
  special issue in Bengali)
Samatat, 21–2, Calcutta, 1974, pp. 151–4
Satyajit Ray's Art, Delhi, Clarion, 1980, pp. 101–32 (with Firoze Rangoonwalla)
Satyajit Ray Retrospective Souvenir: The Second Decade, Swapan Majumdar
  ed., Calcutta, 1979, pp. 23–6 (with Iqbal Masud)
Sequence, 'Ray on music', Dhaka, spring 1975, pp. 14–6, 36
Sunday Observer, Bombay, 25 November 1984 (with Rinki Bhattacharya)
Sunday Statesman, Calcutta, 25 August and 1 September 1985 (with
  Kiranmoy Raha)
Times of India Magazine, Bombay, October 1988, pp. 33, 35 (with Ella
  Dutta; 150th anniversary issue)
Unpublished interview with Amarnath Jayatilaka, 1962

Rest of World

American Film, Washington DC, July–August 1978, pp. 39–50 (discussion at

the American Film Institute's Center for Advanced Film Studies)
October 1985, p. 35 (with Andrew Robinson)

Asia, New York, July–August 1981, pp. 10–11 (with Muriel Peters)

Asia Magazine, Hong Kong, 5 August 1962, pp. 4, 7, 8

Cahiers du Cinéma, Paris, October 1969, pp. 9–10 (with Jacques Aumont on the making of *The Adventures of Goopy and Bagha*)
February 1981, pp. 6–12 (with Daniele Dubroux and Serge le Peron)
July–August 1987, pp. 58–60, 62–4 (with Charles Tesson)

Cineaste, 'The politics of humanism', II, 1, New York, 1982, pp. 24–9 (with Udayan Gupta)

Cinématographe, Paris, October 1982, pp. 72–6 (with Emmanuel Decaux and Bruno Villien)

Film, 'The oriental master', London, Federation of Film Societies, winter 1970, pp. 7–8 (statement by Ray)
January 1974, p. 9 (statement by Ray about *Distant Thunder* at a press conference in Berlin)

Film Comment, New York, Summer 1968, pp. 4–15 (with James Blue on direction of the non-actor)
September–October 1976, pp. 52–4 (with John Hughes)

Film Quarterly, Berkeley, winter 1958, pp. 4–7 (with Hugh Grey)

Films and Filming, London, August 1982, pp. 12–22 (with Andrew Robinson)

Hughes, Robert, ed., *Film: Book 1, The Audience and the Filmmaker*, New York, Grove Press, 1959, p. 56 (answers four questions also put to ten other directors)

Image et Son, Paris, November 1964, pp. 71–8 (with Guy Gauthier)

Nouvel Observateur, Paris, 5 April 1985, pp. 54–5 (with France Huser)

Positif, Paris, January 1970, pp. 19–28 (with Peter Cargin and Bernard Cohn)
May 1979, pp. 9–22 (with Michel Ciment)
June 1979, pp. 33–6 (with Karen Jaehne on *The Chess Players*)

Revue du cinéma, Lausanne, July–August 1971, pp. 16–17 (with B.D. Garga)

Rivista del Cinematografo, Rome, October 1965, p. 556 (with Leo A. Murray)

Screen International, London, 12 May 1984, pp. 130–2 (with Swapan Mullick on *The Home and the World*)

Sight and Sound, London, summer 1970, pp. 114–20 (with Folke Isaksson)
winter 1972/3, pp. 31–3 (with Christian Braad Thomsen mainly on *Days and Nights in the Forest*, *The Adversary* and *Company Limited*)

Stills, London, autumn 1981, pp. 40–8 (with Wendy Allen and Roger Spikes)

SELECT ARTICLES ABOUT SATYAJIT RAY

India

Reviews of individual films by Ray are excluded below; they appear in most newspapers and magazines in Calcutta at the time of release as well as in major newspapers and magazines published from other major cities. The films are also reviewed in numerous film journals.

Ajkal, Ujjal Chakravarti, '*Sujan*, Cinema, Satyajit', Calcutta, 31 May 1986, p. 3

Anandalok, 'Manikdar kache ekta part cheyechilam, denni', Calcutta, 10 December 1988, pp. 55–69 (interview with Soumitra Chatterjee)

Chitrabhash, Dipendu Chakravarti, 'The world of the unwanted', XVIII, 2, Calcutta, 1983, p. 3

Dipendu Chakravarti, 'Identity Crisis of Bengali Youth', January–June 1984, p. 40

January–June 1985 (special issue on *Ghare Baire* in Bengali)

Cinema in India, Swapan Mullick, 'The master', Bombay, January 1987, pp. 18–23

Cine Technique, Ritwik Ghatak, 'Ekmatra Satyajit Ray', Calcutta, March 1972

Close-up, M.R. Menon, 'The art and films of Satyajit Ray: a study', 7–8, Bombay, 1971, pp. 5–17

Eksan, Anil Chowdhury, 'Pather Panchalir *nepathye*' ('The background to *Pather Panchali*'), Calcutta, autumn 1983, pp. 297–317

Anil Chowdhury, 'Aparajitar *katha*' ('The story of *Aparajito*'), autumn 1984, pp. 328–51

Siddhartha Ghosh, 'Science fiction', autumn 1988, pp. 119–76 (pp. 158–67 relates to Ray)

Eve's Weekly, Lekha J. Dhar, 'A Ray in her life', Bombay, 27 July–2 August 1985, pp. 40–2 (profile of Bijoya Ray)

Film Frame, Chidananda Das Gupta, 'Ray and his work', Colombo, December 1969, pp. 43–5

Film World, Lester James Peries, 'Ray and the critics', Bombay, October–November 1970, p. 33

Subrata Banerjee, 'Satyajit Ray: film-maker and man', Bombay, April–May 1971, pp. 31–5 (profile)

Ranjan Banerjee, 'Satyajit Ray: why one of the world's greatest?', Bombay, August 1972, pp. 40–3 (critical assessment)

Filmaker (sic), Bombay, January–March 1976, p. 3 (profile)

Filmfare, 'Bombay honours the far-famed Satyajit Ray', Bombay, 1 July 1960, pp. 19–23 (profile)

Verinder Raj Anand, 'Satyajit Ray and I', Bombay, 19 July 1968, pp. 27, 29 (discusses working methods)

Amitabha Bhattacharya, 'Pather Panchali: after 25 years, still a masterpiece', Bombay, 1–15 September 1980

Gentleman, Bidyut Sarkar, 'A Ray of hope', Bombay, December 1981, pp. 24–31 (profile)

Illustrated Weekly of India, Rajbans Khanna, 'Ray's Wajid Ali Shah', Bombay, 22 October 1978, pp. 49–53 (review of *Shatranj ke Khilari*)

Jyotirmoy Datta, 'Satyajit Ray, 65', Bombay, 18 May 1986, pp. 36–9 (profile)

Anuradha Dutt, 'Sheer grace', Bombay, 17 May 1987, pp. 56–7 (profile of Karuna Banerjee)

Bijoya Ray, 'My husband, Satyajit Ray', Bombay, 20 November 1988, pp. 52–3

India magazine, Marie Seton, 'The vision of Satyajit Ray', Delhi, September 1981, pp. 22–32 (profile)

Indian Post, Nisha Puri, 'I will be resuming work very shortly', Bombay, 9 August 1987 (profile)

Maadhyam, Rothin Sinha, Bombay, May–June 1981, pp. 5–8 (critical assessment)

Movie Montage, Soumitra Chatterjee, 'Apu *theke* Gangacharan', Calcutta, January 1982, pp. 1–14 (diary of the shooting of *Asani Sanket*)

Namaskaar, Subhra and Jayabrato Chatterjee, 'Satyajit Ray: the man behind the mask', Bombay, February–March 1983, pp. 31–5 (profile)

Of Age, Ujjal Chakravarti, I, 11, 12, 13, 14, 17, 18, 19, 20, 21, 22, 23 and II, 2, 3, 4, 5, 7, 8, 14, 16, 17, 18, 20, 23, Calcutta, 1986–7 (discusses various aspects of Ray's technique and style)

Probe India, Amita Malik, 'Nargis vs Satyajit Ray', Allahabad, October 1980, pp. 10–16 (discusses Ray's depiction of India abroad, includes interview with Nargis Dutt)

Quest, Asish Barman, 'Problems of identification and the art of Satyajit Ray', Bombay, July–September 1958, pp. 77–80

Raha, Kiranmoy, 'Satyajit Ray's Calcutta', unpublished article, 1975

Sananda, Aparna Sen, Calcutta, 5 May 1988, p. 4

Satyajit Ray Retrospective Souvenir: The First Decade, R.P. Gupta, 'Those coffee house days', Swapan Majumdar ed., Calcutta, 1975 pp. 15–8

Screen, Phoni K. De, 'Does Satyajit Ray peddle poverty?', Bombay, 30 January 1981

Phoni K. De, 'How *Pather Panchali* was screened in Brussels', Bombay, 9 April 1982

Hameeduddin Mahmood, 'Sathe—Satyajit—*Sadgati*', Bombay, 18 June 1982 (discusses *Sadgati*)

Splice, Buddhadeb Das Gupta, 'Satyajit Ray: artist of social awareness', 3, Calcutta, 1987, pp. 31–4

Akos Ostör, 'Cinema and society in India and Senegal', pp. 7–27

Star Dust, Sumantra Ghosal, 'The Ray of genius', Bombay, May 1977 (describes the making of *The Chess Players*)

Statesman, Lila Majumdar, 'Classic detective, prim and proper', Calcutta, 6 November 1988 (review of *The Adventures of Feluda*)

Sunday, R.P. Gupta, 'Three decades of Satyajit Ray's *Pather Panchali*', Calcutta, 5–11 January 1986, pp. 22–7

Sunil Gangopadhyay (Ganguli), 'Arrayed with honour', 12–18 February 1989, pp. 76–7

Sunday Observer, Bombay, 14 April 1985 (quotes Ray's comments on the death of Marie Seton)

Time and Tide, Delhi, June 1969, pp. 55–63 (critical assessment, especially of the Apu Trilogy)

Times of India, Gautam Adikari, 'The renaissance man: the other side of Satyajit Ray', Bombay, 2 April 1983 (profile)

Week, Pralay Sur, 'Portrait of a Genius', 19–25 February 1989, pp. 45–9

Rest of World

Reviews of individual films by Ray are excluded below; those films which have been released in Europe and the US have been reviewed in most major newspapers and magazines.

American Cinematographer, Andrew Robinson, 'Satyajit Ray at work', Los Angeles, September 1983, pp. 72–80 (describes the making of *The Home and the World*)

Atlantic, Terrence Rafferty, 'Rooms with views', Washington DC, April 1985, pp. 132–3 (critical assessment)

Bianco e nero, Prabhat Mukherjee, '*Chi ha ucciso* Satyajit Ray?', Rome, January–April 1970, pp. 199–202 (critical assessment)

Biografägern, Johan Bergengren, '*En Indisk filmpoet*', 4–5, Stockholm, pp. 8, 19

Cahiers du Cinéma (in English), Georges Sadoul, 'From film to film', 3, New York, 1966, pp. 12–19, 62 (notes of conversations with Ray about his life and work written as autobiography by Sadoul, with an introduction by Sadoul)

Cahiers du Cinéma, Paris, January 1969, pp. 38–50 (translations of three articles by Ray, and 'Ray at the Cinemathèque' by Jacques Aumont)

Charles Tesson, 'Les complaintes du sentier', September 1981, pp. 27–31 (critical assessment)

Charles Tesson, 'Journal de bord d'un cinéaste', October 1982 (review of *Ecrits sur le Cinéma*)

Cinéma 75, Henri Micciollo, Paris, September–October 1975, pp. 120–2 (critical assessment)

Cinéma 81, Henri Micciollo, Paris, March 1981, pp. 40–53 (critical assessment – same as introductory chapter of Micciollo's *Satyajit Ray*)

Corine McMullin, March 1981, pp. 54–61 (profile)

Joël Magny, March 1981, pp. 62–3 (critical assessment)

Cinema Nuovo, 114–15, Rome, 15 September 1957, pp. 142–3 (profile after winning the Golden Lion at Venice)

Cinestudio, J.L. Martinez Montalban, '*Un autor, un cine*', Madrid, pp. 19–24 (critical assessment)

Film, Douglas McVay, 'The Ray Trilogy', London, Federation of Film Societies, March–April 1960, pp. 20–4 (critical assessment)

Mansel Stimpson, 'Ray: the complete artist', July 1974, p. 12 (critical assesment)

Film-rutan, Arne Svensson, 2, Stockholm, 1964, p. 67 (critical assessment)

Films and Filming, Alan Stanbrook, 'The world of Ray', London, November 1965, pp. 55–8 (critical assessment)

Roy Armes, 'Satyajit Ray: astride two cultures', London, August 1982, pp. 6–11 (critical assessment)

Guardian, John Rosselli, 'Poet of the cinema', London, 13 July 1963 (profile)

Marie Seton, 28 September 1977 (discusses making of *The Chess Players*)

Derek Malcolm, 'The world of Ray', 18–19 February 1989 (discusses *An Enemy of the People*)

Image et Son, Guy Gauthier, Paris, November 1964, pp. 69–70

Raphael Bassan, 'Satyajit Ray: *cinéaste des contrastes*', May 1982, pp. 71–83

Independent, Andrew Robinson, 'A small family film business', London, 25 July 1987 (profile)

Ivory, James, sleeve-note for original sound-track of *Shakespeare Wallah* (describes Ray's method of composition)

Journal of South Asian Literature, Peter J. Bertocci, 'Bengali cultural themes in Satyajit Ray's *The World of Apu*: an anthropological perspective', Michigan, winter 1983–4, pp. 15–33

Life, Asian edn., 'A new role for Ray?', 19 August 1968, pp. 57–60 (discusses mainly *The Adventures of Goopy and Bagha*)

Listener, Gavin Millar, 'The master of Indian cinema', London, 18 March 1982
Andrew Robinson, 'Two of a kind', London, 10 July 1986 (discusses Ray and Tagore)

London Magazine, Andrew Robinson, 'The inner eye: aspects of Satyajit Ray', October 1982, pp. 85–92 (critical assessment)
Andrew Robinson, 'Satyajit Ray and Calcutta', December 1987–January 1988, pp. 59–74

Los Angeles Times, Deborah Caulfield, 'Satyajit Ray questions *E.T.* origins', 16 March 1983

Monthly Film Bulletin, Andrew Robinson, 'Bridging the Home and the World', London, September 1984, p. 292

Movie, Rakesh Mathur, 'Satyajit Ray: visions of India', 46, London, Orbis Publishing, pp. 908–11 (critical assessment)

New York Herald Tribune, Richard C. Wald, 'There's no mystery to making a movie', 21 September 1958 (profile)
Barry Hyams, 'India's one-man film crusade', 8 July 1962 (profile)

New York Post, Archer Winsten, 22 September 1958 (profile)
Archer Winsten, 3 July 1967 (profile)

New York Review of Books, Ian Buruma, 'The last Bengali renaissance man', 19 November 1987, pp. 12–16 (profile)

New York Times, Howard Thompson, ' "Little Road" into the big world', 7 September 1958 (profile)
Mel Gussow, 'Ray and Rohmer Discuss Film-making', October 1972 (Ray and Rohmer comment independently of each other)
Bernard Weinraub, 'Satyajit Ray finds a freedom in film', 3 August 1973 (profile)
Joseph Lelyveld, 'Satyajit Ray's films take new directions', 21 October 1975 (profile)
Tom Buckley, 'Satyajit Ray tells of the trials of Indian film-making', 14 April 1978 (profile)
Joan Mellen, 'Satyajit Ray treats history as a multi-level chess game', 4 June 1978 (profile, mainly about *The Chess Players*)
Barbara Crossette, 'All the films of Satyajit Ray at the Modern', 26 June 1981 (profile)
Barbara Crossette, 'Satyajit Ray gives Ibsen a Bengali spin . . .', 7 May 1989
Andrew Robinson, '. . . and reflects on life and art', 7 May 1989 (profile)

New Yorker (anonymous but known to be by James Ivory), 'Maestro', 22 July 1967, pp. 25–7 (profile)

Newsweek, David Ansen, 'The eyes of Satyajit Ray', 20 July 1981, pp. 69–70 (critical assessment)

Positif, Michel Ciment, '*Le monde de* Satyajit Ray', Paris, March 1964, pp. 29–34 (critical assessment)

Bernard Cohn and Patrick Dujarric, '*Quelques films de* Satyajit Ray, *inédits en France*', January 1970, pp. 29–34 (critical assessment)

Michel Ciment, '*Tous les feux du bengale*', Paris, June 1979, pp. 17–22 (critical assessment)

Radio Times, Andrew Robinson, 'In the picture', London, 28 May–3 June 1988 (profile)

Sight and Sound, Eric Rhode, 'Satyajit Ray: a study', London, summer 1961, pp. 133–6 (critical assessment)

Marie Seton, '*Kanchenjungha*', spring 1962, pp. 198–202 (describes the making of *Kanchenjungha*)

Amita Malik, 'Toughs and taxi-drivers', autumn 1962, p. 179 (discusses Ray's preparations for *Abhijan*)

Amita Malik, 'Reluctant god', winter 1965/66, pp. 21–2 (critical assessment)

Penelope Houston, 'Ray's *Charulata*', winter 1965/66, pp. 31–3 (critical assessment of Ray's films in the light of *Charulata*)

Chidananda Das Gupta, 'Ray and Tagore', winter 1966/67, pp. 30–4

Derek Malcolm, 'Satyajit Ray', spring 1982, pp. 106–09 (profile)

Bibekananda Roy, 'Ray off set', winter 1983/84 (discusses work other than film-making), pp. 52–5

Andrew Robinson, 'Bombay, Colombo, Calcutta', summer 1985, pp. 182–6

Derek Malcolm, 'Dr. Stockman in Calcutta', spring 1989, pp. 92–3

Stills, Andrew Robinson, 'Ray in Tollywood', London, May–June 1983, p. 9 (discusses the making of *The Home and the World*)

Tiempo de Cine, Emir Rodriguez Monegal, '*La Trilogia de* Satyajit Ray: *un artista integro*', Buenos Aires, July–September 1961, pp. 4–6 (critical assessment)

Time, 'The gold standard', 17 February 1958 (discusses difficulties of getting *Pather Panchali* distributed in the USA)

Times, Andrew Robinson, 'A man who reveals truths with details', London, 9 August 1984, p. 8 (profile)

Peter Ackroyd, 'The very nature of cinema', London, August 1984 (review of the television film *Satyajit Ray: Portrait of a Director*)

Times Literary Supplement, Eric Rhode, 'A feeling for India', London, 8 July 1977, p. 823 (review of *Our Films Their Films*)

OTHER ARTICLES

Asia, Satti Khanna, 'A major motion picture event from India', New York, July–August 1981, pp. 8–13 (discusses Indian cinema and Ray's place in it)

Chitrabhas, Calcutta, 1981 (organ of the North Calcutta Film Society; special issue in English in memory of Bansi Chandragupta)

Cinema Visions, Gene Moskowitz, 'Things are looking up but . . .', II, 1, Bombay, 1981, pp. 19–21 (comments on Indian cinema)

Henri Micciollo, 'Unfamiliarity breeds contempt', II, I, Bombay, 1981, pp. 36–40 (comments on Indian cinema)

Illustrated Weekly of India, Ashokamitran, 'The great dream bazaar', Bombay, 13 October 1985, pp. 44–5 (discusses impact of *Pather Panchali* in Calcutta in 1955)

Gaston Roberge, 'The cinema of subversion', Bombay, 13 October 1985, pp. 38–41 (discusses the Apu Trilogy)

Andrew Robinson, 'The elusive genius', Bombay, 5 July 1987, pp. 8–15 (profile of V.S. Naipaul with comments on Ray)

London Magazine, Hugo Williams, 'Monsoon diary', March 1964, pp. 39–42 (discusses Ray as part of a visit to India)

Nandy, Ashis, 'An intelligent critic's guide to Indian cinema', paper delivered at a seminar in Jodhpur, December 1987 (published in *Deep Focus*, 1 and 2, Bombay, 1988)

New York Post, Archer Winsten, 18 November 1961 (quotes letter from Edward Harrison with Ray in India)

New York Times, Howard Taubman, 'Calcutta boasts a cultural role', 28 April 1968 (discusses Ray as part of Calcutta life)

James Ivory, 'Years pass: the star gets very fat', 27 March 1966 (discusses film-making in India)

New Yorker, Ved Mehta, 'City of dreadful night', 21 March 1970, pp. 87–97 (profile of Ray as part of a portrait of Calcutta)

Sight and Sound, Lindsay Anderson, 'Panorama at Cannes', London, summer 1956, pp. 16–21 (discusses *Pather Panchali*)

Marie Seton, 'Journey through India', spring 1957, pp. 198–202 (briefly discusses *Pather Panchali*)

South Asia Research, Andrew Robinson, 'Selected Letters of Sukumar Ray', London, November 1987, pp. 169–236 (translation of letters written from Britain 1911–3)

Spectator, Andrew Robinson, 'The Lewis Carroll of Calcutta', London, 19–26 December 1987, p. 47–9 (discusses Sukumar Ray)

Time, 20 September 1963 (discusses Ray as part of a new generation of world film-makers)

Washington Post, 'To kiss and go naked', 2 September 1969 (discusses Indian attitude to screen nudity)

Index